Take Responsibility for Workers and Families Act

H. R. 6379

116th CONGRESS

2d Session

Thirteen Colony Press

Thirteen Colony Press
c/o Sastrugi Press LLC
PO Box 1297, Jackson, WY 83001, United States
www.sastrugipress.com
CIP data available
U.S. Congress House of Representatives
Take Responsibility for Workers and Families Act / U.S. Congress House of Representatives
—1st United States edition
p. cm.
1. Civics 2. Politics 3. Government
The House of Representatives presented H.R. 6379 as the third bill to provide relief to the United States from the COVID-19 pandemic, including material beyond the scope of the pandemic.
ISBN-13: 978-1-944986-99-5 (paperback)
Thirteen Colony Press is an imprint of Sastrugi Press LLC.
ISBN-13: 978-1-944986-99-5(paperback)
Printed in the United States of America when bought in the United States of America.
10 9 8 7 6 5 4 3 2 1
Sastrugi Press
00213

Publisher's Note

The original House of Representatives bill has been reformatted to fit the digital and print copies as you see here for easier reading. Thank you for choosing Thirteen Colony Press.

Contents

TITLE I—FEDERAL BENEFIT ENHANCEMENTS 379

CONTENTS

CONTENTS

Take Responsibility for Workers and Families Act, Overview

The Take Responsibility for Workers & Families Act

House Democrats' more than $2.5 trillion bill boldly addresses the impacts of the coronavirus crisis on families, businesses, and communities by rebuilding our health care system to test and treat everyone and tightening the safety net to support families, shore up small businesses, and help governments maintain services

Making health care affordable and accessible – Eliminates cost-sharing for coronavirus treatments and vaccines for all patients, including the uninsured. To further ensure affordable health care, the legislation increases subsidies on the individual market, provides a new Open Enrollment period, protects access to health insurance for furloughed and newly unemployed workers, and provides new incentives for states to expand Medicaid.

Bolstering the health care system – Provides more than $150 billion to support America's hospitals, Community Health Centers, and government medical programs as they treat coronavirus patients. To further support providers, the legislation offers an additional $80 billion in low-interest loans to hospitals, suspends the Medicare sequester, and takes other important actions to pump funding into the health care system.

Protecting frontline response workers – Requires health care facilities implement clear infectious disease protocols and provide necessary protective equipment to keep frontline health care workers safe. The legislation also provides child care assistance to health care workers and emergency personnel.

Putting money in the pockets of individuals and families – Provides Americans with a direct cash infusion: $1,500 of immediate assistance per individual, up to $7,500 for a family of five. This benefit would be available to anyone with an individual taxpayer identification number, as well as to our nation's retirees and unemployed individuals.

Enhancing unemployment compensation — Creates a temporary Federal Pandemic Unemployment Compensation of $600 a week for any worker affected by COVID-19 and eligible for unemployment compensation benefits. Combined with existing benefits, this replaces 100 percent of wages for the average worker. The legislation also expands eligibility to self-employed workers, individuals whose contracts were cancelled, and new entrants to the job market.

Expanding paid leave and family medical leave – Builds on the *Families First Coronavirus Response Act* by expanding paid sick days and family medical leave to ensure nearly every worker has access to these crucial benefits.

Ensuring food security – Expands and funds additional Supplemental Nutrition Assistance Programs benefits, helping to ensure that families will be able to afford to eat during the coronavirus pandemic.

Supporting small businesses – Streamlines aid for small businesses and provides more than $500 billion in grants and interest-free loans, some with forgivable components, to help Main Street businesses as they cope with the economic disruption caused by the coronavirus pandemic.

Assisting states and local governments – Stabilizes the finances of states and local governments with $200 billion in stabilization funding for states and $15 billion to local governments through the Community Development Block Grant program, allowing them to maintain public services even as revenue falls because of the pandemic. The legislation also authorizes the Federal Reserve to purchase state and local government bonds intended to fight the Coronavirus outbreak.

Standing with America's students – Pumps nearly $60 billion into schools and universities, with $50 billion directly provided to states to help them stabilize their funding for schools and nearly $10 billion to help alleviate the harm caused by coronavirus on higher education institutions, while providing them with added flexibility to continuing operating during the crisis. The legislation also helps current borrowers with their student debt burden.

Upholding our Constitutional imperatives – Ensures that states can carry out this year's election with $4 billion in grant funding for states through the Election Assistance Commission and a national requirement for both 15 days of early voting and no-excuse absentee vote-by-mail, including mailing a ballot to all registered voters in an emergency.

H.R. 6379, Take Responsibility for Workers and Families Act, Title-By-Title Summary

H.R. 6379, Take Responsibility for Workers and Families Act

Title-By-Title Summary

House Democrats' more than $2.5 trillion bill boldly addresses the impacts of the coronavirus crisis on families, businesses, and communities

DIVISION A – Third Coronavirus Preparedness and Response Supplemental Appropriations Act, 2020

Prepared by the Democratic staff of the House Committee on Appropriations

Title I – Agriculture, Rural Development, Food and Drug Administration, and Related Agencies

American Agriculture Safeguards – Provides $55 million to ensure the Animal and Plant Health Inspection Service can continue working with the Department of Homeland Security's Customs and Border Protection during the coronavirus emergency to keep foreign animal and plant pests and diseases from entering the U.S. Provides $45 million to ensure the Agricultural Marketing Service can continue grading commodities, to protect the food supply chain in America.

Food Safety – Includes $33 million to ensure uninterrupted meat and poultry inspections by the Food Safety and Inspection Service to protect the safety of the U.S. food supply during the coronavirus outbreak.

Farm Service Agency – Includes $3 million to ensure FSA has funds for staff to review expected increase in loan servicing and new loan applications in response to the pandemic.

Rural Business Assistance – Includes loan authority for up to $1 billion for the USDA Business and Industry Loan Program to help rural businesses access credit and mitigate the impacts of the coronavirus outbreak.

ReConnect program and Distance Learning and Telemedicine (DLT) – Provides $258 million for the ReConnect program and $25 million for DLT to expand investments in telemedicine and broadband to assist in managing the coronavirus pandemic. These critical investments enhance the ability for individuals to receive healthcare through telemedicine and for students to utilize broadband service for education resources.

The Emergency Food Assistance Program (TEFAP) – $450 million to help local food banks meet increased demand for low-income Americans during the emergency. Including funding provided by the Families First Coronavirus Response Act, TEFAP's total is $850 million.

Food Distribution Program on Indian Reservations (FDPIR) – $100 million to support income-eligible households living on Indian reservations and American Indian households residing in approved areas. Many of these households participate in FDPIR as an alternative to the Supplemental Nutrition Assistance Program.

Supplemental Nutrition Assistance Program (SNAP) – Provides such sums as may be necessary, in addition to base funds, to support anticipated increases in participation and to cover program cost increases related to flexibilities provided to SNAP by the Families First Coronavirus Response Act.

Child Nutrition Programs (CNP) – Includes $9 billion to cover program cost increases related to flexibilities provided to Child Nutrition Programs by the Families First Coronavirus Response Act.

Nutrition Assistance for U.S. Territories – Provides $200 million for USDA to provide nutrition assistance grants to Puerto Rico, American Samoa, and the Commonwealth of the Northern Mariana Islands.

Foreign Agricultural Service – Includes $4 million for emergency evacuations of USDA Foreign Agricultural Service staff and dependents around the world.

Food and Drug Administration – Provides $80 million for FDA's continued efforts to maintain our national drug and device product inventory through outreach to medical product manufacturers to identify and mitigate potential supply chain interruptions. Funds will also assist FDA's enforcement work against counterfeit and misbranded products and its review of emergency use authorizations for medical products, such as diagnostics. Additionally, funds will facilitate the development and review, both pre-market and post-market, of medical countermeasures, devices, therapies, and vaccines to combat the coronavirus.

Marketing Assistance Loans – Includes language allowing USDA to extend the term of a marketing assistance loan for any loan commodity to 12 months.

Title II – Commerce, Justice, Science, and Related Agencies

Economic Development Administration – $2 billion for Economic Adjustment Assistance for

areas responding to economic injury as a result of coronavirus.

Minority Business Development Agency – $15 million for Business Centers and Specialty Centers, to assist minority business enterprises to prevent, prepare for, and respond to coronavirus.

National Institute of Standards and Technology (NIST) research – $6 million for research and other measures to prevent, prepare for, and respond to coronavirus, including for measurement science to support testing for such virus.

NIST Manufacturing Extension Partnership program – $50 million to help small and medium-sized manufacturers prevent, prepare for, and respond to coronavirus, while waiving the cost share requirement.

NIST National Network for Manufacturing Innovation (also known as "Manufacturing USA") – $25 million to support development and manufacturing of medical countermeasures and biomedical equipment and supplies. These funds will effectively go to the National Institute for Innovation in Manufacturing Biopharmaceuticals (NIIMBL), which won a Commerce Department competition a few years ago and has been funded through this program ever since.

NOAA Operations, Research, and Facilities – $33.2 million to prevent, prepare for, and respond to coronavirus.

Bureau of Prisons – $100 million to prevent, prepare for, and respond to coronavirus.

Violence Against Women Act (VAWA) programs – $300 million, including $100 million for grants to combat violence against women, $25 million for transitional housing assistance grants, $100 million for sexual assault victims assistance, $25 million for rural domestic violence and child abuse enforcement assistance, $25 million for legal assistance for victims, and $25 million to support families in the justice system.

Byrne Justice Assistance Grants – $1 billion to help prevent, prepare for, and respond to coronavirus, including for purchasing personal protective equipment. Funds are to be distributed under the same requirements, conditions, compliance, and certification as 2016, thus preventing DOJ from blocking any of these funds from going to sanctuary jurisdictions.

Juvenile Justice Programs – $100 million, including $75 million for part B state formula grants, and $25 million for delinquency prevention grants.

NASA Safety, Security, and Mission Services – $100 million to prevent, prepare for, and respond to coronavirus.

NASA Construction and Environmental Compliance and Restoration – $100 million to prevent, prepare for, and respond to coronavirus.

National Science Foundation (NSF) Research and Related Activities – $100 million to prevent, prepare for, and respond to coronavirus, domestically and internationally, including to fund research grants and other necessary expenses.

NSF Agency Operations and Award Management – $2 million to prevent, prepare for, and respond to coronavirus.

Legal Services Corporation – $100 million to address legal needs arising from coronavirus. **Emergency Paid Leave for Census Workers** – Section 10203 would clarify the application and classification of emergency paid leave for temporary Census Bureau employees.

Title III – Defense

Active, National Guard and Reserve – $3.48 billion to provide the Active, National Guard and Reserve with the necessary tools to fight COVID 19. This includes funding for personal protection equipment for service members as they perform their mission as well as funding for increasing deployment of the National Guard and deployment of the U.S.N.S. Mercy and the U.S.N.S. Comfort for medical support to overwhelmed civilian hospitals.

Defense Health Program – $3.8 billion for medical countermeasures, diagnostics, and medical care for eligible service members, dependents, and retirees. This amount includes funding for diagnostics, vaccines, and anti-virals, procuring additional medical equipment, and support for the Military Health System by expanding military treatment facilities to ensure maximum capacity of the direct care system.

Defense Production Act – $500 million to assist industry in ramping up manufacturing for medical personal protective equipment and to maintain the industrial base in the future.

Title IV – Energy and Water Development, and Related Agencies Army

Corps of Engineers – $70 million to support activities to prevent, prepare for, and respond to coronavirus, including the continued operation of Corps projects across the country.

Bureau of Reclamation – $20.6 million for the Bureau of Reclamation, including $500,000 for the Central Utah Project Completion Account, to support activities to prevent, prepare for, and respond to coronavirus.

Department of Energy – $127.5 million to support activities to prevent, prepare for, and respond to coronavirus, including:

- $99.5 million for the Office of Science
- $28 million to support remote access for Department personnel.

Nuclear Regulatory Commission – $3.3 million to support activities to prevent, prepare for, and respond to coronavirus.

In addition –

to fund the operations, facilities, and equipment at national labs to support research on the coronavirus and develop treatment approaches such as a vaccine; and

Allows funds to be used to reimburse amounts used to prevent, prepare for, and respond to the coronavirus before the date of enactment of the bill.

• Allows the Department of Energy to modify its contracts during declared national emergencies and pandemics to address contract workers whose job duties cannot be performed remotely.

Title V – Financial Services and General Government Assisting Small Businesses – Provides critically needed funding to keep small businesses afloat during this unprecedented economic disruption, including:

• **Small Business Economic Injury Grants** – $100 billion in grants to small businesses that can demonstrate losses due to the outbreak.

• **Small Business Disaster Loans** – Provides for an additional $184 billion in low-interest economic injury disaster loans to help small businesses that have suffered financial losses as a result of the coronavirus outbreak.

• **Small Business Debt Relief** – Provides small businesses with relief from SBA loan payments, including principal, interest, and fees, for six months.

Telemedicine and Telehealth – $200 million for the Federal Communications Commission to provide health care providers with connected devices to facilitate telemedicine services and free up hospital beds.

Distance Learning – $2 billion for the Federal Communications Commission to provide broadband hotspots and connected devices to facilitate distance learning and connectivity.

Low-Income Broadband Access – $1 billion for the Federal Communications Commission to expand access to broadband for low-income Americans.

Federal Facilities – $275 million to clean and disinfect Federal buildings to keep employees and visitors safe.

Technology Modernization Fund – Provides $3 billion for technology-related modernization projects designed to cut costs and drive efficiencies across the Federal government.

Tax Credits and Delay in Tax Filing – $602 million for implementation of tax credits and to postpone the April 15th filing deadline.

Supporting Community Financial Institutions – $200 million for economic support and recovery in distressed communities throughout the U.S. by providing financial and technical assistance to community development financial institutions.

Elections – $4 billion for Election Administration Grants to states for contingency planning, preparation, and resilience of elections for federal office.

Oversight – $100 million to establish and support a COVID-19 Stimulus Accountability and Transparency Board to conduct oversight, monitor spending, provide transparency to the public, and help prevent fraud, waste, and abuse.

Postal Service – $25 billion for revenue forgone due to the coronavirus pandemic.

Title VI – Homeland Security

Personal Protective Equipment – $178 million for the purchase of personal protective equipment for components of the Department of Homeland Security to prevent, prepare for, and respond to coronavirus.

Transportation Security Administration – $100 million to prevent, prepare for, and respond to coronavirus, including $54 million for enhanced sanitation at airport security checkpoints, $26 million for overtime and travel costs for TSA officers, and $20 million for the purchase of explosive trace detection swabs.

Coast Guard – $141 million to prevent, prepare for, and respond to coronavirus through the activation of Coast Guard Reserve personnel and for building capacity and capability for information technology systems and infrastructure to support

telework and remote access.
Cybersecurity and Infrastructure Security Agency – $14.4 million to assist interagency critical infrastructure coordination, enhance analytic capabilities supporting coronavirus response, and related activities.
Federal Emergency Management Agency – $2.345 billion to prevent, prepare for, and respond to coronavirus, including $45 million for facilities and information technology; $200 million for the Emergency Food and Shelter Program; $100 million for Assistance to Firefighters Grants for the purchase of personal protective equipment; and $2 billion for assistance under the nationwide emergency declaration. In addition –
• Extends the deadline for states to meet the requirements of the REAL ID Act to October 1, 2021.
• Allows FEMA to continue paying personnel who reach normal overtime and premium pay caps while working on the coronavirus response.
• Adjusts the Federal cost share for assistance under the nationwide emergency declaration to 100 percent.
• Prohibits the use of funds provided in the bill from being used for other purposes.
• Clarifies and expands the scope of eligibility for FEMA emergency assistance to fill gaps identified by first responders, emergency managers, and nonprofit organizations active in the pandemic response.
• In recognition that several government offices have closed in response to the coronavirus that are responsible for reviewing and adjudicating work authorization requests or that impact American citizens, intending immigrants, and workers' ability to live and work in the United States, to include those with a Deferred Action for Childhood Arrivals status or Temporary Protected Status, a provision is included to automatically extend their current status or work authorization.

Title VII – Interior, Environment, and Related Agencies

Bureau of Indian Affairs Bureau of Indian Affairs – Provides $453 million for essential Tribal governmental services to help prepare for and respond to the pandemic, ensure continuation of government operations, and to aid individual Native Americans. This includes:
• No less than $407 million to be made available to focus efforts at the Tribal level;
• Assistance to individuals suffering loss of income; and
• Funds to deep clean facilities and/or quarantine facilities.
Bureau of Indian Education – Provides $69 million for education-related needs, including salaries, equipment, online curriculum development, and other associated costs.
Office of the Secretary – Provides $158 million for additional department-wide IT/teleworking/cybersecurity needs, personal protective equipment, law enforcement, and other high priority requirements. The bill provides transfer authority to provide maximum flexibility, with the amounts to be distributed as follows:
• **Bureau of Land Management** – Provides $32 million for personal protective equipment, additional IT/telework equipment, emergency law enforcement overtime, and other needs to sustain operations.
• **U.S. Fish and Wildlife Service** – Provides $29 million for personal protective equipment for first responders and staff, cleaning, training, law enforcement interdiction, emergency management on refuges, to sustain critical operations, and information technology.

• **National Park Service** – Provides $32 million for personal protective equipment, additional teleworking equipment, and law enforcement.
• **U.S. Geological Survey** – Provides $31 million for biosurveillance of wildlife and environmental persistence studies, research, cleaning, global mineral and material supply chain disruption/risk/vulnerability assessments, to sustain critical operations, and information technology.
• **Bureau of Ocean Energy Management, Bureau of Safety and Environmental Enforcement, Office of Surface Mining Reclamation** – Provides $2.5 million for protective equipment, cleaning supplies for buildings and facilities.
• **Office of Solicitor** – Provides $650,000 for additional IT/teleworking equipment and personal protective equipment.
• **Office of Inspector General** – Provides $1 million to perform oversight, accountability, and evaluation of programs, projects, or activities to prevent, prepare for, and respond to coronavirus.
• Provides $9 million for Personal Preparedness Equipment for firefighters.
• Provides $17 million for IT/teleworking/cybersecurity equipment through the Working
Capital Fund.
Insular Affairs – Provides $55 million to purchase equipment and medical supplies, and to support the general government response to coronavirus in the Insular Areas.
Environmental Protection Agency – Provides $7.2 million for EPA, of which $3 million is to reduce the risk of environmental transmission of coronavirus, and $4.2 million is for protecting the EPA workforce from spread of coronavirus.
Forest Service – Provides $70.6 million to support large-scale teleworking requirements, Personal Protective Equipment, enhanced cleaning and disinfecting of facilities, and restarts research activities. This includes:
• $3 million to restore research activities;
• $10 million for IT support for telework;
• $7.8 million for Personal Protective Equipment for law enforcement and firefighters; and • $49.8 million for facility cleaning.
Indian Health Service – Provides $1.032 billion for Indian Health Service and Tribally-operated health facilities, Urban Indian Organizations, and Tribal Epidemiology Centers to conduct surveillance, provide health care (including telehealth), establish mobile isolation units, purchase equipment and supplies, and for other needs. This includes:
• No less than $10 million for the Catastrophic Health Emergency Fund; • No less than $24 million for Tribal Epidemiology Centers;
• No less than $30 million for Urban Indian Organizations;
• No less than $50 million for Purchased/Referred Care; and
• No less than $125 million for an Electronic Health Records system.
Agency for Toxic Substance and Disease Registry – Provides $12.5 million to reduce the risk of environmental transmission of coronavirus through better tracking of infections and outreach on methods to safely sanitize cruise ships, homes, and daycare facilities while also protecting vulnerable subpopulations such as pregnant women and children.
Institute of American Indian and Alaska Natives – Provides $78,000 for education-related needs, including salaries, equipment, online curriculum development, and other associated costs.

Smithsonian Institution – Provides $7.5 million for cleaning, security, information technology, and staff overtime.

Kennedy Center – Provides $35 million for emergency needs for operation of the presidential monument.

National Endowment for the Arts – Provides $300 million for the National Endowment for the Arts for grants to support the general operations of recipients; language to allow fiscal year 2019 and 2020 grant funds to be used for general operations; and language to permit the waiver of matching requirements for fiscal year 2019 and 2020 recipients.

National Endowment for the Humanities – Provides $300 million for the National Endowment for the Humanities for grants to support the general operations of recipients; language to allow fiscal year 2019 and 2020 grant funds to be used for general operations; and language to permit the waiver of matching requirements for fiscal year 2019 and 2020 recipients.

Title VIII – Labor, Health and Human Services, Education, and Related Agencies Department of Labor – $1.4 billion to support workforce training and worker protection

activities related to coronavirus, including:

• $1.36 billion to support workers impacted by coronavirus, including older Americans, homeless veterans and Job Corps students;

• $30 million for the Occupational Safety and Health Administration for workplace protection activities in response to coronavirus, including $10 million for Susan Harwood training grants that protect and educate workers; and

• $10 million for enforcement and worker protection activities at the Wage and Hour Division and the Employee Benefits Security Administration, and $15 million for the Employment and Training Administration to administer unemployment insurance activities.

Health Resources and Services Administration – $1.9 billion to support expanded health care services for underserved populations, including:

• $1.3 billion for Health Centers to expand the capacity to provide testing, triage, and care for COVID-19 and other health care services at approximately 1,000 existing health centers across the country;

• $100 million to support rural hospitals to respond to the increased need for clinical services and equipment to meet the needs of patients with COVID-19, as well as to address financial and workforce challenges related to the impact of COVID-19;

• $330 million to develop a telephonic and virtual care platform that aggregates willing providers including physicians, nurses, telehealth platforms, health systems, rural health clinics, Federally-Qualified Health Centers, and others to facilitate the furnishing of telephonic and virtual health care services;

• $15 million to provide technical assistance to rural hospitals and clinics and to support existing telehealth projects to link COVID-19 patients with infectious disease specialists;

• $90 million to Ryan White HIV/AIDS clinics to support extended operational hours, increased staffing hours, additional equipment, and additional home delivered meals and transportation needs of clients, who disproportionately suffer from co-morbidities and underlying immunosuppression that puts them at greater risk for COVID-19 complications

• $15 million for tribes, tribal organizations, urban Indian health organizations, or health service providers to tribes; and

• $5 million to expand the capacity of Poison Control Centers to respond to an increase in calls related to COVID-19.

Centers for Disease Control and Prevention – $5.5 billion to support federal, state, and local public health agencies to prevent, prepare for, and respond to the coronavirus, including:

• $2 billion to support States, locals, territories, and tribes to conduct public health activities such as:

• surveillance for coronavirus;

• laboratory testing to detect positive cases;

• contact tracing to identify additional positive cases;

• infection control at the local level to prevention additional cases; o mitigation to prevent additional cases; and

o other public health preparedness and response activities.

• $1 billion for global disease detection and emergency response;

• $1 billion for the Infectious Diseases Rapid Response Reserve Fund, which supports immediate response activities during outbreaks;

• $500 million for public health data surveillance and analytics infrastructure modernization; and

• Support of CDC's continuing efforts to contain and combat the virus, including repatriation and quarantine efforts, purchase and distribution of diagnostic test kits (including to state and local public health agencies) and support for laboratory testing, workforce training programs, combatting antimicrobial resistance and antibiotic resistant bacteria as a result of secondary infection related to COVID-19, and communicating with and informing public, state, local, and tribal governments and healthcare institutions.

National Institutes of Health –$800 million to expand COVID-19-related research on the NIH campus and at academic institutions across the country, including on vaccines, treatments, diagnostics, and complications of the virus.

Assistant Secretary for Preparedness and Response – $100 billion for hospitals to reimburse health care related expenses or lost revenue directly attributable to the public health emergency resulting from coronavirus; $4.5 billion to reimburse the Department of Veterans Affairs for expenses incurred to provide medical care to civilians; and more than $6 billion for medical response efforts, including:

• More than $3 billion for Biomedical Advanced Research and Development Authority (BARDA) to support research and development of vaccines, therapeutics, and diagnostics to prevent or treat the effects of coronavirus, including:

• $1 billion for innovations in manufacturing platforms to support a U.S.-sourced supply chain of vaccines, therapeutics, and small molecule active pharmaceutical ingredients;

• At least $500 million to support U.S.-based next generation manufacturing facilities;

• More than $1.6 billion for the Strategic National Stockpile to procure pharmaceuticals, personal protective equipment (PPE), and other medical supplies, which can be distributed to State and local health agencies in areas with shortages;

• Increased medical surge capacity at additional health facilities;

• Enhancements to the U.S. Commissioned Corps; and

• Workforce modernization and increased telehealth access and infrastructure to enhance access to digital healthcare delivery.

Public Health Emergency Fund – $5 billion to deposit in a permanent emergency fund to ensure the Department of Health and Human Services is able to respond to a broad range of public health threats and protect the American people.

Substance Abuse and Mental Health Services Administration – $435 million to increase mental health support during this challenging time, to support substance abuse treatment, and to offer increased outreach to homeless individuals, including:

• $200 million for additional grants to Community Behavioral Health Clinics;
• $60 million for additional services to homeless individuals;
• $10 million for mental health support to children;
• $50 million for suicide prevention programs, including the Suicide Lifeline
• $15 million for tribes, tribal organizations, urban Indian health organizations, or health
service providers to tribes; and
• $100 million for emergency response grants to address immediate behavioral health needs as a result of COVID-19.

Agency for Healthcare Research and Quality – $80 million to support evaluations and research related to the health care system's response to COVID-19 and new telehealth investments.

Centers for Medicare & Medicaid Services Program Management – $550 million to provide additional infection control investigations of health care facilities—prioritizing nursing home facilities in localities with community transmission of coronavirus—as well as to support implementation and operations of CMS programs related to the coronavirus response.

Administration for Children and Families – $12.6 billion to provide supportive and social services for families and children through programs including:

• $6 billion for Child Care and Development Block Grants;
• $1 billion for Head Start;
• $2.5 billion for Community Service Block Grants;
• $1.4 billion for the Low-Income Home Energy Assistance Program (LIHEAP); • $1.5 billion to support paying water bills for low income families;
• $100 million for Family Violence Prevention and Services;
• $100 million for Runaway and Homeless Youth Programs; and
• $2 million for the National Domestic Violence Hotline.

Administration for Community Living – $1.2 billion to provide direct services such as home- delivered and prepackaged meals, and supportive services for seniors and disabled individuals, and their caregivers, including:

• $750 million for Senior Nutrition;
• $200 million Home and Community Based Support Services;
• $100 million for Family Caregivers;
• $20 million for Elder Justice and the Long-Term Ombudsman program; • $50 million for Aging and Disability Resource Centers; and
• $85 million for Centers for Independent Living.

Department of Education – $59.8 billion to support the educational needs of States, school districts, and institutions of higher education in response to coronavirus, including:

• $50 billion for a State Fiscal Stabilization Fund for grants to States to support statewide and local funding for elementary and secondary schools and public

postsecondary institutions. This flexible funding can support:
• costs associated with making up instructional time, including teacher, school leader, and classified school employee personnel costs;
• providing school-based supports for impacted students, families, and staff, including counseling, mental health services, family engagement efforts, and the coordination of physical health services;
• costs associated with sanitation and cleaning for schools and school transportation;
• professional development for school-based staff on trauma-informed care to restore the learning environment;
• purchasing educational technology, including assistive technology, that aids in regular and substantive interactions between students and their classroom instructor;
• coordination efforts between State educational agencies and public health departments for emergency planning, response, and recovery;
o authorized activities under education statutes including ESEA, IDEA, McKinney-Vento Homeless Assistance Act and the Perkins Act;
• training and professional development for college and university faculty and staff to use technology and services related to distance education;
• general expenditures for institutions of higher education for expenses associated with a disruption in services or operations related to coronavirus; and,
• emergency financial aid to postsecondary students for housing, food, technology, health care, and child care.
• $200 million for Project SERV to provide grants to school districts and institutions of higher education to recover from traumatic events and disruption related to coronavirus;
• $9.5 billion to help alleviate burdens associated with the coronavirus for both colleges and students, including $1.5 billion for Historically Black Colleges and Universities and Minority Serving Institutions and $8 billion for other institutions of higher education;
• $75 million to support borrowers impacted by coronavirus and to ensure that they receive accurate and helpful information from the Department of Education and student loan servicers about their options;
• $7 million for Gallaudet University to help defray costs associated with a disruption in university operations due to coronavirus and provide support to students;
• $13 million for Howard University to help provide needed institutional and student supports as a result of coronavirus;
• $11 million for Office of the Inspector General for oversight of funding provided in this Act; and
• $10 million for Program Administration to support continued services at the Department of Education through teleworking.

Corporation for Public Broadcasting – $300 million in stabilization funding to support public telecommunication entities.

Institute of Museum and Library Services – $500 million to support libraries and museums with costs and expenses associated with coronavirus, including providing technology and resources for their communities.

Corporation for National and Community Service – $250 million to support continued services and assistance to grantees.

Railroad Retirement Board – $10 million to support the processing of unemployment benefits under the Railroad Unemployment Insurance Act.

Social Security Administration Operating Expenses – $510 million to support the necessary telework and communication needs, continuing salaries and benefits of Federal employees in cases of office closures, and to issue emergency assistance payments.

Title IX – Legislative Branch

House of Representatives – $25 million to support the House's ramp up for teleworking, which includes the purchase of laptops and other teleworking devices as well as IT improvements to deal with the added demand on the network. In addition, this funding will also support the purchase of pandemic kits for Member offices (including district offices), Leadership offices, and Committees. In addition, the legislation provides authority for the Chief Administrative Officer (CAO) to pay contractor staff their normal wages for up to 16 weeks if their job is impacted by the coronavirus.

Office of the Attending Physician (OAP) – $400,000 for OAP to purchase N95 masks, surgical masks, gloves, swabs, testing that OAP sends out to its vendor, and personal protective equipment (PPE).

Capitol Police – $12 million for the Capitol Police to cover expenses related to increased teleworking and contract support for a reduced on-site workforce. In addition, this funding will

support overtime to cover potential staffing shortfalls for the Capitol complex and Dignitary Protection officers.

Architect of the Capitol (AOC) – $25 million to provide and supply important cleaning services across the Capitol grounds, including for the Library of Congress. Provides authority for the AOC to pay contractor staff their normal wages for up to 16 weeks if they are furloughed because of the coronavirus.

Government Accountability Office (GAO) – $50 million for GAO to conduct audits and investigations into spending of the substantial resources provided in this and earlier coronavirus bills to ensure that assistance is going to those who need it and that it is spent efficiently.

Title X – Military Construction, Veterans Affairs, and Related Agencies

Healthcare Access for Veterans – $17.2 billion to support the surge in demand for healthcare services at VA hospitals and clinics and for veterans seeking care at community emergency rooms and urgent care clinics. This includes the purchase of medical equipment, coronavirus test kits, and personal protective equipment, as well as establishing and expanding telehealth visits and support, including tele-ICU and teleradiology capabilities.

In addition –

- Supports the needs of vulnerable veteran populations, including Healthcare for Homeless Veterans, Supportive Services for Veterans Families program, as well as caring for COVID-19 positive veterans within VA-run nursing homes and community living centers.
- Supports the development of alternative sites of care and the procurement of mobile treatment centers.
- Supports increased outreach to veterans and expands 24-hour operations of the crisis response and continuity of operations within VA's Office of Emergency Management.

Information Technology Systems – $3 billion to procure equipment, expand bandwidth, and other necessary supports to address increases in telework, telemedicine, call center volume, and overall demand for services.

Armed Forces Retirement Home – $2.8 million to support personnel expenses for healthcare, security, and food service, as well as for medical supplies and equipment to care for residents.

Title XI – State, Foreign Operations, and Related Programs

State Operations – $315 million for consular operations, emergency evacuations of State Department staff and dependents, and other emergency preparedness needs at embassies around the world.

USAID Operations – $95 million for emergency evacuations of USAID Mission staff and dependents, and other emergency preparedness needs in missions around the world and in Washington, D.C.

Humanitarian Assistance – $600 million to respond to humanitarian needs arising in countries coping with a coronavirus disease outbreak.

Peace Corps – $90 million to recall all of its 6,128 overseas volunteers and unanticipated costs for evacuations; chartered flights; return volunteer health care; increased administration costs; and relocation of U.S. direct hires on authorized/ordered departure.

In addition –

- Provides for additional paid leave to address employee hardships resulting from coronavirus, abroad and domestically for Department of State and USAID direct hires.
- Provides supplementary authority to equip the Department of State, in exceptional circumstances, to also provide medical services or related support for private U.S. persons or third country nationals abroad unable otherwise to obtain such services or support.
- Provides immediate authority to hire doctors, due to limited numbers and the inability of doctors who typically cover broader regions to travel.
- Provides the Department of State authority to obligate and expend the passport and immigrant visa security surcharges to cover shortfalls and loss in fee revenue to pay the costs of providing consular services during fiscal years 2020 and 2021.
- Requires an update to strategy to respond to the coronavirus outbreak and regular reporting on the use of funding.

Title XII – Transportation, Housing and Urban Development, and Related Agencies

Department of Transportation (DOT) –

DOT, Operating Administrations – $30.3 million in budgetary resources to support activities by the Office of the Secretary, Federal Aviation Administration, Federal Motor Carrier Safety Administration, Federal Railroad Administration, and Maritime Administration to prevent, prepare for, and respond to coronavirus. Funding would support increased needs for telework and information technology, inspection equipment, and preparing and equipping the National Defense Reserve Fleet, Ready Reserve Fleet, the United States Merchant Marine Academy.

Aviation, Airport and Airline Worker Relief – To keep airport workers safe and employed: $10 billion in grants to airports, $40 billion in grants to airlines and their ground support contractors, up to $21 billion in loans to airlines, $100 million in grants to maintain a minimal level of scheduled air service to small communities, and $3 million for an Office of Airline Industry Financial Oversight. To keep the environment clean and livable: $1 billion to eliminate high-polluting aircraft and $100 million in research into sustainable aviation fuels.

15

FRA, Amtrak – $1.018 billion to support Amtrak's ability to operate passenger rail service on Northeast Corridor, state-supported, and long-distance routes, and to protect Amtrak workers. This includes $239 million to assist states in making FAST Act required payments to Amtrak for state-supported routes.

FTA, Transit – $25 billion for grants to transit agencies nationwide for operating expenses of those agencies to ensure continued operation of transit services. In addition –

- Distributes funds to transit agencies nationwide, ensuring they can maintain crucial services.
- Allows agencies to make payments to furloughed workers and maintains key worker protections.
- Eliminates requirements that transit agencies "match" federal funds.
- Allows agencies to use federal funds to compensate for lost revenues.

Department of Housing and Urban Development (HUD) –

Management and Administration – $20 million to support activities by the Administrative Support Offices and Program Offices to prevent, prepare for, and respond to coronavirus. Funding would also support program administration and oversight for the $158.8 billion in emergency assistance provided to state, local, and tribal governments and housing authorities through this Act.

Tenant-Based Rental Assistance – $1.5 billion to allow public housing agencies (PHAs) to respond to coronavirus and the ability to keep over 2.2 million families stably housed even when facing a loss of income. Allows PHAs the flexibility necessary for the safe and effective administration of these funds while maintaining fair housing, nondiscrimination, labor standards, and environmental protections.

Public Housing Operating Fund – $720 million for PHAs to carry out coronavirus response for the operation and management of almost 1 million public housing units. Allows PHAs the flexibility necessary for the safe and effective administration of these funds while maintaining fair housing, nondiscrimination, labor standards, and environmental protections.

Native American Programs – $350 million to address the needs of Indian tribes and tribally designated housing entities in preventing, responding to, and preparing for coronavirus. This includes $250 million in formula funding through the Native American Housing Block Grants program and $100 million in imminent threat grants through the Indian Community Development Block Grant program.

Housing Opportunities for Persons with AIDS – $130 million to maintain operations, rental assistance, supportive services, and other necessary actions to mitigate the impact of coronavirus on low-income persons with HIV/AIDS.

Community Development Block Grant – $15 billion for coronavirus response and to mitigate the impacts in our communities: up to $8 billion to be distributed by formula to current grantees, $5 billion awarded directly to States, based on public health needs and other factors, and the remainder to be awarded on a rolling basis via a formula that prioritizes the risk of transmission of coronavirus, number of coronavirus cases, and economic and housing market disruptions resulting from coronavirus. The legislation also waives the public services cap to allow communities to respond to the impacts of the pandemic.

Homeless Assistance Grants – $5 billion for Emergency Solutions Grants to address the impact of coronavirus among individuals and families who are homeless or at risk of homelessness and to support additional homeless assistance, prevention, and diversion activities to mitigate the impacts of the pandemic.

Emergency Rental Assistance – $100 billion to provide emergency assistance to help low- income renters at risk of homelessness avoid eviction due to the economic impact of the coronavirus pandemic.

Housing Assistance Fund – $35 billion for State housing finance agencies to provide housing or utility assistance to individuals and families to prevent foreclosure, eviction, mortgage delinquency, or loss of housing or critical utilities as a result of the coronavirus pandemic.

Assisted Housing Stability – A total of $1.1 billion for HUD multi-family housing programs to prevent, prepare for and respond to coronavirus and ensure the continuation of rental contracts and necessary support services, including:

- Project-Based Rental Assistance – $1 billion;
- Section 202 Housing for the Elderly – $75 million; and
- Section 811 Housing for Persons with Disabilities – $25 million.

Office of Fair Housing and Equal Opportunity – $7 million to address fair housing issues resulting from coronavirus. This includes $4 million for the Fair Housing Assistance Program and $3 million for the Fair Housing Initiatives Program.

DOT and HUD Oversight –

Inspectors General – $10 million total for the DOT and HUD Inspectors General to conduct audits and investigations to ensure transparency and efficiency within the agencies as they prevent, prepare for, and respond to coronavirus.

Title XIII – General Provisions

Technical budgetary provisions.

DIVISION B – Emergency Family and Medical Leave Expansion Act

Prepared by the Democratic staff of the House Committee on Education and Labor

Section 20001. References. This section clarifies that references in this Division to amend or repeal provisions are to be considered to be made to provisions of the Family and Medical Leave Act of 1993, as amended by the Emergency Family and Medical Leave Expansion Act.

Section 20002. Employer Clarification. This section clarifies that public agencies are covered under the Family and Medical Leave Act of 1993, regardless of the number of employees.

Section 20003. Emergency Leave Extension. This section extends the availability of Emergency Family and Medical Leave benefits from December 31, 2020 to December 31, 2021.

Section 20004. Emergency Leave Definitions. This section provides private sector and public sector employees who have been on the job for at least 30 calendar days with the right take up to 12 weeks of job-protected leave under the Family and Medical Leave Act, *regardless of the size of their employers.* Employees can take this leave to (1) self-quarantine, (2) care for a family member who is quarantined, (3) care for a child whose school has closed or child care provider is unavailable due to COVID-19, or (4) care for a family member who is individual with a disability or senior citizen whose place of care or direct care provider is unavailable.

Section 20005. Regulatory Authorities. This section strips the Labor Secretary of authority to issue regulations to carve out employees of small businesses with fewer than 50 employees or to issue regulations to carve health care providers and emergency responders from the right to leave. Any regulations that have been issued under that authority shall have no effect.

Section 20006. Relationship to Leave. This section ensures that workers with part-time schedules are provided 10 workweeks of paid leave, clarifies that paid sick leave provided under the *Families First Coronavirus Response Act* can be taken concurrently with unpaid emergency FMLA leave, and provides that only employees can decide to take unpaid leave concurrently with any other paid leave they have available. This section also ensures that emergency FMLA leave does not count towards an employee's 12 weeks of non-emergency unpaid FMLA leave.

Section 20007. Wage Rate. After two workweeks of unpaid leave, employees will receive a benefit from their employers that will be no less than two-thirds of the employee's usual pay, up to $200 a day. This section ensures that workers received at least the applicable minimum wage in their area.

Section 20008. Notice. This section requires that employees provide their employers with notice that they will need to take leave to care for a child, senior citizen, or individual with a disability as is practicable.

Section 20009. Amendments to the Emergency Family and Medical Leave Expansion Act.

• Clarifies that employees who work under a multiemployer collective agreement and whose employers pay into a multiemployer plan are provided with leave.

• Eliminates provisions that give employers of health care providers and emergency responders the ability to exclude their employees from emergency FMLA leave.

• Eliminates provisions that state that employees do not have a private right of action against violating employers with fewer than 50 employees.

DIVISION C – Emergency Paid Sick Leave Act Amendments

Prepared by the Democratic staff of the House Committee on Education and Labor

Section 30001. References. This section clarifies that references in this Division to amend or repeal provisions are to be considered to be made to provisions of Division E of the *Family First Coronavirus Response Act.*

Section 30002. Paid Sick Time Requirement. This section requires private and public sector employers, regardless of their size, to provide emergency paid sick leave. Eligible full-time employees are entitled to two workweeks (80 hours) of emergency paid sick leave. Eligible part- time employees are entitled to the hours of emergency paid sick leave that equals the typical number of hours that they work in a typical two-week period. Employees can use this leave to seek a diagnosis, receive treatment, care for a family member, care for a child whose school has closed or child care provider is unavailable due to COVID-19. Employees will receive emergency paid sick leave in addition to any existing employer-provided paid leave. This section eliminates an employer's ability to exclude health care providers and emergency responders from emergency paid sick leave.

Section 30003. Prohibited Acts. This section makes a technical correction to the provision that prohibits employers from firing, discharging or discriminating against an employee for taking leave or filing a complaint against an employer for violating the provisions in this act.

Section 30004. Sunset. This section extends the availability of emergency paid sick leave from December 31, 2020 to December 31, 2021.

Section 30005. Definitions. This section eliminates the large employer exemption and clarifies that nonprofit organizations are covered employers. This provision ensures that full-time and part-time employees earn full wage replacement (up to

$511 per day) for all emergency paid sick leave uses.

Section 30006. Regulatory Authorities. This section eliminates the Department of Labor's authority to issue regulations to exempt employers with fewer than 50 employees, health care providers, and emergency responders from this Division's emergency paid leave provision. This section also eliminates the Labor Department's broad authority to issue regulations to align Divisions C, E and G for the Family First Coronavirus Response Act. Any such regulations issued by the Department shall have no force and effect.

DIVISION D – COVID–19 Workers First Protection Act of 2020

Section 40001. Short Title. The short title for the bill is the COVID-19 Workers First Protection Act of 2020.

Section 40002. Emergency Temporary and Permanent Standards. This section requires the Occupational Safety and Health Administration (OSHA) to issue an Emergency Temporary Standard (ETS) within 7 days, requiring employers within the health care sector, emergency medical services (paramedic and firefighters), and any other sectors which either OSHA or the Centers for Disease Control and Prevention (CDC) designate at elevated risk, to develop and implement a comprehensive infectious disease exposure control plan to protect health care workers from exposure to the SARS-CoV-2 virus that causes COVID-19. The ETS shall be based on the guidelines issued by the Centers for Disease Control and Prevention, and the National Institute for Occupational Safety and Health, which are designed to prevent the transmission of infectious agents in healthcare settings and relevant scientific research on novel pathogens. In addition, the ETS may not be less protective than the infectious disease precautions for novel pathogens issued by any OSHA state plan.

OSHA shall issue a comprehensive permanent infectious disease standard within two years to protect employees from occupational exposure to infectious pathogens, including novel pathogens.

This section allows OSHA to exercise discretion in enforcement if it determines that, due to shortages, it is not feasible for an employer to comply with requirements for personal protective or other equipment, provided the employer makes a good-faith effort to comply and implements alternative measures to protect employees.

OSHA state plan states are required to issue an ETS within 14 days of enactment, that is at least as effective as the standard issued by federal OSHA. In the 24 Federal OSHA states, the ETS also applies to state and local governments for health care, emergency response and other covered workers.

Section 40003. Surveillance, Tracking and Investigation of Work-related Cases of COVID- 19 Among Health Care Workers. This section requires the CDC, in conjunction with the National Institute for Occupational Safety and Health, to collect and, as appropriate, investigate reports of work-related transmission of COVID-19 to health care and other workers, and make recommendations on needed actions or guidance based on those reports and investigations.

DIVISION E – Workforce Emergency Response

Prepared by the Democratic staff of the House Committee on Education and Labor

Section 50001. Workforce Response Activities. This section provides increased flexibility needed for State and local areas to provide continuity of services during the COVID-19 national emergency through rapid response activities.

DIVISION F – Family Support Provisions

Prepared by the Democratic staff of the House Committee on Ways and Means and the House Committee on Energy and Commerce

Section 101. Support Continued Safe Operation of Foster Care and Child Welfare Programs and Provide Additional Support to Older Foster Youth During the Emergency.

Older foster youth are especially vulnerable during the pandemic, as they don't have the same parental safety net as most young adults. This section would temporarily provide additional funding to assist older foster youth and expand eligibility to more former foster youth and suspend caps on housing assistance and requirements to make progress in college. The section would also provide for flexible administration of child welfare courts, foster care, and other child welfare programs, in order to comply with all public health restrictions.

Section 102. Allow Home Visiting Programs to Continue Serving Families Safely.

The legislation would modify federal rules to allow mothers and their infants to continue participating in the Maternal, Infant and Early Childhood Home Visiting Program, using virtual visits and with other temporary changes to comply with public health directives. Home visitors would also educate families on emergency preparedness and be able to provide necessary materials to maintain a safe and sanitary home, such as diapers and soap.

Section 103. Waive Federal Rules and Penalties to Allow State Child Support Enforcement Programs and Comply with Current Public Health Requirements.

Child support programs would have more flexible options to comply with social distancing and shelter-in-place guidelines and states would be held harmless from the federal financial penalties and associated with their inability to comply with certain requirements, including for maintaining staff capacity at statewide branches, meeting the 90% Paternity Establishment Percentage, and missing deadlines for filing reports and payments. During the crisis, states would also have more discretion to determine non-payment enforcement measures against unemployed noncustodial parents.

Section 104. Temporarily Suspend Temporary Assistance for Needy Families Program (TANF) Rules Inconsistent with Current Realities. During the emergency, state TANF programs would not be required to comply with the federal Work Participation Rate in order to allow TANF parents to follow public health guidance on social distancing, local shelter-in-place orders, and other requirements associated with maintaining public health and safety during the pandemic. The federal time limit on benefit receipt would also be temporarily suspended, to allow families to receive emergency help during the emergency without affecting future eligibility.

DIVISION G – Health Policies

Prepared by the Democratic staff of the House Committees on Energy and Commerce, Ways and Means, and Education and Labor

TITLE I – MEDICAID

Sec. 101 – Increasing Federal support to State Medicaid programs during economic downturns. Creates a mechanism that will automatically increase federal payments to state Medicaid programs if a state experiences an increase in the state unemployment rate.

Sec. 102 – Limitation on additional Secretarial action with respect to Medicaid supplemental payments reporting requirements. Prevents the Secretary of Health and Human

Services (HHS) from finalizing the Medicaid Fiscal Accountability Regulation

(MFAR) until two years after the end of the public health emergency.

Sec. 103 – Authority to award Medicaid HCBS grants to respond to the COVID-19 public health emergency. Authorizes the Secretary to award grants to states to support activities that strengthen their home- and community-based services (HCBS) benefit.

Sec. 104 – Delay in reduction of FMAP for Medicaid personal care services furnished without an electronic visit verification system. This section, for the duration of the public health emergency, suspends reductions in the federal medical assistance percentage (FMAP) for states that are not in full compliance with the electronic visit verification requirements

Sec. 105 – Coverage at no cost sharing of COVID-19 vaccine and treatment. Ensures that adult Medicaid beneficiaries receiving traditional Medicaid benefits have access to a future COVID-19 vaccine without any out-of-pocket costs. It also includes children enrolled in stand- alone CHIP programs to the vaccines for children program to ensure that they are able to receive COVID-19 vaccinations.

Sec. 106 – Optional coverage at no cost sharing of COVID-19 treatment and vaccines under Medicaid for uninsured individuals. Ensures that uninsured individuals whom states opt to cover through the new Medicaid eligibility pathway will be able to receive testing, treatment and immunizations for COVID-19 without cost-sharing.

Sec. 107 – Temporary increase in Medicaid Federal financial participation for telehealth services. This section, for the duration of the public health emergency, provides a 1 percent increase to the FMAP for telehealth services for state Medicaid programs that cover telehealth services to the same extent as they are required to be covered by Medicare.

Sec. 108 – Extension of full Federal medical assistance percentage to urban Indian organizations. Ensures that tribal providers, including urban Indian organizations, are able to receive 100 percent FMAP.

Sec. 109 – Medicaid coverage for citizens of Freely Associated States. Restores Medicaid eligibility to the citizens of the Freely Associated States.

Sec. 110 – Increased FMAP for medical assistance to newly eligible individuals. Allows states that expanded Medicaid after 2014 to benefit from the enhanced FMAP that was available to states that expanded in 2014.

Sec. 111 – Renewal of application of Medicare payment rate floor to primary care services furnished under Medicaid and inclusion of additional providers. Ensures that primary care providers are paid no less than they would be paid under Medicare for the duration of the public health emergency.

Sec. 112 – Temporary increase in Medicaid DSH allotments. Increases Medicaid disproportionate share hospital (DSH) allotments by 2.5 percent for the duration of the public health emergency.

Sec. 113 – Temporary allowance for medical assistance under Medicaid for inmates during 30-day period preceding release. Confers Medicaid eligibility on incarcerated individuals who are otherwise eligible to enroll 30 days prior to their release.

Sec. 114 – Extension of existing section 1115 demonstration projects. Authorizes the Secretary to extend expiring section 1115 demonstration waivers through 2021 so that state Medicaid programs can prioritize responding to public health emergency.

Sec. 115 - Preventing Medicaid disproportionate share hospital (DSH) cuts.

Cancels the Medicaid DSH cuts for fiscal year 2020, and reduces the DSH cuts for fiscal year 2021 to $4 billion. It also delays the start of the fiscal year 2021 cuts until December 1, 2020.

Sec. 116 - Extension of money follows the person rebalancing demonstration. This section fully finds money follows the person for fiscal year 2020 and provides $75 million for the first two months of fiscal year 2021.

Sec. 117 - Extension of protections for Medicaid recipients of home and community-based services against spousal impoverishment. This section ensures that protections against spousal impoverishment continue to apply to spouses of recipients of home- and community-based services through November 30, 2020.

Sec. 118 - Extension of the community mental health services demonstration program. This section extends the community mental health services demonstration until November 30, 2020.

TITLE II – MEDICARE

Sec. 201 – Coverage of the COVID-19 vaccine under the Medicare program without any cost-sharing. Provides for coverage of the COVID-19 vaccine and its administration under Medicare at no out of-pocket cost to patients under Medicare Part B when such a vaccine is available. The payment amount under part B for the administration of the COVID-19 vaccine will be the same as would be allocated for the administration of a flu vaccine.

Sec. 202 – Holding Medicare beneficiaries harmless for specified COVID-19 treatment services furnished under Part A or Part B of the Medicare program. Establishes zero cost- sharing (out-of-pocket costs) for COVID-19 treatment under Medicare Parts A and B.

Sec. 203 – Medicare sequester delay. Places a moratorium on the two percent Medicare sequester beginning on May 1, 2020, for the duration of the COVID-19 emergency period.

Sec. 204 – Enhancing Medicare telehealth services for federally qualified health centers and rural health clinics during the emergency period. Allows Federally Qualified Health Centers (FQHCs) and Rural Health Clinics (RHCs) to be paid for furnishing telehealth services to beneficiaries in their home or other setting during the COVID-19 emergency period. Medicare would pay for these services at a rate similar to the national average payment rates for comparable telehealth services under the Physician Fee Schedule.

Sec. 205 – Guaranteed issue of certain Medigap policies. Adds guaranteed issue protections for beneficiaries enrolling in supplemental Medigap plans to prevent insurance companies from denying coverage based on pre-existing conditions or health status.

Sec. 206 – Ensuring communications accessibility for residents of skilled nursing facilities during the COVID-19 emergency period. Ensures skilled nursing facilities provide a means for residents to conduct "televisitation" with loved ones while in-person visits are not possible during the COVID-19 emergency period.

Sec. 207 – Medicare hospital inpatient prospective payment system add-on payment for COVID-19 patients during the emergency period. Provides an outlier payment for inpatient claims for any amount over the traditional Medicare payment to cover excess costs hospitals incur for more expensive COVID-19 patients.

Sec. 208 – Coverage of treatments for COVID–19 at no cost sharing under the Medicare Advantage program. Establishes zero cost-sharing (out-of-pocket costs) for COVID-19 treatment under Medicare Advantage.

Sec. 209 – Establishing a risk corridor program for Medicare Advantage plans during the COVID-19 emergency. Establishes a risk corridor programs to help mitigate potential increased cost of claims experienced by Medicare Advantage plans as a result of the COVID-19 emergency.

Sec. 210 – Requiring coverage under Medicare PDPs and MA-PD plans, without the imposition of cost sharing or utilization management requirements, of drugs intended to treat COVID-19 during certain emergencies. Requires Part D prescription drug plans (PDPs) to include on their formularies any outpatient drug that has been authorized, approved, or licensed to treat COVID-19. In addition, this legislation will make clear that Part D plans may not require any copayments, coinsurance, or out-of-pocket costs for this treatment or use prior authorization, step therapy, or any other utilization management tools before covering this therapy. This provision will be in effect for the duration of the plan year of the public health emergency.

Sec. 211 – Requiring Medicare PDPs and MA–PD plans to allow during the COVID-19 emergency period for fills and refills of covered part D drugs for up to a 3-month supply. Requires Part D PDPs to allow beneficiaries to obtain up to three-month supply of their Part D prescription drugs during the COVID-19 public health emergency. This provision will be in effect for the duration of the COVID-19 public health emergency.

Sec. 212 – Extension of the work geographic index floor under the Medicare program.

Extends the work Geographic Pricing Cost Index (GPCI) 1.0 floor for Medicare physician payments through November 30, 2020.

Sec. 213 – Extension of funding for quality measure endorsement, input, and selection.

Extends funding for quality measure endorsement, input, and selection through November 30, 2020.

Sec. 214 – Extension of funding outreach and assistance for low-income programs. Extends funding for outreach and assistance for low-income programs (State Health Insurance Assistance Programs, Area Agencies on Aging, the National Center for Benefits and Outreach Enrollment, and the Aging and Disability Resource Centers) through November 30, 2020.

TITLE III – PRIVATE INSURANCE

Sec. 301 – Special enrollment period through exchanges; federal exchange outreach and educational activities. Provides for a two-month open enrollment period to allow individuals who are uninsured, for whatever reason, to enroll in coverage. Currently, Americans can only enroll in an ACA plan during open enrollment period, or because of a qualifying life event if they were previously insured. This package would establish a one-time special enrollment for the ACA Marketplace. allowing Americans who are uninsured to get insured in the face of COVID- 19, and, if eligible, have premium tax credits help make premiums affordable

Sec. 302 – Short term limited duration insurance rule prohibition. Prohibits the relevant Secretaries from implementing, enforcing, or in any way give effect to a final rule by the Department of Health and Human Services, the Department of Treasury, and the Department of Labor that expanded short-term, limited-duration health insurance plans.

Sec. 303 – Rapid coverage of preventative services and vaccines for COVID-19. Requires individual and group health plans to cover any preventative vaccine and any drugs to treat COVID-19 at zero cost-sharing within 15 days of receiving an "A" or "B" rating by United States Preventive Services Task Force (USPSTF) or a recommendation from the Advisory Committee on Immunization Practices (ACIP).

Sec. 304 – Coverage of COVID-19 related treatment at no cost sharing. Waives cost-sharing for patients' treatment related to COVID-19 who are enrolled in private insurance coverage. The Federal government is required to reimburse insurers for the forgone cost-sharing.

Sec. 305 – Requiring prescription drug refill notifications during emergencies. Requires group health plans and health insurance issuers offering group or individual health insurance coverage to notify patients if their plan permits advance prescription drug refills pursuant to public health preparedness guidelines or recommendations issued by the Center for Disease

Control and Prevention (CDC) and provide patients with options for receiving an advance drug refill.

Sec. 306 – Improvement of certain notifications provided to qualified beneficiaries by group health plans in the case of qualifying events. Improves the information provided to workers who lose their employer-sponsored coverage so that they are aware of all affordable coverage options, including coverage available under the ACA.

Sec. 307 – Subsidies for COBRA. Provides subsidies to allow workers to maintain their employer-sponsored coverage if they become eligible for COBRA or are subject to a temporary furlough.

Sec. 308 – Risk corridor program. Establishes a two-year risk corridors program to provide payments to individual and small group market plans for extreme losses and help mitigate premium increases for consumers.

Sec. 309 – Coverage of in vitro diagnostic products. Clarifies coverage requirements for in vitro diagnostic tests in compliance with the Food and Drug Administration's (FDA) guidance on diagnostic tests for COVID-19 during a public health emergency.

Sec. 310 – Sense of Congress Regarding Surprise Medical Bills. Sense of Congress that during the COVID-19 pandemic health care providers should refrain from balance billing consumers for out-of-network claims related to COVID-19 testing or treatment, and insurance companies should do their utmost to secure access to in-network treatment for their plan participants.

TITLE IV – PROVISIONS RELATING TO OLDER AMERICANS ACT OF 1965

Sec. 401 – Combating Hunger for Older Americans During Coronavirus Crisis. This provision relaxes the definition of "home-bound" so that individuals who are quarantined/staying home due to COVID-19 can receive home-delivered meals, allows flexibility in nutrition standards to ensure continuity of service, and allows flexibility of funding between home- delivered and congregate meals.

Sec. 402 – Access of the State Long-Term Care Ombudsman to residents of long-term care facilities during the COVID-19 public health emergency in fiscal year 2020. This provision clarifies the authority of the long-term care ombudsmen program authorized under the OAA to maintain contact (in appropriate format) with patients in long-term care facilities throughout the duration of COVID-19.

Sec. 403 – Continuity of service and opportunities for participants in community service activities under Title V of the Older Americans Act of 1965. This provision provides flexibility for administrative costs and allows the Secretary to increase the cap on length of participation in SCESP for older workers whose service is interrupted due to the COVID-19 national emergency.

TITLE V – PUBLIC HEALTH POLICIES

SUBTITLE A – IMPROVING PUBLIC HEALTH AND MEDICAL RESPONSE

Sec. 501 – Reimbursement for additional health services relating to coronavirus. Amends the Families First Coronavirus Response Act to allow the National Disaster Medical System to also reimburse for costs related to COVID-19 treatment expenses.

Sec. 502 – Public health data system transformation. Requires the HHS to expand, enhance, and improve public health data systems used by the CDC. Requires HHS to award grants to State, local, Tribal, or territorial public health departments for the modernization of public health data systems in order to assist public health departments in assessing current data infrastructure capabilities and gaps; to improve secure public health data collection, transmission, exchange, maintenance, and analysis; to enhance the interoperability of public health data systems; to support and train related personnel; to support earlier disease and health condition detection; and to develop and disseminate related information and improved electronic case reporting.

Sec. 503 – Reporting on COVID-19 testing and results. Amends the Families First Coronavirus Response Act to require state and local governments, laboratories, and health systems to provide real-time reporting on testing and results, including positive and negative results, as well as any reporting on cases and severe outcomes resulting from COVID-19. In addition, this section would require entities receiving funds through this division to provide regular and real-time reporting to their respective State Emergency Operations Center on COVID-19 testing and results.

Sec. 504 – CDC COVID response line. Requires CDC to maintain a toll-free telephone number to address public health questions related COVID-19.

Sec. 505 – Awareness campaign. Requires the CDC to award grants for the purposes of increasing evidence-based awareness of COVID-19, availability of diagnostic testing, as well as countering stigma associated with the disease.

Sec. 506 – Additional resources for the Medical Reserve Corps. Increases authorization levels for the Assistant Secretary of Preparedness and Response (ASPR's) Medical Reserve Corps (MRC). The MRC network comprises approximately 175,000 volunteers in roughly 850 community-based units located throughout the United States and its territories. Providing increased resources for the Medical Reserve Corps would enable HHS to expand the MRC network.

Sec. 507 – Flexibility for members of National Health Service Corps providers during emergency period. Currently, National Health Service Corps (NHSC) participants providers must abide by strict hour/location requirements in order to meet the terms of their loan agreements. This section would allow NHSC participants flexibility in their hours and location requirements in order to provide care where and how they are needed during a public health emergency.

Sec. 508 – Ready Reserve Corps. Provides the United States Public Health Corps the authority to stand up the Ready Reserve Corps. These health care providers will provide additional surge capacity to parts of the country in need of additional medical providers due to COVID-19.

Sec. 509 – Nation limiting liability for volunteer health care professionals. Currently, federal and state Good Samaritan laws provide some civil liability protections for volunteer health care providers, but only if they are licensed in the state where the

services are performed. This section
would extend narrow liability protections to medical volunteers who have crossed state lines in order to provide surge services related to COVID-19.

SUBTITLE B – TRIBAL HEALTH

Sec. 521 – Improving State, local, and tribal public health security. Extends eligibility for
the CDC's Public Health Emergency Preparedness (PHEP) program to Tribes.

Sec. 522 – Provision of items to tribal programs and facilities. Guarantees Indian Health Service (IHS) and other Tribal health organizations direct access to the Strategic National Stockpile, just like all fifty other states.

SUBTITLE C – MEDICAL PRODUCT SUPPLY CHAIN IMPROVEMENTS

Sec. 531 – Shortages of Essential Devices. Requires manufacturers of essential medical devices, including personal protective equipment and testing devices, determined by the Secretary to be critical to preventing, screening, diagnosing, treating, or mitigating the spread of a disease, to report to FDA on any permanent discontinuances, interruptions in manufacturing, or other situations or circumstances that are likely to lead to a shortage or meaningful disruption in supply in a public health emergency. Early reporting will allow FDA to work to mitigate shortages more quickly.

Sec. 532 – Authority to Destroy Counterfeit Devices. Extends FDA's administrative destruction authority to medical devices. This would allow FDA to destroy certain imported medical devices in instances where FDA believes such medical devices are adulterated, misbranded, or unapproved and may pose a threat to the public health as they currently do for drugs.

Sec. 533 - Requiring the Strategic National Stockpile to Include Certain Types of Medical Supplies. Requires the Secretary to include personal protective equipment, ancillary medical supplies, and other supplies required for the administration of drugs, vaccines and other biological products, medical devices, and diagnostic tests in the Strategic National Stockpile.

Sec. 534 – Reporting Requirement for Drug Manufacturers. Requires drug manufacturers and active pharmaceutical ingredient (API) manufacturers to report quarterly on the volume of drugs they manufacture, prepare, propagate, compound, or process for commercial distribution prior to being imported or offered for import into the United States. Reports must include the number of dosage units for each finished drug product, or amount of active pharmaceutical ingredient. Also requires all facilities involved with the manufacturing of drugs and API to register.

Sec. 535 – National Centers of Excellence in Continuous Pharmaceutical Manufacturing:
Directs FDA to designate National Centers of Excellence in Continuous Pharmaceutical Manufacturing (NCEs). NCEs will work with FDA and industry to craft a national framework for continuous manufacturing implementation, including supporting additional research and
development of this technology, workforce development, standardization, and collaborating with manufacturers to support adoption of continuous manufacturing.

SUBTITLE D – PUBLIC HEALTH EXTENDERS

Sec. 541 – Extension for Community Health Centers, the National Health Service Corps, and Teaching Health Centers that Operate GME Programs. Extends funding for Community Health Centers, the National Health Service Corps, and

Teaching Centers that Operate GME Programs through November 30, 2020.

Sec. 542 – Diabetes Programs. Extends funding for the Special Diabetes Program and Special Diabetes Program for Indians through November 30, 2020.

SUBTITLE E – OTHER EXTENDERS

Sec. 551 – Extension of Sexual Risk Avoidance Education Program. Extends funding for
Sexual Risk Avoidance Education program through November 30, 2020.

Sec. 552 – Extension of Personal Responsibility Education Program. Extends funding for Personal Responsibility Education program through November 30, 2020.

SUBTITLE F- MISCELLANEOUS

Sec. 561 – Health Provider Loan Program. Establishes a loan program to help eligible health care organizations with anticipated revenue loss or higher operating costs as a result of COVID- 19. Eligible health care organizations include hospitals, critical access hospitals, skilled nursing facilities, physician practices, home health providers, community health centers, ambulatory surgical care center, or hospices that participate in Medicare or Medicaid.

DIVISION H – Emergency Coronavirus Pandemic Unemployment Compensation Act of 2020

Prepared by the Democratic staff of the House Committee on Ways and Means

TITLE I

Section 101. Supplemental Federal Pandemic Unemployment Compensation. The federal government would provide a temporary Federal Pandemic Unemployment Compensation (FPUC) of $600 a week for any worker eligible for state or federal unemployment compensation (UC) benefits. The FPUC would be paid in addition to and at the same time as (but not necessarily in the same check) regular state or federal UC benefits. The FPUC, combined with the underlying state unemployment benefit, would replace 100 percent of wages for the average U.S. worker. The federal supplement would not affect eligibility for other benefits like Medicaid, CHIP, SNAP. State UC programs would be fully reimbursed for the cost of administering the supplement and for the cost of the supplement itself.

Sections 102-105. Expansion of "Work Sharing" Programs to Provide Partial Benefits to Individuals with Reduced Hours. The federal government would temporarily provide full funding for short-time compensation or "work sharing" programs, in which employers voluntarily make an agreement with the state unemployment office to prevent layoffs by reducing employee hours, and workers with reduced hours are eligible for partial state UC benefits. States currently bear the full cost of these arrangements. Workers in these programs would also be eligible for Federal Pandemic Unemployment Compensation in the amount of $300. States would receive $100 million for work sharing program promotion and enrollment of employers, and for implementation or improved administration.

Section 106. 13 Week Emergency Benefit Extension in All States. All states would be eligible to provide an additional 13 weeks of unemployment benefits to workers who need beyond what is provided for in state and federal law. In states that had triggered Extended Benefits due to high and rising unemployment, up to 59 weeks of benefits would be available. In states that had not, 39 weeks would be available.

TITLE II

Section 201. Unemployment Compensation for Self-Employed Workers. Self-employed individuals who are unable to work due to the COVID-19 emergency would be eligible for a federal unemployment compensation payment equal to one-quarter of the state's average weekly benefit amount plus the Federal Pandemic Unemployment Compensation ($600), or a total of about $675 a week, on average. Individuals would apply for the benefit at the state UC office, and states would be fully reimbursed for the cost of benefits and administration. Self-employed workers are not covered by regular state unemployment compensation.

Unemployment Compensation for Individuals Who Had Been About to Start Work.

Individuals who had a contract for work canceled due to a COVID-19 work site shutdown would be eligible for a federal unemployment compensation benefit equal to one-quarter of the state's average weekly benefit amount plus the Federal Pandemic Unemployment Compensation ($600), or about $675 a week, on average, for the number of weeks that the contracted job was scheduled to last. Individuals would apply for the benefit at the state UC office, and states would be fully reimbursed for the cost of benefits and administration.

Unemployment Compensation for Job Entrants. Individuals who are available for work, but for the limitations of the pandemic, and do not have enough recent work experience to qualify for state unemployment compensation (recent college graduate and individuals whose recent work does not meet state minimum earnings requirements, for example) would receive a federal payment of $300 a week, administered by state unemployment offices. Individuals would apply for the benefit at the state UC office, and states would be fully reimbursed for the cost of benefits and administration.

TITLE III

Section 301. Unemployment Compensation Support for Nonprofit Organizations and State,

Tribal, and Local Governments. Most nonprofits, Indian Tribes, and governmental entities do 30

not pay per-worker unemployment taxes and instead have "reimbursable arrangements" with state unemployment programs, which require them to reimburse the state for 100 percent of the cost of unemployment compensation paid to their furloughed or laid off workers. During the period of the national emergency, the federal government would pay 50 percent of the reimbursement for those workers so that their employers could follow public health recommendations. Workers at these organizations are also eligible for the Federal Pandemic Unemployment Compensation supplement ($600 a week).

TITLE IV

Waives 7-Day Waiting Period for Railroad Worker Unemployment and Sickness Benefits.

This provision would parallel the provision from the Family First Coronavirus Response Act by waiving the waiting week for unemployment and sickness benefits under the Railroad Unemployment Insurance Act.

Enhanced Unemployment Compensation Under the Railroad Unemployment Insurance Act. For railroad workers receiving unemployment benefits under the Railroad Unemployment Insurance Act, this provision would provide a temporary recovery benefit of $1,200 every two weeks (per registration period) in addition to their regular benefits. This recovery benefit supplemental would not affect eligibility for other benefits like Medicaid, CHIP, and SNAP.

13-Week Railroad Unemployment Benefit Extension. This provision would provide an additional 13 weeks of unemployment benefits to railroad workers who are receiving regular unemployment benefits during the current benefit year.

Eliminating the Sequester for Railroad Unemployment and Sickness Benefits. This provision would eliminate the Balanced Budget and Emergency Deficit Control Act sequester that automatically cuts unemployment and sickness benefits provided to railroad workers under the Railroad Unemployment Insurance Act. This change would allow railroad workers to receive the full benefit amounts to which they are entitled and would create parity with the treatment of other unemployment insurance benefit programs.

DIVISION I – Financial Services

Prepared by the Democratic staff of the House Committee on Financial Services Title I: Protect Consumers, Renters, Homeowners, and People Experiencing Homelessness

- **Sec. 101. Suspension of requirements regarding tenant contributions.** This section suspends rental payments for households receiving federal rental assistance through HUD or USDA and authorizes such sums as may be necessary to ensure that all housing providers do not experience a loss of rental income as a result of this policy. The suspension applies until six months after the date on which the Federal Emergency Management Agency terminates the emergency declaration made by President Trump on March 13, 2020.
- **Sec. 102. Temporary moratorium on eviction filings.** This section places a temporary nationwide ban on landlords from filing evictions on renters, except in some limited circumstances. The ban applies until six months after the date on which the Federal Emergency Management Agency terminates the emergency declaration made by President Trump on March 13, 2020.
- **Sec. 103. Suspension of other consumer loan payments.** This provision suspends changes to consumer agreements or legal actions for nonpayments on consumer loans during the crisis and prohibits creditors and third party debt collectors from charging late fees, higher interest, or pursuing consumers who fall delinquent on all non-mortgage related loans, while allowing for consumers to keep making payments during the crisis.
- **Sec. 104. Emergency rental assistance.** This section authorizes $100 billion to help non- assisted renters who meet certain economic conditions cover their rent and utility payments.
- **Sec. 105. Emergency homeless assistance.** This section authorizes $15.5 billion in emergency homeless assistance to enable state and local governments to finance housing and health related services for the hundreds of thousands of people currently experiencing homelessness.
- **Sec. 106. Participation of Indian Tribes and tribally designated housing entities in Continuum of Care Program.** This section enables tribes and tribally designated housing entities to receive McKinney-Vento Homeless Assistance Grant funding.
- **Sec. 107. Housing Assistance Fund.** This section authorizes a $35 billion fund that would be allocated to states, territories, and D.C. by the Treasury Secretary to help homeowners with mortgage and utility payments, including principal reduction.
- **Sec. 108. Mortgage forbearance.** This provision prohibits foreclosures and repossessions for the duration of the pandemic and 180 days thereafter, and requires mortgage forbearance for homeowners for up to year, including a prohibition on fees

or additional interest during the term of the forbearance, as well as loan repayment options at the end of the forbearance. This section also requires mortgage forbearance for multifamily rental property owners who comply with requirements to halt evictions and late fees for the duration of the forbearance, and creates a Federal Reserve credit facility for mortgage servicers to ensure continued liquidity during the pandemic in light of the required forbearance. Finally, this section extends the "GSE patch" for an additional year until January 1, 2022.

• **Sec. 109. Bankruptcy protections.** This section establishes a $100,000 floor for the homestead exemption for all debtors, and prevents tens of thousands of current Chapter 13 cases from failing because debtors have lost income during the crisis by providing that the debtor may request that the court grant a discharge of all dischargeable debts provided for in the plan under certain conditions and by permitting debtors to extend the term of their plans in order to have additional time to pay critical debts.

• **Sec. 110. Debt collection.** This provision prohibits debt collectors from taking any adverse action on consumers, small businesses, or non-profits during the pandemic period, and for the following 120 days. Debt collectors are prohibited from suing, reporting to a credit reporting agency, or taking any other adverse legal action against consumers, small businesses, or non-profits during the covered period, including on deficiency judgments or confessions of judgment.

• **Sec. 111. Disaster Protection for Workers' Credit.** This section suspends most negative consumer credit reporting during the COVID-19 pandemic and other declared major disasters plus 120 days. Consumers with continued hardship after the 120 day post-pandemic or major disaster period may apply for additional time. Credit score furnishers are also prohibited from creating and/or implementing new credit scoring models that would lower existing consumer credit scores during the COVID-19 pandemic or during other major disaster periods. This section also permanently prohibits reporting consumer medical debt arising from the cost of treatment for COVID-19 or medical expenses arising out of other declared major disasters.

• **Sec. 112. Student loans.** This provision provides immediate relief to private student loan borrowers by having the Department of Treasury make private student loan payments on behalf of the borrower during the pandemic period, and six months thereafter, with up to $10,000 in relief, with the borrower staying current for credit reporting purposes, and any remaining portion of the unused $10,000 going to the private student loan borrower upon resumption of borrower payments.

• **Sec. 113. Waiver of in-person appraisal requirements.** This section authorizes the use of alternative appraisal methods to avoid in-person contact, and requires rulemaking by FHA and FHFA to provide further flexibility in mortgage processing requirements to avoid in-person interactions.

• **Sec. 114. Supplemental funding for community development block grants.** This section provides $15 billion for Community Development Block Grants to allow state and local governments to have a flexible resource to address the needs of their communities when mitigating the impacts of COVID-19, including establishing teams to perform mobile testing of vulnerable populations, such as people experiencing homelessness.

• **Sec. 115. COVID-19 Emergency Housing Relief.** This section suspends work and community service requirements in federal housing programs to ensure that residents do not feel compelled to leave their homes to comply, and provides additional flexibilities to housing providers to respond to the coronavirus pandemic.

- **Sec. 116. Supplemental funding for service coordinators to assist elderly households.** This section provides $300 million for servicer coordinators to assist elderly households living in HUD-assisted housing during the coronavirus pandemic.
- **Sec. 117. Fair housing.** This section authorizes $300 million to ensure individuals are protected from housing-related hate crimes and increasing forms of housing discrimination from Coronavirus-motivated bias through adequate and accessible housing discrimination complaint intake, investigations, and public education of housing rights, as well as robust enforcement of the Fair Housing Act.
- **Sec. 118. HUD counseling program authorization.** This section authorizes $700 million for HUD's housing counseling program to respond to an expected increase in demand for such services as homeowners struggle to make their mortgage payments on time.
- Sec. **119. Defense Production Act of 1950.** This section authorizes $3 billion for activities under Title I and Title III of the Defense Production Act. This provision also allows funds that remain at the end of the current fiscal year to carry over into fiscal year 2021 and provides for quarterly reports on how the funds are spent.

Title II. Provide Assistance to Small Businesses and Community Financial Institutions

- **Sec. 201. Small Business Credit Facility.** This provision directs the Federal Reserve to establish a lending facility for small businesses to provide direct loans to small businesses, including independent contractors and small farms. In addition, another facility
- **Sec. 202. Small Business Financial Assistance Program.** This provision directs the Department of Treasury to establish a $50 billion lending program for small businesses. The program also provides for zero interest loans to small businesses that could be forgiven later as determined by the Secretary of Treasury.
- **Sec. 203. Loan and Payment Relief for Affected Small Businesses and Non-Profits.** This provision supports small businesses that are struggling with the decision to stay open in the face of significant declines in consumer demand and with paying their bills.
- **Sec. 204. Reauthorization of the State Small Business Credit Initiative Act of 2010.** This provision reauthorizes the state small business credit initiative and authorize $10 billion to promote recovery post-pandemic. This program was initially created in 2010 to support small businesses in the wake of the 2008 recession and provides states with grants to finance new and existing small business growth.
- **Sec. 205. Funding of the Initiative to Build Growth Equity Funds for Minority Businesses.** This section authorizes $3 billion in grants through the Minority Business Development Agency.
- **Sec. 206. Community Development Financial Institutions Fund Supplemental Appropriation Authorization.** This section authorizes the CDFI Fund an additional $1 billion in funding for fiscal year 2020.
- **Sec. 207. Minority Depository Institutions.** This section provides additional support to Minority Depository Institutions (MDIs) and Community Development Financial Institutions (CDFIs).
- **Sec. 208. Loans to MDIs and CDFIs.** This section requires the Federal Reserve to issue zero percent loans to certain MDIs and CDFIs during the Pandemic period.

Post- pandemic, the Federal Reserve is required to provide reasonable loan terms to financial institutions under its discount window lending program.
- **Sec. 209 Insurance of Transaction Accounts.** This provision reauthorizes the Transaction Account Program at the FDIC and NCUA to provide support to community banks and credit unions.

Title III. Support to State and Local Governments
- **Sec. 301. Support State and Local Government Financing.** This provision authorizes the Federal Reserve to purchase state and local bonds, and mandate the establishment of a facility to support the market for state and local borrowing intended to fight the Coronavirus outbreak. The Federal Reserve also is required to purchase a sufficient quantity of such bonds that the issuing cost of bonds would be held to a minimum level equivalent to the federal funds rate, providing secure funding and low issuing costs for state and municipal bonds, which have faced unprecedented disruption in recent weeks and are expected to face severe distress in the coming months.
- **Sec. 302. Waive Matching Requirements for State, Territory and Local Governments to use Federal funds.** This provision allows federal financial regulators to temporarily waive requirements that a state, territory or local government provide matching or cost-sharing funds on existing federal grants and extends the waiver authority to subgrantees for before receiving a new federal grant or supplemental funds. It also allows for states, territories, or localities to request to reprogramming authority for awarded grant funds to direct them towards unemployment, childcare, and healthcare needs resulting from the COVID-19 emergency.

Title IV. Protect Financial Stability and Transparent Markets
- **Sec. 401. Temporary halt to rulemakings unrelated to COVID-19.** This provision temporarily prohibits federal financial regulators from adopting rules not directly related to responding to the coronavirus response through the length of the crisis.
- **Sec. 402. Temporary ban on stock buybacks.** This provision imposes a temporary ban on stock buybacks for all companies throughout the length of the coronavirus crisis.
- **Sec. 403. Disclosures related to supply chain disruption risk.** This provision requires public companies to disclose in their annual reports risks to the disruption of their supply chains, including the risks disruptions would have on the workforce, and to develop and disclose supply chain disruption contingency plans.
- **Sec. 404. Disclosures related to global pandemic risk.** This provision requires public companies to disclose their risks and exposures to public health crises that the World Health Organization classifies as "pandemics," including the expected impacts on covered companies' workforces and the steps they are taking to mitigate these risks.
- **Sec. 405. Oversight of Federal aid related to COVID-19.** This provision establishes a COVID-19 Aid Congressional Oversight Panel and authorizes the Special Inspector General to coordinate audits and investigations in connection with federal aid provided to corporations related to COVID-19. They are required to collect and report on diversity data from those recipients of federal aid.
- **Sec. 406. International Financial Institutions.** This provision: authorizes U.S. participation in the 19th replenishment of the World Bank's International Development Association (IDA-19), to which the U.S. has pledged $3 billion; authorizes U.S. participation in the 15th replenishment of the African Development Fund (AfDF-15), to which the U.S. has pledged $514 million; and authorizes U.S. participation in the

7th general capital increase for the African Development Bank, to which the U.S. has pledged approximately $437 million of paid-in capital.

- **Sec. 407. Conditions on federal aid to corporations.** This provision imposes conditions on beneficiaries of government assistance in connection with COVID-19 including: requiring all companies receiving federal aid to maintain workforce levels, worker pay, and all collective bargaining agreements, and provide at minimum 14 days of paid leave throughout the duration of the crisis. Additionally, this provision imposes a ban on all stock buybacks, executive bonuses, golden parachutes, and federal lobbying until all federal aid in connection to COVID-19 is repaid to the federal government. The section requires all accelerated filers receiving federal aid to permanently require worker representation on their corporate boards, and to annually disclose information related to human capital management, political spending, and country-by-country tax reporting, and how federal aid funds are being used to help its workers. Lastly, the provision requires all companies receiving federal aid in connection with COVID-19 to guarantee a $15 minimum wage to all its workers by January 1, 2021 and permanently limits executive compensation to a 50:1 ratio to median worker pay.
- **Sec. 408. Authority for warrants and debt instruments.** This provision conditions the granting of aid related to COVID-19 on purchasing senior preferred voting stock, warrants for common stock, and senior debt instruments in companies receiving federal aid related to COVID-19. The bill also prohibits the federal government from purchasing or guaranteeing assets from foreign corporations.
- **Sec. 409. Authorization to Participate in the New Arrangements to Borrow of the International Monetary Fund.** This provision authorizes the Secretary of the Treasury to extend and increase U.S. participation in the International Monetary Fund's (IMF) emergency backstop facility, known as the New Arrangements to Borrow, to bolster the IMF's ability to respond to the global economic effects of the pandemic.
- **Sec. 410. International Finance Corporation.** This provision authorizes the Secretary of the Treasury to vote in favor of resolutions to increase the capital stock of the International Finance Corporation (IFC), the World Bank's private sector arm, and to vote in favor of an amendment to the IFC's Articles of Agreement to preserve the U.S. veto over future capital increases of the IFC.
- **Sec. 411. Oversight and Reports.** This provision authorizes the Special Inspector General for the Troubled Asset Relief Program and the Congressional COVID-19 Aid Oversight Panel to oversee financial assistance provided in Division Y. In addition the Treasury and GAO are required to produce certain reports to Congress, including collecting and reporting on diversity data from recipients of federal aid.

Title. V. Pandemic Planning and Guidance for Consumers and Regulators

- **Section 501: Financial Literacy Education Commission Emergency Response.** This section provides financial literacy education, including information on access to banking services and other financial products, for individuals seeking information and resources as they recover from any financial distress caused by the coronavirus disease (COVID- 19) outbreak and future major disasters.
- **Section 502: Interagency Guidance for Consumers.** This section requires financial regulatory agencies to issue interagency regulatory guidance on preparedness, flexibility, and relief options for consumers in pandemics and major disasters.

• **Sec. 503. SEC Pandemic Guidance for Investors.** This section requires the Securities and Exchange Commission to issue regulatory guidance on preparedness, flexibility, relief, and investor protection during pandemics and major disasters, including all relevant disclosures. This section requires the SEC to engage in testing with regulated entities on their effectiveness in responding to potential pandemics or major disasters and requires the SEC to issue a report including the results of such testing along with any legislative recommendations the SEC may have related to pandemic preparedness.

• **Sec. 504. National Strategy.** This provision updates the national strategy of the United States on pandemics and the National Planning Frameworks to require that preparedness and recovery planning include a pre-crisis menu of options focused on economic, monetary, and consumer financial issues.

DIVISION J – Education Relief and Other Programs

Prepared by the Democratic staff of the House Committee on Education and Labor

Title I – EDUCATION PROVISIONS Sec. 100101. Short title; table of contents.

This section provides the short title "COVID-19 Pandemic Education Relief Act of 2020".

Sec. 100102. Definitions.

This section provides for various definitions including terms such as "coronavirus" and a "qualifying emergency". A qualifying emergency means a public health emergency related to coronavirus as declared by the Secretary of Health and Human Services, an event related to coronavirus for which the President has declared a major disaster or an emergency under the Stafford Disaster Relief and Emergency Assistance Act, or a national emergency related to coronavirus as declared by the President.

Sec. 100103. Campus-Based Aid Waivers.

This section requires the Secretary of Education to waive the match requirement for institutions of higher education (IHEs) under the campus-based aid programs, including the Supplemental Educational Opportunity Grants (SEOG) and the Federal-Work Study (FWS) program for award years 2019-2020 and 2020-2021. Private, for-profit businesses participating in FWS must still provide a funding match. This section also allows an IHE participating in SEOG and FWS to transfer up to 100 percent of an IHE's unexpended funds under FWS to SEOG during a qualifying emergency. Unallocated funds are not permitted to transfer from SEOG to FWS.

Sec. 100104. Use of Supplemental Educational Opportunity Grants for Emergency Aid.

This section allows an IHE to use any amount of their allocation under SEOG to provide emergency financial aid grants to assist undergraduates or graduate students for unexpected expenses and unmet financial need during a qualifying emergency. In order to determine the amount of need, an IHE may waive the amount of need calculation as required under the *Higher Education Act of 1965* (HEA), allow for a student to receive a grant that is not more than the maximum Federal Pell Grant for the applicable award year (i.e., $6,195 for award year 2019- 2020; $6,345 for award year 2020-2021), and may work with a scholarship-granting organization to accept applications and disperse funds as long as such organization disperses the full amount of the grant provided by the IHE to recipients. Such aid will not be treated as other financial assistance for the purposes of the need calculation under the HEA.

Sec. 100105. Federal Work-Study During a Qualifying Emergency.

This section allows an IHE to continue to make FWS payments to affected work-study students for a time period not to exceed one academic year during which an affected student was unable to fulfill their work-study obligation for all or part of such academic year during a qualifying emergency. IHEs may make payments to affected students equal to or less than the amount of wages the student would have otherwise received, and such aid may be provided as a one-time grant or in multiple payments. Payments cannot be made to students who were not eligible for FWS or who were not completing their work requirements prior to the qualifying emergency. Such payments must meet the match requirements under FWS, unless such requirement has been waived by the Secretary of Education.

An affected student is a student who is enrolled at a FWS-participating IHE, received a work- study award during the academic year in which the qualifying emergency occurred, and was prevented from fulfilling their work obligations due to such emergency.

Sec. 100106. Adjustment of Subsidized Loan Usage Limits.

This section requires the Secretary of Education to exclude any semester that a student is unable to complete as a result of a qualifying emergency from the student's subsidized loan usage limits.

Sec. 100107. Exclusion from Federal Pell Grant Duration Limit.

This section requires Secretary of Education to exclude any semester that a student is unable to complete as a result of a qualifying emergency from the student's lifetime Pell Grant eligibility limit.

Sec. 100108. Institutional Refunds and Federal Loan Flexibility.

This section requires the Secretary of Education to waive Return of Title IV requirements for IHEs if a student withdraws in the middle of a term as a result of a qualifying emergency. A similar waiver is provided for students. The Secretary of Education is further required to cancel the obligation to repay any direct loans taken out for that term. Each IHE receiving a waiver under this section is required to report to the Secretary of Education on the number of students covered by such waivers, the amount of grant or loan assistance associated with each such student, and the total amount of funds that the IHE does not return.

This section specifies that, in the case of a qualifying emergency, an IHE may provide a student with an approved leave of absence instead of requiring the student to return to the same point in their academic program where they left off, which means the IHE can accelerate the student upon the student's return.

Sec. 100109. Satisfactory Academic Progress.

This section specifies that an IHE may exclude attempted credits that were not completed due to a qualifying emergency from Satisfactory Academic Progress calculations.

Sec. 100110. Continuing Education at Affected Foreign Institutions.

This section allows the Secretary of Education to permit foreign IHEs participating in the direct loan program to provide any part of an otherwise eligible program via distance education for the duration of an emergency or disaster as declared by the applicable government and the following payment period. An otherwise eligible program that is offered via distance education by a foreign IHE between March 1, 2020 and date of enactment is deemed eligible for the purposes of participating in the Direct Loan program for the duration of such emergency and the following payment period.

This section further allows the Secretary of Education to permit foreign IHEs to enter into agreements (written arrangements) with public and private, non-profit

IHEs located in the United States (U.S.) to allow a student at such foreign IHE to take courses with an institution in the U.S. Proprietary graduate medical, nursing, or veterinary foreign IHEs may enter into agreements with public; private, non-profit; and proprietary U.S.-based IHEs for the duration of such emergency or disaster and the following payment period. Institutions that utilize either of these provisions must inform the Secretary of Education of such use by June 30, 2020 for 2019-2020 and not later than 30 days after such use for the following award years.

The Secretary of Education must submit a report to the authorizing committees that identifies each foreign institution that utilizes such provisions not later than 180 days after the date of enactment and every 180 days thereafter for the duration of such emergency or disaster and the following payment period.

Sec. 100111. HBCU Capital Financing.

This section authorizes the Secretary of Education to defer payments for Historically Black Colleges and Universities (HBCUs) receiving a loan under the HBCU Capital Financing program during a qualifying emergency. During the deferment, the Secretary of Education will make principal and interest payments that are due under the loan agreement and the institution will not be required to pay any periodic installments. The institution will be required to repay the Secretary of Education for the payments made on its behalf after the loan has been paid in full, except that the institution will have at least one full fiscal year after the end of the emergency before the institution must begin to repay the Secretary of Education. The authority to grant a new loan deferment under this section expires at the end of the qualifying emergency. However, any modification made to a loan or insurance agreement under this section will last for the duration of the period covered by the loan or insurance agreement. The Secretary of Education must submit a report to the authorizing committees every six months identifying each institution that received a deferment.

Sec. 100112. Waiver Authority and Reporting Requirement for Institutional Aid.

This section authorizes the Secretary of Education to waive certain requirements for institutions receiving assistance under the title III (i.e., Strengthening Institutions Program (SIP) and programs for minority-serving institutions such as Historically Black Colleges and Universities (HBCUs) and Tribally Controlled Colleges and Universities (TCCUs)) and title V (i.e., Hispanic-Serving Institutions (HSIs)) during a qualifying emergency. Waivers will apply from the beginning of the emergency through September 30 of the fiscal year following the end of the emergency. The Secretary of Education is authorized to waive the following:

- Certain eligibility data requirements for programs under title III and title V of the HEA;
- Wait-out periods for programs under title III of the HEA;
- Allotment requirements and references to prior year data for HBCUs and predominantly
black institutions (PBIs);
- Funding allocation rules and references to prior year data for masters, professional, and
graduate programs at HBCUs; and
- Restrictions on the use of allotments for construction and maintenance for PBIs and HBCUs.

This section authorizes the Secretary of Education to waive any statutory or regulatory provision to ensure that formula calculations do not adversely affect institutions receiving assistance under the aforementioned programs at the time of the qualifying emergency. This provision applies to formula calculations for fiscal year 2020 and for the period from the beginning of the emergency through September 30 of the fiscal year following the end of the emergency.

This section authorizes institutions to carry over unexpended funds received under title III, title V, and subpart 4 of Part A of title VII (i.e., masters programs for HBCUs and PBIs). Institutions may carry over funds that were not expended during the first five years of a grant into the succeeding five-year period.

The Secretary of Education must submit a report to Congress every six months identifying each grant recipient that receives a modification under this section.

Sec. 100113. Authorized Uses and Other Modifications for Grants.

This section authorizes the Secretary of Education to modify the required and allowable uses of funds for grants awarded under the following programs: SIP, TRIO programs, GEAR UP, and programs for HBCUs, TCCUs, HSIs, and other MSIs. Modifications will be made at the request of grant recipients as a result of a qualifying emergency and will apply from the beginning of the emergency through September 30 of the fiscal year following the end of the emergency.

This section authorizes the Secretary of Education to modify any federal share or other financial matching requirement for any grant awarded on a competitive basis, as well as non-competitive grants awarded to HBCUs, TCCUs, and PBIs.

Modifications will be made at the request of grant recipients as a result of a qualifying emergency and will apply from the beginning of the emergency through September 30 of the fiscal year following the end of the emergency. The Secretary of Education must submit a report to Congress every six months identifying each grant recipient that receives a modification.

Sec. 100114. Service Obligations for Teachers.

This section allows the Secretary of Education to modify the categories of extenuating circumstances for which a TEACH grant recipient who is unable to fulfill all or part of their service obligation is excused from fulfilling that portion of service. Further, this section requires the Secretary of Education to consider teaching service that is part-time or temporarily interrupted during a qualifying emergency to be full-time for the purposes of the TEACH grant service obligations. The Secretary of Education is also required to waive the requirement that teaching service must be consecutive under the Teacher Loan Forgiveness program if that teaching service is temporarily interrupted due to a qualifying emergency and the borrower resumes such service to complete their five-year obligation after the qualifying emergency.

Sec. 100115. Payments for Student Loan Borrowers as a Result of a National Emergency.

This section amends the *Higher Education Act of 1965* (HEA) by adding two sections to Part G of Title IV.

Sec. 493E. Payments for Student Loan Borrowers During a National Emergency.

This section requires the Secretary of Education, upon the enactment of this Act, to make payments on behalf of FFEL, Perkins and direct loans borrowers for each month during the national emergency period. Payments made by the Secretary of Education will be equal to the total amount due on each borrower's loans for that month based on the payment plan selected by the borrower. A national emergency is defined a public health emergency related to coronavirus as declared by the Secretary of Health and Human Services or a national emergency related to coronavirus as declared by the President.

Interest due on loans during the national emergency will not capitalize at any time during the emergency. Payments made by the Secretary of Education will be considered as qualifying payments toward Public Service Loan Forgiveness and forgiveness under income-driven repayment plans, and as on-time payments for the purposes of rehabilitating defaulted loans. The Secretary of Education will ensure that consumer reporting agencies treat loans during this period as if the borrowers were making regularly scheduled payments themselves.

The Secretary of Education shall provide a notice to all borrowers on a monthly basis, starting within 15 days of the enactment of this Act, informing borrowers of the actions taken under this section, providing borrowers with a method to opt-out, and notifying the borrower that benefits under this section are temporary and will end after the national emergency ends. All involuntary collection activity will be halted between the date of enactment of this Act and the end of the national emergency.

After the conclusion of the national emergency, the Secretary of Education shall provide a 90- day transition period during which borrowers will receive at least 3 notices indicating when their payment obligations will resume. Missed payments during this transition period will not result in fees or penalties or be reported to the consumer reporting agency or otherwise impact the borrower's credit history.

This section directs lenders and guaranty agencies that hold FFEL loans to verify borrower-level payment amounts to facilitate the implementation of this section and authorizes the Secretary of Education to establish a payment schedule for loans not held by the Secretary of Education. This section allows the Secretary of Education to waive the requirements of the *Paperwork Reduction Act*, the master calendar and negotiated rulemaking requirements under the HEA, and the notice and comment requirements under the *Privacy Act of 1974*, except that notices under the *Privacy Act* shall be published within six months of enactment of this Act.

This section authorizes and appropriates $50,000,000 for fiscal year 2020 for costs associated with implementation and coordination of this section and such sums as may be necessary to provide the payments and interest cancellation provided under this section. Amounts made available under this section shall be in addition to any other available funding and shall remain available until expended.

Sec. 493F. Minimum Relief for Student Loan Borrowers as a Result of a National Emergency.

This section ensures that every borrower receives at least $10,000 in benefits from Section 493E, except in cases where the borrower's remaining outstanding balance at the end of the national emergency is less than $10,000, in which case the borrower's remaining debt is paid off. This section requires the Secretary, within 90 days of the end of the national emergency, to reduce each borrower's balance by an amount that is equal to the lesser of (1) $10,000 minus the benefits received through section 493E(b) of the HEA, as added by this section and (2) the borrower's remaining outstanding balance. Holders of FFEL loans are required to provide information to the Secretary of Education necessary to calculate benefits under this section.

Sec. 100116. Rule of Construction.

This section states that, unless provided in the Act, nothing in this Act can be construed to provide additional authority to the Secretary of Education to waive any provision of ESEA, the Individuals with Disabilities Education Act, the HEA, and Perkins CTE.

Title II – Other Programs

Sec. 100201. Provisions Related to the Corporation for National and Community Service.

This section allows current AmeriCorps volunteers to receive their Segal AmeriCorps Education Award if their service year is disrupted or suspended due to the COVID-19 national emergency; provides flexibility for the Corporation for National and Community Service to carry over funding from the current fiscal year; ensures grantees offering AmeriCorps service opportunities through fixed price grants do not have to return funds to CNCS if their volunteers fail to have the number of volunteers or service hours completed during the service year due to the COVID-19 national emergency; and allows volunteers in the National Civilian Community Corps to re-enroll for an additional year of service if their service is disrupted, and allows CNCS to increase the age limits of NCCC to 26 for individuals who are reenrolling.

DIVISION K – Agriculture Provisions

Prepared by the Democratic staff of the House Committee on Agriculture

Title I – Commodity Support and Other Agriculture Programs

Sec. 110101. Supplemental Dairy Margin Coverage.

This section provides necessary cash flow assistance to small and mid-sized dairies that have grown over the last seven years by establishing supplemental margin coverage based on the difference between 2019 actual production and Dairy Margin Coverage (DMC) production history. This supplemental coverage works in the same manner as farm bill DMC.

Section 110102. Targeted Purchases.

This section supports providing healthy food to families in need by directing the purchase and donation of food originally destined for the food service industry to food assistance programs, including The Emergency Food Assistance Program. This $300 million targeted purchase initiative supports perishable products within the supply chain that otherwise have no clear market.

Title II – Supplemental Nutrition Assistance Program

Sec. 110201. SNAP Funding.

This section ensures sufficient funds for SNAP to meet potential need during this public health emergency.

Sec. 110202. SNAP Allotments.

This section provides for a 15% increase in the maximum SNAP allotment for individuals and households enrolled in SNAP. It also increases the minimum SNAP benefit from $18 to $30. The section also provides additional funding for States to administer SNAP for the current and next fiscal year, so States are better able to meet the expected increased need for SNAP. This section provides flexibilities for State agencies on quality control monitoring through September 30, 2021.

Sec. 110203. SNAP Rules.

This section prevents USDA from finalizing or implementing three rules that would reduce SNAP benefits and access. Those three rules are requirements for able bodied adults without dependents, revision of categorical eligibility, and standardization of state heating and cooling standard utility allowances.

Sec. 110204. SNAP Hot Food Purchases.

This section provides a waiver so individuals and households with SNAP may purchase hot foods during this public health emergency.

Sec. 110205. Food Distribution Program on Indian Reservations.

This section waives the matching requirement for the additional funds provided to the Food Distribution Program on Indian Reservations, to reduce barriers to accessing the funds in a timely manner.

DIVISION L – Access Act

Prepared by the Democratic staff of the Committee on House Administration

Sec. 120001. Short Title.

The "American Coronavirus/COVID-19 Election Safety and Security Act" or the "ACCESS Act".

Sec. 120002. Requirements for Federal Election Contingency Plans in Response to Natural Disasters and Emergencies.

• Requires states and jurisdictions to establish and make publicly available contingency plans that enable voting in federal elections during a state of emergency, public health emergency or national emergency and to update such plans at least every 5 years.

• Requires contingency plans to include initiatives to provide equipment and resources necessary to protect the health and safety of poll workers and voters and to recruit poll workers from resilient and unaffected populations.

• Permits the Attorney General to bring a civil action in an appropriate United States District Court as may be necessary to carry out the requirements of this section and permits a private right of action.

Sec. 120003. Early Voting and Voting By Mail.

• Requires at least 15 consecutive days of early voting for federal elections. Goes into effect in the November 2020 election and for each succeeding federal election.

• Requires the early voting period to be no less than 10 hours each day, to have uniform hours for each day, and to allow for voting prior to 9:00am and after 5:00pm.

• Requires polling places with early voting periods to be located within walking distance of a stop on a public transportation route and to be available in rural areas of states.

• Directs the Election Assistance Commission to issue election administration standards for early voting that include standards for nondiscriminatory geographic placement of polling places and that permit deviation (provided there is adequate public notice) in the case of unforeseen circumstances.

• Requires states to begin processing and scanning ballots cast during the early voting period at least 14 days prior to election day.

• Ensures that every voter can access no-excuse absentee vote-by-mail, postage prepaid and with a self-sealing envelope. Goes into effect in the November 2020 election and for each succeeding federal election.

• Prohibits states from imposing additional conditions or requirements on the eligibility of a voter to cast an absentee ballot such as notarization or witness signatures, and prohibits requiring identification to obtain an absentee ballot.

• Requires states to conduct signature verification of voters submitting an absentee ballot with due process protections. Requires election officials to provide voter with notice and an opportunity to cure if there is a discrepancy in signatures or a missing signature, and to submit to Congress no later than 120 days after each federal election cycle a report containing information on invalidated ballots.

• Ensures that every voter can submit an online request for an absentee ballot.

•Requires states to deliver an absentee ballot and related voting materials if a voter's request for such materials is received prior to 5 days before election day.

• With respect to the COVID-19 pandemic and all future emergencies declared between 120 days before election day and 30 days before election day, requires states to automatically mail absentee ballots and balloting materials to all registered voters no later than two weeks before election day. Requires a voter to sign an affirmation that the voter has not and will not cast another ballot.

- Provides standards for ballots cast by mail.
- Ensures that absentee ballots and related voting materials are accessible to voters with disabilities.
- Ensures the providing of pre-paid postage for all absentee ballots and self-sealing return envelopes.
- Requires that submitted absentee ballots be accepted and processed if postmarked on or before election day.
- Permits voters to return absentee ballots by casting it at a polling place on election day, by submitting it at a designated ballot drop-off location, or by designating another person to return the ballot to the post office, a ballot drop-off location, a tribally designated building or an election office.
- Requires states to begin processing and scanning ballots cast by mail at least 14 days prior to election day.
- Requires states to establish an absentee ballot tracking program. Goes into effect in the November 2020 election and for each succeeding federal election.
- Ensures that provisional ballots from eligible voters at incorrect polling places be counted and requires states to establish uniform and nondiscriminatory standards for issuing, handling and counting provisional ballots. Goes into effect in the November 2020 election and for each succeeding federal election.
- Provides voters with a private right of action for violations of requirements under Subtitle C of Title III under the Help America Vote Act of 2002.

Sec. 120004. Postage-Free Absentee Ballots.

- Ensures that absentee ballots in federal elections are transmitted to voters expeditiously and with prepaid postage.

Sec. 120005. Requiring Transmission of Blank Absentee Ballots Under UOCAVA To Certain Voters.

- Amends the Uniformed and Overseas Citizens Absentee Voting Act (UOCAVA) to require states to transmit blank absentee ballots by mail and electronically to qualified individuals. Goes into effect in the November 2020 election and for each succeeding federal election.
- Defines qualified individuals as voters who have requested an absentee ballot but have not received it at least 2 days before election day, voters who reside in an area where an emergency has been declared within 5 days of election day and have not already requested an absentee ballot, voters who will be absent on election day due to professional or volunteer service, voters who are hospitalized or expect to be on election day, or voters who have a disability and reside in a state that does not offer secure remote ballot marking.
- Requires blank absentee ballots transmitted to qualified voters to comply with the language requirements under section 203 of the Voting Rights Act of 1965 and the disability requirements under section 508 of the Rehabilitation Act of 1973.
- Requires qualified individuals to provide the state with an affirmation in electronic form that they are qualified, that they have not and will not cast another ballot and that they acknowledge the consequences of stating a material misstatement of fact.
- Requires blank absentee ballots transmitted to qualified individuals to have prepaid

postage.
• Prohibits states from refusing to accept and process an absentee ballot from a qualified individual based on notarization or witness signature, paper type, or envelope type requirements.
Sec. 120006. Voter Registration.
• Amends the National Voter Registration Act of 1993 to ensure that voters can register to vote online and can submit an EAC-prescribed mail voter registration application online.
• Requires states to establish technological security measures to protect information provided through online voter registration services.
• Ensures that online voter registrations services are available to individuals with disabilities.
• Ensures that online voter registration services are also available through the use of an automated telephone-based system.
• Amends the Help America Vote Act of 2002 to ensure that all eligible individuals can register to vote on the same day that they vote. Goes into effect in the November 2020 election and for each succeeding federal election.
• Amends the National Voter Registration Act of 1993 to prohibit states from requiring voter registration applicants to provide more than the last 4 digits of their social security numbers. Goes into effect in the November 2020 election and for each succeeding federal election.
Sec. 120007. Accommodations for Voters Residing In Indian Lands.
• Permits an Indian Tribe to designate buildings as ballot pickup and collection locations and to designate one building per precinct located within Indian lands at no cost to the Indian Tribe.
• Requires states or political subdivisions to collect ballots from designated locations and to provide Indian Tribes with accurate precinct maps for all precincts located within Indian lands at least 60 days before an election.
• Requires states or political subdivisions to provide absentee ballots for federal elections to each individual who is registered to vote and who resides on Indian lands without requiring a residential address or a mail-in or absentee ballot request.
• Ensures that voters living on Indian lands may use the address of a designated building for ballot pickup and collection as their residential and mailing address if such building is in the same precinct of the voter, and if the building is not in the same precinct, may use the address of another tribally designated building within Indian lands.
• Requires that states or political subdivisions covered under section 203 of the Voting Rights Act of 1965 provide all applicable language accessibility requirements.
46
• Permits the Attorney General to bring a civil action in an appropriate United States District Court as may be necessary to carry out the requirements of this section and permits a private right of action.
• Goes into effect in the November 2020 election and for each succeeding federal election.
Sec. 120008. Payments by Election Assistance Commission to States to Assist With Costs of
Compliance.
• Requires the Election Assistance Commission to make payments to eligible states

for the costs of complying with the ACCESS Act, including the costs for pre-paying the postage on absentee ballots and balloting material, for public education campaigns regarding the requirements of the ACCESS Act, and for voluntarily electing to comply with the ACCESS Act in the 2020 primary elections.

- For party-run primaries, requires the Election Assistance Commission to make payments to eligible political parties for costs incurred in transmitting absentee ballots and balloting materials in accordance with the ACCESS Act in the 2020 primary elections.
- Requires states to pass through funds to local jurisdictions or Tribal Governments.
- Requires states and political parties of states to submit an application to the Election Assistance Commission to receive payment assistance.
- In the case of an emergency, permits states to submit a payment request to the Election Assistance Commission and requires that payment be made to the states no later than 7 days after receipt of the request.
- Requires states to submit reports to the Election Assistance Commission no later than 6 months after the end of each fiscal year on the activities conducted with the funds provided.
- Requires the Election Assistance Commission to submit a report on such payments each fiscal year to the Committee on House Administration of the House of Representatives and the Committee on Rules and Administration of the Senate.

Sec. 120009. Grants to States for Conducting Risk-Limiting Audits of Results of Elections.

- Permits the Election Assistance Commission to make grants to eligible states to conduct risk-limiting audits with respect to federal general elections. Goes into effect in the November 2020 election and for each succeeding federal election.
- Authorizes the appropriation of $20 million for fiscal year 2020 for risk-limiting audit grants.
- Authorizes a GAO analysis no later than 6 months after the first grants are awarded on the extent to which risk-limiting audits improve the administration and security of elections.

Sec. 120010. Additional Appropriations for The Election Assistance Commission.

- Authorizes the additional appropriation of $3 million to the Election Assistance Commission for fiscal year 2020 in order for the Commission to provide additional assistance and resources to states to improve election administration.

DIVISION M – Oversight and Accountability

Prepared by the Democratic staff of the House Committee on Oversight and Reform

Sec. 130001. Coronavirus Accountability and Transparency Committee. This section would establish a Coronavirus Accountability and Transparency Committee of independent Inspectors General to coordinate audits and investigations of the spending under the Act and the response to the Coronavirus Pandemic. It would ensure that Inspectors General have the authorities and funding necessary to effectively and efficiently conduct oversight and requires extensive public reporting through Oversight.gov.

Sec. 130002. GAO Oversight and Accountability Responsibilities. This section would provide authority to the independent Government Accountability Office (GAO) to provide oversight over the implementation of the Act and other efforts to respond to the coronavirus pandemic. It would require GAO to provide public updates on its oversight efforts and would authorize $50 million to enable GAO to perform its duties effectively.

DIVISION N – U.S. Postal Service Provisions

Prepared by the Democratic staff of the House Committee on Oversight and Reform

Sec. 140001. Elimination of Postal Service Debt, Additional Borrowing Authority. This section would eliminate the current debt of the Postal Service. This would reset the Postal Service's borrowing authority to the level in current law—$15 billion—by eliminating its current $11 billion debt to the Department of Treasury. The proposal would require Treasury to lend to the Postal Service if requested and eliminate the $3 billion annual borrowing limit in current law. The Postal Service has indicated that this money will likely be required to continue operations during the crisis through the end of the fiscal year.

Sec. 140002. Prioritization of Delivery for Medical Purposes. This section would require the Postal Service to prioritize the delivery of medical products, including pharmaceuticals. It would authorize the Postal Service to establish temporary delivery points during the crisis and allow it to institute flexible delivery in the event its operations or employees are impacted by the coronavirus outbreak.

DIVISION O – Federal Workforce Provisions

Prepared by the Democratic staff of the House Committee on Oversight and Reform

Sec. 150001. Reimbursement for Child and Family Care. Federal employees who are required to report to work face a sudden need to care for children or sick family members at home. This section would provide federal employees up to $2,000 per child or dependent per month in reimbursements for such care.

Sec. 150002. Federal Contractor Equity. Federal contractors have growing concerns that they may not be able to meet contract requirements as a direct result of coronavirus-related contingencies. This section would direct the Office of Management and Budget to issue guidance to ensure that federal contracting officials adjust contacts so contractors are not held accountable for contract provisions made impossible by coronavirus-related activities.

Sec. 150003. Weather and Safety Leave. This section would allow agencies to provide administrative leave to federal employees who cannot access their offices and for whom telework is not possible.

Sec. 150004. Telework Requirements. Maximum telework flexibilities are not currently being implemented across the government. This section would require agency leaders to allow telework for all eligible federal employees during the coronavirus pandemic. It also would clarify that during the epidemic, having a child or dependent at home does not disqualify a location as an acceptable work location. The provisions would require agencies to expand telework by creating incentives to increase its use and disincentives to reducing it.

Sec. 150005. Pay Differential for Duty Related to the Coronavirus. This section would provide hazardous duty pay to federal workers who provide direct patient care and emergency services to individuals who have contracted coronavirus and to workers who have frequent, unavoidable contact with the public, such as Transportation Security Officers.

Sec. 150006. Workers' Compensation for Certain Federal Employees Who Contract the Coronavirus. This section would create a presumption that the coronavirus was contracted in the workplace for employees whose duties require substantial contact with the public.

DIVISION P – Federal Employee Collective Bargaining and Official Time

Prepared by the Democratic Staff of the Committee on Oversight and Reform

Sec. 1. Short Title. The short title of this division is "Protecting Collective Bargaining and Official Time for Federal Workers Act."

Sec. 2. Findings. Federal employee unions protect the rights of federal workers, and collective bargaining is essential to the union process. Congress has declared that "labor organizations and collective bargaining in the civil service are in the public interest." Yet, the Administration has issued Executive Orders that attempt to dismantle federal unions and undermine their collective bargaining rights.

Sec. 3. Nullification of Executive Orders Related to Federal Employee Collective Bargaining. The following Executive Orders and presidential memorandum are rescinded:

(1) Executive Order 13837 (relating to the use of official time);
(2) Executive Order 13836 (relating to federal collective bargaining);
(3) Executive Order 13839 (relating to the Merit Systems Protection Board);
(4) The Presidential Memorandum on the Delegation of Certain Authority under the Federal Service Labor-Management Relations Statute, issued to
the Secretary of Defense on January 29, 2020.

DIVISION Q – Veteran Coronavirus Response Act of 2020

Prepared by the Democratic staff of the House Committee on Veterans' Affairs

Section 170008 – Increase of Amount of Department of Veterans Affairs Payment for Aid and Attendance During Emergency Period Resulting From COVD-19 Pandemic.

• This provision increases the amount of available aid and attendance for veterans in need of in-home care by adding twenty-five percent to the existing aid and attendance monthly benefit for those who need assistance with daily activities or are housebound.

Section 170009 – Treatment of Work Injury Compensation Claims Filed by Employees of the Department of Veterans Affairs for COVID-19.

• All VA employees, including VA clinicians shall be treated as employees under Chapter 81 of title 5 for the purpose of filing a work compensation claim due for COVID-19.

• All VA employees who contract COVID-19 are presumed to have contracted COVID-19
due to VA employment for the purpose of filing a work compensation claim.

Section 170010 – Deferral of Certain Debts Arising from Laws Administered by the Secretary of Veterans Affairs

• Prohibits the Secretary from collecting payments for benefit debts, including through offsets of active VA benefits, establishing new benefit debts, sending notices regarding benefit debts to individuals or consumer reporting agencies, allowing interest to accrue on benefit debts, or applying administrative fees on benefit debts.

• The restrictions above are in effected during the COVID-19 public health emergency period and for 60 days following the end of the emergency period.

• Allows the Secretary to continue to collect payment regarding a benefit debt if the debtor elects to make such payment.

DIVISION R – Aviation Worker Relief

Prepared by the Democratic staff of the House Committee on Transportation and

Infrastructure

Sec. 1. Short title; table of contents. Aviation Worker Relief Act of 2020.

Sec. 2. Definitions. Inherits definitions from section 40102(a) of title 49, United States Code,

except with regards to "contractor" and "employee." 50

Title I – Aviation Worker Relief

Sec. 101. Pandemic relief for aviation workers. Provides $37 bn in grants to employees of mainline, regional, and cargo airlines, passing to workers through each carrier, with each carrier receiving what it reported as its total payroll costs in 2Q+3Q19 **(JOBS SAVED: 750,000).** Provides $3 bn in grants to employees of ground support and catering contractors, based on their sworn financial statements regarding payroll costs in 2Q+3Q19 **(JOBS SAVED: ~210,000).** Provides $21 bn in unsecured loans to air carriers.

Sec. 102. Procedures for financial assistance. Allows loans to be zero-interest to start, but requires that over time loans must provide for payment of interest at rates commensurate with the level of risk assumed by the Government. Grants the Government's claim in any bankruptcy proceeding with respect to outstanding payments superpriority status, making it superior to any claims of other secured or unsecured creditors.

Sec. 103. Terms and conditions. Prohibits airlines from repurchasing shares of stock or using financial assistance to issue dividends to shareholders. Caps CEOs' pay at no more than 50 times the median pay of their employees, and caps CEOs' golden parachutes. Retains the Government's right to fully participate in capital gains realized by airlines receiving assistance. Requires each airline receiving assistance to support U.S. jobs by ensuring no additional aircraft heavy maintenance work is outsourced to repair stations abroad.

Sec. 104. Reports. Mandates a report and update on the financial status of the air carrier industry, including a description of each grant or loan issued under section 101, on Oct. 1, 2020, and one year following the passage of this bill.

Sec. 105. Coordination. Provides for coordination among Secretaries of the Treasury and Transportation in providing relief.

Title II – Labor Protections

Sec. 201. Assistance irrespective of labor costs. Prohibits the Administration from conditioning

any financial assistance on an airline's reduction of labor costs.

Sec. 202. Collective bargaining and snap-back. For any concession or alternation made to a collective bargaining agreement (CBA) as a result of COVID-19, including to rates or pay, rules, or working conditions, this section requires such changes be reversed or renegotiated later to reflect changing economic circumstances (i.e., "snap-back" mechanism).

Sec. 203. Protection of organizing activity. Requires airlines to remain neutral in any communications with employees with respect to any union organizing campaign.

Sec. 204. Working and travel conditions. Ensures carriers follow Centers for Disease Control and Prevention and public health authority guidelines for providing safe conditions for workers and travelers, including but not limited to providing adequate personal protective equipment, full cleaning and sanitary conditions of all planes and facilities, and any other necessary actions.

Sec. 205. Labor union representation on air carrier boards. Requires each airline receiving assistance to designate at least one seat on its board for a representative of one or more labor unions representing the airline's employees, to be selected by a union.

Sec. 206. Furloughed worker protections. Ensures their healthcare and welfare plans (at active employee rates) remain in place for any furloughed workers. Ensures furloughed time counts as years of service for employee retirement and welfare plans. Ensures furloughed employees receive all employer 401(k) nonelective contributions attributable to furloughed time upon return to work and are permitted penalty free hardship withdrawals from 401(k) plans while on furlough.

Sec. 207. Healthcare for unprotected workers. Provides comprehensive health care coverage to both direct and subcontracted employees providing aviation services at airports, in addition to their regular rate of wages, in the form of cash, health insurance, or a combination of the two that is sufficient to support affordable and quality health insurance. Also requires certification that for unprotected workers, the air carrier currently, and that any contractor or subcontractor that provides airline catering services to it, provides health insurance benefits equal to or greater than hourly health and wage fringe benefits rate published by Department of Labor for all hours worked by each airlines catering employee and will continue to do so for at least 5 years after receipt of such stimulus.

Sec. 208. Employee wages and leave. Requires carriers to maintain at least $15 minimum wage for all employees or contracted workers for a period of 10 years upon receipt of financial assistance. Provides paid sick and paid family medical leave to actively encourage sick workers to stay home whether caring for themselves or a family member during illness or quarantine or school closings. Ensures carriers meet their funding obligations under all defined-benefit pension plans. Provides layoff protection via back pay/wage replacement for airline and airport workers and contractors if carriers reduce staff or hours, resulting in a reduction in compensation.

Sec. 209. Limitation on rejection of collective bargaining agreements. Limits a carrier's use of 11 U.S.C. 1113 to discharge a collective bargaining agreement for 10 years from the last date the carrier received Federal financial assistance.

Sec. 210. Increased wage priority. Increases wage priority in bankruptcy for employees to $20,000 indexed for inflation regardless of when accrued.

Sec. 211. Rejection of collective bargaining agreements. Imposes limits on the ability of employers to seek emergency concessions in bankruptcy outside of the normal section 1113 process and for no more than a brief period of time, and amends sections 1113 and 365 of chapter 11 of the bankruptcy code to make clear that breach or rejection of a CBA gives rise to an unsecured claim for damages (as with rejection of any executory contract).

Title III – Airline Industry Financial Oversight

Sec. 301. Creation of Office of Airline Industry Financial Oversight. Sets up an Office of Airline Financial Oversight within the Department of Transportation (DOT).

Sec. 302. Responsibilities of Office of Airline Industry Financial Oversight. Requires the Office in established in Sec. 301, to continually assess, and impose minimum capital and funding requirements for, an airline's financial fitness to guard against future "black swan" events such as Covid-19, ensuring we never have to do this again. Requires airlines to conduct financial stress tests to evaluate their preparedness for and resiliency following such an event.

Sec. 303. Access to information. Provides that the employees of the office may inspect any financial records of an air carrier that they deem appropriate.

Sec. 304. Reports to Congress. Ensures accountability and transparency by requiring the office to report to Congress annually on measures taken by the office during the preceding 12-month period to ensure the adequacy of airlines' financial sustainability.

Sec. 305. Rulemaking authority. Authorizes the Secretary of Transportation to issue such regulations as are necessary to effectuate the office's oversight.

Sec. 306. Authorization of appropriations. Authorizes appropriations of $3 million per year from FY20-23 for operation of the office.

Title IV – Airport Relief

Sec. 401. Emergency Pandemic Funding for Airports. Provides $10 billion for airports to use on, infrastructure projects, cleaning, sanitization, janitorial services, staffing, workforce retention, airport operations, emergency response, debt service payments and other needs. Also requires airports retain 90 percent of their workforce and to provide relief to airport concessionaires **(JOBS SAVED: ~1.2 million)**.

Sec. 402. Maintaining Pre-crisis Airport Improvement Program Levels. Ensures that airports that have experienced a lower number of passenger traffic from the coronavirus COVID-19 crisis do not see lower Airport Improvement Program (AIP) formula funds.

Sec. 403. National Aviation Preparedness Plan. Requires the DOT to develop a national aviation-preparedness plan for communicable diseases, which the Government Accountability Office recommended in 2015, to ensure that airports and other aviation stakeholders are better prepared for a future crisis involving communicable diseases.

Title V – Small Community Air Service

Sec. 501. Continuation of certain air service. Requires the Secretary of Transportation to ensure that any small community that received air service as of March 1, 2020, continues receiving an adequate level of air service. Also authorizes the Secretary of Transportation to issue limited antitrust immunities for airlines to cooperate for purposes of ensuring that small communities receive an adequate level of air service during the period of the pandemic.

Sec. 502. Tolling of EAS limitations. Limits toll enforcement of eligibility for participation in the Essential Air Service program through the end of the period of the President's declaration of a national emergency.

Sec. 503. Sunset. Sunsets this title six months after the last effective date of a national emergency declared.

Title VI – Consumer Protections

Sec. 601. Airline price gouging during disaster or emergency. Requires airlines to waive all change or cancellation fees throughout the entirety of any declared national emergency. Prohibits carriers from charging fare differences for itinerary changes during such an emergency. Further prohibits price gouging for flights from airports during a national emergency or those airports servicing a disaster area or subject to restricted travel, including country-wide bans imposed on air travel during a pandemic.

Sec. 602. Airline refunds during national disasters or emergencies. Requires carriers to offer both a monetary refund of fares, including ancillary fees paid, and travel credit or voucher for any flights cancelled by the carrier or passenger during a national emergency. If a travel credit or voucher is selected, said credit or voucher

cannot expire for at least one year after the date of the original flight.
Sec. 603. Conditions on airline ancillary fees. Requires clear and separate reporting by carriers to the DOT of all carrier-imposed ancillary fees charged to consumers.
Title VII – Environmental Protections
Sec. 701. Sustainable Aviation Fuel Development Program. Provides grants to airports, air carriers and other entities to offset the cost of producing, transporting or storing sustainable aviation fuels.
Sec. 702. Airline Assistance to Recycle and Save Program. DOT is authorized to purchase inefficient airplanes that the airlines are retiring in exchange for airlines' commitment to purchasing newer fuel-efficient airplanes.
Sec. 703. Airline Carbon Emissions Offsets and Goals. Expands the FAA's Voluntary Airport Low Emissions (VALE) program, which airports use to purchase low emission vehicles, refueling and recharging stations, and other airport air quality improvements, to all commercial airports. It will continue to prioritize funding for airports in compromised air quality areas of the country.
Sec. 704. Airline Carbon Emissions Offsets and Goals. Requires air carries receiving assistance to fully offset their carbon emissions starting 2025. Also requires these carriers to reduce their own carbon emissions by 25 percent by 2035 and 50 percent by 2050. Requires continuous audits and reports to ensure air carriers are meeting their targets.
Sec. 705. Research and Development of Sustainable Aviation Fuels. Provides $500 million in additional funding over five years for FAA research and development of sustainable aviation fuels.
Sec. 706. Transparency regarding carbon emissions. Requires airlines and ticket agents to tell prospective purchasers of airline tickets how much carbon emissions are attributed to their flights.
Sec. 707. Study on Certain Climate Change Mitigation Efforts. Requires a study by the National Academies to conduct a study on climate change mitigation efforts within the civil aviation and aerospace industries.
Title VIII – Miscellaneous
Sec. 801. Separability. Ensures that the remainder of this division remains in force in the event
that a particular provision is declared invalid.
Sec. 802. Application of Law. Temporarily suspends application of Buy American requirements to Government procurements during a public health emergency or pendency of an emergency declaration following a natural disaster.

DIVISION S – Small Business Administration

Prepared by the Democratic staff of the House Committee on Small Business

Assisting Small Businesses – Authorizes critically needed funding to keep small businesses afloat during this unprecedented economic disruption, including:

- **Small Business Economic Injury Grants** – Authorizes $100 billion in grants to small businesses that can demonstrate losses due to the outbreak.
- **Small Business Disaster Loans** – Authorizes an additional $184 billion in low-interest economic injury disaster loans to help small businesses that have suffered financial losses as a result of the coronavirus outbreak.
- **Small Business Payroll Support** – Authorizes $300 billion in guaranteed, forgivable loans to cover short-term payroll costs.
- **Small Business Debt Relief** – Provides small businesses with relief from SBA loan

payments, including principal, interest, and fees, for six months.
- **Increasing Access to Capital** – Eliminates fees and increases guarantees on SBA-backed 7(a) and 504 loans to increase access to capital for struggling firms.
- **Minority Business Development Agency** – Authorizes additional resources for the Minority Business Development Agency.
- **Small Business Investment Companies** – Provides additional leverage to SBICs to deploy to start ups and potential high-growth firms.
- **Entrepreneurial Support** – Authorizes $265 million for Small Business Development Centers, Women's Business Centers, Veterans Business Outreach Centers, and SCORE chapters to provide counseling and support to impacted entrepreneurs and small businesses. Authorizes $57 million for Microloan program technical assistance and lending.
- **Language Support** – Authorizes $25 million for SBA to provide resources and services in languages other than English.

DIVISION T – Revenue Provisions

Prepared by the Democratic staff of the House Committee on Ways and Means

TITLE I – Health-Related Tax Relief

Sec. 101. Payroll Tax Credit for COVID-19 Charity Care Provided by Hospitals. Our hospitals face an acute challenge during this crisis, taking on the responsibility of addressing an overwhelming increase in demand for services, regardless of a patient's ability to pay. This provision would alleviate some of the financial strain on hospitals that treat COVID-19-affected patients by providing them a substantial tax credit to offset the charity care they provide. More specifically, the credit would be an amount equal to 90 percent of the COVID-related charity care furnished by a hospital in 2020. Finally, eligible hospitals would be able to claim this credit against their quarterly payroll taxes, with any excess credits being refundable. The credit applies to charity care furnished after January 31, 2020 through December 31, 2020. The amount of the credit would be taken into account for future Medicare DSH payments relating to hospital cost reporting periods occurring in 2020.

Sec. 102. Payroll Tax Credit for COVID-19 Hospital Facility Expenditures. Similarly, to meet the increased demand for COVID-19 testing and treatment, hospitals will need to acquire necessary equipment, beds, and, in some circumstances, retrofit or build temporary structures to treat and house affected patients. This provision would assist hospitals by offsetting the cost of "scaling up" their resources in order to care for COVID-19-affected patients. More specifically, the credit would be an amount equal to 90 percent of an eligible hospital's capital expenditures in 2020 related to the purchase or construction of a temporary structure, the lease of a structure, or the retrofitting of any existing structure, and any depreciable property used in those structures to treat affected patients. Eligible hospitals would be able to claim this credit against their payroll taxes, with any excess credits being refundable. The credit applies to expenditures paid or incurred after January 31, 2020 through December 31, 2020.

Sec. 103. Help Families Whose Incomes Are Fluctuating Not Pay ACA Penalties. People who lose their jobs or have reduced hours may have trouble predicting their annual income.

56

Under the ACA, families must predict their incomes and pay tax credits based on their predictions. The ACA had protections for families that guessed their incomes incorrectly, and the Republicans have since stripped these protections. This provision would reinstate the protections that were in the ACA for families with fluctuating incomes to prevent these families from paying large penalties.

Sec. 104. Improving Affordability by Reducing Premium Costs for Consumers. Democrats have long prioritized getting Americans insured and providing access affordable health care, particularly in light of the health care costs Americans face with COVID-19 and economic uncertainty. This provision increases affordability by expanding eligibility for the ACA's premium tax credits beyond the current 400 percent of the federal poverty level (FPL), and increases the size of the tax credits for individuals and families below 400 percent of FPL. These actions would increase the number of Americans with health insurance while lowering premiums for millions of middle-class Americans.

TITLE II – Economic Stimulus Subtitle A – Economic Assistance Payments

Sec. 201. Economic Assistance to Individuals. This provision provides $1,500 of immediate assistance per individual, up to $7,500 for a family of five.

Households with 2020 income over $150,000 for a joint filer, $112,500 for a head of household filer, and $75,000 for a single filer will be required to pay back part or all of the assistance payment over three years. For these households, the payment is a zero-interest loan.

This benefit will also be available to our nation's retirees. The Social Security Administration would issue payments immediately to all adult Social Security and Supplemental Security Income beneficiaries in the coming weeks, and the Internal Revenue Service would issue payments to all other individuals.

Families do not need earned income to qualify for the assistance, so unemployed individuals still qualify. Filers can qualify as long as they have an individual taxpayer identification number. The payments will not count as income or resources for purposes of eligibility for other federal assistance programs; the payments would also be exempt the Treasury Offset Program and other levies.

Subtitle B – Earned Income Tax Credit

For 2020 and 2021, this provision would allow an individual with no qualifying children to claim the EITC if the individual is between ages 19 and 25 and is not a full-time student. It also allows individuals to claim the credit until they reach age 66. It increases the maximum credit, the earned income, and the phaseout amounts and indexes the earned income amount to inflation. It permanently modifies the EITC rules to allow families with children who do not meet the identification requirements for the EITC (for instance, if they do not have a valid Social Security Number) to claim the no-child EITC; allows credit eligibility in certain cases of married individuals living apart; and repeals provisions that would deny the credit to taxpayers due to excess investment income. Finally, it permanently provides an EITC match for Puerto Rico and other U.S. territories.

Subtitle C – Child Tax Credit

For 2020 through 2025, this provision removes the earned income component for calculating the refundable credit (i.e., the credit is fully refundable regardless of income) and eliminates the $1,400 cap on refundability. It increases the value of the credit from $2,000 to $3,000 and also provides a larger credit of $3,600 for children under the age of 6. Residents of Puerto Rico are able to claim the credit by filing a return with the IRS, and for the other U.S. territories, payments will be made for them to distribute in a manner that replicates the U.S. child tax credit.

Subtitle D – Dependent Care Assistance

For 2020 and 2021, this provision would double the CDCTC, increase the income threshold above which the CDCTC is phased out from $15,000 to $120,000, and adjust these amounts for inflation. It would also make the credit refundable and modify the phase-out calculation. For 2020 and 2021, the provision would increase the exclusion for employer-provided dependent care assistance from $5,000 to $10,500 and adjusts this amount for inflation.

Subtitle E – Net Operating Losses

Sec. 241. Net Operating Loss Carrybacks. Before the Republican tax bill, businesses with current losses and profits in earlier years could claim a tax refund by carrying back the loss. This provision would temporarily allow businesses to carry back losses from 2018, 2019 and 2020 to any of the last five years. The provision also suspends the 80% taxable income limitation for 2018, 2019 and 2020. Net operating loss carrybacks and the suspension of the 80% taxable income limitation do not apply to disqualified taxpayers. Disqualified taxpayers include corporations subject to the limitations on deductibility on excessive executive compensation and on golden parachute payments, and corporations that that have returned more than 5% of the fair market value of their stock to shareholders in the form of stock buybacks and pay dividends. Special rules apply to life insurance companies, as well as to real estate investment trusts and for losses attributable to excess interest expense.

Subtitle F – Employee Retention Credit

Sec. 251. Employee Retention Credit. In order to incentivize employers to keep their employees on payroll rather than laying off those employees, this section would offer a fully refundable tax credit, tied to the payment of employee wages, against the employer's share of Social Security taxes. All eligible employers would be permitted to claim an 80 percent credit on wages up to $10,000 per employee. Eligible employers must have no more than $41.5 million in gross receipts or no more than 1,500 full-time equivalent employees to qualify. They must also have experienced a 20 percent loss in gross receipts in the current calendar quarter compared to the prior year calendar quarter. An eligible employer can no longer claim the credit if their trade or business earns greater than 90 percent of the gross receipts it had in the same calendar quarter in the prior year. The credit applies to wages paid from January 31, 2020 to December 31, 2020.

Subtitle G – Credits for Paid Sick and Family Leave

Sec. 263. Fund Mandated Paid Leave for Governmental Employers. This provision would ensure that governmental employers, including public universities, can receive tax credits for the costs of providing mandated paid sick and family leave as passed in the Families First Coronavirus Response Act.

Sec. 264. Tax Credits for Mandated Paid Leave. This provision expands the tax credits for paid sick leave and paid family leave in the Families First Coronavirus Response Act. These changes align with changes made to the respective mandates in the Act, applying a $511 per day limitation for all types of paid sick leave to the payroll tax credit for employers and to the individual tax credit for self-employed workers. It also limits the paid sick leave and paid family and medical leave employer credits to employers with up to 500 full-time employees. Additionally, this provision allows governmental employers to access both the paid sick leave and paid family leave credits, regardless of employer size.

TITLE III – Administrative

Sec. 301. Delay of certain deadlines. This provision extends the April 15th filing date to July 15th, providing individuals more time to file their tax returns given the limitations caused by the COVID-19 emergency. This extension aligns with the extended filing and payment dates for federal income taxes already announced by the Internal Revenue Service. This provision also allows all individuals to postpone estimated tax payments due from the date of enactment until October 15, 2020. There is no cap on the amount of tax payments postponed, and any individual required to make estimated tax payments can take advantage of the postponement. This delay should increase the available cash flow for individuals experiencing cash shortfalls as a result of the COVID-19 emergency.

TITLE IV – Retirement Provisions

Sec. 401. Special Rules for Use of Retirement Funds: This provision provides early distribution and loan relief for retirement plans during the coronavirus relief period. Specifically, this provision would:

- Waive penalty of 10% on early withdrawals
- Allow individuals three years to repay distributions
- Allow individuals to include distributions in income ratably over three years
- Increase loan limitations to lesser of $100,000 or 100% of participants vested account balance (this doubles current loan limits)
- Loan repayment beginning dates delayed one year

Sec. 402. Plan Funding Rules. With the volatility in the markets and the low interest rate environment – and at a time when many businesses revenues are being devastated, many employers are struggling to meet their contribution requirements to their pension plans. To address this issue, this provision provides funding relief for single employer defined benefit pension plans. Specifically, this provision provides companies with more time to meet their funding obligations by delaying the due date for any contribution otherwise due during 2020 until January 1, 2021. At that time, contributions due earlier would be due with interest. The provision also provides that a plan's status for benefit restrictions as of December 31, 2019 will apply throughout 2020.

Sec. 403. Temporary Waiver of Required Minimum Distribution Rules for Certain Retirement Plans and Accounts: Under current law, generally at the age of 72, individuals must take a required minimum distribution ("RMD") from their defined contribution plans and IRAs. Due to the market downturn, the balances in these accounts have sharply decreased – in many instances, the market has reduced taxpayers' accounts more than what their RMD would have been for 2020. This provision waives the required minimum distributions for 2020, allowing individuals to keep funds in their retirement plans.

Sec. 404. Modification of Special Rules for Minimum Funding Standards for Community Newspapers. Community newspapers are generally family-owned, non-publicly traded, independent newspapers. The recently enacted SECURE Act provided pension funding relief for a number of community newspaper plan sponsors by increasing the interest rate to calculate those funding obligations to 8%. Additionally, the SECURE Act provided for a longer amortization period of 30 years from 7 years. These two changes reduced the annual amount these struggling community newspaper employers are required to contribute to their pension plan. This provision expands the SECURE Act relief to additional community newspapers.

Sec. 405. Application of Cooperative and Small Employer Charity Pension

Plan Rules to Certain Charitable Employers whose primary Exempt Purpose is Providing services with respect to Mothers and Children. This provision provides that a pension plan sponsored by a non-profit employer meeting certain conditions will be subject to the pension funding rules applicable to "Cooperative and Small Employer Charity Pension Plans" (CSEC
Plans). Specifically, it amends the definition of CSEC Plans to provide that a pension plan will be CSEC plan if, as of January 1, 2000, the plan was sponsored by an employer that (i) is exempt from taxation under Code section 501(c)(3), (ii) has been in existence since 1938, (iii) conducts medical research directly or indirectly through grant making, and (iv) has as its primary exempt purpose providing services with respect to mothers and children. This section is effective for plan years beginning after December 31, 2018.

Sec. 406. Extended Amortization for Single Employer Plans. In light of an ongoing pattern of interest rate and market volatility, the current-law requirement to amortize funding shortfalls over seven years is no longer appropriate. Pension plans, participants, and plan sponsors need more stability and a longer period over which to pay for long-term liabilities that can stretch out for more than 50 years. Accordingly, under this proposal, the following rules would apply to all single employer pension plans, effective for plan years beginning after December 31, 2019:

- All shortfall amortization bases for all plan years beginning before January 1, 2020 (and all shortfall amortization installments determined with respect to such bases) shall be reduced to zero.
- All shortfalls would be amortized over 15 years, rather than seven years.

Sec. 407. Extension of Pension Funding Stabilization Percentages for Single Employer Plans. In 2012, 2014, and 2015, Congress provided for pension interest rate smoothing in order to address concerns that historically low interest rates were creating inflated pension funding obligations, diverting corporate assets away from jobs and business recovery. Under interest rate smoothing, the interest rates used to value pension liabilities must be within 10% of 25-year interest rate averages. The smoothed interest rates will begin phasing out in 2021, with the 10% corridor around the 25-year interest rate averages increasing five percentage points each year until interest rates need only be within 30% of the 25-year averages. Because of this phase-out, smoothing will soon cease to have much effect. In order to preserve the stabilizing effects of smoothing, the 10% interest rate corridor would be reduced to 5%, effective in 2020. Additionally, the phase-out of the 5% corridor would be delayed until 2026, at which point the corridor would, as under current law, increase by 5 percentage points each year until it attains 30% in 2030, where it would stay. Finally, a 5% floor would be put on the 25-year interest rate averages. This floor would establish stability and predictability on a longer term basis, so that interest rate variations do not create excessive volatility. In addition, this floor would protect funding rules from the extremes of interest rate movements.

TITLE V – REHABILITATION FOR MULTIEMPLOYER PENSIONS

Sec. 501-508. Pension Plan Relief (The Butch Lewis Act). More than a million Americans participate in multiemployer pension plans that are quickly running out of money. This provision addresses the worsening crisis that threatens the retirement savings of workers and retirees who – year after year – gave up wage increases in order to fund their pension plans. The health of these pension plans suffers under economic stress. This provision would help shore up the financial health of these plans, and the retirees who depend on them.

DIVISION U – Consumer Protection and Telecommunications Provisions

Prepared by the Democratic staff of the House Committee on Energy and Commerce

Section 102. Anti-Price Gouging During COVID-19 Emergency. This section provides the Federal Trade Commission and State attorneys general the authority to seek civil penalties from individuals and companies engaging in price gouging of goods and services during the COVID- 19 public health emergency.

Section 201. Broadband Hotspots and Connected Devices for Schools and Libraries During COVID-19 Emergency. This section authorizes increased funding and provides flexibility to the Federal Communication Commission's (FCC) E-Rate program to enable schools and libraries, including tribal schools and libraries, to offer broadband hotspots and connected devices to facilitate distance learning and connectivity during the COVID-19 public health emergency.

Section 301. Expansion of Low-Income Broadband Subsidies During COVID-19 Emergency. This section authorizes increased funding and provides flexibility for the FCC's Lifeline program to expand access to broadband for low-income Americans during the COVID- 19 public health emergency.

Section 401. Telecommunications Consumer Protections During COVID-19 Emergency.

This section makes certain practices, including the stopping of telephone or broadband services, if a consumer is unable to pay for reasons related to the COVID-19 emergency, unlawful during the COVID-19 public health emergency.

Section 501. Public Safety Use of the T-Band. This section repeals the requirement on the FCC to reallocate and auction the T-Band (470-512 MHz), which allows first responders to continue the use of the band for their public safety communications.

DIVISION V – GROW Act

Section 101. Short Title. The short title for the bill is the "Giving Retirement Options to

Workers Act of 2020."

Section 102. Composite Plans. Reforms the multiemployer pension system by "composite plans." These new plans are composed of features of a traditional defined benefit plan and certain attributes of a 401(k)-style defined contribution plan. The composite plan option is intended to establish a hybrid model of providing lifetime income to multiemployer plan participants while offering employers greater certainty and stability.

DIVISION W – Other Matters

Prepared by the Democratic staff of the House Committee on the Judiciary

Protecting Small Business and Consumer Debtors in Bankruptcy – Ensures that more small businesses and consumer debtors have access to a fresh start through the bankruptcy system during this period of economic disruption, including:

- **Qualifying More Small Businesses for Streamlined Bankruptcy Protections** – Expands the eligibility for small businesses to qualify for reorganization under the streamlined process under subchapter V to chapter 11 of the Bankruptcy Code.
- **Expanding Consumer Bankruptcy Relief** – Includes protections for consumers by extending their payment plans from five to seven years and preventing financial assistance from the federal government related to the COVID-19 pandemic—such

as direct cash deposits—from being treated as "income" for purposes of filing bankruptcy.

DIVISION X - Other Matters

Sec. 199991. Home Energy and Water Service Continuity. This section requires that states and utilities receiving funds pursuant to the Act adopt or maintain in force policies to prevent the shutoff of electricity, home heating and cooling, and drinking and wastewater services to residential customers during the COVID-19 public health emergency.

Sec. 199992. Low-Income Household Drinking Water and Wastewater Assistance. This section provides financial assistance to low income and other adversely affected consumers to assist with payments for drinking water and wastewater expenses by authorizing $1.5 billion for grants to states, territories and Indian Tribes.

Sec. 199993. Delay of Strategic Petroleum Reserve (SPR) Oil Sales Required by Law. This section delays for one year the sale of oil from the SPR required by Section 404 of the Bipartisan Budget Act of 2015. The price of crude oil has fallen to its lowest level in nearly two decades, so selling oil from the SPR now would result in a significant loss of value to the taxpayer.

Sec. 199994. Expansion of DOL Authority to Postpone Certain Deadlines. This section

Sec. 199995. Access to Information from Institutions of Higher Education. This section would clarify that colleges and universities are permitted to provide the Census Bureau information about students living on campus for purposes of responding to the 2020 Census. With many colleges closed due to the coronavirus outbreak, this section would ensure that the Census Bureau will still be able to get an accurate of count of students by receiving information directly from schools. This section would require schools to provide ten days of public notice and an opportunity for students to opt-out before transmitting this information. This section would apply only to the 2020 Census.

Sec. 199996. State Stabilization Fund – $200 billion to provides States, territories and tribes with funding to cover revenue lost because of coronavirus. The funding will be provided in two tranches, with the first tranche immediate and the second to follow based on unemployment rates or on July 1, whichever trigger is hit first. Of the funding in the first tranche, $10 billion is set aside for tribes, $1 billion for territories, and $2.5 billion for small states.

Take Responsibility for Workers and Families Act, Complete Bill Text

16th CONGRESS
2d Session
H. R. 6379
Making emergency supplemental appropriations for the fiscal year ending September 30, 2020, and for other purposes.
IN THE HOUSE OF REPRESENTATIVES
March 23, 2020
Mrs. Lowey (for herself, Mr. Neal, Mr. Pallone, Mr. DeFazio, Mr. Scott of Virginia, Ms. Velázquez, Ms. Waters, Mrs. Carolyn B. Maloney of New York, and Ms. Lofgren) introduced the following bill; which was referred to the Committee on Appropriations, and in addition to the Committees on the Budget, and Ways and Means, for a period to be subsequently determined by the Speaker, in each case for consideration of such provisions as fall within the jurisdiction of the committee concerned
A BILL
Making emergency supplemental appropriations for the fiscal year ending September 30, 2020, and for other purposes.
Be it enacted by the Senate and House of Representatives of the United States of America in Congress assembled,
SECTION 1. SHORT TITLE.
This Act may be cited as the "Take Responsibility for Workers and Families Act".

SEC. 2. TABLE OF CONTENTS.
The table of contents is as follows:

SION ACT
DIVISION C—EMERGENCY PAID SICK LEAVE ACT AMENDMENTS
DIVISION D—COVID-19 WORKERS FIRST PROTECTION ACT OF 2020
DIVISION E—COVID-19 WORKFORCE EMERGENCY RESPONSE ACT OF 2020
DIVISION F—FAMILY SUPPORT PROVISIONS
DIVISION G—HEALTH POLICIES
Title I—Medicaid
Title II—Medicare
Title III—Private Insurance
Title IV—Provisions relating to Older Americans Act of 1965
Title V—Public health policies
DIVISION H—EMERGENCY CORONAVIRUS PANDEMIC UNEMPLOYMENT COMPENSATION ACT OF 2020
Title I—Federal Benefit Enhancements
Title II—Expanded Eligibility for Unemployment Compensation
Title III—Relief for Governmental and Nonprofit Entities
Title IV—Emergency Assistance for Rail Workers
DIVISION I—FINANCIAL SERVICES
Title I—Protecting Consumers, Renters, Homeowners and People Experiencing Homelessness
Title II—Assisting Small Businesses and Community Financial Institutions
Title III—Supporting State, Territory, and Local Governments
Title IV—Promoting Financial Stability and Transparent Markets
Title V—Pandemic Planning and Guidance for Consumers and Regulators
DIVISION J—EDUCATION RELIEF AND OTHER PROGRAMS
Title I—Education provisions
Title II—Other programs
DIVISION K—AGRICULTURE PROVISIONS
Title I—Commodity Support and other Agriculture Programs
Title II—Supplemental Nutrition Assistance Program
DIVISION L—ACCESS ACT
DIVISION M—OVERSIGHT AND ACCOUNTABILITY
DIVISION N—U.S. POSTAL SERVICE PROVISIONS
DIVISION O—FEDERAL WORKFORCE PROVISIONS
DIVISION P—FEDERAL EMPLOYEE COLLECTIVE BARGAINING AND OFFICIAL TIME
DIVISION Q—VETERAN CORONAVIRUS RESPONSE ACT OF 2020
DIVISION R—AVIATION WORKER RELIEF
Title I—Aviation Worker Relief
Title II—Labor Protections
Title III—Airline Industry Financial Oversight
Title IV—Airport Relief

Title V—Small Community Air Service
Title VI—Consumer Protections
Title VII—Environmental Protections
Title VIII—Miscellaneous
DIVISION S—SMALL BUSINESS ADMINISTRATION
DIVISION T—REVENUE PROVISIONS
Title I—Health-related tax relief
Title II—Economic Stimulus
Title III—Administrative
Title IV—Retirement provisions
Title V—Rehabilitation for Multiemployer Pensions
DIVISION U—CONSUMER PROTECTION AND TELECOMMUNICATIONS PROVISIONS
Title I—COVID–19 Price Gouging Prevention
Title II—E–Rate Support for Wi-Fi Hotspots and Connected Devices
Title III—Emergency Lifeline Benefit for Broadband Service
Title IV—Continued Connectivity
Title V—Don't Break Up the T–Band
DIVISION V—GROW ACT
DIVISION W—OTHER MATTERS
DIVISION X—OTHER MATTERS
DIVISION Y—ADDITIONAL OTHER MATTERS

SEC. 3. REFERENCES.

Except as expressly provided otherwise, any reference to "this Act" contained in any division of this Act shall be treated as referring only to the provisions of that division.

DIVISION A—THIRD CORONAVIRUS PREPAREDNESS AND RESPONSE SUPPLEMENTAL APPROPRIATIONS ACT, 2020

TITLE I

—AGRICULTURE, RURAL DEVELOPMENT, FOOD AND DRUG ADMINISTRATION, AND RELATED AGENCIES

DEPARTMENT OF AGRICULTURE

Animal And Plant Health Inspection Service

salaries and expenses

For an additional amount for "Salaries and Expenses", $55,000,000, to prevent, prepare for, and respond to coronavirus, to supplement amounts otherwise available for the Agricultural Quarantine Inspection Program: Provided, That such amount is designated by the Congress as being for an emergency requirement pursuant to section 251(b)(2)(A)(i) of the Balanced Budget and Emergency Deficit Control Act of 1985.

Agricultural Marketing Service

marketing services

For an additional amount for "Marketing Services", $45,000,000, to prevent, prepare for, and respond to coronavirus, to supplement amounts otherwise available for commodity grading, inspection, and audit activities: Provided, That such amount is designated by the Congress as being for an emergency requirement pursuant to section 251(b)(2)(A)(i) of the Balanced Budget and Emergency Deficit Control Act of 1985.

Food Safety And Inspection Service

For an additional amount for "Food Safety and Inspection Service", $33,000,000, to prevent, prepare for, and respond to coronavirus, for the support of temporary and intermittent workers, temporary inspection relocation, and overtime inspection costs: Provided, That such amount is designated by the Congress as being for an emergency requirement pursuant to section 251(b)(2)(A)(i) of the Balanced Budget and Emergency Deficit Control Act of 1985.

Farm Service Agency

salaries and expenses

For an additional amount for "Salaries and Expenses", $3,000,000, to prevent, prepare for, and respond to coronavirus, for temporary staff and overtime expenses: Provided, That such amount is designated by the Congress as being for an emergency requirement pursuant to section 251(b)(2)(A)(i) of the Balanced Budget and Emergency Deficit Control Act of 1985.

Rural Business—Cooperative Service

rural business program account

For an additional amount for "Rural Business Program Account", $20,500,000, to remain available until September 30, 2021, to prevent, prepare for, and respond to coronavirus, for the cost of loans for rural business development programs authorized by section 310B and described in subsection (g) of section 310B of the Consolidated Farm and Rural Development Act: Provided, That such amount is designated by the Congress as being for an emergency requirement pursuant to section 251(b)(2)(A)(i) of the Balanced Budget and Emergency Deficit Control Act of 1985.

Rural Utilities Service

distance learning, telemedicine, and broadband program

For an additional amount for "Distance Learning, Telemedicine, and Broadband Program", $25,000,000, to remain available until September 30, 2021, to prevent, prepare for, and respond to coronavirus, for grants for telemedicine and distance learning services in rural areas as authorized by 7 U.S.C. 950aaa et seq.: Provided, That such amount is designated by the Congress as being for an emergency requirement pursuant to section 251(b)(2)(A)(i) of the Balanced Budget and Emergency Deficit Control Act of 1985.

Food And Nutrition Service

commodity assistance program

For an additional amount for "Commodity Assistance Program", for the emergency food assistance program as authorized by section 27(a) of the Food and Nutrition Act of 2008 (7 U.S.C. 2036(a)) and section 204(a)(1) of the Emergency Food Assistance Act of 1983 (7 U.S.C. 7508(a)(1)), $450,000,000, to remain available through September 30, 2021, to prevent, prepare for, and respond to coronavirus: Provided, That of the funds made available, the Secretary may use up to $200,000,000 for costs associated with the distribution of commodities: Provided further, That such amount is designated by the Congress as being for an emergency requirement pursuant to section 251(b)(2)(A)(i) of the Balanced Budget and Emergency Deficit Control Act of 1985.

Foreign Agricultural Service

salaries and expenses

For an additional amount for "Salaries and Expenses", $4,000,000, to prevent, prepare for, and respond to coronavirus: Provided, That such amount is designated by the Congress as being for an emergency requirement pursuant to section 251(b)(2)(A)(i) of the Balanced Budget and Emergency Deficit Control Act of 1985.

DEPARTMENT OF HEALTH AND HUMAN SERVICES

Food And Drug Administration

salaries and expenses

For an additional amount for "Salaries and Expenses", $80,000,000, to remain available until expended, to prevent, prepare for, and respond to coronavirus, for efforts on potential medical product shortages, enforcement work against counterfeit or misbranded products, work on Emergency Use Authorizations, pre- and post-market work on medical countermeasures, therapies, vaccines and research, and related administrative activities: Provided, That such amount is designated by the Congress as being for an emergency requirement pursuant to section 251(b)(2)(A)(i) of the Balanced Budget and Emergency Deficit Control Act of 1985.

GENERAL PROVISIONS—THIS TITLE

Sec. 10101. For an additional amount for grants under the pilot program established under section 779 of Public Law 115–141, to prevent, prepare for, and respond to coronavirus, $258,000,000, to remain available until September 30, 2021: Provided, That at least 90 percent of the households to be served by a project receiving a grant shall be in a rural area without sufficient access to broadband: Provided further, That for purposes of such pilot program, a rural area without sufficient access to broadband shall be defined as 10 Mbps downstream and 1 Mbps upstream, and such definition shall be reevaluated and redefined, as necessary, on an annual basis by the Secretary of Agriculture: Provided further, That an entity to which a grant is made under the pilot program shall not use a grant to overbuild or duplicate broadband expansion efforts made by any entity that has received a broadband loan from the Rural Utilities Service: Provided further, That priority consideration for grants shall be given to previous applicants now eligible as a result of adjusted eligibility requirements: Provided further, That not more than three percent of the funds made available in this paragraph may be used for administrative costs to carry out the program: Provided further, That such amount is designated by the Congress as being for an emergency requirement pursuant to section 251(b)(2)(A)(i) of the Balanced Budget and Emergency Deficit Control Act of 1985.

Sec. 10102. The first amount under "Child Nutrition Programs" in Division B of the Further Consolidated Appropriations Act, 2020 (P.L. 116–94) is amended by striking "$23,615,098,000" and inserting "$32,615,098,000".

Sec. 10103. The matter under the heading "Supplemental Nutrition Assistance Program" in division B of the Further Consolidated Appropriations Act, 2020 (Public Law 116–94) is amended by inserting before ": Provided," the following: "and for an additional amount, such sums as may be necessary to remain available through September 30, 2022, which shall be placed in reserve for use only in such amounts and at such times as may become necessary to carry out program operations".

Sec. 10104. For an additional amount for "Supplemental Nutrition Assistance Program", to supplement funds otherwise available for the Food Distribution Program on Indian Reservations, $100,000,000, to remain available through September 30, 2021, to prevent, prepare for, and respond to coronavirus: Provided, That of the total amount available, $50,000,000 is for administrative expenses, including facility improvements and equipment upgrades, and $50,000,000 is for the costs relating to additional food purchases: Provided further, That such amount is designated by the Congress as being for an emergency requirement pursuant to section 251(b)(2)(A)(i) of the Balanced Budget and Emergency Deficit Control Act of 1985.

Sec. 10105. In addition to amounts otherwise made available, $200,000,000, to remain available through September 30, 2021, to prevent, prepare for, and respond to coronavirus, shall be available for the Secretary of Agriculture to provide grants to the Commonwealth of the Northern Mariana Islands, Puerto

Rico, and American Samoa for nutrition assistance: Provided, That such amount is designated by the Congress as being for an emergency requirement pursuant to section 251(b)(2)(A)(i) of the Balanced Budget and Emergency Deficit Control Act of 1985.
Sec. 10106. The Secretary may extend the term of a marketing assistance loan authorized by section 1201 of the Agricultural Act of 2014 (7 U.S.C. 9033) for any loan commodity to 12 months: Provided, That the authority made available pursuant to this section shall expire on September 30, 2020: Provided further, That amounts made available by this section are designated by the Congress as being for an emergency requirement pursuant to section 251(b)(2)(A)(i) of the Balanced Budget and Emergency Deficit Control Act of 1985.
Sec. 10107. Notwithstanding any other provision of law, funds made available under each heading in this title shall only be used for the purposes specifically described under that heading.

TITLE II

—COMMERCE, JUSTICE, SCIENCE, AND RELATED AGENCIES
DEPARTMENT OF COMMERCE
Economic Development Administration
economic development assistance programs
(including transfers of funds)
For an additional amount for "Economic Development Assistance Programs" for necessary expenses related to responding to economic injury as a result of coronavirus, $2,000,000,000, to remain available until September 30, 2022: Provided, That such amount shall be for economic adjustment assistance as authorized by section 209 of the Public Works and Economic Development Act of 1965 (42 U.S.C. 3149): Providedfurther, That within the amount appropriated, up to 2 percent of funds appropriated in this paragraph may be transferred to "Salaries and Expenses" for administration and oversight activities: Providedfurther, That the Secretary of Commerce is authorized to appoint and fix the compensation of such temporary personnel as may be necessary to implement the requirements under this heading, without regard to the provisions of title 5, United States Code, governing appointments in competitive service: Providedfurther, That the Secretary of Commerce is authorized to appoint such temporary personnel, after serving continuously for 2 years, to positions in the Economic Development Administration in the same manner that competitive service employees with competitive status are considered for transfer, reassignment, or promotion to such positions, and an individual appointed under this proviso shall become a career-conditional employee, unless the employee has already completed the service requirements for career tenure: Providedfurther, That within the amount appropriated in this paragraph, $4,000,000 shall be transferred to "Office of Inspector General" for carrying out investigations and audits related to the funding provided

under this heading: Provided further, That such amount is designated by the Congress as being for an emergency requirement pursuant to section 251(b)(2)(A)(i) of the Balanced Budget and Emergency Deficit Control Act of 1985.

Minority Business Development Agency

minority business development

For an additional amount for "Minority Business Development" for necessary expenses for the Business Centers and Specialty Centers, including any cost sharing requirements that may exist, for assisting minority business enterprises to prevent, prepare for, and respond to coronavirus, including identifying and accessing local, State, and Federal government assistance related to such virus, $15,000,000, to remain available until September 30, 2021: Provided, That such amount is designated by Congress as being for an emergency requirement pursuant to section 251(b)(2)(A)(i) of the Balanced Budget and Emergency Deficit Control Act of 1985.

National Institute Of Standards And Technology

scientific and technical research and services

For an additional amount for "Scientific and Technical Research and Services" for necessary expenses to prevent, prepare for, and respond to coronavirus, $6,000,000, to remain available until September 30, 2021, including for measurement science to support testing for such virus (or viral strains mutating therefrom) and biomanufacturing: Provided, That such amount is designated by the Congress as being for an emergency requirement pursuant to section 251(b)(2)(A)(i) of the Balanced Budget and Emergency Deficit Control Act of 1985.

industrial technology services

For an additional amount for "Industrial Technology Services" for necessary expenses, $75,000,000, to remain available until September 30, 2021, of which $50,000,000 shall be for the Hollings Manufacturing Extension Partnership to assist manufacturers to prevent, prepare for, and respond to coronavirus, and of which $25,000,000 shall be for the National Network for Manufacturing Innovation (also known as "Manufacturing USA") to support development and manufacturing of medical countermeasures and biomedical equipment and supplies: Provided, That none of the funds provided under this heading shall be subject to cost share requirements under 15 U.S.C. 278k(e)(2) or 15 U.S.C. 278s(e)(7)(A): Provided further, That such amount is designated by the Congress as being for an emergency requirement pursuant to section 251(b)(2)(A)(i) of the Balanced Budget and Emergency Deficit Control Act of 1985.

National Oceanic And Atmospheric Administration

operations, research, and facilities

For an additional amount for "Operations, Research, and Facilities" for necessary expenses to prevent, prepare for, and respond to coronavirus, $33,200,000, to remain available until September 30, 2021: Provided, That such amount is designated by the Congress as being for an emergency requirement pursuant to section 251(b)(2)(A)(i) of the Balanced Budget and Emergency

Deficit Control Act of 1985.

DEPARTMENT OF JUSTICE

Federal Prison System

salaries and expenses

For an additional amount for "Salaries and Expenses", $100,000,000, to remain available until September 30, 2021, for necessary expenses to prevent, prepare for, and respond to coronavirus, including for maintaining correctional operations, including overtime costs, temporary facilities, purchase and rental of equipment, medical services and supplies, and emergency preparedness: Provided, That such amount is designated by the Congress as being for an emergency requirement pursuant to section 251(b)(2)(A)(i) of the Balanced Budget and Emergency Deficit Control Act of 1985.

State And Local Law Enforcement Activities

office on violence against women

violence against women prevention and prosecution programs

For an additional amount for "Violence Against Women Prevention and Prosecution Programs", $300,000,000, to remain available until expended, of which—

(1) $100,000,000 is for grants to combat violence against women, as authorized by part T of the Omnibus Crime Control and Safe Streets Acts of 1968;

(2) $25,000,000 is for transitional housing assistance grants for victims of domestic violence, dating violence, stalking, or sexual assault as authorized by section 40299 of the Violent Crime Control and Law Enforcement Act of 1994 ("1994 Act");

(3) $100,000,000 is for sexual assault victims assistance, as authorized by section 41601 of the 1994 Act;

(4) $25,000,000 is for rural domestic violence and child abuse enforcement assistance grants, as authorized by section 40295 of the 1994 Act;

(5) $25,000,000 is for legal assistance for victims, as authorized by section 1201 of the Victims of Trafficking and Violence Protection Act of 2000 (Public Law 106–386; "2000 Act"); and

(6) $25,000,000 is for grants to support families in the justice system, as authorized by section 1301 of the 2000 Act:

Provided, That such amount is designated by the Congress as being for an emergency requirement pursuant to section 251(b)(2)(A)(i) of the Balanced Budget and Emergency Deficit Control Act of 1985.

state and local law enforcement assistance

For an additional amount for "State and Local Law Enforcement Assistance", $1,000,000,000, to remain available until September 30, 2021, to prevent, prepare for, and respond to coronavirus, including for the purchase of personal protective equipment, for the Edward Byrne Memorial Justice Assistance Grant program as authorized by subpart 1 of part E of title I of the Omnibus Crime Control and Safe Streets Acts of 1968 ("1968 Act"), (except that the allocation provisions under sections 505(a) through (e) and the special rules for Puerto Rico under section 505(g), and section 1001(c), of the 1968 Act, shall not apply for purposes of this Act), to be distributed in relative proportion to fiscal year 2016 allocations: Provided, That awards made using amounts provided in this paragraph shall be made only with the same requirements, conditions, compliance, and certification as fiscal year 2016: Providedfurther, That such amount is designated by the Congress as being for an emergency requirement pursuant to section 251(b)(2)(A)(i) of the Balanced Budget and Emergency Deficit Control Act of 1985.

juvenile justice programs

For an additional amount for "Juvenile Justice Programs", $100,000,000, to remain available until September 30, 2021, to prevent, prepare for, and respond to coronavirus, of which $75,000,000 shall be for programs authorized by section 221 of the Juvenile Justice and Delinquency Prevention Act of 1974 ("the 1974 Act"), and $25,000,000 for delinquency prevention, as authorized by section 261 of the 1974 Act: Provided, That such amount is designated by the Congress as being for an emergency requirement pursuant to section 251(b)(2)(A)(i) of the Balanced Budget and Emergency Deficit Control Act of 1985.

SCIENCE

National Aeronautics And Space Administration

safety, security and mission services

For an additional amount for "Safety, Security and Mission Services", $100,000,000, to remain available until September 30, 2021, to prevent, prepare for, and respond to coronavirus: Provided, That such amount is designated by the Congress as being for an emergency requirement pursuant to section 251(b)(2)(A)(i) of the Balanced Budget and Emergency Deficit Control Act of 1985.

construction and environmental compliance and restoration

For an additional amount for "Construction and Environmental Compliance and Restoration", $100,000,000, to remain available until September 30, 2021, to prevent, prepare for, and respond to coronavirus: Provided, That such amount is designated by the Congress as being for an emergency requirement pursuant to section 251(b)(2)(A)(i) of the Balanced Budget and Emergency Deficit Control Act of 1985.

National Science Foundation

research and related activities

For an additional amount for "Research and Related Activities", $100,000,000, to remain available until September 30, 2021, to prevent, prepare for, and respond to coronavirus, domestically and internationally, including to fund research grants and other necessary expenses: Provided, That such amount is designated by the Congress as being for an emergency requirement pursuant to section 251(b)(2)(A)(i) of the Balanced Budget and Emergency Deficit Control Act of 1985.

agency operations and award management

For an additional amount for "Agency Operations and Award Management", $2,000,000, to prevent, prepare for, and respond to coronavirus, domestically and internationally, including to administer research grants and other necessary expenses: Provided, That such amount is designated by the Congress as being for an emergency requirement pursuant to section 251(b)(2)(A)(i) of the Balanced Budget and Emergency Deficit Control Act of 1985.

RELATED AGENCIES

Legal Services Corporation

payment to the legal services corporation

For an additional amount for "Payment to the Legal Services Corporation" to carry out the purposes of the Legal Services Corporation Act by providing for necessary expenses to prevent, prepare for, and respond to coronavirus, $100,000,000, to remain available until September 30, 2021: Provided, That none of the funds appropriated in this Act to the Legal Services Corporation shall be expended for any purpose prohibited or limited by, or contrary to any of the provisions of, sections 501, 502, 503, 504, 505, and 506 of Public Law 105–119, and all funds appropriated in this Act to the Legal Services Corporation shall be subject to the same terms and conditions set forth in such sections, except that all references in sections 502 and 503 to 1997 and 1998 shall be deemed to refer instead to 2020 and 2021, respectively, and except that sections 501 and 503 of Public Law 104–134 (referenced by Public Law 105–119) shall not apply to the amount made available under this heading: Providedfurther, That for the purposes of this Act, the Legal Services Corporation shall be considered an agency of the United States Government: Providedfurther, That such amount is designated by the Congress as being for an emergency requirement pursuant to section 251(b)(2)(A)(i) of the Balanced Budget and Emergency Deficit Control Act of 1985.

GENERAL PROVISIONS—THIS TITLE

Sec. 10201. (a) Amounts provided by the Department of Commerce Appropriations Act, 2020, for the Hollings Manufacturing Extension Partnership under the heading "National Institute of Standards and Technology—Industrial Technology Services" shall not be subject to cost share requirements under 15 U.S.C. 278k(e)(2).

(b) Subsection (a) shall not apply to the extent that a Manufacturing Extension Partnership Center receives funding from a State that is conditioned upon the application of a Federal cost sharing requirement to the Center.

Sec. 10202. (a) Funds appropriated in this title for the National Science Foundation may be made available to restore amounts, either directly or through reimbursement, for obligations incurred by the National Science Foundation for research grants and other necessary expenses to prevent, prepare for, and respond to coronavirus, domestically or internationally, prior to the date of enactment of this Act.

(b) Grants or cooperative agreements made by the National Science Foundation under this title, to carry out research grants and other necessary expenses to prevent, prepare for, and respond to coronavirus, domestically or internationally, shall include amounts to reimburse costs for these purposes incurred between January 20, 2020, and the date of issuance of such grants or agreements.

Sec. 10203. (a) (1) Section 110(b)(2)(C) of the Family and Medical Leave Act of 1993 (as added by division C of the Families First Coronavirus Response Act) and section 5110(5)(C) of the Families First Coronavirus Response Act (relating to varying schedule hours calculation) shall not apply to the Bureau of the Census regarding any employee hired pursuant to section 23(c) of title 13, United States Code.

(2) Any such employee shall be entitled to 40 hours of paid leave under division E of the Families First Coronavirus Response Act.

(b) With respect to any temporary employee of the Bureau of the Census, including any employee hired pursuant to section 23(c) of title 13, United States Code, the Bureau may classify any leave provided by the Bureau pursuant to the amendments made by division C of the Families First Coronavirus Response Act or division E of such Act to such an employee (based on such employee's status as an employee of the Bureau) as any leave category necessary to comport with the Bureau's leave system.

Sec. 10204. Notwithstanding any other provision of law, funds made available under each heading in this title shall only be used for the purposes specifically described under that heading.

TITLE III

—DEPARTMENT OF DEFENSE

DEPARTMENT OF DEFENSE

Military Personnel

military personnel, army

For an additional amount for Military Personnel, Army, $37,900,000, for necessary expenses to prevent, prepare for, and respond to coronavirus: Provided, That such amount is designated by the Congress as being for an emergency requirement pursuant to section 251(b)(2)(A)(i) of the Balanced Budget and Emergency Deficit Control Act of 1985.

military personnel, navy

For an additional amount for Military Personnel, Navy, $37,900,000, for necessary expenses to prevent, prepare for, and respond to coronavirus: Provided, That such amount is designated by the Congress as being for an emergency requirement pursuant to section 251(b)(2)(A)(i) of the Balanced Budget and Emergency Deficit Control Act of 1985.

military personnel, marine corps

For an additional amount for Military Personnel, Marine Corps, $9,900,000, for necessary expenses to prevent, prepare for, and respond to coronavirus: Provided, That such amount is designated by the Congress as being for an emergency requirement pursuant to section 251(b)(2)(A)(i) of the Balanced Budget and Emergency Deficit Control Act of 1985.

military personnel, air force

For an additional amount for Military Personnel, Air Force, $37,900,000, for necessary expenses to prevent, prepare for, and respond to coronavirus: Provided, That such amount is designated by the Congress as being for an emergency requirement pursuant to section 251(b)(2)(A)(i) of the Balanced Budget and Emergency Deficit Control Act of 1985.

national guard personnel, army

For an additional amount for National Guard Personnel, Army, $804,529,000, for necessary expenses to prevent, prepare for, and respond to coronavirus: Provided, That such amount is designated by the Congress as being for an emergency requirement pursuant to section 251(b)(2)(A)(i) of the Balanced Budget and Emergency Deficit Control Act of 1985.

national guard personnel, air force

For an additional amount for National Guard Personnel, Air Force, $402,063,000, for necessary expenses to prevent, prepare for, and respond to coronavirus: Provided, That such amount is designated by the Congress as being for an emergency requirement pursuant to section 251(b)(2)(A)(i) of the Balanced Budget and Emergency Deficit Control Act of 1985.

Operation And Maintenance

operation and maintenance, army

For an additional amount for "Operation and Maintenance, Army", $105,300,000, to remain available until September 30, 2021, to prevent, prepare for, and respond to coronavirus: Provided, That such amount is designated by the Congress as being for an emergency requirement pursuant to section 251(b)(2)(A)(i) of the Balanced Budget and Emergency Deficit Control Act of 1985.

operation and maintenance, navy

For an additional amount for "Operation and Maintenance, Navy", $568,408,000, to remain available until September 30, 2021, to prevent, prepare for, and respond to coronavirus: Provided, That such amount is designated by the Congress as being for an emergency requirement pursuant to section 251(b)(2)(A)(i) of the Balanced Budget and Emergency Deficit Control Act of 1985.

operation and maintenance, marine corps

For an additional amount for "Operation and Maintenance, Marine Corps", $70,000,000, to remain available until September 30, 2021, to prevent, prepare for, and respond to coronavirus: Provided, That such amount is designated by the Congress as being for an emergency requirement pursuant to section 251(b)(2)(A)(i) of the Balanced Budget and Emergency Deficit Control Act of 1985.

operation and maintenance, air force

For an additional amount for "Operation and Maintenance, Air Force",

$154,000,000, to remain available until September 30, 2021, to prevent, prepare for, and respond to coronavirus: Provided, That such amount is designated by the Congress as being for an emergency requirement pursuant to section 251(b)(2)(A)(i) of the Balanced Budget and Emergency Deficit Control Act of 1985.

operation and maintenance, defense-wide

For an additional amount for "Operation and Maintenance, Defense-Wide", $927,800,000, to remain available until September 30, 2021, to prevent, prepare for, and respond to coronavirus: Provided, That such amount is designated by the Congress as being for an emergency requirement pursuant to section 251(b)(2)(A)(i) of the Balanced Budget and Emergency Deficit Control Act of 1985.

operation and maintenance, army reserve

For an additional amount for "Operation and Maintenance, Army Reserve", $48,000,000, to remain available until September 30, 2021, to prevent, prepare for, and respond to coronavirus: Provided, That such amount is designated by the Congress as being for an emergency requirement pursuant to section 251(b)(2)(A)(i) of the Balanced Budget and Emergency Deficit Control Act of 1985.

operation and maintenance, army national guard

For an additional amount for "Operation and Maintenance, Army National Guard", $194,002,000, to remain available until September 30, 2021, to prevent, prepare for, and respond to coronavirus: Provided, That such amount is designated by the Congress as being for an emergency requirement pursuant to section 251(b)(2)(A)(i) of the Balanced Budget and Emergency Deficit Control Act of 1985.

operation and maintenance, air national guard

For an additional amount for "Operation and Maintenance, Air National Guard", $79,406,000, to remain available until September 30, 2021, to prevent, prepare for, and respond to coronavirus: Provided, That such amount is designated by the Congress as being for an emergency requirement pursuant to section 251(b)(2)(A)(i) of the Balanced Budget and Emergency Deficit Control Act of 1985.

Procurement

defense production act purchases

For an additional amount for "Defense Production Act Purchases", $500,000,000 to remain available until September 30, 2022, to prevent, prepare for, and respond to coronavirus: Provided, That the Secretary of Defense may waive the requirements of 50 U.S.C. 5433(a)(6) on a case-by-case basis upon three days prior written notification to the Committees on Appropriations and Banking, Housing, and Urban Affairs of the Senate, and the Committees on Appropriations and Financial Services of the House of Representatives. Provided further, That such amount is designated by the Congress as being for an emergency requirement pursuant to section 251(b)(2)(A)(i) of the

Balanced Budget and Emergency Deficit Control Act of 1985.
Other Department Of Defense Programs
defense health program
For an additional amount for "Defense Health Program", $3,805,500,000, to prevent, prepare for, and respond to coronavirus; of which $3,561,500,000 shall be for operation and maintenance to remain available until September 30, 2020; and of which $244,000,000, to remain available for obligation until September 30, 2021, shall be for research, development, test and evaluation: Provided, That such amount is designated by the Congress as being for an emergency requirement pursuant to section 251(b)(2)(A)(i) of the Balanced Budget and Emergency Deficit Control Act of 1985.
General Provisions—This Title
Sec. 10301. Notwithstanding any other provision of law, funds made available under each heading in this title shall only be used for the purposes specifically described under that heading.
Sec. 10302. Upon the determination of the Secretary of Defense that such action is necessary in the national interest, the Secretary may transfer up to $500,000,000 between the appropriations or funds made available to the Department of Defense for expenses relating to the use of the National Guard in response to coronavirus: Provided, That such funds may only be transferred among military personnel and operation and maintenance accounts for the National Guard provided for in this title: Provided further, That the Secretary shall notify the Congress promptly of each transfer made pursuant to the authority in this section: Provided further, That the authority provided in this section is in addition to any other transfer authority available to the Department of Defense and is subject to the same terms and conditions as the authority provided in section 8005 of the Department of Defense Appropriations Act, 2020: Provided further, That the transfer authority in sections 8005 and 9002 of the Department of Defense Appropriations Act, 2020, shall not apply to amounts appropriated or otherwise made available in this title.
Sec. 10303. Notwithstanding section 2208(l)(3) of title 10, United States Code, during fiscal year 2020, the amount of advance billings rendered or imposed by Defense working capital funds may exceed $1,000,000,000. In the preceding sentence, the term "advance billing" has the meaning given the term in section 2208(l)(4) of such title.

TITLE IV

—ENERGY AND WATER DEVELOPMENT AND RELATED AGENCIES
CORPS OF ENGINEERS—CIVIL
DEPARTMENT OF THE ARMY
Corps Of Engineers—Civil
operation and maintenance

For an additional amount for "Operation and Maintenance", $50,000,000, to remain available until September 30, 2021, to prevent, prepare for, and respond to coronavirus: Provided, That such amount is designated by the Congress as being for an emergency requirement pursuant to section 251(b)(2)(A)(i) of the Balanced Budget and Emergency Deficit Control Act of 1985.

expenses

For an additional amount for "Expenses", $20,000,000, to remain available until September 30, 2021, to prevent, prepare for, and respond to coronavirus: Provided, That such amount is designated by the Congress as being for an emergency requirement pursuant to section 251(b)(2)(A)(i) of the Balanced Budget and Emergency Deficit Control Act of 1985.

DEPARTMENT OF THE INTERIOR

Bureau Of Reclamation

water and related resources

(including transfer of funds)

For an additional amount for "Water and Related Resources", $12,500,000, to remain available until September 30, 2021, to prevent, prepare for, and respond to coronavirus: Provided, That $500,000 of the funds provided under this paragraph shall be transferred to the Central Utah Project Completion Account to prevent, prepare for, and respond to coronavirus: Provided further, That such amount is designated by the Congress as being for an emergency requirement pursuant to section 251(b)(2)(A)(i) of the Balanced Budget and Emergency Deficit Control Act of 1985.

policy and administration

For an additional amount for "Policy and Administration", $8,100,000, to remain available until September 30, 2021, for necessary expenses to prevent, prepare for, and respond to coronavirus: Provided, That such amount is designated by the Congress as being for an emergency requirement pursuant to section 251(b)(2)(A)(i) of the Balanced Budget and Emergency Deficit Control Act of 1985.

DEPARTMENT OF ENERGY

ENERGY PROGRAMS

Science

For an additional amount for "Science", $99,500,000, to remain available until September 30, 2021, to prevent, prepare for, and respond to coronavirus, for necessary expenses related to providing support and access to scientific user facilities in the Office of Science, including equipment, enabling technologies, and personnel associated with the operations of those scientific user facilities: Provided, That such amount is designated by the Congress as being for an emergency requirement pursuant to section 251(b)(2)(A)(i) of the Balanced Budget and Emergency Deficit Control Act of 1985.

Departmental Administration

(including transfer of funds)

For an additional amount for "Departmental Administration", $28,000,000, to remain available until September 30, 2021, for necessary expenses related to supporting remote access for personnel to prevent, prepare for, and respond to coronavirus: Provided, That funds appropriated under this paragraph in this Act may be transferred to, and merged with, other appropriation accounts of the Department of Energy for necessary expenses related to supporting remote access for personnel to prevent, prepare for, and respond to coronavirus: Provided further, That such amount is designated by the Congress as being for an emergency requirement pursuant to section 251(b)(2)(A)(i) of the Balanced Budget and Emergency Deficit Control Act of 1985.

INDEPENDENT AGENCIES

Nuclear Regulatory Commission

salaries and expenses

For an additional amount for "Salaries and Expenses", $3,300,000, to remain available until September 30, 2021, to prevent, prepare for, and respond to coronavirus: Provided, That the amount provided in this paragraph shall not be derived from fee revenues notwithstanding 42 U.S.C. 2214: Provided further, That such amount is designated by the Congress as being for an emergency requirement pursuant to section 251(b)(2)(A)(i) of the Balanced Budget and Emergency Deficit Control Act of 1985.

GENERAL PROVISIONS—THIS TITLE

Sec. 10401. Notwithstanding any other provision of law, funds made available under each heading in this title shall only be used for the purposes specifically described under that heading.

Sec. 10402. Funds appropriated in this title may be made available to restore amounts, either directly or through reimbursement, for obligations incurred for the same purposes to prevent, prepare for, and respond to coronavirus prior to the date of enactment of this Act.

Sec. 10403. Notwithstanding any other provision of law, and subject to the availability of appropriations, the Secretary of Energy, or designee, may include in or modify the terms and conditions of any Department of Energy contract, or other agreement, to authorize the Department to reimburse any contractor paid leave the contractor provides to its employees as the Secretary deems necessary to ensure the effective response to a declared national emergency or pandemic event. Such authority shall apply only to a contractor whose employees cannot perform work on a federally owned or leased facility or site due to Federal Government directed closures or other restrictions, and who cannot telework because their job duties cannot be performed remotely. As determined by the Secretary, or designee, this authority also shall apply to subcontractors: Provided, That amounts provided by this section are designated by the Congress as being for an emergency requirement pursuant to section 251(b)(2)(A)(i) of the Balanced Budget and Emergency Deficit Control Act of 1985.

TITLE V

—FINANCIAL SERVICES AND GENERAL GOVERNMENT

DEPARTMENT OF THE TREASURY

Departmental Offices

salaries and expenses

For an additional amount for "Salaries and Expenses", $100,000,000 to remain available until expended, for the necessary expenses to establish and support a Coronavirus Accountability and Transparency Committee to conduct oversight of funds provided in this Act in order to monitor spending, provide transparency to the public, and help prevent fraud, waste, and abuse: Provided , That not less frequently than monthly, and until all such funds are expended, the Secretary of the Treasury shall publish on a dedicated portion of the website established under section 2 of the Federal Funding Accountability and Transparency Act of 2006 (31 U.S.C. 6101 note), for any funds made available to or expended by a Federal agency or component of a Federal agency that were provided in Public Law 116–123, Public Law 116–127, or in the Take Responsibility for Workers and Families Act—

(1) for each appropriations account, including an expired or unexpired appropriations account, the amount—

(A) of budget authority appropriated;

(B) that is obligated;

(C) of unobligated balances; and

(D) of any other budgetary resources;

(2) from which accounts and in what amount—

(A) appropriations are obligated for each program activity; and

(B) outlays are made for each program activity;

(3) from which accounts and in what amount—

(A) appropriations are obligated for each object class; and

(B) outlays are made for each object class; and

(4) for each program activity, the amount—

(A) obligated for each object class; and

(B) of outlays made for each object class.

Provided further , That the information required to be published pursuant to the preceding proviso shall be published in such a format that allows such information to be sorted by the public law that provided the relevant obligational authority: Provided further, That such amounts are designated by the Congress as being for an emergency requirement pursuant to section 251(b)(2)(A)(i) of the Balanced Budget and Emergency Deficit Control Act of 1985.

community development financial institutions fund program account

For an additional amount for "Community Development Financial Institutions Fund Program Account", $200,000,000, to remain available until September 30, 2020, to promote economic recovery due to the impact of coronavirus through financial assistance and technical assistance under subparagraphs (A) and (B) of section 108(a)(1), respectively, of Public Law 103–325 (12

U.S.C. 4707(a)(1)(A) and (B)), except that subsections (d) and (e) of section 108 of Public Law 103–325 shall not apply to the provision of such financial assistance and technical assistance: Provided , That up to $10,000,000 may be transferred to and merged with "Administrative Expenses" for administrative expenses to carry out financial assistance and technical assistance: Provided further , That such amount is designated by the Congress as being for an emergency requirement pursuant to section 251(b)(2)(A)(i) of the Balanced Budget and Emergency Deficit Control Act of 1985.

Internal Revenue Service

taxpayer services

For an additional amount for "Taxpayer Services", $236,000,000, to remain available until September 30, 2021, to prevent, prepare for, and respond to coronavirus: Provided , That not later than 30 days after the date of the enactment of this Act, the Commissioner of the Internal Revenue Service shall submit to the Committees on Appropriations of the House of Representatives and the Senate a spend plan for such funds: Provided further , That such amounts are designated by the Congress as being for an emergency requirement pursuant to section 251(b)(2)(A)(i) of the Balanced Budget and Emergency Deficit Control Act of 1985.

enforcement

For an additional amount for "Enforcement", $42,000,000, to remain available until September 30, 2021, to prevent, prepare for, and respond to coronavirus: Provided , That not later than 30 days after the date of the enactment of this Act, the Commissioner of the Internal Revenue Service shall submit to the Committees on Appropriations of the House of Representatives and the Senate a spend plan for such funds: Provided further , That such amounts are designated by the Congress as being for an emergency requirement pursuant to section 251(b)(2)(A)(i) of the Balanced Budget and Emergency Deficit Control Act of 1985.

operations support

For an additional amount for "Operations Support", $324,000,000, to remain available until September 30, 2021, to prevent, prepare for, and respond to coronavirus: Provided , That not later than 30 days after the date of the enactment of this Act, the Commissioner of the Internal Revenue Service shall submit to the Committees on Appropriations of the House of Representatives and the Senate a spend plan for such funds: Provided further , That such amount is designated by the Congress as being for an emergency requirement pursuant to section 251(b)(2)(A)(i) of the Balanced Budget and Emergency Deficit Control Act of 1985.

Administrative Provisions—Internal Revenue Service

(including transfer of funds)

Sec. 10501. In addition to the authority provided in section 101 of title I of division C of Public Law 116–93, the funds provided to the Internal Revenue Service in this Act may be transferred among accounts of the Internal Revenue

Service to prevent, prepare for, and respond to coronavirus. On the date of any such transfer, the Commissioner shall notify the Committees on Appropriations of the House of Representatives and Senate of such transfer.

THE JUDICIARY

The Supreme Court Of The United States

salaries and expenses

For an additional amount for "Salaries and Expenses", $500,000, to remain available until September 30, 2020, for necessary expenses to prevent, prepare for, and respond to coronavirus: Provided, That such amount is designated by the Congress as being for an emergency requirement pursuant to section 251(b)(2)(A)(i) of the Balanced Budget and Emergency Deficit Control Act of 1985.

Courts Of Appeals, District Courts, And Other Judicial Services

salaries and expenses

For an additional amount for "Salaries and Expenses", $6,000,000 to remain available until September 30, 2020, for necessary expenses to prevent, prepare for, and respond to coronavirus: Provided , That such amount is designated by the Congress as being for an emergency requirement pursuant to section 251(b)(2)(A)(i) of the Balanced Budget and Emergency Deficit Control Act of 1985.

defender services

For an additional amount for "Defender Services", $1,000,000, to remain available until September 30, 2020, to prevent, prepare for, and respond to coronavirus: Provided, That such amount is designated by the Congress as being for an emergency requirement pursuant to section 251(b)(2)(A)(i) of the Balanced Budget and Emergency Deficit Control Act of 1985.

DISTRICT OF COLUMBIA

Federal Funds

federal payment for emergency planning and security costs in the district of columbia

For an additional amount for the "Federal Payment for Emergency Planning and Security Costs in the District of Columbia" for the Federal payment of necessary expenses, as determined by the Mayor of the District of Columbia in written consultation with the elected county or city officials of surrounding jurisdictions, $11,000,000, to remain available until September 30, 2020, to prevent, prepare for, and respond to coronavirus: Provided , That such amounts are designated by the Congress as being for an emergency requirement pursuant to section 251(b)(2)(A)(i) of the Balanced Budget and Emergency Deficit Control Act of 1985.

INDEPENDENT AGENCIES

Election Assistance Commissions

salaries and expenses

For an additional amount for "Salaries and Expenses", $5,000,000, to assist States with contingency planning, preparation, and resilience of elections for

Federal office: Provided, That such amount is designated by the Congress as being for an emergency requirement pursuant to section 251(b)(2)(A)(i) of the Balanced Budget and Emergency Deficit Control Act of 1985.

election administration grants

For an additional amount for payments by the Election Assistance Commission to States for contingency planning, preparation, and resilience of elections for Federal office, $4,000,000,000 to remain available until September 30, 2021: Provided , That under this heading the term "State" means each of the 50 States, the District of Columbia, the Commonwealth of Puerto Rico, Guam, American Samoa, the United States Virgin Islands, and the Commonwealth of the Northern Mariana Islands: Provided further, That the amount of the payments made to a State under this heading shall be consistent with section 103 of the Help America Vote Act of 2002 (52 U.S.C. 20903): Provided further , That for the purposes of the preceding proviso, each reference to "$5,000,000" in section 103 shall be deemed to refer to "$7,500,000": Provided further , That not less than 50 percent of the amount of the payment made to a State under this heading shall be allocated in cash or in kind to the units of local government which are responsible for the administration of elections for Federal office in the State: Provided further , That such amount is designated by the Congress as being for an emergency requirement pursuant to section 251(b)(2)(A)(i) of the Balanced Budget and Emergency Deficit Control Act of 1985.

Federal Communications Commission

salaries and expenses

For an additional amount for "Salaries and Expenses", $200,000,000, to remain available until September 30, 2020, to prevent, prepare for, and respond to coronavirus by providing to health care providers telecommunications services, information services, and devices necessary to enable the provision of telehealth services during an emergency period, as defined in section 1135(g)(1) of the Social Security Act (42 U.S.C. 1320b–5(g)(1)): Provided , That the Federal Communications Commission may rely on the rules of the Commission under part 54 of title 47, Code of Federal Regulations, in administering such amount if the Commission determines that such administration is in the public interest and upon the advance notification of the Committees on Appropriations of the House of Representatives and the Senate: Provided further , That such amount is designated by the Congress as being for an emergency requirement pursuant to section 251(b)(2)(A)(i) of the Balanced Budget and Emergency Deficit Control Act of 1985.

emergency connectivity fund

For an additional amount for the "Emergency Connectivity Fund", as authorized under title II of division U of the Take Responsibility for Workers and Families Act, for the provision of Wi-fi hotspots and connected devices to schools and libraries, $2,000,000,000, to remain available until September 30, 2021: Provided , That such amount is designated by the Congress as being for an emergency requirement pursuant to section 251(b)(2)(A)(i) of the Balanced Budget and Emergency Deficit Control Act of 1985.

emergency broadband connectivity fund

For an additional amount for the "Emergency Broadband Connectivity Fund", as authorized under title III of division U of the Take Responsibility for Workers and Families Act, for the provision of an emergency lifeline broadband benefit, $1,000,000,000, to remain available until September 30, 2021: Provided , That such amount is designated by the Congress as being for an emergency requirement pursuant to section 251(b)(2)(A)(i) of the Balanced Budget and Emergency Deficit Control Act of 1985.

General Services Administration

real property activities

federal buildings fund

building operations

For an additional amount, to be deposited in the "Federal Buildings Fund", $275,000,000, to remain available until expended, to prevent, prepare for, and respond to coronavirus: Provided , That such funds may be used to reimburse costs incurred for the purposes provided under this heading: Provided further , That amounts made available under this heading shall be in addition to any other amounts available for such purposes: Provided further , That such amount is designated by the Congress as being for an emergency requirement pursuant to section 251(b)(2)(A)(i) of the Balanced Budget and Emergency Deficit Control Act of 1985.

technology modernization fund

For an additional amount for the "Technology Modernization Fund", $3,000,000,000, to remain available until September 20, 2022, for technology-related modernization activities to prevent, prepare for, and respond to coronavirus: Provided , That such amount is designated by the Congress as being for an emergency requirement pursuant to section 251(b)(2)(A)(i) of the Balanced Budget and Emergency Deficit Control Act of 1985.

Office Of Personnel Management

salaries and expenses

For an additional amount for "Salaries and Expenses", $12,100,000, to prevent, prepare for, and respond to coronavirus: Provided , That such amount is designated by the Congress as being for an emergency requirement pursuant to section 251(b)(2)(A)(i) of the Balanced Budget and Emergency Deficit Control Act of 1985.

Small Business Administration

economic injury grants

For an additional amount for the cost of providing economic recovery grants for small businesses impacted by coronavirus as authorized by section 190009 of the Take Responsibility for Workers and Families Act, $100,000,000,000, to remain available until September 30, 2021: Provided , That such amount is designated by the Congress as being for an emergency requirement pursuant to section 251(b)(2)(A)(i) of the Balanced Budget and Emergency Deficit Control Act of 1985.

disaster loans program account

For an additional amount for the "Disaster Loans Program Account" for the cost of direct loans authorized by section 7(b) of the Small Business Act, including to carry out the requirements of section 190016 of the Take Responsibility for Workers and Families Act (relating to economic injury disaster loan improvements), $25,739,000,000, to remain available until expended: Provided , That up to $739,000,000 may be transferred to and merged with "Small Business Administration—Salaries and Expenses": Provided further , That for purposes of section 7(b)(2)(D) of the Small Business Act, coronavirus shall be deemed to be a disaster and amounts available under "Disaster Loans Program Account" for the cost of direct loans in any fiscal year may be used to make economic injury disaster loans under such section in response to the coronavirus: Provided further , That none of the funds provided under this heading in this Act may be used for indirect administrative expenses: Provided further , That such amount is designated by the Congress as being for an emergency requirement pursuant to section 251(b)(2)(A)(i) of the Balanced Budget and Emergency Deficit Control Act of 1985: Provided further , That amounts repurposed under this heading that were previously designated by the Congress as an emergency requirement pursuant to the Balanced Budget and Emergency Deficit Control Act of 1985 are designated by the Congress as an emergency requirement pursuant to section 251(b)(2)(A)(i) of the Balanced Budget and Emergency Deficit Control Act of 1985.

small business debt relief

For an additional amount for the cost of loan debt relief as authorized by section 190011 of the Take Responsibility for Workers and Families Act, $16,800,000,000 to remain available until September 30, 2021: Provided , That such amount is designated by the Congress as being for an emergency requirement pursuant to section 251(b)(2)(A)(i) of the Balanced Budget and Emergency Deficit Control Act of 1985.

business loans program account

For an additional amount for "Business Loans Program Account", for the cost of direct loans and loan guarantees, $304,407,000,000, to remain available until expended, of which $7,000,000 shall be for the cost of direct loans, $299,400,000,000 shall be for the cost of payroll protection loans as authorized by section 190002(a) of the Take Responsibility for Workers and Families Act, and $5,000,000,000 shall be for the cost of guaranteed loans under section 503 of the Small Business Investment Act of 1958 and section 7(a) of the Small Business Act, including to carry out the requirements of section 190012 (relating to temporary fee reductions), section 190013 (relating to guarantee amounts), and section 190014 (relating to maximum loan amount and program levels for 7(a) loans) of the Take Responsibility for Workers and Families Act: Provided further, That for the period of fiscal years 2020 through 2021, guarantees of trust certificates authorized by section 5(g) of the Small Business Act shall not exceed a principal amount of $60,000,000,000: Provided , That for the period of fiscal years 2020 through 2021, commitments for general business loans authorized under section 7(a) of the Small Business Act shall not exceed $75,000,000,000: Provided further , That amounts provide in this paragraph for the cost of guaranteed loans under section 7(a) of the Small Business Act are in addition to amounts otherwise available for the same purposes: Provided further , That notwithstanding any other provision of law, no amounts made available under this heading shall be available for transfer to another budget account: Provided further , That such amount is designated by the Congress as being for an emergency requirement pursuant to section 251(b)(2)(A)(i) of the Balanced Budget and Emergency Deficit Control Act of 1985.

entrepreneurial development programs

For an additional amount for "Entrepreneurial Development Programs" as authorized under section 190003 of the Take Responsibility for Workers and Families Act, $265,000,000, to remain available until September 30, 2021, of which $240,000,000 shall be for grants to small business development centers: Provided , That such amount is designated by the Congress as being for an emergency requirement pursuant to section 251(b)(2)(A)(i) of the Balanced Budget and Emergency Deficit Control Act of 1985.

office of inspector general

For an additional amount for "Office of Inspector General" for carrying out the provisions of the Inspector General Act of 1978, $25,000,000, to remain available until expended, for oversight and audit of programs, grants, and projects funded under this title: Provided, That such amount is designated by the Congress as being for an emergency requirement pursuant to section 251(b)(2)(A)(i) of the Balanced Budget and Emergency Deficit Control Act of 1985.

salaries and expenses

For an additional amount for "Salaries and Expenses", $775,000,000, to remain available until September 30, 2021, of which $50,000,000 shall be for marketing, management, and technical assistance under section 7(m) of the Small Business Act (15 U.S.C. 636(m)(4)) by intermediaries that make microloans under the microloan program, and of which $25,000,000 shall be for resources and services in languages other than English, as authorized in section 190010 of the Take Responsibility for Workers and Families Act: Provided , That such amount is designated by the Congress as being for an emergency requirement pursuant to section 251(b)(2)(A)(i) of the Balanced Budget and Emergency Deficit Control Act of 1985.

Administrative Provision—Small Business Administration

Sec. 10502. Notwithstanding section 7(b)(2)(D) of the Small Business Act, the Small Business Administration shall issue a disaster declaration for each

State and territory for coronavirus.

United States Postal Service

payment to postal service fund

For payment to the "Postal Service Fund", for revenue forgone due to the coronavirus pandemic, $25,000,000,000, to remain available until September 30, 2022: Provided , That such amount is designated by the Congress as being for an emergency requirement pursuant to section 251(b)(2)(A)(i) of the Balanced Budget and Emergency Deficit Control Act of 1985.

GENERAL PROVISION—THIS TITLE

Sec. 10503. Notwithstanding any other provision of law, funds made available under each heading in this title shall only be used for the purposes specifically described under that heading.

TITLE VI

DEPARTMENT OF HOMELAND SECURITY

Management Directorate

operations and support

For an additional amount for "Operations and Support", $178,000,000, for the purchase of personal protective equipment and related supplies for components of the Department of Homeland Security to prevent, prepare for, and respond to coronavirus: Provided, That such amount is designated by the Congress as being for an emergency requirement pursuant to section 251(b)(2)(A)(i) of the Balanced Budget and Emergency Deficit Control Act of 1985.

Transportation And Security Administration

operations and support

For an additional amount for "Operations and Support", $100,000,000, to prevent, prepare for, and respond to coronavirus; of which $54,000,000 is for enhanced sanitation at airport security checkpoints; of which $26,000,000 is for overtime and travel costs for Transportation Security Officers; and of which $20,000,000 is for the purchase of explosive trace detection swabs: Provided, That such amount is designated by the Congress as being for an emergency requirement pursuant to section 251(b)(2)(A)(i) of the Balanced Budget and Emergency Deficit Control Act of 1985.

Coast Guard

operations and support

For an additional amount for "Operations and Support", $141,000,000, to prevent, prepare for, and respond to coronavirus through activation of Coast Guard Reserve personnel under section 12302 of title 10, United States Code and for purchases to increase the capability and capacity of information technology systems and infrastructure to support telework and remote access: Provided, That such amount is designated by the Congress as being for an emergency requirement pursuant to section 251(b)(2)(A)(i) of the Balanced Budget and Emergency Deficit Control Act of 1985.

Cybersecurity And Infrastructure Security Agency
operations and support
For an additional amount for "Operations and Support", $14,400,000, to prevent, prepare for, and respond to coronavirus through interagency critical infrastructure coordination and related activities: Provided, That such amount is designated by the Congress as being for an emergency requirement pursuant to section 251(b)(2)(A)(i) of the Balanced Budget and Emergency Deficit Control Act of 1985.
Federal Emergency Management Agency
operations and support
For an additional amount for "Operations and Support", $45,000,000, for facilities and information technology to prevent, prepare for, and respond to coronavirus: Provided, That such amount is designated by the Congress as being for an emergency requirement pursuant to section 251(b)(2)(A)(i) of the Balanced Budget and Emergency Deficit Control Act of 1985.
federal assistance
For an additional amount for "Federal Assistance", $200,000,000, for the emergency food and shelter program under title III of the McKinney-Vento Homeless Assistance Act (42 U.S.C. 11331 et seq.): Provided, That notwithstanding sections 315 and 316(b) of such Act, funds made available under this section shall be disbursed by the Emergency Food and Shelter Program National Board not later than 30 days after the date on which such funds become available: Provided further, That such funds may be used to reimburse jurisdictions or local recipient organizations for costs incurred in providing services on or after January 1, 2020: Provided further, That such amount is designated by the Congress as being for an emergency requirement pursuant to section 251(b)(2)(A)(i) of the Balanced Budget and Emergency Deficit Control Act of 1985.
For an additional amount for "Federal Assistance", to supplement funds otherwise available for the "Assistance to Firefighters Grants" $100,000,000, to remain available until September 30, 2021, for the purchase of personal protective equipment and related supplies to prevent, prepare for, and respond to coronavirus: Provided, That such amount is designated by the Congress as being for an emergency requirement pursuant to section 251(b)(2)(A)(i) of the Balanced Budget and Emergency Deficit Control Act of 1985.
disaster relief fund
For an additional amount for "Disaster Relief Fund", $2,000,000,000, to remain available until expended: Provided, That such amount is designated by the Congress as being for an emergency requirement pursuant to section 251(b)(2)(A)(i) of the Balanced Budget and Emergency Deficit Control Act of 1985.
General Provisions—This Title
Sec. 10601. Notwithstanding any other provision of law, funds made available under each heading in this title, except for "Federal Emergency Management

Agency—Disaster Relief Fund", shall only be used for the purposes specifically described under that heading.

Sec. 10602. (a) Assistance provided under the emergency declaration issued by the President on March 13, 2020, pursuant to section 501(b) of the Robert T. Stafford Disaster Relief and Emergency Assistance Act (42 U.S.C. 5121–5207), and under any subsequent major declaration under section 401 of such Act that supersedes such emergency declaration, shall be at a 100 percent Federal cost share.

(b) Amounts repurposed under this section that were previously designated by the Congress, respectively, as an emergency requirement or as being for disaster relief pursuant to the Balanced Budget and Emergency Deficit Control Act are designated by the Congress as being for an emergency requirement pursuant to section 251(b)(2)(A)(i) of the Balanced Budget and Emergency Deficit Control Act of 1985 or as being for disaster relief pursuant to section 251(b)(2)(D) of the Balanced Budget and Emergency Deficit Control Act of 1985.

Sec. 10603. Notwithstanding any other provision of law, any amounts appropriated for "Department of Homeland Security—Federal Emergency Management Agency—Disaster Relief Fund" in this Act are available only for the purposes for which they were appropriated.

Sec. 10604. (a) For calendar year 2020 and calendar year 2021, any provision of law limiting the aggregate amount of premium pay or overtime payable on a biweekly or calendar year basis, or establishing an aggregate limitation on pay, shall not apply to any premium pay or overtime that is funded, either directly or through reimbursement, by the "Federal Emergency Management Agency—Disaster Relief Fund" related to an emergency or major disaster declared in calendar year 2020.

(b) Pay exempted from otherwise applicable limits under this section shall not cause the aggregate pay for the calendar year to exceed the rate of basic pay payable for a position at level II of the Executive Schedule under section 5313 of title 5, United States Code.

(c) Notwithstanding any other provisions of law, an Executive agency shall not be liable for damages, fees, interests, or costs of any kind as a result of any delay occurring prior to the date of enactment of this Act in payments made pursuant to this section.

(d) This section shall take effect as if enacted on December 31, 2019.

(e) Amounts repurposed under this section that were previously designated by the Congress, respectively, as an emergency requirement or as being for disaster relief pursuant to the Balanced Budget and Emergency Deficit Control Act are designated by the Congress as being for an emergency requirement pursuant to section 251(b)(2)(A)(i) of the Balanced Budget and Emergency Deficit Control Act of 1985 or as being for disaster relief pursuant to section 251(b)(2)(D) of the Balanced Budget and Emergency Deficit Control Act of 1985.

Sec. 10605. The Secretary of Homeland Security, under the authority granted under section 205(b) of the REAL ID Act of 2005 (Public Law 109–13; 49 U.S.C. 30301 note) shall extend the deadline by which States are required to meet the driver license and identification card issuance requirements under section 202(a)(1) of such Act until not earlier than September 30, 2021.

Sec. 10606. (a) For the emergency declared on March 13, 2020, by the President under section 501 of the Robert T. Stafford Disaster Relief and Emergency Assistance Act (42 U.S.C. 5191) the President may provide assistance for—

(1) activities, costs, and purchases of State and local jurisdictions including—

(A) activities eligible for assistance under sections 301, 415, 416, and 426 of the Robert T. Stafford Disaster Relief and Emergency Assistance Act (42 U.S.C. 5141, 5182, 5183, 5189d);

(B) backfill costs for first responders and other essential employees who are ill or quarantined;

(C) increased operating costs for essential government services due to such emergency, including costs for implementing continuity plans;

(D) costs of providing guidance and information to the public and for call centers to disseminate such guidance and information;

(E) costs associated with establishing virtual services;

(F) costs for establishing and operating remote test sites;

(G) training provided specifically in anticipation of or in response to the event on which such emergency declaration is predicated;

(H) personal protective equipment and other critical supplies for first responders; and

(I) public health and medical supplies; and

(2) activities and costs of nonprofit organizations including—

(A) operating and equipment costs for blood donation activities, including personnel costs; and

(B) establishing and operating public call centers in support of government operations, including personnel costs.

(b) The activities specified in subsection (a) may also be eligible for assistance under any major disaster declared by the President under section 401 of such Act that supersedes the emergency declaration described in such subsection.

(c) Nothing in this section shall be construed to make ineligible any assistance that would otherwise be eligible under section 502 of such Act.

Sec. 10607. (a) During the public health emergency declared pursuant to section 319 of the Public Health Service Act (42 U.S.C. 247d) with respect to the COVID–19 pandemic, the Secretary of Homeland Security, Secretary of State, Attorney General or Secretary of Labor, as appropriate, shall temporarily suspend or modify any procedural requirement with which an applicant, petitioner, or other person or entity must otherwise comply under the immigration laws, as defined in section 101(a)(17) of the Immigration and Nationality Act (8 U.S.C. 1101(a)(17)), or any regulation pertaining thereto, when necessary to—

(1) promote government efficiency;
(2) ensure the timely and fair adjudication of applications or petitions;
(3) prevent hardship to applicants, petitioners, beneficiaries, or other persons or entities, including by granting automatic or other extensions or renewals when necessary to protect individuals from lapses in status or work authorization; or
(4) protect the public interest.
(b) Notwithstanding any other provision law, the requirements of chapter 5 of title 5, U.S. Code (commonly known as the Administrative Procedure Act), or any other law relating to rulemaking, information collection or publication in the Federal Register shall not apply to any action taken under the authority of this section.
(c) Specific Authority For Expiring Statuses Or Work Authorization.—Notwithstanding any provision of the Immigration and Nationality Act or any other provision of law, with respect to any alien whose status, whether permanent, temporary, or deferred, or employment authorization has expired within the 30 days preceding the date of the enactment of this act, or will expire by the later of one year from the date of enactment of this act or 90 days from the rescission of the March 13, 2020, Presidential Proclamation declaring a national emergency, the Secretary of Homeland Security shall automatically extend such status or work authorization for the same time period as the alien's status or work authorization.
(d) The amounts made available by this section are designated by the Congress as being for an emergency requirement pursuant to section 251(b)(2)(A)(i) of the Balanced Budget and Emergency Deficit Control Act of 1985
Sec. 10608. (a) Amounts provided for "Coast Guard—Operations and Support" in the Consolidated Appropriations Act, 2020 (Public Law 116–93) may be available for pay and benefits of Coast Guard Yard and Vessel Documentation personnel, Non-Appropriated Funds personnel, and for Morale, Welfare and Recreation Programs.
(b) Any amounts repurposed under subsection (a) that were previously designated by the Congress as an emergency requirement or as being for Overseas Contingency Operations/Global War on Terrorism pursuant to the Balanced Budget and Emergency Deficit Control Act of 1985 are designated by the Congress as being for an emergency requirement pursuant to section 251(b)(2)(A)(i) of the Balanced Budget and Emergency Deficit Control Act of 1985 or as for Overseas Contingency Operations/Global War on Terrorism pursuant to section 251(b)(2)(A)(ii) of the Balanced Budget and Emergency Deficit Control Act of 1985.

TITLE VII

—INTERIOR, ENVIRONMENT, AND RELATED AGENCIES
DEPARTMENT OF THE INTERIOR

Bureau Of Indian Affairs
operation of indian programs
(including transfer of funds)

For an additional amount for "Operation of Indian Programs", $453,000,000, to remain available until September 30, 2021, to prevent, prepare for, and respond to coronavirus, including to support public safety and justice programs, welfare and social service programs (including assistance to individuals), and for aid to Tribal governments: Provided, That of such sums, funds may be used for executive direction to carry out cleaning of facilities, to purchase personal protective equipment, and to obtain information technology: Provided further, That the limitation on welfare assistance funds included in the matter preceding the first proviso under this heading in the Further Consolidated Appropriations Act, 2020 (Public Law 116–94) shall not apply to amounts provided for such programs in this paragraph: Provided further, That assistance received hereunder shall not be included in the calculation of funds received by those Tribal governments who participate in the "Small and Needy" program: Provided further, That amounts provided under this heading in this Act may be made available for distribution through Tribal priority allocations for Tribal response and capacity building activities related to the purposes identified under this heading in this Act: Provided further, That such amounts, if transferred to Tribes and Tribal organizations under the Indian Self-Determination and Education Assistance Act: (1) will be transferred on a one-time basis, (2) are non-recurring funds that are not part of the amount required by 25 U.S.C. 5325, and (3) may only be used for the purposes identified under this heading in this Act, notwithstanding any other provision of law: Provided further, That such amount is designated by the Congress as being for an emergency requirement pursuant to section 251(b)(2)(A)(i) of the Balanced Budget and Emergency Deficit Control Act of 1985.

Bureau Of Indian Education
operation of indian education programs

For an additional amount for "Operation of Indian Education Programs", $69,000,000, to remain available until September 30, 2021, to prevent, prepare for, and respond to coronavirus, including, in addition to amounts otherwise available, support for Tribally-Controlled Colleges and Universities, salaries, transportation, and information technology: Provided, That of the amounts provided in this paragraph, not less than $20,000,000 shall be for Tribally-Controlled Colleges and Universities: Provided further, That such amount is designated by the Congress as being for an emergency requirement pursuant to section 251(b)(2)(A)(i) of the Balanced Budget and Emergency Deficit Control Act of 1985.

Departmental Offices
Office Of The Secretary
departmental operations
(including transfers of funds)

For an additional amount for "Departmental Operations" for necessary expenses to prevent, preapre for, and respond to coronavirus, $158,400,000, to remain available until September 30, 2021: Provided, That the amounts made available in this paragraph shall be used to absorb increased operational costs associated with the coronavirus outbreak including but not limited to: purchase of equipment and supplies to disinfect and clean buildings and public areas, support law enforcement and emergency management operations, biosurveillance of wildlife and environmental persistence studies, employee overtime and special pay expenses, and for other response, mitigation, or recovery activities associated with the coronavirus outbreak: Provided further, That the amounts made available by this paragraph may be transferred between the Office of the Secretary and any Department of the Interior component bureau or office that received funding in division D of the Further Consolidated Appropriations Act, 2020 (Public Law 116–94): Provided further, That concurrent with any such transfer the Secretary shall notify the House and Senate Committees on Appropriations in writing and provide a detailed description of and justification for each transfer: Provided further, That as soon as practicable after the date of enactment of this Act, the Secretary shall transfer $1,000,000 to the Office of the Inspector General, "Salaries and Expenses" account for oversight activities related to the implementation of programs, activities, or projects funded herein: Provided further, That expenditure of amounts made available herein may be made through direct expenditure or cooperative agreement: Provided further, That such amount is designated by the Congress as being for an emergency requirement pursuant to section 251(b)(2)(A)(i) of the Balanced Budget and Emergency Deficit Control Act of 1985.

Insular Affairs

For an additional amount for "Assistance to Territories", $55,000,000, to remain available until September 30, 2021, to prevent, prepare for, and respond to coronavirus, domestically or internationally, for territorial assistance, specifically for general technical assistance: Provided, That such amount is designated by the Congress as being for an emergency requirement pursuant to section 251(b)(2)(A)(i) of the Balanced Budget and Emergency Deficit Control Act of 1985.

ENVIRONMENTAL PROTECTION AGENCY

Science And Technology

For an additional amount for "Science and Technology", $2,250,000, to remain available until September 30, 2021, to prevent, prepare for, and respond to coronavirus, of which $750,000 shall be for necessary expenses for cleaning and disinfecting equipment or facilities of, or for use by, the Environmental Protection Agency, and $1,500,000 shall be for research on methods to reduce the risks from environmental transmission of coronavirus via contaminated surfaces or materials: Provided, That such amount is designated by the Congress as being for an emergency requirement pursuant to section 251(b)

(2)(A)(i) of the Balanced Budget and Emergency Deficit Control Act of 1985.

Environmental Programs And Management

For an additional amount for "Environmental Programs and Management", $3,910,000, to remain available until September 30, 2021, to prevent, prepare for, and respond to coronavirus, of which $2,410,000 shall be for necessary expenses for cleaning and disinfecting equipment or facilities of, or for use by, the Environmental Protection Agency, and operational continuity of Environmental Protection Agency programs and related activities, and $1,500,000 shall be for expediting registration and other actions related to pesticides to address coronavirus: Provided, That such amount is designated by the Congress as being for an emergency requirement pursuant to section 251(b)(2)(A)(i) of the Balanced Budget and Emergency Deficit Control Act of 1985.

Buildings And Facilities

For an additional amount for "Buildings and Facilities", $300,000, to remain available until September 30, 2021, to prevent, prepare for, and respond to coronavirus: Provided, That such funds shall be for necessary expenses for cleaning and disinfecting equipment or facilities of, or for use by, the Environmental Protection Agency: Provided further, That such amount is designated by the Congress as being for an emergency requirement pursuant to section 251(b)(2)(A)(i) of the Balanced Budget and Emergency Deficit Control Act of 1985.

Hazardous Substance Superfund

For an additional amount for "Hazardous Substance Superfund", $770,000, to remain available until September 30, 2021, to prevent, prepare for, and respond to coronavirus: Provided, That such funds shall be for necessary expenses for cleaning and disinfecting equipment or facilities of, or for use by, the Environmental Protection Agency: Provided further, That such amount is designated by the Congress as being for an emergency requirement pursuant to section 251(b)(2)(A)(i) of the Balanced Budget and Emergency Deficit Control Act of 1985.

DEPARTMENT OF AGRICULTURE

Forest Service

forest and rangeland research

For an additional amount for "Forest and Rangeland Research", $3,000,000, to remain available until September 30, 2021, for the reestablishment of abandoned or failed experiments associated with coronavirus restrictions: Provided, That such amount is designated by the Congress as being for an emergency requirement pursuant to section 251(b)(2)(A)(i) of the Balanced Budget and Emergency Deficit Control Act of 1985.

national forest system

For an additional amount for"National Forest System", $33,800,000, to remain available until September 30, 2021, to prevent, prepare for, and respond to coronavirus, including for personal protective equipment, for cleaning and disinfecting public recreation amenities, and for necessary expenses related to cybersecurity, the provision of telework ready equipment, and Information Technology help desk personnel: Provided, That such amount is designated by the Congress as being for an emergency requirement pursuant to section 251(b)(2)(A)(i) of the Balanced Budget and Emergency Deficit Control Act of 1985.

capital improvement and maintenance

For an additional amount for "Capital Improvement and Maintenance", $26,800,000, to remain available until September 30, 2021, for necessary expenses related to cybersecurity, the provision of telework ready equipment, and Information Technology help desk personnel, and for the cleaning, disinfecting, and janitorial services to prevent, prepare for, and respond to coronavirus: Provided, That such amount is designated by the Congress as being for an emergency requirement pursuant to section 251(b)(2)(A)(i) of the Balanced Budget and Emergency Deficit Control Act of 1985.

wildland fire management

For an additional amount for "Wildland Fire Management" to supplement amounts otherwise available for Preparedness, $7,000,000, to remain available until September 30, 2021, for personal protective equipment and necessary expenses of first responders to prevent, prepare for, and respond to coronavirus: Provided, That such amount is designated by the Congress as being for an emergency requirement pursuant to section 251(b)(2)(A)(i) of the Balanced Budget and Emergency Deficit Control Act of 1985.

DEPARTMENT OF HEALTH AND HUMAN SERVICES

Indian Health Service

indian health services

For an additional amount for "Indian Health Services", $1,032,000,000, to remain available until September 30, 2021, for preparedness, response, surveillance, and health service activities for coronavirus, including for public health support, electronic health record modernization, telehealth and other IT upgrades, Purchased/Referred care, Catastrophic Health Emergency Fund, community health representatives, Urban Indian Organizations, Tribal Epidemiology Centers, and other activities to protect the safety of patients and staff: Provided, That none of the funds appropriated by this Act to the Indian Health Service for the Electronic Health Record system shall be made available for obligation to execute a Request for Proposal for selection of core components appropriate to support the initial capacity of the system unless the Committees on Appropriations of the House of Representatives and the Senate have been briefed 90 days in advance of such execution of a Request for Proposal: Provided further, That of the amount provided in this paragraph, not less than $450,000,000 shall be distributed through Tribal shares and contracts with Urban Indian Organizations: Provided further, That any amounts provided in this paragraph not allocated pursuant to the preceding proviso shall be allocated at the discretion of the Director of the Indian Health

Service: Provided further, That such amounts may be used to supplement amounts otherwise available under "Indian Health Facilities": Provided further, That such amounts, if transferred to Tribes and Tribal organizations under the Indian Self-Determination and Education Assistance Act, will be transferred on a one-time basis and that these non-recurring funds are not part of the amount required by 25 U.S.C. 5325, and that such amounts may only be used for the purposes identified under this heading notwithstanding any other provision of law: Provided further, That such amount is designated by the Congress as being for an emergency requirement pursuant to section 251(b)(2)(A)(i) of the Balanced Budget and Emergency Deficit Control Act of 1985.

Agency For Toxic Substances And Disease Registry

toxic substances and environmental public health

For an additional amount for "Toxic Substances and Environmental Public Health", $12,500,000, to remain available until September 30, 2021, to monitor, prevent, prepare for, and respond to coronavirus and other emerging infectious diseases, domestically or internationally; of which $7,500,000 shall be for necessary expenses of the Geospatial Research, Analysis and Services Program (GRASP) to support spatial analysis and GIS mapping of infectious disease hot spots, including cruise ships; and $5,000,000 shall be for necessary expenses for awards for Pediatric Environmental Health Specialties Units and state health departments to provide guidance and outreach on safe practices for home, school, and daycare facilities disinfection for facilities that have experienced or want to prevent coronavirus and other emerging infectious disease cases: Provided, That such amount is designated by the Congress as being for an emergency requirement pursuant to section 251(b)(2)(A)(i) of the Balanced Budget and Emergency Deficit Control Act of 1985.

INSTITUTE OF AMERICAN INDIAN AND ALASKA NATIVE CULTURE

Payment To The Institute

For an additional amount for "Payment to the Institute", $78,000, to remain available until September 30, 2021, to prevent, prepare for, and respond to coronavirus: Provided, That such amount is designated by the Congress as being for an emergency requirement pursuant to section 251(b)(2)(A)(i) of the Balanced Budget and Emergency Deficit Control Act of 1985.

SMITHSONIAN INSTITUTION

Salaries And Expenses

For an additional amount for "Salaries and Expenses", $7,500,000, to remain available until September 30, 2021, for cleaning, security, information technology, and staff overtime, to prevent, prepare for, and respond to coronavirus: Provided, That such amount is designated by the Congress as being for an emergency requirement pursuant to section 251(b)(2)(A)(i) of the Balanced Budget and Emergency Deficit Control Act of 1985.

John F. Kennedy Center For The Performing Arts

operations and maintenance

For an additional amount for "Operations and Maintenance", $35,000,000, to remain available until September 30, 2021, for operations and maintenance requirements related to the consequences of coronavirus: Provided, That notwithstanding the provisions of 20 U.S.C. 76h et seq., funds provided in this Act shall be made available to cover operating expenses required to ensure the continuity of the John F. Kennedy Center for the Performing Arts and its affiliates, including for employee compensation and benefits, grants, contracts, payments for rent or utilities, fees for artists or performers, information technology, and other administrative expenses: Provided further, That no later than October 31, 2020, the Board of Trustees of the Center shall submit a report to the Committees on Appropriations of the House of Representatives and Senate that includes a detailed explanation of the distribution of the funds provided herein: Provided further, That such amount is designated by the Congress as being for an emergency requirement pursuant to section 251(b)(2)(A)(i) of the Balanced Budget and Emergency Deficit Control Act of 1985.

National Foundation On The Arts And The Humanities

National Endowment For The Arts

grants and administration

For an additional amount for "Grants and Administration", $300,000,000, to remain available until September 30, 2021, for grants to respond to the impacts of coronavirus: Provided, That such funds are available under the same terms and conditions as grant funding appropriated to this heading in P.L. 116–94: Provided further, That 40 percent of such funds shall be distributed to State arts agencies and regional arts organizations and 60 percent of such funds shall be for direct grants: Provided further, That such amount is designated by the Congress as being for an emergency requirement pursuant to section 251(b)(2)(A)(i) of the Balanced Budget and Emergency Deficit Control Act of 1985.

National Endowment For The Humanities

grants and administration

For an additional amount for "Grants and Administration", $300,000,000, to remain available until September 30, 2021, for grants to respond to the impacts of coronavirus: Provided, That such funds are available under the same terms and conditions as grant funding appropriated to this heading in Public Law 116–94: Provided further, That 40 percent of such funds shall be distributed to state humanities councils and 60 percent of such funds shall be for direct grants: Provided further, That such amount is designated by the Congress as being for an emergency requirement pursuant to section 251(b)(2)(A)(i) of the Balanced Budget and Emergency Deficit Control Act of 1985.

GENERAL PROVISIONS

Sec. 10701. Notwithstanding any other provision of law, funds made available under the heading "National Foundation on the Arts and the Humanities—National Endowment for the Arts—Grants and Administration" for each of fiscal years 2019 and 2020 for grants for the purposes described in section 5(c) of the National Foundation on the Arts and Humanities Act of 1965 (20 U.S.C. 954(c)) may also be used by the recipients of such grants for purposes of the general operations of such recipients and the matching requirements under subsections (e), (g)(4)(A), and (p)(3) of section 5 of the National Foundation on the Arts and Humanities Act of 1965 (20 U.S.C. 954) may be waived with respect to such grants.

Sec. 10702. Notwithstanding any other provision of law, funds made available under the heading "National Foundation on the Arts and the Humanities—National Endowment for the Humanities—Grants and Administration" for each of fiscal years 2019 and 2020 for grants for the purposes described in section 7(c) and 7(h)(1) of the National Foundation on the Arts and Humanities Act of 1965 may also be used by the recipients of such grants for purposes of the general operations of such recipients and the matching requirements under subsection (h)(2)(A) of section 7 of the National Foundation on the Arts and Humanities Act of 1965 may be waived with respect to such grants.

TITLE VIII

—DEPARTMENTS OF LABOR, HEALTH AND HUMAN SERVICES, AND EDUCATION, AND RELATED AGENCIES

DEPARTMENT OF LABOR

Employment And Training Administration

training and employment services

For an additional amount for "Training and Employment Services", $960,000,000, to remain available until September 30, 2021, to prevent, prepare for, and respond to coronavirus through activities under the Workforce Innovation and Opportunity Act (referred to in this Act as "WIOA") as follows:

(1) $212,000,000 for grants to States for adult employment and training activities, including supportive services and needs-related payments;

(2) $227,000,000 for grants to States for youth activities, including supportive services;

(3) $261,000,000 for grants to States for dislocated worker employment and training activities, including supportive services and needs-related payments;

(4) $250,000,000 for the Dislocated Worker Assistance National Reserve, of which $150,000,000 shall be for the Strengthening Community College Training Grant program as outlined under the heading "Training and Employment Services" in paragraph (2)(A)(ii) of title I of division A of Public Law 116–94 to assist community colleges in meeting the educational and training needs of their communities as a result of coronavirus;

(5) $10,000,000 for Migrant and Seasonal Farmworker programs, including for emergency supportive services to farmworkers, of which $500,000 shall be available for the collection and dissemination of electronic and printed materials related to coronavirus:

Provided, That such amount is designated by the Congress as being for an emergency requirement pursuant to section 251(b)(2)(A)(i) of the Balanced Budget and Emergency Deficit Control Act of 1985.

job corps

For an additional amount for "Job Corps", $100,000,000, to remain available until September 30, 2021, to prevent, prepare for, and respond to coronavirus, including for student services: Provided, That such amount is designated by the Congress as being for an emergency requirement pursuant to section 251(b)(2)(A)(i) of the Balanced Budget and Emergency Deficit Control Act of 1985.

state unemployment insurance and employment service operations

For an additional amount for "State Unemployment and Insurance and Employment Service Operations", $150,000,000, to remain available until September 30, 2021, to prevent, prepare for, and respond to coronavirus through grants to States in accordance with section 6 of the Wagner-Peyser Act: Provided, That such amount is designated by the Congress as being for an emergency requirement pursuant to section 251(b)(2)(A)(i) of the Balanced Budget and Emergency Deficit Control Act of 1985.

community service employment for older americans

For an additional amount for "Community Service Employment for Older Americans", $120,000,000, to remain available until September 30, 2021, to prevent, prepare for, and respond to coronavirus: Provided, That funds made available under this heading in this Act may, in accordance with section 517(c) of the Older Americans Act of 1965, be recaptured and reobligated: Provided further, That such amount is designated by the Congress as being for an emergency requirement pursuant to section 251(b)(2)(A)(i) of the Balanced Budget and Emergency Deficit Control Act of 1985.

program administration

For an additional amount for "Program Administration", $15,000,000, to remain available until September 30, 2020, to prevent, prepare for, and respond to coronavirus, including for the administration, oversight, and coordination of unemployment insurance activities related thereto: Provided, That such amount is designated by the Congress as being for an emergency requirement pursuant to section 251(b)(2)(A)(i) of the Balanced Budget and Emergency Deficit Control Act of 1985.

Employee Benefits Security Administration

salaries and expenses

For an additional amount for "Employee Benefits Security Administration", $3,000,000, to remain available until September 30, 2020, to prevent, prepare for, and respond to coronavirus, including for the administration, oversight, and coordination of worker protection activities related thereto: Provided, That such amount is designated by the Congress as being for an emergency requirement pursuant to section 251(b)(2)(A)(i) of the Balanced Budget and Emergency Deficit Control Act of 1985.

Wage And Hour Division

salaries and expenses

For an additional amount for "Wage and Hour Division", $6,500,000, to remain available until September 30, 2020, to prevent, prepare for, and respond to coronavirus, including for the administration, oversight, and coordination of worker protection activities related thereto: Provided, That such amount is designated by the Congress as being for an emergency requirement pursuant to section 251(b)(2)(A)(i) of the Balanced Budget and Emergency Deficit Control Act of 1985.

Occupational Safety And Health Administration

salaries and expenses

For an additional amount for "Occupational Safety and Health Administration", $30,000,000, to remain available until September 30, 2021, for worker protection activities to prevent, prepare for, and respond to coronavirus: Provided, That of that amount, $10,000,000 shall be available for Susan Harwood training grants: Provided further, That such amount is designated by the Congress as being for an emergency requirement pursuant to section 251(b)(2)(A)(i) of the Balanced Budget and Emergency Deficit Control Act of 1985.

Departmental Management

Office Of Inspector General

salaries and expenses

For an additional amount for "Office of Inspector General", $1,500,000, to remain available until September 30, 2022, for oversight of activities supported with funds appropriated to the Department of Labor: Provided, That such amount is designated by the Congress as being for an emergency requirement pursuant to section 251(b)(2)(A)(i) of the Balanced Budget and Emergency Deficit Control Act of 1985.

Veterans Employment And Training

For an additional amount for "Veterans Employment and Training," $15,000,000, to remain available through September 30, 2021, to prevent, prepare for, and respond to coronavirus, including for programs to assist homeless veterans and veterans at risk of homelessness: Provided, That such amount is designated by the Congress as being for an emergency requirement pursuant to section 251(b)(2)(A)(i) of the Balanced Budget and Emergency Deficit Control Act of 1985.

DEPARTMENT OF HEALTH AND HUMAN SERVICES

Health Resources And Services Administration

primary health care

For an additional amount for "Primary Health Care", $1,300,000,000, to remain available until September 30, 2021, for necessary expenses to prevent, prepare for, and respond to coronavirus, for grants and cooperative agreements under the Health Centers Program, as defined by section 330 of the Public Health Service Act, and for eligible entities under the Native Hawaiian Health Care

Improvement Act, including maintenance of current health care center capacity and staffing levels: Provided, That sections 330(r)(2)(B), 330(e)(6)(A)(iii), and 330(e)(6)(B)(iii) shall not apply to funds provided under this heading in this Act: Provided further, That such amount is designated by the Congress as being for an emergency requirement pursuant to section 251(b)(2)(A)(i) of the Balanced Budget and Emergency Deficit Control Act of 1985.

ryan white hiv/aids program

For an additional amount for "Ryan White HIV/AIDS Program", $90,000,000, to remain available through September 30, 2021, to prevent, prepare for, and respond to coronavirus: Provided, That awards from funds provided under this heading in this Act shall be through modifications to existing contracts and supplements to existing grants and cooperative agreements under parts A, B, C, D, F, and section 2692(a) of title XXVI of the Public Health Service Act: Provided further, That such supplements shall be awarded using a data-driven methodology determined by the Secretary of Health and Human Services: Provided further, That sections 2604(c), 2612(b), and 2651(c) of the Public Health Service Act shall not apply to funds provided under this heading in this Act: Provided further, That such amount is designated by the Congress as being for an emergency requirement pursuant to section 251(b)(2)(A)(i) of the Balanced Budget and Emergency Deficit Control Act of 1985.

health care systems

For an additional amount for "Health Care Systems", $5,000,000, to remain available until September 30, 2021 to prevent, prepare for, and respond to coronavirus, for activities authorized under sections 1271 and 1273 of the Public Health Service Act to improve the capacity of poison control centers to respond to increased calls and communications: Provided, That such amount is designated by the Congress as being for an emergency requirement pursuant to section 251(b)(2)(A)(i) of the Balanced Budget and Emergency Deficit Control Act of 1985.

rural health

For an additional amount for "Rural Health", $460,000,000, to remain available through September 30, 2021, to prevent, prepare for, and respond to coronavirus, including telephonic and virtual care for the underinsured, and for continuation and expansion of telehealth and rural health activities under sections 330A and 330I of the Public Health Service Act and section 711 of the Social Security Act: Provided, That of the amount provided under this heading in this Act, not less than $15,000,000 shall be allocated to tribes, tribal organizations, urban Indian health organizations, or health service providers to tribes: Provided further, That such amount is designated by the Congress as being for an emergency requirement pursuant to section 251(b)(2)(A)(i) of the Balanced Budget and Emergency Deficit Control Act of 1985.

Centers For Disease Control And Prevention

cdc–wide activities and program support

For an additional amount for "CDC–Wide Activities and Program Support",

$5,500,000,000, to remain available until September 30, 2024, to prevent, prepare for, and respond to coronavirus, domestically or internationally: Provided, That not less than $2,000,000,000 of the amount provided shall be for grants to or cooperative agreements with States, localities, territories, tribes, tribal organizations, urban Indian health organizations, or health service providers to tribes, for such purposes including to carry out surveillance, epidemiology, laboratory capacity, infection control, mitigation, communications, and other preparedness and response activities: Provided further, That every grantee that received a Public Health Emergency Preparedness grant for fiscal year 2019 shall receive not less than 100 percent of that grant level from funds provided in the first proviso under this heading in this Act, and not less than $125,000,000 of such funds shall be allocated to tribes, tribal organizations, urban Indian health organizations, or health service providers to tribes: Provided further, That the Director of the Centers for Disease Control and Prevention ("CDC") may satisfy the funding thresholds outlined in the preceding two provisos by making awards through other grant or cooperative agreement mechanisms: Provided further, That of the amount provided under this heading in this Act, not less than $1,000,000,000 shall be for global disease detection and emergency response: Provided further, That of the amount provided under this heading in this Act, $500,000,000 shall be for public health data surveillance and analytics infrastructure modernization: Provided further, That funds appropriated under this heading in this Act may be used for grants for the rent, lease, purchase, acquisition, construction, alteration, or renovation of non-Federally owned facilities to improve preparedness and response capability at the State and local level: Provided further, That funds may be used for purchase and insurance of official motor vehicles in foreign countries: Provided further, That such amount is designated by the Congress as being for an emergency requirement pursuant to section 251(b)(2)(A)(i) of the Balanced Budget and Emergency Deficit Control Act of 1985.

National Institutes Of Health

national heart, lung, and blood institute

For an additional amount for "National Heart, Lung, and Blood Institute", $103,400,000, to remain available until September 30, 2024, to prevent, prepare for, and respond to coronavirus, domestically or internationally: Provided, That such amount is designated by the Congress as being for an emergency requirement pursuant to section 251(b)(2)(A)(i) of the Balanced Budget and Emergency Deficit Control Act of 1985.

national institute of allergy and infectious diseases

For an additional amount for "National Institute of Allergy and Infectious Diseases", $550,000,000, to remain available until September 30, 2024, to prevent, prepare for, and respond to coronavirus, domestically or internationally: Provided, That such amount is designated by the Congress as being for an emergency requirement pursuant to section 251(b)(2)(A)(i) of the Balanced Budget and Emergency Deficit Control Act of 1985.

national institute of environmental health sciences
For an additional amount for "National Institute of Environmental Health Sciences", $10,000,000, to remain available until September 30, 2024, for worker-based training to prevent and reduce exposure of hospital employees, emergency first responders, and other workers who are at risk of exposure to coronavirus through their work duties: Provided, That such amount is designated by the Congress as being for an emergency requirement pursuant to section 251(b)(2)(A)(i) of the Balanced Budget and Emergency Deficit Control Act of 1985.
national institute of biomedical imaging and bioengineering
For an additional amount for "National Institute of Biomedical Imaging and Bioengineering", $60,000,000, to remain available until September 30, 2024, to prevent, prepare for, and respond to coronavirus, domestically or internationally: Provided, That such amount is designated by the Congress as being for an emergency requirement pursuant to section 251(b)(2)(A)(i) of the Balanced Budget and Emergency Deficit Control Act of 1985.
national library of medicine
For an additional amount for "National Library of Medicine", $10,000,000, to remain available until September 30, 2024, to prevent, prepare for, and respond to coronavirus, domestically or internationally: Provided, That such amount is designated by the Congress as being for an emergency requirement pursuant to section 251(b)(2)(A)(i) of the Balanced Budget and Emergency Deficit Control Act of 1985.
national center for advancing translational sciences
For an additional amount for "National Center for Advancing Translational Sciences", $36,000,000, to remain available until September 30, 2024, to prevent, prepare for, and respond to coronavirus, domestically or internationally: Provided, That such amount is designated by the Congress as being for an emergency requirement pursuant to section 251(b)(2)(A)(i) of the Balanced Budget and Emergency Deficit Control Act of 1985.
office of the director
For an additional amount for "Office of the Director", $30,000,000, to remain available until September 30, 2024, to prevent, prepare for, and respond to coronavirus, domestically or internationally: Provided, That the funds provided under this heading in this Act shall be available for the Common Fund established under section 402A(c)(1) of the Public Health Service Act: Provided further, That such amount is designated by the Congress as being for an emergency requirement pursuant to section 251(b)(2)(A)(i) of the Balanced Budget and Emergency Deficit Control Act of 1985.
Substance Abuse And Mental Health Services Administration
health surveillance and program support
For an additional amount for "Health Surveillance and Program Support", $435,000,000, to remain available until September 30, 2021, to prevent, prepare for, and respond to coronavirus, for program support and cross-cutting

activities that supplement activities funded under the headings "Mental Health", "Substance Abuse Treatment", and "Substance Abuse Prevention" in carrying out titles III, V, and XIX of the Public Health Service Act ("PHS Act"): Provided, That $200,000,000 of the funds made available under this heading in this Act shall be for grants to communities and community organizations who meet criteria for Certified Community Behavioral Health Clinics pursuant to section 223(a) of Public Law 113–93: Provided further, That $60,000,000 of the funds made available under this heading in this Act shall be for services to the homeless population: Provided further, That $10,000,000 of the funds made available under this heading in this Act shall be for the National Child Traumatic Stress Network: Provided further, That not less than $50,000,000 of the funds made available under this heading in this Act shall be for suicide prevention programs: Provided further, That not less than $100,000,000 of the amount made available under this heading in this Act is available for State Emergency Response Grants authorized under section 501(o) of the PHS Act: Provided further, That not less than $15,000,000 of the amount made available under this heading in this Act shall be allocated to tribes, tribal organizations, urban Indian health organizations, or health or behavioral health service providers to tribes: Provided further, That such amount is designated by the Congress as being for an emergency requirement pursuant to section 251(b)(2)(A)(i) of the Balanced Budget and Emergency Deficit Control Act of 1985.

Agency For Healthcare Research And Quality

For an additional amount for "Healthcare Research and Quality", $80,000,000, to remain available until September 30, 2024, to prevent, prepare for, and respond to coronavirus, to carry out titles III and IX of the Public Health Service Act, part A of title XI of the Social Security Act, and section 1013 of the Medicare Prescription Drug, Improvement, and Modernization Act of 2003: Provided, That section 947(c) of the Public Health Service Act shall not apply to funds made available under this heading in this Act: Provided further, That such amount is designated by the Congress as being for an emergency requirement pursuant to section 251(b)(2)(A)(i) of the Balanced Budget and Emergency Deficit Control Act of 1985.

Centers For Medicare & Medicaid Services

program management

For an additional amount for "Program Management", $550,000,000, to remain available until September 30, 2022 to prevent, prepare for, and respond to coronavirus, of which $100,000,000 shall be for necessary expenses of the survey and certification program, prioritizing nursing home facilities in localities with community transmission of coronavirus: Provided, That such amount is designated by the Congress as being for an emergency requirement pursuant to section 251(b)(2)(A)(i) of the Balanced Budget and Emergency Deficit Control Act of 1985.

Administration For Children And Families

low income home energy assistance

For an additional amount for "Low Income Home Energy Assistance", $1,400,000,000, to remain available until September 30, 2021, for making payments under subsection (b) of section 2602 of the Low-Income Home Energy Assistance Act of 1981 (42 U.S.C. 8621 et seq.): Provided, That of the amount provided under this heading in this Act, $700,000,000 shall be allocated as though the total appropriation for such payments for fiscal year 2020 was less than $1,975,000,000: Provided further, That section 2607(b)(2)(B) of such Act (42 U.S.C. 8626(b)(2)(B)) shall not apply to funds made available under this heading in this Act: Provided further, That such amount is designated by the Congress as being for an emergency requirement pursuant to section 251(b)(2)(A)(i) of the Balanced Budget and Emergency Deficit Control Act of 1985.

payments to states for the child care and development block grant

For an additional amount for "Payments to States for the Child Care and Development Block Grant", $6,000,000,000, to remain available until September 30, 2021, to prevent, prepare for, and respond to coronavirus, including for Federal administrative expenses, which shall be used to supplement, not supplant State, Territory, and Tribal general revenue funds for child care assistance for low-income families without regard to requirements in section 658E(c)(3)(D), section 658E(c)(3)(E), section 658G(a), or section 658G(c) of the Child Care and Development Block Grant Act ("CCDBG Act"): Provided, That funds made available under this heading in this Act may also be used for costs of waiving family copayments and covering costs typically paid through family copayments, continued payments and assistance to child care providers in cases of decreased enrollment, child absences, or provider closures related to coronavirus, and to ensure child care providers are able to remain open or reopen as appropriate and applicable: Provided further, That States, Territories, and Tribes are encouraged to place conditions on payments to child care providers that ensure that child care providers use a portion of funds received to continue to pay the salaries and wages of staff: Provided further, That such funds may be used for mobilizing emergency child care services, for providing temporary assistance to eligible child care providers to support costs associated with coronavirus, and for supporting child care resource and referral services: Provided further, That States, Territories, and Tribes are authorized to use funds appropriated under this heading to provide child care assistance to health care sector employees, emergency responders, sanitation workers, and other workers deemed essential during the response to coronavirus by public officials, without regard to the income eligibility requirements of section 658P(4) of the CCDBG Act: Provided further, That the Secretary shall remind States that CCDBG State plans do not need to be amended prior to utilizing existing authorities in the CCDBG Act for the purposes provided herein: Provided further, That funds appropriated under this heading in this Act shall be available to eligible child care providers under section 658P(6) of the CCDBG Act, even if such providers were not receiving

CCDBG assistance prior to the public health emergency as a result of the coronavirus, for the purposes of cleaning and sanitation, and other activities necessary to maintain or resume the operation of programs: Provided further, That obligations incurred for the purposes provided herein prior to the date of enactment of this Act may be charged to funds appropriated under this heading in this Act: Provided further, That such amount is designated by the Congress as being for an emergency requirement pursuant to section 251(b)(2)(A)(i) of the Balanced Budget and Emergency Deficit Control Act of 1985.

children and families services programs

For an additional amount for "Children and Families Services Programs", $5,202,000,000, to remain available until September 30, 2021, which shall be used as follows:

(1) $1,000,000,000 for making payments under the Head Start Act to be allocated in an amount that bears the same ratio to such portion as the number of enrolled children served by the agency involved bears to the number of enrolled children by all Head Start agencies: Provided, That none of the funds appropriated in this paragraph shall be included in the calculation of the "base grant" in subsequent fiscal years, as such term is defined in sections 640(a)(7)(A), 641A(h)(1)(B), or 645(d)(3) of the Head Start Act: Provided further, That funds appropriated in this paragraph are not subject to the allocation requirements of section 640(a) of the Head Start Act and in addition to allowable uses of fund in 45 CFR 1301–1305, shall be allowable for developing and implementing procedures and systems to improve the coordination, preparedness and response efforts with State, local, tribal, an territorial public health departments, and other relevant agencies; cost of meals and snacks not reimbursed by the Secretary of Agriculture; mental health services and supports; mental health crisis response and intervention services; training and professional development for staff on infectious disease management; purchasing necessary supplies and contracted services to sanitize and clean facilities and vehicles, if applicable; and other costs that are necessary to maintain and resume the operation of programs, such as substitute staff, technology infrastructure, or other emergency assistance: Provided further, That up to $600,000,000 shall be available for the purpose of operating supplemental summer programs through non-competitive grant supplements to existing grantees determined to be most ready to operate those programs by the Office of Head Start: Provided further, That not more than $15,000,000 shall be available for Federal administrative expenses and shall remain available through September 30, 2021: Provided further, That obligations incurred for the purposes provided herein prior to the date of enactment of this subdivision may be charged to funds appropriated under this heading.

(2) $2,500,000,000 for activities to carry out the Community Services Block Grant Act: Provided, That of the amount made available in this paragraph in this Act, $50,000,000 shall be available for Statewide activities in accordance

with section 675C(b)(1) of such Act: Provided further, That of the amount made available in this paragraph in this Act, $25,000,000 shall be available for grants to support the procurement and distribution of diapers through non-profit organizations: Provided further, That of the amount made available in this paragraph in this Act, $25,000,000 shall be available for administrative expenses in accordance with section 675C(b)(2) of such Act: Provided further, That each State, territory, or tribe shall allocate not less than xx percent of its formula award to non-profit organizations: Provided further, That for services furnished under such Act during fiscal years 2020 and 2021, States may apply the last sentence of section 673(2) of such Act by substituting "200 percent" for "125 percent".
(3) $2,000,000, for the National Domestic Violence Hotline as authorized by Section 303(b) of the Family Violence Prevention and Services Act: Provided, That the Secretary may use amounts made available in the preceding proviso for providing hotline services remotely.
(4) $100,000,000 for Family Violence Prevention and Services formula grants as authorized by Section 303(a) of the Family Violence and Prevention and Services Act: Provided, That the Secretary may use amounts made available in the preceding proviso for providing temporary housing and in-person assistance to victims of family, domestic, and dating violence: Provided further, That for funds obligated during the period of any public health emergency declared under section 319 of the Public Health Service Act with respect to coronavirus, the Secretary may waive the matching funds requirement in section 306(c)(4) of such Act.
(5) $100,000,000 for carrying out activities under the Runaway and Homeless Youth Act: Provided, That amounts made available in the preceding proviso shall be used to supplement, not supplant, existing funds and shall be available without regard to matching requirements.
(6) $1,500,000,000 for necessary expenses for grants for assisting low-income households, as defined by the grantee, in paying their water and wastewater utility costs: Provided, That eligible grantees shall be those identified in section 2003 of the Social Security Act, and funds appropriated in this paragraph shall be allocated among such entities proportionately to the size of the allotment to each such entity under such section;
Provided further, That such amount is designated by the Congress as being for an emergency requirement pursuant to section 251(b)(2)(A)(i) of the Balanced Budget and Emergency Deficit Control Act of 1985.
Administration For Community Living
aging and disability services programs
For an additional amount for "Aging and Disability Services Programs", $1,205,000,000, to remain available until September 30, 2021, to prevent, prepare for, and respond to coronavirus: Provided, That of the amount made available under this heading in this Act, $1,070,000,000 shall be for activities authorized under the Older Americans Act of 1965 ("OAA"), including

$200,000,000 for supportive services under part B of title III; $720,000,000 for nutrition services under subparts 1 and 2 of part C of title III; $30,000,000 for nutrition services under title VI; $100,000,000 for support services for family caregivers under part E of title III; and $20,000,000 for elder rights protection activities, including the long-term ombudsman program under title VII of such Act: Provided further, That of the amount made available under this heading in this Act, $50,000,000 shall be for aging and disability resource centers authorized in sections 202(b) and 411 of the OAA: Provided further, That of the amount made available under this heading in this Act, $85,000,000 shall be available for centers for independent living that have received grants funded under part C of chapter I of title VII of the Rehabilitation Act of 1973: Provided further, That to facilitate State use of funds provided under this heading in this Act, matching requirements under sections 304(d)(1)(D) and 373(g)(2) of the OAA shall not apply to funds made available under this heading: Provided further, That the transfer authority under section 308(b)(4)(A) of the OAA shall apply to funds made available under this heading in this Act by substituting "100 percent" for "40 percent": Provided further, That the State Long-Term Care Ombudsman shall have continuing direct access (or other access through the use of technology) to residents of long-term care facilities, during any portion of the public health emergency relating to coronavirus as of the date of enactment of this Act and ending on September 30, 2020, to provide services described in section 712(a)(3)(B) of the OAA: Provided further, That such amount is designated by the Congress as being for an emergency requirement pursuant to section 251(b)(2)(A)(i) of the Balanced Budget and Emergency Deficit Control Act of 1985.

Office Of The Secretary

public health and social services emergency fund

For an additional amount for "Public Health and Social Services Emergency Fund", $6,077,000,000, to remain available until September 30, 2024, to prevent, prepare for, and respond to coronavirus, domestically or internationally, including the development of necessary countermeasures and vaccines, prioritizing platform-based technologies with U.S.-based manufacturing capabilities, the purchase of vaccines, therapeutics, diagnostics, and necessary medical supplies, as well as medical surge capacity, workforce modernization, enhancements to the U.S. Commissioned Corps, telehealth access and infrastructure, initial advanced manufacturing, and related administrative activities: Provided, That no less than $1,000,000,000 shall be dedicated to the development, translation and demonstration at scale of innovations in manufacturing platforms to support vitally necessary medical countermeasures to support a reliable U.S.-sourced supply chain of: (a) vaccines, (b) therapeutics, (c) small molecule APIs (active pharmaceutical ingredients), including construction costs: Provided further, That the Secretary of Health and Human Services shall purchase vaccines developed using funds made available under this heading in this Act to respond to an outbreak or pandemic related to coronavirus in quantities determined by the Secretary to be adequate to address the public health need: Provided further, That products purchased by the Federal government with funds made available under this heading, including vaccines, therapeutics, and diagnostics, shall be purchased in accordance with Federal Acquisition Regulation guidance on fair and reasonable pricing: Provided further, That the Secretary may take such measures authorized under current law to ensure that vaccines, therapeutics, and diagnostics developed from funds provided in this Act will be affordable in the commercial market Provided further, That in carrying out the preceding proviso, the Secretary shall not take actions that delay the development of such products: Provided further, That products purchased with funds appropriated in this paragraph may, at the discretion of the Secretary of Health and Human Services, be deposited in the Strategic National Stockpile under section 319F–2 of the Public Health Service Act ("PHS Act"): Provided further, That funds appropriated under this heading in this Act may be transferred to, and merged with, the fund authorized by section 319F–4, the Covered Countermeasure Process Fund, of the PHS Act: Provided further, That funds appropriated under this heading in this Act may be used for grants for the construction, alteration, or renovation of non-Federally owned facilities to improve preparedness and response capability at the State and local level: Provided further, That funds appropriated under this heading in this Act may be used for the construction, alteration, or renovation of non-Federally owned facilities for the production of vaccines, therapeutics, and diagnostics where the Secretary determines that such a contract is necessary to secure sufficient amounts of such supplies: Provided further, That of the amount provided under this heading in this Act, $1,635,000,000 shall be for expenses necessary to carry out section 319F–2(a) of the PHS Act: Provided further, That of the amount provided under this heading in this Act, not less than $500,000,000 shall be available to the Biomedical Advanced Research and Development Authority for acquisition, construction, or renovation of privately owned U.S.-based next generation manufacturing facilities: Provided further, That not later than seven days after the date of enactment of this Act, and weekly thereafter until the Secretary declares the public health emergency related to coronavirus no longer exists, the Secretary shall report to the Committees on Appropriations of the House of Representatives and the Senate on the current inventory of personal protective equipment in the Strategic National Stockpile, including the numbers of face shields, gloves, goggles and glasses, gowns, head covers, masks, and respirators, as well as deployment of personal protective equipment during the previous week, reported by state and other jurisdiction: Provided further, That after the date that a report is required to be submitted pursuant to the preceding proviso, amounts made available for "Department of Health and Human Services—Office of the Secretary—General Departmental Management" in Public Law 116–94 for salaries and expenses of the Immediate Office of the Secretary shall be reduced by

$250,000 for each day that such report has not been submitted: Provided further, That such amount is designated by the Congress as being for an emergency requirement pursuant to section 251(b)(2)(A)(i) of the Balanced Budget and Emergency Deficit Control Act of 1985.

For an additional amount for "Public Health and Social Services Emergency Fund", $100,000,000,000, to remain available until expended, for making payments, through grants or other payment mechanisms, to covered entities to cover or reimburse health care related expenses or lost revenues attributable to the COVID–19 outbreak, including such expenses or losses occurring after January 20, 2020: Provided, That these funds may not be used to reimburse expenses or losses that have been reimbursed from other sources or that other sources are obligated to reimburse: Provided further, That, in this paragraph, the term "covered entity" means an entity that provides medical diagnoses or health care services relating to actual or possible cases of COVID–19: Provided further, That the Secretary of Health and Human Services shall, on a rolling basis, review applications and make payments under this paragraph and shall prioritize making such payments for charity care furnished, covered entities with high volumes of health care related expenses or lost revenues directly attributable to COVID–19, building or construction of temporary structures, leasing of properties, medical supplies and equipment including personal protective equipment and testing supplies, increased workforce and trainings, emergency operation centers, construction of or retrofitting facilities, forgone revenue unlikely to be earned in the future, and surge capacity: Provided further, That no covered entity may be restricted from receiving a payment under this paragraph based on any factor that is unrelated to its qualifications to perform the services required for receipt of the payment: Provided further, That payments under this paragraph shall be made in consideration of the most efficient payment systems to provide emergency payment: Provided further, That, in this paragraph, the term "payment" means a pre-payment, prospective payment, or retrospective payment: Provided further, That to be eligible for a payment under this paragraph, a covered entity shall submit to the Secretary of Health and Human Services an application that includes a statement justifying the need of the entity for the payment and the covered entity shall have a valid tax identification number: Provided further, That, not later than 3 years after final payments are made under this paragraph, the Secretary of Health and Human Services shall instruct the Office of the Inspector General or Comptroller General of the United States to audit such payments: Provided further, That such amount is designated by the Congress as being for an emergency requirement pursuant to section 251(b)(2)(A)(i) of the Balanced Budget and Emergency Deficit Control Act of 1985.

For an additional amount for "Public Health and Social Services Emergency Fund", $4,500,000,000, to remain available until September 30, 2022, to prevent, prepare for, and respond to coronavirus, to reimburse the Department of Veterans Affairs for expenses incurred by the Veterans Affairs health care system to provide medical care to civilians: Provided, That funds provided under this paragraph shall be made available only if the Secretary of Health and Human Services certifies to the Committees on Appropriations of the House of Representatives and the Senate that such funds are necessary to reimburse the Department of Veterans Affairs for expenses incurred to provide health care to civilians: Provided further, That the Secretary shall notify the Committees on Appropriations of the House of Representatives and the Senate prior to such certification: Provided further, That such amount is designated by the Congress as being for an emergency requirement pursuant to section 251(b)(2)(A)(i) of the Balanced Budget and Emergency Deficit Control Act of 1985.

public health emergency fund

For an additional amount for the "Public Health Emergency Fund", $5,000,000,000, to remain available until expended, to prevent, prepare for, and respond to coronavirus, to be deposited into the Public Health Emergency Fund, as established under section 319(b) of the Public Health Service Act: Provided, That products purchased with funds appropriated under this heading in this Act may, at the discretion of the Secretary of Health and Human Services, be deposited in the Strategic National Stockpile under section 319F–2 of the Public Health Service Act: Provided further, That such amount is designated by the Congress as being for an emergency requirement pursuant to section 251(b)(2)(A)(i) of the Balanced Budget and Emergency Deficit Control Act of 1985 such amount is designated by the Congress as being for an emergency requirement pursuant to section 251(b)(2)(A)(i) of the Balanced Budget and Emergency Deficit Control Act of 1985.

DEPARTMENT OF EDUCATION

State Fiscal Stabilization Fund

For an additional amount for "State Fiscal Stabilization Fund", $50,000,000,000, to remain available until September 30, 2022, to prevent, prepare for, and respond to coronavirus: Provided, That the Secretary of Education (referred to under this heading as "Secretary") shall make grants to the Governor of each State for support of elementary, secondary, and postsecondary education and, as applicable, early childhood education programs and services: Provided further, That of the amount made available, the Secretary shall first allocate up to one-half of 1 percent to the outlying areas and one-half of 1 percent to the Bureau of Indian Education (BIE) for activities consistent with this heading under such terms and conditions as the Secretary may determine: Provided further, That of the amount made available, the Secretary shall allocate 1 percent of funds to provide grants to States with the highest coronavirus burden to support activities under this heading: Provided further, That the Secretary shall issue a notice inviting applications not later than 30 days of enactment of this Act and approve or deny applications not later than 30 days after receipt: Provided further, That the Secretary may reserve up to $30,000,000 for administration and oversight of the activities under this heading: Provided further, That the Secretary shall allocate 61 percent of the remaining funds made available to carry out this heading to the States on the basis of their relative population of individuals aged 5 through 24 and allocate 39 percent on the basis of their relative number of children counted under section 1124(c) of the Elementary and Secondary Education Act of 1965 (referred to under this heading as "ESEA") as State grants: Provided further, That State grants shall support statewide elementary, secondary, and postsecondary activities; subgrants to local educational agencies; and, subgrants to public institutions of higher education: Provided further, That States shall allocate not less than 30 percent of the funds received under the sixth proviso as subgrants to local educational agencies on the basis of their relative number of children counted under section 1124(c) of the ESEA: Provided further, That States shall allocate not less than 30 percent of the funds received under the sixth proviso as subgrants to public institutions of higher education on the basis of the relative share of full-time equivalent students who received Pell Grants at the institution in the previous award year and of the total enrollment of full-time equivalent students at the institution in the previous award year: Provided further, That the Governor shall return to the Secretary any funds received that the Governor does not award to local educational agencies and public institutions of higher education or otherwise commit within two years of receiving such funds, and the Secretary shall reallocate such funds to the remaining States in accordance with the sixth proviso: Provided further, That Governors shall use State grants to maintain or restore State fiscal support for elementary, secondary and postsecondary education: Provided further, That funds for local educational agencies may be used for any activity authorized by the ESEA, the Individuals with Disabilities Education Act, the McKinney-Vento Homeless Assistance Act (Title VII, Subpart B), the Adult Education and Family Literacy Act or the Carl D. Perkins Career and Technical Education Act of 2006 ("the Perkins Act"): Provided further, That a State or local educational agency receiving funds under this heading may use the funds for activities coordinated with State, local, tribal, and territorial public health departments to detect, prevent, or mitigate the spread of infectious disease or otherwise respond to coronavirus; support online learning by purchasing educational technology and internet access for students, which may include assistive technology or adaptive equipment, that aids in regular and substantive educational interactions between students and their classroom instructor; provide ongoing professional development to staff in how to effectively provide quality online academic instruction; provide assistance for children and families to promote equitable participation in quality online learning; plan and implement activities related to summer learning, including providing classroom instruction or quality online learning during the summer months; plan for and coordinate during long-term closures, provide technology for quality online learning to all students, and how to support the needs of low-income students, racial and ethnic minorities, students with disabilities, English learners, students experiencing homelessness, and children in foster care, including how to address learning gaps that are created or exacerbated due to long-term closures; and other activities that are necessary to maintain the operation of and continuity of services in local educational agencies, including maintaining employment of existing personnel: Provided further, That a public institution of higher education that receives funds under this heading shall use funds for education and general expenditures and grants to students for expenses directly related to coronavirus and the disruption of campus operations (which may include emergency financial aid to students for food, housing, technology, health care, and child care costs that shall not be required to be repaid by such students) or for the acquisition of technology and services directly related to the need for distance learning and the training of faculty and staff to use such technology and services (which shall not include paying contractors a portion of tuition revenue or for pre-enrollment recruitment activities): Provided further, That priority shall be given to under-resourced institutions, institutions with high burden due to the coronavirus, and institutions who do not possess distance education capabilities at the time of enactment of this Act: Provided further, That an institution of higher education may not use funds received under this heading to increase its endowment or provide funding for capital outlays associated with facilities related to athletics, sectarian instruction, or religious worship: Provided further, That funds may be used to support hourly workers, such as education support professionals, classified school employees, and adjunct and contingent faculty: Provided further, That a Governor of a State desiring to receive an allocation under this heading shall submit an application at such time, in such manner, and containing such information as the Secretary may reasonably require: Provided further, That a State's application shall include assurances that the State will maintain support for elementary and secondary education in fiscal year 2020, fiscal year 2021, and fiscal year 2022 at least at the level of such support that is the average of such State's support for elementary and secondary education in the 3 fiscal years preceding the date of enactment of this Act: Provided further, That a State's application shall include assurances that the State will maintain State support for higher education (not including support for capital projects or for research and development or tuition and fees paid by students) in fiscal year 2020, fiscal year 2021, and fiscal year 2022 at least at the level of such support that is the average of such State's support for higher education (which shall include State and local government funding to institutions of higher education and state need-based financial aid) in the 3 fiscal years preceding the date of enactment of this Act: Provided further, That in such application, the Governor shall provide baseline data that demonstrates the State's current status in each of the areas described in such assurances in the preceding provisos: Provided further, That a State's application shall include assurances that the State will not construe any provisions under this heading as displacing any otherwise applicable provision of any collective-bargaining agreement between an eligible entity and a labor organization as defined by section 2(5) of the National Labor Relations Act (29 U.S.C. 152(5)) or analogous State law: Provided further, That a State's application shall include assurances that the State shall maintain the wages, benefits, and other terms and conditions of employment set forth in any collective-bargaining agreement between the eligible entity and a labor organization, as defined in the preceding proviso: Provided further, That a State receiving funds under this heading shall submit a report to the Secretary, at such time and in such manner as the Secretary may require, that describes the use of funds provided under this heading: Provided further, That no recipient of funds under this heading shall use funds to provide financial assistance to students to attend private elementary or secondary schools, unless such funds are used to provide special education and related services to children with disabilities, as authorized by the Individuals with Disabilities Education Act: Provided further, That the terms "elementary education" and "secondary education" have the meaning given such terms under State law: Provided further, That the term "institution of higher education" has the meaning given such term in section 101 of the Higher Education Act of 1965: Provided further, That the term "fiscal year" shall have the meaning given such term under State law: Provided further, That such amount is designated by the Congress as being for an emergency requirement pursuant to section 251(b)(2)(A)(i) of the Balanced Budget and Emergency Deficit Control Act of 1985.

Safe Schools And Citizenship Education

For an additional amount for "Safe Schools and Citizenship Education", to supplement funds otherwise available for the "Project School Emergency Response to Violence program", $200,000,000, to remain available until September 30, 2020, to prevent, prepare for, and respond to coronavirus, including to help elementary, secondary and postsecondary schools clean and disinfect affected schools, and assist in counseling and distance learning and associated costs: Provided, That such amount is designated by the Congress as being for an emergency requirement pursuant to section 251(b)(2)(A)(i) of the Balanced Budget and Emergency Deficit Control Act of 1985.

Gallaudet University

For an additional amount for "Gallaudet University", $7,000,000, to remain available until September 30, 2020, to prevent, prepare for, and respond to coronavirus, including to help defray the expenses (which may include lost revenue, reimbursement for expenses already incurred, technology costs associated with a transition to distance learning, faculty and staff trainings, and payroll) directly caused by coronavirus and to enable grants to students for expenses directly related to coronavirus and the disruption of university operations (which may include food, housing, transportation, technology, health care, and child care): Provided, That such amount is designated by the Congress as being for an emergency requirement pursuant to section 251(b)

(2)(A)(i) of the Balanced Budget and Emergency Deficit Control Act of 1985.

Student Aid Administration

For an additional amount for "Student Aid Administration", $75,000,000, to remain available until September 30, 2020, to prevent, prepare for, and respond to coronavirus in carrying out part D of title I, and subparts 1, 3, 9 and 10 of part A, and parts B, C, D, and E of title IV of the HEA, and subpart 1 of part A of title VII of the Public Health Service Act to support essential services directly related to coronavirus: Provided, That not later than 30 days after the date of enactment of this Act, the Secretary shall, using outbound communications, provide all Federal student loan borrowers a notice of their options to lower or delay payments as a result of the coronavirus by enrolling in income-driven repayment, deferment, or forbearance, and including a brief description of such options: Provided further, That such amount is designated by the Congress as being for an emergency requirement pursuant to section 251(b)(2)(A)(i) of the Balanced Budget and Emergency Deficit Control Act of 1985.

Higher Education

For an additional amount for "Higher Education", $9,500,000,000, to remain available until September 30, 2020, to prevent, prepare for, and respond to coronavirus, including under parts A and B of title III, part A of title V, subpart 4 of part A of title VII, and part B of title VII of the Higher Education Act, which may be used to defray expenses (including lost revenue, reimbursement for expenses already incurred, technology costs associated with a transition to distance education, faculty and staff trainings, and payroll) incurred by institutions of higher education and for grants to students for any component of the student's cost of attendance (as defined under section 472 of the Higher Education Act), including food, housing, course materials, technology, health care, and child care as follows:

(1) $1,500,000,000 for parts A and B of title III, part A of title V, and subpart 4 of part A of title VII to address needs directly related to coronavirus: Provided, That the Secretary of Education shall allow institutions to use prior awards under the authorities covered by the preceding proviso to prevent, prepare for, and respond to coronavirus;

(2) $8,000,000,000 for part B of title VII of the Higher Education Act for institutions of higher education (as defined in section 101 or 102(c) of the Higher Education Act) to address needs directly related to coronavirus: Provided, That such funds shall be available to the Secretary only for payments to help defray the expenses incurred by such institutions of higher education that were forced to close campuses or alter delivery of instruction as a result of coronavirus: Provided further, That any non-profit, private institution of higher education that is not otherwise eligible for a grant of at least $1,000,000, shall be eligible to receive an amount equal to whichever is lesser of the total loss of revenue and increased costs associated with the coronavirus or $1,000,000: Provided further, That funds may be used to make payments to

such institutions to provide emergency grants to students who attend such institutions for academic years beginning on or after July 1, 2019: Provided further, That such payments shall be made in accordance with criteria established by the Secretary and made publicly available without regard to section 437 of the General Education Provisions Act, section 553 of title 5, United States Code, or part B of title VII of the HEA: Provided further, That institutions receiving funds under the heading State Fiscal Stabilization Fund (not including amounts provided through state-based financial aid) shall not be eligible for additional funding for part B of title VII under this heading: Provided further, That such payments shall not be used to increase endowments or provide funding for capital outlays associated with facilities related to athletics, sectarian instruction, or religious worship: Provided further, That such amounts is designated by the Congress as being for an emergency requirement pursuant to section 251(b)(2)(A)(i) of the Balanced Budget and Emergency Deficit Control Act of 1985.

Howard University

For an additional amount for "Howard University", $13,000,000, to remain available until September 30, 2020, to prevent, prepare for, and respond to coronavirus, including to help defray the expenses (which may include lost revenue, reimbursement for expenses already incurred, technology costs associated with a transition to distance learning, faculty and staff trainings, and payroll) directly caused by coronavirus and to enable grants to students for expenses directly related to coronavirus and the disruption of university operations (which may include food, housing, transportation, technology, health care, and child care): Provided, That such amount is designated by the Congress as being for an emergency requirement pursuant to section 251(b)(2)(A)(i) of the Balanced Budget and Emergency Deficit Control Act of 1985.

Departmental Management

program administration

For an additional amount for "Program Administration", $10,000,000, to remain available until September 30, 2020, to prevent, prepare for, and respond to coronavirus: Provided, That such funds shall only be used to support network bandwidth and capacity for telework for Departmental staff and the cleaning of facilities as a result of coronavirus: Provided further, That such amount is designated by the Congress as being for an emergency requirement pursuant to section 251(b)(2)(A)(i) of the Balanced Budget and Emergency Deficit Control Act of 1985.

office of the inspector general

For an additional amount for the "Office of Inspector General", $11,000,000, to remain available until September 30, 2022, to prevent, prepare for, and respond to coronavirus, including for salaries and expenses necessary for oversight and audit of programs, grants, and projects funded in this Act to respond to coronavirus Provided, That such amount is designated by the Congress as being for an emergency requirement pursuant to section 251(b)

(2)(A)(i) of the Balanced Budget and Emergency Deficit Control Act of 1985.

RELATED AGENCIES

Corporation For National And Community Service

For an additional amount for the "Corporation for National and Community Service", $250,000,000, to remain available until September 30, 2020, to prevent, prepare for, and respond to coronavirus: Provided, That such amount is designated by the Congress as being for an emergency requirement pursuant to section 251(b)(2)(A)(i) of the Balanced Budget and Emergency Deficit Control Act of 1985.

Administrative Provision—Corporation For National And Community Service

Sec. 10801. (a) (1) The remaining unobligated balances of funds as of September 30, 2020, from amounts provided to "Corporation for National and Community Service—Operating Expenses" in title IV of Division A of the Further Consolidated Appropriations Act, 2020 (Public Law 116–94), are hereby permanently rescinded.

(2) In addition to any amounts otherwise provided, there is hereby appropriated on September 30, 2020, for an additional amount for fiscal year 2020, an amount equal to the unobligated balances rescinded pursuant to paragraph (1): Provided, That amounts made available pursuant to this paragraph shall remain available until September 30, 2021, and shall be available for the same purposes and under the same authorities that they were originally made available in Public Law 116–94.

(b) (1) The remaining unobligated balances of funds as of September 30, 2020, from amounts provided to "Corporation for National and Community Service—Salaries and Expenses" in title IV of Division A of the Further Consolidated Appropriations Act, 2020 (Public Law 116–94), are hereby permanently rescinded.

(2) In addition to any amounts otherwise provided, there is hereby appropriated on September 30, 2020, for an additional amount for fiscal year 2020, an amount equal to the unobligated balances rescinded pursuant to paragraph (1): Provided, That amounts made available pursuant to this paragraph shall remain available until September 30, 2021, and shall be available for the same purposes and under the same authorities that they were originally made available in Public Law 116–94.

(c) (1) The remaining unobligated balances of funds as of September 30, 2020, from amounts provided to "Corporation for National and Community Service—Office of Inspector General" in title IV of Division A of the Further Consolidated Appropriations Act, 2020 (Public Law 116–94), are hereby permanently rescinded.

(2) In addition to any amounts otherwise provided, there is hereby appropriated on September 30, 2020, for an additional amount for fiscal year 2020, an amount equal to the unobligated balances rescinded pursuant to paragraph (1): Provided, That amounts made available pursuant to this paragraph shall

remain available until September 30, 2021, and shall be available for the same purposes and under the same authorities that they were originally made available in Public Law 116–94.

Corporation For Public Broadcasting

For an additional amount for "Corporation for Public Broadcasting", $300,000,000, to remain available until September 30, 2020, to prevent, prepare for, and respond to coronavirus, including for fiscal stabilization grants to public telecommunications entities, with no deduction for administrative or other costs of the Corporation, to maintain programming and services and preserve small and rural stations threatened by declines in non-Federal revenues, of which $50,000,000 shall be used to support the public television system: Provided, That such amount is designated by the Congress as being for an emergency requirement pursuant to section 251(b)(2)(A)(i) of the Balanced Budget and Emergency Deficit Control Act of 1985.

Institute Of Museum And Library Services

For an additional amount for "Institute of Museum and Library Services", $500,000,000, to remain available until September 30, 2021, to prevent, prepare for, and respond to coronavirus, including grants to States, museums, territories and tribes to expand digital network access, purchase tablets and other internet-enabled devices, for operational expenses, and provide technical support services: Provided, That any matching funds requirements for States, museums, or tribes are waived: Provided further, That such amount is designated by the Congress as being for an emergency requirement pursuant to section 251(b)(2)(A)(i) of the Balanced Budget and Emergency Deficit Control Act of 1985.

Railroad Retirement Board

limitation on administration

For an additional amount for "Limitation on Administration", $10,000,000, to remain available until September 30, 2020, to prevent, prepare for, and respond to coronavirus, including the purchase of information technology equipment to improve the mobility of the workforce, and to provide for additional hiring or overtime hours as needed to administer the Railroad Unemployment Insurance Act: Provided, That such amount is designated by the Congress as being for an emergency requirement pursuant to section 251(b)(2)(A)(i) of the Balanced Budget and Emergency Deficit Control Act of 1985.

Social Security Administration

limitation on administrative expenses

For an additional amount for "Limitation on Administrative Expenses", $510,000,000, to remain available until September 30, 2021, for necessary expenses to prevent, prepare for, and respond to coronavirus, including paying the salaries and benefits of employees affected as a result of office closures, telework, phone and communication services for employees, overtime costs, and supplies, and for resources necessary for processing disability and retirement workloads and backlogs, of which the amount made available under this heading in this Act, $210,000,000 shall be for the purposes of issuing emergency assistance payments: Provided further, That such amount is designated by the Congress as being for an emergency requirement pursuant to section 251(b)(2)(A)(i) of the Balanced Budget and Emergency Deficit Control Act of 1985.

GENERAL PROVISIONS—THIS TITLE

Sec. 10802. Notwithstanding any other provision of law, funds made available under each heading in this title shall only be used for the purposes specifically described under that heading.

Sec. 10803. (a) Funds appropriated in this title may be made available to restore amounts, either directly or through reimbursement, for obligations incurred by agencies of the Department of Health and Human Services to prevent, prepare for, and respond to coronavirus, domestically or internationally, prior to the date of enactment of this Act. This subsection shall not apply to obligations incurred by the Infectious Diseases Rapid Response Reserve Fund.

(b) Grants or cooperative agreements with States, localities, territories, tribes, tribal organizations, urban Indian health organizations, or health service providers to tribes, under this title, to carry out surveillance, epidemiology, laboratory capacity, infection control, mitigation, communications, and other preparedness and response activities to prevent, prepare for, and respond to coronavirus shall include amounts to reimburse costs for these purposes incurred between January 20, 2020, and the date of enactment of this Act.

Sec. 10804. Funds appropriated by this title may be used by the Secretary of the Health and Human Services to appoint, without regard to the provisions of sections 3309 through 3319 of title 5 of the United States Code, candidates needed for positions to perform critical work relating to coronavirus for which—

(1) public notice has been given; and

(2) the Secretary has determined that such a public health threat exists.

Sec. 10805. Funds made available by this title may be used to enter into contracts with individuals for the provision of personal services (as described in section 104 of part 37 of title 48, Code of Federal Regulations (48 CFR 37.104)) to support the prevention of, preparation for, or response to coronavirus, domestically and internationally, subject to prior notification to the Committees on Appropriations of the House of Representatives and the Senate: Provided, That such individuals may not be deemed employees of the United States for the purpose of any law administered by the Office of Personnel Management: Provided further, That the authority made available pursuant to this section shall expire on September 30, 2024.

Sec. 10806. Of the funds appropriated by this title under the heading "Public Health and Social Services Emergency Fund", $4,000,000 shall be transferred to, and merged with, funds made available under the heading "Office of the Secretary, Office of Inspector General", and shall remain available until expended, for oversight of activities supported with funds appropriated to the Department of Health and Human Services in this Act: Provided, That the Inspector General of the Department of Health and Human Services shall consult with the Committees on Appropriations of the House of Representatives and the Senate prior to obligating such funds: Provided further, That the transfer authority provided by this section is in addition to any other transfer authority provided by law.

Sec. 10807. Of the funds provided under the heading "CDC–Wide Activities and Program Support", $1,000,000,000, to remain available until expended, shall be available to the Director of the CDC for deposit in the Infectious Diseases Rapid Response Reserve Fund established by section 231 of division B of Public Law 115–245.

Sec. 10808. (a) Premium Pay Authority.—If services performed by an employee of the Department of Health and Human Services during fiscal year 2020 are determined by the head of the agency to be primarily related to preparation, prevention, or response to SARS–CoV–2 or another coronavirus with pandemic potential, any premium pay for such services shall be disregarded in calculating the aggregate of such employee's basic pay and premium pay for purposes of a limitation under section 5547(a) of title 5, United States Code, or under any other provision of law, whether such employee's pay is paid on a biweekly or calendar year basis.

(b) Overtime Authority.—Any overtime pay for such services shall be disregarded in calculating any annual limit on the amount of overtime pay payable in a calendar or fiscal year.

(c) Applicability Of Aggregate Limitation On Pay.—With regard to such services, any pay that is disregarded under either subsection (a) or (b) shall be disregarded in calculating such employee's aggregate pay for purposes of the limitation in section 5307 of such title 5.

(d) Limitation Of Pay Authority.—

(1) Pay that is disregarded under subsection (a) or (b) shall not cause the aggregate of the employee's basic pay and premium pay for the applicable calendar year to exceed the rate of basic pay payable for a position at level II of the Executive Schedule under section 5313 of title 5, United States Code, as in effect at the end of such calendar year.

(2) For purposes of applying this subsection to an employee who would otherwise be subject to the premium pay limits established under section 5547 of title 5, United States Code, "premium pay" means the premium pay paid under the provisions of law cited in section 5547(a).

(3) For purposes of applying this subsection to an employee under a premium pay limit established under an authority other than section 5547 of title 5, United States Code, the agency responsible for administering such limit shall determine what payments are considered premium pay.

(e) Effective Date.—This section shall take effect as if enacted on February 2, 2020.

(f) Treatment Of Additional Pay.—If application of this section results in the payment of additional premium pay to a covered employee of a type that is normally creditable as basic pay for retirement or any other purpose, that additional pay shall not—

(1) be considered to be basic pay of the covered employee for any purpose; or

(2) be used in computing a lump-sum payment to the covered employee for accumulated and accrued annual leave under section 5551 or section 5552 of title 5, United States Code.

Sec. 10809. (a) Funds appropriated for "Department of Health and Human Services—Centers for Disease Control and Prevention—CDC-Wide Activities and Program Support"" in title III of the Coronavirus Preparedness and Response Supplemental Appropriations Act, 2020 (Public Law 116–123) shall be paid to "Department of Homeland Security—Countering Weapons of Mass Destruction Office—Federal Assistance" for costs incurred under other transaction authority and related to screening for coronavirus, domestically or internationally, including costs incurred prior to the enactment of such Act.

(b) The amounts repurposed under subsection (a) that were previously designated by the Congress as an emergency requirement pursuant to section 251(b)(2)(A)(i) of the Balanced Budget and Emergency Deficit Control Act of 1985 are designated by the Congress as an emergency requirement pursuant to such section of such Act.

TITLE IX

—LEGISLATIVE BRANCH

SENATE

Contingent Expenses Of The Senate

sergeant at arms and doorkeeper of the senate

For an additional amount for "Sergeant at Arms and Doorkeeper of the Senate", $1,000,000, to remain available until expended, to prevent, prepare for, and respond to coronavirus: Provided, That such amount is designated by the Congress as being for an emergency requirement pursuant to section 251(b)(2)(A)(i) of the Balanced Budget and Emergency Deficit Control Act of 1985.

miscellaneous items

For an additional amount for "Miscellaneous Items", $9,000,000, to remain available until expended, to prevent, prepare for, and respond to coronavirus: Provided, That such amount is designated by the Congress as being for an emergency requirement pursuant to section 251(b)(2)(A)(i) of the Balanced Budget and Emergency Deficit Control Act of 1985.

HOUSE OF REPRESENTATIVES

Salaries And Expenses

For an additional amount for "Salaries and Expenses", $25,000,000, to remain available until September 30, 2021, except that $5,000,000 shall remain available until expended, for necessary expenses of the House of Representatives to prevent, prepare for, and respond to coronavirus, to be allocated in accordance with a spend plan submitted to the Committee on Appropriations of the House of Representatives by the Chief Administrative Officer and approved by such Committee: Provided, That such amount is designated by the Congress as being for an emergency requirement pursuant to section 251(b)(2)(A)(i) of the Balanced Budget and Emergency Deficit Control Act of 1985.

JOINT ITEMS

Office Of The Attending Physician

For an additional amount for "Office of the Attending Physician", $400,000, to remain available until expended, to prevent, prepare for, and respond to coronavirus: Provided, That such amount is designated by the Congress as being for an emergency requirement pursuant to section 251(b)(2)(A)(i) of the Balanced Budget and Emergency Deficit Control Act of 1985.

CAPITOL POLICE

Salaries

For an additional amount for "Salaries", $12,000,000, to remain available until September 30, 2021, to prevent, prepare for, and respond to coronavirus: Provided, That amounts provided in this paragraph may be transferred between Capitol Police "Salaries" and "General Expenses" for the purposes provided herein without the approval requirement of section 1001 of the Legislative Branch Appropriations Act, 2014 (2 U.S.C. 1907a): Provided further, That such amount is designated by the Congress as being for an emergency requirement pursuant to section 251(b)(2)(A)(i) of the Balanced Budget and Emergency Deficit Control Act of 1985.

ARCHITECT OF THE CAPITOL

Capital Construction And Operations

For an additional amount for "Capital Construction and Operations", $25,000,000, to remain available until September 30, 2021, for necessary expenses of the Architect of the Capitol to prevent, prepare for, and respond to coronavirus, including the purchase and distribution of cleaning and sanitation products throughout all facilities and grounds under the care of the Architect of the Capitol, wherever located, including any related services and operational costs: Provided, That such amount is designated by the Congress as being for an emergency requirement pursuant to section 251(b)(2)(A)(i) of the Balanced Budget and Emergency Deficit Control Act of 1985.

LIBRARY OF CONGRESS

Salaries And Expenses

For an additional amount for "Salaries and Expenses", $700,000, to remain available until September 30, 2020, to be made available to the Little Scholars Child Development Center, subject to approval by the Committees on Appropriations of the Senate and House of Representatives, and the Senate Committee on Rules and Administration, and the Committee on House

Administration: Provided, That such amount is designated by the Congress as being for an emergency requirement pursuant to section 251(b)(2)(A)(i) of the Balanced Budget and Emergency Deficit Control Act of 1985.

GOVERNMENT ACCOUNTABILITY OFFICE

Salaries And Expenses

For an additional amount for "Salaries and Expenses", $50,000,000, to remain available until expended, for audits and investigations relating to coronavirus: Provided, That, not later than 90 days after the date of enactment of this Act, the Government Accountability Office shall submit to the Committees on Appropriations of the House of Representatives and the Senate a spend plan specifying funding estimates and a timeline for such audits and investigations: Provided further, That such amount is designated by the Congress as being for an emergency requirement pursuant to section 251(b)(2)(A)(i) of the Balanced Budget and Emergency Deficit Control Act of 1985.

General Provisions—This Title

SOURCE OF FUNDS USED FOR PAYMENT OF SALARIES AND EXPENSES OF SENATE EMPLOYEE CHILD CARE CENTER

Sec. 10901. The Secretary of the Senate shall reimburse the Senate Employee Child Care Center for personnel costs incurred starting on April 1, 2020, for employees of such Center who have been ordered to cease working due to measures taken in the Capitol complex to combat coronavirus, not to exceed $84,000 per month, from amounts in the appropriations account "MISCELLANEOUS ITEMS" within the contingent fund of the Senate.

SOURCE OF FUNDS USED FOR PAYMENT OF SALARIES AND EXPENSES OF LITTLE SCHOLARS CHILD DEVELOPMENT CENTER

Sec. 10902. The Library of Congress shall reimburse Little Scholars Child Development Center for salaries for employees incurred from April 1, 2020, to September 30, 2020, for employees of such Center who have been ordered to cease working due to measures taken in the Capitol complex to combat coronavirus, not to exceed $113,000 per month, from amounts in the appropriations account "Library of Congress—Salaries and Expenses".

SOURCE OF FUNDS USED FOR PAYMENT OF SALARIES AND EXPENSES OF HOUSE OF REPRESENTATIVES CHILD CARE CENTER

Sec. 10903. (a) Authorizing Use Of Revolving Fund Or Appropriated Funds.—Section 312(d)(3)(A) of the Legislative Branch Appropriations Act, 1992 (2 U.S.C. 2062(d)(3)(A)) is amended—

(1) in subparagraph (A), by striking the period at the end and inserting the following: ", and, at the option of the Chief Administrative Officer during an emergency situation, the payment of the salary of other employees of the Center."; and

(2) by adding at the end the following new subparagraph:

"(C) During an emergency situation, the payment of such other expenses for activities carried out under this section as the Chief Administrative Officer determines appropriate.".

(b) Effective Date.—The amendment made by subsection (a) shall apply with respect to fiscal year 2020 and each succeeding fiscal year.

PAYMENTS TO ENSURE CONTINUING AVAILABILITY OF GOODS AND SERVICES DURING THE CORONAVIRUS EMERGENCY

Sec. 10904. (a) Authorization To Make Payments.—Notwithstanding any other provision of law and subject to subsection (b), during an emergency situation, the Chief Administrative Officer of the House of Representatives may make payments under contracts with vendors providing goods and services to the House in amounts and under terms and conditions other than those provided under the contract in order to ensure that those goods and services remain available to the House throughout the duration of the emergency.

(b) Conditions.—

(1) APPROVAL REQUIRED.—The Chief Administrative Officer may not make payments under the authority of subsection (a) without the approval of the Committee on House Administration of the House of Representatives.

(2) AVAILABILITY OF APPROPRIATIONS.—The authority of the Chief Administrative Officer to make payments under the authority of subsection (a) is subject to the availability of appropriations to make such payments.

(c) Applicability.—This section shall apply with respect to fiscal year 2020 and each succeeding fiscal year.

AUTHORIZING PAYMENTS UNDER SERVICE CONTRACTS DURING THE CORONAVIRUS EMERGENCY

Sec. 10905. (a) Authorizing Payments.—Notwithstanding section 3324(a) of title 31, United States Code, or any other provision of law and subject to subsection (b), if the employees of a contractor with a service contract with the Architect of the Capitol are furloughed or otherwise unable to work during closures, stop work orders, or reductions in service arising from or related to the impacts of coronavirus, the Architect of the Capitol may continue to make the payments provided for under the contract for the weekly salaries and benefits of such employees for not more than 16 weeks.

(b) Availability Of Appropriations.—The authority of the Architect of the Capitol to make payments under the authority of subsection (a) is subject to the availability of appropriations to make such payments.

(c) Regulations.—The Architect of the Capitol shall promulgate such regulations as may be necessary to carry out this section.

MASS MAILINGS AS FRANKED MAIL

Sec. 10906. (a) Waiver Of Restrictions To Respond To Threats To Life Safety.—

(1) Section 3210(a)(6)(D) of title 39, United States Code, is amended by striking the period at the end of the first sentence and inserting the following: ", and in the case of the Commission, to waive this paragraph in the case of mailings sent in response to or to address threats to life safety.".

(2) EFFECTIVE DATE.—The amendments made by this subsection shall apply with respect to mailings sent on or after the date of the enactment of

this Act.

TECHNICAL CORRECTION

Sec. 10907. In the matter preceding the first proviso under the heading "Library of Congress—Salaries and Expenses" in division E of the Further Consolidated Appropriations Act, 2020 (Public Law 116–94), strike "$504,164,000" and insert "$510,164,000".

TITLE X

MILITARY CONSTRUCTION, VETERANS AFFAIRS, AND RELATED AGENCIES

DEPARTMENT OF VETERANS AFFAIRS

Veterans Benefits Administration

general operating expenses, veterans benefits administration

For an additional amount for "General Operating Expenses, Veterans Benefits Administration", $13,000,000, to remain available until September 30, 2021, to prevent, prepare for, and respond to coronavirus: Provided, That such amount is designated by the Congress as being for an emergency requirement pursuant to section 251(b)(2)(A)(i) of the Balanced Budget and Emergency Deficit Control Act of 1985.

Veterans Health Administration

medical services

For an additional amount for "Medical Services", $14,432,000,000, to remain available until September 30, 2021, to prevent, prepare for, and respond to coronavirus, including related impacts on health care delivery: Provided, That such amount is designated by the Congress as being for an emergency requirement pursuant to section 251(b)(2)(A)(i) of the Balanced Budget and Emergency Deficit Control Act of 1985.

medical community care

For an additional amount for "Medical Community Care", $2,100,000,000, to remain available until September 30, 2021, to prevent, prepare for, and respond to coronavirus, including related impacts on health care delivery: Provided, That such amount is designated by the Congress as being for an emergency requirement pursuant to section 251(b)(2)(A)(i) of the Balanced Budget and Emergency Deficit Control Act of 1985.

medical support and compliance

For an additional amount for "Medical Support and Compliance", $100,000,000, to remain available until September 30, 2021, to prevent, prepare for, and respond to coronavirus, including related impacts on health care delivery: Provided, That such amount is designated by the Congress as being for an emergency requirement pursuant to section 251(b)(2)(A)(i) of the Balanced Budget and Emergency Deficit Control Act of 1985.

medical facilities

For an additional amount for "Medical Facilities", $605,613,000, to remain available until September 30, 2021, to prevent, prepare for, and respond to coronavirus, including related impacts on health care delivery: Provided, That such amount is designated by the Congress as being for an emergency requirement pursuant to section 251(b)(2)(A)(i) of the Balanced Budget and Emergency Deficit Control Act of 1985.

Departmental Administration

general administration

For an additional amount for "General Administration", $6,000,000, to remain available until September 30, 2021, to prevent, prepare for, and respond to coronavirus: Provided, That such amount is designated by the Congress as being for an emergency requirement pursuant to section 251(b)(2)(A)(i) of the Balanced Budget and Emergency Deficit Control Act of 1985.

information technology systems

For an additional amount for "Information Technology Systems", $3,000,000,000, to remain available until September 30, 2021, to prevent, prepare for, and respond to coronavirus, including related impacts on health care delivery: Provided, That such amount is designated by the Congress as being for an emergency requirement pursuant to section 251(b)(2)(A)(i) of the Balanced Budget and Emergency Deficit Control Act of 1985.

office of inspector general

For an additional amount for "Office of Inspector General", $14,300,000, to remain available until September 30, 2022, for oversight of activities funded by this title and administered by the Department of Veterans Affairs: Provided, That such amount is designated by the Congress as being for an emergency requirement pursuant to section 251(b)(2)(A)(i) of the Balanced Budget and Emergency Deficit Control Act of 1985.

Armed Forces Retirement Home

trust fund

For an additional amount for "Armed Forces Retirement Home Trust Fund", $2,800,000, to remain available until September 30, 2021, to prevent, prepare for, and respond to coronavirus, to be paid from funds available in the Armed Forces Retirement Home Trust Fund: Provided, That of the amounts made available under this heading from funds available in the Armed Forces Retirement Home Trust Fund, $2,800,000 shall be paid from the general fund of the Treasury to the Trust Fund: Provided further, That the Chief Executive Officer of the Armed Forces Retirement Home shall submit to the Committees on Appropriations of the House of Representatives and the Senate monthly reports detailing obligations, expenditures, and planned activities: Provided further, That such amount is designated by the Congress as being for an emergency requirement pursuant to section 251(b)(2)(A)(i) of the Balanced Budget and Emergency Deficit Control Act of 1985.

TITLE XI

—DEPARTMENT OF STATE, FOREIGN OPERATIONS, AND RELATED PROGRAMS

DEPARTMENT OF STATE

Administration Of Foreign Affairs

diplomatic programs

For an additional amount for "Diplomatic Programs", $315,000,000, to remain available until September 30, 2022, for necessary expenses to prevent, prepare for, and respond to coronavirus, including for evacuation expenses, emergency preparedness, and maintaining consular operations: Provided, That such amount is designated by the Congress as being for an emergency requirement pursuant to section 251(b)(2)(A)(i) of the Balanced Budget and Emergency Deficit Control Act of 1985.

UNITED STATES AGENCY FOR INTERNATIONAL DEVELOPMENT

Funds Appropriated To The President

operating expenses

For an additional amount for "Operating Expenses", $95,000,000, to remain available until September 30, 2022, for necessary expenses to prevent, prepare for, and respond to coronavirus: Provided, That such amount is designated by the Congress as being for an emergency requirement pursuant to section 251(b)(2)(A)(i) of the Balanced Budget and Emergency Deficit Control Act of 1985.

BILATERAL ECONOMIC ASSISTANCE

Funds Appropriated To The President

international disaster assistance

For an additional amount for "International Disaster Assistance", $300,000,000, to remain available until expended, for necessary expenses to prevent, prepare for, and respond to coronavirus: Provided, That such amount is designated by the Congress as being for an emergency requirement pursuant to section 251(b)(2)(A)(i) of the Balanced Budget and Emergency Deficit Control Act of 1985.

Department Of State

migration and refugee assistance

For an additional amount for "Migration and Refugee Assistance", $300,000,000, to remain available until expended, for necessary expenses to prevent, prepare for, and respond to coronavirus: Provided, That such amount is designated by the Congress as being for an emergency requirement pursuant to section 251(b)(2)(A)(i) of the Balanced Budget and Emergency Deficit Control Act of 1985.

Independent Agencies

peace corps

For an additional amount for "Peace Corps", $90,000,000, to remain available until September 30, 2022, for necessary expenses to prevent, prepare for, and respond to coronavirus: Provided, That such amount is designated by the Congress as being for an emergency requirement pursuant to section 251(b)

(2)(A)(i) of the Balanced Budget and Emergency Deficit Control Act of 1985.
GENERAL PROVISIONS — THIS TITLE
(including transfer of funds)
Sec. 11101. The authorities and limitations of section 402 of the Coronavirus Preparedness and Response Supplemental Appropriations Act (division A of Public Law 116–123) shall apply to funds appropriated by this title as follows:
(1) subsections (a), (d), (e) and (f) shall apply to funds under the heading "Diplomatic Programs"; and
(2) subsections (c), (d), (e), and (f) shall apply to funds under the heading "International Disaster Assistance".
Sec. 11102. Funds appropriated by this title under the headings "Diplomatic Programs", "Operating Expenses", and "Peace Corps" may be used to reimburse such accounts administered by the Department of State, the United States Agency for International Development, and the Peace Corps for obligations incurred to prevent, prepare for, and respond to coronavirus prior to the date of enactment of this Act.
Sec. 11103. Section 7064(a) of the Department of State, Foreign Operations, and Related Programs Appropriations Act, 2020 (division G of Public Law 116–94), is amended by striking "$100,000,000" and inserting in lieu thereof "$110,000,000", and by adding before the period at the end the following ": Provided, That no amounts may be used that were designated by the Congress for Overseas Contingency Operations/Global War on Terrorism pursuant to the Concurrent Resolution on the Budget or the Balanced Budget and Emergency Deficit Control Act of 1985".
Sec. 11104. The reporting requirements of section 406(b) of the Coronavirus Preparedness and Response Supplemental Appropriations Act, 2020 (division A of Public Law 116–123) shall apply to funds appropriated by this title: Provided, That the requirement to jointly submit such reports shall not apply to the Director of the Peace Corps: Provided further, That reports required by such section may be consolidated and shall include information on all funds made available to such executive agency to prevent, prepare for, and respond to coronavirus.
Sec. 11105. Notwithstanding any other provision of law, and in addition to leave authorized under any other provision of law, the Secretary of State, the Administrator of the United States Agency for International Development, or the head of another Federal agency with employees under Chief of Mission Authority, may, in order to prevent, prepare for, and respond to coronavirus, provide additional paid leave to address employee hardships resulting from coronavirus: Provided, That this authority shall apply to leave taken since January 29, 2020, and may be provided abroad and domestically: Provided further, That the head of such agency shall consult with the Committee on Appropriations and the Committee on Foreign Affairs of the House of Representatives and the Committee on Appropriations and the Committee on Foreign Relations of the Senate prior to the initial implementation of such

authority: Provided further, That the authority made available pursuant to this section shall expire on September 30, 2022.

Sec. 11106. The Secretary of State, to prevent, prepare for, and respond to coronavirus, may exercise the authorities of section 3(j) of the State Department Basic Authorities Act of 1956 (22 U.S.C. 2670(j)) to provide medical services or related support for private United States citizens, nationals, and permanent resident aliens abroad, or third country nationals connected to United States persons or the diplomatic or development missions of the United States abroad who are unable to obtain such services or support otherwise: Provided, That such assistance shall be provided on a reimbursable basis to the extent feasible: Provided further, That such reimbursements may be credited to the applicable Department of State appropriation, to remain available until expended: Provided further, That the Secretary shall prioritize providing medical services or related support to individuals eligible for the health program under section 904 of the Foreign Service Act of 1980 (22 U.S.C. 4084): Provided further, That the authority made available pursuant to this section shall expire on September 30, 2022.

Sec. 11107. Notwithstanding section 6(b) of the Department of State Authorities Act of 2006 (Public Law 109–472), during fiscal years 2020 and 2021, passport and immigrant visa surcharges collected in any fiscal year pursuant to the fourth paragraph under the heading "Diplomatic and Consular Programs" in title IV of the Consolidated Appropriations Act, 2005 (division B of Public Law 108–447 (8 U.S.C. 1714)) may be obligated and expended on the costs of providing consular services: Provided, That such funds should be prioritized for American citizen services.

Sec. 11108. The Secretary of State is authorized to enter into contracts with individuals for the provision of personal services (as described in section 104 of part 37 of title 48, Code of Federal Regulations and including pursuant to section 904 of the Foreign Service Act of 1980 (22 U.S.C. 4084)) to prevent, prepare for, and respond to coronavirus, within the United States, subject to prior consultation with, and the regular notification procedures of, the Committee on Appropriations and the Committee on Foreign Affairs of the House of Representatives and the Committee on Appropriations and the Committee on Foreign Relations of the Senate: Provided, That such individuals may not be deemed employees of the United States for the purpose of any law administered by the Office of Personnel Management: Provided further, That not later than 15 days after utilizing this authority, the Secretary of State shall provide a report to such committees on the overall staffing needs for the Office of Medical Services: Provided further, That the authority made available pursuant to this section shall expire on September 30, 2022.

Sec. 11109. The matter under the heading "Emergencies in the Diplomatic and Consular Service" in title I of the Department of State, Foreign Operations, and Related Programs Appropriations Act, 2020 (division G of Public Law 116–94) is amended by striking "$1,000,000" and inserting in lieu thereof

"$5,000,000".

Sec. 11110. The first proviso under the heading "Millennium Challenge Corporation" in title III of the Department of State, Foreign Operations, and Related Programs Appropriations Act, 2020 (division G of Public Law 116–94) is amended by striking "$105,000,000" and inserting in lieu thereof "$107,000,000".

Sec. 11111. Notwithstanding any other provision of law, any oath of office required by law may, in particular circumstances that could otherwise pose health risks, be administered remotely, subject to appropriate verification: Provided, That prior to exercising the authority of this section, the Secretary of State shall submit a report to the Committee on Appropriations and the Committee on Foreign Relations of the Senate and the Committee on Appropriations and the Committee on Foreign Affairs of the House of Representatives describing the process and procedures for administering such oaths, including appropriate verification: Provided further, That the authority made available pursuant to this section shall expire on September 30, 2021.

Sec. 11112. (a) Purposes.—For purposes of strengthening the ability of foreign countries to prevent, prepare for, and respond to coronavirus and to the adverse economic impacts of coronavirus, in a manner that would protect the United States from the spread of coronavirus and mitigate an international economic crisis resulting from coronavirus that may pose a significant risk to the economy of the United States, each paragraph of subsection (b) shall take effect upon enactment of this Act.

(b) Coronavirus Responses.—

(1) INTERNATIONAL DEVELOPMENT ASSOCIATION REPLENISHMENT.—The International Development Association Act (22 U.S.C. 284 et seq.) is amended by adding at the end the following new section:

"SEC. 31. NINETEENTH REPLENISHMENT.

"(a) In General.—The United States Governor of the International Development Association is authorized to contribute on behalf of the United States $3,004,200,000 to the nineteenth replenishment of the resources of the Association, subject to obtaining the necessary appropriations.

"(b) Authorization Of Appropriations.—In order to pay for the United States contribution provided for in subsection (a), there are authorized to be appropriated, without fiscal year limitation, $3,004,200,000 for payment by the Secretary of the Treasury.".

(2) INTERNATIONAL FINANCE CORPORATION AUTHORIZATION.—The International Finance Corporation Act (22 U.S.C. 282 et seq.) is amended by adding at the end the following new section:

"SEC. 18. CAPITAL INCREASES AND AMENDMENT TO THE ARTICLES OF AGREEMENT.

"(a) Votes Authorized.—The United States Governor of the Corporation is

authorized to vote in favor of—
"(1) a resolution to increase the authorized capital stock of the Corporation by 16,999,998 shares, to implement the conversion of a portion of the retained earnings of the Corporation into paid-in capital, which will result in the United States being issued an additional 3,771,899 shares of capital stock, without any cash contribution;
"(2) a resolution to increase the authorized capital stock of the Corporation on a general basis by 4,579,995 shares; and
"(3) a resolution to increase the authorized capital stock of the Corporation on a selective basis by 919,998 shares.
"(b) Amendment Of The Articles .—The United States Governor of the Corporation is authorized to agree to and accept an amendment to article II, section 2(c)(ii) of the Articles of Agreement of the Corporation that would increase the vote by which the Board of Governors of the Corporation may increase the capital stock of the Corporation from a four-fifths majority to an eighty-five percent majority.".
(3) AFRICAN DEVELOPMENT BANK.—The African Development Bank Act (22 U.S.C. 290i et seq.) is amended by adding at the end the following new section:

"SEC. 1345. SEVENTH CAPITAL INCREASE.
"(a) Subscription Authorized.—
"(1) IN GENERAL.—The United States Governor of the Bank may subscribe on behalf of the United States to 532,023 additional shares of the capital stock of the Bank.
"(2) LIMITATION.—Any subscription by the United States to the capital stock of the Bank shall be effective only to such extent and in such amounts as are provided in advance in appropriations Acts.
"(b) Authorizations Of Appropriations.—
"(1) IN GENERAL.—In order to pay for the increase in the United States subscription to the Bank under subsection (a), there are authorized to be appropriated, without fiscal year limitation, $7,286,587,008 for payment by the Secretary of the Treasury.
"(2) SHARE TYPES.—Of the amount authorized to be appropriated under paragraph (1)—
"(A) $437,190,016 shall be for paid in shares of the Bank; and
"(B) $6,849,396,992 shall be for callable shares of the Bank.".
(4) AFRICAN DEVELOPMENT FUND.—The African Development Fund Act (22 U.S.C. 290g et seq.) is amended by adding at the end the following new section:

"SEC. 226. FIFTEENTH REPLENISHMENT.
"(a) In General.—The United States Governor of the Fund is authorized to contribute on behalf of the United States $513,900,000 to the fifteenth

replenishment of the resources of the Fund, subject to obtaining the necessary appropriations.

"(b) Authorization Of Appropriations.—In order to pay for the United States contribution provided for in subsection (a), there are authorized to be appropriated, without fiscal year limitation, $513,900,000 for payment by the Secretary of the Treasury.".

(5) INTERNATIONAL MONETARY FUND AUTHORIZATION FOR NEW ARRANGEMENTS TO BORROW.—

(A) IN GENERAL.—Section 17 of the Bretton Woods Agreements Act (22 U.S.C. 286e–2) is amended—

(i) in subsection (a)—

(I) by redesignating paragraphs (3), (4), and (5) as paragraphs (4), (5), and (6), respectively;

(II) by inserting after paragraph (2) the following new paragraph:

"(3) In order to carry out the purposes of a one-time decision of the Executive Directors of the International Monetary Fund (the Fund) to expand the resources of the New Arrangements to Borrow, established pursuant to the decision of January 27, 1997, referred to in paragraph (1), the Secretary of the Treasury is authorized to make loans, in an amount not to exceed the dollar equivalent of 28,202,470,000 of Special Drawing Rights, in addition to any amounts previously authorized under this section, except that prior to activation of the New Arrangements to Borrow, the Secretary of the Treasury shall report to Congress whether supplementary resources are needed to forestall or cope with an impairment of the international monetary system and whether the Fund has fully explored other means of funding to the Fund."; and

(III) in paragraph (5), as so redesignated, by striking "paragraph (3)" and inserting "paragraph (4)".

(ii) in paragraph (6), as so redesignated, by striking "December 16, 2022" and inserting "December 31, 2025"; and

(iii) in subsection (e)(1) by striking "(a)(2)," each place such term appears and inserting "(a)(2), (a)(3)".

(B) The amounts provided by the amendments made by this section are designated by the Congress as being for an emergency requirement pursuant to section 251(b)(2)(A)(i) of the Balanced Budget and Emergency Deficit Control Act of 1985.

TECHNICAL CORRECTIONS

Sec. 11113. (a) Environment Cooperation Commissions; North American Development Bank.—Section 601 of the United States-Mexico-Canada Agreement Implementation Act (Public Law 116–113; 134 Stat. 78) is amended by inserting ", other than sections 532 and 533 of such Act and part 2 of subtitle D of title V of such Act (as amended by section 831 of this Act)," before "is repealed".

(b) Protective Orders.—Section 422 of the United States-Mexico-Canada Agreement Implementation Act (134 Stat. 64) is amended in subsection (a)

(2)(A) by striking "all that follows through ', the administering authority'" and inserting "all that follows through 'Agreement, the administering authority'".

(c) Dispute Settlement.—Subsection (j) of section 504 of the United States-Mexico-Canada Agreement Implementation Act (134 Stat. 76) is amended in the item proposed to be inserted into the table of contents of such Act relating to section 414 by striking "determination" and inserting "determinations".

(d) Effetive Date.—Each amendment made by this section shall take effect as if included in the enactment of the United States-Mexico-Canada Agreement Implementation Act.

(e) North American Development Bank: Limitation On Callable Capital Subscriptions.—The Secretary of the Treasury may subscribe without fiscal year limitation to the callable capital portion of the United States share of capital stock of the North American Development Bank in an amount not to exceed $1,020,000,000. The authority in the preceding sentence shall be in addition to any other authority provided by previous Acts.

(f) The amounts provided by the amendments made by this section are designated by the Congress as being for an emergency requirement pursuant to section 251(b)(2)(A)(i) of the Balanced Budget and Emergency Deficit Control Act of 1985.

Sec. 11114. Notwithstanding any other provision of law, funds made available under each heading in this title shall only be used for the purposes specifically described under that heading.

TITLE XII

TRANSPORTATION, HOUSING AND URBAN DEVELOPMENT, AND RELATED AGENCIES

DEPARTMENT OF TRANSPORTATION

Office Of The Secretary

salaries and expenses

For an additional amount for "Salaries and Expenses", $1,753,000, to remain available until September 30, 2020, to prevent, prepare for, and respond to coronavirus, including necessary expenses for operating costs and capital outlays: Provided, That such amounts are in addition to any other amounts made available for this purpose: Provided further, That obligations of amounts under this heading in this Act shall not be subject to the limitation on obligations under the heading "Office of the Secretary—Working Capital Fund" in division H of the Further Consolidated Appropriations Act, 2020 (Public Law 116–94): Provided further, That such amount is designated by the Congress as being for an emergency requirement pursuant to section 251(b)(2)(A)(i) of the Balanced Budget and Emergency Deficit Control Act of 1985.

payment to air carriers

In addition to funds made available to the "Payment to Air Carriers" program in Public Law 116–94 to carry out the essential air service program under sections 41731 through 41742 of title 49, United States Code, $100,000,000, to be derived from the general fund and made available to the Essential Air Service and Rural Improvement Fund, to remain available until expended: Provided, That in determining between or among carriers competing to provide service to a community, the Secretary may consider the relative subsidy requirements of the carriers: Provided further, That basic essential air service minimum requirements shall not include the 15-passenger capacity requirement under section 41732(b)(3) of such title: Provided further, That none of the funds in this Act or any other Act shall be used to enter into a new contract with a community located less than 40 miles from the nearest small hub airport before the Secretary has negotiated with the community over a local cost share: Provided further, That amounts authorized to be distributed for the essential air service program under section 41742(b) of title 49, United States Code, shall be made available from amounts otherwise provided to the Administrator of the Federal Aviation Administration: Provided further, That the Administrator may reimburse such amounts from fees credited to the account established under section 45303 of such title: Provided further, That such amount is designated by the Congress as being for an emergency requirement pursuant to section 251(b)(2)(A)(i) of the Balanced Budget and Emergency Deficit Control Act of 1985.

office of airline industry financial oversight

For the necessary expenses of the Office of Airline Industry Financial Oversight, as authorized in section 301 of title III of division R of the Take Responsibility for Workers and Families Act, $3,000,000: Provided, That such amount is designated by the Congress as being for an emergency requirement pursuant to section 251(b)(2)(A)(i) of the Balanced Budget and Emergency Deficit Control Act of 1985.

airline assistance to recycle and save program

For the necessary expenses of the Airline Assistance to Recycle and Save Program, as authorized in section 702 of title VII of division R of the Take Responsibility for Workers and Families Act, $1,000,000,000 to remain available until expended: Provided, That such amount is designated by the Congress as being for an emergency requirement pursuant to section 251(b)(2)(A)(i) of the Balanced Budget and Emergency Deficit Control Act of 1985.

pandemic relief for aviation workers

For necessary expenses for providing pandemic relief for aviation workers, $40,000,000,000, to remain available until September 30, 2021 of which $37,000,000,000 shall be for the purposes authorized in section 101(a)(1)(A) of title I of division R of the Take Responsibility for Workers and Families Act, and $3,000,000,000, shall be for the purposes authorized in section 101(a)(1)(B) of title I of division R of the Take Responsibility for Workers and Families Act: Provided, That such amount is designated by the Congress as being for an emergency requirement pursuant to section 251(b)(2)(A)(i) of the Balanced Budget and Emergency Deficit Control Act of 1985.

In addition, for the cost of making direct loans and loan guarantees in accordance with the terms and conditions in sections 101–103 and 105 of title I of division R of the Take Responsibility for Workers and Families Act, such sums as may be necessary to remain available until September 30, 2021: Provided, That such costs, including the cost of modifying such loans, shall be defined by section 502 of the Congressional Budget Act of 1974: Provided further, That subject to section 502 of the Congressional Budget Act of 1974, during fiscal years 2020 and 2021, the aggregate sum of the principle for direct loans and guaranteed loans shall not exceed $21,000,000,000: Provided further, That such amount is designated by the Congress as being for an emergency requirement pursuant to section 251(b)(2)(A)(i) of the Balanced Budget and Emergency Deficit Control Act of 1985.

Federal Aviation Administration

operations

(airport and airway trust fund)

Of the amounts made available from the Airport and Airway Trust Fund for "Federal Aviation Administration—Operations" in title XI of subdivision 1 of division B of the Bipartisan Budget Act of 2018 (Public Law 115–123), not more than $25,000,000 may be used to prevent, prepare for, and respond to coronavirus: Provided, That amounts repurposed under this heading in this Act that were previously designated by the Congress as an emergency requirement pursuant to the Balanced Budget and Emergency Deficit Control Act of 1985 are designated by the Congress as an emergency requirement pursuant to section 251(b)(2)(A)(i) of the Balanced Budget and Emergency Deficit Control Act of 1985.

grants-in-aid for airports

For an additional amount for "Grants-In-Aid for Airports", to enable the Secretary of Transportation to make grants in accordance with the terms and conditions in section 401 of title IV division R of the Take Responsibility for Workers and Families Act, $10,000,000,000, to remain available until expended: Provided, That amounts made available under this heading in this Act shall be derived from the general fund: Provided further, That such amount is designated by the Congress as being for an emergency requirement pursuant to section 251(b)(2)(A)(i) of the Balanced Budget and Emergency Deficit Control Act of 1985.

research, engineering, and development

For an additional amount for "Research, Engineering, and Development", as authorized in section 705 of title VII of division R of the Take Responsibility for Workers and Families Act, $100,000,000, to remain available until expended: Provided, That such amount is designated by the Congress as being for an emergency requirement pursuant to section 251(b)(2)(A)(i) of the Balanced Budget and Emergency Deficit Control Act of 1985.

Federal Motor Carrier Safety Administration

motor carrier safety operations and programs

Of prior year unobligated contract authority and liquidating cash provided for Motor Carrier Safety in the Transportation Equity Act for the 21st Century (Public Law 105–178), SAFETEA–LU (Public Law 109–59), or any other Act, in addition to amounts already appropriated in fiscal year 2020 for "Motor Carrier Safety Operations and Programs" $150,000 in additional obligation limitation is provided and repurposed for obligations incurred to support activities to prevent, prepare for, and respond to coronavirus: Provided, That such amount is designated by the Congress as being for an emergency requirement pursuant to section 251(b)(2)(A)(i) of the Balanced Budget and Emergency Deficit Control Act of 1985.

Federal Railroad Administration

safety and operations

For an additional amount for "Safety and Operations", $250,000, to remain available until September 30, 2021, to prevent, prepare for, and respond to coronavirus: Provided, That such amount is designated by the Congress as being for an emergency requirement pursuant to section 251(b)(2)(A)(i) of the Balanced Budget and Emergency Deficit Control Act of 1985.

northeast corridor grants to the national railroad passenger corporation

(including transfer of funds)

For an additional amount for "Northeast Corridor Grants to the National Railroad Passenger Corporation", $492,000,000, to remain available until September 30, 2021, to prevent, prepare for, and respond to coronavirus, including to enable the Secretary of Transportation to make or amend existing grants to the National Railroad Passenger Corporation for activities associated with the Northeast Corridor as authorized by section 11101(a) of the Fixing America's Surface Transportation Act (division A of Public Law 114–94): Provided, That amounts made available under this heading in this Act may be transferred to and merged with "National Network Grants to the National Railroad Passenger Corporation" to prevent, prepare for, and respond to coronavirus: Provided further, That such amount is designated by the Congress as being for an emergency requirement pursuant to section 251(b)(2)(A)(i) of the Balanced Budget and Emergency Deficit Control Act of 1985.

national network grants to the national railroad passenger corporation

(including transfer of funds)

For an additional amount for "National Network Grants to the National Railroad Passenger Corporation", $526,000,000, to remain available until September 30, 2021, to prevent, prepare for, and respond to coronavirus, including to enable the Secretary of Transportation to make or amend existing grants to the National Railroad Passenger Corporation for activities associated with the National Network as authorized by section 11101(b) of the Fixing America's Surface Transportation Act (division A of Public Law 114–94): Provided, That a State shall not be required to pay the National Railroad Passenger Corporation more than 80 percent of the amount paid in fiscal year

2019 under section 209 of the Passenger Rail Investment and Improvement Act of 2008 (Public Law 110–432) and that not less than $239,000,000 of the amounts made available under this heading in this Act shall be made available for use in lieu of any increase in a State's payment: Provided further, That amounts made available under this heading in this Act may be transferred to and merged with the "Northeast Corridor Grants to the National Railroad Passenger Corporation" to prevent, prepare for, and respond to coronavirus: Provided further, That such amount is designated by the Congress as being for an emergency requirement pursuant to section 251(b)(2)(A)(i) of the Balanced Budget and Emergency Deficit Control Act of 1985.

Federal Transit Administration

transit infrastructure grants

For an additional amount for "Transit Infrastructure Grants" $25,000,000,000, to remain available until September 30, 2021, to prevent, prepare for, and respond to coronavirus: Provided, That the Secretary of Transportation shall provide funds appropriated under this heading in this Act as if such funds were provided under section 5307 of title 49, United States Code, and apportion such funds in accordance with section 5336 of such title (other than subsections (h)(1) and (h)(4)), sections 5311, 5337, and 5340 of title 49, United States Code, and apportion such funds in accordance with such sections, except that funds apportioned under section 5337 shall be added to funds apportioned under section 5307 for administration under section 5307: Provided further, That the Secretary shall allocate the amounts provided in the preceding proviso under sections 5307, 5311, 5337, and 5340 of title 49, United States Code, among such sections in the same ratio as funds were provided in the fiscal year 2020 apportionments: Provided further, That funds apportioned under this heading shall be apportioned not later than 7 days after the date of enactment of this Act: Provided further, That funds shall be apportioned using the fiscal year 2020 apportionment formulas: Provided further, That not more than three-quarters of 1 percent of the funds for transit infrastructure grants shall be available for administrative expenses and ongoing program management oversight as authorized under sections 5334 and 5338(f)(2) of title 49, United States Code, and shall be in addition to any other appropriations for such purpose: Provided further, That notwithstanding subsection (a)(1) or (b) of section 5307 of title 49, United States Code, funds provided under this heading are available for the operating expenses of transit agencies related to the response to a public health emergency as described in section 319 of the Public Health Service Act, including, beginning on January 31, 2020, reimbursement for operating costs to maintain service and lost revenue due to the public health emergency, the purchase of personal protective equipment, and paying the administrative leave of operations personnel due to reductions in service: Provided further, That such operating expenses are not required to be included in a transportation improvement program, long-range transportation, statewide transportation plan, or a statewide transportation improvement program: Provided further, That the Secretary shall not waive the requirements of section 5333 of title 49, United States Code, for funds appropriated under this heading or for funds previously made available under section 5307 of title 49, United States Code, or sections 5311, 5337, or 5340 of such title as a result of the coronavirus: Provided further, That unless otherwise specified, applicable requirements under chapter 53 of title 49, United States Code, shall apply to funding made available under this heading, except that the Federal share of the costs for which any grant is made under this heading shall be, at the option of the recipient, up to 100 percent: Provided further, That the amount made available under this heading shall be derived from the general fund and shall not be subject to any limitation on obligations for transit programs set forth in any Act: Provided further, That such amount is designated by the Congress as being for an emergency requirement pursuant to section 251(b)(2)(A)(i) of the Balanced Budget and Emergency Deficit Control Act of 1985.

Maritime Administration

operations and training

For an additional amount for "Operations and Training", $3,134,000, to remain available until September 30, 2021, to prevent, prepare for, and respond to coronavirus: Provided, That of the amounts made available under this heading in this Act, $1,000,000 shall be for the operations of the United States Merchant Marine Academy: Provided further, That such amount is designated by the Congress as being for an emergency requirement pursuant to section 251(b)(2)(A)(i) of the Balanced Budget and Emergency Deficit Control Act of 1985.

Office Of Inspector General

salaries and expenses

For an additional amount for "Office of Inspector General", $5,000,000, to remain available through September 30, 2021: Provided, That the amount made available under this heading in this Act shall be for necessary expenses of the Office of Inspector General to carry out the provisions of the Inspector General Act of 1978, as amended: Provided further, That the amounts made available under this heading in this Act shall be used to conduct audits and investigations of activities carried out with amounts made available in this Act to the Department of Transportation to prevent, prepare for, and respond to coronavirus: Provided further, That the Inspector General shall have all the necessary authority, in carrying out the duties specified in the Inspector General Act, as amended (5 U.S.C. App 3), to investigate allegations of fraud, including false statements to the Government (18 U.S.C. 1001), by any person or entity that is subject to regulation by the Department of Transportation: Provided further, That such amount is designated by the Congress as being for an emergency requirement pursuant to section 251(b)(2)(A)(i) of the Balanced Budget and Emergency Deficit Control Act of 1985.

General Provisions—Department Of Transportation

Sec. 12101. For amounts made available by this Act under the headings "Northeast Corridor Grants to the National Railroad Passenger Corporation" and "National Network Grants to the National Railroad Passenger Corporation", the Secretary of Transportation may not waive the requirements under section 24312 of title 49, United States Code, and section 24305(f) of title 49, United States Code: Provided, That for amounts made available by this Act under such headings the Secretary shall require the National Railroad Passenger Corporation to comply with the Railway Retirement Act of 1974 (45 U.S.C. 231 et seq.), the Railway Labor Act (45 U.S.C. 151 et seq.), and the Railroad Unemployment Insurance Act (45 U.S.C. 351 et seq.): Provided further, That not later than 7 days after the date of enactment of this Act and each subsequent 7 days thereafter, the Secretary shall notify the House and Senate Committees on Appropriations, the Committee on Transportation and Infrastructure of the House of Representatives, and the Committee on Commerce, Science, and Transportation of the Senate of any National Railroad Passenger Corporation employee furloughs as a result of efforts to prevent, prepare for, and respond to coronavirus: Provided further, That in the event of any National Railroad Passenger Corporation employee furloughs as a result of efforts to prevent, prepare for, and respond to coronavirus, the Secretary shall require the National Railroad Passenger Corporation to provide such employees the opportunity to be recalled to their previously held positions as intercity passenger rail service is restored to March 1, 2020 levels and not later than the date on which intercity passenger rail service has been fully restored to March 1, 2020 levels.

DEPARTMENT OF HOUSING AND URBAN DEVELOPMENT

Management And Administration

administrative support offices

For an additional amount for "Administrative Support Offices", $10,000,000, to remain available until September 30, 2021, to prevent, prepare for, and respond to coronavirus: Provided, That such amount is designated by the Congress as being for an emergency requirement pursuant to section 251(b)(2)(A)(i) of the Balanced Budget and Emergency Deficit Control Act of 1985.

program offices

For an additional amount for "Program Offices", $10,000,000, to remain available until September 30, 2030, to prevent, prepare for, and respond to coronavirus: Provided, That of the sums appropriated under this heading in this Act—

(1) $2,500,000 shall be available for the Office of Public and Indian Housing;

(2) $5,000,000 shall be available for the Office of Community Planning and Development; and

(3) $2,500,000 shall be available for the Office of Housing:

Provided further, That such amount is designated by the Congress as being for an emergency requirement pursuant to section 251(b)(2)(A)(i) of the Balanced Budget and Emergency Deficit Control Act of 1985.

Public And Indian Housing

tenant-based rental assistance

For an additional amount for "Tenant-Based Rental Assistance", $1,500,000,000, to remain available until expended, to provide additional funds for public housing agencies to maintain operations and take other necessary actions to prevent, prepare for, and respond to coronavirus: Provided, That of the amounts made available under this heading in this Act, $1,000,000,000 shall be available for additional administrative and other expenses of public housing agencies in administering their section 8 programs, including Mainstream vouchers, in response to coronavirus: Provided further, That such other expenses shall be new eligible activities to be defined by the Secretary and shall be activities to support or maintain the health and safety of assisted individuals and families, and costs related to retention and support of current participating landlords: Provided further, That amounts made available under paragraph (3) of this heading in division H of the Further Consolidated Appropriations Act, 2020 (Public Law 116–94) may be used for the other expenses as described in the preceding proviso in addition to their other available uses: Provided further, That of the amounts made available under this heading in this Act, $500,000,000 shall be available for adjustments in the calendar year 2020 section 8 renewal funding allocations, including Mainstream vouchers, for public housing agencies that experience a significant increase in voucher per-unit costs due to extraordinary circumstances or that, despite taking reasonable cost savings measures, as determined by the Secretary, would otherwise be required to terminate rental assistance for families as a result of insufficient funding: Provided further, That the Secretary shall allocate amounts provided in the preceding proviso based on need, as determined by the Secretary: Provided further, That for any amounts provided under this heading in prior Acts for tenant-based rental assistance contracts, including necessary administrative expenses, under section 811 of the Cranston-Gonzalez National Affordable Housing Act (42 U.S.C. 8013) that remain available for this purpose after funding renewals and administrative expenses, the Secretary shall award no less than 50 percent of the remaining amounts for the same purpose within 60 days of enactment of this Act: Provided further, That the Secretary may waive, or specify alternative requirements for, any provision of any statute or regulation that the Secretary administers in connection with the use of the amounts made available under this heading and the same heading of Public Law 116–94 (except for requirements related to fair housing, nondiscrimination, labor standards, and the environment), upon a finding by the Secretary that any such waivers or alternative requirements are necessary for the safe and effective administration of these funds to prevent, prepare for, and respond to coronavirus: Provided further, That the Secretary shall notify the public through the Federal Register or other appropriate means to ensure the most expeditious allocation of this funding of any such waiver or alternative requirement in order for such waiver or alternative requirement to take effect, and that such public notice may be provided at a minimum on the Internet at the appropriate Government web site or through other electronic media, as determined by the Secretary: Provided further, That any such waivers or alternative requirements shall remain in effect for the time and duration specified by the Secretary in such public notice and may be extended if necessary upon additional notice by the Secretary: Provided further, That such amount is designated by the Congress as being for an emergency requirement pursuant to section 251(b)(2)(A)(i) of the Balanced Budget and Emergency Deficit Control Act of 1985.

public housing operating fund

For an additional amount for "Public Housing Operating Fund" for 2020 payments to public housing agencies for the operation and management of public housing, as authorized by section 9(e) of the United States Housing Act of 1937 (42 U.S.C. 1437g(e)), $720,000,000, to remain available until September 30, 2021: Provided, That such amount shall be combined with the amount appropriated for the same purpose under the same heading of Public Law 116–94, and distributed to all public housing agencies pursuant to the Operating Fund formula at part 990 of title 24, Code of Federal Regulations: Provided further, That for the period from the enactment of this Act through December 31, 2020, such combined total amount may be used for eligible activities under subsections (d)(1) and (e)(1) of such section 9 and for other expenses to prevent, prepare for, and respond to coronavirus, including activities to support or maintain the health and safety of assisted individuals and families, and activities to support education and child care for impacted families: Provided further, That amounts made available under the headings "Public Housing Operating Fund" and "Public Housing Capital Fund" in prior Acts, except for any set-asides listed under such headings, may be used for all of the purposes described in the preceding proviso: Provided further, That the expanded uses and funding flexibilities described in the previous two provisos shall be available to all public housing agencies through December 31, 2020, except that the Secretary may extend the period under which such flexibilities shall be available in additional 12 month increments upon a finding that individuals and families assisted by the public housing program continue to require expanded services due to the coronavirus pandemic: Provided further, That the Secretary may waive, or specify alternative requirements for, any provision of any statute or regulation that the Secretary administers in connection with the use of such combined total amount of funds made available under the headings "Public Housing Operating Fund" and "Public Housing Capital Fund" in prior Acts (except for requirements related to fair housing, nondiscrimination, labor standards, and the environment), upon a finding by the Secretary that any such waivers or alternative requirements are necessary for the safe and effective administration of these funds to prevent, prepare for, and respond to coronavirus: Provided further, That the Secretary shall notify the public through the Federal Register or other appropriate means to ensure the most expeditious allocation of this funding of any such waiver or alternative requirement in order for such waiver or alternative requirement to take effect, and that such public notice may be provided at a minimum on the Internet at the appropriate Government web site or through other electronic media, as determined by the Secretary: Provided further, That any such waivers or alternative requirements shall remain in effect for the time and duration specified by the Secretary in such public notice and may be extended if necessary upon additional notice by the Secretary: Provided further , That amounts repurposed under this heading that were previously designated by the Congress as an emergency requirement pursuant to the Balanced Budget and Emergency Deficit Control Act of 1985 are designated by the Congress as an emergency requirement pursuant to section 251(b)(2)(A)(i) of the Balanced Budget and Emergency Deficit Control Act of 1985 Provided further, That such amount is designated by the Congress as being for an emergency requirement pursuant to section 251(b)(2)(A)(i) of the Balanced Budget and Emergency Deficit Control Act of 1985.

native american programs

For an additional amount for "Native American Programs", $350,000,000, to remain available until September 30, 2024, to prevent, prepare for, and respond to coronavirus, of which—

(1) $250,000,000 shall be for the Native American Housing Block Grants program, as authorized under title I of the Native American Housing Assistance and Self-Determination Act of 1996 ("NAHASDA") (25 U.S.C. 4111 et seq.): Provided, That amounts made available in this paragraph shall be distributed according to the same funding formula used in fiscal year 2020: Provided further, That such amounts may be used to cover the cost of and reimbursement of allowable costs to prevent, prepare for, and respond to coronavirus incurred by a recipient regardless of the date on which such costs were incurred: Provided further, That the Secretary may waive, or specify alternative requirements for, any provision of any statute or regulation that the Secretary administers in connection with the use of amounts made available in this paragraph and in paragraph (1) under this heading in division H of the Further Consolidated Appropriations Act, 2020 (Public Law 116–94) (except for requirements related to fair housing, nondiscrimination, labor standards, and the environment), upon a finding by the Secretary that any such waivers or alternative requirements are necessary to expedite or facilitate the use of such amounts, including to prevent, prepare for, and respond to coronavirus: Provided further, That any such waivers shall apply retroactively to activities to prevent, prepare for, and respond to coronavirus carried out with any amounts described in the preceding proviso; and

(2) $100,000,000 shall be for grants to Indian tribes for carrying out the Indian Community Development Block Grant program, as authorized under title I of the Housing and Community Development Act of 1974 (42 U.S.C. 5301 et seq.) with respect to Indian tribes for use to respond to emergencies

that constitute imminent threats to health and safety: Provided, That, notwithstanding section 106(a)(1) of such Act, the Secretary shall prioritize, without competition, allocations of such amounts for activities and projects to prevent, prepare for, and respond to coronavirus: Provided further, That not to exceed 20 percent of any grant made with amounts made available in this paragraph shall be expended for planning and management development and administration: Provided further, That such amounts may be used to cover the cost of and reimbursement of allowable costs to prevent, prepare for, and respond to coronavirus incurred by a recipient regardless of the date on which such costs were incurred: Provided further, That, notwithstanding section 105(a)(8) of the Housing and Community Development Act of 1974 (42 U.S.C. 5301 et seq.), there shall be no percent limitation on the use of amounts for public services activities to prevent, prepare for, and respond to coronavirus: Provided further, That the preceding proviso shall apply to all such activities funded with amounts made available in this paragraph and in paragraph (4) under this heading in division H of the Further Consolidated Appropriations Act, 2020 (Public Law 116–94): Provided further, That the Secretary may waive, or specify alternative requirements for, any provision of any statute or regulation that the Secretary administers in connection with the use of amounts made available in this paragraph and in paragraph (4) under this heading in division H of the Further Consolidated Appropriations Act, 2020 (Public Law 116–94) (except for requirements related to fair housing, nondiscrimination, labor standards, and the environment), upon a finding by the Secretary that any such waivers or alternative requirements are necessary to expedite or facilitate the use of such amounts, including to prevent, prepare for, and respond to coronavirus: Provided further, That any such waivers shall apply retroactively to activities to prevent, prepare for, and respond to coronavirus carried out with any amounts described in the preceding proviso: Provided further, That such amount is designated by the Congress as being for an emergency requirement pursuant to section 251(b)(2)(A)(i) of the Balanced Budget and Emergency Deficit Control Act of 1985.

Community Planning And Development

housing opportunities for persons with aids

For an additional amount for carrying out the "Housing Opportunities for Persons with AIDS" program, as authorized by the AIDS Housing Opportunity Act (42 U.S.C. 12901 et seq.), $130,000,000, to remain available until September 30, 2021, except that amounts allocated pursuant to section 854(c)(5) of such Act shall remain available until September 30, 2022, to provide additional funds to maintain operations and for rental assistance, supportive services, and other necessary actions, in order to prevent, prepare for, and respond to the coronavirus: Provided, That not less than $100,000,000 of the amount provided under this heading in this Act shall be allocated pursuant to the formula in section 854 of such Act using the same data elements as utilized pursuant to that same formula in fiscal year 2020:

Provided further, That up to $20,000,000 of the amount provided under this heading in this Act shall be to provide an additional one-time, non-renewable award to grantees currently administering existing contracts for permanent supportive housing that initially were funded under section 854(c)(5) of such Act from funds made available under this heading in fiscal year 2010 and prior years: Provided further, That such awards shall be made proportionally to their existing grants: Provided further, That, notwithstanding section 858(b)(3)(B) of such Act (42 U.S.C. 12907(b)(3)(B)), housing payment assistance for rent, mortgage, or utilities payments may be provided for a period of up to 24 months: Provided further, That such awards are not required to be spent on permanent supportive housing: Provided further, That, to protect persons who are living with HIV/AIDS, such amounts provided under this heading in this Act may be used to self-isolate, quarantine, or to provide other coronavirus infection control services as recommended by the Centers for Disease Control and Prevention for household members not living with HIV/AIDS: Provided further, That such amounts may be used to provide relocation services, including to provide lodging at hotels, motels, or other locations in order to satisfy the objectives of the preceding proviso: Provided further, That, notwithstanding section 856(g) of such Act (42 U.S.C. 12905(g)), a grantee may use up to 6 percent of its award under this Act for administrative purposes, and a project sponsor may use up to 10 percent of its sub-award under this Act for administrative purposes: Provided further, That such amounts provided under this heading in this Act may be used to reimburse allowable costs consistent with the purposes of this heading incurred by a grantee or project sponsor regardless of the date on which such costs were incurred: Provided further, That any regulatory waivers the Secretary may issue may be deemed to be effective as of the date a grantee began preparing for coronavirus: Provided further, That any additional activities or authorities authorized under this heading in this Act may also apply at the discretion and upon notice of the Secretary to all amounts made available under this same heading in Public Law 116–94 if such amounts are used by grantees for the purposes described under this heading: Provided further, That up to 2 percent of amounts made available under this heading in this Act may be used, without competition, to increase prior awards made to existing technical assistance providers to provide an immediate increase in capacity building and technical assistance available to grantees under this heading and under the same heading in prior Acts: Provided further, That such amount is designated by the Congress as being for an emergency requirement pursuant to section 251(b)(2)(A)(i) of the Balanced Budget and Emergency Deficit Control Act of 1985.

community development fund

For an additional amount for "Community Development Fund", $15,000,000,000, for assistance under the community development block grant program under title I of the Housing and Community Development

Act of 1974 (42 U.S.C. 5301 et seq.) to prevent, prepare for, and respond to coronavirus, to remain available until September 30, 2022: Provided, That up to $8,000,000,000 of the amount made available under this heading shall be distributed pursuant to section 106 of such Act (42 U.S.C. 5306) to grantees that received allocations pursuant to that same formula in fiscal year 2020, and that such allocations shall be made within 30 days of enactment of this Act: Provided further, That, in addition to amounts allocated pursuant to the preceding proviso, an additional $5,000,000,000 shall be allocated directly to States to prevent, prepare for, and respond to coronavirus within the State, including activities within entitlement and nonentitlement communities, based on public health needs, risk of transmission of coronavirus, number of coronavirus cases compared to the national average, and economic and housing market disruptions, and other factors, as determined by the Secretary, using best available data and that such allocations shall be made within 45 days of enactment of this Act: Provided further, That any remaining amounts shall be distributed directly to the State or unit of general local government, at the discretion of the Secretary, according to a formula based on factors to be determined by the Secretary, prioritizing risk of transmission of coronavirus, number of coronavirus cases compared to the national average, and economic and housing market disruptions resulting from coronavirus: Provided further, That such allocations may be made on a rolling basis as additional needs develop and data becomes available: Provided further, That the Secretary shall make all such allocations based on the best available data at the time of allocation: Provided further, That amounts made available in the preceding provisos may be used to reimburse allowable costs consistent with the purposes of this heading in this Act incurred by a State or locality regardless of the date on which such costs were incurred: Provided further, That section 116(b) of such Act (42 U.S.C. 5316(b)) and any implementing regulations, which require grantees to submit their final statements of activities no later than August 16 of a given fiscal year, shall not apply to final statements submitted in accordance with sections 104(a)(2) and (a)(3) of such Act (42 U.S.C. 5304(a)(2) and (a)(3)) and comprehensive housing affordability strategies submitted in accordance with section 105 of the Cranston-Gonzalez National Affordable Housing Act (42 U.S.C. 12705) for fiscal years 2019 and 2020: Provided further, That such final statements and comprehensive housing affordability strategies shall instead be submitted not later than August 16, 2021: Provided further, That the Secretary may waive, or specify alternative requirements for, any provision of any statute or regulation that the Secretary administers in connection with the use of amounts made available under this heading and for fiscal years 2019 and 2020 (except for requirements related to fair housing, nondiscrimination, labor standards, and the environment), if the Secretary finds that good cause exists for the waiver or alternative requirement and such waiver or alternative requirement would not be inconsistent with the overall purpose of title I of the Housing and Community Development Act of 1974 , including for the purposes of addressing the impact of coronavirus: Provided further, That any such waiver or alternative requirement shall not take effect before the expiration of the 5-day period that begins on the date on which the Secretary notifies the public through the Federal Register or other appropriate means, including by means of the Internet at the appropriate Government web site or through other electronic media, as determined by the Secretary: Provided further, That of the amounts made available under this heading, up to $10,000,000 shall be made available for capacity building and technical assistance to support the use of such amounts to expedite or facilitate infectious disease response: Provided further, That, notwithstanding sections 104(a)(2), (a)(3), and (c) of the Housing and Community Development Act of 1974 (42 U.S.C. 5304(a)(2), (a)(3), and (c)) and section 105 of the Cranston-Gonzalez National Affordable Housing Act (42 U.S.C. 12705), a grantee may not be required to amend its statement of activities in order to engage in activities to prevent, prepare, and respond to coronavirus or the economic and housing disruption caused by such virus, but shall make public a report within 180 days of the end of the crisis which fully accounts for those activities: Provided further, That a grantee may not be required to hold in-person public hearings in connection with citizen participation plan, but shall provide citizens with notice and a reasonable opportunity to comment of no less than 15 days: Provided further, That such procedures shall apply to grants from amounts made available under this heading and for fiscal years 2019 and 2020: Provided further, That, during the period that national or local health authorities recommend social distancing and limiting public gatherings for public health reasons, a grantee may carry out virtual public hearings to fulfill applicable public hearing requirements for all grants from funds made available under this heading in this and prior Acts: Provided further, That any such virtual hearings shall provide reasonable notification and access for citizens in accordance with the grantee's certifications, timely responses from local officials to all citizen questions and issues, and public access to all questions and responses: Provided further, That, notwithstanding subsection 105(a)(8) of the Housing and Community Development Act of 1974 (42 U.S.C. 5305(a)(8)), there shall be no percent limitation for the use of funds for public services activities to prevent, prepare, and respond to coronavirus or the economic and housing disruption caused by it: Provided further, That the preceding proviso shall apply to all such activities carried out with grants of funds made available under this heading and for fiscal years 2019 and 2020: Provided further, That the Secretary shall ensure there are adequate procedures in place to prevent any duplication of benefits as defined by section 312 of the Robert T. Stafford Disaster Relief and Emergency Assistance Act (42 U.S.C. 5155) and act in accordance with section 1210 of the Disaster Recovery Reform Act of 2018 (division D of Public Law 115–254; 132 Stat. 3442) and section 312 of the Robert T. Stafford Disaster Relief and Emergency Assistance Act (42 U.S.C. 5115): Provided further, That such amount is designated by the

Congress as being for an emergency requirement pursuant to section 251(b)(2)(A)(i) of the Balanced Budget and Emergency Deficit Control Act of 1985.

homeless assistance grants

For an additional amount for "Homeless Assistance Grants", $5,000,000,000, to remain available until September 30, 2022, for the Emergency Solutions Grants program as authorized under subtitle B of title IV of the McKinney-Vento Homeless Assistance Act (42 U.S.C. 11371 et seq.), as amended, to prevent, prepare for, and respond to coronavirus among individuals and families who are homeless, receiving homeless assistance, or at risk of homelessness and to support additional homeless assistance and homelessness prevention activities to mitigate the impacts created by coronavirus: Provided, That up to $1,500,000,000 of the amount appropriated under this heading in this Act shall be distributed pursuant to 24 CFR 576.3 to grantees that received allocations pursuant to that same formula in fiscal year 2020, and that such allocations shall be made within 30 days of enactment of this Act: Provided further, That, in addition to amounts allocated in the preceding proviso, an additional $1,500,000,000 shall be allocated directly to a State or unit of general local government by a formula to be developed by the Secretary and that such allocations shall be made within 45 days of enactment of this Act: Provided further, That such formula shall allocate such amounts for the benefit of unsheltered homeless, sheltered homeless, and those at risk of homelessness to geographical areas with the greatest need based on the risk of increasing transmission of coronavirus, rising rates of sheltered and unsheltered homelessness, and disruptions to economic and housing markets and other factors, as determined by the Secretary: Provided further, That not less than every 60 days thereafter, the Secretary shall allocate a minimum of an additional $500,000,000: Provided further, That amounts in the preceding proviso shall be allocated by a formula to be developed by the Secretary which takes into consideration the factors contained in the third proviso under this heading, in addition to the best available data on the number of coronavirus cases and disruptions in economic and housing markets, and other factors as determined by the Secretary: Provided further, That such amounts may be used to reimburse allowable costs consistent with the purposes of this heading incurred by a State or locality regardless of the date on which such costs were incurred: Provided further, That individuals and families who are very low-income (as such term is defined in section 3(b) of the United States Housing Act of 1937 (42 U.S.C. 1437a(b)) shall be considered "at risk of homelessness" and eligible for homelessness prevention assistance if they meet the criteria in subparagraphs (B) and (C) of section 401(1) of the McKinney-Vento Homeless Act (42 U.S.C. 11360(1)(B) and (C)): Provided further, That any individuals and families who are low-income (as such term is defined in section 3(b) of the United States Housing Act of 1937 (42 U.S.C. 1437a(b)) shall be eligible for rental assistance: Provided further, That recipients may deviate from applicable procurement standards when procuring goods and services consistent with the purposes of this heading: Provided further, That a recipient may use up to 10 percent of its allocation for administrative purposes: Provided further, That the use of such amounts shall not be subject to the consultation, citizen participation, or match requirements that otherwise apply to the Emergency Solutions Grants program, except that a recipient must publish how it has and will utilize its allocation at a minimum on the Internet at the appropriate Government web site or through other electronic media: Provided further, That the spending cap established pursuant to section 415(b) of the McKinney-Vento Homeless Act (42 U.S.C. 11374) shall not apply to such amounts: Provided further, That such amounts may be used to provide temporary emergency shelters (through leasing of existing property, temporary structures, or other means) for the purposes described under this heading, and that such temporary emergency shelters shall not be subject to the minimum periods of use required by section 416(c)(1) of such Act (42 U.S.C. 11375(c)(1)): Provided further, That Federal habitability and environmental review standards and requirements shall not apply to the use of such amounts for those temporary emergency shelters that have been determined by Federal, State, or local health officials to be necessary to prevent and mitigate the spread of coronavirus: Provided further, That such amounts may be used for training on infectious disease prevention and mitigation and to provide hazard pay, including for time worked prior to enactment of this Act, for staff working directly to prevent and mitigate the spread of coronavirus among persons who are homeless or at risk of homelessness, and that such activities shall not be considered administrative costs for purposes of the 10 percent cap: Provided further, That in administering the amounts made available under this heading in this Act, the Secretary may waive, or specify alternative requirements for, any provision of any statute or regulation (except for any requirements related to fair housing, nondiscrimination, labor standards, and the environment) that the Secretary administers in connection with the obligation or use by the recipient of these amounts, if the Secretary finds that good cause exists for the waiver or alternative requirement and such waiver or alternative requirement is consistent with the purposes described under this heading: Provided further, That any such waivers shall be deemed to be effective as of the date a State or unit of local government began preparing for coronavirus and shall apply to the use of amounts provided under this heading and amounts provided under the same heading in fiscal year 2020 used by recipients for the purposes described under this heading: Provided further, That the Secretary shall notify the public through the Federal Register or other appropriate means, 5 days before the effective date, of any such waiver or alternative requirement, and that such public notice may be provided on the Internet at the appropriate Government web site or through other electronic media, as determined by the Secretary: Provided further, That up to 1 percent of amounts made available under this heading in this Act may be used to increase prior awards made to existing technical assistance providers with experience in providing health care services in order to provide an immediate increase in capacity building and technical assistance to recipients of the Emergency Solutions Grants program under this heading and under the same heading in fiscal years 2018, 2019 and 2020: Provided further, That none of the funds provided under this heading may be used to require people experiencing homelessness to receive treatment or perform any other prerequisite activities as a condition for receiving shelter, housing, or other services: Provided further, That such amount is designated by the Congress as being for an emergency requirement pursuant to section 251(b)(2)(A)(i) of the Balanced Budget and Emergency Deficit Control Act of 1985.

emergency rental assistance

For and additional amount for "Emergency Rental Assistance", as authorized in section 104 of title I of division I of the Take Responsibility for Workers and Families Act, $100,000,000,000, to remain available until expended: Provided, That such amount is designated by the Congress as being for an emergency requirement pursuant to section 251(b)(2)(A)(i) of the Balanced Budget and Emergency Deficit Control Act of 1985.

housing assistance fund

For an additional amount for the "Housing Assistance Fund", as authorized in section 107 of title I of division I of the Take Responsibility for Workers and Families Act, $35,000,000,000, to remain available until expended: Provided, That such amount is designated by the Congress as being for an emergency requirement pursuant to section 251(b)(2)(A)(i) of the Balanced Budget and Emergency Deficit Control Act of 1985.

Housing Programs

assisted housing stability

For an additional amount for assistance to owners or sponsors of properties receiving project-based assistance pursuant to section 202 of the Housing Act of 1959 (12 U.S.C. 17012), section 811 of the Cranston-Gonzalez National Affordable Housing Act (42 U.S.C. 8013), or section 8 of the United States Housing Act of 1937, as amended, (42 U.S.C. 1437f), $1,100,000,000, to remain available until expended, unless otherwise specified: Provided, That such amounts shall be used to prevent, prepare for, and respond to coronavirus: Provided further, That of the amounts made available under this heading in this Act:

(1) $1,000,000,000 shall be for "Project-Based Rental Assistance" to supplement funds already available for expiring or terminating section 8 project-based subsidy contracts (including section 8 moderate rehabilitation contracts), for amendments to section 8 project-based subsidy contracts (including section 8 moderate rehabilitation contracts), for contracts entered into pursuant to section 441 of the McKinney-Vento Homeless Assistance Act (42 U.S.C. 11401), for renewal of section 8 contracts for units in projects that are subject to approved plans of action under the Emergency Low Income

Housing Preservation Act of 1987 or the Low-Income Housing Preservation and Resident Homeownership Act of 1990, and for administrative and other expenses associated with project-based activities and assistance funded under this paragraph;

(2) $75,000,000, to remain available until September 30, 2022, shall be for "Housing for the Elderly" to supplement funds already available for project rental assistance for the elderly under section 202(c)(2) of such Housing Act of 1959, including amendments to contracts for such assistance and renewal of expiring contracts for such assistance for up to a 1-year term, for senior preservation rental assistance contracts, including renewals, as authorized by section 811(e) of the American Housing and Economic Opportunity Act of 2000, as amended, and for supportive services associated with the housing for the elderly as authorized by such section 202: Provided further, That funds made available under this paragraph shall be used to provide emergency assistance for continuation of contracts for project rental assistance and amendment to such contracts, supportive services, existing service coordinators, one-time grants to hire additional service coordinators, other staffing, rent supports, and emergency preparedness relating to coronavirus; and

(3) $25,000,000, to remain available until September 30, 2023, shall be for "Housing for Persons with Disabilities" to supplement funds already available for project rental assistance for supportive housing for persons with disabilities under section 811(d)(2) of such Cranston-Gonzalez National Affordable Housing Act, for project assistance contracts pursuant to section 202(h) of the Housing Act of 1959 (Public Law 86–372; 73 Stat. 667), including amendments to contracts for such assistance and renewal of expiring contracts for such assistance for up to a 1-year term, for project rental assistance to State housing finance agencies and other appropriate entities as authorized under section 811(b)(3) of the Cranston-Gonzalez National Housing Act, and for supportive services associated with the housing for persons with disabilities as authorized by section 811(b)(1) of such Act:

Provided further, That for the purposes of addressing the impact of coronavirus, the Secretary may waive, or specify alternative requirements for, any provision of any statute or regulation that the Secretary administers in connection with the use of amounts made available under this heading in this Act (except for requirements related to fair housing, nondiscrimination, labor standards, and the environment) upon a finding by the Secretary that any such waivers or alternative requirements are necessary to expedite or facilitate the use of such amounts: Provided further, That the Secretary shall notify the public through the Federal Register or other appropriate means of any such waiver or alternative requirement in order for such waiver or alternative requirement to take effect, and that such public notice may be provided at minimum on the Internet at the appropriate Government web site or through other electronic media, as determined by the Secretary: Provided further, That up to

1 percent of the amounts provided under paragraphs (1), (2) and (3) may be used to make new awards or increase prior awards made to existing technical assistance providers, without competition, to provide an immediate increase in capacity building and technical assistance available to recipients of amounts identified in the preceding proviso, to remain available until September 30, 2024: Provided further, That such amount is designated by the Congress as being for an emergency requirement pursuant to section 251(b)(2)(A)(i) of the Balanced Budget and Emergency Deficit Control Act of 1985.

Fair Housing And Equal Opportunity

fair housing activities

For an additional amount for "Fair Housing Activities", $7,000,000, to remain available until September 30, 2021, for contracts, grants, and other assistance, as authorized by title VIII of the Civil Rights Act of 1968, as amended by the Fair Housing Amendments Act of 1988, and section 561 of the Housing and Community Development Act of 1987, to prevent, prepare for, and respond to coronavirus, of which $4,000,000 shall be for the Fair Housing Assistance Program Partnership for Special Enforcement grants to address fair housing issues relating to coronavirus, and $3,000,000 shall be for the Fair Housing Initiatives Program for education and outreach activities under such section 561 to educate the public about fair housing issues related to coronavirus: Provided, That such amount is designated by the Congress as being for an emergency requirement pursuant to section 251(b)(2)(A)(i) of the Balanced Budget and Emergency Deficit Control Act of 1985.

Office Of Inspector General

For an additional amount for "Office of Inspector General", $5,000,000, to remain available until September 30, 2021: Provided, That the amount made available under this heading in this Act shall be for necessary salaries and expenses of the Office of Inspector General in carrying out the Inspector General Act of 1978 and to conduct audits and investigations of activities carried out with amounts made available in this Act to the Department of Housing and Urban Development to prevent, prepare for, and respond to coronavirus: Provided further, That the Inspector General shall have independent authority over all personnel issues within this office: Provided further, That such amount is designated by the Congress as being for an emergency requirement pursuant to section 251(b)(2)(A)(i) of the Balanced Budget and Emergency Deficit Control Act of 1985.

TITLE XIII

GENERAL PROVISIONS—THIS DIVISION

Sec. 13101. Not later than 30 days after the date of enactment of this Act, the head of each executive agency that receives funding in this Act, or that received funding in the Coronavirus Preparedness and Response Supplemental Appropriations Act, 2020 (division A of Public Law 116–123) or the Second

Coronavirus Preparedness and Response Supplemental Appropriations Act, 2020 (division A of Public Law 116–127), shall provide a report detailing the anticipated uses of all such funding to the Committees on Appropriations of the House of Representatives and the Senate: Provided, That each report shall include estimated personnel and administrative costs, as well as the total amount of funding apportioned, allotted, obligated, and expended, to date: Provided further, That each such report shall be updated and submitted to such Committees every 60 days until all funds are expended or expire: Provided further, That reports submitted pursuant to this section shall satisfy the requirements of section 1701 of division A of Public Law 116–127.

Sec. 13102. Each amount appropriated or made available by this Act is in addition to amounts otherwise appropriated for the fiscal year involved.

Sec. 13103. In this Act, the term "coronavirus" means SARS–CoV–2 or another coronavirus with pandemic potential.

Sec. 13104. No part of any appropriation contained in this Act shall remain available for obligation beyond the current fiscal year unless expressly so provided herein.

Sec. 13105. Unless otherwise provided for by this Act, the additional amounts appropriated by this Act to appropriations accounts shall be available under the authorities and conditions applicable to such appropriations accounts for fiscal year 2020.

Sec. 13106. Each amount designated in this Act by the Congress as being for an emergency requirement pursuant to section 251(b)(2)(A)(i) of the Balanced Budget and Emergency Deficit Control Act of 1985 shall be available (or rescinded or transferred, if applicable) only if the President subsequently so designates all such amounts and transmits such designations to the Congress.

Sec. 13107. Any amount appropriated by this Act, designated by the Congress as an emergency requirement pursuant to section 251(b)(2)(A)(i) of the Balanced Budget and Emergency Deficit Control Act of 1985 and subsequently so designated by the President, and transferred pursuant to transfer authorities provided by this Act shall retain such designation.

Sec. 13108. Notwithstanding any other provision of law, and subject to the availability of appropriations, funds made available by this Act or any other Act may be used to modify the terms and conditions of a contract, or other agreement, without consideration, to authorize a federal agency to reimburse at contract billing rates not to exceed an average of 40 hours per week any contractor paid leave, including sick leave, the contractor provides to its employees to ensure the effective response to the declared national emergency for the coronavirus pandemic event. Such authority shall apply only to a contractor whose employees cannot perform work on a federally owned or leased facility or site due to Federal Government directed closures or other restrictions, and who cannot telework because their job duties cannot be performed remotely during the declared national emergency for the coronavirus pandemic event. This authority also shall apply to subcontractors.

The amounts made available by this section are designated by the Congress as an emergency requirement pursuant to section 251(b)(2)(A)(i) of the Balanced Budget and Emergency Deficit Control Act of 1985.

This division may be cited as the "Third Coronavirus Preparedness and Response Supplemental Appropriations Act, 2020" .

DIVISION B—EMERGENCY FAMILY AND MEDICAL LEAVE EXPANSION ACT

SEC. 20001. REFERENCES.

Except as otherwise expressly provided, whenever in this division an amendment or repeal is expressed in terms of an amendment to, or repeal of, a section or other provision, the reference shall be considered to be made to a section or other provision of the Family and Medical Leave Act of 1993 (29 U.S.C. 2601 et seq.), as amended by the Emergency Family and Medical Leave Expansion Act (Public Law 116–127).

SEC. 20002. EMPLOYER CLARIFICATION.

Section 101(4) is amended by adding at the end the following:

"(C) CLARIFICATION.—Subparagraph (A)(i) shall not apply with respect to a public agency described in subparagraph (A)(iii).".

SEC. 20003. EMERGENCY LEAVE EXTENSION.

Section 102(a)(1)(F) is amended by striking "December 31, 2020" and inserting "December 31, 2021".

SEC. 20004. EMERGENCY LEAVE DEFINITIONS.

(a) Eligible Employee.—Section 110(a)(1) is amended in subparagraph (A), by striking "sections 101(2)(A) and 101(2)(B)(ii)" and inserting "section 101(2)".

(b) Employer Threshold.—Section 110(a)(1)(B) is amended by striking "fewer than 500 employees" and inserting "1 or more employees".

(c) Parent.—Section 110(a)(1) is amended by adding at the end the following:

"(C) PARENT.—In lieu of the definition in section 101(7), the term 'parent', with respect to an employee, means any of the following:

"(i) A biological, foster, or adoptive parent of the employee.

"(ii) A stepparent of the employee.

"(iii) A parent-in-law of the employee.

"(iv) A parent of a domestic partner of the employee.

"(v) A legal guardian or other person who stood in loco parentis to an employee when the employee was a child.".

(d) Qualifying Need Related To A Public Health Emergency.—Section 110(a)(2)(A) is amended to read as follows:

"(A) QUALIFYING NEED RELATED TO A PUBLIC HEALTH EMERGENCY.—The term 'qualifying need related to a public health emergency', with respect to leave, means that the employee is unable to perform the functions of the position of such employee due to a need for leave for any of the following:

"(i) To comply with a recommendation or order by a public official having jurisdiction or a health care provider on the basis that the physical presence of the employee on the job would jeopardize the health of others because of—

"(I) the exposure of the employee to COVID–19; or

"(II) exhibition of symptoms of COVID–19 by the employee.

"(ii) To care for a family member of an eligible employee with respect to whom a public official having jurisdiction or a health care provider makes a determination that the presence of such family member in the community would jeopardize the health of other individuals in the community because of—

"(I) the exposure of the family member to COVID–19; or

"(II) exhibition of symptoms of COVID–19 by the family member.

"(iii) To care for the son or daughter of such employee if the school or place of care has been closed, or the child care provider of such son or daughter is unavailable, due to a public health emergency.

"(iv) To care for a family member who meets criteria of 101(12)(B) or is a senior citizen, if the place of care for such family member is closed, or the direct care provider is unavailable, due to a public health emergency.".

(e) Family Member.—Section 110(a)(2) is amended by adding at the end the following:

"(E) FAMILY MEMBER.—The term 'family member', with respect to an employee, means any of the following:

"(i) A parent of the employee.

"(ii) A spouse of the employee.

"(iii) A sibling of the employee.

"(iv) Next of kin of the employee or a person for whom the employee is next of kin.

"(v) A son or daughter of the employee.

"(vi) A grandparent or grandchild of the employee.

"(vii) An domestic partner of the employee.

"(F) DOMESTIC PARTNER.—

"(i) IN GENERAL.—The term 'domestic partner', with respect to an individual, means another individual with whom the individual is in a committed relationship.

"(ii) COMMITTED RELATIONSHIP DEFINED.—The term 'committed relationship' means a relationship between 2 individuals, each at least 18 years of age, in which each individual is the other individual's sole domestic partner and both individuals share responsibility for a significant measure of each other's common welfare. The term includes any such relationship between 2 individuals that is granted legal recognition by a State or political subdivision of a State as a marriage or analogous relationship, including a civil union or domestic partnership.".

SEC. 20005. REGULATORY AUTHORITIES.

(a) In General.—Section 110(a) is amended by striking paragraph (3).

(b) Force Or Effect Of Regulations.—Any regulation issued under section 110(a)(3), as in effect on the day before the date of the enactment of this Act, shall have no force or effect.

SEC. 20006. RELATIONSHIP TO PAID LEAVE.

Section 110(b) is amended—

(1) in paragraph (1)—

(A) in the header, by striking "10 DAYS" and inserting "2 WORKWEEKS";

(B) in subparagraph (A), by striking "10 days" and inserting "2 workweeks";

(C) in subparagraph (B), by inserting, ", including leave provided under section 5102 of the Emergency Paid Sick Leave Act (Public Law 116–127)," after "medical or sick leave"; and

(D) by inserting at the end the following:

"(C) EMPLOYER REQUIREMENT.—An employer may not require an employee to substitute any leave described in subparagraph (B) for leave under section 102(a)(1)(F).

"(D) RELATIONSHIP TO OTHER FAMILY AND MEDICAL LEAVE.—Leave taken under subparagraph (F) of section 102(a)(1) shall not count towards the 12 weeks of leave to which an employee is entitled under subparagraphs (A) through (E) of such section."; and

(2) in paragraph (2)(A), by striking "10 days" and inserting "2 workweeks".

SEC. 20007. WAGE RATE.

Section 110(b)(2)(B)(I) is amended to read as follows:

"(I) an amount that is not less than the greater of—

"(aa) the minimum wage rate in effect under section 6(a)(1) of the Fair Labor Standards Act of 1938 (29 U.S.C. 206(a)(1));

"(bb) the minimum wage rate in effect for such employee in the applicable State or locality, whichever is greater, in which the employee is employed; or

"(cc) two thirds of an employee's regular rate of pay (as determined under section 7(e) of the Fair Labor Standards Act of 1938 (29 U.S.C. 207(e)); and".

SEC. 20008. NOTICE.

Section 110(c) is amended by inserting "or subsection (a)(2)(A)(iv)" after "for the purpose described in subsection (a)(2)(A)(iii)".

SEC. 20009. AMENDMENTS TO THE EMERGENCY FAMILY AND MEDICAL LEAVE EXPANSION ACT.

The Emergency Family and Medical Leave Expansion Act (Public Law 116–127) is amended—

(1) in section 3103(b), by striking "Employees" and inserting, "Notwithstanding section 102(a)(1)(A) of the Family and Medical Leave Act of 1993 (29 U.S.C. 2612(a)(1)(A)), employees"; and

(2) by striking sections 3104 and 3105.

DIVISION C—EMERGENCY PAID SICK LEAVE ACT AMENDMENTS

SEC. 30001. REFERENCES.

Except as otherwise expressly provided, whenever in this division an amendment or repeal is expressed in terms of an amendment to, or repeal of, a section or other provision, the reference shall be considered to be made to a section or other provision of division E of the Families First Coronavirus Response Act (Public Law 116–127).

SEC. 30002. PAID SICK TIME REQUIREMENT.

(a) Uses.—Section 5102(a) is amended to read as follows:

"(a) In General.—An employer shall provide to each employee employed by the employer paid sick time for any of the following uses:

"(1) To self-isolate because the employee is diagnosed with COVID–19.

"(2) To obtain a medical diagnosis or care if such employee is experiencing the symptoms of COVID–19.

"(3) To comply with a recommendation or order by a public official with jurisdiction or a health care provider on the basis that the physical presence of the employee on the job would jeopardize the health of others because of—

"(A) the exposure of the employee to COVID–19; or

"(B) exhibition of symptoms of COVID–19 by the employee; or

"(4) To care for or assist a family member of the employee—

"(A) who—

"(i) is self-isolating because such family member has been diagnosed with COVID–19; or

"(ii) is experiencing symptoms of COVID–19 and needs to obtain medical diagnosis or care.

"(B) with respect to whom a public official with jurisdiction or a health care provider makes a determination that the presence of the family member in the community would jeopardize the health of other individuals in the community because of—

"(i) the exposure of such family member to the COVID–19; or

"(ii) exhibition of symptoms of COVID–19 by such family member.

"(5) To care for the son or daughter of such employee if the school or place of care has been closed, or the child care provider of such son or daughter is unavailable, due to COVID–19.".

(b) Employers With Existing Policies.—Section 5102 by adding at the end the following:

"(f) Employers With Existing Policies.—With respect to an employer that provides paid leave on the day before the date of enactment of this Act—

"(1) the paid sick time under this Act shall be made available to employees of the employer in addition to such paid leave; and

"(2) the employer may not change such paid leave on or after such date of enactment to avoid being subject to paragraph (1).".

SEC. 30003. PROHIBITED ACTS.
Section 5104(1) is amended by striking "and" at the end and inserting "or".

SEC. 30004. SUNSET.
Section 5109 is amended by striking "December 31, 2020" and inserting "December 31, 2021".

SEC. 30005. DEFINITIONS.
(a) Employee.—Section 5110(1)(A)(i) is amended—
(1) by striking "terms" and inserting "term"; and
(2) by striking "paragraph (5)(A)" and inserting "paragraph (2)(A)".
(b) Employer.—Section 5110(2)(B) is amended—
(1) by striking "terms" and inserting "term";
(2) by amending subclause (I) of clause (i) to read as follows:
"(I) means any person engaged in commerce or in any industry or activity affecting commerce that employs 1 or more employees;"; and
(3) by amending clause (ii) to read as follows:
"(ii) PUBLIC AGENCY AND NON-PROFIT ORGANIZATIONS.— For purposes of clause (i)(III) and (i)(I), a public agency and a nonprofit organization shall be considered to be a person engaged in commerce or in an industry or activity affecting commerce.".
(c) FMLA Terms.—Section 5110(4) is amended to read as follows:
"(4) FMLA TERMS.—The terms 'health care provider', 'next of kin', 'son or daughter', and 'spouse' have the meanings given such terms in section 101 of the Family and Medical Leave Act of 1993 (29 U.S.C. 2611).".
(d) Paid Sick Time.—Section 5110(5) is amended—
(1) in subparagraph (A)—
(A) in clause (i), by striking "section 2(a)" and inserting "section 5102(a)"; and
(B) in clause (ii), by striking "exceed" and all that follows and inserting "exceed $511 per day and $5,110 in the aggregate.";
(2) in subparagraph (B)—
(A) by striking the following:
"(B) REQUIRED COMPENSATION.—
"(i) IN GENERAL.—Subject to subparagraph (A)(ii),"; and inserting the following:
"(B) REQUIRED COMPENSATION.—Subject to subparagraph (A)(ii),"; and
(B) by striking clause (ii); and
(3) in subparagraph (C), by striking " section 2(a)" and inserting "section 5102(a)".
(a) Additional Definitions.—Section 5110 is amended by adding at the end the following:
"(6) DOMESTIC PARTNER.—
"(A) IN GENERAL.—The term 'domestic partner', with respect to an individual, means another individual with whom the individual is in a

committed relationship.

"(B) COMMITTED RELATIONSHIP DEFINED.—The term 'committed relationship' means a relationship between 2 individuals, each at least 18 years of age, in which each individual is the other individual's sole domestic partner and both individuals share responsibility for a significant measure of each other's common welfare. The term includes any such relationship between 2 individuals that is granted legal recognition by a State or political subdivision of a State as a marriage or analogous relationship, including a civil union or domestic partnership.

"(7) FAMILY MEMBER.—The term 'family member', with respect to an employee, means any of the following:

"(A) A parent of the employee.

"(B) A spouse of the employee.

"(C) A son or daughter of the employee.

"(D) A sibling of the employee.

"(E) A next of kin of the employee or a person for whom the employee is next of kin.

"(F) A grandparent or grandchild of the employee.

"(G) A domestic partner of the employee.

"(8) FFCRA TERMS.—The terms 'child care provider' and 'school' have the meanings given such terms in section 110(a)(2) of the Family and Medical and Leave Act of 1993.

"(9) PARENT.—The term 'parent', with respect to an employee, means any of the following:

"(A) A biological, foster, or adoptive parent of the employee.

"(B) A stepparent of the employee.

"(C) A parent-in-law of the employee.

"(D) A parent of a domestic partner of the employee.

"(E) A legal guardian or other person who stood in loco parentis to an employee when the employee was a child.".

SEC. 30006. REGULATORY AUTHORITIES.

(a) In General.—Division E is amended by striking section 5111.

(b) Force Or Effect Of Regulations.—Any regulation issued under section 5111 of division E of the Families First Coronavirus Response Act (Public Law 116–127), as in effect on the day before the date of the enactment of this Act, shall have no force or effect.

DIVISION D—COVID–19 WORKERS FIRST PROTECTION ACT OF 2020

SEC. 40001. SHORT TITLE.

This division may be cited as the "COVID–19 Workers First Protection Act of 2020".

SEC. 40002. EMERGENCY TEMPORARY AND PERMANENT STANDARDS.

(a) Emergency Temporary Standard.—

(1) IN GENERAL.—In consideration of the grave risk presented by COVID–19 and the need to strengthen protections for employees, pursuant to section 6(c)(1) of the Occupational Safety and Health Act of 1970 (29 U.S.C. 655(c)(1)) and notwithstanding the provisions of law and the Executive Order listed in paragraph (7), not later than 7 days after the date of enactment of this Act, the Secretary of Labor shall, in consultation with the Director of the Centers for Disease Control and Prevention, the Director of the National Institute for Occupational Safety and Health, the Commissioner of the Food and Drug Administration, and the persons described in paragraph (2), promulgate an emergency temporary standard to protect from occupational exposure to SARS–CoV–2—

(A) employees of health care sector employers;

(B) employees of employers in the paramedic and emergency medical services, including such services provided by firefighters and other emergency responders; and

(C) employees in other sectors and occupations whom the Centers for Disease Control and Prevention or the Occupational Safety and Health Administration identifies as having elevated risk.

(2) CONSULTATION.—In developing the standard under this subsection, the Secretary shall consult with professional associations and representatives of the employees in the occupations and sectors described in subparagraphs (A) through (C) of paragraph (1) and the employers of such employees.

(3) ENFORCEMENT DISCRETION.—If the Secretary of Labor determines it is not feasible for an employer to comply with a requirement of the standard promulgated under this subsection (such as a shortage of the necessary personal protective equipment), the Secretary may exercise discretion in the enforcement of such requirement if the employer demonstrates that the employer—

(A) is exercising due diligence to come into compliance with such requirement; and

(B) is implementing alternative methods and measures to protect employees.

(4) EXTENSION OF STANDARD.—Notwithstanding paragraphs (2) and (3) of section 6(c) of the Occupational Safety and Health Act of 1970 (29 U.S.C. 655(c)), the emergency temporary standard promulgated under

this subsection shall be in effect until the date on which the final standard promulgated under subsection (b) is in effect.

(5) STATE PLAN ADOPTION.—With respect to a State with a State plan that has been approved by the Secretary of Labor under section 18 of the Occupational Safety and Health Act of 1970 (29 U.S.C. 667), not later than 14 days after the date of enactment of this Act, such State shall promulgate an emergency temporary standard that is at least as effective in protecting from occupational exposure to SARS–CoV–2 the employees in the occupations and sectors described in subparagraphs (A) through (C) of paragraph (1) as the emergency temporary standard promulgated under this subsection.

(6) EMPLOYER DEFINED.—For purposes of the standard promulgated under this subsection, the term "employer" under section 3 of the Occupational Safety and Health Act of 1970 (29 U.S.C. 652) includes any State or political subdivision of a State, except for those already subject to the jurisdiction of a State plan approved under Section 18(b) of the Occupational Safety and Health Act of 1970.

(7) INAPPLICABLE PROVISIONS OF LAW AND EXECUTIVE ORDER.—The requirements of chapter 6 of title V, United States Code (commonly referred to as the "Regulatory Flexibility Act"), subchapter I of chapter 35 of title 44, United States Code (commonly referred to as the "Paperwork Reduction Act"), and Executive Order 12866 (58 Fed. Reg. 190; relating to regulatory planning and review), as amended, shall not apply to the standard promulgated under this subsection.

(b) Permanent Standard.—Not later than 24 months after the date of enactment of this Act, the Secretary of Labor shall promulgate a final standard—

(1) to protect employees from occupational exposure to infectious pathogens, including novel pathogens; and

(2) that shall be effective and enforceable in the same manner and to the same extent as a standard promulgated under section 6(b) of the Occupational Safety and Health Act of 1970 (29 U.S.C. 655(b)).

(c) Requirements.—Each standard promulgated under this section shall—

(1) require the employers of the employees in the occupations and sectors described in subparagraphs (A) through (C) of subsection (a)(1) to develop and implement a comprehensive infectious disease exposure control plan;

(2) provide no less protection for novel pathogens than precautions mandated by standards adopted by a State plan that has been approved by the Secretary of Labor under section 18 of the Occupational Safety and Health Act of 1970 (296 U.S.C. 667); and

(3) incorporate, as appropriate—

(A) guidelines issued by the Centers for Disease Control and Prevention, and the National Institute for Occupational Safety and Health, which are designed to prevent the transmission of infectious agents in healthcare settings; and

(B) relevant scientific research on novel pathogens.

SEC. 40003. SURVEILLANCE, TRACKING, AND INVESTIGATION OF WORK-RELATED CASES OF COVID–19 AMONG HEALTH CARE WORKERS.

The Director of the Centers for Disease Control and Prevention, in conjunction with the Director of the National Institute for Occupational Safety and Health, shall—

(1) collect and analyze case reports and other data on COVID–19, to identify and evaluate the extent, nature, and source of COVID–19 among employees in the occupations and sectors described in subparagraphs (A) through (C) of section 2(a)(1);

(2) investigate, as appropriate, individual cases of COVID–19 among such employees to evaluate the source of exposure and adequacy of infection and exposure control programs and measures;

(3) provide regular periodic reports on COVID–19 disease among such employees to the public; and

(4) based on such reports and investigations make recommendations on needed actions or guidance to protect such employees from COVID–19.

DIVISION E—COVID–19 WORKFORCE EMERGENCY RESPONSE ACT OF 2020

SEC. 50001. SHORT TITLE.

(a) Short Title.—This Act may be cited as the "Workforce Emergency Response Act of 2020".

SEC. 50002. DEFINITIONS.

In this Act:

(1) CORONAVIRUS.—The term "coronavirus" means coronavirus as defined in section 506 of the Coronavirus Preparedness and Response Supplemental Appropriations Act, 2020 (Public Law 116–123).

(2) COVID–19 NATIONAL EMERGENCY.—The term "COVID–19 national emergency" means the national emergency declared by the President under the National Emergencies Act (50 U.S.C. 1601 et seq.) on March 13, 2020, with respect to the coronavirus.

(3) SECRETARY.—The term "Secretary" means the Secretary of Labor.

(4) WIOA TERMS.—Except as otherwise provided, the terms in this Act have the meanings given the terms in section 3 of the Workforce Innovation and Opportunity Act (29 U.S.C. 3102).

SEC. 50003. WORKFORCE RESPONSE ACTIVITIES.

(a) In General.—The purpose of this section is to provide the increased flexibility needed for State and local areas to provide continuity of services during the COVID–19 national emergency.

(b) Administrative Costs.—Notwithstanding section 128(b)(4) of the Workforce Innovation and Opportunity Act (29 U.S.C. 3163(b)(4)), of the funds allocated to a local area, including a single State local area, under subtitle B of title I of such Act (29 U.S.C. 3151 et seq.) that remain unobligated for program year 2019, an amount up to 20 percent may be used for the administrative costs of carrying out local workforce investment activities under chapter 2 or chapter 3 of subtitle B of title I of such Act (29 U.S.C. 3151 et seq.), as long as any amount used under this subsection that exceeds the amount authorized for administrative costs under section 128(b)(4)(A) of such Act (29 U.S.C. 3163(b)(4)) is used to respond to the COVID–19 national emergency.

(c) Rapid Response Activities.—

(1) STATEWIDE RAPID RESPONSE.—Of the reserved by a Governor under section 128(a) of the Workforce Innovation and Opportunity Act (29 U.S.C. 3163(a)) for statewide activities that remain unobligated for program year 2019, such funds may be used for the statewide rapid response activities described in section 134(a)(2)(A) of such Act (29 U.S.C. 3174(a)(2)(A)) for responding to the COVID–19 national emergency.

(2) LOCAL BOARDS.—Of the funds reserved by a Governor under section

133(a)(2) of such Act (29 U.S.C. 3173(a)(2)) that remain unobligated for program year 2019, such funds may be distributed by the Governor not later than 30 days after the date of enactment of this Act to local boards most impacted by the coronavirus, at the determination of the Governor, for rapid response activities related to responding to the COVID–19 national emergency.

DIVISION F—FAMILY SUPPORT PROVISIONS

SEC. 60001. CONTINUED SAFE OPERATION OF CHILD WELFARE PROGRAMS AND SUPPORT FOR OLDER FOSTER YOUTH.

(a) Funding Increases.—

(1) GENERAL PROGRAM.—The dollar amount specified in section 477(h)(1) of the Social Security Act for fiscal year 2020 is deemed to be $185,900,000.

(2) EDUCATION AND TRAINING VOUCHERS.—The dollar amount specified in section 477(h)(2) of such Act for fiscal year 2020 is deemed to be $78,000,000.

(b) Programmatic Flexibility.—With respect to the period that begins on March 1, 2020, and ends with the close of calendar year 2020:

(1) ELIMINATION OF AGE LIMITATIONS ON ELIGIBILITY FOR ASSISTANCE.—Eligibility for services or assistance under a State program operated pursuant to section 477 of the Social Security Act shall be provided without regard to the age of the recipient.

(2) SUSPENSION OF WORK AND EDUCATION REQUIREMENTS UNDER THE EDUCATION AND TRAINING VOUCHER PROGRAM.—Section 477(i)(3) of the Social Security Act shall be applied and administered without regard to any work or education requirement.

(3) AUTHORITY TO WAIVE LIMITATION ON PERCENTAGE OF FUNDS USED FOR HOUSING ASSISTANCE.—The Secretary of Health and Human Services (in this subsection referred to as the "Secretary") may apply and administer section 477 of the Social Security Act without regard to subsection (b)(3)(B) of such section.

(4) AUTHORITY TO WAIVE RULES CONFLICTING WITH NEEDED ASSISTANCE AND SERVICES.—The Secretary may waive any requirement imposed by or under part B or E of title IV of the Social Security Act (including any limitation on the ability of contractors pursuant to such part B or E to apply for no-cost contract extensions) that the Secretary deems to be in conflict with using funds made available pursuant to this section or other statutes for the provision of financial, education, work, housing, and other assistance and services needed in response to the public health emergency declared by the Secretary pursuant to section 319 of the Public Health Service Act on January 31, 2020, entitled "Determination that a Public Health Emergency Exists Nationwide as the Result of the 2019 Novel Coronavirus".

(5) AUTHORITY OF STATES TO DETERMINE HOW DAILY ACTIVITIES MAY BE CONDUCTED REMOTELY.—The Secretary may allow a State to determine how daily activities under the State plan developed under part B of title IV of the Social Security Act and the State program funded under section 477 of such Act may be conducted through electronic means to comply with public health guidelines relating to social distancing, including conducting any required court proceedings pertaining to children in care. In making any such determination, the State shall work to ensure that the safety and health

of each child in care remains paramount.

(6) COUNTING OF REMOTE CASEWORKER VISITS AS IN-PERSON VISITS.—In the case of a foster child who has attained 18 years of age and with respect to whom foster care maintenance payments are being made under a State plan approved under part E of title IV of the Social Security Act, caseworker contact with the child that includes visual and auditory contact and which is conducted solely by electronic means is deemed an in-person visit to the child by the caseworker for purposes of section 424(f)(1)(A) of such Act if the child is visited by the caseworker in person not less than once every 6 months while in such care.

(7) ELIMINATION OF EDUCATION AND EMPLOYMENT REQUIREMENTS FOR CERTAIN FOSTER YOUTH.—The Secretary may waive the applicability of subclauses (I) through (IV) of section 475(8)(B)(iv) of the Social Security Act.

(c) State Defined.—In subsection (a), the term "State" has the meaning given the term in section 1101(a) of the Social Security Act for purposes of title IV of the Social Security Act, and includes an Indian tribe, tribal organization, or tribal consortium with an application and plan approved under this section 477(j) of such Act for fiscal year 2020.

SEC. 60002. ALLOWING HOME VISITING PROGRAMS TO CONTINUE SERVING FAMILIES SAFELY.

(a) In General.—For purposes of section 511 of the Social Security Act, during the period that begins on February 1, 2020, and ends with the close of calendar year 2020—

(1) a virtual home visit shall be considered a home visit;

(2) funding for, and staffing levels of, a program conducted pursuant to such section shall not be reduced on account of reduced enrollment in the program; and

(3) funds provided for such a program may be used—

(A) to train home visitors in conducting a virtual home visit and in emergency preparedness and response planning for families served;

(B) for the acquisition by families enrolled in the program of such technological means as are needed to conduct and support a virtual home visit; and

(C) to provide emergency supplies (such as diapers, formula, non-perishable food, water, hand soap and hand sanitizer) to families served.

(b) Virtual Home Visit Defined.—In subsection (a), the term "virtual home visit" means a visit that is conducted solely by electronic means.

(c) Authority To Delay Deadlines.—

(1) IN GENERAL.—The Secretary of Health and Human Services may extend the deadline by which a requirement of section 511 of the Social Security Act must be met, by such period of time as the Secretary deems appropriate.

(2) GUIDANCE.—The Secretary shall provide to eligible entities funded under section 511 of the Social Security Act information on the parameters

used in extending a deadline under paragraph (1) of this subsection.

SEC. 60003. EMERGENCY FLEXIBILITY FOR CHILD SUPPORT PROGRAMS.

(a) In General.—With respect to the period that begins on March 1, 2020, and ends with the close of calendar year 2021:

(1) The Secretary of Health and Human Services (in this subsection referred to as the "Secretary") may increase any percentage in effect for purposes of section 455(a)(1) of the Social Security Act to not more than 100 percent.

(2) On application of an Indian tribe therefor, the Secretary may waive any matching funds requirement imposed on the tribe under section 455(f) of such Act.

(3) Paragraphs (2) and (8) of section 409(a) of such Act shall have no force or effect.

(4) The Secretary may exempt a State from any requirement of section 466 of such Act.

(5) The Secretary may not impose a penalty or take any other adverse action against a State pursuant to section 452(g)(1) of such Act for failure to achieve a paternity establishment percentage of less than 90 percent.

(6) The Secretary may not find that the paternity establishment percentage for a State is not based on reliable data for purposes of section 452(g)(1) of such Act, and the Secretary may not determine that the data which a State submitted pursuant to section 452(a)(4)(C)(i) of such Act and which is used in determining a performance level is not complete or reliable for purposes of section 458(b)(5)(B) of such Act, on the basis of the failure of the State to submit OCSE Form 396 or 34 in a timely manner.

(7) The Secretary may not impose a penalty or take any other adverse action against a State for failure to comply with section 454A(g)(1)(A)(i) of such Act.

(8) The Secretary may not disapprove a State plan submitted pursuant to part D of title IV of such Act for failure of the plan to meet the requirement of section 454(1) of such Act, and may not impose a penalty or take any other adverse action against a State with such a plan that meets that requirement for failure to comply with that requirement.

(9) To the extent that a preceding provision of this section applies with respect to a provision of law applicable to a program operated by an Indian tribe or tribal organization (as defined in subsections (e) and (l) of section 4 of the Indian Self-Determination and Education Assistance Act (25 U.S.C. 450b)), that preceding provision shall apply with respect to the Indian tribe or tribal organization.

(b) State Defined.—In subsection (a), the term "State" has the meaning given the term in section 1101(a) of the Social Security Act for purposes of title IV of such Act.

SEC. 60004. EMERGENCY FLEXIBILITY FOR STATE TANF

PROGRAMS.
(a) State Programs.—Sections 407 and 408(a)(7) of the Social Security Act shall have no force or effect during the applicable period, and paragraphs (3), (9), (14), and (15) of section 409(a) of such Act shall not apply with respect to conduct engaged in during the period.
(b) Tribal Programs.—The minimum work participation requirements and time limits established under section 412(c) of the Social Security Act shall have no force or effect during the applicable period, and the penalties established under such section shall not apply with respect to conduct engaged in during the period.
(c) Penalty For Noncompliance.—
(1) IN GENERAL.—If the Secretary of Health and Human Services finds that a State or an Indian tribe has imposed a work requirement as a condition of receiving assistance, or a time limit on the provision of assistance, under a program funded under part A of title IV of the Social Security Act or any program funded with qualified State expenditures (as defined in section 409(a)(7)(B)(i) of such Act) during the applicable period, or has imposed a penalty for failure to comply with a work requirement during the period, the Secretary shall reduce the grant payable to the State under section 403(a)(1) of such Act or the grant payable to the tribe under section 412(a)(1) of such Act, as the case may be, for fiscal year 2021 by an amount equal to 5 percent of the State or tribal family assistance grant, as the case may be.
(2) APPLICABILITY OF CERTAIN PROVISIONS.—For purposes of subsections (c) and (d) of section 409 of the Social Security Act, paragraph (1) of this subsection shall be considered to be included in section 409(a) of such Act.
(d) Definitions.—In this section:
(1) APPLICABLE PERIOD.—The term "applicable period" means the period that begins on March 1, 2020, and ends with the close of calendar year 2020.
(2) WORK REQUIREMENT.—The term "work requirement" means a requirement to engage in a work activity (as defined in section 407(d) of the Social Security Act).
(3) OTHER TERMS.—Each other term has the meaning given the term in section 419 of the Social Security Act. DIVISION G—HEALTH POLICIES

TITLE I—MEDICAID

SEC. 70101. INCREASING FEDERAL SUPPORT TO STATE MEDICAID PROGRAMS DURING ECONOMIC DOWNTURNS.
(a) In General.—Section 1905 of the Social Security Act (42 U.S.C. 1396d) is amended—
(1) in subsection (b), by striking "and (ff)" and inserting "(ff), and (gg)"; and
(2) by adding at the end the following new subsection:

"(gg) Increased FMAP During Economic Downturns.—

"(1) IN GENERAL.—Notwithstanding subsection (b), (y), or (z)(2), if a fiscal quarter that begins on or after January 1, 2020, is an economic downturn quarter (as defined in paragraph (2)) with respect to a State, then the Federal medical assistance percentage applicable to amounts expended by the State for medical assistance for services furnished during such quarter shall be increased in accordance with paragraphs (3) and (4).

"(2) ECONOMIC DOWNTURN QUARTER.—

"(A) IN GENERAL.—

"(i) IN GENERAL.—In this subsection, the term 'economic downturn quarter' means, with respect to a State, a fiscal quarter during which the State's unemployment rate for the quarter exceeds the percentage determined for the State and quarter under clause (ii).

"(ii) THRESHOLD PERCENTAGE.—The percentage determined under this clause for a State and fiscal quarter is the percentage equal to the lower of—

"(I) the State unemployment rate at the 20th percentile of the distribution of the State's quarterly unemployment rates for the 60-quarter period preceding the quarter involved, increased by 1 percentage point; and

"(II) the State's average quarterly unemployment rate for the 12-quarter period preceding the quarter involved, increased by 1 percentage point.

"(B) UNEMPLOYMENT DATA.—

"(i) IN GENERAL.—Except as provided in clause (ii), for purposes of determining unemployment rates for a State and a quarter under this paragraph, the Secretary shall use data from the Local Area Unemployment Statistics from the Bureau of Labor Statistics.

"(ii) APPLICATION TO CERTAIN TERRITORIES.—In the case of the Virgin Islands, Guam, the Northern Mariana Islands, or American Samoa, the Secretary shall use data from the U–6 unemployment measure of the Bureau of Labor Statistics to make any necessary determinations under subparagraph (A).

"(3) FMAP INCREASE DURING ECONOMIC DOWNTURN QUARTER.—

"(A) IN GENERAL.—During a fiscal quarter that is an economic downturn quarter with respect to a State, the Federal medical assistance percentage otherwise determined for the State and quarter under subsection (b) and, if applicable, the Federal medical assistance percentage applicable under subsection (y), (z)(2), or (ff) with respect to medical assistance furnished by the State during such quarter to individuals described in either such subsection shall be increased by the number of percentage points (rounded to the nearest tenth of a percentage point) equal to the product of—

"(i) the number of percentage points (rounded to the nearest tenth of a percentage point) by which the unemployment rate for the State and quarter exceeds the percentage determined for the State and quarter under paragraph (2)(A)(ii); and

"(ii) 4.8.

"(B) APPLICATION OF COVID-19 FMAP INCREASE.—Any increase applicable to the Federal medical assistance percentage of a State for a fiscal quarter under subparagraph (A) shall be in addition to any increase to such percentage for such quarter made pursuant to section 6008(a) of the Families First Coronavirus Response Act.

"(C) LIMITATION.—In no case shall an increase to the Federal medical assistance percentage of a State under this paragraph result in a Federal medical assistance percentage that exceeds 95 percent.

"(D) SCOPE OF APPLICATION.—Any increase to the Federal medical assistance percentage of a State for a fiscal quarter under this paragraph shall only apply with respect to payments for amounts expended by the State for medical assistance for services furnished during such quarter and shall not apply with respect to—

"(i) disproportionate share hospital payments described in section 1923;

"(ii) payments under title IV or XXI;

"(iii) any payments under this title that are based on the enhanced FMAP described in section 2105(b); or

"(iv) any payments under this title that are based on a Federal medical assistance percentage determined for a State under subsection (aa) (but only to the extent that such Federal medical assistance percentage is higher than the economic recovery FMAP).

"(4) ADVANCE PAYMENT; RETROSPECTIVE ADJUSTMENT.—

"(A) IN GENERAL.—Prior to the beginning of each fiscal quarter that begins on or after July 1, 2020, the Secretary shall, with respect to each State—

"(i) determine the increase (if any) that is expected to apply to the Federal medical assistance percentage of such State for such quarter under this subsection based on the projections made for the State and quarter under subparagraph (B); and

"(ii) shall apply such increase to the Federal medical assistance percentage of the State for purposes of making payments to the State for amounts expended during such quarter as medical assistance under the State plan.

"(B) PROJECTION OF STATE UNEMPLOYMENT RATES.—Prior to the beginning of each fiscal quarter that begins on or after July 1, 2020, the Secretary, acting through the Chief Actuary of the Centers for Medicare & Medicaid Services, shall, using the most recently available data described in paragraph (2)(B), make projections with respect to—

"(i) the unemployment rates for each State for such quarter;

"(ii) the threshold percentages described in paragraph (2)(A)(ii) for each State for such quarter; and

"(iii) the national unemployment rate for such quarter.

"(C) RETROSPECTIVE ADJUSTMENT.—As soon as practicable after final unemployment data becomes available for a fiscal quarter that begins on or after July 1, 2020, the Secretary shall, with respect to each State—

"(i) make a final determination of the increase (if any) applicable to the

Federal medical assistance percentage of the State for the quarter under this subsection; and

"(ii) in accordance with subsection (d)(2) of section 1903, reduce or increase the amount payable to the State under subsection (a) of such section for a subsequent fiscal quarter to the extent of any overpayment or underpayment which the Secretary determines was made as a result of a miscalculation of the increase applicable to the Federal medical assistance percentage of the State for such prior fiscal quarter under this subsection.

"(5) RETROSPECTIVE APPLICATION OF OVER-THE-LIMIT FMAP INCREASES.—

"(A) IN GENERAL.—If a State has excess percentage points with respect to an economic downturn quarter and an applicable FMAP (as determined under subparagraph (B)), the State may elect to apply such excess percentage points to increase such applicable FMAP for one or more quarters during the look-back period for the State and economic downturn quarter in accordance with this paragraph.

"(B) EXCESS PERCENTAGE POINTS.—For purposes of this paragraph, the number of excess percentage points for a State, economic downturn quarter, and an applicable FMAP shall be equal to the number of percentage points by which—

"(i) the applicable FMAP for the State and quarter (after application of paragraph (3) but without regard to subparagraph (C) of such paragraph); exceeds

"(ii) 95 percent.

"(C) EFFECT OF APPLICATION OF EXCESS PERCENTAGE POINTS.—If a State elects to apply excess percentage points to an applicable FMAP to a quarter during a look-back period under this paragraph, the Secretary shall determine the additional amount of payment under section 1903(a) to which the State would have been entitled for such quarter if the applicable FMAP (as so increased) had been in effect for such quarter, and shall treat such additional amount as an underpayment for such quarter.

"(D) DISTRIBUTION OF EXCESS PERCENTAGE POINTS.—A State that has excess percentage points with respect to an economic downturn quarter and applicable FMAP may elect to divide such points among more than 1 quarter during the look-back period for such State and quarter provided that no excess percentage point (or fraction of an excess percentage point) is applied to the applicable FMAP of more than 1 quarter.

"(E) LIMITATIONS.—

"(i) NO INCREASES OVER 100 PERCENT.—A State may not increase an applicable FMAP for any quarter during a look-back period under this paragraph if such increase would result in the applicable FMAP for such quarter exceeding 100 percent.

"(ii) SCOPE OF APPLICATION.—Any increase to an applicable FMAP of a State for a fiscal quarter under this paragraph—

"(I) shall only apply with respect to payments for amounts expended by the State for medical assistance for services furnished during such quarter to which such applicable FMAP is applicable; and

"(II) shall not apply with respect to payments described in paragraph (3)(D).

"(F) DEFINITIONS.—In this paragraph:

"(i) APPLICABLE FMAP.—The term 'applicable FMAP' means, with respect to a State and fiscal quarter—

"(I) the Federal medical assistance percentage determined for the State and quarter under subsection (b);

"(II) the Federal medical assistance percentage applicable under subsection (y);

"(III) the Federal medical assistance percentage applicable under subsection (z)(2); or

"(IV) the Federal medical assistance percentage determined for the State and quarter under subsection (ff).

"(ii) LOOK-BACK PERIOD.—The term 'look-back period' means, with respect to a State and a fiscal quarter that is an economic downturn quarter for the State, the period of 4 fiscal quarters that ends with the fourth quarter which precedes the most recent fiscal quarters that was not an economic downturn quarter for the State.

"(6) REQUIREMENT FOR ALL STATES.—A State may not receive an increase in the Federal medical assistance percentage for such State under this subsection, with respect to a fiscal quarter, if—

"(A) eligibility standards, methodologies, or procedures under the State plan or a waiver of such plan are more restrictive during such quarter than the eligibility standards, methodologies, or procedures, respectively, under such plan (or waiver) as in effect on the last day of the most recent fiscal quarter that was not an economic downturn quarter for the State;

"(B) the amount of any premium imposed by the State pursuant to section 1916 or 1916A during such quarter, with respect to an individual enrolled under such plan (or waiver), exceeds the amount of such premium as of the date described in subparagraph (A); or

"(C) the State fails to provide that an individual who is enrolled for benefits under such plan (or waiver) as of the date described in subparagraph (A) or enrolls for benefits under such plan (or waiver) during the period beginning with such date and ending with the day before the first day of the next quarter that is not an economic downturn quarter for the State shall be treated as eligible for such benefits for not less than 12 months (or, if such period is less than 12 months, throughout such period) unless the individual requests a voluntary termination of eligibility or the individual ceases to be a resident of the State.".

(b) Exclusion Of Economic Downturn FMAP Increases From Territorial Caps.—Section 1108 of the Social Security Act (42 U.S.C. 1308) is amended—

(1) in subsection (f), in the matter preceding paragraph (1), by striking

"subsection (g) and section 1935(e)(1)(B)" and inserting "subsections (g) and (h) and section 1935(e)(1)(B)"; and
(2) by adding at the end the following:
"(h) Exclusion From Caps Of Amounts Attributable To Economic Downturn FMAP.—The portion of any payment made to a territory for a fiscal year that is attributable to an increase in the Federal medical assistance percentage for a fiscal quarter during such year under section 1905(gg) shall not be taken into account for purposes of applying payment limits under subsections (f) and (g).".

SEC. 70102. LIMITATION ON ADDITIONAL SECRETARIAL ACTION WITH RESPECT TO MEDICAID SUPPLEMENTAL PAYMENTS REPORTING REQUIREMENTS.
(a) In General.—Notwithstanding any other provision of law, during the period that begins on the date of enactment of this section and ends the date that is 2 years after the last day of the emergency period defined in paragraph (1)(B) of section 1135(g) of the Social Security Act (42 U.S.C. 1320b–5(g)), the Secretary of Health and Human Services shall not take any action (through promulgation of regulation, issue of regulatory guidance, or otherwise) to—
(1) finalize or otherwise implement provisions contained in the proposed rule published on November 18, 2019, on pages 63722 through 63785 of volume 84, Federal Register (relating to parts 430, 433, 447, 455, and 457 of title 42, Code of Federal Regulations); or
(2) promulgate or implement any rule or provision similar to the provisions described in paragraph (1) pertaining to the Medicaid program established under title XIX of the Social Security Act (42 U.S.C. 1396 et seq.) or the State Children's Health Insurance Program established under title XXI of such Act (42 U.S.C. 1397aa et seq.).
(b) Continuation Of Other Secretarial Authority.—Nothing in this section shall be construed as prohibiting the Secretary during the period described in subsection (a) from taking any action (through promulgation of regulation, issuance of regulatory guidance, or other administrative action) to enforce a provision of law in effect as of the date of enactment of this section with respect to the Medicaid program established under title XIX of the Social Security Act (42 U.S.C. 1396 et seq.) or the State Children's Health Insurance Program established under title XXI of such Act (42 U.S.C. 1397aa et seq.), or to promulgate or implement a new rule or provision during such period with respect to such programs, other than a rule or provision described in subsection (a) and subject to the prohibition set forth in that subsection.

SEC. 70103. AUTHORITY TO AWARD MEDICAID HCBS GRANTS TO RESPOND TO THE COVID–19 PUBLIC HEALTH EMERGENCY.
(a) In General.—The Secretary is authorized to award grants to States in accordance with this section to enhance access to home and community-

based services during the COVID–19 public health emergency period.
(b) Definitions.—In this section:
(1) COVID–19 PUBLIC HEALTH EMERGENCY PERIOD.—The term "COVID–19 public health emergency period" means the portion of the emergency period defined in paragraph (1)(B) of section 1135(g) of the Social Security Act (42 U.S.C. 1320b–5(g)) beginning on or after the date of the enactment of this Act.
(2) ELIGIBLE INDIVIDUAL.—The term "eligible individual" means an individual who is eligible for or enrolled for medical assistance under a State Medicaid program.
(3) HOME AND COMMUNITY-BASED SERVICES.—The term "home and community-based services" means, with respect to a State Medicaid program, home and community-based services (including home health and personal care services) that are provided under the State's qualified HCBS program or that could be provided under such a program but are otherwise provided under the Medicaid program.
(4) INDIAN TRIBE.—The term "Indian tribe" means an Indian tribe, a tribal organization, or an urban Indian organization (as such terms are defined in section 4 of the Indian Health Care Improvement Act (25 U.S.C. 1603)), and includes a tribal consortium of Indian tribes or tribal organizations (as so defined).
(5) MEDICAID PROGRAM.—The term "Medicaid program" means, with respect to a State, the State program under title XIX of the Social Security Act (42 U.S.C. 1396 et seq.) (including any waiver or demonstration under such title or under section 1115 of such Act (42 U.S.C. 1315) relating to such title).
(6) SECRETARY.—The term "Secretary" means the Secretary of Health and Human Services.
(7) STATE.—The term "State" has the meaning given such term for purposes of title XIX of the Social Security Act (42 U.S.C. 1396 et seq.).
(8) QUALIFIED HCBS PROGRAM.—The term "qualified HCBS program" means a program providing home and community-based services operating under a State Medicaid program, whether or not operating under waiver authority.
(c) Grants To States.—
(1) IN GENERAL.—During the COVID–19 public health emergency period, the Secretary may award grants to States with applications meeting the requirements of paragraph (2).
(2) APPLICATION REQUIREMENTS.—A State seeking a grant under this section shall submit an application to the Secretary at such time, in such form and manner, and containing such information as the Secretary shall require.
(3) LIMITATIONS.—
(A) TERMINATION OF AUTHORITY.—The Secretary shall not award any grants under this section with respect to a State that submits an application after the date that is 60 days after the end of the COVID–19 public health

emergency period.
(B) USE OF FUNDS.—A State to which a grant is made under this section shall only use grant funds in accordance with subsection (d).
(C) MAINTENANCE OF STATE EFFORT.—Federal funds paid to a State pursuant to this section must be used to supplement, but not supplant, the level of State funds expended for home and community-based services for eligible individuals programs in effect for such individuals at the time the grant is awarded under this section.
(4) MONTHLY GRANT PAYMENT AMOUNTS.—
(A) IN GENERAL.—Subject to paragraph (5), the Secretary shall pay to each State that is awarded a grant under this section, for each month during the State's grant period (as defined in subparagraph (C)), an amount equal to 15 percent of the amount determined for the State under subparagraph (B).
(B) AVERAGE MONTHLY HCBS EXPENDITURES.—The amount determined for a State under this subparagraph is the amount equal to—
(i) the sum of—
(I) the average annual amount of State expenditures under title XIX of the Social Security Act (42 U.S.C. 1396 et seq.) that are attributable to providing medical assistance for home and community-based services for the 3 most recent fiscal years for which data is available; and
(II) the average annual amount, if any, received by the State pursuant to an MFP demonstration project conducted under section 6071 of the Deficit Reduction Act of 2005 (42 U.S.C. 1396a note) for the 3 most recent fiscal years for which data is available; divided by
(ii) 12.
(C) GRANT PERIOD DEFINED.—In this paragraph, the term "grant period" means, with respect to a State, the period of months—
(i) beginning with the month in which the Secretary approves the State's application for a grant under this section; and
(ii) ending with the 12th month that begins after the end of the COVID–19 public health emergency period.
(5) GRANTS TO INDIAN TRIBES.—
(A) IN GENERAL.—During the COVID–19 public health emergency period, the Secretary may award grants to an Indian tribe in the same manner, and subject to the same requirements, as apply to a State, except as otherwise provided in this paragraph.
(B) APPLICATION.—Any Indian tribe seeking a grant under this section shall submit to the Secretary an application that includes (in addition to any other information the Secretary shall require) an identification of the population and service area or areas to be served by the activities and programs that will be funded by the grant.
(C) MONTHLY GRANT PAYMENT AMOUNTS.—
(i) IN GENERAL.—The Secretary shall pay to each Indian tribe that is awarded a grant under this section, for each month during the tribe's grant

period (as defined in clause (iii)), an amount equal to 15 percent of the amount determined for the tribe under clause (ii).

(ii) TRIBAL SHARE OF MONTHLY HCBS EXPENDITURES.—The amount determined for an Indian tribe under this clause is equal to the—

(I) the total of the average annual amount of State expenditures made by a State or States under title XIX of the Social Security Act (42 U.S.C. 1396 et seq.) that are attributable to providing medical assistance for home and community-based services to eligible individuals who reside in the service area or areas identified by the tribe pursuant to subparagraph (B) for the 3 most recent fiscal years for which data is available; divided by

(II) 12.

(iii) GRANT PERIOD.—The term "grant period" has the same meaning with respect to an Indian tribe as the term has with respect to a State under paragraph (4)(C).

(D) REDUCTION OF STATE GRANT AMOUNTS.—If any State in which lies a service area or areas identified by an Indian tribe in a successful grant application pursuant to subparagraph (B) is also awarded a grant under this section, the Secretary shall reduce the amount payable to such State each month under paragraph (4) by the portion of the amount payable to the Indian tribe under this paragraph that is attributable to expenditures by the State.

(d) Permissible Uses Of Funds.—

(1) IN GENERAL.—A State to which a grant is made under this section may use grant funds—

(A) to work with community partners such as Area Agencies on Aging, Independent Living Centers, non-profit home and community based service providers, and other entities providing home and community-based services;

(B) during the COVID–19 public health emergency period, for the purposes described in paragraph (2); and

(C) after the end of such period, for the purposes described in paragraph (3).

(2) PERMISSIBLE USES DURING THE EMERGENCY PERIOD.—The purposes described in this paragraph for which a State may use grant funds awarded under this section are the following:

(A) To increase rates for home health and direct service worker agencies to provide home and community-based services under the State Medicaid program, provided that any agency or individual that receives payment under such an increased rate increases the compensation it pays its home health or direct service workers.

(B) To provide paid sick leave, paid family leave, and paid medical leave for home health workers and direct service workers.

(C) To provide hazard pay, overtime pay, and shift differential pay for home health workers and direct service workers.

(D) To provide home and community-based services to eligible individuals who are on waiting lists for programs approved under sections 1115 or 1915 of the Social Security Act (42 U.S.C. 1315, 1396n).

(E) To purchase emergency supplies and equipment necessary to enhance access to services and to protect the health and well-being of home health workers and direct service workers.

(F) To pay for home health worker and direct service worker travel to conduct home and community-based services.

(G) To recruit new direct service workers and home health workers.

(H) To support family care providers of eligible individuals with needed supplies and equipment and pay.

(I) To pay for training for direct service workers and home health workers that is specific to the COVID–19 public health emergency.

(J) To pay for assistive technologies, staffing, and other costs incurred during the public health emergency in order to facility community integration and ensure an individual's person-centered service plan continue to be fully implemented.

(K) To support direct service workers and home health workers going to nursing facilities, hospitals, institutions, and quarantine settings to provide services to eligible individuals who usually receive home and community-based services and have chosen to temporarily move to a more restrictive setting.

(L) To prepare information and public health and educational materials in accessible formats about prevention, treatment, recovery and other aspects of COVID–19 for eligible individuals, their families, and the general community served by home health and direct service agencies, including formats accessible to people with low literacy or intellectual disabilities.

(M) To pay for American sign language interpreters to assist in providing home and community-based services to eligible individuals and to inform the general public about COVID–19.

(N) To allow for day service providers to shift to providing home-based services.

(O) To pay for COVID–19 testing in home settings.

(P) To pay for other expenses deemed appropriate by the Secretary and which meet the criteria of the home and community-based settings rule.

(3) PERMISSIBLE USES AFTER THE EMERGENCY PERIOD.—The purpose described in this paragraph for which a State may use grant funds awarded under this section is to assist eligible individuals who had to relocate to a nursing facility or institutional setting from their homes during the COVID–19 public health emergency period in—

(A) moving back to their homes (including by paying for moving costs);

(B) resuming home and community-based services;

(C) receiving mental health services and necessary rehabilitative service to regain skills lost while relocated during the public health emergency period; and

(D) continuing home and community-based services for eligible individuals who were served from a waiting list for such services during the public health emergency period.

(e) Reporting Requirements.—

(1) STATE REPORTING REQUIREMENTS.—Not later than 18 months after the end of the COVID–19 public health emergency period, any State that received a grant under this section shall submit a report to the Secretary that contains the following information:

(A) Activities and programs that were funded using grant amounts.

(B) The number of eligible individuals who were served by such activities and programs.

(C) The number of eligible individuals who were able to resume home and community-based services as a result of such activities and programs.

(2) HHS REPORT.—Not later than 18 months after the end of the COVID–19 public health emergency period, the Secretary shall issue a public summary of the grants awarded under this section.

(f) Appropriation.—

(1) IN GENERAL.—Subject to paragraph (2), there are appropriated for fiscal year 2020 from any funds in the Treasury not otherwise appropriated such sums as are necessary to carry out this section, to remain available until expended.

(2) AVAILABILITY OF APPROPRIATIONS.—Amounts made available under paragraph (1) shall not be available for the awarding of grants to States that do not submit an application for such a grant before the date described in subsection (c)(3)(A).

(3) UNUSED GRANT FUNDS.—A State that receives a grant under this section shall return to the Secretary any portion of such grant that is unused as of the date that is 1 year after the last day of the COVID–19 public health emergency period, and such returned portion shall revert to the Treasury.

(g) Providing Home And Community-Based Services In Acute Care Hospitals.—Section 1902(h) of the Social Security Act (42 U.S.C. 1396a(h)) is amended—

(1) by inserting "(1)" after "(h)";

(2) by inserting ", home and community-based services provided under subsection (c), (d), or (i) of section 1915 or under a waiver under section 1115, self-directed personal assistance services provided pursuant to a written plan of care under section 1915(j), and home and community-based attendant services and supports under section 1915(k)" before the period; and

(3) by adding at the end the following:

"(2) Nothing in this title, title XVIII, or title XI shall be construed as prohibiting receipt of any care or services specified in paragraph (1) in an acute care hospital that are—

"(A) identified in an individual's person-centered plan of services and supports (or comparable plan of care);

"(B) provided to meet needs of the individual that are not met through the provision of hospital services;

"(C) not a substitute for services that the hospital is obligated to provide through its conditions of participation or under Federal or State law; and

"(D) designed to ensure smooth transitions between acute care settings and home and community-based settings, and to preserve the individual's functions.".

SEC. 70104. DELAY IN REDUCTION OF FMAP FOR MEDICAID PERSONAL CARE SERVICES FURNISHED WITHOUT AN ELECTRONIC VISIT VERIFICATION SYSTEM.

Section 1903(l) of the Social Security Act (42 U.S.C. 1396b(l)) is amended—

(1) in paragraph (1)—

(A) by striking "January 1, 2020" and inserting "the date that is 6 months after the end of the emergency period described in section 1135(g)(1)(B)"; and

(B) in subparagraph (A), by inserting "(if applicable)" after "percentage points" each place it appears; and

(2) in paragraph (4)(A)(i), by inserting before the semicolon the following: "(if applicable) or for calendar quarters occurring during the period beginning on the date that is 6 months after the end of the emergency period described in section 1135(g)(1)(B) and ending on the date that is 1 year after the end of such period".

SEC. 70105. COVERAGE AT NO COST SHARING OF COVID–19 VACCINE AND TREATMENT.

(a) Medicaid.—

(1) IN GENERAL.—Section 1905(a)(4) of the Social Security Act (42 U.S.C. 1396d(a)(4)) is amended—

(A) by striking "and (D)" and inserting "(D)"; and

(B) by striking the semicolon at the end and inserting "; (E) a COVID–19 vaccine licensed under section 351 of the Public Health Service Act and the administration of such vaccine; and (F) items and services furnished for the treatment of COVID–19 or a condition that may complicate the treatment of COVID–19;".

(2) PROHIBITION OF COST SHARING.—

(A) IN GENERAL.—Subsections (a)(2) and (b)(2) of section 1916 of the Social Security Act (42 U.S.C. 1396o), as amended by section 6004(a)(2)(A) of the Families First Coronavirus Response Act, are each amended—

(i) in subparagraph (F), by striking "or" at the end;

(ii) in subparagraph (G), by striking "; and" and inserting ", or"; and

(iii) by adding at the end the following subparagraphs:

"(H) a COVID–19 vaccine licensed under section 351 of the Public Health Service Act and the administration of such vaccine, or

"(I) any item or service furnished for the treatment of COVID–19 or a condition that may complicate the treatment of COVID–19; and".

(B) APPLICATION TO ALTERNATIVE COST SHARING.—Section 1916A(b)(3)(B) of the Social Security Act (42 U.S.C. 1396o–1(b)(3)(B)), as amended by section 6004(a)(2)(B) of the Families First Coronavirus Response Act, is amended—

(i) in clause (xi), by striking “any visit” and inserting “any service”; and

(ii) by adding at the end the following clauses:

“(xii) A COVID–19 vaccine licensed under section 351 of the Public Health Service Act and the administration of such vaccine.

“(xiii) An item or service furnished for the treatment of COVID–19 or a condition that may complicate the treatment of COVID–19.”.

(C) CLARIFICATION.—The amendments made this subsection shall apply with respect to a State plan of a territory in the same manner as a State plan of one of the 50 States.

(b) State Pediatric Vaccine Distribution Program.—Section 1928 of the Social Security Act (42 U.S.C. 1396s) is amended—

(1) in subsection (a)(1)—

(A) in subparagraph (A), by striking “; and” and inserting a semicolon;

(B) in subparagraph (B), by striking the period and inserting “; and”; and

(C) by adding at the end the following subparagraph:

“(C) each vaccine-eligible child (as defined in subsection (b)) is entitled to receive a COVID–19 vaccine from a program-registered provider (as defined in subsection (h)(8)) without charge for—

“(i) the cost of such vaccine; or

“(ii) the administration of such vaccine.”;

(2) in subsection (c)(2)—

(A) in subparagraph (C)(ii), by inserting “, but may not impose a fee for the administration of a COVID–19 vaccine” before the period; and

(B) by adding at the end the following subparagraph:

“(D) The provider will provide and administer an approved COVID–19 vaccine to a vaccine-eligible child in accordance with the same requirements as apply under the preceding subparagraphs to the provision and administration of a qualified pediatric vaccine to such a child.”; and

(3) in subsection (d)(1), in the first sentence, by inserting “, including with respect to a COVID–19 vaccine licensed under section 351 of the Public Health Service Act” before the period.

(c) CHIP.—

(1) IN GENERAL.—Section 2103(c) of the Social Security Act (42 U.S.C. 1397cc(c)), as amended by section 6004(b)(1) of the Families First Coronavirus Response Act, is amended by adding at the end the following paragraph:

“(11) COVERAGE OF COVID–19 VACCINES AND TREATMENT.—The child health assistance provided to a targeted low-income child shall include coverage of—

“(A) any COVID–19 vaccine licensed under section 351 of the Public Health Service Act and the administration of such vaccine; and

"(B) any item or service furnished for the treatment of COVID–19 or a condition that may complicate the treatment of COVID–19.".

(2) PROHIBITION OF COST SHARING.—Section 2103(e)(2) of the Social Security Act (42 U.S.C. 1397cc(e)(2)), as amended by section 6004(b)(3) of the Families First Coronavirus Response Act, is amended—

(A) in the paragraph header, by inserting "A COVID–19 VACCINE, COVID–19 TREATMENT," before "OR PREGNANCY-RELATED ASSISTANCE"; and

(B) by striking "visits described in section 1916(a)(2)(G), or" and inserting "services described in section 1916(a)(2)(G), vaccines described in section 1916(a)(2)(H), items or services described in section 1916(a)(2)(I), or".

(d) Conforming Amendments.—Section 1937 of the Social Security Act (42 U.S.C. 1396u–7) is amended—

(1) in subsection (a)(1)(B), by inserting ", under subclause (XXIII) of section 1902(a)(10)(A)(ii)," after "section 1902(a)(10)(A)(i)"; and

(2) in subsection (b)(5), by adding before the period the following: ", and, effective on the date of the enactment of the Take Responsibility for Workers and Families Act, must comply with subparagraphs (F) through (I) of subsections (a)(2) and (b)(2) of sections 1916 and 1916A".

(e) Effective Date.—The amendments made by this section shall take effect on the date of enactment of this Act and shall apply with respect to a COVID–19 vaccine beginning on the date that such vaccine is licensed under section 351 of the Public Health Service Act (42 U.S.C. 262).

SEC. 70106. OPTIONAL COVERAGE AT NO COST SHARING OF COVID–19 TREATMENT AND VACCINES UNDER MEDICAID FOR UNINSURED INDIVIDUALS.

(a) In General.—Section 1902(a)(10) of the Social Security Act (42 U.S.C. 1396a(a)(10) is amended, in the matter following subparagraph (G), by striking "and any visit described in section 1916(a)(2)(G)" and inserting the following: ", any COVID–19 vaccine that is administered during any such portion (and the administration of such vaccine), any item or service that is furnished during any such portion for the treatment of COVID–19 or a condition that may complicate the treatment of COVID–19, and any services described in section 1916(a)(2)(G)".

(b) Definition Of Uninsured Individual.—Subsection (ss) of section 1902 of the Social Security Act (42 U.S.C. 1396a), as added by section 6004(a)(3)(C) of the Families First Coronavirus Response Act, is amended to read as follows:

"(ss) Uninsured Individual Defined.—For purposes of this section, the term 'uninsured individual' means, notwithstanding any other provision of this title, any individual who is not covered by minimum essential coverage (as defined in section 5000A(f)(1) of the Internal Revenue Code of 1986).".

(c) Clarification Regarding Emergency Services For Certain Individuals.—Section 1903(v)(2) of the Social Security Act (42 U.S.C. 1396b(v)(2)) is amended by adding at the end the following flush sentence:

"For purposes of subparagraph (A), care and services described in such subparagraph include any in vitro diagnostic product described in section 1905(a)(3)(B) that is administered during any portion of the emergency period described in such section beginning on or after the date of the enactment of this sentence (and the administration of such product), any COVID–19 vaccine that is administered during any such portion (and the administration of such vaccine), any item or service that is furnished during any such portion for the treatment of COVID–19 or a condition that may complicate the treatment of COVID–19, and any services described in section 1916(a)(2)(G).".

(d) Inclusion Of COVID–19 Concern As An Emergency Condition.—Section 1903(v)(3) of the Social Security Act (42 U.S.C. 1396b(v)(3)) is amended by adding at the end the following flush sentence:

"Such term includes any indication that an alien described in paragraph (1) may have contracted COVID–19.".

SEC. 70107. TEMPORARY INCREASE IN MEDICAID FEDERAL FINANCIAL PARTICIPATION FOR TELEHEALTH SERVICES.

(a) In General.—Subject to subsection (b), for each calendar quarter occurring during the period beginning on the first day of the emergency period defined in paragraph (1)(B) of section 1135(g) of the Social Security Act (42 U.S.C. 1320b–5(g)) and ending on the last day of the calendar quarter in which the last day of such emergency period occurs, in the case of a State that has expenditures for telehealth services furnished during such quarter for which payment may be made to the State under section 1903(a) of the Social Security Act (42 U.S.C. 1396b(a)), the percentage of Federal financial participation otherwise required to be paid to such State under such section for such amounts expended shall be increased by one percentage point.

(b) Requirements.—A State described in subsection (a) may not receive the percentage increase in Federal financial participation described in such subsection with respect to a calendar quarter unless the State provides for telehealth services under the State plan approved under such title XIX (or a waiver of such plan) during such quarter in the same manner and to the same extent that telehealth services are covered under section 1834(m) of the Social Security Act (42 U.S.C. 1395m(m)), including pursuant to any waiver under section 1135 of such Act (42 U.S.C. 1320b–5). Nothing in the preceding sentence shall be construed as requiring a State to pay for telehealth services furnished to an individual eligible under the State plan (or waiver) at a rate that would exceed the payment amount that otherwise would be made under the State plan (or waiver) for such services.

SEC. 70108. EXTENSION OF FULL FEDERAL MEDICAL ASSISTANCE PERCENTAGE TO INDIAN HEALTH CARE PROVIDERS.

Section 1905 of the Social Security Act (42 U.S.C. 1396d) is amended—

(1) in subsection (a)(9), by inserting "and including such services furnished in any location by or through an Indian health care provider (as defined in section 1932(h)(4)(A))" before the semicolon; and

(2) in subsection (b)—

(A) by inserting "(whether or not such services are provided within such a facility)" following "received through an Indian Health Service facility,"; and

(B) by striking "Indian Health Care Improvement Act)" and inserting "Indian Health Care Improvement Act), or through an Urban Indian organization (as defined in section 4 of the Indian Health Care Improvement Act) pursuant to a grant or contract with the Indian Health Service under title V of the Indian Health Care Improvement Act".

SEC. 70109. MEDICAID COVERAGE FOR CITIZENS OF FREELY ASSOCIATED STATES.

(a) In General.—Section 402(b)(2) of the Personal Responsibility and Work Opportunity Reconciliation Act of 1996 (8 U.S.C. 1612(b)(2)) is amended by adding at the end the following new subparagraph:

"(G) MEDICAID EXCEPTION FOR CITIZENS OF FREELY ASSOCIATED STATES.—With respect to eligibility for benefits for the designated Federal program defined in paragraph (3)(C) (relating to the Medicaid program), section 401(a) and paragraph (1) shall not apply to any individual who lawfully resides in 1 of the 50 States or the District of Columbia in accordance with the Compacts of Free Association between the Government of the United States and the Governments of the Federated States of Micronesia, the Republic of the Marshall Islands, and the Republic of Palau and shall not apply, at the option of the Governor of Puerto Rico, the Virgin Islands, Guam, the Northern Mariana Islands, or American Samoa as communicated to the Secretary of Health and Human Services in writing, to any individual who lawfully resides in the respective territory in accordance with such Compacts.".

(b) Exception To 5-Year Limited Eligibility.—Section 403(d) of such Act (8 U.S.C. 1613(d)) is amended—

(1) in paragraph (1), by striking "or" at the end;

(2) in paragraph (2), by striking the period at the end and inserting "; or"; and

(3) by adding at the end the following new paragraph:

"(3) an individual described in section 402(b)(2)(G), but only with respect to the designated Federal program defined in section 402(b)(3)(C).".

(c) Definition Of Qualified Alien.—Section 431(b) of such Act (8 U.S.C. 1641(b)) is amended—

(1) in paragraph (6), by striking "; or" at the end and inserting a comma;

(2) in paragraph (7), by striking the period at the end and inserting ", or"; and

(3) by adding at the end the following new paragraph:

"(8) an individual who lawfully resides in the United States in accordance with a Compact of Free Association referred to in section 402(b)(2)(G), but only with respect to the designated Federal program defined in section 402(b)(3)(C) (relating to the Medicaid program).".

(d) Conforming Amendments.—Section 1108 of the Social Security Act (42 U.S.C. 1308), as amended by section 101(b), is further amended—

(1) in subsection (f), in the matter preceding paragraph (1), by striking "subsections (g) and (h) and section 1935(e)(1)(B)" and inserting "subsections (g), (h), and (i) and section 1935(e)(1)(B)"; and

(2) by adding at the end the following:

"(i) Exclusion Of Medical Assistance Expenditures For Citizens Of Freely Associated States.—Expenditures for medical assistance provided to an individual described in section 431(b)(8) of the Personal Responsibility and Work Opportunity Reconciliation Act of 1996 (8 U.S.C. 1641(b)(8)) shall not be taken into account for purposes of applying payment limits under subsections (f) and (g).".

(e) Effective Date.—The amendments made by this section shall apply to benefits for items and services furnished on or after the date of the enactment of this Act.

SEC. 70110. INCREASED FMAP FOR MEDICAL ASSISTANCE TO NEWLY ELIGIBLE INDIVIDUALS.

(a) In General.—Section 1905(y)(1) of the Social Security Act (42 U.S.C. 1396d(y)(1)) is amended—

(1) in subparagraph (A), by striking "2014, 2015, and 2016" and inserting "each of the first 3 consecutive 12-month periods in which the State provides medical assistance to newly eligible individuals";

(2) in subparagraph (B), by striking "2017" and inserting "the fourth consecutive 12-month period in which the State provides medical assistance to newly eligible individuals";

(3) in subparagraph (C), by striking "2018 " and inserting "the fifth consecutive 12-month period in which the State provides medical assistance to newly eligible individuals";

(4) in subparagraph (D), by striking "2019" and inserting "the sixth consecutive 12-month period in which the State provides medical assistance to newly eligible individuals"; and

(5) in subparagraph (E), by striking "2020 and each year thereafter" and inserting "the seventh consecutive 12-month period in which the State provides medical assistance to newly eligible individuals and each such period thereafter".

(b) Effective Date.—The amendments made by subsection (a) shall take effect as if included in the enactment of the Patient Protection and Affordable Care Act.

SEC. 70111. RENEWAL OF APPLICATION OF MEDICARE PAYMENT RATE FLOOR TO PRIMARY CARE SERVICES FURNISHED UNDER MEDICAID AND INCLUSION OF ADDITIONAL PROVIDERS.

(a) Renewal Of Payment Floor; Additional Providers.—

(1) IN GENERAL.—Section 1902(a)(13) of the Social Security Act (42 U.S.C. 1396a(a)(13)) is amended by striking subparagraph (C) and inserting the

following:

"(C) payment for primary care services (as defined in subsection (jj)) at a rate that is not less than 100 percent of the payment rate that applies to such services and physician under part B of title XVIII (or, if greater, the payment rate that would be applicable under such part if the conversion factor under section 1848(d) for the year involved were the conversion factor under such section for 2009), and that is not less than the rate that would otherwise apply to such services under this title if the rate were determined without regard to this subparagraph, and that are—

"(i) furnished in 2013 and 2014, by a physician with a primary specialty designation of family medicine, general internal medicine, or pediatric medicine; or

"(ii) furnished during the period beginning on the first day of the first month beginning after the date of the enactment of the Take Responsibility for Workers and Families Act and ending on the last day of the calendar quarter during which the last day of the emergency period described in section 1135(g)(1)(B) occurs—

"(I) by a physician with a primary specialty designation of family medicine, general internal medicine, pediatric medicine, or obstetrics and gynecology, but only if the physician self-attests that the physician is board-certified in family medicine, general internal medicine, pediatric medicine, or obstetrics and gynecology, respectively;

"(II) by a physician with a primary specialty designation of a family medicine subspecialty, an internal medicine subspecialty, a pediatric subspecialty, or a subspecialty of obstetrics and gynecology, without regard to the board that offers the designation for such a subspecialty, but only if the physician self-attests that the physician is board-certified in such a subspecialty;

"(III) by an advanced practice clinician, as defined by the Secretary, that works under the supervision of—

"(aa) a physician described in subclause (I) or (II); or

"(bb) a nurse practitioner or a physician assistant (as such terms are defined in section 1861(aa)(5)(A)) who is working in accordance with State law, or a certified nurse-midwife (as defined in section 1861(gg)(2)) who is working in accordance with State law;

"(IV) by a rural health clinic, Federally-qualified health center, or other health clinic that receives reimbursement on a fee schedule applicable to a physician described in subclause (I) or (II), an advanced practice clinician described in subclause (III), or a nurse practitioner, physician assistant, or certified nurse-midwife described in subclause (III)(bb), for services furnished by—

"(aa) such a physician, nurse practitioner, physician assistant, or certified nurse-midwife, respectively; or

"(bb) an advanced practice clinician supervised by such a physician, nurse practitioner, physician assistant, or certified nurse-midwife; or

"(V) by a nurse practitioner, physician assistant, or certified nurse-midwife described in subclause (III)(bb), in accordance with procedures that ensure that the portion of the payment for such services that the nurse practitioner, physician assistant, or certified nurse-midwife is paid is not less than the amount that the nurse practitioner, physician assistant, or certified nurse-midwife would be paid if the services were provided under part B of title XVIII;".

(2) CONFORMING AMENDMENTS.—Section 1905(dd) of the Social Security Act (42 U.S.C. 1396d(dd)) is amended—

(A) by striking "Notwithstanding" and inserting the following:

"(1) IN GENERAL.—Notwithstanding";

(B) by inserting "or furnished during the additional period specified in paragraph (2)," after "2015,"; and

(C) by adding at the end the following:

"(2) ADDITIONAL PERIOD.—For purposes of paragraph (1), the additional period specified in this paragraph is the period with respect to which section 1902(a)(13)(C)(ii) applies.".

(b) Improved Targeting Of Primary Care.—Section 1902(jj) of the Social Security Act (42 U.S.C. 1396a(jj)) is amended—

(1) by redesignating paragraphs (1) and (2) as subparagraphs (A) and (B), respectively, and moving the margin of each such subparagraph, as so redesignated, 2 ems to the right;

(2) by striking "For purposes of" and inserting the following:

"(1) IN GENERAL.—For purposes of"; and

(3) by adding at the end the following:

"(2) EXCLUSIONS.—Such term does not include any services described in subparagraph (A) or (B) of paragraph (1) if such services are provided in an emergency department of a hospital during the period described in subsection (a)(13)(C)(ii).".

(c) Ensuring Payment By Managed Care Entities.—

(1) IN GENERAL.—Section 1903(m)(2)(A) of the Social Security Act (42 U.S.C. 1396b(m)(2)(A)) is amended—

(A) in clause (xii), by striking "and" after the semicolon;

(B) in clause (xiii)—

(i) by moving the margin of such clause 2 ems to the left; and

(ii) by striking the period at the end and inserting "; and"; and

(C) by inserting after clause (xiii) the following:

"(xiv) such contract provides that (I) payments to health care providers specified in section 1902(a)(13)(C) for furnishing primary care services defined in section 1902(jj) during a year or period specified in section 1902(a)(13)(C) are at least equal to the amounts set forth and required by the Secretary by regulation, (II) the entity shall, upon request, provide documentation to the State that is sufficient to enable the State and the Secretary to ensure compliance with subclause (I), and (III) the Secretary shall approve payments described in subclause (I) that are furnished through an agreed-upon capitation, partial capitation, or other value-based payment arrangement if the agreed-upon capitation, partial capitation, or other value-based payment arrangement is based on a reasonable methodology and the entity provides documentation to the State that is sufficient to enable the State and the Secretary to ensure compliance with subclause (I).".

(2) CONFORMING AMENDMENT.—Section 1932(f) of the Social Security Act (42 U.S.C. 1396u–2(f)) is amended by inserting "and clause (xiv) of section 1903(m)(2)(A)" before the period.

(3) EFFECTIVE DATE.—The amendments made by this subsection shall apply with respect to contracts entered into on or after the date of the enactment of this Act.

SEC. 70112. TEMPORARY INCREASE IN MEDICAID DSH ALLOTMENTS.

(a) In General.—Section 1923(f)(3) of the Social Security Act (42 U.S.C. 1396r–4(f)(3)) is amended—

(1) in subparagraph (A), by striking "and subparagraph (E)" and inserting "and subparagraphs (E) and (F)"; and

(2) by adding at the end the following new subparagraph:

"(F) TEMPORARY INCREASE IN ALLOTMENTS DURING CERTAIN PUBLIC HEALTH EMERGENCY.—The DSH allotment for any State is—

"(i) for fiscal year 2020, equal to 102.5 percent of the DSH allotment that would be determined under this paragraph for the State for fiscal year 2020 without application of this subparagraph, notwithstanding subparagraphs (B) and (C); and

"(ii) for a subsequent fiscal year (if any) during which the emergency period defined in paragraph (1)(B) of section 1135(g) of the Social Security Act is in effect, equal to 102.5 percent of the DSH allotment determined under this subparagraph for the State for the previous fiscal year.

For each fiscal year after fiscal year 2020 during which the emergency period described in clause (ii) is not in effect, the DSH allotment for a State for such fiscal year is equal to the DSH allotment that would have been determined under this paragraph for such fiscal year if this subparagraph had not been enacted.".

(b) Sense Of Congress.—It is the sense of Congress that a State should prioritize making payments under the State plan of the State under title XIX of the Social Security Act (42 U.S.C. 1396 et seq.) (or a waiver of such plan) to disproportionate share hospitals that have a higher share of COVID–19 patients relative to other such hospitals in the State.

SEC. 70113. TEMPORARY ALLOWANCE FOR MEDICAL ASSISTANCE UNDER MEDICAID FOR INMATES DURING 30-DAY PERIOD PRECEDING RELEASE.

The subdivision (A) following paragraph (30) of section 1905(a) of the Social Security Act (42 U.S.C. 1396d(a)) is amended by inserting "and except during the 30-day period preceding the date of release of such individual from such public institution, but only if such 30-day period occurs during the emergency period described in section 1135(g)(1)(B)" after "medical institution".

SEC. 70114. EXTENSION OF EXISTING SECTION 1115 DEMONSTRATION PROJECTS.

(a) Applicability.—This section shall apply with respect to demonstration projects operated by States pursuant to section 1115(a) of the Social Security Act (42 U.S.C. 1315(a)) to promote the objectives of title XIX or XXI of the Social Security Act with a project term set to end on or before December 31, 2020.

(b) Approval Of Extension.—Upon request by a State, the Secretary of Health and Human Services shall approve an extension of the waiver and expenditure authorities for a demonstration project described in subsection (a) for a period up to and including December 31, 2021, to ensure continuity of programs and funding during the emergency period described in section 1135(g)(1)(B) of the Social Security Act (42 U.S.C. 42 U.S.C. 1320b–5(g)(1)(B)).

(c) Extension Terms And Conditions.— (1) The approval pursuant to this section shall extend the terms and conditions that applied to the demonstration project to the extension period. Financial terms and conditions shall continue at levels equivalent to the prior demonstration or program year. All demonstration program components shall be extended to operate through ffthe end of the extension term. In its request for an extension, the state shall identify operational and programmatic changes necessary to continue and stabilize programs into the extension period and shall work with the Secretary of Health and Human Services to implement such changes.

(2) Notwithstanding the foregoing, the State may request, and the Secretary of Health and Human Services may approve, modifications to a demonstration project's terms and conditions to address the impact of the federally designated public health emergency with respect to COVID–19. Such modifications may, at the option of the State, become effective retroactive to the start of the calendar quarter in which the first day of the emergency period described in paragraph (1)(B) of section 1135(g) of the Social Security Act 42 U.S.C. 42 U.S.C. 1320b–5(g)) occurs.

(d) Budget Neutrality.—Budget neutrality for extensions under this section shall be deemed to have been met at the conclusion of the extension period, and States receiving extensions under this section shall not be required to submit a budget neutrality analysis for the extension period.

(e) Expedited Application Process.—The Federal and State public notice and comment procedures or other time constraints otherwise applicable to demonstration project amendments shall be waived to expedite a State's extension request pursuant to this section. The Secretary of Health and Human Services shall approve the extension application within 45 days of a State's submission of its request, or such other timeframe as is mutually agreed to with the State.

(f) Continuation Of Secretarial Authority Under Declared Emergency.—This section does not restrict the Secretary of Health and Human Services from exercising existing flexibilities through demonstration projects operated pursuant to section 1115 of the Social Security Act (42 U.S.C. 1315) in conjunction with the COVID–19 public health emergency.

(g) Rule Of Construction.—Nothing in this section shall authorize the Secretary of Health and Human Service to approve or extend a waiver that fails to meet the requirements of section 1115 of the Social Security Act (42 U.S.C. 1315).

SEC. 70115. MODIFICATION OF REDUCTIONS IN MEDICAID DSH ALLOTMENTS.

Section 1923(f)(7)(A) of the Social Security Act (42 U.S.C. 1396r–4(f)(7)(A)) is amended—

(1) in clause (i), in the matter preceding subclause (I), by striking "For the period beginning May 23, 2020, and ending September 30, 2020, and for each of fiscal years 2021 through 2025" and inserting "For the period beginning December 1, 2020, and ending September 30, 2021, and for each of fiscal years 2022 through 2025"; and

(2) in clause (ii)—

(A) in subclause (I), by striking "for the period beginning May 23, 2020, and ending September 30, 2020" and inserting "for the period beginning December 1, 2020, and ending September 30, 2021"; and

(B) in subclause (II), by striking "for each of fiscal years 2021 through 2025" and inserting "for each of fiscal years 2022 through 2025".

SEC. 70116. EXTENSION OF MONEY FOLLOWS THE PERSON REBALANCING DEMONSTRATION.

(a) In General.—Section 6071(h)(1) of the Deficit Reduction Act of 2005 (42 U.S.C. 1396a note) is amended—

(1) in subparagraph (F), by striking "and" at the end; and

(2) by striking subparagraph (G) and inserting the following:

"(G) $450,000,000 for fiscal year 2020; and

"(H) $75,206,000 for the period beginning on October 1, 2020, and ending on November 30, 2020.".

(b) Effective Date.—The amendments made by subsection (a) shall take effect as if included in the enactment of the Further Consolidated Appropriations Act, 2020 (Public Law 116–94).

SEC. 70117. EXTENSION OF PROTECTION FOR MEDICAID RECIPIENTS OF HOME AND COMMUNITY-BASED SERVICES AGAINST SPOUSAL IMPOVERISHMENT.

(a) In General.—Section 2404 of Public Law 111–148 (42 U.S.C. 1396r–5 note) is amended by striking "May 22, 2020" and inserting "November 30, 2020".

(b) Rule Of Construction.—Nothing in section 2404 of Public Law 111–148 (42 U.S.C. 1396r–5 note) or section 1902(a)(17) or 1924 of the Social Security Act (42 U.S.C. 1396a(a)(17), 1396r–5) shall be construed as prohibiting a State from applying an income or resource disregard under a methodology authorized under section 1902(r)(2) of such Act (42 U.S.C. 1396a(r)(2))—

(1) to the income or resources of an individual described in section 1902(a)(10)(A)(ii)(VI) of such Act (42 U.S.C. 1396a(a)(10)(A)(ii)(VI)) (including a disregard of the income or resources of such individual's spouse); or

(2) on the basis of an individual's need for home and community-based services authorized under subsection (c), (d), (i), or (k) of section 1915 of such Act (42 U.S.C. 1396n) or under section 1115 of such Act (42 U.S.C. 1315).

SEC. 70118. EXTENSION OF THE COMMUNITY MENTAL HEALTH SERVICES DEMONSTRATION PROGRAM.

Section 223(d)(3) of the Protecting Access to Medicare Act of 2014 (42 U.S.C. 1396a note) is amended by striking "May 22, 2020" and inserting "November 30, 2020".

TITLE II—MEDICARE

SEC. 70201. COVERAGE OF THE COVID-19 VACCINE UNDER THE MEDICARE PROGRAM WITHOUT ANY COST-SHARING.

(a) Medical And Other Health Services.—Section 1861(s)(10)(A) of the Social Security Act (42 U.S.C. 1395x(s)(10)(A)) is amended by inserting ", and COVID-19 vaccine and its administration" after "influenza vaccine and its administration".

(b) Part B Deductible.—Section 1833(b) of the Social Security Act (42 U.S.C. 1395l(b)) is amended, in the first sentence—

(1) by striking "and" before "(11)"; and (B) by inserting before the period at the end the following: ", and (11)

(2) by inserting before the period at the end the following: ", and (12) such deductible shall not apply with respect a COVID-19 vaccine and its administration described in section 1861(s)(10)(A)".

(c) Waiving Cost-Sharing Under Medicare Advantage.—Section 1852(a)(1)(B) of the Social Security Act (42 U.S.C. 1395w–22(a)(1)(B)) is amended—

(1) in clause (iv)—

(A) by redesignating subclause (VI) as subclause (VII); and

(B) by inserting after subclause (V) the following new subclause:

"(VI) COVID-19 vaccines and the administration of such vaccines, as described in section 1861(s)(10)(A)."; and

(2) in clause (v), by striking "subclauses (IV) and (V)" and inserting "subclauses (IV), (V), and (VI)".

(d) Implementation.—Notwithstanding any other provision of law, the Secretary of Health and Human Services may implement the amendments made by subsection (c) by program instruction or otherwise.

(e) Payment For Administration Of COVID-19 Vaccine.—The payment amount under part B of title XVIII of the Social Security Act for the administration of a COVID-19 vaccine pursuant to the amendment made by subsection (a) shall be the same as the payment amount under such part for the administration of an influenza vaccine, pneumococcal vaccine, and a hepatitis B vaccine.

(f) Authority For Roster Billing.—Notwithstanding any other provision of law, the Secretary of Health and Human Services may, by program instruction or otherwise, include a COVID-19 vaccine as a vaccine with respect to which the Secretary permits roster billing for purposes of payment under part B of title XVIII of the Social Security Act.

(g) Effective Date.—The amendments made by this section shall take effect on the date of enactment of this Act and shall apply with respect to a COVID-19 vaccine beginning on the date that such vaccine is licensed under section 351 of the Public Health Service Act (42 U.S.C. 262).

SEC. 70202. HOLDING MEDICARE BENEFICIARIES HARMLESS FOR SPECIFIED COVID-19 TREATMENT SERVICES FURNISHED UNDER PART A OR PART B OF THE MEDICARE PROGRAM.

(a) In General.—Notwithstanding any other provision of law, in the case of a specified COVID-19 treatment service (as defined in subsection (b)) furnished to an individual entitled to benefits under part A or enrolled under part B of title XVIII of the Social Security Act (42 U.S.C. 1395 et seq.) for which payment is made under such part A or such part B, the Secretary of Health and Human Services (in this section referred to as the "Secretary") shall provide that—

(1) any cost-sharing required (including any deductible, copayment, or coinsurance) applicable to such individual under such part A or such part B with respect to such item or service is paid by the Secretary; and

(2) the provider of services or supplier (as defined in section 1861 of the Social Security Act (42 U.S.C. 1395x)) does not hold such individual liable for such requirement.

(b) Definition Of Specified COVID-19 Treatment Services.—For purposes of this section, the term "specified COVID-19 treatment service" means any item or service furnished to an individual for which payment may be made under part A or part B of title XVIII of the Social Security Act (42 U.S.C. 1395 et seq.) if such item or service is included in a claim with an ICD-10-CM code relating to COVID-19 (as described in the document entitled "ICD-10-CM Official Coding Guidelines - Supplement Coding encounters related to COVID-19 Coronavirus Outbreak" published on February 20, 2020, or as otherwise specified by the Secretary).

(c) Recovery Of Cost-Sharing Amounts Paid By The Secretary In The Case Of Supplemental Insurance Coverage.—

(1) IN GENERAL.—In the case of any amount paid by the Secretary pursuant to subsection (a)(1) that the Secretary determines would otherwise have been paid by a group health plan or health insurance issuer (as such terms are defined in section 2791 of the Public Health Service Act (42 U.S.C. 300gg–91)), a private entity offering a medicare supplemental policy under section 1882 of the Social Security Act (42 U.S.C. 1395ss), any other health plan offering supplemental coverage, a State plan under title XIX of the Social Security Act, or the Secretary of Defense under the TRICARE program,

such plan, issuer, private entity, other health plan, State plan, or Secretary of Defense, as applicable, shall pay to the Secretary, not later than 1 year after such plan, issuer, private entity, other health plan, State plan, or Secretary of Defense receives a notice under paragraph (3), such amount in accordance with this subsection.

(2) REQUIRED INFORMATION.—Not later than 9 months after the date of the enactment of this Act, each group health plan, health insurance issuer, private entity, other health plan, State plan, and Secretary of Defense described in paragraph (1) shall submit to the Secretary such information as the Secretary determines necessary for purposes of carrying out this subsection. Such information so submitted shall be updated by such plan, issuer, private entity, other health plan, State plan, or Secretary of Defense, as applicable, at such time and in such manner as specified by the Secretary.

(3) REVIEW OF CLAIMS AND NOTIFICATION.—The Secretary shall establish a process under which claims for items and services for which the Secretary has paid an amount pursuant to subsection (a)(1) are reviewed for purposes of identifying if such amount would otherwise have been paid by a plan, issuer, private entity, other health plan, State plan, or Secretary of Defense described in paragraph (1). In the case such a claim is so identified, the Secretary shall determine the amount that would have been otherwise payable by such plan, issuer, private entity, other health plan, State plan, or Secretary of Defense and notify such plan, issuer, private entity, other health plan, State plan, or Secretary of Defense of such amount.

(4) ENFORCEMENT.—The Secretary may impose a civil monetary penalty in an amount determined appropriate by the Secretary in the case of a plan, issuer, private entity, other health plan, or State plan that fails to comply with a provision of this section. The provisions of section 1128A of the Social Security Act shall apply to a civil monetary penalty imposed under the previous sentence in the same manner as such provisions apply to a penalty or proceeding under subsection (a) or (b) of such section.

(d) Funding.—The Secretary shall provide for the transfer to the Centers for Medicare & Medicaid Program Management Account from the Federal Hospital Insurance Trust Fund and the Federal Supplementary Trust Fund (in such portions as the Secretary determines appropriate) $100,000,000 for purposes of carrying out this section.

(e) Report.—Not later than 3 years after the date of the enactment of this Act, the Inspector General of the Department of Health and Human Services shall submit to Congress a report containing an analysis of amounts paid pursuant to subsection (a)(1) compared to amounts paid to the Secretary pursuant to subsection (c).

(f) Implementation.—Notwithstanding any other provision of law, the Secretary may implement the provisions of this section by program instruction or otherwise.

SEC. 70203. MEDICARE SEQUESTER DELAY.

During the period beginning on May 1, 2020, and ending on such date the emergency period described in section 1135(g)(1)(B) of the Social Security Act (42 U.S.C. 1320b–5(g)(1)(B)) ends, the Medicare program under title XVIII of the Social Security Act (42 U.S.C. 1395 et seq.) shall be exempt from reduction under any sequestration order issued pursuant to section 254 of the Balanced Budget and Emergency Deficit Control Act of 1985 before, on, or after the date of enactment of this Act.

SEC. 70204. ENHANCING MEDICARE TELEHEALTH SERVICES FOR FEDERALLY QUALIFIED HEALTH CENTERS AND RURAL HEALTH CLINICS DURING THE EMERGENCY PERIOD.

Section 1834(m) of the Social Security Act (42 U.S.C. 1395m(m)) is amended—

(1) in the first sentence of paragraph (1), by striking "The Secretary" and inserting "Subject to paragraph (8), the Secretary";

(2) in paragraph (2)(A), by striking "The Secretary" and inserting "Subject to paragraph (8), the Secretary";

(3) in paragraph (4)—

(A) in subparagraph (A), by striking "The term" and inserting "Subject to paragraph (8),the term"; and

(B) in subparagraph (F)(i), by striking "The term" and inserting "Subject to paragraph (8), the term"; and

(4) by adding at the end the following new paragraph:

"(8) ENHANCING TELEHEALTH SERVICES FOR FEDERALLY QUALIFIED HEALTH CENTERS AND RURAL HEALTH CLINICS DURING THE EMERGENCY PERIOD.—

"(A) IN GENERAL.—During the emergency period described in section 1135(g)(1)(B)—

"(i) the Secretary shall pay for telehealth services that are furnished via a telecommunications system by a Federally qualified health center or a rural health clinic to an eligible telehealth individual enrolled under this part notwithstanding that the Federally qualified health center or rural clinic providing the telehealth service is not at the same location as the beneficiary;

"(ii) the amount of payment to a Federally qualified health center or rural health clinic that serves as a distant site for such a telehealth service shall be determined under subparagraph (B); and

"(iii) for purposes of this subsection—

"(I) the term 'distant site' includes a Federally qualified health center or rural health clinic that furnishes a telehealth service to an eligible telehealth individual; and

"(II) the term 'telehealth services' includes a rural health clinic service or Federally qualified health center service that is furnished using telehealth to the extent that payment codes corresponding to services identified by the Secretary under clause (i) or (ii) of paragraph (4)(F) are listed on the corresponding claim for such rural health clinic service or Federally qualified health center service.

"(B) SPECIAL PAYMENT RULE.—The Secretary shall develop and implement payment methods that apply under this subsection to a Federally qualified health center or rural health clinic that serves as a distant site that furnishes a telehealth service to an eligible telehealth individual during such emergency period. Such payment methods shall be based on payment rates that are similar to the national average payment rates for comparable telehealth services under the physician fee schedule under section 1848. Notwithstanding any other provision of law, the Secretary may implement such payment methods through program instruction or otherwise.".

SEC. 70205. GUARANTEED ISSUE OF CERTAIN MEDIGAP POLICIES.

(a) Guaranteed Issue Of Medigap Policies To All Medigap-Eligible Medicare Beneficiaries.—

(1) IN GENERAL.—Section 1882(s) of the Social Security Act (42 U.S.C. 1395ss(s)) is amended—

(A) in paragraph (2)(A), by striking "65 years of age or older and is enrolled for benefits under part B" and inserting "entitled to, or enrolled for, benefits under part A and enrolled for benefits under part B";

(B) in paragraph (2)(D), by striking "who is 65 years of age or older as of the date of issuance and";

(C) in paragraph (3)(B)(ii), by striking "is 65 years of age or older and"; and

(D) in paragraph (3)(B)(vi), by striking "at age 65".

(2) ADDITIONAL ENROLLMENT PERIOD FOR CERTAIN INDIVIDUALS.—

(A) ONE-TIME ENROLLMENT PERIOD.—

(i) IN GENERAL.—In the case of a specified individual, the Secretary shall establish a one-time enrollment period described in clause (iii) during which such an individual may enroll in any medicare supplemental policy of the individual's choosing.

(ii) APPLICATION.—The provisions of—

(I) paragraph (2) of section 1882(s) of the Social Security Act (42 U.S.C. 1395ss(s)) shall apply with respect to a specified individual who is described in subclause (I) of subparagraph (B)(iii) as if references in such paragraph (2) to the 6 month period described in subparagraph (A) of such paragraph were references to the one-time enrollment period established under clause (i); and

(II) paragraph (3) of such section shall apply with respect to a specified individual who is described in subclause (II) of subparagraph (B)(iii) as if references in such paragraph (3) to the period specified in subparagraph (E) of such paragraph were references to the one-time enrollment period established under clause (i).

(iii) PERIOD.—The enrollment period established under clause (i) shall be the 6-month period beginning on January 1, 2024.

(B) SPECIFIED INDIVIDUAL.—For purposes of this paragraph, the term "specified individual" means an individual who—

(i) is entitled to hospital insurance benefits under part A of title XVIII of the

Social Security Act (42 U.S.C. 1395c et seq.) pursuant to section 226(b) or section 226A of such Act (42 U.S.C. 426(b); 426–1);

(ii) is enrolled for benefits under part B of such Act (42 U.S.C. 1395j et seq.); and

(iii) (I) would not, but for the amendments made by subparagraphs (A) and (B) of paragraph (1) and the provisions of this paragraph (if such provisions applied to such individual), be eligible for the guaranteed issue of a medicare supplemental policy under paragraph (2) of section 1882(s) of such Act (42 U.S.C. 1395ss(s)); or

(II) would not, but for the amendments made by subparagraphs (C) and (D) of paragraph (1) and the provisions of this paragraph (if such provisions applied to such individual), be eligible for the guaranteed issue of a medicare supplemental policy under paragraph (3) of such section.

(C) OUTREACH PLAN.—

(i) IN GENERAL.—The Secretary shall develop an outreach plan to notify specified individuals of the one-time enrollment period established under subparagraph (A).

(ii) CONSULTATION.—In implementing the outreach plan developed under clause (i), the Secretary shall consult with consumer advocates, brokers, insurers, the National Association of Insurance Commissioners, and State Health Insurance Assistance Programs.

(3) EFFECTIVE DATE.—The amendments made by paragraph (1) shall apply to medicare supplemental policies effective on or after January 1, 2024.

(b) Guaranteed Issue Of Medigap Policies For Medicare Advantage Enrollees.—

(1) IN GENERAL.—Section 1882(s)(3) of the Social Security Act (42 U.S.C. 1395ss(s)(3)), as amended by subsection (a), is further amended—

(A) in subparagraph (B), by adding at the end the following new clause:

"(vii) The individual—

"(I) was enrolled in a Medicare Advantage plan under part C for not less than 12 months;

"(II) subsequently disenrolled from such plan;

"(III) elects to receive benefits under this title through the original Medicare fee-for-service program under parts A and B; and

"(IV) has not previously elected to receive benefits under this title through the original Medicare fee-for-service program pursuant to disenrollment from a Medicare Advantage plan under part C.";

(B) by striking subparagraph (C)(iii) and inserting the following:

"(iii) Subject to subsection (v)(1), for purposes of an individual described in clause (vi) or (vii) of subparagraph (B), a medicare supplemental policy described in this subparagraph shall include any medicare supplemental policy."; and

(C) in subparagraph (E)—

(i) in clause (iv), by striking "and" at the end;

(ii) in clause (v), by striking the period at the end and inserting "; and"; and

(iii) by adding at the end the following new clause—

"(vi) in the case of an individual described in subparagraph (B)(vii), the annual, coordinated election period (as defined in section 1851(e)(3)(B)) or a continuous open enrollment period (as defined in section 1851(e)(2)) during which the individual disenrolls from a Medicare Advantage plan under part C.".

(2) EFFECTIVE DATE.—The amendments made by paragraph (1) shall apply to medicare supplemental policies effective on or after January 1, 2024.

SEC. 70206. ENSURING COMMUNICATIONS ACCESSIBILITY FOR RESIDENTS OF SKILLED NURSING FACILITIES DURING THE COVID-19 EMERGENCY PERIOD.

(a) In General.—Section 1819(c)(3) of the Social Security Act (42 U.S.C. 1395i–3(c)(3)) is amended—

(1) in subparagraph (D), by striking "and" at the end;

(2) in subparagraph (E), by striking the period and inserting "; and"; and

(3) by adding at the end the following new subparagraph:

"(F) provide for reasonable access to the use of a telephone, including TTY and TDD services (as defined for purposes of section 483.10 of title 42, Code of Federal Regulations (or a successor regulation)), and the internet (to the extent available to the facility) and inform each such resident (or a representative of such resident) of such access and any changes in policies or procedures of such facility relating to limitations on external visitors.".

(b) COVID-19 Provisions.—

(1) GUIDANCE.—Not later than 15 days after the date of the enactment of this Act, the Secretary of Health and Human Service shall issue guidance on steps skilled nursing facilities may take to ensure residents have access to televisitation during the emergency period defined in section 1135(g)(1)(B) of the Social Security Act (42 U.S.C. 1320b–5(g)(1)(B)).

(2) REVIEW OF FACILITIES.—The Secretary of Health and Human Services shall take such steps as determined appropriate by the Secretary to ensure that residents of skilled nursing facilities and relatives of such residents are made aware of the access rights described in section 1819(c)(3)(F) of the Social Security Act (42 U.S.C. 1395i–3(c)(3)(F)).

SEC. 70207. MEDICARE HOSPITAL INPATIENT PROSPECTIVE PAYMENT SYSTEM OUTLIER PAYMENTS FOR COVID-19 PATIENTS DURING CERTAIN EMERGENCY PERIOD.

(a) In General.—Section 1886(d)(5)(A) of the Social Security Act (42 U.S.C. 1395ww(d)(5)(A)) is amended—

(1) in clause (ii), by striking "For cases" and inserting "Subject to clause (vii), for cases";

(2) in clause (iii), by striking "The amount" and inserting "Subject to clause (vii), the amount";

(3) in clause (iv), by striking "The total amount" and inserting "Subject to clause (vii), the total amount"; and

(4) by adding at the end the following new clause:
"(vii) For discharges that have a primary or secondary diagnosis of COVID-19 and that occur during the emergency period described in section 1135(g)(1)(B), the amount of any additional payment under clause (ii) for a subsection (d) hospital for such a discharge shall be determined as if—
"(I) clause (ii) was amended by striking 'plus a fixed dollar amount determined by the Secretary';
"(II) the reference in clause (iii) to 'approximate the marginal cost of care beyond the cutoff point applicable under clause (i) or (ii)' were a reference to 'approximate the marginal cost of care beyond the cutoff point applicable under clause (i), or, in the case of an additional payment requested under clause (ii), be equal to 100 percent of the amount by which the costs of the discharge for which such additional payment is so requested exceed the applicable DRG prospective payment rate'; and
"(III) clause (iv) does not apply.".
(b) Exclusion From Reduction In Average Standardized Amounts Payable To Hospitals Located In Certain Areas.—Section 1886(d)(3)(B) of the Social Security Act (42 U.S.C. 1395ww(d)(3)(B)) is amended by inserting before the period the following: ", other than additional payments described in clause (vii) of such paragraph".
(c) Application To Site Neutral IPPS Payment Rates.—Section 1886(m)(6)(B) of the Social Security Act (42 U.S.C. 1395ww(m)(6)(B)) is amended—
(1) in clause (i)—
(A) in the matter preceding subclause (I), by striking "In this paragraph" and inserting "Subject to clause (ii), in this paragraph";
(B) in subclause (I), by striking "clause (iii)" and inserting "clause (iv)"; and
(C) in subclause (II), by striking "clause (ii)" and inserting "clause (iii)";
(2) in clause (ii), in the matter preceding subclause (I), by striking "clause (iv)" and inserting "clause (v)";
(3) in clause (iii)(I), by striking "clause (ii)" and inserting "clause (iii)";
(4) in clause (iv), by striking "clause (ii)(I)" and inserting "clause (iii)(I)";
(5) by redesignating clauses (ii) through (iv) as clauses (iii) through (v), respectively; and
(6) by inserting after clause (i) the following new clause:
"(ii) EXCEPTION.—Notwithstanding clause (i), the term 'applicable site neutral payment rate' means—
"(I) for discharges that have a primary or secondary diagnosis of COVID-19 and that occur during any portion of the emergency period described in section 1135(g)(1)(B) occurring during a cost reporting period described in clause (i)(I), the greater of the blended payment rate specified in clause (iv) or the percent described in clause (iii)(II); and
"(II) for discharges that have a primary or secondary diagnosis of COVID-19 and that occur during any portion of the emergency period described in section 1135(g)(1)(B) occurring during a cost reporting period described in

clause (i)(II), the percent described in clause (iii)(II).".

(d) Implementation.—Notwithstanding any other provision of law, the Secretary of Health and Human Services may implement the amendments made by this section by program instruction or otherwise.

SEC. 70208. COVERAGE OF TREATMENTS FOR COVID–19 AT NO COST SHARING UNDER THE MEDICARE ADVANTAGE PROGRAM.

(a) In General.—Section 1852(a)(1)(B) of the Social Security Act (42 U.S.C. 1395w–22(a)(1)(B)) is amended by adding at the end the following new clause:

"(vii) SPECIAL COVERAGE RULES FOR SPECIFIED COVID–19 TREATMENT SERVICES.—Notwithstanding clause (i), in the case of a specified COVID-19 treatment service (as defined in section 70202(b) of the Take Responsibility for Workers and Families Act) that is furnished during a plan year occurring during any portion of the emergency period defined in section 1135(g)(1)(B) beginning on or after the date of the enactment of this clause, a Medicare Advantage plan may not, with respect to such service, impose—

"(I) any cost-sharing requirement (including a deductible, copayment, or coinsurance requirement); and

"(II) in the case such service is a critical specified COVID-19 treatment service (including ventilator services and intensive care unit services), any prior authorization or other utilization management requirement.

A Medicare Advantage plan may not take the application of this clause into account for purposes of a bid amount submitted by such plan under section 1854(a)(6).".

(b) Reimbursement Of Medicare Advantage Plans For Elimination Of Cost Sharing.—Section 1853 of the Social Security Act (42 U.S.C. 1395w–23) is amended by adding at the end the following new subsection:

"(p) Additional Payment To Account For Cost Sharing Elimination For COVID-19 Treatment Services.—

"(1) IN GENERAL.—A Medicare Advantage plan shall notify the Secretary of the total dollar amount of cost sharing that, but for the application of section 1852(a)(1)(B)(vii), would have been required under such plan for specified COVID-19 treatment services (as defined in section 70202(b) of the Take Responsibility for Workers and Families Act) furnished during a plan year described in such section to individuals enrolled in the plan. The Secretary shall make periodic and timely payments in accordance with this subsection to such plan that, in the aggregate, equal such total dollar amount.

"(2) TIMING OF PAYMENT.—Payments by the Secretary under this subsection shall be made beginning March 1, 2021, for amounts described in such paragraph that would have been required under such plan for specified COVID-19 treatment services furnished during plan year 2020. Payments by the Secretary under this subsection for such amounts that would have been so required under such plan for such services furnished during a plan year subsequent to plan year 2020 shall be made beginning March 1 of the plan year following such subsequent plan year.

"(3) NON-APPLICATION.—Section 1853(c)(7) shall not apply with respect to the application of this subsection.

"(4) APPROPRIATION.—There are transferred to the Centers for Medicare & Medicaid Program Management Fund, out of any monies in the Treasury not otherwise obligated, such sums as may be necessary to the Secretary for purposes of making payments under this subsection.".

(c) Implementation.—Notwithstanding any other provision of law, the Secretary of Health and Human Services may implement the amendments made by this section by program instruction or otherwise.

SEC. 70209. ESTABLISHING A RISK CORRIDOR PROGRAM FOR MEDICARE ADVANTAGE PLANS DURING THE COVID-19 EMERGENCY.

(a) In General.—Section 1853 of the Social Security Act (42 U.S.C. 1395w–23), as amended by section 70208(b), is further amended by adding at the end the following new subsection:

"(q) Risk Corridor Program During The COVID-19 Emergency.—

"(1) IN GENERAL.—The Secretary shall establish and administer a program of risk corridors for each plan year, any portion of which occurs during the emergency period defined in section 1135(g)(1)(B), under which the Secretary shall make payments to MA organizations offering a Medicare Advantage plan based on the ratio of the allowable costs of the plan to the aggregate premiums of the plan.

"(2) PAYMENT METHODOLOGY.—The Secretary shall provide under the program established under paragraph (1) that if the allowable costs for a Medicare Advantage plan for any plan year are more than 105 percent of the target amount, the Secretary shall pay to the plan an amount equal to 75 percent of the allowable costs in excess of 105 percent of the target amount.

"(3) TIMING.—

"(A) SUBMISSION OF INFORMATION BY PLANS.—With respect to a plan year for which the program described in paragraph (1) is established and administered, not later than July 1 of the succeeding plan year each MA organization offering a Medicare Advantage plan shall submit to the Secretary such information as the Secretary may require for purposes of carrying out such program.

"(B) PAYMENT.—The Secretary shall pay to an MA organization offering a Medicare Advantage plan eligible to receive a payment under the program with respect to a plan year the amount provided under paragraph (2) for such plan year not later than 60 days after such organization submits information with respect to such plan and plan year under subparagraph (A).

"(4) DEFINITIONS.—

"(A) ALLOWABLE COSTS.—

"(i) IN GENERAL.—The amount of allowable costs of a MA organization offering a Medicare Advantage plan for a plan year is an amount equal to the total costs (other than administrative costs) of such plan in providing benefits covered by such plan, but only to the extent that such costs are incurred with respect to such benefits for items and services that are benefits under the original medicare fee-for-service program option.

"(ii) REDUCTIONS.—Allowable costs for a Medicare Advantage plan for a plan year shall be reduced by any payment made under subsection (p) with respect to such plan and such plan year.

"(B) TARGET AMOUNT.—The target amount described in this paragraph is, with respect to a Medicare Advantage plan and a plan year, the total amount of payments paid to the MA organization for the plan for benefits under the original medicare fee-for-service program option for the plan year, taking into account amounts paid by the Secretary and enrollees, based upon the bid amount submitted under section 1854, reduced by the total amount of administrative expenses for the year assumed in such bid.

"(5) FUNDING.—There are appropriated to the Centers for Medicare & Medicaid Services Program Management Account, out of any monies in the Treasury not otherwise obligated, such sums as may be necessary for purposes of carrying out this subsection.".

(b) Implementation.—Notwithstanding any other provision of law, the Secretary of Health and Human Service may implement the amendments made by this section by program instruction or otherwise.

SEC. 70210. REQUIRING COVERAGE UNDER MEDICARE PDPS AND MA–PD PLANS, WITHOUT THE IMPOSITION OF COST SHARING OR UTILIZATION MANAGEMENT REQUIREMENTS, OF DRUGS INTENDED TO TREAT COVID-19 DURING CERTAIN EMERGENCIES.

(a) Coverage Requirement.—

(1) IN GENERAL.—Section 1860D–4(b)(3) of the Social Security Act (42 U.S.C. 1395w–104(b)(3)) is amended by adding at the end the following new subparagraph:

"(I) REQUIRED INCLUSION OF DRUGS INTENDED TO TREAT COVID-19.—

"(i) IN GENERAL.—Notwithstanding any other provision of law, a PDP sponsor offering a prescription drug plan shall, with respect to a plan year, any portion of which occurs during the period described in clause (ii), be required to—

"(I) include in any formulary—

"(aa) all covered part D drugs with a medically accepted indication (as defined in section 1860D–2(e)(4)) to treat COVID-19 that are marketed in the United States; and

"(bb) all drugs authorized under section 564 or 564A of the Federal Food Drug and Cosmetic Act to treat COVID-19; and

"(II) not impose any prior authorization or other utilization management requirement with respect to such drugs described in item (aa) or (bb) of

subclause (I) (other than such a requirement that limits the quantity of drugs due to safety).
"(ii) PERIOD DESCRIBED.—For purposes of clause (i), the period described in this clause is the period during which there exists the public health emergency declared by the Secretary pursuant to section 319 of the Public Health Service Act on January 31, 2020, entitled 'Determination that a Public Health Emergency Exists Nationwide as the Result of the 2019 Novel Coronavirus' (including any renewal of such declaration pursuant to such section).".
(b) Elimination Of Cost Sharing.—
(1) ELIMINATION OF COST-SHARING FOR DRUGS INTENDED TO TREAT COVID-19 UNDER STANDARD AND ALTERNATIVE PRESCRIPTION DRUG COVERAGE.—Section 1860D–2 of the Social Security Act (42 U.S.C. 1395w–102) is amended—
(A) in subsection (b)—
(i) in paragraph (1)(A), by striking "The coverage" and inserting "Subject to paragraph (8), the coverage";
(ii) in paragraph (2)—
(I) in subparagraph (A), by inserting after "Subject to subparagraphs (C) and (D)" the following: "and paragraph (8)";
(II) in subparagraph (C)(i), by striking "paragraph (4)" and inserting "paragraphs (4) and (8)"; and
(III) in subparagraph (D)(i), by striking "paragraph (4)" and inserting "paragraphs (4) and (8)";
(iii) in paragraph (4)(A)(i), by striking "The coverage" and inserting "Subject to paragraph (8), the coverage"; and
(iv) by adding at the end the following new paragraph:
"(8) ELIMINATION OF COST-SHARING FOR DRUGS INTENDED TO TREAT COVID-19.—The coverage does not impose any deductible, copayment, coinsurance, or other cost-sharing requirement for drugs described in section 1860D–4(b)(3)(I)(i)(I) with respect to a plan year, any portion of which occurs during the period during which there exists the public health emergency declared by the Secretary pursuant to section 319 of the Public Health Service Act on January 31, 2020, entitled 'Determination that a Public Health Emergency Exists Nationwide as the Result of the 2019 Novel Coronavirus' (including any renewal of such declaration pursuant to such section)."; and
(B) in subsection (c), by adding at the end the following new paragraph:
"(4) SAME ELIMINATION OF COST-SHARING FOR DRUGS INTENDED TO TREAT COVID-19.—The coverage is in accordance with subsection (b)(8).".
(2) ELIMINATION OF COST-SHARING FOR DRUGS INTENDED TO TREAT COVID-19 DISPENSED TO INDIVIDUALS WHO ARE SUBSIDY ELIGIBLE INDIVIDUALS.—Section 1860D–14(a) of the Social Security Act

(42 U.S.C. 1395w–114(a)) is amended—
(A) in paragraph (1)—
(i) in subparagraph (D)—
(I) in clause (ii), by striking "In the case of" and inserting "Subject to subparagraph (F), in the case of"; and
(II) in clause (iii), by striking "In the case of" and inserting "Subject to subparagraph (F), in the case of"; and
(ii) by adding at the end the following new subparagraph:
"(F) ELIMINATION OF COST-SHARING FOR DRUGS INTENDED TO TREAT COVID-19.—Coverage that is in accordance with section 1860D–2(b)(8)."; and
(B) in paragraph (2)—
(i) in subparagraph (B), by striking "A reduction" and inserting "Subject to subparagraph (F), a reduction";
(ii) in subparagraph (D), by striking "The substitution" and inserting "Subject to subparagraph (F), the substitution";
(iii) in subparagraph (E), by inserting after "Subject to" the following: "subparagraph (F) and"; and
(iv) by adding at the end the following new subparagraph:
"(F) ELIMINATION OF COST-SHARING FOR DRUGS INTENDED TO TREAT COVID-19.—Coverage that is in accordance with section 1860D–2(b)(8).".
(c) Implementation.—Notwithstanding any other provision of law, the Secretary of Health and Human Services may implement the amendments made by this section by program instruction or otherwise.

SEC. 70211. REQUIRING MEDICARE PDPS AND MA–PD PLANS TO ALLOW DURING THE COVID-19 EMERGENCY PERIOD FOR FILLS AND REFILLS OF COVERED PART D DRUGS FOR UP TO A 3-MONTH SUPPLY.

(a) In General.—Section 1860D–4(b) of the Social Security Act (42 U.S.C. 1395w–104(b)) is amended by adding at the end the following new paragraph:
"(4) ENSURING ACCESS DURING COVID-19 PUBLIC HEALTH EMERGENCY PERIOD.—
"(A) IN GENERAL.—During the emergency period described in section 1135(g)(1)(B), subject to subparagraph (B), a prescription drug plan or MA–PD plan shall, notwithstanding any cost and utilization management, medication therapy management, or other such programs under this part, permit a part D eligible individual enrolled in such plan to obtain in a single fill or refill, at the option of such individual, the total day supply (not to exceed a 90-day supply) prescribed for such individual for a covered part D drug.
"(B) SAFETY EDIT EXCEPTION.—A prescription drug plan or MA–PD plan may not permit a part D eligible individual to obtain a single fill or refill inconsistent with an applicable safety edit.".
(b) Implementation.—Notwithstanding any other provision of law, the

Secretary of Health and Human Services may implement the amendment made by this section by program instruction or otherwise.
SEC. 70212. EXTENSION OF THE WORK GEOGRAPHIC INDEX FLOOR UNDER THE MEDICARE PROGRAM.
Section 1848(e)(1)(E) of the Social Security Act (42 U.S.C. 1395w–4(e)(1)(E)) is amended by striking "May 23, 2020" and inserting "December 1, 2020".
SEC. 70213. EXTENSION OF FUNDING FOR QUALITY MEASURE ENDORSEMENT, INPUT, AND SELECTION.
(a) In General.—Section 1890(d)(2) of the Social Security Act (42 U.S.C. 1395aaa(d)(2)) is amended—
(1) in the first sentence, by striking "and $4,830,000 for the period beginning on October 1, 2019, and ending on May 22, 2020" and inserting "$25,170,000 for fiscal year 2020, and $5,013,699 for the period beginning on October 1, 2020, and ending on November 30, 2020"; and
(2) in the third sentence, by striking "for each of fiscal years 2018 and 2019 and for the period beginning on October 1, 2019, and ending on May 22, 2020" and inserting "for each of fiscal years 2018 through 2020 and for the period beginning on October 1, 2020, and ending on November 30, 2020".
(b) Effective Date.—The amendments made by subsection (a) shall take effect as if included in the enactment of the Further Consolidated Appropriations Act, 2020 (Public Law 116–94).
SEC. 70214. EXTENSION OF FUNDING OUTREACH AND ASSISTANCE FOR LOW-INCOME PROGRAMS.
(a) Additional Funding For State Health Insurance Programs.—Subsection (a)(1)(B) of section 119 of the Medicare Improvements for Patients and Providers Act of 2008 (42 U.S.C. 1395b–3 note) is amended—
(1) in clause (xi), by striking "and" at the end;
(2) in clause (xii), by striking the period at the end and inserting a semicolon; and
(3) by inserting after clause (xii) the following new clauses:
"(xiii) for the period beginning on May 23, 2020, and ending on September 30, 2020, of $5,383,562; and
"(xiv) for the period beginning on October 1, 2020, and ending on November 30, 2020, of $2,506,849.".
(b) Additional Funding For Area Agencies On Aging.—Subsection (b)(1)(B) of such section 119, as so amended, is amended—
(1) in clause (xi), by striking "and" at the end;
(2) in clause (xii), by striking the period at the end and inserting a semicolon; and
(3) by inserting after clause (xii) the following new clauses:
"(xiii) for the period beginning on May 23, 2020, and ending on September 30, 2020, of $5,383,562; and
"(xiv) for the period beginning on October 1, 2020, and ending on November 30, 2020, of $2,506,849.".

(c) Additional Funding For Aging And Disability Resource Centers.—Subsection (c)(1)(B) of such section 119, as so amended, is amended—

(1) in clause (xi), by striking "and" at the end;

(2) in clause (xii), by striking the period at the end and inserting a semicolon; and

(3) by inserting after clause (xii) the following new clauses:

"(xiii) for the period beginning on May 23, 2020, and ending on September 30, 2020, of $1,794,521; and

"(xiv) for the period beginning on October 1, 2020, and ending on November 30, 2020, of $835,616.".

(d) Additional Funding For Contract With The National Center For Benefits And Outreach Enrollment.—Subsection (d)(2) of such section 119, as so amended, is amended—

(1) in clause (xi), by striking "and" at the end;

(2) in clause (xii), by striking the period at the end and inserting a semicolon; and

(3) by inserting after clause (xii) the following new clauses:

"(xiii) for the period beginning on May 23, 2020, and ending on September 30, 2020, of $5,383,562; and

"(xiv) for the period beginning on October 1, 2020, and ending on November 30, 2020, of $2,506,849.".

TITLE III—PRIVATE INSURANCE

SEC. 70301. SPECIAL ENROLLMENT PERIOD THROUGH EXCHANGES; FEDERAL EXCHANGE OUTREACH AND EDUCATIONAL ACTIVITIES.

(a) Special Enrollment Period Through Exchanges.—Section 1311(c) of the Patient Protection and Affordable Care Act (42 U.S.C. 18031(c)) is amended—

(1) in paragraph (6)—

(A) in subparagraph (C), by striking at the end "and";

(B) in subparagraph (D), by striking at the end the period and inserting "; and"; and

(C) by adding at the end the following new subparagraph:

"(E) subject to subparagraph (B) of paragraph (8), the special enrollment period described in subparagraph (A) of such paragraph."; and

(2) by adding at the end the following new paragraph:

"(8) SPECIAL ENROLLMENT PERIOD FOR CERTAIN PUBLIC HEALTH EMERGENCY.—

"(A) IN GENERAL.—The Secretary shall, subject to subparagraph (B), require an Exchange to provide—

"(i) for a special enrollment period during the emergency period described in section 1135(g)(1)(B) of the Social Security Act—

"(I) which shall begin on the date that is one week after the date of the enactment of this paragraph and which, in the case of an Exchange established or operated by the Secretary within a State pursuant to section 1321(c), shall be an 8-week period; and

"(II) during which any individual who is otherwise eligible to enroll in a qualified health plan through the Exchange may enroll in such a qualified health plan; and

"(ii) that, in the case of an individual who enrolls in a qualified health plan through the Exchange during such enrollment period, the coverage period under such plan shall begin, at the option of the individual, on April 1, 2020, or on the first day of the month following the day the individual selects a plan through such special enrollment period.

"(B) EXCEPTION.—The requirement of subparagraph (A) shall not apply to a State-operated or State-established Exchange if such Exchange, prior to the date of the enactment of this paragraph, established or otherwise provided for a special enrollment period to address access to coverage under qualified health plans offered through such Exchange during the emergency period described in section 1135(g)(1)(B) of the Social Security Act.".

(b) Federal Exchange Outreach And Educational Activities.—Section 1321(c) of the Patient Protection and Affordable Care Act (42 U.S.C. 18041(c)) is amended by adding at the end the following new paragraph:

"(3) OUTREACH AND EDUCATIONAL ACTIVITIES.—

"(A) IN GENERAL.—In the case of an Exchange established or operated by the Secretary within a State pursuant to this subsection, the Secretary shall carry out outreach and educational activities for purposes of informing potential enrollees in qualified health plans offered through the Exchange of the availability of coverage under such plans and financial assistance for coverage under such plans. Such outreach and educational activities shall be provided in a manner that is culturally and linguistically appropriate to the needs of the populations being served by the Exchange (including hard-to-reach populations, such as racial and sexual minorities, limited English proficient populations, and young adults).

"(B) LIMITATION ON USE OF FUNDS.—No funds appropriated under this paragraph shall be used for expenditures for promoting non-ACA compliant health insurance coverage.

"(C) NON-ACA COMPLIANT HEALTH INSURANCE COVERAGE.—For purposes of subparagraph (B):

"(i) The term 'non-ACA compliant health insurance coverage' means health insurance coverage, or a group health plan, that is not a qualified health plan.

"(ii) Such term includes the following:

"(I) An association health plan.

"(II) Short-term limited duration insurance.

"(D) FUNDING.—Out of any funds in the Treasury not otherwise appropriated, there are hereby appropriated $25,000,000 to carry out this paragraph. Funds appropriated under this subparagraph shall remain available until expended.".

(c) Implementation.—The Secretary of Health and Human Services may implement the provisions of (including amendments made by) this section through subregulatory guidance, program instruction, or otherwise.

SEC. 70302. SHORT-TERM LIMITED DURATION INSURANCE RULE PROHIBITION.

The Secretary of Health and Human Services, the Secretary of the Treasury, and the Secretary of Labor may not take any action to implement, enforce, or otherwise give effect to the rule entitled "Short-Term, Limited Duration Insurance" (83 Fed. Reg. 38212 (August 3, 2018)), and the Secretaries may not promulgate any substantially similar rule.

SEC. 70303. RAPID COVERAGE OF PREVENTIVE SERVICES AND VACCINES FOR COVID-19.

(a) In General.—In the case of a qualifying COVID-19 preventive service, notwithstanding section 2713(b) of the Public Health Service Act (42 U.S.C. 300gg–13(b)) (including the regulations under section 2590.715–2713 of title 29, Code of Federal Regulations, section 54.9815–2713 of title 26, Code of Federal Regulations, and section 147.130 of title 45, Code of Federal Regulations), the Secretary of Health and Human Services, Secretary of Labor, and Secretary of the Treasury shall apply to group health plans and health insurance issuers offering group or individual health insurance coverage the requirement under section 2713(a) of the Public Health Service Act (42 U.S.C. 300gg–13(a)), with respect to such services, as if such section 2713(a)—

(1) required the coverage of such service under such plans and such coverage be effective not later than the specified date (as defined in subsection (b)(2)) with respect to such service; and

(2) applied to grandfathered health plans (as defined in section 1251(e) of the Patient Protection and Affordable Care Act (42 U.S.C. 18011(e))).

(b) Definitions.—For purposes of this section:

(1) QUALIFYING COVID-19 PREVENTIVE SERVICE.—The term "qualifying COVID-19 preventive service" means an item, service, or immunization that is intended to prevent or mitigate COVID-19 and that is—

(A) an evidence-based item or service that has in effect a rating of "A" or "B" in the current recommendations of the United States Preventive Services Task Force; or

(B) an immunization that has in effect a recommendation from the Advisory Committee on Immunization Practices of the Centers for Disease Control and Prevention with respect to the individual involved.

(2) SPECIFIED DATE.—The term "specified date" means—

(A) with respect to a qualifying COVID-19 preventive service described in paragraph (1)(A), the date that is 15 business days after the date on which a rating, as described in such paragraph, is made with respect to such service; and

(B) with respect to a qualifying COVID-19 preventive service described in paragraph (1)(B), the date that is 15 business days after the date on which a recommendation, as described in such paragraph, is made relating to the service.

(3) ADDITIONAL TERMS.—The terms "group health plan"; "health

insurance issuer"; "group health insurance coverage", and "individual health insurance coverage" have the meanings given such terms in section 2791 of the Public Health Service Act (42 U.S.C. 300gg–91), section 733 of the Employee Retirement Income Security Act (29 U.S.C. 1191b), and section 9832 of the Internal Revenue Code of 1986, as applicable.

(c) Implementation.—The Secretary of Health and Human Services, Secretary of Labor, and Secretary of the Treasury may implement the provisions of this section through program instruction, subregulatory guidance, or otherwise.

SEC. 70304. COVERAGE OF COVID-19 RELATED TREATMENT AT NO COST SHARING.

(a) In General.—A group health plan and a health insurance issuer offering group or individual health insurance coverage (including a grandfathered health plan (as defined in section 1251(e) of the Patient Protection and Affordable Care Act)) shall provide coverage, and shall not impose any cost sharing (including deductibles, copayments, and coinsurance) requirements, for the following items and services furnished during any portion of the emergency period defined in paragraph (1)(B) of section 1135(g) of the Social Security Act (42 U.S.C. 1320b–5(g)) beginning on or after the date of the enactment of this Act:

(1) Medically necessary items and services (including in-person or telehealth visits in which such items and services are furnished) that are furnished to an individual who has been diagnosed with (or after provision of the items and services is diagnosed with) COVID-19 to treat or mitigate the effects of COVID-19.

(2) Medically necessary items and services (including in-person or telehealth visits in which such items and services are furnished) that are furnished to an individual who is presumed to have COVID-19 but is never diagnosed as such, if the following conditions are met:

(A) Such items and services are furnished to the individual to treat or mitigate the effects of COVID-19 or to mitigate the impact of COVID-19 on society.

(B) Health care providers have taken appropriate steps under the circumstances to make a diagnosis, or confirm whether a diagnosis was made, with respect to such individual, for COVID-19, if possible.

(b) Items And Services Related To COVID-19.—For purposes of this section—

(1) not later than one week after the date of the enactment of this section, the Secretary of Health and Human Services, Secretary of Labor, and Secretary of the Treasury shall jointly issue guidance specifying applicable diagnoses and medically necessary items and services related to COVID-19; and

(2) such items and services shall include all items or services that are relevant to the treatment or mitigation of COVID-19, regardless of whether such items or services are ordinarily covered under the terms of a group health plan or group or individual health insurance coverage offered by a health insurance issuer.

(c) Reimbursement To Plans And Coverage For Waiving Cost-Sharing.—

(1) IN GENERAL.—A group health plan or a health insurance issuer offering group or individual health insurance coverage (including a grandfathered health plan (as defined in section 1251(e) of the Patient Protection and Affordable Care Act)) that does not impose cost sharing requirements as described in subsection (a) shall notify the Secretary of Health and Human Services, Secretary of Labor, and Secretary of the Treasury (through a joint process established jointly by the Secretaries) of the total dollar amount of cost-sharing that, but for the application of subsection (a), would have been required under such plans and coverage for items and services related to COVID-19 furnished during the period to which subsection (a) applies to enrollees, participants, and beneficiaries in the plan or coverage to whom such subsection applies, but which was not imposed for such items and services so furnished pursuant to such subsection and the Secretary of Health and Human Services, in coordination with the Secretary of Labor and the Secretary of the Treasury, shall make payments in accordance with this subsection to the plan or issuer equal to such total dollar amount.

(2) METHODOLOGY FOR PAYMENTS.—The Secretary of Health and Human Service, in coordination with the Secretary of Labor and the Secretary of the Treasury shall establish a payment system for making payments under this subsection. Any such system shall make payment for the value of cost sharing not imposed by the plan or issuer involved.

(3) TIMING OF PAYMENTS.—Payments made under paragraph (1) shall be made no later than May 1, 2021, for amounts of cost sharing waivers with respect to 2020. Payments under this subsection with respect to such waivers with respect to a year subsequent to 2020 that begins during the period to which subsection (a) applies shall be made no later than May of the year following such subsequent year.

(4) APPROPRIATIONS.—There is authorized to be appropriated, and there is appropriated, out of any monies in the Treasury not otherwise appropriated, such funds as are necessary to carry out this subsection.

(d) Enforcement.—

(1) APPLICATION WITH RESPECT TO PHSA, ERISA, AND IRC.—The provisions of this section shall be applied by the Secretary of Health and Human Services, Secretary of Labor, and Secretary of the Treasury to group health plans and health insurance issuers offering group or individual health insurance coverage as if included in the provisions of part A of title XXVII of the Public Health Service Act, part 7 of the Employee Retirement Income Security Act of 1974, and subchapter B of chapter 100 of the Internal Revenue Code of 1986, as applicable.

(2) PRIVATE RIGHT OF ACTION.—An individual with respect to whom an action is taken by a group health plan or health insurance issuer offering group or individual health insurance coverage in violation of subsection (a) may commence a civil action against the plan or issuer for appropriate relief. The previous sentence shall not be construed as limiting any enforcement

mechanism otherwise applicable pursuant to paragraph (1).

(e) Implementation.—The Secretary of Health and Human Services, Secretary of Labor, and Secretary of the Treasury may implement the provisions of this section through sub-regulatory guidance, program instruction or otherwise.

(f) Terms.—The terms "group health plan"; "health insurance issuer"; "group health insurance coverage", and "individual health insurance coverage" have the meanings given such terms in section 2791 of the Public Health Service Act (42 U.S.C. 300gg–91), section 733 of the Employee Retirement Income Security Act of 1974 (29 U.S.C. 1191b), and section 9832 of the Internal Revenue Code of 1986, as applicable.

SEC. 70305. REQUIRING PRESCRIPTION DRUG REFILL NOTIFICATIONS DURING EMERGENCIES.

(a) ERISA.—

(1) IN GENERAL.—Subpart B of part 7 of subtitle B of title I of the Employee Retirement Income Security Act of 1974 (29 U.S.C. 1185 et seq.) is amended by adding at the end the following new section:

"SEC. 716. PROVISION OF PRESCRIPTION DRUG REFILL NOTIFICATIONS DURING EMERGENCIES.

"(a) In General.—A group health plan, and a health insurance issuer offering health insurance coverage in connection with a group health plan, that provides benefits for prescription drugs under such plan or such coverage shall provide to each individual enrolled under such plan or such coverage who resides in an emergency area during an emergency period, not later than 5 business days after the date of the beginning of such period with respect to such area (or, the case of the emergency period described in section 70305(d)(2) of the Take Responsibility for Workers and Families Act, not later than 5 business days after the date of the enactment of this section), a notification—

"(1) of whether such plan or coverage will waive, during such period with respect to such an individual, any time restrictions under such plan or coverage on any authorized refills for such drugs to enable such refills in advance of when such refills would otherwise have been permitted under such plan or coverage; and

"(2) in the case that such plan or coverage will waive such restrictions during such period with respect to such an individual, that contains information on how such an individual may obtain such a refill.

"(b) Emergency Area; Emergency Period.—For purposes of this section, an 'emergency area' is a geographical area in which, and an 'emergency period' is the period during which, there exists—

"(1) an emergency or disaster declared by the President pursuant to the National Emergencies Act or the Robert T. Stafford Disaster Relief and Emergency Assistance Act; and

"(2) a public health emergency declared by the Secretary pursuant to section 319 of the Public Health Service Act.".

(2) CLERICAL AMENDMENT.—The table of contents of the Employee

Retirement Income Security Act of 1974 is amended by inserting after the item relating to section 714 the following:

"Sec. 715. Additional market reforms.

"Sec. 716. Provision of prescription drug refill notifications during emergencies.".

(b) PHSA.—Subpart II of part A of title XXVII of the Public Health Service Act (42 U.S.C. 300gg–11 et seq.) is amended by adding at the end the following new section:

"SEC. 2730. PROVISION OF PRESCRIPTION DRUG REFILL NOTIFICATIONS DURING EMERGENCIES.

"(a) In General.—A group health plan, and a health insurance issuer offering group or individual health insurance coverage, that provides benefits for prescription drugs under such plan or such coverage shall provide to each individual enrolled under such plan or such coverage who resides in an emergency area during an emergency period, not later than 5 business days after the date of the beginning of such period with respect to such area (or, the case of the emergency period described in section 70305(d)(2) of the Take Responsibility for Workers and Families Act, not later than 5 business days after the date of the enactment of this section), a notification—

"(1) of whether such plan or coverage will waive, during such period with respect to such an individual, any time restrictions under such plan or coverage on any authorized refills for such drugs to enable such refills in advance of when such refills would otherwise have been permitted under such plan or coverage; and

"(2) in the case that such plan or coverage will waive such restrictions during such period with respect to such an individual, that contains information on how such an individual may obtain such a refill.

"(b) Emergency Area; Emergency Period.—For purposes of this section, an 'emergency area' is a geographical area in which, and an 'emergency period' is the period during which, there exists—

"(1) an emergency or disaster declared by the President pursuant to the National Emergencies Act or the Robert T. Stafford Disaster Relief and Emergency Assistance Act; and

"(2) a public health emergency declared by the Secretary pursuant to section 319.".

(c) IRC.—

(1) IN GENERAL.—Subchapter B of chapter 100 of the Internal Revenue Code of 1986 is amended by adding at the end the following new section:

"SEC. 9816. PROVISION OF PRESCRIPTION DRUG REFILL NOTIFICATIONS DURING EMERGENCIES.

"(a) In General.—A group health plan that provides benefits for prescription drugs under such plan shall provide to each individual enrolled under such plan who resides in an emergency area during an emergency period, not later than 5 business days after the date of the beginning of such period with respect to such area (or, the case of the emergency period described in section 70305(d)(2) of the Take Responsibility for Workers and Families Act, not later than 5 business days after the date of the enactment of this section), a notification—

"(1) of whether such plan will waive, during such period with respect to such an individual, any time restrictions under such plan on any authorized refills for such drugs to enable such refills in advance of when such refills would otherwise have been permitted under such plan; and

"(2) in the case that such plan will waive such restrictions during such period with respect to such an individual, that contains information on how such an individual may obtain such a refill.

"(b) Emergency Area; Emergency Period.—For purposes of this section, an 'emergency area' is a geographical area in which, and an 'emergency period' is the period during which, there exists—

"(1) an emergency or disaster declared by the President pursuant to the National Emergencies Act or the Robert T. Stafford Disaster Relief and Emergency Assistance Act; and

"(2) a public health emergency declared by the Secretary pursuant to section 319 of the Public Health Service Act.".

(2) CLERICAL AMENDMENT.—The table of sections for subchapter B of chapter 100 of the Internal Revenue Code of 1986 is amended by adding at the end the following new item:

"Sec. 9816. Provision of prescription drug refill notifications during emergencies.".

(d) Effective Date.—The amendments made by this section shall apply with respect to—

(1) emergency periods beginning on or after the date of the enactment of this Act; and

(2) the emergency period relating to the public health emergency declared by the Secretary of Health and Human Services pursuant to section 319 of the Public Health Service Act on January 31, 2020, entitled "Determination that a Public Health Emergency Exists Nationwide as the Result of the 2019 Novel Coronavirus".

SEC. 70306. IMPROVEMENT OF CERTAIN NOTIFICATIONS PROVIDED TO QUALIFIED BENEFICIARIES BY GROUP HEALTH PLANS IN THE CASE OF QUALIFYING EVENTS.

(a) Employee Retirement Income Security Act Of 1974.—

(1) IN GENERAL.—Section 606 of the Employee Retirement Income Security Act of 1974 (29 U.S.C. 1166) is amended—

(A) in subsection (a)(4), in the matter following subparagraph (B), by striking "under this subsection" and inserting "under this part in accordance with the notification requirements under subsection (c)"; and

(B) in subsection (c)—

(i) by striking "For purposes of subsection (a)(4), any notification" and

inserting For purposes of subsection (a)(4)—
"(1) any notification";
(ii) by striking ", whichever is applicable, and any such notification" and inserting of subsection (a), whichever is applicable;
"(2) any such notification"; and
(iii) by striking "such notification is made" and inserting such notification is made; and
"(3) any such notification shall, with respect to each qualified beneficiary with respect to whom such notification is made, include information regarding any Exchange established under title I of the Patient Protection and Affordable Care Act through which such a qualified beneficiary may be eligible to enroll in a qualified health plan (as defined in section 1301 of the Patient Protection and Affordable Care Act), including—
"(A) the publicly accessible Internet website address for such Exchange;
"(B) the publicly accessible Internet website address for the Find Local Help directory maintained by the Department of Health and Human Services on the healthcare.gov Internet website (or a successor website);
"(C) a clear explanation that—
"(i) an individual who is eligible for continuation coverage may also be eligible to enroll, with financial assistance, in a qualified health plan offered through such Exchange, but, in the case that such individual elects to enroll in such continuation coverage and subsequently elects to terminate such continuation coverage before the period of such continuation coverage expires, such individual will not be eligible to enroll in a qualified health plan offered through such Exchange during a special enrollment period; and
"(ii) an individual who elects to enroll in continuation coverage will remain eligible to enroll in a qualified health plan offered through such Exchange during an open enrollment period and may be eligible for financial assistance with respect to enrolling in such a qualified health plan;
"(D) information on consumer protections with respect to enrolling in a qualified health plan offered through such Exchange, including the requirement for such a qualified health plan to provide coverage for essential health benefits (as defined in section 1302(b) of the Patient Protection and Affordable Care Act) and the requirements applicable to such a qualified health plan under part A of title XXVII of the Public Health Service Act; and
"(E) information on the availability of financial assistance with respect to enrolling in a qualified health plan, including the maximum income limit for eligibility for a premium tax credit under section 36B of the Internal Revenue Code of 1986.".
(2) EFFECTIVE DATE.—The amendments made by paragraph (1) shall apply with respect to qualifying events occurring on or after the date that is 14 days after the date of the enactment of this Act.
(b) Public Health Service Act.—
(1) IN GENERAL.—Section 2206 of the Public Health Service Act (42 U.S.C.

300bb–6) is amended—

(A) by striking "In accordance" and inserting the following:

"(a) In General.—In accordance";

(B) by striking "of such beneficiary's rights under this subsection" and inserting "of such beneficiary's rights under this title in accordance with the notification requirements under subsection (b)"; and

(C) by striking "For purposes of paragraph (4)," and all that follows through "such notification is made." and inserting the following:

"(b) Rules Relating To Notification Of Qualified Beneficiaries By Plan Administrator.—For purposes of subsection (a)(4)—

"(1) any notification shall be made within 14 days of the date on which the plan administrator is notified under paragraph (2) or (3) of subsection (a), whichever is applicable;

"(2) any such notification to an individual who is a qualified beneficiary as the spouse of the covered employee shall be treated as notification to all other qualified beneficiaries residing with such spouse at the time such notification is made; and

"(3) any such notification shall, with respect to each qualified beneficiary with respect to whom such notification is made, include information regarding any Exchange established under title I of the Patient Protection and Affordable Care Act through which such a qualified beneficiary may be eligible to enroll in a qualified health plan (as defined in section 1301 of the Patient Protection and Affordable Care Act), including—

"(A) the publicly accessible Internet website address for such Exchange;

"(B) the publicly accessible Internet website address for the Find Local Help directory maintained by the Department of Health and Human Services on the healthcare.gov Internet website (or a successor website);

"(C) a clear explanation that—

"(i) an individual who is eligible for continuation coverage may also be eligible to enroll, with financial assistance, in a qualified health plan offered through such Exchange, but, in the case that such individual elects to enroll in such continuation coverage and subsequently elects to terminate such continuation coverage before the period of such continuation coverage expires, such individual will not be eligible to enroll in a qualified health plan offered through such Exchange during a special enrollment period; and

"(ii) an individual who elects to enroll in continuation coverage will remain eligible to enroll in a qualified health plan offered through such Exchange during an open enrollment period and may be eligible for financial assistance with respect to enrolling in such a qualified health plan;

"(D) information on consumer protections with respect to enrolling in a qualified health plan offered through such Exchange, including the requirement for such a qualified health plan to provide coverage for essential health benefits (as defined in section 1302(b) of the Patient Protection and Affordable Care Act) and the requirements applicable to such a qualified health plan under part A of title XXVII; and

"(E) information on the availability of financial assistance with respect to enrolling in a qualified health plan, including the maximum income limit for eligibility for a premium tax credit under section 36B of the Internal Revenue Code of 1986.".

(2) EFFECTIVE DATE.—The amendments made by paragraph (1) shall apply with respect to qualifying events occurring on or after the date that is 14 days after the date of the enactment of this Act.

(c) Internal Revenue Code Of 1986.—

(1) IN GENERAL.—Section 4980B(f)(6) of the Internal Revenue Code of 1986 is amended—

(A) in subparagraph (D)—

(i) in clause (ii), by striking "under subparagraph (C)" and inserting "under clause (iii)"; and

(ii) by redesignating clauses (i) and (ii) as subclauses (I) and (II), respectively, and moving the margin of each such subclause, as so redesignated, 2 ems to the right;

(B) by redesignating subparagraphs (A) through (D) as clauses (i) through (iv), respectively, and moving the margin of each such clause, as so redesignated, 2 ems to the right;

(C) by striking "In accordance" and inserting the following:

"(A) IN GENERAL.—In accordance";

(D) by inserting after "of such beneficiary's rights under this subsection" the following: "in accordance with the notification requirements under subparagraph (C)"; and

(E) by striking "The requirements of subparagraph (B)" and all that follows through "such notification is made." and inserting the following:

"(B) ALTERNATIVE MEANS OF COMPLIANCE WITH REQUIREMENT FOR NOTIFICATION OF MULTIEMPLOYER PLANS BY EMPLOYERS.—The requirements of subparagraph (A)(ii) shall be considered satisfied in the case of a multiemployer plan in connection with a qualifying event described in paragraph (3)(B) if the plan provides that the determination of the occurrence of such qualifying event will be made by the plan administrator.

"(C) RULES RELATING TO NOTIFICATION OF QUALIFIED BENEFICIARIES BY PLAN ADMINISTRATOR.—For purposes of subparagraph (A)(iv)—

"(i) any notification shall be made within 14 days (or, in the case of a group health plan which is a multiemployer plan, such longer period of time as may be provided in the terms of the plan) of the date on which the plan administrator is notified under clause (ii) or (iii) of subparagraph (A), whichever is applicable;

"(ii) any such notification to an individual who is a qualified beneficiary as the spouse of the covered employee shall be treated as notification to all other qualified beneficiaries residing with such spouse at the time such notification is made; and

"(iii) any such notification shall, with respect to each qualified beneficiary with respect to whom such notification is made, include information regarding any Exchange established under title I of the Patient Protection and Affordable Care Act through which such a qualified beneficiary may be eligible to enroll in a qualified health plan (as defined in section 1301 of the Patient Protection and Affordable Care Act), including—

"(I) the publicly accessible Internet website address for such Exchange;

"(II) the publicly accessible Internet website address for the Find Local Help directory maintained by the Department of Health and Human Services on the healthcare.gov Internet website (or a successor website);

"(III) a clear explanation that—

"(aa) an individual who is eligible for continuation coverage may also be eligible to enroll, with financial assistance, in a qualified health plan offered through such Exchange, but, in the case that such individual elects to enroll in such continuation coverage and subsequently elects to terminate such continuation coverage before the period of such continuation coverage expires, such individual will not be eligible to enroll in a qualified health plan offered through such Exchange during a special enrollment period; and

"(bb) an individual who elects to enroll in continuation coverage will remain eligible to enroll in a qualified health plan offered through such Exchange during an open enrollment period and may be eligible for financial assistance with respect to enrolling in such a qualified health plan;

"(IV) information on consumer protections with respect to enrolling in a qualified health plan offered through such Exchange, including the requirement for such a qualified health plan to provide coverage for essential health benefits (as defined in section 1302(b) of the Patient Protection and Affordable Care Act) and the requirements applicable to such a qualified health plan under part A of title XXVII of the Public Health Service Act; and

"(V) information on the availability of financial assistance with respect to enrolling in a qualified health plan, including the maximum income limit for eligibility for a premium tax credit under section 36B.".

(2) EFFECTIVE DATE.—The amendments made by paragraph (1) shall apply with respect to qualifying events occurring on or after the date that is 14 days after the date of the enactment of this Act.

(d) Model Notices.—Not later than 14 days after the date of the enactment of this Act, the Secretary of the Labor, in consultation with the Secretary of the Treasury and the Secretary of Health and Human Services, shall—

(1) update the model Consolidated Omnibus Budget Reconciliation Act of 1985 (referred to in this subsection as "COBRA") continuation coverage general notice and the model COBRA continuation coverage election notice developed by the Secretary of Labor for purposes of facilitating compliance of group health plans with the notification requirements under section 606 of the Employee Retirement Income Security Act of 1974 (29 U.S.C. 1166) to

include the information described in paragraph (3) of subsection (c) of such section 606, as added by subsection (a)(1);
(2) provide an opportunity for consumer testing of each such notice, as so updated, to ensure that each such notice is clear and understandable to the average participant or beneficiary of a group health plan; and
(3) rename the model COBRA continuation coverage general notice and the model COBRA continuation coverage election notice as the "model COBRA continuation coverage and Affordable Care Act coverage general notice" and the "model COBRA continuation coverage and Affordable Care Act coverage election notice", respectively.
SEC. 70307. PRESERVING HEALTH BENEFITS FOR WORKERS.
(a) Premium Assistance For COBRA Continuation Coverage For Individuals And Their Families.—
(1) PROVISION OF PREMIUM ASSISTANCE.—
(A) REDUCTION OF PREMIUMS PAYABLE.—In the case of any premium for a period of coverage beginning on or after the date of the enactment of this Act for COBRA continuation coverage with respect to any assistance eligible individual, such individual shall be treated for purposes of any COBRA continuation provision as having paid the amount of such premium if such individual pays (or a person other than such individual's employer pays on behalf of such individual) 0 percent of the amount of such premium (as determined without regard to this subsection).
(B) PLAN ENROLLMENT OPTION.—
(i) IN GENERAL.—Notwithstanding the COBRA continuation provisions, an assistance eligible individual may, not later than 90 days after the date of notice of the plan enrollment option described in this subparagraph, elect to enroll in coverage under a plan offered by the employer involved, or the employee organization involved (including, for this purpose, a joint board of trustees of a multiemployer trust affiliated with one or more multiemployer plans), that is different than coverage under the plan in which such individual was enrolled at the time the qualifying event occurred, and such coverage shall be treated as COBRA continuation coverage for purposes of the applicable COBRA continuation coverage provision.
(ii) REQUIREMENTS.—An assistance eligible individual may elect to enroll in different coverage as described in clause (i) only if—
(I) the employer involved has made a determination that such employer will permit assistance eligible individuals to enroll in different coverage as provided for this subparagraph;
(II) the premium for such different coverage does not exceed the premium for coverage in which the individual was enrolled at the time the qualifying event occurred;
(III) the different coverage in which the individual elects to enroll is coverage that is also offered to the active employees of the employer at the time at which such election is made; and

(IV) the different coverage is not—
(aa) coverage that provides only dental, vision, counseling, or referral services (or a combination of such services);
(bb) a flexible spending arrangement (as defined in section 106(c)(2) of the Internal Revenue Code of 1986); or
(cc) coverage that provides coverage for services or treatments furnished in an on-site medical facility maintained by the employer and that consists primarily of first-aid services, prevention and wellness care, or similar care (or a combination of such care).
(C) PREMIUM REIMBURSEMENT.—For provisions providing the payment of such premium, see section 6432 of the Internal Revenue Code of 1986, as added by paragraph (12).
(2) LIMITATION OF PERIOD OF PREMIUM ASSISTANCE.—
(A) ELIGIBILITY FOR ADDITIONAL COVERAGE.—Paragraph (1)(A) shall not apply with respect to any assistance eligible individual for months of coverage beginning on or after—
(i) the earlier of the first date that such individual is eligible for coverage under any other group health plan (other than coverage consisting of only dental, vision, counseling, or referral services (or a combination thereof), coverage under a flexible spending arrangement (as defined in section 106(c)(2) of the Internal Revenue Code of 1986), coverage of treatment that is furnished in an on-site medical facility maintained by the employer and that consists primarily of first-aid services, prevention and wellness care, or similar care (or a combination thereof)), is eligible for benefits under title XVIII of the Social Security Act, or enrolls in a qualified health plan (as defined in section 1301(a) of the Patient Protection and Affordable Care Act (42 U.S.C. 18021(a)) offered through an Exchange established under title I of the Patient Protection and Affordable Care Act; and
(ii) the earliest of—
(I) the date which is 9 months after the first day of the first month that paragraph (1)(A) applies with respect to such individual;
(II) the date following the expiration of the maximum period of continuation coverage required under the applicable COBRA continuation coverage provision; or
(III) the date following the expiration of the period of continuation coverage allowed under paragraph (4)(B)(ii).
(B) TIMING OF ELIGIBILITY FOR ADDITIONAL COVERAGE.—For purposes of subparagraph (A)(i), an individual shall not be treated as eligible for coverage under a group health plan before the first date on which such individual could be covered under such plan.
(C) NOTIFICATION REQUIREMENT.—An assistance eligible individual shall notify in writing the group health plan with respect to which paragraph (1)(A) applies if such paragraph ceases to apply by reason of subparagraph (A)(i). Such notice shall be provided to the group health plan in such time

and manner as may be specified by the Secretary of Labor.

(3) ASSISTANCE ELIGIBLE INDIVIDUAL.—For purposes of this section, the term "assistance eligible individual" means any qualified beneficiary if—

(A) at any time during the emergency period described in section 1135(g)(1)(B) of the Social Security Act (42 U.S.C. 1320b–5(g)(1)(B)) such qualified beneficiary is eligible for COBRA continuation coverage by reason of qualifying event specified in section 603(2) of the Employee Retirement Income Security Act of 1974, section 4980B(f)(3)(B) of the Internal Revenue Code of 1986, section 2203(2) of the Public Health Service Act, or section 8905a of title 5, United States Code; and

(B) such qualified beneficiary elects such coverage.

(4) EXTENSION OF ELECTION PERIOD AND EFFECT ON COVERAGE.—

(A) IN GENERAL.—For purposes of applying section 605(a) of the Employee Retirement Income Security Act of 1974, section 4980B(f)(5)(A) of the Internal Revenue Code of 1986, section 2205(a) of the Public Health Service Act, and section 8905a(c)(2) of title 5, United States Code, in the case of—

(i) an individual who does not have an election of COBRA continuation coverage in effect on the date of the enactment of this Act but who would be an assistance eligible individual if such election were so in effect; or

(ii) an individual who elected COBRA continuation coverage on or after the first date of the emergency period described in section 1135(g)(1)(B) of the Social Security Act (42 U.S.C. 1320b–5(g)(1)(B)) and disenrolled from such coverage before the date of the enactment of this Act;

such individual may elect the COBRA continuation coverage under the COBRA continuation coverage provisions containing such sections during the period beginning on the date of the enactment of this Act and ending 60 days after the date on which the notification required under paragraph (7)(C) is provided to such individual.

(B) COMMENCEMENT OF COVERAGE; NO REACH-BACK.—Any COBRA continuation coverage elected by a qualified beneficiary during an extended election period under subparagraph (A)—

(i) shall commence with the first period of coverage beginning on or after the date of the enactment of this Act; and

(ii) shall not extend beyond the period of COBRA continuation coverage that would have been required under the applicable COBRA continuation coverage provision if the coverage had been elected as required under such provision.

(5) EXPEDITED REVIEW OF DENIALS OF PREMIUM ASSISTANCE.—In any case in which an individual requests treatment as an assistance eligible individual and is denied such treatment by the group health plan, the Secretary of Labor (or the Secretary of Health and Human Services in connection with COBRA continuation coverage which is provided other than pursuant to part 6 of subtitle B of title I of the Employee Retirement Income Security Act of 1974), in consultation with the Secretary of the Treasury, shall provide

for expedited review of such denial. An individual shall be entitled to such review upon application to such Secretary in such form and manner as shall be provided by such Secretary. Such Secretary shall make a determination regarding such individual's eligibility within 15 business days after receipt of such individual's application for review under this paragraph. Either Secretary's determination upon review of the denial shall be de novo and shall be the final determination of such Secretary. A reviewing court shall grant deference to such Secretary's determination. The provisions of this paragraph, paragraphs (1) through (4), and paragraph (7) shall be treated as provisions of title I of the Employee Retirement Income Security Act of 1974 for purposes of part 5 of subtitle B of such title.

(6) DISREGARD OF SUBSIDIES FOR PURPOSES OF FEDERAL AND STATE PROGRAMS.—Notwithstanding any other provision of law, any premium reduction with respect to an assistance eligible individual under this subsection shall not be considered income or resources in determining eligibility for, or the amount of assistance or benefits provided under, any other public benefit provided under Federal law or the law of any State or political subdivision thereof.

(7) NOTICES TO INDIVIDUALS.—

(A) GENERAL NOTICE.—

(i) IN GENERAL.—In the case of notices provided under section 606(a)(4) of the Employee Retirement Income Security Act of 1974 (29 U.S.C. 1166(4)), section 4980B(f)(6)(D) of the Internal Revenue Code of 1986, section 2206(4) of the Public Health Service Act (42 U.S.C. 300bb–6(4)), or section 8905a(f)(2)(A) of title 5, United States Code, with respect to individuals who, during the period described in paragraph (3)(A), become entitled to elect COBRA continuation coverage, the requirements of such sections shall not be treated as met unless such notices include an additional notification to the recipient of—

(I) the availability of premium reduction with respect to such coverage under this subsection; and

(II) the option to enroll in different coverage if the employer permits assistance eligible individuals to elect enrollment in different coverage (as described in paragraph (1)(B)).

(ii) ALTERNATIVE NOTICE.—In the case of COBRA continuation coverage to which the notice provision under such sections does not apply, the Secretary of Labor, in consultation with the Secretary of the Treasury and the Secretary of Health and Human Services, shall, in consultation with administrators of the group health plans (or other entities) that provide or administer the COBRA continuation coverage involved, provide rules requiring the provision of such notice.

(iii) FORM.—The requirement of the additional notification under this subparagraph may be met by amendment of existing notice forms or by inclusion of a separate document with the notice otherwise required.

(B) SPECIFIC REQUIREMENTS.—Each additional notification under subparagraph (A) shall include—

(i) the forms necessary for establishing eligibility for premium reduction under this subsection;

(ii) the name, address, and telephone number necessary to contact the plan administrator and any other person maintaining relevant information in connection with such premium reduction;

(iii) a description of the extended election period provided for in paragraph (4)(A);

(iv) a description of the obligation of the qualified beneficiary under paragraph (2)(C) to notify the plan providing continuation coverage of eligibility for subsequent coverage under another group health plan or eligibility for benefits under title XVIII of the Social Security Act and the penalty provided under section 6720C of the Internal Revenue Code of 1986 for failure to so notify the plan;

(v) a description, displayed in a prominent manner, of the qualified beneficiary's right to a reduced premium and any conditions on entitlement to the reduced premium;

(vi) a description of the option of the qualified beneficiary to enroll in different coverage if the employer permits such beneficiary to elect to enroll in such different coverage under paragraph (1)(B);

(vii) information regarding any Exchange established under title I of the Patient Protection and Affordable Care Act through which a qualified beneficiary may be eligible to enroll in a qualified health plan, including—

(I) the publicly accessible internet website address for such Exchange;

(II) the publicly accessible internet website address for the Find Local Help directory maintained by the Department of Health and Human Services on the healthcare.gov internet website (or a successor website);

(III) a clear explanation that—

(aa) an individual who is eligible for continuation coverage may also be eligible to enroll, with financial assistance, in a qualified health plan offered through such Exchange, but, in the case that such individual elects to enroll in such continuation coverage and subsequently elects to terminate such continuation coverage before the period of such continuation coverage expires, such individual will not be eligible to enroll in a qualified health plan offered through such Exchange during a special enrollment period; and

(bb) an individual who elects to enroll in continuation coverage will remain eligible to enroll in a qualified health plan offered through such Exchange during an open enrollment period and may be eligible for financial assistance with respect to enrolling in such a qualified health plan;

(IV) information on consumer protections with respect to enrolling in a qualified health plan offered through such Exchange, including the requirement for such a qualified health plan to provide coverage for essential health benefits (as defined in section 1302(b) of such Act (42 U.S.C. 18022(b))) and the requirements applicable to such a qualified health plan under part A of title XXVII of the Public Health Service Act (42 U.S.C. 300gg et seq.); and

(V) information on the availability of financial assistance with respect to enrolling in a qualified health plan, including the maximum income limit for eligibility for a premium tax credit under section 36B of the Internal Revenue Code of 1986.

(C) NOTICE IN CONNECTION WITH EXTENDED ELECTION PERIODS.—In the case of any assistance eligible individual (or any individual described in paragraph (4)(A)) who became entitled to elect COBRA continuation coverage before the date of the enactment of this Act, the administrator of the group health plan (or other entity) involved shall provide (within 60 days after the date of enactment of this Act) for the additional notification required to be provided under subparagraph (A) and failure to provide such notice shall be treated as a failure to meet the notice requirements under the applicable COBRA continuation provision.

(D) MODEL NOTICES.—Not later than 30 days after the date of enactment of this Act—

(i) the Secretary of the Labor, in consultation with the Secretary of the Treasury and the Secretary of Health and Human Services, shall prescribe models for the additional notification required under this paragraph (other than the additional notification described in clause (ii)); and

(ii) in the case of any additional notification provided pursuant to subparagraph (A) under section 8905a(f)(2)(A) of title 5, United States Code, the Office of Personnel Management shall prescribe a model for such additional notification.

(8) REGULATIONS.—The Secretary of the Treasury may prescribe such regulations or other guidance as may be necessary or appropriate to carry out the provisions of this subsection, including the prevention of fraud and abuse under this subsection, except that the Secretary of Labor and the Secretary of Health and Human Services may prescribe such regulations (including interim final regulations) or other guidance as may be necessary or appropriate to carry out the provisions of paragraphs (5), (7), and (9).

(9) OUTREACH.—The Secretary of Labor, in consultation with the Secretary of the Treasury and the Secretary of Health and Human Services, shall provide outreach consisting of public education and enrollment assistance relating to premium reduction provided under this subsection. Such outreach shall target employers, group health plan administrators, public assistance programs, States, insurers, and other entities as determined appropriate by such Secretaries. Such outreach shall include an initial focus on those individuals electing continuation coverage who are referred to in paragraph (7)(C). Information on such premium reduction, including enrollment, shall also be made available on websites of the Departments of Labor, Treasury, and Health and Human Services.

(10) DEFINITIONS.—For purposes of this section:

(A) ADMINISTRATOR.—The term "administrator" has the meaning given such term in section 3(16)(A) of the Employee Retirement Income Security Act of 1974.

(B) COBRA CONTINUATION COVERAGE.—The term "COBRA continuation coverage" means continuation coverage provided pursuant to part 6 of subtitle B of title I of the Employee Retirement Income Security Act of 1974 (other than under section 609), title XXII of the Public Health Service Act, section 4980B of the Internal Revenue Code of 1986 (other than subsection (f)(1) of such section insofar as it relates to pediatric vaccines), or section 8905a of title 5, United States Code, or under a State program that provides comparable continuation coverage. Such term does not include coverage under a health flexible spending arrangement under a cafeteria plan within the meaning of section 125 of the Internal Revenue Code of 1986.

(C) COBRA CONTINUATION PROVISION.—The term "COBRA continuation provision" means the provisions of law described in subparagraph (B).

(D) COVERED EMPLOYEE.—The term "covered employee" has the meaning given such term in section 607(2) of the Employee Retirement Income Security Act of 1974.

(E) QUALIFIED BENEFICIARY.—The term "qualified beneficiary" has the meaning given such term in section 607(3) of the Employee Retirement Income Security Act of 1974.

(F) GROUP HEALTH PLAN.—The term "group health plan" has the meaning given such term in section 607(1) of the Employee Retirement Income Security Act of 1974.

(G) STATE.—The term "State" includes the District of Columbia, the Commonwealth of Puerto Rico, the Virgin Islands, Guam, American Samoa, and the Commonwealth of the Northern Mariana Islands.

(H) PERIOD OF COVERAGE.—Any reference in this subsection to a period of coverage shall be treated as a reference to a monthly or shorter period of coverage with respect to which premiums are charged with respect to such coverage.

(11) REPORTS.—

(A) INTERIM REPORT.—The Secretary of the Treasury shall submit an interim report to the Committee on Education and Labor, the Committee on Ways and Means, and the Committee on Energy and Commerce of the House of Representatives and the Committee on Health, Education, Labor, and Pensions and the Committee on Finance of the Senate regarding the premium reduction provided under this subsection that includes—

(i) the number of individuals provided such assistance as of the date of the report; and

(ii) the total amount of expenditures incurred (with administrative expenditures noted separately) in connection with such assistance as of the date of the report.

(B) FINAL REPORT.—As soon as practicable after the last period of COBRA continuation coverage for which premium reduction is provided under this section, the Secretary of the Treasury shall submit a final report to each Committee referred to in subparagraph (A) that includes—
(i) the number of individuals provided premium reduction under this section;
(ii) the average dollar amount (monthly and annually) of premium reductions provided to such individuals; and
(iii) the total amount of expenditures incurred (with administrative expenditures noted separately) in connection with premium reduction under this section.
(12) COBRA PREMIUM ASSISTANCE.—
(A) IN GENERAL.—Subchapter B of chapter 65 of the Internal Revenue Code of 1986 is amended by adding at the end the following new section:
"SEC. 6432. COBRA PREMIUM ASSISTANCE.
"(a) In General.—The person to whom premiums are payable under COBRA continuation coverage shall be reimbursed as provided in subsection (c) for the amount of premiums not paid by assistance eligible individuals by reason of section 70307 of the Take Responsibility for Workers and Families Act.
"(b) Person Entitled To Reimbursement.—For purposes of subsection (a), except as otherwise provided by the Secretary, the person to whom premiums are payable under COBRA continuation coverage shall be treated as being—
"(1) in the case of any group health plan which is a multiemployer plan (as defined in section 3(37) of the Employee Retirement Income Security Act of 1974), the plan,
"(2) in the case of any group health plan not described in paragraph (1)—
"(A) which is subject to the COBRA continuation provisions contained in—
"(i) this title,
"(ii) the Employee Retirement Income Security Act of 1974,
"(iii) the Public Health Service Act, or
"(iv) title 5, United States Code, or
"(B) under which some or all of the coverage is not provided by insurance, the employer maintaining the plan, and
"(3) in the case of any group health plan not described in paragraph (1) or (2), the insurer providing the coverage under the group health plan.
"(c) Method Of Reimbursement.—Except as otherwise provided by the Secretary—
"(1) TREATMENT AS PAYMENT OF PAYROLL TAXES.—Each person entitled to reimbursement under subsection (a) (and filing a claim for such reimbursement at such time and in such manner as the Secretary may require) shall be treated for purposes of this title and section 1324(b)(2) of title 31, United States Code, as having paid to the Secretary, on the date that the assistance eligible individual's premium payment is received, payroll taxes in an amount equal to the portion of such reimbursement which relates to such premium. To the extent that the amount treated as paid under the preceding

sentence exceeds the amount of such person's liability for such taxes, the Secretary shall credit or refund such excess in the same manner as if it were an overpayment of such taxes.

"(2) OVERSTATEMENTS.—Any overstatement of the reimbursement to which a person is entitled under this section (and any amount paid by the Secretary as a result of such overstatement) shall be treated as an underpayment of payroll taxes by such person and may be assessed and collected by the Secretary in the same manner as payroll taxes.

"(3) REIMBURSEMENT CONTINGENT ON PAYMENT OF REMAINING PREMIUM.—No reimbursement may be made under this section to a person with respect to any assistance eligible individual until after the reduced premium required under section 70307 of such Act with respect to such individual has been received.

"(d) Definitions.—For purposes of this section—

"(1) PAYROLL TAXES.—The term 'payroll taxes' means—

"(A) amounts required to be deducted and withheld for the payroll period under section 3402 (relating to wage withholding),

"(B) amounts required to be deducted for the payroll period under section 3102 (relating to FICA employee taxes), and

"(C) amounts of the taxes imposed for the payroll period under section 3111 (relating to FICA employer taxes).

"(2) PERSON.—The term 'person' includes any governmental entity.

"(e) Reporting.—Each person entitled to reimbursement under subsection (a) for any period shall submit such reports (at such time and in such manner) as the Secretary may require, including—

"(1) an attestation of involuntary termination of employment for each covered employee on the basis of whose termination entitlement to reimbursement is claimed under subsection (a),

"(2) a report of the amount of payroll taxes offset under subsection (a) for the reporting period and the estimated offsets of such taxes for the subsequent reporting period in connection with reimbursements under subsection (a), and

"(3) a report containing the TINs of all covered employees, the amount of subsidy reimbursed with respect to each covered employee and qualified beneficiaries, and a designation with respect to each covered employee as to whether the subsidy reimbursement is for coverage of 1 individual or 2 or more individuals.

"(f) Regulations.—The Secretary shall issue such regulations or other guidance as may be necessary or appropriate to carry out this section, including—

"(1) the requirement to report information or the establishment of other methods for verifying the correct amounts of reimbursements under this section, and

"(2) the application of this section to group health plans that are multiemployer plans (as defined in section 3(37) of the Employee Retirement Income Security

Act of 1974).”.

(B) SOCIAL SECURITY TRUST FUNDS HELD HARMLESS.—In determining any amount transferred or appropriated to any fund under the Social Security Act, section 6432 of the Internal Revenue Code of 1986 shall not be taken into account.

(C) CLERICAL AMENDMENT.—The table of sections for subchapter B of chapter 65 of the Internal Revenue Code of 1986 is amended by adding at the end the following new item:

“Sec. 6432. COBRA premium assistance.”.

(D) EFFECTIVE DATE.—The amendments made by this paragraph shall apply to premiums to which subsection (a)(1)(A) applies.

(E) SPECIAL RULE.—

(i) IN GENERAL.—In the case of an assistance eligible individual who pays, with respect to the first period of COBRA continuation coverage to which subsection (a)(1)(A) applies or the immediately subsequent period, the full premium amount for such coverage, the person to whom such payment is payable shall—

(I) make a reimbursement payment to such individual for the amount of such premium paid in excess of the amount required to be paid under subsection (a)(1)(A); or

(II) provide credit to the individual for such amount in a manner that reduces one or more subsequent premium payments that the individual is required to pay under such subsection for the coverage involved.

(ii) REIMBURSING EMPLOYER.—A person to which clause (i) applies shall be reimbursed as provided for in section 6432 of the Internal Revenue Code of 1986 for any payment made, or credit provided, to the employee under such clause.

(iii) PAYMENT OF CREDITS.—Unless it is reasonable to believe that the credit for the excess payment in clause (i)(II) will be used by the assistance eligible individual within 180 days of the date on which the person receives from the individual the payment of the full premium amount, a person to which clause (i) applies shall make the payment required under such clause to the individual within 60 days of such payment of the full premium amount. If, as of any day within the 180-day period, it is no longer reasonable to believe that the credit will be used during that period, payment equal to the remainder of the credit outstanding shall be made to the individual within 60 days of such day.

(13) PENALTY FOR FAILURE TO NOTIFY HEALTH PLAN OF CESSATION OF ELIGIBILITY FOR PREMIUM ASSISTANCE.—

(A) IN GENERAL.—Part I of subchapter B of chapter 68 of the Internal Revenue Code of 1986 is amended by adding at the end the following new section:

“SEC. 6720C. PENALTY FOR FAILURE TO NOTIFY HEALTH PLAN OF CESSATION OF ELIGIBILITY FOR COBRA PREMIUM ASSISTANCE.

"(a) In General.—Any person required to notify a group health plan under section 70307 of the Take Responsibility for Workers and Families Act who fails to make such a notification at such time and in such manner as the Secretary of Labor may require shall pay a penalty of 110 percent of the premium reduction provided under such section after termination of eligibility under such subsection.

"(b) Reasonable Cause Exception.—No penalty shall be imposed under subsection (a) with respect to any failure if it is shown that such failure is due to reasonable cause and not to willful neglect.".

(B) CLERICAL AMENDMENT.—The table of sections of part I of subchapter B of chapter 68 of such Code is amended by adding at the end the following new item:

"Sec. 6720C. Penalty for failure to notify health plan of cessation of eligibility for COBRA premium assistance.".

(14) COORDINATION WITH HCTC.—

(A) IN GENERAL.—Section 35(g)(9) of the Internal Revenue Code of 1986 is amended to read as follows:

"(9) COBRA PREMIUM ASSISTANCE.—In the case of an assistance eligible individual who receives premium reduction for COBRA continuation coverage under section 70307 of the Take Responsibility for Workers and Families Act for any month during the taxable year, such individual shall not be treated as an eligible individual, a certified individual, or a qualifying family member for purposes of this section or section 7527 with respect to such month.".

(B) EFFECTIVE DATE.—The amendment made by subparagraph (A) shall apply to taxable years ending after the date of the enactment of this Act.

(15) EXCLUSION OF COBRA PREMIUM ASSISTANCE FROM GROSS INCOME.—

(A) IN GENERAL.—Part III of subchapter B of chapter 1 of the Internal Revenue Code of 1986 is amended by inserting after section 139B the following new section:

"SEC. 139I. COBRA PREMIUM ASSISTANCE.

"In the case of an assistance eligible individual (as defined in section 70307 of the Take Responsibility for Workers and Families Act), gross income does not include any premium reduction provided under subsection (a) of such section.".

(B) CLERICAL AMENDMENT.—The table of sections for part III of subchapter B of chapter 1 of such Code is amended by inserting after the item relating to section 139B the following new item:

"Sec. 139I. COBRA premium assistance.".

(C) EFFECTIVE DATE.—The amendments made by this paragraph shall apply to taxable years ending after the date of the enactment of this Act.

(b) Preserving Affordable Coverage For Furloughed Workers.—

(1) IN GENERAL.—The Secretary of Labor, in coordination with the Secretary of the Treasury, shall establish a process whereby the premium assistance

under subsection (a) shall be available to an individual who has been subject to a furlough at any time during the emergency period described in section 1135(g)(1)(B) of the Social Security Act (42 U.S.C. 1320b–5(g)(1)(B)).

(2) FURLOUGH DEFINED.—

(A) IN GENERAL.—In this subsection, the term "furlough" means a temporary cessation of work at the will of the employer during which an individual remains employed and covered under a group health plan.

(B) GROUP HEALTH PLAN DEFINED.—In this paragraph, the term "group health plan" has the meaning given such term in section 607(1) of the Employee Retirement Income Security Act of 1974.

(3) TREATMENT WITH RESPECT TO INTERNAL REVENUE CODE OF 1986.—For purposes of sections 6432, 6720C, 35(g)(9), and 139I of the Internal Revenue Code of 1986, any premium assistance provided pursuant to any process established under this subsection to individuals who have been subject to a furlough shall be treated in the same manner as premium assistance for COBRA continuation coverage.

(c) Elimination Of Premium Subsidy For High-Income Individuals.—

(1) RECAPTURE OF SUBSIDY FOR HIGH-INCOME INDIVIDUALS.—If—

(A) premium assistance is provided under this section with respect to any COBRA continuation coverage which covers the taxpayer, the taxpayer's spouse, or any dependent (within the meaning of section 152 of the Internal Revenue Code of 1986, determined without regard to subsections (b)(1), (b)(2), and (d)(1)(B) thereof) of the taxpayer during any portion of the taxable year, and

(B) the taxpayer's modified adjusted gross income for such taxable year exceeds $125,000 ($250,000 in the case of a joint return),

then the tax imposed by chapter 1 of such Code with respect to the taxpayer for such taxable year shall be increased by the amount of such assistance.

(2) PHASE-IN OF RECAPTURE.—

(A) IN GENERAL.—In the case of a taxpayer whose modified adjusted gross income for the taxable year does not exceed $145,000 ($290,000 in the case of a joint return), the increase in the tax imposed under paragraph (1) shall not exceed the phase-in percentage of such increase (determined without regard to this paragraph).

(B) PHASE-IN PERCENTAGE.—For purposes of this subsection, the term "phase-in percentage" means the ratio (expressed as a percentage) obtained by dividing—

(i) the excess of described in subparagraph (B) of paragraph (1), by

(ii) $20,000 ($40,000 in the case of a joint return).

(3) OPTION FOR HIGH-INCOME INDIVIDUALS TO WAIVE ASSISTANCE AND AVOID RECAPTURE.—Notwithstanding subsection (a)(3), an individual shall not be treated as an assistance eligible individual for purposes of this section and section 6432 of the Internal Revenue Code of 1986 if such individual—

(A) makes a permanent election (at such time and in such form and manner as the Secretary of the Treasury may prescribe) to waive the right to the premium assistance provided under this section, and

(B) notifies the entity to whom premiums are reimbursed under section 6432(a) of such Code of such election.

(4) MODIFIED ADJUSTED GROSS INCOME.—For purposes of this subsection, the term "modified gross income" means the adjusted gross income (as defined in section 62 of the Internal Revenue Code of 1986) of the taxpayer for the taxable year increased by any amount excluded from gross income under section 911, 931, or 933 of such Code.

(5) CREDITS NOT ALLOWED AGAINST TAX, ETC.—For purposes determining regular tax liability under section 26(b) of such Code, the increase in tax under this subsection shall not be treated as a tax imposed under chapter 1 of such Code.

(6) REGULATIONS.—The Secretary of the Treasury shall issue such regulations or other guidance as are necessary or appropriate to carry out this subsection, including requirements that the entity to whom premiums are reimbursed under section 6432(a) of the Internal Revenue Code of 1986 report to the Secretary, and to each assistance eligible individual, the amount of premium assistance provided under subsection (a) with respect to each such individual.

(7) EFFECTIVE DATE.—The provisions of this subsection shall apply to taxable years ending after the date of the enactment of this Act.

SEC. 70308. RISK CORRIDOR PROGRAM.

(a) In General.—The Secretary of Health and Human Services (in this section referred to as the "Secretary") shall establish and administer a program of risk corridors for plan years 2020 and 2021 under which the Secretary shall make payments to health insurance issuers offering health insurance coverage in the individual or small group market based on the ratio of the allowable costs of the coverage to the aggregate premiums of the coverage.

(b) Payment Methodology.—The Secretary shall provide under the program established under subsection (a) that if the allowable costs for a health insurance issuer offering health insurance coverage in the individual or small group market for any plan year are more than 105 percent of the target amount, the Secretary shall pay to the issuer an amount equal to 75 percent of the allowable costs in excess of 105 percent of the target amount.

(c) Information Collection.—The Secretary shall establish a process under which information is collected from health insurance issuers offering health insurance coverage in the individual or small group market for purposes of carrying out this section.

(d) Definitions.—

(1) ALLOWABLE COSTS.—

(A) IN GENERAL.—The amount of allowable costs of a health insurance issuer offering health insurance coverage in the individual or small group market for

any year is an amount equal to the total costs (other than administrative costs) of such issuer in providing benefits covered by such coverage.
(B) CERTAIN REDUCTIONS.—Allowable costs shall reduced by any—
(i) risk adjustment payments received under section 1341 of the Patient Protection and Affordable Care Act (42 U.S.C. 18061);
(ii) reinsurance payments received pursuant to a waiver approved under section 1332 of such Act (42 U.S.C. 18052); and
(iii) payments received pursuant to section 70304.
(2) ADDITIONAL TERMS.—For purposes of this section, the terms "health insurance issuer", "health insurance coverage", "individual market", and "small group market" have the meanings given such terms in section 2791 of the Public Health Service Act (42 U.S.C. 300gg–91).
(3) TARGET AMOUNT.—The target amount of health insurance coverage offered in the individual or small group market for any year is an amount equal to the total premiums (including any premium subsidies under any governmental program), reduced by the administrative costs of the coverage.
(e) Implementation.—The Secretary of Health and Human Services may implement the provisions of this section by subregulatory guidance, program instruction, or otherwise.
(f) Appropriation.—There are appropriated, out of any monies in the Treasury not otherwise obligated, such sums as may be necessary to carry out this section.
SEC. 70309. COVERAGE OF IN VITRO DIAGNOSTIC PRODUCTS.
(a) In General.—Section 6001 of division F of the Families First Coronavirus Response Act (Public Law 116–127) is amended—
(1) by amending subsection (a)(1) to read as follows:
"(1) Qualified in vitro diagnostic products and the administration of such in vitro diagnostic products."; and
(2) in subsection (d)—
(A) by striking "Terms.—The terms" and inserting the following: Terms.—In this section:
"(1) HEALTH INSURANCE TERMS.—The terms"; and
(B) by adding at the end the following:
"(2) QUALIFIED IN VITRO DIAGNOSTIC PRODUCT.—
"(A) The term 'qualified in vitro diagnostic product' means an in vitro diagnostic product (as defined in section 809.3(a) of title 21, Code of Federal Regulations) for the detection of SARS–CoV–2 or the diagnosis of the virus that causes COVID–19 that is approved, cleared, or authorized under section 510(k), 513, 515, or 564 of the Federal Food, Drug, and Cosmetic Act (21 U.S.C. 360(k), 360c, 360e, and 360bbb–3).
"(B) Such term includes an in vitro diagnostic test that—
"(i) subject to subparagraph (C), is developed and used in a laboratory certified to perform high-complexity testing pursuant to section 353 of the Public Health Service Act (42 U.S.C. 263a) and with respect to which such

laboratory—

"(I) validates prior to use for the detection of SARS–CoV–2 or the diagnosis of the virus that causes COVID–19, including by obtaining confirmation of validation using an assay authorized under section 564 of the Federal Food, Drug, and Cosmetic Act (21 U.S.C. 360bbb–3);

"(II) notifies the Secretary of such use; and

"(III) includes a statement together with the results of the test that reads: 'This test has not been FDA cleared or approved. This test has been authorized by FDA under an emergency use authorization for use by authorized laboratories. This test has been authorized only for the detection of nucleic acid from SARS-CoV-2, not for any other viruses or pathogens';

"(ii) is developed and used in a laboratory certified to perform high-complexity testing pursuant to section 353 of the Public Health Service Act (42 U.S.C. 263a) and such laboratory—

"(I) is operating under an authorization of the State (as defined in section 2 of the Public Health Service Act (42 U.S.C. 201)) in which such laboratory is located and such State has notified the Secretary of its intention to review tests intended to diagnose SARS–CoV–2 or diagnose the virus that causes COVID–19 to be used in such State;

"(II) has notified the Secretary of such use for such purpose in such State; and

"(III) includes a statement together with the results of the test that reads: 'This test was developed for use as a part of a response to the public health emergency declared to address the outbreak of COVID–19. This test has not been reviewed by the Food and Drug Administration'; or

"(iii) is developed by a commercial test manufacturer that, with respect to such test—

"(I) validates such test prior to use to detect SARS–CoV–2 or diagnose the virus that causes COVID–19, including by obtaining confirmation of validation using an assay authorized under section 564 of the Federal Food, Drug, and Cosmetic Act (21 U.S.C. 360bbb–3);

"(II) notifies the Secretary of such use; and

"(III) includes a statement together with the results of the test that reads: 'This test has not been FDA cleared or approved. This test has been authorized by FDA under an emergency use authorization for use by authorized laboratories. This test has been authorized only for the detection of nucleic acid from SARS-CoV-2, not for any other viruses or pathogens'.

"(C) Such term shall not include a test described in clause (i) or (iii) of subparagraph (B) if—

"(i) the emergency use authorization request submitted by a laboratory or manufacturer described in such respective clause with respect to such test has been denied; or

"(ii) such laboratory or manufacturer does not submit such a request within 15 business days of the notification under subclause (II) of such respective subparagraph.".

(b) Conforming Amendment.—Subparagraph (B) of section 1905(a)(3) of the Social Security Act (42 U.S.C. 1396d(a)(3)), as added by section 6004(a)(1) of division F of the Families First Coronavirus Response Act) is amended to read as follows:

"(B) qualified in vitro diagnostic products (as defined in section 6001(d) of division F of the Families First Coronavirus Response Act) and the administration of such in vitro diagnostic products;".

SEC. 70310. SENSE OF CONGRESS REGARDING SURPRISE MEDICAL BILLS.

(a) Findings.—Congress finds the following:

(1) Surprise medical bills can be financially devastating for consumers.

(2) Surprise medical bills are often unavoidable and occur in situations where consumers have no ability to reasonably choose an in-network provider or insurance company networks are too narrow for consumers to be able to access seamless in-network care.

(3) Consumers and their financial stability should not be caught in the middle between insurance companies and health care providers.

(4) It is imperative that Congress enacts a comprehensive, long-term solution to protect consumers and end surprise medical billing.

(5) During the COVID-19 pandemic, consumers across the country will increasingly require emergency or unanticipated health care services and at the same time may have limited access to in-network providers due to the increased demand on the health care system and it is critical that they are not deterred from seeking care due to the threat of a surprise medical bill.

(6) The virus is now spreading faster in the United States than anywhere else in the world and experts indicate that day by day, more hospital beds will be full, more resources will be depleted, and the virus will claim more lives.

(b) Sense Of Congress.—It is the sense of the Congress that, during the COVID-19 pandemic—

(1) heath care providers should refrain from balance billing consumers for out-of-network claims related to COVID-19 testing or treatment and insurance companies should do their utmost to secure access to in-network treatment for their plan participants, including providing adequate reimbursement rates for services; and

(2) consumers' cost-sharing should be limited to what they would have paid if the providers testing or treating them for COVID-19 were in-network for their insurance plan.

TITLE IV—PROVISIONS RELATING TO OLDER AMERICANS ACT OF 1965

SEC. 70401. COMBATING HUNGER FOR OLDER AMERICANS DURING CORONAVIRUS CRISIS.

(a) Home Delivered Nutrition Services Criteria Applicable Under The Older Americans Act Of 1965 During Fiscal Year 2020 To Respond To The COVID-19 Public Health Emergency.—For purposes of State agencies determining the delivery of nutrition services under subpart 2 of part C of title III of the Older Americans Act of 1965 (42 U.S.C. 3030f et seq.), during the portion of COVID-19 public health emergency declared under section 319 of the Public Health Service Act (42 U.S.C. 247d) that occurs in the period beginning on the date of the enactment of this Act and ending on September 30, 2020, the State agencies shall include among individuals receiving delivery because they are homebound an individual age 60 and older, or an individual with a disability (of any age), who is unable to obtain nutrition because the individual is under a quarantine, practicing social distancing, or otherwise unable to leave home, due to the emergency.

(b) Congregate Nutrition Services Criteria Applicable Under The Older Americans Act Of 1965 During Fiscal Year 2020 To Respond To The COVID-19 Public Health Emergency.— If a State demonstrates, to the satisfaction of the Assistant Secretary (as defined in section 102 of the Older Americans Act of 1965 (42 U.S.C.3002), that funds received by the State and attributable to funds appropriated under paragraph (1) or (2) of section 303(b) of the Older Americans Act of 1965 (42 U.S.C. 3023(b)), including funds transferred under subparagraph (A) of paragraph (4) of such section without regard to the exception referring to subparagraph (B) specified in such subparagraph (A), for fiscal year 2020 are insufficient to satisfy the need for services under subpart I or subpart II of part C of title III of the Older Americans Act of 1965 (42 U.S.C. 3030d–2 et seq.) in fiscal year 2020 during the COVID-19 public health emergency declared under section 319 of the Public Health Service Act (42 U.S.C. 247d), the Assistant Secretary shall allow State and area agencies on aging, without prior approval, to transfer up to 100 percent of the funds so received between subpart 1 and subpart 2 of such part C for use the State or area agency on aging considers appropriate to meet the needs of the area served.

(c) Waiver.—To facilitate implementation of subparts 1 and 2 of part C of title III of the Older Americans Act of 1965 (42 U.S.C. 3030e et seq.) during any portion of the COVID-19 public health emergency declared under section 319 of the Public Health Service Act (42 U.S.C. 247d) that occurs in the period beginning on the date of the enactment of this Act and ending on September 30, 2020, the Assistant Secretary for Aging may waive the requirements for emergency meals to comply with the requirements of clauses (i) and (ii) of section 339(2)(A) of the Older Americans Act of 1965 (42 U.S.C. 3030g–21(2)(A)).

SEC. 70402. ACCESS OF THE STATE LONG-TERM CARE OMBUDSMAN TO RESIDENTS OF LONG-TERM CARE FACILITIES DURING THE COVID-19 PUBLIC HEALTH EMERGENCY IN FISCAL YEAR 2020.

During any portion of the COVID-19 public health emergency declared under section 319 of the Public Health Service Act (42 U.S.C. 247d) that occurs in the period beginning on the date of the enactment of this Act and ending on September 30, 2020, the State Long-Term Care Ombudsman shall have continuing direct access (or other access through the use of technology to the greatest extent practicable) to residents of long-term care facilities to provide the services described in section 712(a)(3)(B) of the Older Americans Act of 1965 (42 U.S.C. 3058h(a)(3)(B)).

SEC. 70403. CONTINUITY OF SERVICE AND OPPORTUNITIES FOR PARTICIPANTS IN COMMUNITY SERVICE ACTIVITIES UNDER TITLE V OF THE OF THE OLDER AMERICANS ACT OF 1965.

To ensure continuity of service and opportunities for participants in community service activities under title V of the of the Older Americans Act of 1965 (42 U.S.C. 3056–3056p), the Secretary of Labor—

(1) (A) may allow for individuals participating in such activities as of March 1, 2020, to extend their participation for a period that exceeds the period described in section 518(a)(3)(B)(i) of such Act if the Secretary determines such extension is appropriate due to the effects of the COVID-19 public heath emergency declared under section 319 of the Public Health Service Act (42 U.S.C. 247d), and

(B) may extend the average participation cap for eligible individuals applicable to grantees under section 502(b)(1)(C) of such Act to a cap the Secretary determines is appropriate due to the effects of the COVID-19 public heath emergency declared under section 319 of the Public Health Service Act (42 U.S.C. 247d), and

(2) may increase the amount available to pay the authorized administrative costs to an amount not to exceed 20 percent of the grant amount if the Secretary determines that such increase is necessary to adequately respond to the additional administrative needs to respond to the COVID-19 public health emergency declared under section 319 of the Public Health Service Act (42 U.S.C. 247d).

TITLE V—PUBLIC HEALTH POLICIES

Subtitle A—Improving Public Health And Medical Response

SEC. 70501. REIMBURSEMENT FOR ADDITIONAL HEALTH SERVICES RELATING TO CORONAVIRUS.

Title V of division A of the Families First Coronavirus Response Act (Public Law 116–127) is amended under the heading "Department of Health and Human Services—Office of the Secretary—Public Health and Social Services Emergency Fund" is amended by inserting ", or treatment related to SARS–CoV–2 or COVID–19 for uninsured individuals" after "or visits described in paragraph (2) of such section for uninsured individuals".

SEC. 70502. PUBLIC HEALTH DATA SYSTEM TRANSFORMATION.

Subtitle C of title XXVIII of the Public Health Service Act (42 U.S.C. 300hh–31 et seq.) is amended by adding at the end the following:

"SEC. 2822. PUBLIC HEALTH DATA SYSTEM TRANSFORMATION.

"(a) Expanding CDC And Public Health Department Capabilities.—

"(1) IN GENERAL.—The Secretary, acting through the Director of the Centers for Disease Control and Prevention, shall—

"(A) conduct activities to expand, enhance, and improve applicable public health data systems used by the Centers for Disease Control and Prevention, related to the interoperability and improvement of such systems (including as it relates to preparedness for, prevention and detection of, and response to public health emergencies); and

"(B) award grants or cooperative agreements to State, local, Tribal, or territorial public health departments for the expansion and modernization of public health data systems, to assist public health departments in—

"(i) assessing current data infrastructure capabilities and gaps to improve and increase consistency in data collection, storage, analysis and, as appropriate, to improve dissemination of public health-related information;

"(ii) improving secure public health data collection, transmission, exchange, maintenance, and analysis;

"(iii) improving the secure exchange of data between the Centers for Disease Control and Prevention, State, local, Tribal, and territorial public health departments, public health organizations, and health care providers, including by public health officials in multiple jurisdictions within such State, as appropriate, and by simplifying and supporting reporting by health care providers, as applicable, pursuant to State law, including through the use of health information technology;

"(iv) enhancing the interoperability of public health data systems (including systems created or accessed by public health departments) with health information technology, including with health information technology certified under section 3001(c)(5);

"(v) supporting and training data systems, data science, and informatics personnel;

"(vi) supporting earlier disease and health condition detection, such as through near real-time data monitoring, to support rapid public health responses;

"(vii) supporting activities within the applicable jurisdiction related to the expansion and modernization of electronic case reporting; and

"(viii) developing and disseminating information related to the use and importance of public health data.

"(2) DATA STANDARDS.—In carrying out paragraph (1), the Secretary, acting through the Director of the Centers for Disease Control and Prevention, shall, as appropriate and in consultation with the Office of the National Coordinator for Health Information Technology, designate data and technology standards (including standards for interoperability) for public health data systems, with deference given to standards published by consensus-based standards development organizations with public input and voluntary consensus-based standards bodies.

"(3) PUBLIC-PRIVATE PARTNERSHIPS.—The Secretary may develop and utilize public-private partnerships for technical assistance, training, and related implementation support for State, local, Tribal, and territorial public health departments, and the Centers for Disease Control and Prevention, on the expansion and modernization of electronic case reporting and public health data systems, as applicable.

"(b) Requirements.—

"(1) HEALTH INFORMATION TECHNOLOGY STANDARDS.—The Secretary may not award a grant or cooperative agreement under subsection (a)(1)(B) unless the applicant uses or agrees to use standards endorsed by the National Coordinator for Health Information Technology pursuant to section 3001(c)(1) or adopted by the Secretary under section 3004.

"(2) WAIVER.—The Secretary may waive the requirement under paragraph (1) with respect to an applicant if the Secretary determines that the activities under subsection (a)(1)(B) cannot otherwise be carried out within the applicable jurisdiction.

"(3) APPLICATION.—A State, local, Tribal, or territorial health department applying for a grant or cooperative agreement under this section shall submit an application to the Secretary at such time and in such manner as the Secretary may require. Such application shall include information describing—

"(A) the activities that will be supported by the grant or cooperative agreement; and

"(B) how the modernization of the public health data systems involved will support or impact the public health infrastructure of the health department, including a description of remaining gaps, if any, and the actions needed to address such gaps.

"(c) Strategy And Implementation Plan.—Not later than 180 days after the date of enactment of this section, the Secretary, acting through the Director of the Centers for Disease Control and Prevention, shall submit to the Committee on Health, Education, Labor, and Pensions of the Senate and the Committee on Energy and Commerce of the House of Representatives a coordinated strategy and an accompanying implementation plan that identifies and demonstrates the measures the Secretary will utilize to—

"(1) update and improve applicable public health data systems used by the Centers for Disease Control and Prevention; and

"(2) carry out the activities described in this section to support the improvement of State, local, Tribal, and territorial public health data systems.

"(d) Consultation.—The Secretary, acting through the Director of the Centers for Disease Control and Prevention, shall consult with State, local, Tribal, and territorial health departments, professional medical and public health associations, associations representing hospitals or other health care entities, health information technology experts, and other appropriate public or private entities regarding the plan and grant program to modernize public health data systems pursuant to this section. Activities under this subsection may include the provision of technical assistance and training related to the exchange of information by such public health data systems used by relevant health care and public health entities at the local, State, Federal, Tribal, and territorial levels, and the development and utilization of public-private partnerships for implementation support applicable to this section.

"(e) Report To Congress.—Not later than 1 year after the date of enactment of this section, the Secretary shall submit a report to the Committee on Health, Education, Labor, and Pensions of the Senate and the Committee on Energy and Commerce of the House of Representatives that includes—

"(1) a description of any barriers to—

"(A) public health authorities implementing interoperable public health data systems and electronic case reporting;

"(B) the exchange of information pursuant to electronic case reporting; or

"(C) reporting by health care providers using such public health data systems, as appropriate, and pursuant to State law;

"(2) an assessment of the potential public health impact of implementing electronic case reporting and interoperable public health data systems; and

"(3) a description of the activities carried out pursuant to this section.

"(f) Electronic Case Reporting.—In this section, the term 'electronic case reporting' means the automated identification, generation, and bilateral exchange of reports of health events among electronic health record or health information technology systems and public health authorities.

"(g) Authorization Of Appropriations.—To carry out this section, there are authorized to be appropriated $100,000,000 for each of fiscal years 2021 through 2025.".

SEC. 70503. REPORTING ON COVID-19 TESTING AND RESULTS.

State and local governments, laboratories, and health systems receiving funds or assistance pursuant to division A of the Families First Coronavirus Response Act (Public Law 116–127) or pursuant to division A of this Act shall ensure that—

(1) the respective State Emergency Operations Center and State and local public health departments, receive regular and real-time reporting on data, in a timely manner, on testing and results, including positive and negative laboratory results, as well as reporting on cases and severe outcomes resulting from COVID-19, as determined by the Director of the Centers for Disease Control and Prevention; and

(2) such data is transmitted in a regular and timely manner to the Centers for Disease Control and Prevention.

SEC. 70504. CENTERS FOR DISEASE CONTROL AND PREVENTION COVID-19 RESPONSE LINE.

(a) In General.—During the public health emergency declared by the Secretary of Health and Human Services pursuant to section 319 of the Public Health Service Act (42 U.S.C. 247d) on January 31, 2020 with respect to COVID-19, the Secretary, acting through the Director of the Centers for Disease Control and Prevention, shall maintain a toll-free telephone number to address public health queries, including questions concerning COVID-19.

(b) Authorization Of Appropriations.—To carry out this section, there is authorized to be appropriated $10,000,000, to remain available until expended.

SEC. 70505. AWARENESS CAMPAIGN.

The Secretary of Health and Human Services, acting through the Director of the Centers for Disease Control and Prevention and in coordination with other offices and agencies, as appropriate, shall award competitive grants or contracts to one or more public or private entities to carry out a national campaign, based on available scientific evidence, to increase awareness and knowledge of COVID-19, including countering stigma associated with COVID-19 and improving information on the availability of diagnostic testing and other related services at community health centers.

SEC. 70506. ADDITIONAL FUNDING FOR MEDICAL RESERVE CORPS.

Section 2813 of the Public Health Service Act (42 U.S.C. 300hh–15) is amended by striking "$11,200,000 for each of fiscal years 2019 through 2023" and inserting "$31,200,000 for each of fiscal years 2020 and 2021 and $11,200,000 for each of fiscal years 2022 and 2023".

SEC. 70507. FLEXIBILITY FOR MEMBERS OF NATIONAL HEALTH SERVICE CORPS DURING EMERGENCY PERIOD.

Subsection (a) of section 333 of the Public Health Service Act (42 U.S.C. 254f) is amended by adding at the end the following new paragraph:

"(4) During an emergency period (as defined in section 1135(g)(1) of the Social Security Act, the Secretary may, notwithstanding this subpart and subpart III, assign members of the Corps to provide such health services at such places and for such number of hours as the Secretary determines necessary to respond to the emergency, provided that—

"(A) the members voluntarily agree to such assignment and hours;

"(B) the places to which such members are assigned are within a reasonable distance of the places to which the respective members were assigned or were to be assigned absent a waiver under this paragraph; and

"(C) the minimum number of hours required are the same as were required prior to the date of enactment of this paragraph.".

SEC. 70508. READY RESERVE CORPS.

(a) Commissioned Corps And Ready Reserve Corps.—Section 203 of the Public Health Service Act (42 U.S.C. 204) is amended—

(1) in subsection (a)(1), by striking " a Ready Reserve Corps for service in time of national emergency" and inserting ", for service in time of a public health or national emergency, a Ready Reserve Corps"; and

(2) in subsection (c)—

(A) in the heading, by striking "Research" and inserting "Reserve Corps";

(B) in paragraph (1), by inserting "during public health or national emergencies" before the period;

(C) in paragraph (2)—

(i) in the matter preceding subparagraph (A), by inserting ", consistent with paragraph (1)" after "shall";

(ii) in subparagraph (C), by inserting "during such emergencies" after "members"; and

(iii) in subparagraph (D), by inserting ", consistent with subparagraph (C)" before the period; and

(D) by adding at the end the following:

"(3) STATUTORY REFERENCES TO RESERVE.—A reference in any Federal statute, except in the case of subsection (b), to the 'Reserve Corps' of the Public Health Service or to the 'reserve' of the Public Health Service shall be deemed to be a reference to the Ready Reserve Corps.".

(b) Deployment Readiness.—Section 203A(a)(1)(B) of the Public Health Service Act (42 U.S.C. 204a(a)(1)(B)) is amended by striking "Active Reserves" and inserting "Ready Reserve Corps".

(c) Retirement Of Commissioned Officers.—Section 211 of the Public Health Service Act (42 U.S.C. 212) is amended—

(1) by striking "(in the case of an officer in the Reserve Corps)" each place it appears;

(2) by striking "the Service" each place it appears and inserting "the Regular Corps";

(3) in subsection (c)—

(A) in paragraph (1)—

(i) by striking "or an officer of the Reserve Corps"; and

(ii) by inserting "or under section 221(a)(19)" after "subsection (a)"; and

(B) in paragraph (2), by striking "Regular or Reserve Corps" and inserting "Regular Corps or Ready Reserve Corps"; and

(4) in subsection (f), by striking "the Regular or Reserve Corps of".

(d) Rights, Privileges, Etc. Of Officers And Surviving Beneficiaries.—Section 221 of the Public Health Service Act (42 U.S.C. 213a) is amended—

(1) in subsection (a), by adding at the end the following:

"(19) Chapter 1223, Retired Pay for Non-Regular Service.

"(20) Section 12601, Compensation: Reserve on active duty accepting from any person.

"(21) Section 12684, Reserves: separation for absence without authority or sentence to imprisonment."; and

(2) in subsection (b)—

(A) by striking "Secretary of Health, Education, and Welfare or his designee" and inserting "Secretary of Health and Human Services or the designee of such secretary";

(B) by striking "(b) The authority vested" and inserting the following:

"(b) (1) The authority vested";

(C) by striking "For purposes of" and inserting the following:

"(2) For purposes of"; and

(D) by adding at the end the following:

"(3) For purposes of paragraph (19) of subsection (a), the terms 'Military department', 'Secretary concerned', and 'Armed forces' in such title 10 shall be deemed to include, respectively, the Department of Health and Human

Services, the Secretary of Health and Human Services, and the Commissioned Corps.".

SEC. 70509. LIMITATION ON LIABILITY FOR VOLUNTEER HEALTH CARE PROFESSIONALS DURING COVID-19 EMERGENCY RESPONSE.

(a) Limitation On Liability.—Except as provided in subsection (b), a health care professional shall not be liable under Federal or State law for any harm caused by an act or omission of the professional in the provision of health care services during the public health emergency with respect to COVID–19 declared by the Secretary of Health and Human Services (referred to in this section as the "Secretary") pursuant to section 319 of the Public Health Service Act (42 U.S.C. 247d) on January 31, 2020, if—

(1) the professional is providing health care services in response to such public health emergency, as a volunteer; and

(2) the act or omission occurs—

(A) in the course of providing health care services;

(B) in the health care professional's capacity as a volunteer;

(C) in the course of providing health care services that are within the scope of the license, registration, or certification of the volunteer, as defined by the State of licensure, registration, or certification; and

(D) in a good faith belief that the individual being treated is in need of health care services.

(b) Exceptions.—Subsection (a) does not apply if—

(1) the harm was caused by an act or omission constituting willful or criminal misconduct, gross negligence, reckless misconduct, or a conscious flagrant indifference to the rights or safety of the individual harmed by the health care professional; or

(2) the health care professional rendered the health care services under the influence (as determined pursuant to applicable State law) of alcohol or an intoxicating drug.

(c) Preemption.—

(1) IN GENERAL.—This section preempts the laws of a State or any political subdivision of a State to the extent that such laws are inconsistent with this section, unless such laws provide greater protection from liability.

(2) VOLUNTEER PROTECTION ACT.—Protections afforded by this section are in addition to those provided by the Volunteer Protection Act of 1997 (Public Law 105–19).

(d) Definitions.—In this section—

(1) the term "harm" includes physical, nonphysical, economic, and noneconomic losses;

(2) the term "health care professional" means an individual who is licensed, registered, or certified under Federal or State law to provide health care services;

(3) the term "health care services" means any services provided by a health care professional, or by any individual working under the supervision of a

health care professional that relate to—

(A) the diagnosis, prevention, or treatment of COVID-19; or

(B) the assessment or care of the health of a human being for COVID-19; and

(4) the term "volunteer" means a health care professional who, with respect to the health care services rendered, does not receive compensation or any other thing of value in lieu of compensation, which compensation—

(A) includes a payment under any insurance policy or health plan, or under any Federal or State health benefits program; and

(B) excludes receipt of items to be used exclusively for rendering health care services in the health care professional's capacity as a volunteer described in subsection (a)(1) and excludes any reimbursement for travel to the site where the volunteer services are being rendered and any payments in cash or kind to cover room and board, if services are being rendered more than 75 miles from the volunteer's principal place of residence.

(e) Applicability.—This section applies only with respect to a claim for a harm caused by an act or omission occurring—

(1) on or after the date of enactment of this Act; and

(2) during the period of the public health emergency declared by the Secretary of Health and Human Services pursuant to section 319 of the Public Health Service Act (42 U.S.C. 247d) on January 31, 2020 with respect to COVID-19.

Subtitle B—Tribal Health

SEC. 70521. IMPROVING STATE, LOCAL, AND TRIBAL PUBLIC HEALTH SECURITY.

Section 319C–1 of the Public Health Service Act (42 U.S.C. 247d–3a) is amended—

(1) in the section heading, by striking "AND LOCAL" and inserting ", LOCAL, AND TRIBAL";

(2) in subsection (b)—

(A) in paragraph (1)—

(i) in subparagraph (B), by striking "or" at the end;

(ii) in subparagraph (C), by striking "and" at the end and inserting "or"; and

(iii) by adding at the end the following:

"(D) be an Indian tribe, tribal organization, or a consortium of Indian tribes or tribal organizations; and"; and

(B) in paragraph (2)—

(i) in the matter preceding subparagraph (A), by inserting ", as applicable" after "including";

(ii) in subparagraph (A)(viii)—

(I) by inserting "and tribal" after "with State";

(II) by striking "(as defined in section 8101 of the Elementary and Secondary Education Act of 1965)" and inserting "and tribal educational agencies (as defined in sections 8101 and 6132, respectively, of the Elementary and Secondary Education Act of 1965)"; and

(III) by inserting "and tribal" after "and State";

(iii) in subparagraph (G), by striking "and tribal" and inserting "tribal, and urban Indian organization"; and

(iv) in subparagraph (H), by inserting ", Indian tribes, and urban Indian organizations" after "public health";

(3) in subsection (e), by inserting "Indian tribes, tribal organizations, urban Indian organizations," after "local emergency plans,";

(4) in subsection (h)—

(A) in paragraph (1)(A)—

(i) by striking "through 2023" and inserting "and 2020"; and

(ii) by inserting before the period "; and $690,000,000 for each of fiscal years 2021 through 2023 for awards pursuant to paragraph (3) (subject to the authority of the Secretary to make awards pursuant to paragraphs (4) and (5)) and paragraph (8), of which not less than $5,000,000 shall be reserved each fiscal year for awards under paragraph (8)";

(B) in the heading of paragraph (3), by inserting "FOR STATES" after "AMOUNT"; and

(C) by adding at the end the following:

"(8) TRIBAL ELIGIBLE ENTITIES.—

"(A) DETERMINATION OF FUNDING AMOUNT.—

"(i) IN GENERAL.—The Secretary shall award at least 10 cooperative agreements under this section, in amounts not less than the minimum amount determined under clause (ii), to eligible entities described in subsection (b)(1)(D) that submits to the Secretary an application that meets the criteria of the Secretary for the receipt of such an award and that meets other reasonable implementation conditions established by the Secretary, in consultation with Indian tribes, for such awards. If the Secretary receives more than 10 applications under this section from eligible entities described in subsection (b)(1)(D) that meet the criteria and conditions described in the previous sentence, the Secretary, in consultation with Indian tribes, may make additional awards under this section to such entities.

"(ii) MINIMUM AMOUNT.—In determining the minimum amount of an award pursuant to clause (i), the Secretary, in consultation with Indian tribes, shall first determine an amount the Secretary considers appropriate for the eligible entity.

"(B) AVAILABLE UNTIL EXPENDED.—Amounts provided to a tribal eligible entity under a cooperative agreement under this section for a fiscal year and remaining unobligated at the end of such year shall remain available to such entity during the entirety of the performance period, for the purposes for which said funds were provided.

"(C) NO MATCHING REQUIREMENT.—Subparagraphs (B), (C), and (D) of paragraph (1) shall not apply with respect to cooperative agreements awarded under this section to eligible entities described in subsection (b)(1)(D)."; and

(5) by adding at the end the following:

"(l) Special Rules Related To Tribal Eligible Entities.—

"(1) MODIFICATIONS.—After consultation with Indian tribes, the Secretary may make necessary and appropriate modifications to the program under this section to facilitate the use of the cooperative agreement program by eligible entities described in subsection (b)(1)(D).

"(2) WAIVERS.—

"(A) IN GENERAL.—Except as provided in subparagraph (B), the Secretary may waive or specify alternative requirements for any provision of this section (including regulations) that the Secretary administers in connection with this section if the Secretary finds that the waiver or alternative requirement is necessary for the effective delivery and administration of this program with respect to eligible entities described in subsection (b)(1)(D).

"(B) EXCEPTION.—The Secretary may not waive or specify alternative requirements under subparagraph (A) relating to labor standards or the environment.

"(3) CONSULTATION.—The Secretary shall consult with Indian tribes and tribal organizations on the design of this program with respect to such tribes and organizations to ensure the effectiveness of the program in enhancing the security of Indian tribes with respect to public health emergencies.

"(4) REPORTING.—

"(A) IN GENERAL.—Not later than 2 years after the date of enactment of this subsection, and as an addendum to the biennial evaluations required under subsection (k), the Secretary, in coordination with the Director of the Indian Health Service, shall—

"(i) conduct a review of the implementation of this section with respect to eligible entities described in subsection (b)(1)(D), including any factors that may have limited its success; and

"(ii) submit a report describing the results of the review described in clause (i) to—

"(I) the Committee on Indian Affairs, the Committee on Health, Education, Labor, and Pensions, and the Committee on Appropriations of the Senate; and

"(II) the Subcommittee on Indigenous People of the Committee on Natural Resources, the Committee on Energy and Commerce, and the Committee on Appropriations of the House of Representatives.

"(B) ANALYSIS OF TRIBAL PUBLIC HEALTH EMERGENCY INFRASTRUCTURE LIMITATION.—The Secretary shall include in the initial report submitted under subparagraph (A) a description of any public health emergency infrastructure limitation encountered by eligible entities described in subsection (b)(1)(D).".

SEC. 70522. PROVISION OF ITEMS TO INDIAN PROGRAMS AND FACILITIES.

(a) Strategic National Stockpile.—Section 319F–2(a)(3)(G) of the Public Health Service Act (42 U.S.C. 247d–6b(a)(3)(G)) is amended by inserting ", and, in the case that the Secretary deploys the stockpile under this subparagraph, ensure, in coordination with the applicable States and programs and facilities, that appropriate drugs, vaccines and other biological products, medical devices, and other supplies are deployed by the Secretary directly to health programs or facilities operated by the Indian Health Service, an Indian tribe, a tribal organization (as those terms are defined in section 4 of the Indian Self-Determination and Education Assistance Act (25 U.S.C. 5304)), or an inter-tribal consortium (as defined in section 501 of the Indian Self-Determination and Education Assistance Act (25 U.S.C. 5381)) or through an urban Indian organization (as defined in section 4 of the Indian Health Care Improvement Act), while avoiding duplicative distributions to such programs or facilities" before the semicolon.

(b) Distribution Of Qualified Pandemic Or Epidemic Products To IHS Facilities.—Title III of the Public Health Service Act (42 U.S.C. 241 et seq.) is amended by inserting after section 319F–4 the following:

"SEC. 319F–5. DISTRIBUTION OF QUALIFIED PANDEMIC OR EPIDEMIC PRODUCTS TO INDIAN PROGRAMS AND FACILITIES.

"In the case that the Secretary distributes qualified pandemic or epidemic products (as defined in section 319F–3(i)(7)) to States or other entities, the Secretary shall ensure, in coordination with the applicable States and programs and facilities, that, as appropriate, such products are distributed directly to health programs or facilities operated by the Indian Health Service, an Indian tribe, a tribal organization (as those terms are defined in section 4 of the Indian Self-Determination and Education Assistance Act (25 U.S.C. 5304)), or an inter-tribal consortium (as defined in section 501 of the Indian Self-Determination and Education Assistance Act (25 U.S.C. 5381)) or through an urban Indian organization (as defined in section 4 of the Indian Health Care Improvement Act), while avoiding duplicative distributions to such programs or facilities.".

Subtitle C—Medical Product Supply Chain Improvements

SEC. 70531. SHORTAGES OF ESSENTIAL DEVICES.

Chapter V of the Federal Food, Drug, and Cosmetic Act (21 U.S.C. 351 et seq.) is amended by inserting after section 520 the following:

"SEC. 520A. DISCONTINUANCE OR INTERRUPTION IN THE PRODUCTION OF ESSENTIAL DEVICES DURING PUBLIC HEALTH EMERGENCIES.

"(a) Notification.—

"(1) IN GENERAL.—A manufacturer or contract terminal sterilizer of an essential device shall notify the Secretary—

"(A) in accordance with paragraph (3), when such manufacturer or sterilizer becomes aware of—

"(i) a permanent discontinuance in the manufacture of the device (except for a permanent discontinuance as a result of an approved modification of the device);

"(ii) an interruption in the manufacture of the device that is likely to lead to a

shortage or meaningful disruption in the supply of that device in the United States; or
"(iii) any other situation or circumstance that is likely to lead to a shortage or meaningful disruption in the supply of that device in the United States; and
"(B) in accordance with paragraph (2)(C), of the reason for such discontinuance, interruption, or other situation or circumstance.
"(2) REQUIRED INCLUSIONS.—A notification under paragraph (1) shall include each of the following:
"(A) The name of the device, including the Device Identifier or National Product Code for the device, if applicable.
"(B) The name of the manufacturer of the device.
"(C) The reason for the notification, including whether any of the following reasons apply:
"(i) Requirements related to complying with quality system regulations.
"(ii) Shortage of a material used in the manufacture of the device.
"(iii) Shortage of a component, part, or accessory of the device.
"(iv) Delay in shipping of the device.
"(v) Increased demand for the device.
"(vi) Natural disaster.
"(vii) Cyber security.
"(viii) Facility closure.
"(ix) Other reasons as the Secretary deems appropriate.
"(D) The estimated duration of the discontinuance, interruption, or other situation or circumstance.
"(E) Any other information the manufacturer deems relevant.
"(3) TIMING.—The notification required under paragraph (1) shall be submitted, in a manner prescribed by the Secretary—
"(A) no later than 6 months prior to the date of the discontinuance, interruption, or other situation or circumstance; or
"(B) if compliance with subparagraph (A) is not possible, as soon as is practicable, and in no case later than 5 business days after the manufacturer becomes aware of an event, situation, or circumstance requiring notification under paragraph (1).
"(b) Distribution.—
"(1) PUBLIC AVAILABILITY.—To the extent practicable, the Secretary shall distribute, through such means as the Secretary deems appropriate, information on any discontinuance, interruption, or other situation or circumstance described in subsection (a) to appropriate organizations, including to hospitals, physicians and other health care providers, patients, and supply chain partners.
"(2) PUBLIC HEALTH EXCEPTION.—The Secretary may choose not to make information collected under this section publicly available pursuant to this section if the Secretary determines that the disclosure of such information would adversely affect public health, such as by increasing the possibility of an

unnecessary over-purchase or other disruption of the availability of medical products to patients.

"(c) Confidentiality.—Nothing in this section shall be construed as authorizing the Secretary to disclose any information that is a trade secret or confidential information subject to section 552(b)(4) of title 5, United States Code, or section 1905 of title 18, United States Code.

"(d) Failure To Meet Requirements.—If a person fails to submit information as required under subsection (a)—

"(1) the Secretary shall issue a letter to such person setting forth the basis for noncompliance and informing such person of a failure to comply;

"(2) within 30 calendar days from the issuance of a letter under paragraph (1), the person who receives such letter shall submit to the Secretary a written response to such letter setting forth the basis for noncompliance and providing information required under subsection (a); and

"(3) not later than 45 calendar days after the issuance of a letter under paragraph (1), the Secretary shall make such letter and any response to such letter under paragraph (2) available to the public on the public website of the Food and Drug Administration, with appropriate redactions made to protect information described in subsection (c), except that, if the Secretary determines that the letter under paragraph (1) was issued in error or, after review of such response, the person had a reasonable basis for not notifying as required under subsection (a), the requirements of this paragraph shall not apply.

"(e) Expedited Inspections And Reviews.—If, based on notifications described in subsection (a) or any other relevant information, the Secretary concludes that there is, or is likely to be, a shortage of a device described in subsection (a), the Secretary may—

"(1) expedite the review of premarket submissions under sections 510(k), 513(f)(2), 515, and 520(m), that could help mitigate or prevent such shortage; or

"(2) expedite an inspection or reinspection of an establishment that could help mitigate or prevent such shortage.

"(f) Effect Of Notification.—The submission of a notification under subsection (a) shall not be construed—

"(1) as an admission that any product that is the subject of such notification violates any provision of this Act; or

"(2) as evidence of the entity's intent to market the product for an indication or use for which the product has not been approved or cleared by the Secretary.

"(g) Identification Of Essential Devices.—

"(1) IN GENERAL.—In the event of, or in advance of, a declaration of a public health emergency pursuant to section 319 of the Public Health Service Act, the Secretary shall designate and make publicly available, including on the public website of the Food and Drug Administration, a list of devices that are critical to preventing, screening, diagnosing, treating, or mitigating the spread

of a disease or condition during such emergency.
"(2) CONSIDERATION.—In developing such list, the Secretary shall take into consideration—
"(A) the medical necessity of devices;
"(B) the urgency to prevent serious injury or death; and
"(C) the availability of other devices.
"(3) UPDATES.—During the course of such public health emergency, the Secretary shall update the list of essential devices as necessary, including adding and removing devices.
"(h) Definitions.—For purposes of this section:
"(1) ESSENTIAL DEVICE.—The term 'essential device' means a device designated in a list in effect under subsection (g).
"(2) MANUFACTURER.—The term 'manufacturer' means the entity that holds the medical device marketing submission, or if a medical device marketing submission is not required, the entity responsible for listing the medical device under section 510.
"(3) MEANINGFUL DISRUPTION.—The term 'meaningful disruption'—
"(A) means a change in production that is reasonably likely to lead to a reduction in the supply of an essential device that is more than negligible and affects the ability to fill orders or meet expected demand for the device of the manufacturer or contract terminal sterilizer involved; and
"(B) does not include, so long as the manufacturer expects to resume operations in a short period of time, not to exceed 6 months, interruptions in—
"(i) manufacturing due to matters such as routine maintenance or insignificant changes; or
"(ii) manufacturing of components or raw materials.
"(4) SHORTAGE.—The term 'shortage', with respect to a device, means a period of time when the demand or projected demand for the device within the United States exceeds the supply of the device or a comparable device of that manufacturer or another manufacturer, including as a result of discontinuance of a device or an interruption in the manufacturing or importation of a device or a component of a device or the device constituent of a combination product.".
SEC. 70532. AUTHORITY TO DESTROY COUNTERFEIT DEVICES.
(a) In General.—Section 801(a) of the Federal Food, Drug, and Cosmetic Act (21 U.S.C. 381(a)) is amended—
(1) in the fourth sentence, by inserting "or counterfeit device" after "counterfeit drug"; and
(2) by striking "The Secretary of the Treasury shall cause the destruction of" and all that follows through "liable for costs pursuant to subsection (c)." and inserting the following: "The Secretary of the Treasury shall cause the destruction of any such article refused admission unless such article is exported, under regulations prescribed by the Secretary of the Treasury, within ninety days of the date of notice of such refusal or within such additional time

as may be permitted pursuant to such regulations, except that the Secretary of Health and Human Services may destroy, without the opportunity for export, any drug or device refused admission under this section, if such drug or device is valued at an amount that is $2,500 or less (or such higher amount as the Secretary of the Treasury may set by regulation pursuant to section 498(a)(1) of the Tariff Act of 1930 (19 U.S.C. 1498(a)(1))) and was not brought into compliance as described under subsection (b). The Secretary of Health and Human Services shall issue regulations providing for notice and an opportunity to appear before the Secretary of Health and Human Services and introduce testimony, as described in the first sentence of this subsection, on destruction of a drug or device under the seventh sentence of this subsection. The regulations shall provide that prior to destruction, appropriate due process is available to the owner or consignee seeking to challenge the decision to destroy the drug or device. Where the Secretary of Health and Human Services provides notice and an opportunity to appear and introduce testimony on the destruction of a drug or device, the Secretary of Health and Human Services shall store and, as applicable, dispose of the drug or device after the issuance of the notice, except that the owner and consignee shall remain liable for costs pursuant to subsection (c).".

(b) Definition.—Section 201(h) of the Federal Food, Drug, and Cosmetic Act (21 U.S.C. 321(h)) is amended—

(1) by redesignating subparagraphs (1), (2), and (3) as clauses (A), (B), and (C), respectively; and

(2) after making such redesignations—

(A) by striking "(h) The term" and inserting "(h)(1) The term"; and

(B) by adding at the end the following:

"(2) The term 'counterfeit device' means a device which, or the container, packaging, or labeling of which, without authorization, bears a trademark, trade name, or other identifying mark, imprint, or symbol, or any likeness thereof, or is manufactured using a design, of a device manufacturer, packer, or distributor other than the person or persons who in fact manufactured, packed, or distributed such device and which thereby falsely purports or is represented to be the product of, or to have been packed or distributed by, such other device manufacturer, packer, or distributor.

"(3) For purposes of subparagraph (2)—

"(A) the term 'manufactured' refers to any of the following activities: manufacture, preparation, propagation, compounding, assembly, or processing; and

"(B) the term 'manufacturer' means a person who is engaged in any of the activities listed in clause (A).".

SEC. 70533. REQUIRING THE STRATEGIC NATIONAL STOCKPILE TO INCLUDE CERTAIN TYPES OF MEDICAL SUPPLIES.

Section 319F–2(a)(1) of the Public Health Service Act (42 U.S.C. 247d–6b(a)(1)) is amended by inserting "(including personal protective equipment, ancillary medical supplies, and other supplies required for the administration of drugs, vaccines and other biological products, medical devices, and diagnostic tests)'" after "other supplies".

SEC. 70534. REPORTING REQUIREMENT FOR DRUG MANUFACTURERS.

(a) Establishments In A Foreign Country.—Section 510(i) of the Federal Food, Drug, and Cosmetic Act (21 U.S.C. 360(i)) is amended by inserting at the end the following new paragraph:

"(5) The requirements of paragraphs (1) and (2) shall apply to establishments within a foreign country engaged in the manufacture, preparation, propagation, compounding, or processing of any drug, including the active pharmaceutical ingredient, that is required to be listed pursuant to subsection (j). Such requirements shall apply regardless of whether the drug, including the active pharmaceutical ingredient, undergoes further manufacture, preparation, propagation, compounding, or processing at a separate establishment outside the United States prior to being imported or offered for import into the United States.".

(b) Listing Of Drugs.—Section 510(j) of the Federal Food, Drug, and Cosmetic Act (21 U.S.C. 360(j)) is amended—

(1) in paragraph (1)—

(A) in subparagraph (D), by striking "and" at the end;

(B) in subparagraph (E), by striking the period at the end and inserting "; and"; and

(C) by adding at the end the following new subparagraph:

"(F) in the case of a drug contained in the applicable list, a certification that the registrant has—

"(i) identified every other establishment where manufacturing is performed for the drug; and

"(ii) notified each known foreign establishment engaged in the manufacture, preparation, propagation, compounding, or processing of the drug, including the active pharmaceutical ingredient, of the inclusion of the drug in the list and the obligation to register.";

(2) by redesignating paragraphs (3) and (4) as paragraphs (4) and (5), respectively; and

(3) by inserting after paragraph (2) the following:

"(3) (A) Subject to subparagraph (B), each person who registers with the Secretary under this section shall report to the Secretary by electronic means in a form and manner as specified by the Secretary, with regard to drugs, once during the month of March of each year, once during the month of June of each year, once during the month of September of each year, and once during the month of December of each year, on the amount of each listed drug that was manufactured, prepared, propagated, compounded, or processed at each establishment registered by such person since the date the person last made a report under this paragraph. Such amount shall include the number of dosage units for each finished drug product intended for distribution in the United States, or amount of active pharmaceutical ingredient intended for distribution in the United States. The Secretary may require information reported under this subparagraph to be further delineated in such manner as the Secretary determines appropriate.

"(B) Notwithstanding subparagraph (A), the Secretary may issue an order exempting certain biological products or categories of biological products licensed under section 351 of the Public Health Service Act from some or all of the reporting requirements under such subparagraph if the Secretary determines that the application of such requirements to such products (or categories thereof) is not necessary to protect the public health.".

(c) Rules Of Construction.—

(1) Nothing in the amendments made by this section shall be construed—

(A) to limit or narrow, in any manner, the meaning or application of the provisions of subsection (i) or (j) of section 510 of the Federal Food, Drug, and Cosmetic Act (21 U.S.C. 360); or

(B) to affect any determination under either such subsection made prior to the date of enactment of this Act.

(2) Nothing in the amendments made by this section shall be construed—

(A) to limit or narrow the ability of the Secretary of Health and Human Services to share confidential commercial information pursuant to a memorandum of understanding, entered into before, on, or after the date of enactment of this section, between the Food and Drug Administration and another Federal department or agency; or

(B) as authorizing the Secretary to disclose any information that is confidential commercial or trade secret information subject to section 552(b)(4) of title 5, United States Code, or section 1905 of title 18, United States Code.

SEC. 70535. NATIONAL CENTERS OF EXCELLENCE IN CONTINUOUS PHARMACEUTICAL MANUFACTURING.

(a) In General.—Section 3016 of the 21st Century Cures Act (21 U.S.C. 399h) is amended to read as follows:

"SEC. 3016. NATIONAL CENTERS OF EXCELLENCE IN CONTINUOUS PHARMACEUTICAL MANUFACTURING.

"(a) In General.—The Secretary of Health and Human Services, acting through the Commissioner of Food and Drugs—

"(1) shall solicit and, beginning not later than one year after the date of enactment of the National Centers of Excellence in Continuous Pharmaceutical Manufacturing Act of 2019, receive requests from institutions of higher education to be designated as a National Center of Excellence in Continuous Pharmaceutical Manufacturing (in this section referred to as a 'National Center of Excellence') to support the advancement and development of continuous manufacturing; and

"(2) shall so designate any institution of higher education that—

"(A) requests such designation; and

"(B) meets the criteria specified in subsection (c).

"(b) Request For Designation.—A request for designation under subsection (a) shall be made to the Secretary at such time, in such manner, and containing such information as the Secretary may require. Any such request shall include a description of how the institution of higher education meets or plans to meet each of the criteria specified in subsection (c).

"(c) Criteria For Designation Described.—The criteria specified in this subsection with respect to an institution of higher education are that the institution has, as of the date of the submission of a request under subsection (a) by such institution—

"(1) physical and technical capacity for research and development of continuous manufacturing;

"(2) manufacturing knowledge-sharing networks with other institutions of higher education, large and small pharmaceutical manufacturers, generic and nonprescription manufacturers, contract manufacturers, and other entities;

"(3) proven capacity to design and demonstrate new, highly effective technology for use in continuous manufacturing;

"(4) a track record for creating and transferring knowledge with respect to continuous manufacturing;

"(5) the potential to train a future workforce for research on and implementation of advanced manufacturing and continuous manufacturing; and

"(6) experience in participating in and leading a continuous manufacturing technology partnership with other institutions of higher education, large and small pharmaceutical manufacturers, generic and nonprescription manufacturers, contract manufacturers, and other entities—

"(A) to support companies with continuous manufacturing in the United States;

"(B) to support Federal agencies with technical assistance, which may include regulatory and quality metric guidance as applicable, for advanced manufacturing and continuous manufacturing;

"(C) with respect to continuous manufacturing, to organize and conduct research and development activities needed to create new and more effective technology, capture and disseminate expertise, create intellectual property, and maintain technological leadership;

"(D) to develop best practices for designing continuous manufacturing; and

"(E) to assess and respond to the workforce needs for continuous manufacturing, including the development of training programs if needed.

"(d) Termination Of Designation.—The Secretary may terminate the designation of any National Center of Excellence designated under this section if the Secretary determines such National Center of Excellence no longer meets the criteria specified in subsection (c). Not later than 60 days before the effective date of such a termination, the Secretary shall provide written notice to the National Center of Excellence, including the rationale for such termination.

"(e) Conditions For Designation.—As a condition of designation as a National

Center of Excellence under this section, the Secretary shall require that an institution of higher education enter into an agreement with the Secretary under which the institution agrees—

"(1) to collaborate directly with the Food and Drug Administration to publish the reports required by subsection (g);

"(2) to share data with the Food and Drug Administration regarding best practices and research generated through the funding under subsection (f);

"(3) to develop, along with industry partners (which may include large and small biopharmaceutical manufacturers, generic and nonprescription manufacturers, and contract manufacturers) and another institution or institutions designated under this section, if any, a roadmap for developing a continuous manufacturing workforce;

"(4) to develop, along with industry partners and other institutions designated under this section, a roadmap for strengthening existing, and developing new, relationships with other institutions; and

"(5) to provide an annual report to the Food and Drug Administration regarding the institution's activities under this section, including a description of how the institution continues to meet and make progress on the criteria listed in subsection (c).

"(f) Funding.—

"(1) IN GENERAL.—The Secretary shall award funding, through grants, contracts, or cooperative agreements, to the National Centers of Excellence designated under this section for the purpose of studying and recommending improvements to continuous manufacturing, including such improvements as may enable the Centers—

"(A) to continue to meet the conditions specified in subsection (e); and

"(B) to expand capacity for research on, and development of, continuing manufacturing.

"(2) CONSISTENCY WITH FDA MISSION.—As a condition on receipt of funding under this subsection, a National Center of Excellence shall agree to consider any input from the Secretary regarding the use of funding that would—

"(A) help to further the advancement of continuous manufacturing through the National Center of Excellence; and

"(B) be relevant to the mission of the Food and Drug Administration.

"(3) AUTHORIZATION OF APPROPRIATIONS.—There is authorized to be appropriated to carry out this subsection $80,000,000 for the period of fiscal years 2021 through 2025.

"(4) RULE OF CONSTRUCTION.—Nothing in this section shall be construed as precluding a National Center for Excellence designated under this section from receiving funds under any other provision of this Act or any other Federal law.

"(g) Annual Review And Reports.—

"(1) ANNUAL REPORT.—Beginning not later than one year after the date on which the first designation is made under subsection (a), and annually thereafter, the Secretary shall—

"(A) submit to Congress a report describing the activities, partnerships and collaborations, Federal policy recommendations, previous and continuing funding, and findings of, and any other applicable information from, the National Centers of Excellence designated under this section; and

"(B) make such report available to the public in an easily accessible electronic format on the website of the Food and Drug Administration.

"(2) REVIEW OF NATIONAL CENTERS OF EXCELLENCE AND POTENTIAL DESIGNEES.—The Secretary shall periodically review the National Centers of Excellence designated under this section to ensure that such National Centers of Excellence continue to meet the criteria for designation under this section.

"(3) REPORT ON LONG-TERM VISION OF FDA ROLE.—Not later than 2 years after the date on which the first designation is made under subsection (a), the Secretary, in consultation with the National Centers of Excellence designated under this section, shall submit a report to the Congress on the long-term vision of the Department of Health and Human Services on the role of the Food and Drug Administration in supporting continuous manufacturing, including—

"(A) a national framework of principles related to the implementation and regulation of continuous manufacturing;

"(B) a plan for the development of Federal regulations and guidance for how advanced manufacturing and continuous manufacturing can be incorporated into the development of pharmaceuticals and regulatory responsibilities of the Food and Drug Administration; and

"(C) appropriate feedback solicited from the public, which may include other institutions, large and small biopharmaceutical manufacturers, generic and nonprescription manufacturers, and contract manufacturers.

"(h) Definitions.—In this section:

"(1) ADVANCED MANUFACTURING.—The term 'advanced manufacturing' means an approach for the manufacturing of pharmaceuticals that incorporates novel technology, or uses an established technique or technology in a new or innovative way (such as continuous manufacturing where the input materials are continuously transformed within the process by two or more unit operations) that enhances drug quality or improves the manufacturing process.

"(2) CONTINUOUS MANUFACTURING.—The term 'continuous manufacturing'—

"(A) means a process where the input materials are continuously fed into and transformed within the process, and the processed output materials are continuously removed from the system; and

"(B) consists of an integrated process that consists of a series of two or more unit operations.

"(3) INSTITUTION OF HIGHER EDUCATION.—The term 'institution of higher education' has the meaning given such term in section 101(a) of the Higher Education Act of 1965 (20 U.S.C. 1001(a)).

"(4) SECRETARY.—The term 'Secretary' means the Secretary of Health and Human Services, acting through the Commissioner of Food and Drugs.".

(b) Transition Rule.—Section 3016 of the 21st Century Cures Act (21 U.S.C. 399h), as in effect on the day before the date of the enactment of this section, shall apply with respect to grants awarded under such section before such date of enactment.

Subtitle D—Public Health Extenders

SEC. 70541. EXTENSION FOR COMMUNITY HEALTH CENTERS, THE NATIONAL HEALTH SERVICE CORPS, AND TEACHING HEALTH CENTERS THAT OPERATE GME PROGRAMS.

(a) Community Health Centers.—Section 10503(b)(1) of the Patient Protection and Affordable Care Act (42 U.S.C. 254b–2(b)(1)) is amended—

(1) in subparagraph (E), by striking "and" at the end;

(2) in subparagraph (F), by striking ", $4,000,000,000 for fiscal year 2019, and $2,575,342,466 for the period beginning on October 1, 2019, and ending on May 22, 2020; and" and inserting a semicolon; and

(3) by adding at the end the following:

"(G) $4,000,000,000 for each of fiscal years 2019 and 2020; and

"(H) $668,493,151 for the period beginning on October 1, 2020, and ending on November 30, 2020; and".

(b) National Health Service Corps.—Section 10503(b)(2) of the Patient Protection and Affordable Care Act (42 U.S.C. 254b–2(b)(2)) is amended—

(1) in subparagraph (F), by striking "and 2019; and" and inserting "through 2020; and"; and

(2) in subparagraph (G), by striking "$199,589,041 for the period beginning on October 1, 2019, and ending on May 22, 2020" and inserting "$51,808,220 for the period beginning on October 1, 2020, and ending on November 30, 2020."

(c) Teaching Health Centers That Operate Graduate Medical Education Programs.—Section 340H(g)(1) of the Public Health Service Act (42 U.S.C. 256h(g)(1)) is amended—

(1) by striking "and 2019" and inserting "through 2020" and;

(2) by striking "$81,445,205 for the period beginning on October 1, 2019, and ending on May 22, 2020" and inserting "$21,141,096 for the period beginning on October 1, 2020, and ending on November 30, 2020".

SEC. 70542. DIABETES PROGRAMS.

(a) Type I.—Section 330B(b)(2)(D) of the Public Health Service Act (42 U.S.C. 254c–2(b)(2)(D)) is amended by striking "and 2019, and $96,575,342 for the period beginning on October 1, 2019, and ending on May 22, 2020" and inserting "through 2020, and $25,068,494 for the period beginning on October 1, 2020, and ending on November 30, 2020".

(b) Indians.—Section 330C(c)(2)(D) of the Public Health Service Act (42 U.S.C. 254c–3(c)(2)(D)) is amended by striking "and 2019, and $96,575,342 for the period beginning on October 1, 2019, and ending on May 22, 2020" and inserting "through 2020, and $25,068,494 for the period beginning on October 1, 2020, and ending on November 30, 2020".

Subtitle E—Other Extenders

SEC. 70551. EXTENSION OF SEXUAL RISK AVOIDANCE EDUCATION PROGRAM.

Section 510 of the Social Security Act (42 U.S.C. 710) is amended—

(1) in subsection (a)—

(A) in paragraph (1), in the matter preceding subparagraph (A), by striking "and 2019 and for the period beginning October 1, 2019, and ending May 22, 2020" and inserting "through 2020 and for the period beginning on October 1, 2020, and ending on November 30, 2020";

(B) in paragraph (2)(A), by striking "and 2019 and for the period beginning October 1, 2019, and ending May 22, 2020" and inserting "through 2020, and for the period beginning on October 1, 2020, and ending on November 30, 2020"; and

(C) in paragraphs (1), (2)(A), and (2)(B)(i), by striking "with respect to such period, for fiscal year 2020" each place it appears and inserting "with respect to such period, for fiscal year 2021"; and

(2) in subsection (f)(1), by striking "and 2019 and $48,287,671 for the period beginning October 1, 2019, and ending May 22, 2020" and inserting "through 2020, and $12,534,247 for the period beginning on October 1, 2020, and ending on November 30, 2020".

SEC. 70552. EXTENSION OF PERSONAL RESPONSIBILITY EDUCATION PROGRAM.

Section 513 of the Social Security Act (42 U.S.C. 713) is amended—

(1) in subsection (a)(1)—

(A) in subparagraph (A), in the matter preceding clause (i), by striking "through 2019 and for the period beginning October 1, 2019, and ending May 22, 2020" and inserting "through 2020 and for the period beginning on October 1, 2020, and ending November 30, 2020"; and

(B) in subparagraph (B)(i), by striking "beginning October 1, 2019, and ending May 22, 2020" and inserting "beginning on October 1, 2020, and ending November 30, 2020";

(2) in subsection (a)(4)(A), by striking "2019" each place it appears and inserting "2020"; and

(3) in subsection (f), by striking "through 2019 and $48,287,671 for the period beginning October 1, 2019, and ending May 22, 2020" and inserting "through 2020, and $12,534,247 for the period beginning on October 1, 2020, and ending on November 30, 2020".

Subtitle F—Miscellaneous

SEC. 70561. HEALTH PROVIDER LOAN PROGRAM.

(a) In General.—Not later than 30 days after the date of enactment of this title, the Secretary shall establish a program under which loans shall be made to eligible health care organizations to assist such organizations with anticipated revenue loss or higher operating costs as a result of the COVID-19 emergency.

(b) Program Requirements.—The Secretary shall establish standards and guidelines for application, loan amount, repayment, and extension, and shall consider the eligible health care organization's financial condition, service in an area heavily impacted by the COVID-19 emergency, or other factors deemed appropriate.

(c) Eligible Health Care Organizations.—To be eligible for a loan under subsection (a), an entity shall—

(1) be a health care provider or supplier that receives assistance or otherwise participates in the Medicare or Medicaid program under title XVIII or XIX of the Social Security Act (42 U.S.C. 1395 and 1396 et seq.), including a hospital, critical access hospital, skilled nursing facility, physician practice, home health provider, community health center, ambulatory surgical care center, or hospice; and

(2) submit to the Secretary an application at such time, in such manner, and containing such information as the Secretary may require.

(d) Terms And Conditions.—

(1) INTEREST.—A loan under this section shall have a rate of interest of not to exceed 2 percent. Interest shall begin to accrue on the date that is 60 days after the date of origination.

(2) TERM.—The term of a loan under this section shall be 1 year minus one day. A borrower shall have the option to extend such term for a total of not to exceed 19 years. Further extensions may be granted if approval by the Secretary.

(3) SECURITY.—An eligible health care organization shall not be required to provide security for a loan under this section.

(4) PAYMENTS.—Loan payments shall be made on a biannual basis.

(e) Definitions.—In this section:

(1) COVID-19 EMERGENCY.—The term "COVID-19 emergency" means the national emergency declared by the President under the National Emergencies Act (50 U.S.C. 1601 et seq.) with respect to the Coronavirus Disease 2019 (COVID-19).

(2) SECRETARY.—The term "Secretary" means the Secretary of Health and Human Services.

(f) Use Of Certain Funds.—Loan recipients may use funds such recipients were awarded under the Public Health and Social Services Emergency Fund or the Health Provider Assistance Fund established under section 562 to repay loans awarded under this section, provided the funds from the Public Health and Social Services Emergency Fund or the Health Provider Assistance Fund were awarded based on foregone revenue.

(g) Clarification.—No individual, employer, or other entity may be restricted from participating in or benefitting from any exemption or benefit under this section, based on any factor that is unrelated to its qualifications to perform the required services.

(h) Appropriations.—There is authorized to be appropriated, and there is appropriated, to carry out this section, $80,000,000,000 for fiscal year 2020, to remain available until expended.

DIVISION G—HEALTH POLICIES

TITLE I—MEDICAID

SEC. 70101. INCREASING FEDERAL SUPPORT TO STATE MEDICAID PROGRAMS DURING ECONOMIC DOWNTURNS.

(a) In General.—Section 1905 of the Social Security Act (42 U.S.C. 1396d) is amended—

(1) in subsection (b), by striking "and (ff)" and inserting "(ff), and (gg)"; and

(2) by adding at the end the following new subsection:

"(gg) Increased FMAP During Economic Downturns.—

"(1) IN GENERAL.—Notwithstanding subsection (b), (y), or (z)(2), if a fiscal quarter that begins on or after January 1, 2020, is an economic downturn quarter (as defined in paragraph (2)) with respect to a State, then the Federal medical assistance percentage applicable to amounts expended by the State for medical assistance for services furnished during such quarter shall be increased in accordance with paragraphs (3) and (4).

"(2) ECONOMIC DOWNTURN QUARTER.—

"(A) IN GENERAL.—

"(i) IN GENERAL.—In this subsection, the term 'economic downturn quarter' means, with respect to a State, a fiscal quarter during which the State's unemployment rate for the quarter exceeds the percentage determined for the State and quarter under clause (ii).

"(ii) THRESHOLD PERCENTAGE.—The percentage determined under this clause for a State and fiscal quarter is the percentage equal to the lower of—

"(I) the State unemployment rate at the 20th percentile of the distribution of the State's quarterly unemployment rates for the 60-quarter period preceding the quarter involved, increased by 1 percentage point; and

"(II) the State's average quarterly unemployment rate for the 12-quarter period preceding the quarter involved, increased by 1 percentage point.

"(B) UNEMPLOYMENT DATA.—

"(i) IN GENERAL.—Except as provided in clause (ii), for purposes of determining unemployment rates for a State and a quarter under this paragraph, the Secretary shall use data from the Local Area Unemployment Statistics from the Bureau of Labor Statistics.

"(ii) APPLICATION TO CERTAIN TERRITORIES.—In the case of the Virgin Islands, Guam, the Northern Mariana Islands, or American Samoa, the Secretary shall use data from the U–6 unemployment measure of the Bureau of Labor Statistics to make any necessary determinations under subparagraph (A).

"(3) FMAP INCREASE DURING ECONOMIC DOWNTURN QUARTER.—

"(A) IN GENERAL.—During a fiscal quarter that is an economic downturn quarter with respect to a State, the Federal medical assistance percentage otherwise determined for the State and quarter under subsection (b) and, if applicable, the Federal medical assistance percentage applicable under subsection (y), (z)(2), or (ff) with respect to medical assistance furnished by the State during such quarter to individuals described in either such subsection shall be increased by the number of percentage points (rounded to the nearest tenth of a percentage point) equal to the product of—

"(i) the number of percentage points (rounded to the nearest tenth of a percentage point) by which the unemployment rate for the State and quarter exceeds the percentage determined for the State and quarter under paragraph (2)(A)(ii); and

"(ii) 4.8.

"(B) APPLICATION OF COVID–19 FMAP INCREASE.—Any increase applicable to the Federal medical assistance percentage of a State for a fiscal quarter under subparagraph (A) shall be in addition to any increase to such percentage for such quarter made pursuant to section 6008(a) of the Families First Coronavirus Response Act.

"(C) LIMITATION.—In no case shall an increase to the Federal medical assistance percentage of a State under this paragraph result in a Federal medical assistance percentage that exceeds 95 percent.

"(D) SCOPE OF APPLICATION.—Any increase to the Federal medical assistance percentage of a State for a fiscal quarter under this paragraph shall only apply with respect to payments for amounts expended by the State for medical assistance for services furnished during such quarter and shall not apply with respect to—

"(i) disproportionate share hospital payments described in section 1923;

"(ii) payments under title IV or XXI;

"(iii) any payments under this title that are based on the enhanced FMAP described in section 2105(b); or

"(iv) any payments under this title that are based on a Federal medical assistance percentage determined for a State under subsection (aa) (but only to the extent that such Federal medical assistance percentage is higher than the economic recovery FMAP).

"(4) ADVANCE PAYMENT; RETROSPECTIVE ADJUSTMENT.—

"(A) IN GENERAL.—Prior to the beginning of each fiscal quarter that begins on or after July 1, 2020, the Secretary shall, with respect to each State—

"(i) determine the increase (if any) that is expected to apply to the Federal medical assistance percentage of such State for such quarter under this subsection based on the projections made for the State and quarter under subparagraph (B); and

"(ii) shall apply such increase to the Federal medical assistance percentage of the State for purposes of making payments to the State for amounts expended during such quarter as medical assistance under the State plan.

"(B) PROJECTION OF STATE UNEMPLOYMENT RATES.—Prior to the beginning of each fiscal quarter that begins on or after July 1, 2020, the

Secretary, acting through the Chief Actuary of the Centers for Medicare & Medicaid Services, shall, using the most recently available data described in paragraph (2)(B), make projections with respect to—

"(i) the unemployment rates for each State for such quarter;

"(ii) the threshold percentages described in paragraph (2)(A)(ii) for each State for such quarter; and

"(iii) the national unemployment rate for such quarter.

"(C) RETROSPECTIVE ADJUSTMENT.—As soon as practicable after final unemployment data becomes available for a fiscal quarter that begins on or after July 1, 2020, the Secretary shall, with respect to each State—

"(i) make a final determination of the increase (if any) applicable to the Federal medical assistance percentage of the State for the quarter under this subsection; and

"(ii) in accordance with subsection (d)(2) of section 1903, reduce or increase the amount payable to the State under subsection (a) of such section for a subsequent fiscal quarter to the extent of any overpayment or underpayment which the Secretary determines was made as a result of a miscalculation of the increase applicable to the Federal medical assistance percentage of the State for such prior fiscal quarter under this subsection.

"(5) RETROSPECTIVE APPLICATION OF OVER-THE-LIMIT FMAP INCREASES.—

"(A) IN GENERAL.—If a State has excess percentage points with respect to an economic downturn quarter and an applicable FMAP (as determined under subparagraph (B)), the State may elect to apply such excess percentage points to increase such applicable FMAP for one or more quarters during the look-back period for the State and economic downturn quarter in accordance with this paragraph.

"(B) EXCESS PERCENTAGE POINTS.—For purposes of this paragraph, the number of excess percentage points for a State, economic downturn quarter, and an applicable FMAP shall be equal to the number of percentage points by which—

"(i) the applicable FMAP for the State and quarter (after application of paragraph (3) but without regard to subparagraph (C) of such paragraph); exceeds

"(ii) 95 percent.

"(C) EFFECT OF APPLICATION OF EXCESS PERCENTAGE POINTS.—If a State elects to apply excess percentage points to an applicable FMAP to a quarter during a look-back period under this paragraph, the Secretary shall determine the additional amount of payment under section 1903(a) to which the State would have been entitled for such quarter if the applicable FMAP (as so increased) had been in effect for such quarter, and shall treat such additional amount as an underpayment for such quarter.

"(D) DISTRIBUTION OF EXCESS PERCENTAGE POINTS.—A State that has excess percentage points with respect to an economic downturn quarter

and applicable FMAP may elect to divide such points among more than 1 quarter during the look-back period for such State and quarter provided that no excess percentage point (or fraction of an excess percentage point) is applied to the applicable FMAP of more than 1 quarter.
"(E) LIMITATIONS.—
"(i) NO INCREASES OVER 100 PERCENT.—A State may not increase an applicable FMAP for any quarter during a look-back period under this paragraph if such increase would result in the applicable FMAP for such quarter exceeding 100 percent.
"(ii) SCOPE OF APPLICATION.—Any increase to an applicable FMAP of a State for a fiscal quarter under this paragraph—
"(I) shall only apply with respect to payments for amounts expended by the State for medical assistance for services furnished during such quarter to which such applicable FMAP is applicable; and
"(II) shall not apply with respect to payments described in paragraph (3)(D).
"(F) DEFINITIONS.—In this paragraph:
"(i) APPLICABLE FMAP.—The term 'applicable FMAP' means, with respect to a State and fiscal quarter—
"(I) the Federal medical assistance percentage determined for the State and quarter under subsection (b);
"(II) the Federal medical assistance percentage applicable under subsection (y);
"(III) the Federal medical assistance percentage applicable under subsection (z)(2); or
"(IV) the Federal medical assistance percentage determined for the State and quarter under subsection (ff).
"(ii) LOOK-BACK PERIOD.—The term 'look-back period' means, with respect to a State and a fiscal quarter that is an economic downturn quarter for the State, the period of 4 fiscal quarters that ends with the fourth quarter which precedes the most recent fiscal quarters that was not an economic downturn quarter for the State.
"(6) REQUIREMENT FOR ALL STATES.—A State may not receive an increase in the Federal medical assistance percentage for such State under this subsection, with respect to a fiscal quarter, if—
"(A) eligibility standards, methodologies, or procedures under the State plan or a waiver of such plan are more restrictive during such quarter than the eligibility standards, methodologies, or procedures, respectively, under such plan (or waiver) as in effect on the last day of the most recent fiscal quarter that was not an economic downturn quarter for the State;
"(B) the amount of any premium imposed by the State pursuant to section 1916 or 1916A during such quarter, with respect to an individual enrolled under such plan (or waiver), exceeds the amount of such premium as of the date described in subparagraph (A); or
"(C) the State fails to provide that an individual who is enrolled for benefits

under such plan (or waiver) as of the date described in subparagraph (A) or enrolls for benefits under such plan (or waiver) during the period beginning with such date and ending with the day before the first day of the next quarter that is not an economic downturn quarter for the State shall be treated as eligible for such benefits for not less than 12 months (or, if such period is less than 12 months, throughout such period) unless the individual requests a voluntary termination of eligibility or the individual ceases to be a resident of the State.".

(b) Exclusion Of Economic Downturn FMAP Increases From Territorial Caps.—Section 1108 of the Social Security Act (42 U.S.C. 1308) is amended—

(1) in subsection (f), in the matter preceding paragraph (1), by striking "subsection (g) and section 1935(e)(1)(B)" and inserting "subsections (g) and (h) and section 1935(e)(1)(B)"; and

(2) by adding at the end the following:

"(h) Exclusion From Caps Of Amounts Attributable To Economic Downturn FMAP.—The portion of any payment made to a territory for a fiscal year that is attributable to an increase in the Federal medical assistance percentage for a fiscal quarter during such year under section 1905(gg) shall not be taken into account for purposes of applying payment limits under subsections (f) and (g).".

SEC. 70102. LIMITATION ON ADDITIONAL SECRETARIAL ACTION WITH RESPECT TO MEDICAID SUPPLEMENTAL PAYMENTS REPORTING REQUIREMENTS.

(a) In General.—Notwithstanding any other provision of law, during the period that begins on the date of enactment of this section and ends the date that is 2 years after the last day of the emergency period defined in paragraph (1)(B) of section 1135(g) of the Social Security Act (42 U.S.C. 1320b–5(g)), the Secretary of Health and Human Services shall not take any action (through promulgation of regulation, issue of regulatory guidance, or otherwise) to—

(1) finalize or otherwise implement provisions contained in the proposed rule published on November 18, 2019, on pages 63722 through 63785 of volume 84, Federal Register (relating to parts 430, 433, 447, 455, and 457 of title 42, Code of Federal Regulations); or

(2) promulgate or implement any rule or provision similar to the provisions described in paragraph (1) pertaining to the Medicaid program established under title XIX of the Social Security Act (42 U.S.C. 1396 et seq.) or the State Children's Health Insurance Program established under title XXI of such Act (42 U.S.C. 1397aa et seq.).

(b) Continuation Of Other Secretarial Authority.—Nothing in this section shall be construed as prohibiting the Secretary during the period described in subsection (a) from taking any action (through promulgation of regulation, issuance of regulatory guidance, or other administrative action) to enforce a provision of law in effect as of the date of enactment of this section with respect to the Medicaid program established under title XIX of the Social Security Act (42 U.S.C. 1396 et seq.) or the State Children's Health Insurance Program established under title XXI of such Act (42 U.S.C. 1397aa et seq.), or to promulgate or implement a new rule or provision during such period with respect to such programs, other than a rule or provision described in subsection (a) and subject to the prohibition set forth in that subsection.

SEC. 70103. AUTHORITY TO AWARD MEDICAID HCBS GRANTS TO RESPOND TO THE COVID–19 PUBLIC HEALTH EMERGENCY.

(a) In General.—The Secretary is authorized to award grants to States in accordance with this section to enhance access to home and community-based services during the COVID–19 public health emergency period.

(b) Definitions.—In this section:

(1) COVID–19 PUBLIC HEALTH EMERGENCY PERIOD.—The term "COVID–19 public health emergency period" means the portion of the emergency period defined in paragraph (1)(B) of section 1135(g) of the Social Security Act (42 U.S.C. 1320b–5(g)) beginning on or after the date of the enactment of this Act.

(2) ELIGIBLE INDIVIDUAL.—The term "eligible individual" means an individual who is eligible for or enrolled for medical assistance under a State Medicaid program.

(3) HOME AND COMMUNITY-BASED SERVICES.—The term "home and community-based services" means, with respect to a State Medicaid program, home and community-based services (including home health and personal care services) that are provided under the State's qualified HCBS program or that could be provided under such a program but are otherwise provided under the Medicaid program.

(4) INDIAN TRIBE.—The term "Indian tribe" means an Indian tribe, a tribal organization, or an urban Indian organization (as such terms are defined in section 4 of the Indian Health Care Improvement Act (25 U.S.C. 1603)), and includes a tribal consortium of Indian tribes or tribal organizations (as so defined).

(5) MEDICAID PROGRAM.—The term "Medicaid program" means, with respect to a State, the State program under title XIX of the Social Security Act (42 U.S.C. 1396 et seq.) (including any waiver or demonstration under such title or under section 1115 of such Act (42 U.S.C. 1315) relating to such title).

(6) SECRETARY.—The term "Secretary" means the Secretary of Health and Human Services.

(7) STATE.—The term "State" has the meaning given such term for purposes of title XIX of the Social Security Act (42 U.S.C. 1396 et seq.).

(8) QUALIFIED HCBS PROGRAM.—The term "qualified HCBS program" means a program providing home and community-based services operating under a State Medicaid program, whether or not operating under waiver authority.

(c) Grants To States.—
(1) IN GENERAL.—During the COVID–19 public health emergency period, the Secretary may award grants to States with applications meeting the requirements of paragraph (2).
(2) APPLICATION REQUIREMENTS.—A State seeking a grant under this section shall submit an application to the Secretary at such time, in such form and manner, and containing such information as the Secretary shall require.
(3) LIMITATIONS.—
(A) TERMINATION OF AUTHORITY.—The Secretary shall not award any grants under this section with respect to a State that submits an application after the date that is 60 days after the end of the COVID–19 public health emergency period.
(B) USE OF FUNDS.—A State to which a grant is made under this section shall only use grant funds in accordance with subsection (d).
(C) MAINTENANCE OF STATE EFFORT.—Federal funds paid to a State pursuant to this section must be used to supplement, but not supplant, the level of State funds expended for home and community-based services for eligible individuals programs in effect for such individuals at the time the grant is awarded under this section.
(4) MONTHLY GRANT PAYMENT AMOUNTS.—
(A) IN GENERAL.—Subject to paragraph (5), the Secretary shall pay to each State that is awarded a grant under this section, for each month during the State's grant period (as defined in subparagraph (C)), an amount equal to 15 percent of the amount determined for the State under subparagraph (B).
(B) AVERAGE MONTHLY HCBS EXPENDITURES.—The amount determined for a State under this subparagraph is the amount equal to—
(i) the sum of—
(I) the average annual amount of State expenditures under title XIX of the Social Security Act (42 U.S.C. 1396 et seq.) that are attributable to providing medical assistance for home and community-based services for the 3 most recent fiscal years for which data is available; and
(II) the average annual amount, if any, received by the State pursuant to an MFP demonstration project conducted under section 6071 of the Deficit Reduction Act of 2005 (42 U.S.C. 1396a note) for the 3 most recent fiscal years for which data is available; divided by
(ii) 12.
(C) GRANT PERIOD DEFINED.—In this paragraph, the term "grant period" means, with respect to a State, the period of months—
(i) beginning with the month in which the Secretary approves the State's application for a grant under this section; and
(ii) ending with the 12th month that begins after the end of the COVID–19 public health emergency period.
(5) GRANTS TO INDIAN TRIBES.—
(A) IN GENERAL.—During the COVID–19 public health emergency period,

the Secretary may award grants to an Indian tribe in the same manner, and subject to the same requirements, as apply to a State, except as otherwise provided in this paragraph.

(B) APPLICATION.—Any Indian tribe seeking a grant under this section shall submit to the Secretary an application that includes (in addition to any other information the Secretary shall require) an identification of the population and service area or areas to be served by the activities and programs that will be funded by the grant.

(C) MONTHLY GRANT PAYMENT AMOUNTS.—

(i) IN GENERAL.—The Secretary shall pay to each Indian tribe that is awarded a grant under this section, for each month during the tribe's grant period (as defined in clause (iii)), an amount equal to 15 percent of the amount determined for the tribe under clause (ii).

(ii) TRIBAL SHARE OF MONTHLY HCBS EXPENDITURES.—The amount determined for an Indian tribe under this clause is equal to the—

(I) the total of the average annual amount of State expenditures made by a State or States under title XIX of the Social Security Act (42 U.S.C. 1396 et seq.) that are attributable to providing medical assistance for home and community-based services to eligible individuals who reside in the service area or areas identified by the tribe pursuant to subparagraph (B) for the 3 most recent fiscal years for which data is available; divided by

(II) 12.

(iii) GRANT PERIOD.—The term "grant period" has the same meaning with respect to an Indian tribe as the term has with respect to a State under paragraph (4)(C).

(D) REDUCTION OF STATE GRANT AMOUNTS.—If any State in which lies a service area or areas identified by an Indian tribe in a successful grant application pursuant to subparagraph (B) is also awarded a grant under this section, the Secretary shall reduce the amount payable to such State each month under paragraph (4) by the portion of the amount payable to the Indian tribe under this paragraph that is attributable to expenditures by the State.

(d) Permissible Uses Of Funds.—

(1) IN GENERAL.—A State to which a grant is made under this section may use grant funds—

(A) to work with community partners such as Area Agencies on Aging, Independent Living Centers, non-profit home and community based service providers, and other entities providing home and community-based services;

(B) during the COVID–19 public health emergency period, for the purposes described in paragraph (2); and

(C) after the end of such period, for the purposes described in paragraph (3).

(2) PERMISSIBLE USES DURING THE EMERGENCY PERIOD.—The purposes described in this paragraph for which a State may use grant funds awarded under this section are the following:

(A) To increase rates for home health and direct service worker agencies to provide home and community-based services under the State Medicaid program, provided that any agency or individual that receives payment under such an increased rate increases the compensation it pays its home health or direct service workers.

(B) To provide paid sick leave, paid family leave, and paid medical leave for home health workers and direct service workers.

(C) To provide hazard pay, overtime pay, and shift differential pay for home health workers and direct service workers.

(D) To provide home and community-based services to eligible individuals who are on waiting lists for programs approved under sections 1115 or 1915 of the Social Security Act (42 U.S.C. 1315, 1396n).

(E) To purchase emergency supplies and equipment necessary to enhance access to services and to protect the health and well-being of home health workers and direct service workers.

(F) To pay for home health worker and direct service worker travel to conduct home and community-based services.

(G) To recruit new direct service workers and home health workers.

(H) To support family care providers of eligible individuals with needed supplies and equipment and pay.

(I) To pay for training for direct service workers and home health workers that is specific to the COVID–19 public health emergency.

(J) To pay for assistive technologies, staffing, and other costs incurred during the public health emergency in order to facility community integration and ensure an individual's person-centered service plan continue to be fully implemented.

(K) To support direct service workers and home health workers going to nursing facilities, hospitals, institutions, and quarantine settings to provide services to eligible individuals who usually receive home and community-based services and have chosen to temporarily move to a more restrictive setting.

(L) To prepare information and public health and educational materials in accessible formats about prevention, treatment, recovery and other aspects of COVID–19 for eligible individuals, their families, and the general community served by home health and direct service agencies, including formats accessible to people with low literacy or intellectual disabilities.

(M) To pay for American sign language interpreters to assist in providing home and community-based services to eligible individuals and to inform the general public about COVID–19.

(N) To allow for day service providers to shift to providing home-based services.

(O) To pay for COVID–19 testing in home settings.

(P) To pay for other expenses deemed appropriate by the Secretary and which meet the criteria of the home and community-based settings rule.

(3) PERMISSIBLE USES AFTER THE EMERGENCY PERIOD.—The purpose described in this paragraph for which a State may use grant funds awarded under this section is to assist eligible individuals who had to relocate to a nursing facility or institutional setting from their homes during the COVID–19 public health emergency period in—

(A) moving back to their homes (including by paying for moving costs);

(B) resuming home and community-based services;

(C) receiving mental health services and necessary rehabilitative service to regain skills lost while relocated during the public health emergency period; and

(D) continuing home and community-based services for eligible individuals who were served from a waiting list for such services during the public health emergency period.

(e) Reporting Requirements.—

(1) STATE REPORTING REQUIREMENTS.—Not later than 18 months after the end of the COVID–19 public health emergency period, any State that received a grant under this section shall submit a report to the Secretary that contains the following information:

(A) Activities and programs that were funded using grant amounts.

(B) The number of eligible individuals who were served by such activities and programs.

(C) The number of eligible individuals who were able to resume home and community-based services as a result of such activities and programs.

(2) HHS REPORT.—Not later than 18 months after the end of the COVID–19 public health emergency period, the Secretary shall issue a public summary of the grants awarded under this section.

(f) Appropriation.—

(1) IN GENERAL.—Subject to paragraph (2), there are appropriated for fiscal year 2020 from any funds in the Treasury not otherwise appropriated such sums as are necessary to carry out this section, to remain available until expended.

(2) AVAILABILITY OF APPROPRIATIONS.—Amounts made available under paragraph (1) shall not be available for the awarding of grants to States that do not submit an application for such a grant before the date described in subsection (c)(3)(A).

(3) UNUSED GRANT FUNDS.—A State that receives a grant under this section shall return to the Secretary any portion of such grant that is unused as of the date that is 1 year after the last day of the COVID–19 public health emergency period, and such returned portion shall revert to the Treasury.

(g) Providing Home And Community-Based Services In Acute Care Hospitals.—Section 1902(h) of the Social Security Act (42 U.S.C. 1396a(h)) is amended—

(1) by inserting "(1)" after "(h)";

(2) by inserting ", home and community-based services provided under

subsection (c), (d), or (i) of section 1915 or under a waiver under section 1115, self-directed personal assistance services provided pursuant to a written plan of care under section 1915(j), and home and community-based attendant services and supports under section 1915(k)" before the period; and

(3) by adding at the end the following:

"(2) Nothing in this title, title XVIII, or title XI shall be construed as prohibiting receipt of any care or services specified in paragraph (1) in an acute care hospital that are—

"(A) identified in an individual's person-centered plan of services and supports (or comparable plan of care);

"(B) provided to meet needs of the individual that are not met through the provision of hospital services;

"(C) not a substitute for services that the hospital is obligated to provide through its conditions of participation or under Federal or State law; and

"(D) designed to ensure smooth transitions between acute care settings and home and community-based settings, and to preserve the individual's functions.".

SEC. 70104. DELAY IN REDUCTION OF FMAP FOR MEDICAID PERSONAL CARE SERVICES FURNISHED WITHOUT AN ELECTRONIC VISIT VERIFICATION SYSTEM.

Section 1903(l) of the Social Security Act (42 U.S.C. 1396b(l)) is amended—

(1) in paragraph (1)—

(A) by striking "January 1, 2020" and inserting "the date that is 6 months after the end of the emergency period described in section 1135(g)(1)(B)"; and

(B) in subparagraph (A), by inserting "(if applicable)" after "percentage points" each place it appears; and

(2) in paragraph (4)(A)(i), by inserting before the semicolon the following: "(if applicable) or for calendar quarters occurring during the period beginning on the date that is 6 months after the end of the emergency period described in section 1135(g)(1)(B) and ending on the date that is 1 year after the end of such period".

SEC. 70105. COVERAGE AT NO COST SHARING OF COVID–19 VACCINE AND TREATMENT.

(a) Medicaid.—

(1) IN GENERAL.—Section 1905(a)(4) of the Social Security Act (42 U.S.C. 1396d(a)(4)) is amended—

(A) by striking "and (D)" and inserting "(D)"; and

(B) by striking the semicolon at the end and inserting "; (E) a COVID–19 vaccine licensed under section 351 of the Public Health Service Act and the administration of such vaccine; and (F) items and services furnished for the treatment of COVID–19 or a condition that may complicate the treatment of COVID–19;".

(2) PROHIBITION OF COST SHARING.—

(A) IN GENERAL.—Subsections (a)(2) and (b)(2) of section 1916 of the Social Security Act (42 U.S.C. 1396o), as amended by section 6004(a)(2)(A) of the Families First Coronavirus Response Act, are each amended—

(i) in subparagraph (F), by striking "or" at the end;

(ii) in subparagraph (G), by striking "; and" and inserting ", or"; and

(iii) by adding at the end the following subparagraphs:

"(H) a COVID–19 vaccine licensed under section 351 of the Public Health Service Act and the administration of such vaccine, or

"(I) any item or service furnished for the treatment of COVID–19 or a condition that may complicate the treatment of COVID–19; and".

(B) APPLICATION TO ALTERNATIVE COST SHARING.—Section 1916A(b)(3)(B) of the Social Security Act (42 U.S.C. 1396o–1(b)(3)(B)), as amended by section 6004(a)(2)(B) of the Families First Coronavirus Response Act, is amended—

(i) in clause (xi), by striking "any visit" and inserting "any service"; and

(ii) by adding at the end the following clauses:

"(xii) A COVID–19 vaccine licensed under section 351 of the Public Health Service Act and the administration of such vaccine.

"(xiii) An item or service furnished for the treatment of COVID–19 or a condition that may complicate the treatment of COVID–19.".

(C) CLARIFICATION.—The amendments made this subsection shall apply with respect to a State plan of a territory in the same manner as a State plan of one of the 50 States.

(b) State Pediatric Vaccine Distribution Program.—Section 1928 of the Social Security Act (42 U.S.C. 1396s) is amended—

(1) in subsection (a)(1)—

(A) in subparagraph (A), by striking "; and" and inserting a semicolon;

(B) in subparagraph (B), by striking the period and inserting "; and"; and

(C) by adding at the end the following subparagraph:

"(C) each vaccine-eligible child (as defined in subsection (b)) is entitled to receive a COVID–19 vaccine from a program-registered provider (as defined in subsection (h)(8)) without charge for—

"(i) the cost of such vaccine; or

"(ii) the administration of such vaccine.";

(2) in subsection (c)(2)—

(A) in subparagraph (C)(ii), by inserting ", but may not impose a fee for the administration of a COVID–19 vaccine" before the period; and

(B) by adding at the end the following subparagraph:

"(D) The provider will provide and administer an approved COVID–19 vaccine to a vaccine-eligible child in accordance with the same requirements as apply under the preceding subparagraphs to the provision and administration of a qualified pediatric vaccine to such a child."; and

(3) in subsection (d)(1), in the first sentence, by inserting ", including with

respect to a COVID–19 vaccine licensed under section 351 of the Public Health Service Act" before the period.

(c) CHIP.—

(1) IN GENERAL.—Section 2103(c) of the Social Security Act (42 U.S.C. 1397cc(c)), as amended by section 6004(b)(1) of the Families First Coronavirus Response Act, is amended by adding at the end the following paragraph:

"(11) COVERAGE OF COVID–19 VACCINES AND TREATMENT.—The child health assistance provided to a targeted low-income child shall include coverage of—

"(A) any COVID–19 vaccine licensed under section 351 of the Public Health Service Act and the administration of such vaccine; and

"(B) any item or service furnished for the treatment of COVID–19 or a condition that may complicate the treatment of COVID–19.".

(2) PROHIBITION OF COST SHARING.—Section 2103(e)(2) of the Social Security Act (42 U.S.C. 1397cc(e)(2)), as amended by section 6004(b)(3) of the Families First Coronavirus Response Act, is amended—

(A) in the paragraph header, by inserting "A COVID–19 VACCINE, COVID–19 TREATMENT," before "OR PREGNANCY-RELATED ASSISTANCE"; and

(B) by striking "visits described in section 1916(a)(2)(G), or" and inserting "services described in section 1916(a)(2)(G), vaccines described in section 1916(a)(2)(H), items or services described in section 1916(a)(2)(I), or".

(d) Conforming Amendments.—Section 1937 of the Social Security Act (42 U.S.C. 1396u–7) is amended—

(1) in subsection (a)(1)(B), by inserting ", under subclause (XXIII) of section 1902(a)(10)(A)(ii)," after "section 1902(a)(10)(A)(i)"; and

(2) in subsection (b)(5), by adding before the period the following: ", and, effective on the date of the enactment of the Take Responsibility for Workers and Families Act, must comply with subparagraphs (F) through (I) of subsections (a)(2) and (b)(2) of sections 1916 and 1916A".

(e) Effective Date.—The amendments made by this section shall take effect on the date of enactment of this Act and shall apply with respect to a COVID–19 vaccine beginning on the date that such vaccine is licensed under section 351 of the Public Health Service Act (42 U.S.C. 262).

SEC. 70106. OPTIONAL COVERAGE AT NO COST SHARING OF COVID–19 TREATMENT AND VACCINES UNDER MEDICAID FOR UNINSURED INDIVIDUALS.

(a) In General.—Section 1902(a)(10) of the Social Security Act (42 U.S.C. 1396a(a)(10) is amended, in the matter following subparagraph (G), by striking "and any visit described in section 1916(a)(2)(G)" and inserting the following: ", any COVID–19 vaccine that is administered during any such portion (and the administration of such vaccine), any item or service that is furnished during any such portion for the treatment of COVID–19 or a condition that may complicate the treatment of COVID–19, and any services described in section 1916(a)(2)(G)".

(b) Definition Of Uninsured Individual.—Subsection (ss) of section 1902 of the Social Security Act (42 U.S.C. 1396a), as added by section 6004(a)(3)(C) of the Families First Coronavirus Response Act, is amended to read as follows:

"(ss) Uninsured Individual Defined.—For purposes of this section, the term 'uninsured individual' means, notwithstanding any other provision of this title, any individual who is not covered by minimum essential coverage (as defined in section 5000A(f)(1) of the Internal Revenue Code of 1986).".

(c) Clarification Regarding Emergency Services For Certain Individuals.—Section 1903(v)(2) of the Social Security Act (42 U.S.C. 1396b(v)(2)) is amended by adding at the end the following flush sentence:

"For purposes of subparagraph (A), care and services described in such subparagraph include any in vitro diagnostic product described in section 1905(a)(3)(B) that is administered during any portion of the emergency period described in such section beginning on or after the date of the enactment of this sentence (and the administration of such product), any COVID–19 vaccine that is administered during any such portion (and the administration of such vaccine), any item or service that is furnished during any such portion for the treatment of COVID–19 or a condition that may complicate the treatment of COVID–19, and any services described in section 1916(a)(2)(G).".

(d) Inclusion Of COVID–19 Concern As An Emergency Condition.—Section 1903(v)(3) of the Social Security Act (42 U.S.C. 1396b(v)(3)) is amended by adding at the end the following flush sentence:

"Such term includes any indication that an alien described in paragraph (1) may have contracted COVID–19.".

SEC. 70107. TEMPORARY INCREASE IN MEDICAID FEDERAL FINANCIAL PARTICIPATION FOR TELEHEALTH SERVICES.

(a) In General.—Subject to subsection (b), for each calendar quarter occurring during the period beginning on the first day of the emergency period defined in paragraph (1)(B) of section 1135(g) of the Social Security Act (42 U.S.C. 1320b–5(g)) and ending on the last day of the calendar quarter in which the last day of such emergency period occurs, in the case of a State that has expenditures for telehealth services furnished during such quarter for which payment may be made to the State under section 1903(a) of the Social Security Act (42 U.S.C. 1396b(a)), the percentage of Federal financial participation otherwise required to be paid to such State under such section for such amounts expended shall be increased by one percentage point.

(b) Requirements.—A State described in subsection (a) may not receive the percentage increase in Federal financial participation described in such subsection with respect to a calendar quarter unless the State provides for telehealth services under the State plan approved under such title XIX (or a waiver of such plan) during such quarter in the same manner and to the same extent that telehealth services are covered under section 1834(m) of the Social Security Act (42 U.S.C. 1395m(m)), including pursuant to any waiver under section 1135 of such Act (42 U.S.C. 1320b–5). Nothing in the preceding sentence shall be construed as requiring a State to pay for telehealth services furnished to an individual eligible under the State plan (or waiver) at a rate that would exceed the payment amount that otherwise would be made under the State plan (or waiver) for such services.

SEC. 70108. EXTENSION OF FULL FEDERAL MEDICAL ASSISTANCE PERCENTAGE TO INDIAN HEALTH CARE PROVIDERS.

Section 1905 of the Social Security Act (42 U.S.C. 1396d) is amended—

(1) in subsection (a)(9), by inserting "and including such services furnished in any location by or through an Indian health care provider (as defined in section 1932(h)(4)(A))" before the semicolon; and

(2) in subsection (b)—

(A) by inserting "(whether or not such services are provided within such a facility)" following "received through an Indian Health Service facility,"; and

(B) by striking "Indian Health Care Improvement Act)" and inserting "Indian Health Care Improvement Act), or through an Urban Indian organization (as defined in section 4 of the Indian Health Care Improvement Act) pursuant to a grant or contract with the Indian Health Service under title V of the Indian Health Care Improvement Act".

SEC. 70109. MEDICAID COVERAGE FOR CITIZENS OF FREELY ASSOCIATED STATES.

(a) In General.—Section 402(b)(2) of the Personal Responsibility and Work Opportunity Reconciliation Act of 1996 (8 U.S.C. 1612(b)(2)) is amended by adding at the end the following new subparagraph:

"(G) MEDICAID EXCEPTION FOR CITIZENS OF FREELY ASSOCIATED STATES.—With respect to eligibility for benefits for the designated Federal program defined in paragraph (3)(C) (relating to the Medicaid program), section 401(a) and paragraph (1) shall not apply to any individual who lawfully resides in 1 of the 50 States or the District of Columbia in accordance with the Compacts of Free Association between the Government of the United States and the Governments of the Federated States of Micronesia, the Republic of the Marshall Islands, and the Republic of Palau and shall not apply, at the option of the Governor of Puerto Rico, the Virgin Islands, Guam, the Northern Mariana Islands, or American Samoa as communicated to the Secretary of Health and Human Services in writing, to any individual who lawfully resides in the respective territory in accordance with such Compacts.".

(b) Exception To 5-Year Limited Eligibility.—Section 403(d) of such Act (8 U.S.C. 1613(d)) is amended—

(1) in paragraph (1), by striking "or" at the end;

(2) in paragraph (2), by striking the period at the end and inserting "; or"; and

(3) by adding at the end the following new paragraph:
"(3) an individual described in section 402(b)(2)(G), but only with respect to the designated Federal program defined in section 402(b)(3)(C).".
(c) Definition Of Qualified Alien.—Section 431(b) of such Act (8 U.S.C. 1641(b)) is amended—
(1) in paragraph (6), by striking "; or" at the end and inserting a comma;
(2) in paragraph (7), by striking the period at the end and inserting ", or"; and
(3) by adding at the end the following new paragraph:
"(8) an individual who lawfully resides in the United States in accordance with a Compact of Free Association referred to in section 402(b)(2)(G), but only with respect to the designated Federal program defined in section 402(b)(3)(C) (relating to the Medicaid program).".
(d) Conforming Amendments.—Section 1108 of the Social Security Act (42 U.S.C. 1308), as amended by section 101(b), is further amended—
(1) in subsection (f), in the matter preceding paragraph (1), by striking "subsections (g) and (h) and section 1935(e)(1)(B)" and inserting "subsections (g), (h), and (i) and section 1935(e)(1)(B)"; and
(2) by adding at the end the following:
"(i) Exclusion Of Medical Assistance Expenditures For Citizens Of Freely Associated States.—Expenditures for medical assistance provided to an individual described in section 431(b)(8) of the Personal Responsibility and Work Opportunity Reconciliation Act of 1996 (8 U.S.C. 1641(b)(8)) shall not be taken into account for purposes of applying payment limits under subsections (f) and (g).".
(e) Effective Date.—The amendments made by this section shall apply to benefits for items and services furnished on or after the date of the enactment of this Act.

SEC. 70110. INCREASED FMAP FOR MEDICAL ASSISTANCE TO NEWLY ELIGIBLE INDIVIDUALS.
(a) In General.—Section 1905(y)(1) of the Social Security Act (42 U.S.C. 1396d(y)(1)) is amended—
(1) in subparagraph (A), by striking "2014, 2015, and 2016" and inserting "each of the first 3 consecutive 12-month periods in which the State provides medical assistance to newly eligible individuals";
(2) in subparagraph (B), by striking "2017" and inserting "the fourth consecutive 12-month period in which the State provides medical assistance to newly eligible individuals";
(3) in subparagraph (C), by striking "2018 " and inserting "the fifth consecutive 12-month period in which the State provides medical assistance to newly eligible individuals";
(4) in subparagraph (D), by striking "2019" and inserting "the sixth consecutive 12-month period in which the State provides medical assistance to newly eligible individuals"; and

(5) in subparagraph (E), by striking “2020 and each year thereafter” and inserting “the seventh consecutive 12-month period in which the State provides medical assistance to newly eligible individuals and each such period thereafter”.

(b) Effective Date.—The amendments made by subsection (a) shall take effect as if included in the enactment of the Patient Protection and Affordable Care Act.

SEC. 70111. RENEWAL OF APPLICATION OF MEDICARE PAYMENT RATE FLOOR TO PRIMARY CARE SERVICES FURNISHED UNDER MEDICAID AND INCLUSION OF ADDITIONAL PROVIDERS.

(a) Renewal Of Payment Floor; Additional Providers.—

(1) IN GENERAL.—Section 1902(a)(13) of the Social Security Act (42 U.S.C. 1396a(a)(13)) is amended by striking subparagraph (C) and inserting the following:

“(C) payment for primary care services (as defined in subsection (jj)) at a rate that is not less than 100 percent of the payment rate that applies to such services and physician under part B of title XVIII (or, if greater, the payment rate that would be applicable under such part if the conversion factor under section 1848(d) for the year involved were the conversion factor under such section for 2009), and that is not less than the rate that would otherwise apply to such services under this title if the rate were determined without regard to this subparagraph, and that are—

“(i) furnished in 2013 and 2014, by a physician with a primary specialty designation of family medicine, general internal medicine, or pediatric medicine; or

“(ii) furnished during the period beginning on the first day of the first month beginning after the date of the enactment of the Take Responsibility for Workers and Families Act and ending on the last day of the calendar quarter during which the last day of the emergency period described in section 1135(g)(1)(B) occurs—

“(I) by a physician with a primary specialty designation of family medicine, general internal medicine, pediatric medicine, or obstetrics and gynecology, but only if the physician self-attests that the physician is board-certified in family medicine, general internal medicine, pediatric medicine, or obstetrics and gynecology, respectively;

“(II) by a physician with a primary specialty designation of a family medicine subspecialty, an internal medicine subspecialty, a pediatric subspecialty, or a subspecialty of obstetrics and gynecology, without regard to the board that offers the designation for such a subspecialty, but only if the physician self-attests that the physician is board-certified in such a subspecialty;

“(III) by an advanced practice clinician, as defined by the Secretary, that works under the supervision of—

“(aa) a physician described in subclause (I) or (II); or

"(bb) a nurse practitioner or a physician assistant (as such terms are defined in section 1861(aa)(5)(A)) who is working in accordance with State law, or a certified nurse-midwife (as defined in section 1861(gg)(2)) who is working in accordance with State law;

"(IV) by a rural health clinic, Federally-qualified health center, or other health clinic that receives reimbursement on a fee schedule applicable to a physician described in subclause (I) or (II), an advanced practice clinician described in subclause (III), or a nurse practitioner, physician assistant, or certified nurse-midwife described in subclause (III)(bb), for services furnished by—

"(aa) such a physician, nurse practitioner, physician assistant, or certified nurse-midwife, respectively; or

"(bb) an advanced practice clinician supervised by such a physician, nurse practitioner, physician assistant, or certified nurse-midwife; or

"(V) by a nurse practitioner, physician assistant, or certified nurse-midwife described in subclause (III)(bb), in accordance with procedures that ensure that the portion of the payment for such services that the nurse practitioner, physician assistant, or certified nurse-midwife is paid is not less than the amount that the nurse practitioner, physician assistant, or certified nurse-midwife would be paid if the services were provided under part B of title XVIII;".

(2) CONFORMING AMENDMENTS.—Section 1905(dd) of the Social Security Act (42 U.S.C. 1396d(dd)) is amended—

(A) by striking "Notwithstanding" and inserting the following:

"(1) IN GENERAL.—Notwithstanding";

(B) by inserting "or furnished during the additional period specified in paragraph (2)," after "2015,"; and

(C) by adding at the end the following:

"(2) ADDITIONAL PERIOD.—For purposes of paragraph (1), the additional period specified in this paragraph is the period with respect to which section 1902(a)(13)(C)(ii) applies.".

(b) Improved Targeting Of Primary Care.—Section 1902(jj) of the Social Security Act (42 U.S.C. 1396a(jj)) is amended—

(1) by redesignating paragraphs (1) and (2) as subparagraphs (A) and (B), respectively, and moving the margin of each such subparagraph, as so redesignated, 2 ems to the right;

(2) by striking "For purposes of" and inserting the following:

"(1) IN GENERAL.—For purposes of"; and

(3) by adding at the end the following:

"(2) EXCLUSIONS.—Such term does not include any services described in subparagraph (A) or (B) of paragraph (1) if such services are provided in an emergency department of a hospital during the period described in subsection (a)(13)(C)(ii).".

(c) Ensuring Payment By Managed Care Entities.—

(1) IN GENERAL.—Section 1903(m)(2)(A) of the Social Security Act (42

U.S.C. 1396b(m)(2)(A)) is amended—
(A) in clause (xii), by striking "and" after the semicolon;
(B) in clause (xiii)—
(i) by moving the margin of such clause 2 ems to the left; and
(ii) by striking the period at the end and inserting "; and"; and
(C) by inserting after clause (xiii) the following:
"(xiv) such contract provides that (I) payments to health care providers specified in section 1902(a)(13)(C) for furnishing primary care services defined in section 1902(jj) during a year or period specified in section 1902(a)(13)(C) are at least equal to the amounts set forth and required by the Secretary by regulation, (II) the entity shall, upon request, provide documentation to the State that is sufficient to enable the State and the Secretary to ensure compliance with subclause (I), and (III) the Secretary shall approve payments described in subclause (I) that are furnished through an agreed-upon capitation, partial capitation, or other value-based payment arrangement if the agreed-upon capitation, partial capitation, or other value-based payment arrangement is based on a reasonable methodology and the entity provides documentation to the State that is sufficient to enable the State and the Secretary to ensure compliance with subclause (I).".
(2) CONFORMING AMENDMENT.—Section 1932(f) of the Social Security Act (42 U.S.C. 1396u–2(f)) is amended by inserting "and clause (xiv) of section 1903(m)(2)(A)" before the period.
(3) EFFECTIVE DATE.—The amendments made by this subsection shall apply with respect to contracts entered into on or after the date of the enactment of this Act.

SEC. 70112. TEMPORARY INCREASE IN MEDICAID DSH ALLOTMENTS.
(a) In General.—Section 1923(f)(3) of the Social Security Act (42 U.S.C. 1396r–4(f)(3)) is amended—
(1) in subparagraph (A), by striking "and subparagraph (E)" and inserting "and subparagraphs (E) and (F)"; and
(2) by adding at the end the following new subparagraph:
"(F) TEMPORARY INCREASE IN ALLOTMENTS DURING CERTAIN PUBLIC HEALTH EMERGENCY.—The DSH allotment for any State is—
"(i) for fiscal year 2020, equal to 102.5 percent of the DSH allotment that would be determined under this paragraph for the State for fiscal year 2020 without application of this subparagraph, notwithstanding subparagraphs (B) and (C); and
"(ii) for a subsequent fiscal year (if any) during which the emergency period defined in paragraph (1)(B) of section 1135(g) of the Social Security Act is in effect, equal to 102.5 percent of the DSH allotment determined under this subparagraph for the State for the previous fiscal year.
For each fiscal year after fiscal year 2020 during which the emergency period

described in clause (ii) is not in effect, the DSH allotment for a State for such fiscal year is equal to the DSH allotment that would have been determined under this paragraph for such fiscal year if this subparagraph had not been enacted.".

(b) Sense Of Congress.—It is the sense of Congress that a State should prioritize making payments under the State plan of the State under title XIX of the Social Security Act (42 U.S.C. 1396 et seq.) (or a waiver of such plan) to disproportionate share hospitals that have a higher share of COVID–19 patients relative to other such hospitals in the State.

SEC. 70113. TEMPORARY ALLOWANCE FOR MEDICAL ASSISTANCE UNDER MEDICAID FOR INMATES DURING 30-DAY PERIOD PRECEDING RELEASE.

The subdivision (A) following paragraph (30) of section 1905(a) of the Social Security Act (42 U.S.C. 1396d(a)) is amended by inserting "and except during the 30-day period preceding the date of release of such individual from such public institution, but only if such 30-day period occurs during the emergency period described in section 1135(g)(1)(B)" after "medical institution".

SEC. 70114. EXTENSION OF EXISTING SECTION 1115 DEMONSTRATION PROJECTS.

(a) Applicability.—This section shall apply with respect to demonstration projects operated by States pursuant to section 1115(a) of the Social Security Act (42 U.S.C. 1315(a)) to promote the objectives of title XIX or XXI of the Social Security Act with a project term set to end on or before December 31, 2020.

(b) Approval Of Extension.—Upon request by a State, the Secretary of Health and Human Services shall approve an extension of the waiver and expenditure authorities for a demonstration project described in subsection (a) for a period up to and including December 31, 2021, to ensure continuity of programs and funding during the emergency period described in section 1135(g)(1)(B) of the Social Security Act (42 U.S.C. 42 U.S.C. 1320b–5(g)(1)(B)).

(c) Extension Terms And Conditions.— (1) The approval pursuant to this section shall extend the terms and conditions that applied to the demonstration project to the extension period. Financial terms and conditions shall continue at levels equivalent to the prior demonstration or program year. All demonstration program components shall be extended to operate through ffthe end of the extension term. In its request for an extension, the state shall identify operational and programmatic changes necessary to continue and stabilize programs into the extension period and shall work with the Secretary of Health and Human Services to implement such changes.

(2) Notwithstanding the foregoing, the State may request, and the Secretary of Health and Human Services may approve, modifications to a demonstration project's terms and conditions to address the impact of the federally designated

public health emergency with respect to COVID–19. Such modifications may, at the option of the State, become effective retroactive to the start of the calendar quarter in which the first day of the emergency period described in paragraph (1)(B) of section 1135(g) of the Social Security Act 42 U.S.C. 42 U.S.C. 1320b–5(g)) occurs.

(d) Budget Neutrality.—Budget neutrality for extensions under this section shall be deemed to have been met at the conclusion of the extension period, and States receiving extensions under this section shall not be required to submit a budget neutrality analysis for the extension period.

(e) Expedited Application Process.—The Federal and State public notice and comment procedures or other time constraints otherwise applicable to demonstration project amendments shall be waived to expedite a State's extension request pursuant to this section. The Secretary of Health and Human Services shall approve the extension application within 45 days of a State's submission of its request, or such other timeframe as is mutually agreed to with the State.

(f) Continuation Of Secretarial Authority Under Declared Emergency.—This section does not restrict the Secretary of Health and Human Services from exercising existing flexibilities through demonstration projects operated pursuant to section 1115 of the Social Security Act (42 U.S.C. 1315) in conjunction with the COVID–19 public health emergency.

(g) Rule Of Construction.—Nothing in this section shall authorize the Secretary of Health and Human Service to approve or extend a waiver that fails to meet the requirements of section 1115 of the Social Security Act (42 U.S.C. 1315).

SEC. 70115. MODIFICATION OF REDUCTIONS IN MEDICAID DSH ALLOTMENTS.

Section 1923(f)(7)(A) of the Social Security Act (42 U.S.C. 1396r–4(f)(7)(A)) is amended—

(1) in clause (i), in the matter preceding subclause (I), by striking "For the period beginning May 23, 2020, and ending September 30, 2020, and for each of fiscal years 2021 through 2025" and inserting "For the period beginning December 1, 2020, and ending September 30, 2021, and for each of fiscal years 2022 through 2025"; and

(2) in clause (ii)—

(A) in subclause (I), by striking "for the period beginning May 23, 2020, and ending September 30, 2020" and inserting "for the period beginning December 1, 2020, and ending September 30, 2021"; and

(B) in subclause (II), by striking "for each of fiscal years 2021 through 2025" and inserting "for each of fiscal years 2022 through 2025".

SEC. 70116. EXTENSION OF MONEY FOLLOWS THE PERSON REBALANCING DEMONSTRATION.

(a) In General.—Section 6071(h)(1) of the Deficit Reduction Act of 2005 (42 U.S.C. 1396a note) is amended—

(1) in subparagraph (F), by striking "and" at the end; and

(2) by striking subparagraph (G) and inserting the following:

"(G) $450,000,000 for fiscal year 2020; and

"(H) $75,206,000 for the period beginning on October 1, 2020, and ending on November 30, 2020.".

(b) Effective Date.—The amendments made by subsection (a) shall take effect as if included in the enactment of the Further Consolidated Appropriations Act, 2020 (Public Law 116–94).

SEC. 70117. EXTENSION OF PROTECTION FOR MEDICAID RECIPIENTS OF HOME AND COMMUNITY-BASED SERVICES AGAINST SPOUSAL IMPOVERISHMENT.

(a) In General.—Section 2404 of Public Law 111–148 (42 U.S.C. 1396r–5 note) is amended by striking "May 22, 2020" and inserting "November 30, 2020".

(b) Rule Of Construction.—Nothing in section 2404 of Public Law 111–148 (42 U.S.C. 1396r–5 note) or section 1902(a)(17) or 1924 of the Social Security Act (42 U.S.C. 1396a(a)(17), 1396r–5) shall be construed as prohibiting a State from applying an income or resource disregard under a methodology authorized under section 1902(r)(2) of such Act (42 U.S.C. 1396a(r)(2))—

(1) to the income or resources of an individual described in section 1902(a)(10)(A)(ii)(VI) of such Act (42 U.S.C. 1396a(a)(10)(A)(ii)(VI)) (including a disregard of the income or resources of such individual's spouse); or

(2) on the basis of an individual's need for home and community-based services authorized under subsection (c), (d), (i), or (k) of section 1915 of such Act (42 U.S.C. 1396n) or under section 1115 of such Act (42 U.S.C. 1315).

SEC. 70118. EXTENSION OF THE COMMUNITY MENTAL HEALTH SERVICES DEMONSTRATION PROGRAM.

Section 223(d)(3) of the Protecting Access to Medicare Act of 2014 (42 U.S.C. 1396a note) is amended by striking "May 22, 2020" and inserting "November 30, 2020".

TITLE II—MEDICARE

SEC. 70201. COVERAGE OF THE COVID-19 VACCINE UNDER THE MEDICARE PROGRAM WITHOUT ANY COST-SHARING.

(a) Medical And Other Health Services.—Section 1861(s)(10)(A) of the Social Security Act (42 U.S.C. 1395x(s)(10)(A)) is amended by inserting ", and COVID-19 vaccine and its administration" after "influenza vaccine and its administration".

(b) Part B Deductible.—Section 1833(b) of the Social Security Act (42 U.S.C. 1395l(b)) is amended, in the first sentence—

(1) by striking “and” before “(11)”; and (B) by inserting before the period at the end the following: “, and (11)

(2) by inserting before the period at the end the following: “, and (12) such deductible shall not apply with respect a COVID-19 vaccine and its administration described in section 1861(s)(10)(A)”.

(c) Waiving Cost-Sharing Under Medicare Advantage.—Section 1852(a)(1)(B) of the Social Security Act (42 U.S.C. 1395w–22(a)(1)(B)) is amended—

(1) in clause (iv)—

(A) by redesignating subclause (VI) as subclause (VII); and

(B) by inserting after subclause (V) the following new subclause:

“(VI) COVID-19 vaccines and the administration of such vaccines, as described in section 1861(s)(10)(A).”; and

(2) in clause (v), by striking “subclauses (IV) and (V)” and inserting “subclauses (IV), (V), and (VI)”.

(d) Implementation.—Notwithstanding any other provision of law, the Secretary of Health and Human Services may implement the amendments made by subsection (c) by program instruction or otherwise.

(e) Payment For Administration Of COVID-19 Vaccine.—The payment amount under part B of title XVIII of the Social Security Act for the administration of a COVID-19 vaccine pursuant to the amendment made by subsection (a) shall be the same as the payment amount under such part for the administration of an influenza vaccine, pneumococcal vaccine, and a hepatitis B vaccine.

(f) Authority For Roster Billing.—Notwithstanding any other provision of law, the Secretary of Health and Human Services may, by program instruction or otherwise, include a COVID-19 vaccine as a vaccine with respect to which the Secretary permits roster billing for purposes of payment under part B of title XVIII of the Social Security Act.

(g) Effective Date.—The amendments made by this section shall take effect on the date of enactment of this Act and shall apply with respect to a COVID-19 vaccine beginning on the date that such vaccine is licensed under section 351 of the Public Health Service Act (42 U.S.C. 262).

SEC. 70202. HOLDING MEDICARE BENEFICIARIES HARMLESS FOR SPECIFIED COVID-19 TREATMENT SERVICES FURNISHED UNDER PART A OR PART B OF THE MEDICARE PROGRAM.

(a) In General.—Notwithstanding any other provision of law, in the case of a specified COVID-19 treatment service (as defined in subsection (b)) furnished to an individual entitled to benefits under part A or enrolled under part B of title XVIII of the Social Security Act (42 U.S.C. 1395 et seq.) for which payment is made under such part A or such part B, the Secretary of Health and Human Services (in this section referred to as the “Secretary”) shall provide that—

(1) any cost-sharing required (including any deductible, copayment, or

coinsurance) applicable to such individual under such part A or such part B with respect to such item or service is paid by the Secretary; and
(2) the provider of services or supplier (as defined in section 1861 of the Social Security Act (42 U.S.C. 1395x)) does not hold such individual liable for such requirement.
(b) Definition Of Specified COVID-19 Treatment Services.—For purposes of this section, the term "specified COVID-19 treatment service" means any item or service furnished to an individual for which payment may be made under part A or part B of title XVIII of the Social Security Act (42 U.S.C. 1395 et seq.) if such item or service is included in a claim with an ICD-10-CM code relating to COVID-19 (as described in the document entitled "ICD-10-CM Official Coding Guidelines - Supplement Coding encounters related to COVID-19 Coronavirus Outbreak" published on February 20, 2020, or as otherwise specified by the Secretary).
(c) Recovery Of Cost-Sharing Amounts Paid By The Secretary In The Case Of Supplemental Insurance Coverage.—
(1) IN GENERAL.—In the case of any amount paid by the Secretary pursuant to subsection (a)(1) that the Secretary determines would otherwise have been paid by a group health plan or health insurance issuer (as such terms are defined in section 2791 of the Public Health Service Act (42 U.S.C. 300gg–91)), a private entity offering a medicare supplemental policy under section 1882 of the Social Security Act (42 U.S.C. 1395ss), any other health plan offering supplemental coverage, a State plan under title XIX of the Social Security Act, or the Secretary of Defense under the TRICARE program, such plan, issuer, private entity, other health plan, State plan, or Secretary of Defense, as applicable, shall pay to the Secretary, not later than 1 year after such plan, issuer, private entity, other health plan, State plan, or Secretary of Defense receives a notice under paragraph (3), such amount in accordance with this subsection.
(2) REQUIRED INFORMATION.—Not later than 9 months after the date of the enactment of this Act, each group health plan, health insurance issuer, private entity, other health plan, State plan, and Secretary of Defense described in paragraph (1) shall submit to the Secretary such information as the Secretary determines necessary for purposes of carrying out this subsection. Such information so submitted shall be updated by such plan, issuer, private entity, other health plan, State plan, or Secretary of Defense, as applicable, at such time and in such manner as specified by the Secretary.
(3) REVIEW OF CLAIMS AND NOTIFICATION.—The Secretary shall establish a process under which claims for items and services for which the Secretary has paid an amount pursuant to subsection (a)(1) are reviewed for purposes of identifying if such amount would otherwise have been paid by a plan, issuer, private entity, other health plan, State plan, or Secretary of Defense described in paragraph (1). In the case such a claim is so identified, the Secretary shall determine the amount that would have been otherwise

payable by such plan, issuer, private entity, other health plan, State plan, or Secretary of Defense and notify such plan, issuer, private entity, other health plan, State plan, or Secretary of Defense of such amount.

(4) ENFORCEMENT.—The Secretary may impose a civil monetary penalty in an amount determined appropriate by the Secretary in the case of a plan, issuer, private entity, other health plan, or State plan that fails to comply with a provision of this section. The provisions of section 1128A of the Social Security Act shall apply to a civil monetary penalty imposed under the previous sentence in the same manner as such provisions apply to a penalty or proceeding under subsection (a) or (b) of such section.

(d) Funding.—The Secretary shall provide for the transfer to the Centers for Medicare & Medicaid Program Management Account from the Federal Hospital Insurance Trust Fund and the Federal Supplementary Trust Fund (in such portions as the Secretary determines appropriate) $100,000,000 for purposes of carrying out this section.

(e) Report.—Not later than 3 years after the date of the enactment of this Act, the Inspector General of the Department of Health and Human Services shall submit to Congress a report containing an analysis of amounts paid pursuant to subsection (a)(1) compared to amounts paid to the Secretary pursuant to subsection (c).

(f) Implementation.—Notwithstanding any other provision of law, the Secretary may implement the provisions of this section by program instruction or otherwise.

SEC. 70203. MEDICARE SEQUESTER DELAY.

During the period beginning on May 1, 2020, and ending on such date the emergency period described in section 1135(g)(1)(B) of the Social Security Act (42 U.S.C. 1320b–5(g)(1)(B)) ends, the Medicare program under title XVIII of the Social Security Act (42 U.S.C. 1395 et seq.) shall be exempt from reduction under any sequestration order issued pursuant to section 254 of the Balanced Budget and Emergency Deficit Control Act of 1985 before, on, or after the date of enactment of this Act.

SEC. 70204. ENHANCING MEDICARE TELEHEALTH SERVICES FOR FEDERALLY QUALIFIED HEALTH CENTERS AND RURAL HEALTH CLINICS DURING THE EMERGENCY PERIOD.

Section 1834(m) of the Social Security Act (42 U.S.C. 1395m(m)) is amended—

(1) in the first sentence of paragraph (1), by striking "The Secretary" and inserting "Subject to paragraph (8), the Secretary";

(2) in paragraph (2)(A), by striking "The Secretary" and inserting "Subject to paragraph (8), the Secretary";

(3) in paragraph (4)—

(A) in subparagraph (A), by striking "The term" and inserting "Subject to paragraph (8),the term"; and

(B) in subparagraph (F)(i), by striking "The term" and inserting "Subject to paragraph (8), the term"; and

(4) by adding at the end the following new paragraph:

"(8) ENHANCING TELEHEALTH SERVICES FOR FEDERALLY QUALIFIED HEALTH CENTERS AND RURAL HEALTH CLINICS DURING THE EMERGENCY PERIOD.—

"(A) IN GENERAL.—During the emergency period described in section 1135(g)(1)(B)—

"(i) the Secretary shall pay for telehealth services that are furnished via a telecommunications system by a Federally qualified health center or a rural health clinic to an eligible telehealth individual enrolled under this part notwithstanding that the Federally qualified health center or rural clinic providing the telehealth service is not at the same location as the beneficiary;

"(ii) the amount of payment to a Federally qualified health center or rural health clinic that serves as a distant site for such a telehealth service shall be determined under subparagraph (B); and

"(iii) for purposes of this subsection—

"(I) the term 'distant site' includes a Federally qualified health center or rural health clinic that furnishes a telehealth service to an eligible telehealth individual; and

"(II) the term 'telehealth services' includes a rural health clinic service or Federally qualified health center service that is furnished using telehealth to the extent that payment codes corresponding to services identified by the Secretary under clause (i) or (ii) of paragraph (4)(F) are listed on the corresponding claim for such rural health clinic service or Federally qualified health center service.

"(B) SPECIAL PAYMENT RULE.—The Secretary shall develop and implement payment methods that apply under this subsection to a Federally qualified health center or rural health clinic that serves as a distant site that furnishes a telehealth service to an eligible telehealth individual during such emergency period. Such payment methods shall be based on payment rates that are similar to the national average payment rates for comparable telehealth services under the physician fee schedule under section 1848. Notwithstanding any other provision of law, the Secretary may implement such payment methods through program instruction or otherwise.".

SEC. 70205. GUARANTEED ISSUE OF CERTAIN MEDIGAP POLICIES.

(a) Guaranteed Issue Of Medigap Policies To All Medigap-Eligible Medicare Beneficiaries.—

(1) IN GENERAL.—Section 1882(s) of the Social Security Act (42 U.S.C. 1395ss(s)) is amended—

(A) in paragraph (2)(A), by striking "65 years of age or older and is enrolled for benefits under part B" and inserting "entitled to, or enrolled for, benefits under part A and enrolled for benefits under part B";

(B) in paragraph (2)(D), by striking "who is 65 years of age or older as of the date of issuance and";
(C) in paragraph (3)(B)(ii), by striking "is 65 years of age or older and"; and
(D) in paragraph (3)(B)(vi), by striking "at age 65".
(2) ADDITIONAL ENROLLMENT PERIOD FOR CERTAIN INDIVIDUALS.—
(A) ONE-TIME ENROLLMENT PERIOD.—
(i) IN GENERAL.—In the case of a specified individual, the Secretary shall establish a one-time enrollment period described in clause (iii) during which such an individual may enroll in any medicare supplemental policy of the individual's choosing.
(ii) APPLICATION.—The provisions of—
(I) paragraph (2) of section 1882(s) of the Social Security Act (42 U.S.C. 1395ss(s)) shall apply with respect to a specified individual who is described in subclause (I) of subparagraph (B)(iii) as if references in such paragraph (2) to the 6 month period described in subparagraph (A) of such paragraph were references to the one-time enrollment period established under clause (i); and
(II) paragraph (3) of such section shall apply with respect to a specified individual who is described in subclause (II) of subparagraph (B)(iii) as if references in such paragraph (3) to the period specified in subparagraph (E) of such paragraph were references to the one-time enrollment period established under clause (i).
(iii) PERIOD.—The enrollment period established under clause (i) shall be the 6-month period beginning on January 1, 2024.
(B) SPECIFIED INDIVIDUAL.—For purposes of this paragraph, the term "specified individual" means an individual who—
(i) is entitled to hospital insurance benefits under part A of title XVIII of the Social Security Act (42 U.S.C. 1395c et seq.) pursuant to section 226(b) or section 226A of such Act (42 U.S.C. 426(b); 426–1);
(ii) is enrolled for benefits under part B of such Act (42 U.S.C. 1395j et seq.); and
(iii) (I) would not, but for the amendments made by subparagraphs (A) and (B) of paragraph (1) and the provisions of this paragraph (if such provisions applied to such individual), be eligible for the guaranteed issue of a medicare supplemental policy under paragraph (2) of section 1882(s) of such Act (42 U.S.C. 1395ss(s)); or
(II) would not, but for the amendments made by subparagraphs (C) and (D) of paragraph (1) and the provisions of this paragraph (if such provisions applied to such individual), be eligible for the guaranteed issue of a medicare supplemental policy under paragraph (3) of such section.
(C) OUTREACH PLAN.—
(i) IN GENERAL.—The Secretary shall develop an outreach plan to notify specified individuals of the one-time enrollment period established under subparagraph (A).

(ii) CONSULTATION.—In implementing the outreach plan developed under clause (i), the Secretary shall consult with consumer advocates, brokers, insurers, the National Association of Insurance Commissioners, and State Health Insurance Assistance Programs.

(3) EFFECTIVE DATE.—The amendments made by paragraph (1) shall apply to medicare supplemental policies effective on or after January 1, 2024.

(b) Guaranteed Issue Of Medigap Policies For Medicare Advantage Enrollees.—

(1) IN GENERAL.—Section 1882(s)(3) of the Social Security Act (42 U.S.C. 1395ss(s)(3)), as amended by subsection (a), is further amended—

(A) in subparagraph (B), by adding at the end the following new clause:

"(vii) The individual—

"(I) was enrolled in a Medicare Advantage plan under part C for not less than 12 months;

"(II) subsequently disenrolled from such plan;

"(III) elects to receive benefits under this title through the original Medicare fee-for-service program under parts A and B; and

"(IV) has not previously elected to receive benefits under this title through the original Medicare fee-for-service program pursuant to disenrollment from a Medicare Advantage plan under part C.";

(B) by striking subparagraph (C)(iii) and inserting the following:

"(iii) Subject to subsection (v)(1), for purposes of an individual described in clause (vi) or (vii) of subparagraph (B), a medicare supplemental policy described in this subparagraph shall include any medicare supplemental policy."; and

(C) in subparagraph (E)—

(i) in clause (iv), by striking "and" at the end;

(ii) in clause (v), by striking the period at the end and inserting "; and"; and

(iii) by adding at the end the following new clause—

"(vi) in the case of an individual described in subparagraph (B)(vii), the annual, coordinated election period (as defined in section 1851(e)(3)(B)) or a continuous open enrollment period (as defined in section 1851(e)(2)) during which the individual disenrolls from a Medicare Advantage plan under part C.".

(2) EFFECTIVE DATE.—The amendments made by paragraph (1) shall apply to medicare supplemental policies effective on or after January 1, 2024.

SEC. 70206. ENSURING COMMUNICATIONS ACCESSIBILITY FOR RESIDENTS OF SKILLED NURSING FACILITIES DURING THE COVID-19 EMERGENCY PERIOD.

(a) In General.—Section 1819(c)(3) of the Social Security Act (42 U.S.C. 1395i–3(c)(3)) is amended—

(1) in subparagraph (D), by striking "and" at the end;

(2) in subparagraph (E), by striking the period and inserting "; and"; and

(3) by adding at the end the following new subparagraph:

"(F) provide for reasonable access to the use of a telephone, including TTY and TDD services (as defined for purposes of section 483.10 of title 42, Code of Federal Regulations (or a successor regulation)), and the internet (to the extent available to the facility) and inform each such resident (or a representative of such resident) of such access and any changes in policies or procedures of such facility relating to limitations on external visitors.".

(b) COVID-19 Provisions.—

(1) GUIDANCE.—Not later than 15 days after the date of the enactment of this Act, the Secretary of Health and Human Service shall issue guidance on steps skilled nursing facilities may take to ensure residents have access to televisitation during the emergency period defined in section 1135(g)(1)(B) of the Social Security Act (42 U.S.C. 1320b–5(g)(1)(B)).

(2) REVIEW OF FACILITIES.—The Secretary of Health and Human Services shall take such steps as determined appropriate by the Secretary to ensure that residents of skilled nursing facilities and relatives of such residents are made aware of the access rights described in section 1819(c)(3)(F) of the Social Security Act (42 U.S.C. 1395i–3(c)(3)(F)).

SEC. 70207. MEDICARE HOSPITAL INPATIENT PROSPECTIVE PAYMENT SYSTEM OUTLIER PAYMENTS FOR COVID-19 PATIENTS DURING CERTAIN EMERGENCY PERIOD.

(a) In General.—Section 1886(d)(5)(A) of the Social Security Act (42 U.S.C. 1395ww(d)(5)(A)) is amended—

(1) in clause (ii), by striking "For cases" and inserting "Subject to clause (vii), for cases";

(2) in clause (iii), by striking "The amount" and inserting "Subject to clause (vii), the amount";

(3) in clause (iv), by striking "The total amount" and inserting "Subject to clause (vii), the total amount"; and

(4) by adding at the end the following new clause:

"(vii) For discharges that have a primary or secondary diagnosis of COVID-19 and that occur during the emergency period described in section 1135(g)(1)(B), the amount of any additional payment under clause (ii) for a subsection (d) hospital for such a discharge shall be determined as if—

"(I) clause (ii) was amended by striking 'plus a fixed dollar amount determined by the Secretary';

"(II) the reference in clause (iii) to 'approximate the marginal cost of care beyond the cutoff point applicable under clause (i) or (ii)' were a reference to 'approximate the marginal cost of care beyond the cutoff point applicable under clause (i), or, in the case of an additional payment requested under clause (ii), be equal to 100 percent of the amount by which the costs of the discharge for which such additional payment is so requested exceed the applicable DRG prospective payment rate'; and

"(III) clause (iv) does not apply.".

(b) Exclusion From Reduction In Average Standardized Amounts Payable To Hospitals Located In Certain Areas.—Section 1886(d)(3)(B) of the Social Security Act (42 U.S.C. 1395ww(d)(3)(B)) is amended by inserting before the period the following: ", other than additional payments described in clause (vii) of such paragraph".

(c) Application To Site Neutral IPPS Payment Rates.—Section 1886(m)(6)(B) of the Social Security Act (42 U.S.C. 1395ww(m)(6)(B)) is amended—

(1) in clause (i)—

(A) in the matter preceding subclause (I), by striking "In this paragraph" and inserting "Subject to clause (ii), in this paragraph";

(B) in subclause (I), by striking "clause (iii)" and inserting "clause (iv)"; and

(C) in subclause (II), by striking "clause (ii)" and inserting "clause (iii)";

(2) in clause (ii), in the matter preceding subclause (I), by striking "clause (iv)" and inserting "clause (v)";

(3) in clause (iii)(I), by striking "clause (ii)" and inserting "clause (iii)";

(4) in clause (iv), by striking "clause (ii)(I)" and inserting "clause (iii)(I)";

(5) by redesignating clauses (ii) through (iv) as clauses (iii) through (v), respectively; and

(6) by inserting after clause (i) the following new clause:

"(ii) EXCEPTION.—Notwithstanding clause (i), the term 'applicable site neutral payment rate' means—

"(I) for discharges that have a primary or secondary diagnosis of COVID-19 and that occur during any portion of the emergency period described in section 1135(g)(1)(B) occurring during a cost reporting period described in clause (i)(I), the greater of the blended payment rate specified in clause (iv) or the percent described in clause (iii)(II); and

"(II) for discharges that have a primary or secondary diagnosis of COVID-19 and that occur during any portion of the emergency period described in section 1135(g)(1)(B) occurring during a cost reporting period described in clause (i)(II), the percent described in clause (iii)(II).".

(d) Implementation.—Notwithstanding any other provision of law, the Secretary of Health and Human Services may implement the amendments made by this section by program instruction or otherwise.

SEC. 70208. COVERAGE OF TREATMENTS FOR COVID–19 AT NO COST SHARING UNDER THE MEDICARE ADVANTAGE PROGRAM.

(a) In General.—Section 1852(a)(1)(B) of the Social Security Act (42 U.S.C. 1395w–22(a)(1)(B)) is amended by adding at the end the following new clause:

"(vii) SPECIAL COVERAGE RULES FOR SPECIFIED COVID–19 TREATMENT SERVICES.—Notwithstanding clause (i), in the case of a specified COVID-19 treatment service (as defined in section 70202(b) of the Take Responsibility for Workers and Families Act) that is furnished during a plan year occurring during any portion of the emergency period defined in section 1135(g)(1)(B) beginning on or after the date of the enactment of this clause, a Medicare Advantage plan may not, with respect to such service, impose—

"(I) any cost-sharing requirement (including a deductible, copayment, or coinsurance requirement); and

"(II) in the case such service is a critical specified COVID-19 treatment service (including ventilator services and intensive care unit services), any prior authorization or other utilization management requirement.

A Medicare Advantage plan may not take the application of this clause into account for purposes of a bid amount submitted by such plan under section 1854(a)(6).".

(b) Reimbursement Of Medicare Advantage Plans For Elimination Of Cost Sharing.—Section 1853 of the Social Security Act (42 U.S.C. 1395w–23) is amended by adding at the end the following new subsection:

"(p) Additional Payment To Account For Cost Sharing Elimination For COVID-19 Treatment Services.—

"(1) IN GENERAL.—A Medicare Advantage plan shall notify the Secretary of the total dollar amount of cost sharing that, but for the application of section 1852(a)(1)(B)(vii), would have been required under such plan for specified COVID-19 treatment services (as defined in section 70202(b) of the Take Responsibility for Workers and Families Act) furnished during a plan year described in such section to individuals enrolled in the plan. The Secretary shall make periodic and timely payments in accordance with this subsection to such plan that, in the aggregate, equal such total dollar amount.

"(2) TIMING OF PAYMENT.—Payments by the Secretary under this subsection shall be made beginning March 1, 2021, for amounts described in such paragraph that would have been required under such plan for specified COVID-19 treatment services furnished during plan year 2020. Payments by the Secretary under this subsection for such amounts that would have been so required under such plan for such services furnished during a plan year subsequent to plan year 2020 shall be made beginning March 1 of the plan year following such subsequent plan year.

"(3) NON-APPLICATION.—Section 1853(c)(7) shall not apply with respect to the application of this subsection.

"(4) APPROPRIATION.—There are transferred to the Centers for Medicare & Medicaid Program Management Fund, out of any monies in the Treasury not otherwise obligated, such sums as may be necessary to the Secretary for purposes of making payments under this subsection.".

(c) Implementation.—Notwithstanding any other provision of law, the Secretary of Health and Human Services may implement the amendments made by this section by program instruction or otherwise.

SEC. 70209. ESTABLISHING A RISK CORRIDOR PROGRAM FOR MEDICARE ADVANTAGE PLANS DURING THE COVID-19

EMERGENCY.

(a) In General.—Section 1853 of the Social Security Act (42 U.S.C. 1395w–23), as amended by section 70208(b), is further amended by adding at the end the following new subsection:

"(q) Risk Corridor Program During The COVID-19 Emergency.—

"(1) IN GENERAL.—The Secretary shall establish and administer a program of risk corridors for each plan year, any portion of which occurs during the emergency period defined in section 1135(g)(1)(B), under which the Secretary shall make payments to MA organizations offering a Medicare Advantage plan based on the ratio of the allowable costs of the plan to the aggregate premiums of the plan.

"(2) PAYMENT METHODOLOGY.—The Secretary shall provide under the program established under paragraph (1) that if the allowable costs for a Medicare Advantage plan for any plan year are more than 105 percent of the target amount, the Secretary shall pay to the plan an amount equal to 75 percent of the allowable costs in excess of 105 percent of the target amount.

"(3) TIMING.—

"(A) SUBMISSION OF INFORMATION BY PLANS.—With respect to a plan year for which the program described in paragraph (1) is established and administered, not later than July 1 of the succeeding plan year each MA organization offering a Medicare Advantage plan shall submit to the Secretary such information as the Secretary may require for purposes of carrying out such program.

"(B) PAYMENT.—The Secretary shall pay to an MA organization offering a Medicare Advantage plan eligible to receive a payment under the program with respect to a plan year the amount provided under paragraph (2) for such plan year not later than 60 days after such organization submits information with respect to such plan and plan year under subparagraph (A).

"(4) DEFINITIONS.—

"(A) ALLOWABLE COSTS.—

"(i) IN GENERAL.—The amount of allowable costs of a MA organization offering a Medicare Advantage plan for a plan year is an amount equal to the total costs (other than administrative costs) of such plan in providing benefits covered by such plan, but only to the extent that such costs are incurred with respect to such benefits for items and services that are benefits under the original medicare fee-for-service program option.

"(ii) REDUCTIONS.—Allowable costs for a Medicare Advantage plan for a plan year shall be reduced by any payment made under subsection (p) with respect to such plan and such plan year.

"(B) TARGET AMOUNT.—The target amount described in this paragraph is, with respect to a Medicare Advantage plan and a plan year, the total amount of payments paid to the MA organization for the plan for benefits under the original medicare fee-for-service program option for the plan year, taking into account amounts paid by the Secretary and enrollees, based upon the bid amount submitted under section 1854, reduced by the total amount of administrative expenses for the year assumed in such bid.

"(5) FUNDING.—There are appropriated to the Centers for Medicare & Medicaid Services Program Management Account, out of any monies in the Treasury not otherwise obligated, such sums as may be necessary for purposes of carrying out this subsection.".

(b) Implementation.—Notwithstanding any other provision of law, the Secretary of Health and Human Service may implement the amendments made by this section by program instruction or otherwise.

SEC. 70210. REQUIRING COVERAGE UNDER MEDICARE PDPS AND MA–PD PLANS, WITHOUT THE IMPOSITION OF COST SHARING OR UTILIZATION MANAGEMENT REQUIREMENTS, OF DRUGS INTENDED TO TREAT COVID-19 DURING CERTAIN EMERGENCIES.

(a) Coverage Requirement.—

(1) IN GENERAL.—Section 1860D–4(b)(3) of the Social Security Act (42 U.S.C. 1395w–104(b)(3)) is amended by adding at the end the following new subparagraph:

"(I) REQUIRED INCLUSION OF DRUGS INTENDED TO TREAT COVID-19.—

"(i) IN GENERAL.—Notwithstanding any other provision of law, a PDP sponsor offering a prescription drug plan shall, with respect to a plan year, any portion of which occurs during the period described in clause (ii), be required to—

"(I) include in any formulary—

"(aa) all covered part D drugs with a medically accepted indication (as defined in section 1860D–2(e)(4)) to treat COVID-19 that are marketed in the United States; and

"(bb) all drugs authorized under section 564 or 564A of the Federal Food Drug and Cosmetic Act to treat COVID-19; and

"(II) not impose any prior authorization or other utilization management requirement with respect to such drugs described in item (aa) or (bb) of subclause (I) (other than such a requirement that limits the quantity of drugs due to safety).

"(ii) PERIOD DESCRIBED.—For purposes of clause (i), the period described in this clause is the period during which there exists the public health emergency declared by the Secretary pursuant to section 319 of the Public Health Service Act on January 31, 2020, entitled 'Determination that a Public Health Emergency Exists Nationwide as the Result of the 2019 Novel Coronavirus' (including any renewal of such declaration pursuant to such section).".

(b) Elimination Of Cost Sharing.—

(1) ELIMINATION OF COST-SHARING FOR DRUGS INTENDED TO TREAT COVID-19 UNDER STANDARD AND ALTERNATIVE

PRESCRIPTION DRUG COVERAGE.—Section 1860D–2 of the Social Security Act (42 U.S.C. 1395w–102) is amended—

(A) in subsection (b)—

(i) in paragraph (1)(A), by striking "The coverage" and inserting "Subject to paragraph (8), the coverage";

(ii) in paragraph (2)—

(I) in subparagraph (A), by inserting after "Subject to subparagraphs (C) and (D)" the following: "and paragraph (8)";

(II) in subparagraph (C)(i), by striking "paragraph (4)" and inserting "paragraphs (4) and (8)"; and

(III) in subparagraph (D)(i), by striking "paragraph (4)" and inserting "paragraphs (4) and (8)";

(iii) in paragraph (4)(A)(i), by striking "The coverage" and inserting "Subject to paragraph (8), the coverage"; and

(iv) by adding at the end the following new paragraph:

"(8) ELIMINATION OF COST-SHARING FOR DRUGS INTENDED TO TREAT COVID-19.—The coverage does not impose any deductible, copayment, coinsurance, or other cost-sharing requirement for drugs described in section 1860D–4(b)(3)(I)(i)(I) with respect to a plan year, any portion of which occurs during the period during which there exists the public health emergency declared by the Secretary pursuant to section 319 of the Public Health Service Act on January 31, 2020, entitled 'Determination that a Public Health Emergency Exists Nationwide as the Result of the 2019 Novel Coronavirus' (including any renewal of such declaration pursuant to such section)."; and

(B) in subsection (c), by adding at the end the following new paragraph:

"(4) SAME ELIMINATION OF COST-SHARING FOR DRUGS INTENDED TO TREAT COVID-19.—The coverage is in accordance with subsection (b)(8).".

(2) ELIMINATION OF COST-SHARING FOR DRUGS INTENDED TO TREAT COVID-19 DISPENSED TO INDIVIDUALS WHO ARE SUBSIDY ELIGIBLE INDIVIDUALS.—Section 1860D–14(a) of the Social Security Act (42 U.S.C. 1395w–114(a)) is amended—

(A) in paragraph (1)—

(i) in subparagraph (D)—

(I) in clause (ii), by striking "In the case of" and inserting "Subject to subparagraph (F), in the case of"; and

(II) in clause (iii), by striking "In the case of" and inserting "Subject to subparagraph (F), in the case of"; and

(ii) by adding at the end the following new subparagraph:

"(F) ELIMINATION OF COST-SHARING FOR DRUGS INTENDED TO TREAT COVID-19.—Coverage that is in accordance with section 1860D–2(b)(8)."; and

(B) in paragraph (2)—

(i) in subparagraph (B), by striking "A reduction" and inserting "Subject to subparagraph (F), a reduction";

(ii) in subparagraph (D), by striking "The substitution" and inserting "Subject to subparagraph (F), the substitution";

(iii) in subparagraph (E), by inserting after "Subject to" the following: "subparagraph (F) and"; and

(iv) by adding at the end the following new subparagraph:

"(F) ELIMINATION OF COST-SHARING FOR DRUGS INTENDED TO TREAT COVID-19.—Coverage that is in accordance with section 1860D–2(b)(8).".

(c) Implementation.—Notwithstanding any other provision of law, the Secretary of Health and Human Services may implement the amendments made by this section by program instruction or otherwise.

SEC. 70211. REQUIRING MEDICARE PDPS AND MA–PD PLANS TO ALLOW DURING THE COVID-19 EMERGENCY PERIOD FOR FILLS AND REFILLS OF COVERED PART D DRUGS FOR UP TO A 3-MONTH SUPPLY.

(a) In General.—Section 1860D–4(b) of the Social Security Act (42 U.S.C. 1395w–104(b)) is amended by adding at the end the following new paragraph:

"(4) ENSURING ACCESS DURING COVID-19 PUBLIC HEALTH EMERGENCY PERIOD.—

"(A) IN GENERAL.—During the emergency period described in section 1135(g)(1)(B), subject to subparagraph (B), a prescription drug plan or MA–PD plan shall, notwithstanding any cost and utilization management, medication therapy management, or other such programs under this part, permit a part D eligible individual enrolled in such plan to obtain in a single fill or refill, at the option of such individual, the total day supply (not to exceed a 90-day supply) prescribed for such individual for a covered part D drug.

"(B) SAFETY EDIT EXCEPTION.—A prescription drug plan or MA–PD plan may not permit a part D eligible individual to obtain a single fill or refill inconsistent with an applicable safety edit.".

(b) Implementation.—Notwithstanding any other provision of law, the Secretary of Health and Human Services may implement the amendment made by this section by program instruction or otherwise.

SEC. 70212. EXTENSION OF THE WORK GEOGRAPHIC INDEX FLOOR UNDER THE MEDICARE PROGRAM.

Section 1848(e)(1)(E) of the Social Security Act (42 U.S.C. 1395w–4(e)(1)(E)) is amended by striking "May 23, 2020" and inserting "December 1, 2020".

SEC. 70213. EXTENSION OF FUNDING FOR QUALITY MEASURE ENDORSEMENT, INPUT, AND SELECTION.

(a) In General.—Section 1890(d)(2) of the Social Security Act (42 U.S.C.

1395aaa(d)(2)) is amended—

(1) in the first sentence, by striking "and $4,830,000 for the period beginning on October 1, 2019, and ending on May 22, 2020" and inserting "$25,170,000 for fiscal year 2020, and $5,013,699 for the period beginning on October 1, 2020, and ending on November 30, 2020"; and

(2) in the third sentence, by striking "for each of fiscal years 2018 and 2019 and for the period beginning on October 1, 2019, and ending on May 22, 2020" and inserting "for each of fiscal years 2018 through 2020 and for the period beginning on October 1, 2020, and ending on November 30, 2020".

(b) Effective Date.—The amendments made by subsection (a) shall take effect as if included in the enactment of the Further Consolidated Appropriations Act, 2020 (Public Law 116–94).

SEC. 70214. EXTENSION OF FUNDING OUTREACH AND ASSISTANCE FOR LOW-INCOME PROGRAMS.

(a) Additional Funding For State Health Insurance Programs.—Subsection (a)(1)(B) of section 119 of the Medicare Improvements for Patients and Providers Act of 2008 (42 U.S.C. 1395b–3 note) is amended—

(1) in clause (xi), by striking "and" at the end;

(2) in clause (xii), by striking the period at the end and inserting a semicolon; and

(3) by inserting after clause (xii) the following new clauses:

"(xiii) for the period beginning on May 23, 2020, and ending on September 30, 2020, of $5,383,562; and

"(xiv) for the period beginning on October 1, 2020, and ending on November 30, 2020, of $2,506,849.".

(b) Additional Funding For Area Agencies On Aging.—Subsection (b)(1)(B) of such section 119, as so amended, is amended—

(1) in clause (xi), by striking "and" at the end;

(2) in clause (xii), by striking the period at the end and inserting a semicolon; and

(3) by inserting after clause (xii) the following new clauses:

"(xiii) for the period beginning on May 23, 2020, and ending on September 30, 2020, of $5,383,562; and

"(xiv) for the period beginning on October 1, 2020, and ending on November 30, 2020, of $2,506,849.".

(c) Additional Funding For Aging And Disability Resource Centers.—Subsection (c)(1)(B) of such section 119, as so amended, is amended—

(1) in clause (xi), by striking "and" at the end;

(2) in clause (xii), by striking the period at the end and inserting a semicolon; and

(3) by inserting after clause (xii) the following new clauses:

"(xiii) for the period beginning on May 23, 2020, and ending on September 30, 2020, of $1,794,521; and "(xiv) for the period beginning on October 1, 2020, and ending on November 30, 2020, of $835,616.".

(d) Additional Funding For Contract With The National Center For Benefits And Outreach Enrollment.—Subsection (d)(2) of such section 119, as so amended, is amended—

(1) in clause (xi), by striking "and" at the end;

(2) in clause (xii), by striking the period at the end and inserting a semicolon; and

(3) by inserting after clause (xii) the following new clauses:

"(xiii) for the period beginning on May 23, 2020, and ending on September 30, 2020, of $5,383,562; and

"(xiv) for the period beginning on October 1, 2020, and ending on November 30, 2020, of $2,506,849.".

TITLE III—PRIVATE INSURANCE

SEC. 70301. SPECIAL ENROLLMENT PERIOD THROUGH EXCHANGES; FEDERAL EXCHANGE OUTREACH AND EDUCATIONAL ACTIVITIES.

(a) Special Enrollment Period Through Exchanges.—Section 1311(c) of the Patient Protection and Affordable Care Act (42 U.S.C. 18031(c)) is amended—

(1) in paragraph (6)—

(A) in subparagraph (C), by striking at the end "and";

(B) in subparagraph (D), by striking at the end the period and inserting "; and"; and

(C) by adding at the end the following new subparagraph:

"(E) subject to subparagraph (B) of paragraph (8), the special enrollment period described in subparagraph (A) of such paragraph."; and

(2) by adding at the end the following new paragraph:

"(8) SPECIAL ENROLLMENT PERIOD FOR CERTAIN PUBLIC HEALTH EMERGENCY.—

"(A) IN GENERAL.—The Secretary shall, subject to subparagraph (B), require an Exchange to provide—

"(i) for a special enrollment period during the emergency period described in section 1135(g)(1)(B) of the Social Security Act—

"(I) which shall begin on the date that is one week after the date of the enactment of this paragraph and which, in the case of an Exchange established or operated by the Secretary within a State pursuant to section 1321(c), shall be an 8-week period; and

"(II) during which any individual who is otherwise eligible to enroll in a qualified health plan through the Exchange may enroll in such a qualified health plan; and

"(ii) that, in the case of an individual who enrolls in a qualified health plan through the Exchange during such enrollment period, the coverage period under such plan shall begin, at the option of the individual, on April 1, 2020, or on the first day of the month following the day the individual selects a plan through such special enrollment period.

"(B) EXCEPTION.—The requirement of subparagraph (A) shall not apply to a State-operated or State-established Exchange if such Exchange, prior to the date of the enactment of this paragraph, established or otherwise provided for a special enrollment period to address access to coverage under qualified health plans offered through such Exchange during the emergency period described in section 1135(g)(1)(B) of the Social Security Act.".

(b) Federal Exchange Outreach And Educational Activities.—Section 1321(c) of the Patient Protection and Affordable Care Act (42 U.S.C. 18041(c)) is amended by adding at the end the following new paragraph:

"(3) OUTREACH AND EDUCATIONAL ACTIVITIES.—

"(A) IN GENERAL.—In the case of an Exchange established or operated by the Secretary within a State pursuant to this subsection, the Secretary shall carry out outreach and educational activities for purposes of informing potential enrollees in qualified health plans offered through the Exchange of the availability of coverage under such plans and financial assistance for coverage under such plans. Such outreach and educational activities shall be provided in a manner that is culturally and linguistically appropriate to the needs of the populations being served by the Exchange (including hard-to-reach populations, such as racial and sexual minorities, limited English proficient populations, and young adults).

"(B) LIMITATION ON USE OF FUNDS.—No funds appropriated under this paragraph shall be used for expenditures for promoting non-ACA compliant health insurance coverage.

"(C) NON-ACA COMPLIANT HEALTH INSURANCE COVERAGE.—For purposes of subparagraph (B):

"(i) The term 'non-ACA compliant health insurance coverage' means health insurance coverage, or a group health plan, that is not a qualified health plan.

"(ii) Such term includes the following:

"(I) An association health plan.

"(II) Short-term limited duration insurance.

"(D) FUNDING.—Out of any funds in the Treasury not otherwise appropriated, there are hereby appropriated $25,000,000 to carry out this paragraph. Funds appropriated under this subparagraph shall remain available until expended.".

(c) Implementation.—The Secretary of Health and Human Services may implement the provisions of (including amendments made by) this section through subregulatory guidance, program instruction, or otherwise.

SEC. 70302. SHORT-TERM LIMITED DURATION INSURANCE RULE PROHIBITION.

The Secretary of Health and Human Services, the Secretary of the Treasury, and the Secretary of Labor may not take any action to implement, enforce, or otherwise give effect to the rule entitled "Short-Term, Limited Duration Insurance" (83 Fed. Reg. 38212 (August 3, 2018)), and the Secretaries may not promulgate any substantially similar rule.

SEC. 70303. RAPID COVERAGE OF PREVENTIVE SERVICES AND VACCINES FOR COVID-19.

(a) In General.—In the case of a qualifying COVID-19 preventive service, notwithstanding section 2713(b) of the Public Health Service Act (42 U.S.C. 300gg–13(b)) (including the regulations under section 2590.715–2713 of title 29, Code of Federal Regulations, section 54.9815–2713 of title 26, Code of Federal Regulations, and section 147.130 of title 45, Code of Federal Regulations), the Secretary of Health and Human Services, Secretary of Labor, and Secretary of the Treasury shall apply to group health plans and health insurance issuers offering group or individual health insurance coverage the requirement under section 2713(a) of the Public Health Service Act (42 U.S.C. 300gg–13(a)), with respect to such services, as if such section 2713(a)—

(1) required the coverage of such service under such plans and such coverage be effective not later than the specified date (as defined in subsection (b)(2)) with respect to such service; and

(2) applied to grandfathered health plans (as defined in section 1251(e) of the Patient Protection and Affordable Care Act (42 U.S.C. 18011(e))).

(b) Definitions.—For purposes of this section:

(1) QUALIFYING COVID-19 PREVENTIVE SERVICE.—The term "qualifying COVID-19 preventive service" means an item, service, or immunization that is intended to prevent or mitigate COVID-19 and that is—

(A) an evidence-based item or service that has in effect a rating of "A" or "B" in the current recommendations of the United States Preventive Services Task Force; or

(B) an immunization that has in effect a recommendation from the Advisory Committee on Immunization Practices of the Centers for Disease Control and Prevention with respect to the individual involved.

(2) SPECIFIED DATE.—The term "specified date" means—

(A) with respect to a qualifying COVID-19 preventive service described in paragraph (1)(A), the date that is 15 business days after the date on which a rating, as described in such paragraph, is made with respect to such service; and

(B) with respect to a qualifying COVID-19 preventive service described in paragraph (1)(B), the date that is 15 business days after the date on which a recommendation, as described in such paragraph, is made relating to the service.

(3) ADDITIONAL TERMS.—The terms "group health plan"; "health insurance issuer"; "group health insurance coverage", and "individual health insurance coverage" have the meanings given such terms in section 2791 of the

Public Health Service Act (42 U.S.C. 300gg–91), section 733 of the Employee Retirement Income Security Act (29 U.S.C. 1191b), and section 9832 of the Internal Revenue Code of 1986, as applicable.

(c) Implementation.—The Secretary of Health and Human Services, Secretary of Labor, and Secretary of the Treasury may implement the provisions of this section through program instruction, subregulatory guidance, or otherwise.

SEC. 70304. COVERAGE OF COVID-19 RELATED TREATMENT AT NO COST SHARING.

(a) In General.—A group health plan and a health insurance issuer offering group or individual health insurance coverage (including a grandfathered health plan (as defined in section 1251(e) of the Patient Protection and Affordable Care Act)) shall provide coverage, and shall not impose any cost sharing (including deductibles, copayments, and coinsurance) requirements, for the following items and services furnished during any portion of the emergency period defined in paragraph (1)(B) of section 1135(g) of the Social Security Act (42 U.S.C. 1320b–5(g)) beginning on or after the date of the enactment of this Act:

(1) Medically necessary items and services (including in-person or telehealth visits in which such items and services are furnished) that are furnished to an individual who has been diagnosed with (or after provision of the items and services is diagnosed with) COVID-19 to treat or mitigate the effects of COVID-19.

(2) Medically necessary items and services (including in-person or telehealth visits in which such items and services are furnished) that are furnished to an individual who is presumed to have COVID-19 but is never diagnosed as such, if the following conditions are met:

(A) Such items and services are furnished to the individual to treat or mitigate the effects of COVID-19 or to mitigate the impact of COVID-19 on society.

(B) Health care providers have taken appropriate steps under the circumstances to make a diagnosis, or confirm whether a diagnosis was made, with respect to such individual, for COVID-19, if possible.

(b) Items And Services Related To COVID-19.—For purposes of this section—

(1) not later than one week after the date of the enactment of this section, the Secretary of Health and Human Services, Secretary of Labor, and Secretary of the Treasury shall jointly issue guidance specifying applicable diagnoses and medically necessary items and services related to COVID-19; and

(2) such items and services shall include all items or services that are relevant to the treatment or mitigation of COVID-19, regardless of whether such items or services are ordinarily covered under the terms of a group health plan or group or individual health insurance coverage offered by a health insurance issuer.

(c) Reimbursement To Plans And Coverage For Waiving Cost-Sharing.—

(1) IN GENERAL.—A group health plan or a health insurance issuer offering

group or individual health insurance coverage (including a grandfathered health plan (as defined in section 1251(e) of the Patient Protection and Affordable Care Act)) that does not impose cost sharing requirements as described in subsection (a) shall notify the Secretary of Health and Human Services, Secretary of Labor, and Secretary of the Treasury (through a joint process established jointly by the Secretaries) of the total dollar amount of cost-sharing that, but for the application of subsection (a), would have been required under such plans and coverage for items and services related to COVID-19 furnished during the period to which subsection (a) applies to enrollees, participants, and beneficiaries in the plan or coverage to whom such subsection applies, but which was not imposed for such items and services so furnished pursuant to such subsection and the Secretary of Health and Human Services, in coordination with the Secretary of Labor and the Secretary of the Treasury, shall make payments in accordance with this subsection to the plan or issuer equal to such total dollar amount.

(2) METHODOLOGY FOR PAYMENTS.—The Secretary of Health and Human Service, in coordination with the Secretary of Labor and the Secretary of the Treasury shall establish a payment system for making payments under this subsection. Any such system shall make payment for the value of cost sharing not imposed by the plan or issuer involved.

(3) TIMING OF PAYMENTS.—Payments made under paragraph (1) shall be made no later than May 1, 2021, for amounts of cost sharing waivers with respect to 2020. Payments under this subsection with respect to such waivers with respect to a year subsequent to 2020 that begins during the period to which subsection (a) applies shall be made no later than May of the year following such subsequent year.

(4) APPROPRIATIONS.—There is authorized to be appropriated, and there is appropriated, out of any monies in the Treasury not otherwise appropriated, such funds as are necessary to carry out this subsection.

(d) Enforcement.—

(1) APPLICATION WITH RESPECT TO PHSA, ERISA, AND IRC.—The provisions of this section shall be applied by the Secretary of Health and Human Services, Secretary of Labor, and Secretary of the Treasury to group health plans and health insurance issuers offering group or individual health insurance coverage as if included in the provisions of part A of title XXVII of the Public Health Service Act, part 7 of the Employee Retirement Income Security Act of 1974, and subchapter B of chapter 100 of the Internal Revenue Code of 1986, as applicable.

(2) PRIVATE RIGHT OF ACTION.—An individual with respect to whom an action is taken by a group health plan or health insurance issuer offering group or individual health insurance coverage in violation of subsection (a) may commence a civil action against the plan or issuer for appropriate relief. The previous sentence shall not be construed as limiting any enforcement mechanism otherwise applicable pursuant to paragraph (1).

(e) Implementation.—The Secretary of Health and Human Services, Secretary of Labor, and Secretary of the Treasury may implement the provisions of this section through sub-regulatory guidance, program instruction or otherwise.

(f) Terms.—The terms "group health plan"; "health insurance issuer"; "group health insurance coverage", and "individual health insurance coverage" have the meanings given such terms in section 2791 of the Public Health Service Act (42 U.S.C. 300gg–91), section 733 of the Employee Retirement Income Security Act of 1974 (29 U.S.C. 1191b), and section 9832 of the Internal Revenue Code of 1986, as applicable.

SEC. 70305. REQUIRING PRESCRIPTION DRUG REFILL NOTIFICATIONS DURING EMERGENCIES.

(a) ERISA.—

(1) IN GENERAL.—Subpart B of part 7 of subtitle B of title I of the Employee Retirement Income Security Act of 1974 (29 U.S.C. 1185 et seq.) is amended by adding at the end the following new section:

"SEC. 716. PROVISION OF PRESCRIPTION DRUG REFILL NOTIFICATIONS DURING EMERGENCIES.

"(a) In General.—A group health plan, and a health insurance issuer offering health insurance coverage in connection with a group health plan, that provides benefits for prescription drugs under such plan or such coverage shall provide to each individual enrolled under such plan or such coverage who resides in an emergency area during an emergency period, not later than 5 business days after the date of the beginning of such period with respect to such area (or, the case of the emergency period described in section 70305(d)(2) of the Take Responsibility for Workers and Families Act, not later than 5 business days after the date of the enactment of this section), a notification—

"(1) of whether such plan or coverage will waive, during such period with respect to such an individual, any time restrictions under such plan or coverage on any authorized refills for such drugs to enable such refills in advance of when such refills would otherwise have been permitted under such plan or coverage; and

"(2) in the case that such plan or coverage will waive such restrictions during such period with respect to such an individual, that contains information on how such an individual may obtain such a refill.

"(b) Emergency Area; Emergency Period.—For purposes of this section, an 'emergency area' is a geographical area in which, and an 'emergency period' is the period during which, there exists—

"(1) an emergency or disaster declared by the President pursuant to the National Emergencies Act or the Robert T. Stafford Disaster Relief and Emergency Assistance Act; and

"(2) a public health emergency declared by the Secretary pursuant to section 319 of the Public Health Service Act.".

(2) CLERICAL AMENDMENT.—The table of contents of the Employee Retirement Income Security Act of 1974 is amended by inserting after the item relating to section 714 the following:

"Sec. 715. Additional market reforms.

"Sec. 716. Provision of prescription drug refill notifications during emergencies.".

(b) PHSA.—Subpart II of part A of title XXVII of the Public Health Service Act (42 U.S.C. 300gg–11 et seq.) is amended by adding at the end the following new section:

"SEC. 2730. PROVISION OF PRESCRIPTION DRUG REFILL NOTIFICATIONS DURING EMERGENCIES.

"(a) In General.—A group health plan, and a health insurance issuer offering group or individual health insurance coverage, that provides benefits for prescription drugs under such plan or such coverage shall provide to each individual enrolled under such plan or such coverage who resides in an emergency area during an emergency period, not later than 5 business days after the date of the beginning of such period with respect to such area (or, the case of the emergency period described in section 70305(d)(2) of the Take Responsibility for Workers and Families Act, not later than 5 business days after the date of the enactment of this section), a notification—

"(1) of whether such plan or coverage will waive, during such period with respect to such an individual, any time restrictions under such plan or coverage on any authorized refills for such drugs to enable such refills in advance of when such refills would otherwise have been permitted under such plan or coverage; and

"(2) in the case that such plan or coverage will waive such restrictions during such period with respect to such an individual, that contains information on how such an individual may obtain such a refill.

"(b) Emergency Area; Emergency Period.—For purposes of this section, an 'emergency area' is a geographical area in which, and an 'emergency period' is the period during which, there exists—

"(1) an emergency or disaster declared by the President pursuant to the National Emergencies Act or the Robert T. Stafford Disaster Relief and Emergency Assistance Act; and

"(2) a public health emergency declared by the Secretary pursuant to section 319.".

(c) IRC.—

(1) IN GENERAL.—Subchapter B of chapter 100 of the Internal Revenue Code of 1986 is amended by adding at the end the following new section:

"SEC. 9816. PROVISION OF PRESCRIPTION DRUG REFILL NOTIFICATIONS DURING EMERGENCIES.

"(a) In General.—A group health plan that provides benefits for prescription drugs under such plan shall provide to each individual enrolled under such plan who resides in an emergency area during an emergency period, not later than 5 business days after the date of the beginning of such period with respect to such area (or, the case of the emergency period described in section 70305(d)(2) of the Take Responsibility for Workers and Families Act, not later than 5 business days after the date of the enactment of this section), a notification—

"(1) of whether such plan will waive, during such period with respect to such an individual, any time restrictions under such plan on any authorized refills for such drugs to enable such refills in advance of when such refills would otherwise have been permitted under such plan; and

"(2) in the case that such plan will waive such restrictions during such period with respect to such an individual, that contains information on how such an individual may obtain such a refill.

"(b) Emergency Area; Emergency Period.—For purposes of this section, an 'emergency area' is a geographical area in which, and an 'emergency period' is the period during which, there exists—

"(1) an emergency or disaster declared by the President pursuant to the National Emergencies Act or the Robert T. Stafford Disaster Relief and Emergency Assistance Act; and

"(2) a public health emergency declared by the Secretary pursuant to section 319 of the Public Health Service Act.".

(2) CLERICAL AMENDMENT.—The table of sections for subchapter B of chapter 100 of the Internal Revenue Code of 1986 is amended by adding at the end the following new item:

"Sec. 9816. Provision of prescription drug refill notifications during emergencies.".

(d) Effective Date.—The amendments made by this section shall apply with respect to—

(1) emergency periods beginning on or after the date of the enactment of this Act; and

(2) the emergency period relating to the public health emergency declared by the Secretary of Health and Human Services pursuant to section 319 of the Public Health Service Act on January 31, 2020, entitled "Determination that a Public Health Emergency Exists Nationwide as the Result of the 2019 Novel Coronavirus".

SEC. 70306. IMPROVEMENT OF CERTAIN NOTIFICATIONS PROVIDED TO QUALIFIED BENEFICIARIES BY GROUP HEALTH PLANS IN THE CASE OF QUALIFYING EVENTS.

(a) Employee Retirement Income Security Act Of 1974.—

(1) IN GENERAL.—Section 606 of the Employee Retirement Income Security Act of 1974 (29 U.S.C. 1166) is amended—

(A) in subsection (a)(4), in the matter following subparagraph (B), by striking "under this subsection" and inserting "under this part in accordance with the notification requirements under subsection (c)"; and

(B) in subsection (c)—

(i) by striking "For purposes of subsection (a)(4), any notification" and inserting For purposes of subsection (a)(4)—

"(1) any notification";

(ii) by striking ", whichever is applicable, and any such notification" and inserting of subsection (a), whichever is applicable;

"(2) any such notification"; and

(iii) by striking "such notification is made" and inserting such notification is made; and

"(3) any such notification shall, with respect to each qualified beneficiary with respect to whom such notification is made, include information regarding any Exchange established under title I of the Patient Protection and Affordable Care Act through which such a qualified beneficiary may be eligible to enroll in a qualified health plan (as defined in section 1301 of the Patient Protection and Affordable Care Act), including—

"(A) the publicly accessible Internet website address for such Exchange;

"(B) the publicly accessible Internet website address for the Find Local Help directory maintained by the Department of Health and Human Services on the healthcare.gov Internet website (or a successor website);

"(C) a clear explanation that—

"(i) an individual who is eligible for continuation coverage may also be eligible to enroll, with financial assistance, in a qualified health plan offered through such Exchange, but, in the case that such individual elects to enroll in such continuation coverage and subsequently elects to terminate such continuation coverage before the period of such continuation coverage expires, such individual will not be eligible to enroll in a qualified health plan offered through such Exchange during a special enrollment period; and

"(ii) an individual who elects to enroll in continuation coverage will remain eligible to enroll in a qualified health plan offered through such Exchange during an open enrollment period and may be eligible for financial assistance with respect to enrolling in such a qualified health plan;

"(D) information on consumer protections with respect to enrolling in a qualified health plan offered through such Exchange, including the requirement for such a qualified health plan to provide coverage for essential health benefits (as defined in section 1302(b) of the Patient Protection and Affordable Care Act) and the requirements applicable to such a qualified health plan under part A of title XXVII of the Public Health Service Act; and

"(E) information on the availability of financial assistance with respect to enrolling in a qualified health plan, including the maximum income limit for eligibility for a premium tax credit under section 36B of the Internal Revenue Code of 1986.".

(2) EFFECTIVE DATE.—The amendments made by paragraph (1) shall apply with respect to qualifying events occurring on or after the date that is 14 days after the date of the enactment of this Act.

(b) Public Health Service Act.—

(1) IN GENERAL.—Section 2206 of the Public Health Service Act (42 U.S.C. 300bb–6) is amended—

(A) by striking "In accordance" and inserting the following:

"(a) In General.—In accordance";

(B) by striking "of such beneficiary's rights under this subsection" and inserting "of such beneficiary's rights under this title in accordance with the notification requirements under subsection (b)"; and

(C) by striking "For purposes of paragraph (4)," and all that follows through "such notification is made." and inserting the following:

"(b) Rules Relating To Notification Of Qualified Beneficiaries By Plan Administrator.—For purposes of subsection (a)(4)—

"(1) any notification shall be made within 14 days of the date on which the plan administrator is notified under paragraph (2) or (3) of subsection (a), whichever is applicable;

"(2) any such notification to an individual who is a qualified beneficiary as the spouse of the covered employee shall be treated as notification to all other qualified beneficiaries residing with such spouse at the time such notification is made; and

"(3) any such notification shall, with respect to each qualified beneficiary with respect to whom such notification is made, include information regarding any Exchange established under title I of the Patient Protection and Affordable Care Act through which such a qualified beneficiary may be eligible to enroll in a qualified health plan (as defined in section 1301 of the Patient Protection and Affordable Care Act), including—

"(A) the publicly accessible Internet website address for such Exchange;

"(B) the publicly accessible Internet website address for the Find Local Help directory maintained by the Department of Health and Human Services on the healthcare.gov Internet website (or a successor website);

"(C) a clear explanation that—

"(i) an individual who is eligible for continuation coverage may also be eligible to enroll, with financial assistance, in a qualified health plan offered through such Exchange, but, in the case that such individual elects to enroll in such continuation coverage and subsequently elects to terminate such continuation coverage before the period of such continuation coverage expires, such individual will not be eligible to enroll in a qualified health plan offered through such Exchange during a special enrollment period; and

"(ii) an individual who elects to enroll in continuation coverage will remain eligible to enroll in a qualified health plan offered through such Exchange during an open enrollment period and may be eligible for financial assistance with respect to enrolling in such a qualified health plan;

"(D) information on consumer protections with respect to enrolling in a qualified health plan offered through such Exchange, including the requirement for such a qualified health plan to provide coverage for essential health benefits (as defined in section 1302(b) of the Patient Protection and Affordable Care Act) and the requirements applicable to such a qualified health plan under part A of title XXVII; and

"(E) information on the availability of financial assistance with respect to enrolling in a qualified health plan, including the maximum income limit for eligibility for a premium tax credit under section 36B of the Internal Revenue Code of 1986.".

(2) EFFECTIVE DATE.—The amendments made by paragraph (1) shall apply with respect to qualifying events occurring on or after the date that is 14 days after the date of the enactment of this Act.

(c) Internal Revenue Code Of 1986.—

(1) IN GENERAL.—Section 4980B(f)(6) of the Internal Revenue Code of 1986 is amended—

(A) in subparagraph (D)—

(i) in clause (ii), by striking "under subparagraph (C)" and inserting "under clause (iii)"; and

(ii) by redesignating clauses (i) and (ii) as subclauses (I) and (II), respectively, and moving the margin of each such subclause, as so redesignated, 2 ems to the right;

(B) by redesignating subparagraphs (A) through (D) as clauses (i) through (iv), respectively, and moving the margin of each such clause, as so redesignated, 2 ems to the right;

(C) by striking "In accordance" and inserting the following:

"(A) IN GENERAL.—In accordance";

(D) by inserting after "of such beneficiary's rights under this subsection" the following: "in accordance with the notification requirements under subparagraph (C)"; and

(E) by striking "The requirements of subparagraph (B)" and all that follows through "such notification is made." and inserting the following:

"(B) ALTERNATIVE MEANS OF COMPLIANCE WITH REQUIREMENT FOR NOTIFICATION OF MULTIEMPLOYER PLANS BY EMPLOYERS.—The requirements of subparagraph (A)(ii) shall be considered satisfied in the case of a multiemployer plan in connection with a qualifying event described in paragraph (3)(B) if the plan provides that the determination of the occurrence of such qualifying event will be made by the plan administrator.

"(C) RULES RELATING TO NOTIFICATION OF QUALIFIED BENEFICIARIES BY PLAN ADMINISTRATOR.—For purposes of subparagraph (A)(iv)—

"(i) any notification shall be made within 14 days (or, in the case of a group health plan which is a multiemployer plan, such longer period of time as may be provided in the terms of the plan) of the date on which the plan administrator is notified under clause (ii) or (iii) of subparagraph (A), whichever is applicable;

"(ii) any such notification to an individual who is a qualified beneficiary as the spouse of the covered employee shall be treated as notification to all other qualified beneficiaries residing with such spouse at the time such notification is made; and

"(iii) any such notification shall, with respect to each qualified beneficiary with respect to whom such notification is made, include information regarding any Exchange established under title I of the Patient Protection and Affordable Care Act through which such a qualified beneficiary may be eligible to enroll in a qualified health plan (as defined in section 1301 of the Patient Protection and Affordable Care Act), including—

"(I) the publicly accessible Internet website address for such Exchange;

"(II) the publicly accessible Internet website address for the Find Local Help directory maintained by the Department of Health and Human Services on the healthcare.gov Internet website (or a successor website);

"(III) a clear explanation that—

"(aa) an individual who is eligible for continuation coverage may also be eligible to enroll, with financial assistance, in a qualified health plan offered through such Exchange, but, in the case that such individual elects to enroll in such continuation coverage and subsequently elects to terminate such continuation coverage before the period of such continuation coverage expires, such individual will not be eligible to enroll in a qualified health plan offered through such Exchange during a special enrollment period; and

"(bb) an individual who elects to enroll in continuation coverage will remain eligible to enroll in a qualified health plan offered through such Exchange during an open enrollment period and may be eligible for financial assistance with respect to enrolling in such a qualified health plan;

"(IV) information on consumer protections with respect to enrolling in a qualified health plan offered through such Exchange, including the requirement for such a qualified health plan to provide coverage for essential health benefits (as defined in section 1302(b) of the Patient Protection and Affordable Care Act) and the requirements applicable to such a qualified health plan under part A of title XXVII of the Public Health Service Act; and

"(V) information on the availability of financial assistance with respect to enrolling in a qualified health plan, including the maximum income limit for eligibility for a premium tax credit under section 36B.".

(2) EFFECTIVE DATE.—The amendments made by paragraph (1) shall apply with respect to qualifying events occurring on or after the date that is 14 days after the date of the enactment of this Act.

(d) Model Notices.—Not later than 14 days after the date of the enactment of this Act, the Secretary of the Labor, in consultation with the Secretary of the Treasury and the Secretary of Health and Human Services, shall—

(1) update the model Consolidated Omnibus Budget Reconciliation Act of 1985 (referred to in this subsection as "COBRA") continuation coverage general notice and the model COBRA continuation coverage election notice developed by the Secretary of Labor for purposes of facilitating compliance

of group health plans with the notification requirements under section 606 of the Employee Retirement Income Security Act of 1974 (29 U.S.C. 1166) to include the information described in paragraph (3) of subsection (c) of such section 606, as added by subsection (a)(1);

(2) provide an opportunity for consumer testing of each such notice, as so updated, to ensure that each such notice is clear and understandable to the average participant or beneficiary of a group health plan; and

(3) rename the model COBRA continuation coverage general notice and the model COBRA continuation coverage election notice as the "model COBRA continuation coverage and Affordable Care Act coverage general notice" and the "model COBRA continuation coverage and Affordable Care Act coverage election notice", respectively.

SEC. 70307. PRESERVING HEALTH BENEFITS FOR WORKERS.

(a) Premium Assistance For COBRA Continuation Coverage For Individuals And Their Families.—

(1) PROVISION OF PREMIUM ASSISTANCE.—

(A) REDUCTION OF PREMIUMS PAYABLE.—In the case of any premium for a period of coverage beginning on or after the date of the enactment of this Act for COBRA continuation coverage with respect to any assistance eligible individual, such individual shall be treated for purposes of any COBRA continuation provision as having paid the amount of such premium if such individual pays (or a person other than such individual's employer pays on behalf of such individual) 0 percent of the amount of such premium (as determined without regard to this subsection).

(B) PLAN ENROLLMENT OPTION.—

(i) IN GENERAL.—Notwithstanding the COBRA continuation provisions, an assistance eligible individual may, not later than 90 days after the date of notice of the plan enrollment option described in this subparagraph, elect to enroll in coverage under a plan offered by the employer involved, or the employee organization involved (including, for this purpose, a joint board of trustees of a multiemployer trust affiliated with one or more multiemployer plans), that is different than coverage under the plan in which such individual was enrolled at the time the qualifying event occurred, and such coverage shall be treated as COBRA continuation coverage for purposes of the applicable COBRA continuation coverage provision.

(ii) REQUIREMENTS.—An assistance eligible individual may elect to enroll in different coverage as described in clause (i) only if—

(I) the employer involved has made a determination that such employer will permit assistance eligible individuals to enroll in different coverage as provided for this subparagraph;

(II) the premium for such different coverage does not exceed the premium for coverage in which the individual was enrolled at the time the qualifying event occurred;

(III) the different coverage in which the individual elects to enroll is coverage that is also offered to the active employees of the employer at the time at which such election is made; and

(IV) the different coverage is not—

(aa) coverage that provides only dental, vision, counseling, or referral services (or a combination of such services);

(bb) a flexible spending arrangement (as defined in section 106(c)(2) of the Internal Revenue Code of 1986); or

(cc) coverage that provides coverage for services or treatments furnished in an on-site medical facility maintained by the employer and that consists primarily of first-aid services, prevention and wellness care, or similar care (or a combination of such care).

(C) PREMIUM REIMBURSEMENT.—For provisions providing the payment of such premium, see section 6432 of the Internal Revenue Code of 1986, as added by paragraph (12).

(2) LIMITATION OF PERIOD OF PREMIUM ASSISTANCE.—

(A) ELIGIBILITY FOR ADDITIONAL COVERAGE.—Paragraph (1)(A) shall not apply with respect to any assistance eligible individual for months of coverage beginning on or after—

(i) the earlier of the first date that such individual is eligible for coverage under any other group health plan (other than coverage consisting of only dental, vision, counseling, or referral services (or a combination thereof), coverage under a flexible spending arrangement (as defined in section 106(c)(2) of the Internal Revenue Code of 1986), coverage of treatment that is furnished in an on-site medical facility maintained by the employer and that consists primarily of first-aid services, prevention and wellness care, or similar care (or a combination thereof)), is eligible for benefits under title XVIII of the Social Security Act, or enrolls in a qualified health plan (as defined in section 1301(a) of the Patient Protection and Affordable Care Act (42 U.S.C. 18021(a)) offered through an Exchange established under title I of the Patient Protection and Affordable Care Act; and

(ii) the earliest of—

(I) the date which is 9 months after the first day of the first month that paragraph (1)(A) applies with respect to such individual;

(II) the date following the expiration of the maximum period of continuation coverage required under the applicable COBRA continuation coverage provision; or

(III) the date following the expiration of the period of continuation coverage allowed under paragraph (4)(B)(ii).

(B) TIMING OF ELIGIBILITY FOR ADDITIONAL COVERAGE.—For purposes of subparagraph (A)(i), an individual shall not be treated as eligible for coverage under a group health plan before the first date on which such individual could be covered under such plan.

(C) NOTIFICATION REQUIREMENT.—An assistance eligible individual shall notify in writing the group health plan with respect to which paragraph (1)(A) applies if such paragraph ceases to apply by reason of subparagraph (A)(i). Such notice shall be provided to the group health plan in such time and manner as may be specified by the Secretary of Labor.

(3) ASSISTANCE ELIGIBLE INDIVIDUAL.—For purposes of this section, the term "assistance eligible individual" means any qualified beneficiary if—

(A) at any time during the emergency period described in section 1135(g)(1)(B) of the Social Security Act (42 U.S.C. 1320b–5(g)(1)(B)) such qualified beneficiary is eligible for COBRA continuation coverage by reason of qualifying event specified in section 603(2) of the Employee Retirement Income Security Act of 1974, section 4980B(f)(3)(B) of the Internal Revenue Code of 1986, section 2203(2) of the Public Health Service Act, or section 8905a of title 5, United States Code; and

(B) such qualified beneficiary elects such coverage.

(4) EXTENSION OF ELECTION PERIOD AND EFFECT ON COVERAGE.—

(A) IN GENERAL.—For purposes of applying section 605(a) of the Employee Retirement Income Security Act of 1974, section 4980B(f)(5)(A) of the Internal Revenue Code of 1986, section 2205(a) of the Public Health Service Act, and section 8905a(c)(2) of title 5, United States Code, in the case of—

(i) an individual who does not have an election of COBRA continuation coverage in effect on the date of the enactment of this Act but who would be an assistance eligible individual if such election were so in effect; or

(ii) an individual who elected COBRA continuation coverage on or after the first date of the emergency period described in section 1135(g)(1)(B) of the Social Security Act (42 U.S.C. 1320b–5(g)(1)(B)) and disenrolled from such coverage before the date of the enactment of this Act;

such individual may elect the COBRA continuation coverage under the COBRA continuation coverage provisions containing such sections during the period beginning on the date of the enactment of this Act and ending 60 days after the date on which the notification required under paragraph (7)(C) is provided to such individual.

(B) COMMENCEMENT OF COVERAGE; NO REACH-BACK.—Any COBRA continuation coverage elected by a qualified beneficiary during an extended election period under subparagraph (A)—

(i) shall commence with the first period of coverage beginning on or after the date of the enactment of this Act; and

(ii) shall not extend beyond the period of COBRA continuation coverage that would have been required under the applicable COBRA continuation coverage provision if the coverage had been elected as required under such provision.

(5) EXPEDITED REVIEW OF DENIALS OF PREMIUM ASSISTANCE.—In any case in which an individual requests treatment as an assistance eligible individual and is denied such treatment by the group health plan, the Secretary of Labor (or the Secretary of Health and Human Services in connection with

COBRA continuation coverage which is provided other than pursuant to part 6 of subtitle B of title I of the Employee Retirement Income Security Act of 1974), in consultation with the Secretary of the Treasury, shall provide for expedited review of such denial. An individual shall be entitled to such review upon application to such Secretary in such form and manner as shall be provided by such Secretary. Such Secretary shall make a determination regarding such individual's eligibility within 15 business days after receipt of such individual's application for review under this paragraph. Either Secretary's determination upon review of the denial shall be de novo and shall be the final determination of such Secretary. A reviewing court shall grant deference to such Secretary's determination. The provisions of this paragraph, paragraphs (1) through (4), and paragraph (7) shall be treated as provisions of title I of the Employee Retirement Income Security Act of 1974 for purposes of part 5 of subtitle B of such title.

(6) DISREGARD OF SUBSIDIES FOR PURPOSES OF FEDERAL AND STATE PROGRAMS.—Notwithstanding any other provision of law, any premium reduction with respect to an assistance eligible individual under this subsection shall not be considered income or resources in determining eligibility for, or the amount of assistance or benefits provided under, any other public benefit provided under Federal law or the law of any State or political subdivision thereof.

(7) NOTICES TO INDIVIDUALS.—

(A) GENERAL NOTICE.—

(i) IN GENERAL.—In the case of notices provided under section 606(a)(4) of the Employee Retirement Income Security Act of 1974 (29 U.S.C. 1166(4)), section 4980B(f)(6)(D) of the Internal Revenue Code of 1986, section 2206(4) of the Public Health Service Act (42 U.S.C. 300bb–6(4)), or section 8905a(f)(2)(A) of title 5, United States Code, with respect to individuals who, during the period described in paragraph (3)(A), become entitled to elect COBRA continuation coverage, the requirements of such sections shall not be treated as met unless such notices include an additional notification to the recipient of—

(I) the availability of premium reduction with respect to such coverage under this subsection; and

(II) the option to enroll in different coverage if the employer permits assistance eligible individuals to elect enrollment in different coverage (as described in paragraph (1)(B)).

(ii) ALTERNATIVE NOTICE.—In the case of COBRA continuation coverage to which the notice provision under such sections does not apply, the Secretary of Labor, in consultation with the Secretary of the Treasury and the Secretary of Health and Human Services, shall, in consultation with administrators of the group health plans (or other entities) that provide or administer the COBRA continuation coverage involved, provide rules requiring the provision of such notice.

(iii) FORM.—The requirement of the additional notification under this subparagraph may be met by amendment of existing notice forms or by inclusion of a separate document with the notice otherwise required.

(B) SPECIFIC REQUIREMENTS.—Each additional notification under subparagraph (A) shall include—

(i) the forms necessary for establishing eligibility for premium reduction under this subsection;

(ii) the name, address, and telephone number necessary to contact the plan administrator and any other person maintaining relevant information in connection with such premium reduction;

(iii) a description of the extended election period provided for in paragraph (4)(A);

(iv) a description of the obligation of the qualified beneficiary under paragraph (2)(C) to notify the plan providing continuation coverage of eligibility for subsequent coverage under another group health plan or eligibility for benefits under title XVIII of the Social Security Act and the penalty provided under section 6720C of the Internal Revenue Code of 1986 for failure to so notify the plan;

(v) a description, displayed in a prominent manner, of the qualified beneficiary's right to a reduced premium and any conditions on entitlement to the reduced premium;

(vi) a description of the option of the qualified beneficiary to enroll in different coverage if the employer permits such beneficiary to elect to enroll in such different coverage under paragraph (1)(B);

(vii) information regarding any Exchange established under title I of the Patient Protection and Affordable Care Act through which a qualified beneficiary may be eligible to enroll in a qualified health plan, including—

(I) the publicly accessible internet website address for such Exchange;

(II) the publicly accessible internet website address for the Find Local Help directory maintained by the Department of Health and Human Services on the healthcare.gov internet website (or a successor website);

(III) a clear explanation that—

(aa) an individual who is eligible for continuation coverage may also be eligible to enroll, with financial assistance, in a qualified health plan offered through such Exchange, but, in the case that such individual elects to enroll in such continuation coverage and subsequently elects to terminate such continuation coverage before the period of such continuation coverage expires, such individual will not be eligible to enroll in a qualified health plan offered through such Exchange during a special enrollment period; and

(bb) an individual who elects to enroll in continuation coverage will remain eligible to enroll in a qualified health plan offered through such Exchange during an open enrollment period and may be eligible for financial assistance with respect to enrolling in such a qualified health plan;

(IV) information on consumer protections with respect to enrolling in a qualified health plan offered through such Exchange, including the requirement for such a qualified health plan to provide coverage for essential health benefits (as defined in section 1302(b) of such Act (42 U.S.C. 18022(b))) and the requirements applicable to such a qualified health plan under part A of title XXVII of the Public Health Service Act (42 U.S.C. 300gg et seq.); and

(V) information on the availability of financial assistance with respect to enrolling in a qualified health plan, including the maximum income limit for eligibility for a premium tax credit under section 36B of the Internal Revenue Code of 1986.

(C) NOTICE IN CONNECTION WITH EXTENDED ELECTION PERIODS.—In the case of any assistance eligible individual (or any individual described in paragraph (4)(A)) who became entitled to elect COBRA continuation coverage before the date of the enactment of this Act, the administrator of the group health plan (or other entity) involved shall provide (within 60 days after the date of enactment of this Act) for the additional notification required to be provided under subparagraph (A) and failure to provide such notice shall be treated as a failure to meet the notice requirements under the applicable COBRA continuation provision.

(D) MODEL NOTICES.—Not later than 30 days after the date of enactment of this Act—

(i) the Secretary of the Labor, in consultation with the Secretary of the Treasury and the Secretary of Health and Human Services, shall prescribe models for the additional notification required under this paragraph (other than the additional notification described in clause (ii)); and

(ii) in the case of any additional notification provided pursuant to subparagraph (A) under section 8905a(f)(2)(A) of title 5, United States Code, the Office of Personnel Management shall prescribe a model for such additional notification.

(8) REGULATIONS.—The Secretary of the Treasury may prescribe such regulations or other guidance as may be necessary or appropriate to carry out the provisions of this subsection, including the prevention of fraud and abuse under this subsection, except that the Secretary of Labor and the Secretary of Health and Human Services may prescribe such regulations (including interim final regulations) or other guidance as may be necessary or appropriate to carry out the provisions of paragraphs (5), (7), and (9).

(9) OUTREACH.—The Secretary of Labor, in consultation with the Secretary of the Treasury and the Secretary of Health and Human Services, shall provide outreach consisting of public education and enrollment assistance relating to premium reduction provided under this subsection. Such outreach shall target employers, group health plan administrators, public assistance programs, States, insurers, and other entities as determined appropriate by such Secretaries. Such outreach shall include an initial focus on those individuals electing continuation coverage who are referred to in paragraph (7)(C). Information on such premium reduction, including enrollment, shall

also be made available on websites of the Departments of Labor, Treasury, and Health and Human Services.

(10) DEFINITIONS.—For purposes of this section:

(A) ADMINISTRATOR.—The term "administrator" has the meaning given such term in section 3(16)(A) of the Employee Retirement Income Security Act of 1974.

(B) COBRA CONTINUATION COVERAGE.—The term "COBRA continuation coverage" means continuation coverage provided pursuant to part 6 of subtitle B of title I of the Employee Retirement Income Security Act of 1974 (other than under section 609), title XXII of the Public Health Service Act, section 4980B of the Internal Revenue Code of 1986 (other than subsection (f)(1) of such section insofar as it relates to pediatric vaccines), or section 8905a of title 5, United States Code, or under a State program that provides comparable continuation coverage. Such term does not include coverage under a health flexible spending arrangement under a cafeteria plan within the meaning of section 125 of the Internal Revenue Code of 1986.

(C) COBRA CONTINUATION PROVISION.—The term "COBRA continuation provision" means the provisions of law described in subparagraph (B).

(D) COVERED EMPLOYEE.—The term "covered employee" has the meaning given such term in section 607(2) of the Employee Retirement Income Security Act of 1974.

(E) QUALIFIED BENEFICIARY.—The term "qualified beneficiary" has the meaning given such term in section 607(3) of the Employee Retirement Income Security Act of 1974.

(F) GROUP HEALTH PLAN.—The term "group health plan" has the meaning given such term in section 607(1) of the Employee Retirement Income Security Act of 1974.

(G) STATE.—The term "State" includes the District of Columbia, the Commonwealth of Puerto Rico, the Virgin Islands, Guam, American Samoa, and the Commonwealth of the Northern Mariana Islands.

(H) PERIOD OF COVERAGE.—Any reference in this subsection to a period of coverage shall be treated as a reference to a monthly or shorter period of coverage with respect to which premiums are charged with respect to such coverage.

(11) REPORTS.—

(A) INTERIM REPORT.—The Secretary of the Treasury shall submit an interim report to the Committee on Education and Labor, the Committee on Ways and Means, and the Committee on Energy and Commerce of the House of Representatives and the Committee on Health, Education, Labor, and Pensions and the Committee on Finance of the Senate regarding the premium reduction provided under this subsection that includes—

(i) the number of individuals provided such assistance as of the date of the report; and

(ii) the total amount of expenditures incurred (with administrative expenditures noted separately) in connection with such assistance as of the date of the report.

(B) FINAL REPORT.—As soon as practicable after the last period of COBRA continuation coverage for which premium reduction is provided under this section, the Secretary of the Treasury shall submit a final report to each Committee referred to in subparagraph (A) that includes—

(i) the number of individuals provided premium reduction under this section;

(ii) the average dollar amount (monthly and annually) of premium reductions provided to such individuals; and

(iii) the total amount of expenditures incurred (with administrative expenditures noted separately) in connection with premium reduction under this section.

(12) COBRA PREMIUM ASSISTANCE.—

(A) IN GENERAL.—Subchapter B of chapter 65 of the Internal Revenue Code of 1986 is amended by adding at the end the following new section:

"SEC. 6432. COBRA PREMIUM ASSISTANCE.

"(a) In General.—The person to whom premiums are payable under COBRA continuation coverage shall be reimbursed as provided in subsection (c) for the amount of premiums not paid by assistance eligible individuals by reason of section 70307 of the Take Responsibility for Workers and Families Act.

"(b) Person Entitled To Reimbursement.—For purposes of subsection (a), except as otherwise provided by the Secretary, the person to whom premiums are payable under COBRA continuation coverage shall be treated as being—

"(1) in the case of any group health plan which is a multiemployer plan (as defined in section 3(37) of the Employee Retirement Income Security Act of 1974), the plan,

"(2) in the case of any group health plan not described in paragraph (1)—

"(A) which is subject to the COBRA continuation provisions contained in—

"(i) this title,

"(ii) the Employee Retirement Income Security Act of 1974,

"(iii) the Public Health Service Act, or

"(iv) title 5, United States Code, or

"(B) under which some or all of the coverage is not provided by insurance, the employer maintaining the plan, and

"(3) in the case of any group health plan not described in paragraph (1) or (2), the insurer providing the coverage under the group health plan.

"(c) Method Of Reimbursement.—Except as otherwise provided by the Secretary—

"(1) TREATMENT AS PAYMENT OF PAYROLL TAXES.—Each person entitled to reimbursement under subsection (a) (and filing a claim for such reimbursement at such time and in such manner as the Secretary may require) shall be treated for purposes of this title and section 1324(b)(2) of title 31,

United States Code, as having paid to the Secretary, on the date that the assistance eligible individual's premium payment is received, payroll taxes in an amount equal to the portion of such reimbursement which relates to such premium. To the extent that the amount treated as paid under the preceding sentence exceeds the amount of such person's liability for such taxes, the Secretary shall credit or refund such excess in the same manner as if it were an overpayment of such taxes.

"(2) OVERSTATEMENTS.—Any overstatement of the reimbursement to which a person is entitled under this section (and any amount paid by the Secretary as a result of such overstatement) shall be treated as an underpayment of payroll taxes by such person and may be assessed and collected by the Secretary in the same manner as payroll taxes.

"(3) REIMBURSEMENT CONTINGENT ON PAYMENT OF REMAINING PREMIUM.—No reimbursement may be made under this section to a person with respect to any assistance eligible individual until after the reduced premium required under section 70307 of such Act with respect to such individual has been received.

"(d) Definitions.—For purposes of this section—

"(1) PAYROLL TAXES.—The term 'payroll taxes' means—

"(A) amounts required to be deducted and withheld for the payroll period under section 3402 (relating to wage withholding),

"(B) amounts required to be deducted for the payroll period under section 3102 (relating to FICA employee taxes), and

"(C) amounts of the taxes imposed for the payroll period under section 3111 (relating to FICA employer taxes).

"(2) PERSON.—The term 'person' includes any governmental entity.

"(e) Reporting.—Each person entitled to reimbursement under subsection (a) for any period shall submit such reports (at such time and in such manner) as the Secretary may require, including—

"(1) an attestation of involuntary termination of employment for each covered employee on the basis of whose termination entitlement to reimbursement is claimed under subsection (a),

"(2) a report of the amount of payroll taxes offset under subsection (a) for the reporting period and the estimated offsets of such taxes for the subsequent reporting period in connection with reimbursements under subsection (a), and

"(3) a report containing the TINs of all covered employees, the amount of subsidy reimbursed with respect to each covered employee and qualified beneficiaries, and a designation with respect to each covered employee as to whether the subsidy reimbursement is for coverage of 1 individual or 2 or more individuals.

"(f) Regulations.—The Secretary shall issue such regulations or other guidance as may be necessary or appropriate to carry out this section, including—

"(1) the requirement to report information or the establishment of other methods for verifying the correct amounts of reimbursements under this section, and

"(2) the application of this section to group health plans that are multiemployer plans (as defined in section 3(37) of the Employee Retirement Income Security Act of 1974).".

(B) SOCIAL SECURITY TRUST FUNDS HELD HARMLESS.—In determining any amount transferred or appropriated to any fund under the Social Security Act, section 6432 of the Internal Revenue Code of 1986 shall not be taken into account.

(C) CLERICAL AMENDMENT.—The table of sections for subchapter B of chapter 65 of the Internal Revenue Code of 1986 is amended by adding at the end the following new item:

"Sec. 6432. COBRA premium assistance.".

(D) EFFECTIVE DATE.—The amendments made by this paragraph shall apply to premiums to which subsection (a)(1)(A) applies.

(E) SPECIAL RULE.—

(i) IN GENERAL.—In the case of an assistance eligible individual who pays, with respect to the first period of COBRA continuation coverage to which subsection (a)(1)(A) applies or the immediately subsequent period, the full premium amount for such coverage, the person to whom such payment is payable shall—

(I) make a reimbursement payment to such individual for the amount of such premium paid in excess of the amount required to be paid under subsection (a)(1)(A); or

(II) provide credit to the individual for such amount in a manner that reduces one or more subsequent premium payments that the individual is required to pay under such subsection for the coverage involved.

(ii) REIMBURSING EMPLOYER.—A person to which clause (i) applies shall be reimbursed as provided for in section 6432 of the Internal Revenue Code of 1986 for any payment made, or credit provided, to the employee under such clause.

(iii) PAYMENT OF CREDITS.—Unless it is reasonable to believe that the credit for the excess payment in clause (i)(II) will be used by the assistance eligible individual within 180 days of the date on which the person receives from the individual the payment of the full premium amount, a person to which clause (i) applies shall make the payment required under such clause to the individual within 60 days of such payment of the full premium amount. If, as of any day within the 180-day period, it is no longer reasonable to believe that the credit will be used during that period, payment equal to the remainder of the credit outstanding shall be made to the individual within 60 days of such day.

(13) PENALTY FOR FAILURE TO NOTIFY HEALTH PLAN OF CESSATION OF ELIGIBILITY FOR PREMIUM ASSISTANCE.—

(A) IN GENERAL.—Part I of subchapter B of chapter 68 of the Internal

Revenue Code of 1986 is amended by adding at the end the following new section:

"SEC. 6720C. PENALTY FOR FAILURE TO NOTIFY HEALTH PLAN OF CESSATION OF ELIGIBILITY FOR COBRA PREMIUM ASSISTANCE.

"(a) In General.—Any person required to notify a group health plan under section 70307 of the Take Responsibility for Workers and Families Act who fails to make such a notification at such time and in such manner as the Secretary of Labor may require shall pay a penalty of 110 percent of the premium reduction provided under such section after termination of eligibility under such subsection.

"(b) Reasonable Cause Exception.—No penalty shall be imposed under subsection (a) with respect to any failure if it is shown that such failure is due to reasonable cause and not to willful neglect.".

(B) CLERICAL AMENDMENT.—The table of sections of part I of subchapter B of chapter 68 of such Code is amended by adding at the end the following new item:

"Sec. 6720C. Penalty for failure to notify health plan of cessation of eligibility for COBRA premium assistance.".

(14) COORDINATION WITH HCTC.—

(A) IN GENERAL.—Section 35(g)(9) of the Internal Revenue Code of 1986 is amended to read as follows:

"(9) COBRA PREMIUM ASSISTANCE.—In the case of an assistance eligible individual who receives premium reduction for COBRA continuation coverage under section 70307 of the Take Responsibility for Workers and Families Act for any month during the taxable year, such individual shall not be treated as an eligible individual, a certified individual, or a qualifying family member for purposes of this section or section 7527 with respect to such month.".

(B) EFFECTIVE DATE.—The amendment made by subparagraph (A) shall apply to taxable years ending after the date of the enactment of this Act.

(15) EXCLUSION OF COBRA PREMIUM ASSISTANCE FROM GROSS INCOME.—

(A) IN GENERAL.—Part III of subchapter B of chapter 1 of the Internal Revenue Code of 1986 is amended by inserting after section 139B the following new section:

"SEC. 139I. COBRA PREMIUM ASSISTANCE.

"In the case of an assistance eligible individual (as defined in section 70307 of the Take Responsibility for Workers and Families Act), gross income does not include any premium reduction provided under subsection (a) of such section.".

(B) CLERICAL AMENDMENT.—The table of sections for part III of subchapter B of chapter 1 of such Code is amended by inserting after the item relating to section 139B the following new item:

"Sec. 139I. COBRA premium assistance.".

(C) EFFECTIVE DATE.—The amendments made by this paragraph shall apply to taxable years ending after the date of the enactment of this Act.

(b) Preserving Affordable Coverage For Furloughed Workers.—

(1) IN GENERAL.—The Secretary of Labor, in coordination with the Secretary of the Treasury, shall establish a process whereby the premium assistance under subsection (a) shall be available to an individual who has been subject to a furlough at any time during the emergency period described in section 1135(g)(1)(B) of the Social Security Act (42 U.S.C. 1320b–5(g)(1)(B)).

(2) FURLOUGH DEFINED.—

(A) IN GENERAL.—In this subsection, the term "furlough" means a temporary cessation of work at the will of the employer during which an individual remains employed and covered under a group health plan.

(B) GROUP HEALTH PLAN DEFINED.—In this paragraph, the term "group health plan" has the meaning given such term in section 607(1) of the Employee Retirement Income Security Act of 1974.

(3) TREATMENT WITH RESPECT TO INTERNAL REVENUE CODE OF 1986.—For purposes of sections 6432, 6720C, 35(g)(9), and 139I of the Internal Revenue Code of 1986, any premium assistance provided pursuant to any process established under this subsection to individuals who have been subject to a furlough shall be treated in the same manner as premium assistance for COBRA continuation coverage.

(c) Elimination Of Premium Subsidy For High-Income Individuals.—

(1) RECAPTURE OF SUBSIDY FOR HIGH-INCOME INDIVIDUALS.—If—

(A) premium assistance is provided under this section with respect to any COBRA continuation coverage which covers the taxpayer, the taxpayer's spouse, or any dependent (within the meaning of section 152 of the Internal Revenue Code of 1986, determined without regard to subsections (b)(1), (b)(2), and (d)(1)(B) thereof) of the taxpayer during any portion of the taxable year, and

(B) the taxpayer's modified adjusted gross income for such taxable year exceeds $125,000 ($250,000 in the case of a joint return),

then the tax imposed by chapter 1 of such Code with respect to the taxpayer for such taxable year shall be increased by the amount of such assistance.

(2) PHASE-IN OF RECAPTURE.—

(A) IN GENERAL.—In the case of a taxpayer whose modified adjusted gross income for the taxable year does not exceed $145,000 ($290,000 in the case of a joint return), the increase in the tax imposed under paragraph (1) shall not exceed the phase-in percentage of such increase (determined without regard to this paragraph).

(B) PHASE-IN PERCENTAGE.—For purposes of this subsection, the term "phase-in percentage" means the ratio (expressed as a percentage) obtained by dividing—

(i) the excess of described in subparagraph (B) of paragraph (1), by

(ii) $20,000 ($40,000 in the case of a joint return).

(3) OPTION FOR HIGH-INCOME INDIVIDUALS TO WAIVE ASSISTANCE AND AVOID RECAPTURE.—Notwithstanding subsection (a)(3), an individual shall not be treated as an assistance eligible individual for purposes of this section and section 6432 of the Internal Revenue Code of 1986 if such individual—

(A) makes a permanent election (at such time and in such form and manner as the Secretary of the Treasury may prescribe) to waive the right to the premium assistance provided under this section, and

(B) notifies the entity to whom premiums are reimbursed under section 6432(a) of such Code of such election.

(4) MODIFIED ADJUSTED GROSS INCOME.—For purposes of this subsection, the term "modified gross income" means the adjusted gross income (as defined in section 62 of the Internal Revenue Code of 1986) of the taxpayer for the taxable year increased by any amount excluded from gross income under section 911, 931, or 933 of such Code.

(5) CREDITS NOT ALLOWED AGAINST TAX, ETC.—For purposes determining regular tax liability under section 26(b) of such Code, the increase in tax under this subsection shall not be treated as a tax imposed under chapter 1 of such Code.

(6) REGULATIONS.—The Secretary of the Treasury shall issue such regulations or other guidance as are necessary or appropriate to carry out this subsection, including requirements that the entity to whom premiums are reimbursed under section 6432(a) of the Internal Revenue Code of 1986 report to the Secretary, and to each assistance eligible individual, the amount of premium assistance provided under subsection (a) with respect to each such individual.

(7) EFFECTIVE DATE.—The provisions of this subsection shall apply to taxable years ending after the date of the enactment of this Act.

SEC. 70308. RISK CORRIDOR PROGRAM.

(a) In General.—The Secretary of Health and Human Services (in this section referred to as the "Secretary") shall establish and administer a program of risk corridors for plan years 2020 and 2021 under which the Secretary shall make payments to health insurance issuers offering health insurance coverage in the individual or small group market based on the ratio of the allowable costs of the coverage to the aggregate premiums of the coverage.

(b) Payment Methodology.—The Secretary shall provide under the program established under subsection (a) that if the allowable costs for a health insurance issuer offering health insurance coverage in the individual or small group market for any plan year are more than 105 percent of the target amount, the Secretary shall pay to the issuer an amount equal to 75 percent of the allowable costs in excess of 105 percent of the target amount.

(c) Information Collection.—The Secretary shall establish a process under which information is collected from health insurance issuers offering health insurance coverage in the individual or small group market for purposes of carrying out this section.

(d) Definitions.—

(1) ALLOWABLE COSTS.—

(A) IN GENERAL.—The amount of allowable costs of a health insurance issuer offering health insurance coverage in the individual or small group market for any year is an amount equal to the total costs (other than administrative costs) of such issuer in providing benefits covered by such coverage.

(B) CERTAIN REDUCTIONS.—Allowable costs shall reduced by any—

(i) risk adjustment payments received under section 1341 of the Patient Protection and Affordable Care Act (42 U.S.C. 18061);

(ii) reinsurance payments received pursuant to a waiver approved under section 1332 of such Act (42 U.S.C. 18052); and

(iii) payments received pursuant to section 70304.

(2) ADDITIONAL TERMS.—For purposes of this section, the terms "health insurance issuer", "health insurance coverage", "individual market", and "small group market" have the meanings given such terms in section 2791 of the Public Health Service Act (42 U.S.C. 300gg–91).

(3) TARGET AMOUNT.—The target amount of health insurance coverage offered in the individual or small group market for any year is an amount equal to the total premiums (including any premium subsidies under any governmental program), reduced by the administrative costs of the coverage.

(e) Implementation.—The Secretary of Health and Human Services may implement the provisions of this section by subregulatory guidance, program instruction, or otherwise.

(f) Appropriation.—There are appropriated, out of any monies in the Treasury not otherwise obligated, such sums as may be necessary to carry out this section.

SEC. 70309. COVERAGE OF IN VITRO DIAGNOSTIC PRODUCTS.

(a) In General.—Section 6001 of division F of the Families First Coronavirus Response Act (Public Law 116–127) is amended—

(1) by amending subsection (a)(1) to read as follows:

"(1) Qualified in vitro diagnostic products and the administration of such in vitro diagnostic products."; and

(2) in subsection (d)—

(A) by striking "Terms.—The terms" and inserting the following: Terms.—In this section:

"(1) HEALTH INSURANCE TERMS.—The terms"; and

(B) by adding at the end the following:

"(2) QUALIFIED IN VITRO DIAGNOSTIC PRODUCT.—

"(A) The term 'qualified in vitro diagnostic product' means an in vitro diagnostic product (as defined in section 809.3(a) of title 21, Code of Federal Regulations) for the detection of SARS–CoV–2 or the diagnosis of the virus that causes COVID–19 that is approved, cleared, or authorized under section 510(k), 513, 515, or 564 of the Federal Food, Drug, and Cosmetic Act (21 U.S.C. 360(k), 360c, 360e, and 360bbb–3).

"(B) Such term includes an in vitro diagnostic test that—

"(i) subject to subparagraph (C), is developed and used in a laboratory certified to perform high-complexity testing pursuant to section 353 of the Public Health Service Act (42 U.S.C. 263a) and with respect to which such laboratory—

"(I) validates prior to use for the detection of SARS–CoV–2 or the diagnosis of the virus that causes COVID–19, including by obtaining confirmation of validation using an assay authorized under section 564 of the Federal Food, Drug, and Cosmetic Act (21 U.S.C. 360bbb–3);

"(II) notifies the Secretary of such use; and

"(III) includes a statement together with the results of the test that reads: 'This test has not been FDA cleared or approved. This test has been authorized by FDA under an emergency use authorization for use by authorized laboratories. This test has been authorized only for the detection of nucleic acid from SARS-CoV-2, not for any other viruses or pathogens';

"(ii) is developed and used in a laboratory certified to perform high-complexity testing pursuant to section 353 of the Public Health Service Act (42 U.S.C. 263a) and such laboratory—

"(I) is operating under an authorization of the State (as defined in section 2 of the Public Health Service Act (42 U.S.C. 201)) in which such laboratory is located and such State has notified the Secretary of its intention to review tests intended to diagnose SARS–CoV–2 or diagnose the virus that causes COVID–19 to be used in such State;

"(II) has notified the Secretary of such use for such purpose in such State; and

"(III) includes a statement together with the results of the test that reads: 'This test was developed for use as a part of a response to the public health emergency declared to address the outbreak of COVID–19. This test has not been reviewed by the Food and Drug Administration'; or

"(iii) is developed by a commercial test manufacturer that, with respect to such test—

"(I) validates such test prior to use to detect SARS–CoV–2 or diagnose the virus that causes COVID–19, including by obtaining confirmation of validation using an assay authorized under section 564 of the Federal Food, Drug, and Cosmetic Act (21 U.S.C. 360bbb–3);

"(II) notifies the Secretary of such use; and

"(III) includes a statement together with the results of the test that reads: 'This test has not been FDA cleared or approved. This test has been authorized by FDA under an emergency use authorization for use by authorized laboratories. This test has been authorized only for the detection of nucleic acid from SARS-CoV-2, not for any other viruses or pathogens'.

"(C) Such term shall not include a test described in clause (i) or (iii) of subparagraph (B) if—

"(i) the emergency use authorization request submitted by a laboratory or manufacturer described in such respective clause with respect to such test has been denied; or

"(ii) such laboratory or manufacturer does not submit such a request within 15 business days of the notification under subclause (II) of such respective subparagraph.".

(b) Conforming Amendment.—Subparagraph (B) of section 1905(a)(3) of the Social Security Act (42 U.S.C. 1396d(a)(3)), as added by section 6004(a)(1) of division F of the Families First Coronavirus Response Act) is amended to read as follows:

"(B) qualified in vitro diagnostic products (as defined in section 6001(d) of division F of the Families First Coronavirus Response Act) and the administration of such in vitro diagnostic products;".

SEC. 70310. SENSE OF CONGRESS REGARDING SURPRISE MEDICAL BILLS.

(a) Findings.—Congress finds the following:

(1) Surprise medical bills can be financially devastating for consumers.

(2) Surprise medical bills are often unavoidable and occur in situations where consumers have no ability to reasonably choose an in-network provider or insurance company networks are too narrow for consumers to be able to access seamless in-network care.

(3) Consumers and their financial stability should not be caught in the middle between insurance companies and health care providers.

(4) It is imperative that Congress enacts a comprehensive, long-term solution to protect consumers and end surprise medical billing.

(5) During the COVID-19 pandemic, consumers across the country will increasingly require emergency or unanticipated health care services and at the same time may have limited access to in-network providers due to the increased demand on the health care system and it is critical that they are not deterred from seeking care due to the threat of a surprise medical bill.

(6) The virus is now spreading faster in the United States than anywhere else in the world and experts indicate that day by day, more hospital beds will be full, more resources will be depleted, and the virus will claim more lives.

(b) Sense Of Congress.—It is the sense of the Congress that, during the COVID-19 pandemic—

(1) heath care providers should refrain from balance billing consumers for out-of-network claims related to COVID-19 testing or treatment and insurance companies should do their utmost to secure access to in-network treatment for their plan participants, including providing adequate reimbursement rates for services; and

(2) consumers' cost-sharing should be limited to what they would have paid if the providers testing or treating them for COVID-19 were in-network for

their insurance plan.

TITLE IV—PROVISIONS RELATING TO OLDER AMERICANS ACT OF 1965

SEC. 70401. COMBATING HUNGER FOR OLDER AMERICANS DURING CORONAVIRUS CRISIS.

(a) Home Delivered Nutrition Services Criteria Applicable Under The Older Americans Act Of 1965 During Fiscal Year 2020 To Respond To The COVID-19 Public Health Emergency.—For purposes of State agencies determining the delivery of nutrition services under subpart 2 of part C of title III of the Older Americans Act of 1965 (42 U.S.C. 3030f et seq.), during the portion of COVID-19 public health emergency declared under section 319 of the Public Health Service Act (42 U.S.C. 247d) that occurs in the period beginning on the date of the enactment of this Act and ending on September 30, 2020, the State agencies shall include among individuals receiving delivery because they are homebound an individual age 60 and older, or an individual with a disability (of any age), who is unable to obtain nutrition because the individual is under a quarantine, practicing social distancing, or otherwise unable to leave home, due to the emergency.

(b) Congregate Nutrition Services Criteria Applicable Under The Older Americans Act Of 1965 During Fiscal Year 2020 To Respond To The COVID-19 Public Health Emergency.— If a State demonstrates, to the satisfaction of the Assistant Secretary (as defined in section 102 of the Older Americans Act of 1965 (42 U.S.C.3002), that funds received by the State and attributable to funds appropriated under paragraph (1) or (2) of section 303(b) of the Older Americans Act of 1965 (42 U.S.C. 3023(b)), including funds transferred under subparagraph (A) of paragraph (4) of such section without regard to the exception referring to subparagraph (B) specified in such subparagraph (A), for fiscal year 2020 are insufficient to satisfy the need for services under subpart I or subpart II of part C of title III of the Older Americans Act of 1965 (42 U.S.C. 3030d–2 et seq.) in fiscal year 2020 during the COVID-19 public health emergency declared under section 319 of the Public Health Service Act (42 U.S.C. 247d), the Assistant Secretary shall allow State and area agencies on aging, without prior approval, to transfer up to 100 percent of the funds so received between subpart 1 and subpart 2 of such part C for use the State or area agency on aging considers appropriate to meet the needs of the area served.

(c) Waiver.—To facilitate implementation of subparts 1 and 2 of part C of title III of the Older Americans Act of 1965 (42 U.S.C. 3030e et seq.) during any portion of the COVID-19 public health emergency declared under section 319 of the Public Health Service Act (42 U.S.C. 247d) that occurs in the period beginning on the date of the enactment of this Act and ending on September

30, 2020, the Assistant Secretary for Aging may waive the requirements for emergency meals to comply with the requirements of clauses (i) and (ii) of section 339(2)(A) of the Older Americans Act of 1965 (42 U.S.C. 3030g–21(2)(A)).

SEC. 70402. ACCESS OF THE STATE LONG-TERM CARE OMBUDSMAN TO RESIDENTS OF LONG-TERM CARE FACILITIES DURING THE COVID-19 PUBLIC HEALTH EMERGENCY IN FISCAL YEAR 2020.

During any portion of the COVID-19 public health emergency declared under section 319 of the Public Health Service Act (42 U.S.C. 247d) that occurs in the period beginning on the date of the enactment of this Act and ending on September 30, 2020, the State Long-Term Care Ombudsman shall have continuing direct access (or other access through the use of technology to the greatest extent practicable) to residents of long-term care facilities to provide the services described in section 712(a)(3)(B) of the Older Americans Act of 1965 (42 U.S.C. 3058h(a)(3)(B)).

SEC. 70403. CONTINUITY OF SERVICE AND OPPORTUNITIES FOR PARTICIPANTS IN COMMUNITY SERVICE ACTIVITIES UNDER TITLE V OF THE OF THE OLDER AMERICANS ACT OF 1965.

To ensure continuity of service and opportunities for participants in community service activities under title V of the of the Older Americans Act of 1965 (42 U.S.C. 3056–3056p), the Secretary of Labor—

(1) (A) may allow for individuals participating in such activities as of March 1, 2020, to extend their participation for a period that exceeds the period described in section 518(a)(3)(B)(i) of such Act if the Secretary determines such extension is appropriate due to the effects of the COVID-19 public heath emergency declared under section 319 of the Public Health Service Act (42 U.S.C. 247d), and

(B) may extend the average participation cap for eligible individuals applicable to grantees under section 502(b)(1)(C) of such Act to a cap the Secretary determines is appropriate due to the effects of the COVID-19 public heath emergency declared under section 319 of the Public Health Service Act (42 U.S.C. 247d), and

(2) may increase the amount available to pay the authorized administrative costs to an amount not to exceed 20 percent of the grant amount if the Secretary determines that such increase is necessary to adequately respond to the additional administrative needs to respond to the COVID-19 public health emergency declared under section 319 of the Public Health Service Act (42 U.S.C. 247d).

TITLE V—PUBLIC HEALTH POLICIES

Subtitle A—Improving Public Health And Medical Response

SEC. 70501. REIMBURSEMENT FOR ADDITIONAL HEALTH SERVICES RELATING TO CORONAVIRUS.

Title V of division A of the Families First Coronavirus Response Act (Public Law 116–127) is amended under the heading "Department of Health and Human Services—Office of the Secretary—Public Health and Social Services Emergency Fund" is amended by inserting ", or treatment related to SARS-CoV-2 or COVID-19 for uninsured individuals" after "or visits described in paragraph (2) of such section for uninsured individuals".

SEC. 70502. PUBLIC HEALTH DATA SYSTEM TRANSFORMATION.

Subtitle C of title XXVIII of the Public Health Service Act (42 U.S.C. 300hh-31 et seq.) is amended by adding at the end the following:

"SEC. 2822. PUBLIC HEALTH DATA SYSTEM TRANSFORMATION.

"(a) Expanding CDC And Public Health Department Capabilities.—

"(1) IN GENERAL.—The Secretary, acting through the Director of the Centers for Disease Control and Prevention, shall—

"(A) conduct activities to expand, enhance, and improve applicable public health data systems used by the Centers for Disease Control and Prevention, related to the interoperability and improvement of such systems (including as it relates to preparedness for, prevention and detection of, and response to public health emergencies); and

"(B) award grants or cooperative agreements to State, local, Tribal, or territorial public health departments for the expansion and modernization of public health data systems, to assist public health departments in—

"(i) assessing current data infrastructure capabilities and gaps to improve and increase consistency in data collection, storage, analysis and, as appropriate, to improve dissemination of public health-related information;

"(ii) improving secure public health data collection, transmission, exchange, maintenance, and analysis;

"(iii) improving the secure exchange of data between the Centers for Disease Control and Prevention, State, local, Tribal, and territorial public health departments, public health organizations, and health care providers, including by public health officials in multiple jurisdictions within such State, as appropriate, and by simplifying and supporting reporting by health care providers, as applicable, pursuant to State law, including through the use of health information technology;

"(iv) enhancing the interoperability of public health data systems (including systems created or accessed by public health departments) with health information technology, including with health information technology certified under section 3001(c)(5);

"(v) supporting and training data systems, data science, and informatics personnel;

"(vi) supporting earlier disease and health condition detection, such as through near real-time data monitoring, to support rapid public health responses;

"(vii) supporting activities within the applicable jurisdiction related to the expansion and modernization of electronic case reporting; and

"(viii) developing and disseminating information related to the use and importance of public health data.

"(2) DATA STANDARDS.—In carrying out paragraph (1), the Secretary, acting through the Director of the Centers for Disease Control and Prevention, shall, as appropriate and in consultation with the Office of the National Coordinator for Health Information Technology, designate data and technology standards (including standards for interoperability) for public health data systems, with deference given to standards published by consensus-based standards development organizations with public input and voluntary consensus-based standards bodies.

"(3) PUBLIC-PRIVATE PARTNERSHIPS.—The Secretary may develop and utilize public-private partnerships for technical assistance, training, and related implementation support for State, local, Tribal, and territorial public health departments, and the Centers for Disease Control and Prevention, on the expansion and modernization of electronic case reporting and public health data systems, as applicable.

"(b) Requirements.—

"(1) HEALTH INFORMATION TECHNOLOGY STANDARDS.—The Secretary may not award a grant or cooperative agreement under subsection (a)(1)(B) unless the applicant uses or agrees to use standards endorsed by the National Coordinator for Health Information Technology pursuant to section 3001(c)(1) or adopted by the Secretary under section 3004.

"(2) WAIVER.—The Secretary may waive the requirement under paragraph (1) with respect to an applicant if the Secretary determines that the activities under subsection (a)(1)(B) cannot otherwise be carried out within the applicable jurisdiction.

"(3) APPLICATION.—A State, local, Tribal, or territorial health department applying for a grant or cooperative agreement under this section shall submit an application to the Secretary at such time and in such manner as the Secretary may require. Such application shall include information describing—

"(A) the activities that will be supported by the grant or cooperative agreement; and

"(B) how the modernization of the public health data systems involved will support or impact the public health infrastructure of the health department, including a description of remaining gaps, if any, and the actions needed to address such gaps.

"(c) Strategy And Implementation Plan.—Not later than 180 days after the date of enactment of this section, the Secretary, acting through the Director of the Centers for Disease Control and Prevention, shall submit to the Committee on Health, Education, Labor, and Pensions of the Senate and the Committee on

Energy and Commerce of the House of Representatives a coordinated strategy and an accompanying implementation plan that identifies and demonstrates the measures the Secretary will utilize to—

"(1) update and improve applicable public health data systems used by the Centers for Disease Control and Prevention; and

"(2) carry out the activities described in this section to support the improvement of State, local, Tribal, and territorial public health data systems.

"(d) Consultation.—The Secretary, acting through the Director of the Centers for Disease Control and Prevention, shall consult with State, local, Tribal, and territorial health departments, professional medical and public health associations, associations representing hospitals or other health care entities, health information technology experts, and other appropriate public or private entities regarding the plan and grant program to modernize public health data systems pursuant to this section. Activities under this subsection may include the provision of technical assistance and training related to the exchange of information by such public health data systems used by relevant health care and public health entities at the local, State, Federal, Tribal, and territorial levels, and the development and utilization of public-private partnerships for implementation support applicable to this section.

"(e) Report To Congress.—Not later than 1 year after the date of enactment of this section, the Secretary shall submit a report to the Committee on Health, Education, Labor, and Pensions of the Senate and the Committee on Energy and Commerce of the House of Representatives that includes—

"(1) a description of any barriers to—

"(A) public health authorities implementing interoperable public health data systems and electronic case reporting;

"(B) the exchange of information pursuant to electronic case reporting; or

"(C) reporting by health care providers using such public health data systems, as appropriate, and pursuant to State law;

"(2) an assessment of the potential public health impact of implementing electronic case reporting and interoperable public health data systems; and

"(3) a description of the activities carried out pursuant to this section.

"(f) Electronic Case Reporting.—In this section, the term 'electronic case reporting' means the automated identification, generation, and bilateral exchange of reports of health events among electronic health record or health information technology systems and public health authorities.

"(g) Authorization Of Appropriations.—To carry out this section, there are authorized to be appropriated $100,000,000 for each of fiscal years 2021 through 2025.".

SEC. 70503. REPORTING ON COVID-19 TESTING AND RESULTS.

State and local governments, laboratories, and health systems receiving funds or assistance pursuant to division A of the Families First Coronavirus Response Act (Public Law 116–127) or pursuant to division A of this Act

shall ensure that—
(1) the respective State Emergency Operations Center and State and local public health departments, receive regular and real-time reporting on data, in a timely manner, on testing and results, including positive and negative laboratory results, as well as reporting on cases and severe outcomes resulting from COVID-19, as determined by the Director of the Centers for Disease Control and Prevention; and
(2) such data is transmitted in a regular and timely manner to the Centers for Disease Control and Prevention.

SEC. 70504. CENTERS FOR DISEASE CONTROL AND PREVENTION COVID-19 RESPONSE LINE.
(a) In General.—During the public health emergency declared by the Secretary of Health and Human Services pursuant to section 319 of the Public Health Service Act (42 U.S.C. 247d) on January 31, 2020 with respect to COVID-19, the Secretary, acting through the Director of the Centers for Disease Control and Prevention, shall maintain a toll-free telephone number to address public health queries, including questions concerning COVID-19.
(b) Authorization Of Appropriations.—To carry out this section, there is authorized to be appropriated $10,000,000, to remain available until expended.

SEC. 70505. AWARENESS CAMPAIGN.
The Secretary of Health and Human Services, acting through the Director of the Centers for Disease Control and Prevention and in coordination with other offices and agencies, as appropriate, shall award competitive grants or contracts to one or more public or private entities to carry out a national campaign, based on available scientific evidence, to increase awareness and knowledge of COVID-19, including countering stigma associated with COVID-19 and improving information on the availability of diagnostic testing and other related services at community health centers.

SEC. 70506. ADDITIONAL FUNDING FOR MEDICAL RESERVE CORPS.
Section 2813 of the Public Health Service Act (42 U.S.C. 300hh–15) is amended by striking "$11,200,000 for each of fiscal years 2019 through 2023" and inserting "$31,200,000 for each of fiscal years 2020 and 2021 and $11,200,000 for each of fiscal years 2022 and 2023".

SEC. 70507. FLEXIBILITY FOR MEMBERS OF NATIONAL HEALTH SERVICE CORPS DURING EMERGENCY PERIOD.
Subsection (a) of section 333 of the Public Health Service Act (42 U.S.C. 254f) is amended by adding at the end the following new paragraph:
"(4) During an emergency period (as defined in section 1135(g)(1) of the Social Security Act, the Secretary may, notwithstanding this subpart and subpart III, assign members of the Corps to provide such health services

at such places and for such number of hours as the Secretary determines necessary to respond to the emergency, provided that—

"(A) the members voluntarily agree to such assignment and hours;

"(B) the places to which such members are assigned are within a reasonable distance of the places to which the respective members were assigned or were to be assigned absent a waiver under this paragraph; and

"(C) the minimum number of hours required are the same as were required prior to the date of enactment of this paragraph.".

SEC. 70508. READY RESERVE CORPS.

(a) Commissioned Corps And Ready Reserve Corps.—Section 203 of the Public Health Service Act (42 U.S.C. 204) is amended—

(1) in subsection (a)(1), by striking " a Ready Reserve Corps for service in time of national emergency" and inserting ", for service in time of a public health or national emergency, a Ready Reserve Corps"; and

(2) in subsection (c)—

(A) in the heading, by striking "Research" and inserting "Reserve Corps";

(B) in paragraph (1), by inserting "during public health or national emergencies" before the period;

(C) in paragraph (2)—

(i) in the matter preceding subparagraph (A), by inserting ", consistent with paragraph (1)" after "shall";

(ii) in subparagraph (C), by inserting "during such emergencies" after "members"; and

(iii) in subparagraph (D), by inserting ", consistent with subparagraph (C)" before the period; and

(D) by adding at the end the following:

"(3) STATUTORY REFERENCES TO RESERVE.—A reference in any Federal statute, except in the case of subsection (b), to the 'Reserve Corps' of the Public Health Service or to the 'reserve' of the Public Health Service shall be deemed to be a reference to the Ready Reserve Corps.".

(b) Deployment Readiness.—Section 203A(a)(1)(B) of the Public Health Service Act (42 U.S.C. 204a(a)(1)(B)) is amended by striking "Active Reserves" and inserting "Ready Reserve Corps".

(c) Retirement Of Commissioned Officers.—Section 211 of the Public Health Service Act (42 U.S.C. 212) is amended—

(1) by striking "(in the case of an officer in the Reserve Corps)" each place it appears;

(2) by striking "the Service" each place it appears and inserting "the Regular Corps";

(3) in subsection (c)—

(A) in paragraph (1)—

(i) by striking "or an officer of the Reserve Corps"; and

(ii) by inserting "or under section 221(a)(19)" after "subsection (a)"; and

(B) in paragraph (2), by striking "Regular or Reserve Corps" and inserting "Regular Corps or Ready Reserve Corps"; and

(4) in subsection (f), by striking "the Regular or Reserve Corps of".

(d) Rights, Privileges, Etc. Of Officers And Surviving Beneficiaries.—Section 221 of the Public Health Service Act (42 U.S.C. 213a) is amended—

(1) in subsection (a), by adding at the end the following:

"(19) Chapter 1223, Retired Pay for Non-Regular Service.

"(20) Section 12601, Compensation: Reserve on active duty accepting from any person.

"(21) Section 12684, Reserves: separation for absence without authority or sentence to imprisonment."; and

(2) in subsection (b)—

(A) by striking "Secretary of Health, Education, and Welfare or his designee" and inserting "Secretary of Health and Human Services or the designee of such secretary";

(B) by striking "(b) The authority vested" and inserting the following:

"(b) (1) The authority vested";

(C) by striking "For purposes of" and inserting the following:

"(2) For purposes of"; and

(D) by adding at the end the following:

"(3) For purposes of paragraph (19) of subsection (a), the terms 'Military department', 'Secretary concerned', and 'Armed forces' in such title 10 shall be deemed to include, respectively, the Department of Health and Human Services, the Secretary of Health and Human Services, and the Commissioned Corps.".

SEC. 70509. LIMITATION ON LIABILITY FOR VOLUNTEER HEALTH CARE PROFESSIONALS DURING COVID-19 EMERGENCY RESPONSE.

(a) Limitation On Liability.—Except as provided in subsection (b), a health care professional shall not be liable under Federal or State law for any harm caused by an act or omission of the professional in the provision of health care services during the public health emergency with respect to COVID–19 declared by the Secretary of Health and Human Services (referred to in this section as the "Secretary") pursuant to section 319 of the Public Health Service Act (42 U.S.C. 247d) on January 31, 2020, if—

(1) the professional is providing health care services in response to such public health emergency, as a volunteer; and

(2) the act or omission occurs—

(A) in the course of providing health care services;

(B) in the health care professional's capacity as a volunteer;

(C) in the course of providing health care services that are within the scope of the license, registration, or certification of the volunteer, as defined by the State of licensure, registration, or certification; and

(D) in a good faith belief that the individual being treated is in need of health care services.
(b) Exceptions.—Subsection (a) does not apply if—
(1) the harm was caused by an act or omission constituting willful or criminal misconduct, gross negligence, reckless misconduct, or a conscious flagrant indifference to the rights or safety of the individual harmed by the health care professional; or
(2) the health care professional rendered the health care services under the influence (as determined pursuant to applicable State law) of alcohol or an intoxicating drug.
(c) Preemption.—
(1) IN GENERAL.—This section preempts the laws of a State or any political subdivision of a State to the extent that such laws are inconsistent with this section, unless such laws provide greater protection from liability.
(2) VOLUNTEER PROTECTION ACT.—Protections afforded by this section are in addition to those provided by the Volunteer Protection Act of 1997 (Public Law 105–19).
(d) Definitions.—In this section—
(1) the term "harm" includes physical, nonphysical, economic, and noneconomic losses;
(2) the term "health care professional" means an individual who is licensed, registered, or certified under Federal or State law to provide health care services;
(3) the term "health care services" means any services provided by a health care professional, or by any individual working under the supervision of a health care professional that relate to—
(A) the diagnosis, prevention, or treatment of COVID-19; or
(B) the assessment or care of the health of a human being for COVID-19; and
(4) the term "volunteer" means a health care professional who, with respect to the health care services rendered, does not receive compensation or any other thing of value in lieu of compensation, which compensation—
(A) includes a payment under any insurance policy or health plan, or under any Federal or State health benefits program; and
(B) excludes receipt of items to be used exclusively for rendering health care services in the health care professional's capacity as a volunteer described in subsection (a)(1) and excludes any reimbursement for travel to the site where the volunteer services are being rendered and any payments in cash or kind to cover room and board, if services are being rendered more than 75 miles from the volunteer's principal place of residence.
(e) Applicability.—This section applies only with respect to a claim for a harm caused by an act or omission occurring—
(1) on or after the date of enactment of this Act; and
(2) during the period of the public health emergency declared by the Secretary of Health and Human Services pursuant to section 319 of the Public Health

Service Act (42 U.S.C. 247d) on January 31, 2020 with respect to COVID-19.
Subtitle B—Tribal Health

SEC. 70521. IMPROVING STATE, LOCAL, AND TRIBAL PUBLIC HEALTH SECURITY.

Section 319C–1 of the Public Health Service Act (42 U.S.C. 247d–3a) is amended—

(1) in the section heading, by striking "AND LOCAL" and inserting ", LOCAL, AND TRIBAL";

(2) in subsection (b)—

(A) in paragraph (1)—

(i) in subparagraph (B), by striking "or" at the end;

(ii) in subparagraph (C), by striking "and" at the end and inserting "or"; and

(iii) by adding at the end the following:

"(D) be an Indian tribe, tribal organization, or a consortium of Indian tribes or tribal organizations; and"; and

(B) in paragraph (2)—

(i) in the matter preceding subparagraph (A), by inserting ", as applicable" after "including";

(ii) in subparagraph (A)(viii)—

(I) by inserting "and tribal" after "with State";

(II) by striking "(as defined in section 8101 of the Elementary and Secondary Education Act of 1965)" and inserting "and tribal educational agencies (as defined in sections 8101 and 6132, respectively, of the Elementary and Secondary Education Act of 1965)"; and

(III) by inserting "and tribal" after "and State";

(iii) in subparagraph (G), by striking "and tribal" and inserting "tribal, and urban Indian organization"; and

(iv) in subparagraph (H), by inserting ", Indian tribes, and urban Indian organizations" after "public health";

(3) in subsection (e), by inserting "Indian tribes, tribal organizations, urban Indian organizations," after "local emergency plans,";

(4) in subsection (h)—

(A) in paragraph (1)(A)—

(i) by striking "through 2023" and inserting "and 2020"; and

(ii) by inserting before the period "; and $690,000,000 for each of fiscal years 2021 through 2023 for awards pursuant to paragraph (3) (subject to the authority of the Secretary to make awards pursuant to paragraphs (4) and (5)) and paragraph (8), of which not less than $5,000,000 shall be reserved each fiscal year for awards under paragraph (8)";

(B) in the heading of paragraph (3), by inserting "FOR STATES" after "AMOUNT"; and

(C) by adding at the end the following:

"(8) TRIBAL ELIGIBLE ENTITIES.—

"(A) DETERMINATION OF FUNDING AMOUNT.—

"(i) IN GENERAL.—The Secretary shall award at least 10 cooperative agreements under this section, in amounts not less than the minimum amount determined under clause (ii), to eligible entities described in subsection (b)(1)(D) that submits to the Secretary an application that meets the criteria of the Secretary for the receipt of such an award and that meets other reasonable implementation conditions established by the Secretary, in consultation with Indian tribes, for such awards. If the Secretary receives more than 10 applications under this section from eligible entities described in subsection (b)(1)(D) that meet the criteria and conditions described in the previous sentence, the Secretary, in consultation with Indian tribes, may make additional awards under this section to such entities.

"(ii) MINIMUM AMOUNT.—In determining the minimum amount of an award pursuant to clause (i), the Secretary, in consultation with Indian tribes, shall first determine an amount the Secretary considers appropriate for the eligible entity.

"(B) AVAILABLE UNTIL EXPENDED.—Amounts provided to a tribal eligible entity under a cooperative agreement under this section for a fiscal year and remaining unobligated at the end of such year shall remain available to such entity during the entirety of the performance period, for the purposes for which said funds were provided.

"(C) NO MATCHING REQUIREMENT.—Subparagraphs (B), (C), and (D) of paragraph (1) shall not apply with respect to cooperative agreements awarded under this section to eligible entities described in subsection (b)(1)(D)."; and

(5) by adding at the end the following:

"(l) Special Rules Related To Tribal Eligible Entities.—

"(1) MODIFICATIONS.—After consultation with Indian tribes, the Secretary may make necessary and appropriate modifications to the program under this section to facilitate the use of the cooperative agreement program by eligible entities described in subsection (b)(1)(D).

"(2) WAIVERS.—

"(A) IN GENERAL.—Except as provided in subparagraph (B), the Secretary may waive or specify alternative requirements for any provision of this section (including regulations) that the Secretary administers in connection with this section if the Secretary finds that the waiver or alternative requirement is necessary for the effective delivery and administration of this program with respect to eligible entities described in subsection (b)(1)(D).

"(B) EXCEPTION.—The Secretary may not waive or specify alternative requirements under subparagraph (A) relating to labor standards or the environment.

"(3) CONSULTATION.—The Secretary shall consult with Indian tribes and tribal organizations on the design of this program with respect to such tribes and organizations to ensure the effectiveness of the program in enhancing the security of Indian tribes with respect to public health emergencies.

"(4) REPORTING.—

"(A) IN GENERAL.—Not later than 2 years after the date of enactment of this subsection, and as an addendum to the biennial evaluations required under subsection (k), the Secretary, in coordination with the Director of the Indian Health Service, shall—

"(i) conduct a review of the implementation of this section with respect to eligible entities described in subsection (b)(1)(D), including any factors that may have limited its success; and

"(ii) submit a report describing the results of the review described in clause (i) to—

"(I) the Committee on Indian Affairs, the Committee on Health, Education, Labor, and Pensions, and the Committee on Appropriations of the Senate; and

"(II) the Subcommittee on Indigenous People of the Committee on Natural Resources, the Committee on Energy and Commerce, and the Committee on Appropriations of the House of Representatives.

"(B) ANALYSIS OF TRIBAL PUBLIC HEALTH EMERGENCY INFRASTRUCTURE LIMITATION.—The Secretary shall include in the initial report submitted under subparagraph (A) a description of any public health emergency infrastructure limitation encountered by eligible entities described in subsection (b)(1)(D).".

SEC. 70522. PROVISION OF ITEMS TO INDIAN PROGRAMS AND FACILITIES.

(a) Strategic National Stockpile.—Section 319F–2(a)(3)(G) of the Public Health Service Act (42 U.S.C. 247d–6b(a)(3)(G)) is amended by inserting ", and, in the case that the Secretary deploys the stockpile under this subparagraph, ensure, in coordination with the applicable States and programs and facilities, that appropriate drugs, vaccines and other biological products, medical devices, and other supplies are deployed by the Secretary directly to health programs or facilities operated by the Indian Health Service, an Indian tribe, a tribal organization (as those terms are defined in section 4 of the Indian Self-Determination and Education Assistance Act (25 U.S.C. 5304)), or an inter-tribal consortium (as defined in section 501 of the Indian Self-Determination and Education Assistance Act (25 U.S.C. 5381)) or through an urban Indian organization (as defined in section 4 of the Indian Health Care Improvement Act), while avoiding duplicative distributions to such programs or facilities" before the semicolon.

(b) Distribution Of Qualified Pandemic Or Epidemic Products To IHS Facilities.—Title III of the Public Health Service Act (42 U.S.C. 241 et seq.) is amended by inserting after section 319F–4 the following:

"SEC. 319F–5. DISTRIBUTION OF QUALIFIED PANDEMIC OR EPIDEMIC PRODUCTS TO INDIAN PROGRAMS AND FACILITIES.

"In the case that the Secretary distributes qualified pandemic or epidemic products (as defined in section 319F–3(i)(7)) to States or other entities, the Secretary shall ensure, in coordination with the applicable States and programs and facilities, that, as appropriate, such products are distributed directly to health programs or facilities operated by the Indian Health Service, an Indian tribe, a tribal organization (as those terms are defined in section 4 of the Indian Self-Determination and Education Assistance Act (25 U.S.C. 5304)), or an inter-tribal consortium (as defined in section 501 of the Indian Self-Determination and Education Assistance Act (25 U.S.C. 5381)) or through an urban Indian organization (as defined in section 4 of the Indian Health Care Improvement Act), while avoiding duplicative distributions to such programs or facilities.".

Subtitle C—Medical Product Supply Chain Improvements

SEC. 70531. SHORTAGES OF ESSENTIAL DEVICES.

Chapter V of the Federal Food, Drug, and Cosmetic Act (21 U.S.C. 351 et seq.) is amended by inserting after section 520 the following:

"SEC. 520A. DISCONTINUANCE OR INTERRUPTION IN THE PRODUCTION OF ESSENTIAL DEVICES DURING PUBLIC HEALTH EMERGENCIES.

"(a) Notification.—

"(1) IN GENERAL.—A manufacturer or contract terminal sterilizer of an essential device shall notify the Secretary—

"(A) in accordance with paragraph (3), when such manufacturer or sterilizer becomes aware of—

"(i) a permanent discontinuance in the manufacture of the device (except for a permanent discontinuance as a result of an approved modification of the device);

"(ii) an interruption in the manufacture of the device that is likely to lead to a shortage or meaningful disruption in the supply of that device in the United States; or

"(iii) any other situation or circumstance that is likely to lead to a shortage or meaningful disruption in the supply of that device in the United States; and

"(B) in accordance with paragraph (2)(C), of the reason for such discontinuance, interruption, or other situation or circumstance.

"(2) REQUIRED INCLUSIONS.—A notification under paragraph (1) shall include each of the following:

"(A) The name of the device, including the Device Identifier or National Product Code for the device, if applicable.

"(B) The name of the manufacturer of the device.

"(C) The reason for the notification, including whether any of the following reasons apply:

"(i) Requirements related to complying with quality system regulations.

"(ii) Shortage of a material used in the manufacture of the device.
"(iii) Shortage of a component, part, or accessory of the device.
"(iv) Delay in shipping of the device.
"(v) Increased demand for the device.
"(vi) Natural disaster.
"(vii) Cyber security.
"(viii) Facility closure.
"(ix) Other reasons as the Secretary deems appropriate.
"(D) The estimated duration of the discontinuance, interruption, or other situation or circumstance.
"(E) Any other information the manufacturer deems relevant.
"(3) TIMING.—The notification required under paragraph (1) shall be submitted, in a manner prescribed by the Secretary—
"(A) no later than 6 months prior to the date of the discontinuance, interruption, or other situation or circumstance; or
"(B) if compliance with subparagraph (A) is not possible, as soon as is practicable, and in no case later than 5 business days after the manufacturer becomes aware of an event, situation, or circumstance requiring notification under paragraph (1).
"(b) Distribution.—
"(1) PUBLIC AVAILABILITY.—To the extent practicable, the Secretary shall distribute, through such means as the Secretary deems appropriate, information on any discontinuance, interruption, or other situation or circumstance described in subsection (a) to appropriate organizations, including to hospitals, physicians and other health care providers, patients, and supply chain partners.
"(2) PUBLIC HEALTH EXCEPTION.—The Secretary may choose not to make information collected under this section publicly available pursuant to this section if the Secretary determines that the disclosure of such information would adversely affect public health, such as by increasing the possibility of an unnecessary over-purchase or other disruption of the availability of medical products to patients.
"(c) Confidentiality.—Nothing in this section shall be construed as authorizing the Secretary to disclose any information that is a trade secret or confidential information subject to section 552(b)(4) of title 5, United States Code, or section 1905 of title 18, United States Code.
"(d) Failure To Meet Requirements.—If a person fails to submit information as required under subsection (a)—
"(1) the Secretary shall issue a letter to such person setting forth the basis for noncompliance and informing such person of a failure to comply;
"(2) within 30 calendar days from the issuance of a letter under paragraph (1), the person who receives such letter shall submit to the Secretary a written response to such letter setting forth the basis for noncompliance and providing information required under subsection (a); and

"(3) not later than 45 calendar days after the issuance of a letter under paragraph (1), the Secretary shall make such letter and any response to such letter under paragraph (2) available to the public on the public website of the Food and Drug Administration, with appropriate redactions made to protect information described in subsection (c), except that, if the Secretary determines that the letter under paragraph (1) was issued in error or, after review of such response, the person had a reasonable basis for not notifying as required under subsection (a), the requirements of this paragraph shall not apply.

"(e) Expedited Inspections And Reviews.—If, based on notifications described in subsection (a) or any other relevant information, the Secretary concludes that there is, or is likely to be, a shortage of a device described in subsection (a), the Secretary may—

"(1) expedite the review of premarket submissions under sections 510(k), 513(f)(2), 515, and 520(m), that could help mitigate or prevent such shortage; or

"(2) expedite an inspection or reinspection of an establishment that could help mitigate or prevent such shortage.

"(f) Effect Of Notification.—The submission of a notification under subsection (a) shall not be construed—

"(1) as an admission that any product that is the subject of such notification violates any provision of this Act; or

"(2) as evidence of the entity's intent to market the product for an indication or use for which the product has not been approved or cleared by the Secretary.

"(g) Identification Of Essential Devices.—

"(1) IN GENERAL.—In the event of, or in advance of, a declaration of a public health emergency pursuant to section 319 of the Public Health Service Act, the Secretary shall designate and make publicly available, including on the public website of the Food and Drug Administration, a list of devices that are critical to preventing, screening, diagnosing, treating, or mitigating the spread of a disease or condition during such emergency.

"(2) CONSIDERATION.—In developing such list, the Secretary shall take into consideration—

"(A) the medical necessity of devices;

"(B) the urgency to prevent serious injury or death; and

"(C) the availability of other devices.

"(3) UPDATES.—During the course of such public health emergency, the Secretary shall update the list of essential devices as necessary, including adding and removing devices.

"(h) Definitions.—For purposes of this section:

"(1) ESSENTIAL DEVICE.—The term 'essential device' means a device designated in a list in effect under subsection (g).

"(2) MANUFACTURER.—The term 'manufacturer' means the entity that holds the medical device marketing submission, or if a medical device marketing submission is not required, the entity responsible for listing the medical device under section 510.

"(3) MEANINGFUL DISRUPTION.—The term 'meaningful disruption'—

"(A) means a change in production that is reasonably likely to lead to a reduction in the supply of an essential device that is more than negligible and affects the ability to fill orders or meet expected demand for the device of the manufacturer or contract terminal sterilizer involved; and

"(B) does not include, so long as the manufacturer expects to resume operations in a short period of time, not to exceed 6 months, interruptions in—

"(i) manufacturing due to matters such as routine maintenance or insignificant changes; or

"(ii) manufacturing of components or raw materials.

"(4) SHORTAGE.—The term 'shortage', with respect to a device, means a period of time when the demand or projected demand for the device within the United States exceeds the supply of the device or a comparable device of that manufacturer or another manufacturer, including as a result of discontinuance of a device or an interruption in the manufacturing or importation of a device or a component of a device or the device constituent of a combination product.".

SEC. 70532. AUTHORITY TO DESTROY COUNTERFEIT DEVICES.

(a) In General.—Section 801(a) of the Federal Food, Drug, and Cosmetic Act (21 U.S.C. 381(a)) is amended—

(1) in the fourth sentence, by inserting "or counterfeit device" after "counterfeit drug"; and

(2) by striking "The Secretary of the Treasury shall cause the destruction of" and all that follows through "liable for costs pursuant to subsection (c)." and inserting the following: "The Secretary of the Treasury shall cause the destruction of any such article refused admission unless such article is exported, under regulations prescribed by the Secretary of the Treasury, within ninety days of the date of notice of such refusal or within such additional time as may be permitted pursuant to such regulations, except that the Secretary of Health and Human Services may destroy, without the opportunity for export, any drug or device refused admission under this section, if such drug or device is valued at an amount that is $2,500 or less (or such higher amount as the Secretary of the Treasury may set by regulation pursuant to section 498(a)(1) of the Tariff Act of 1930 (19 U.S.C. 1498(a)(1))) and was not brought into compliance as described under subsection (b). The Secretary of Health and Human Services shall issue regulations providing for notice and an opportunity to appear before the Secretary of Health and Human Services and introduce testimony, as described in the first sentence of this subsection, on destruction of a drug or device under the seventh sentence of this subsection. The regulations shall provide that prior to destruction, appropriate due process is available to the owner or consignee seeking to

challenge the decision to destroy the drug or device. Where the Secretary of Health and Human Services provides notice and an opportunity to appear and introduce testimony on the destruction of a drug or device, the Secretary of Health and Human Services shall store and, as applicable, dispose of the drug or device after the issuance of the notice, except that the owner and consignee shall remain liable for costs pursuant to subsection (c).".

(b) Definition.—Section 201(h) of the Federal Food, Drug, and Cosmetic Act (21 U.S.C. 321(h)) is amended—

(1) by redesignating subparagraphs (1), (2), and (3) as clauses (A), (B), and (C), respectively; and

(2) after making such redesignations—

(A) by striking "(h) The term" and inserting "(h)(1) The term"; and

(B) by adding at the end the following:

"(2) The term 'counterfeit device' means a device which, or the container, packaging, or labeling of which, without authorization, bears a trademark, trade name, or other identifying mark, imprint, or symbol, or any likeness thereof, or is manufactured using a design, of a device manufacturer, packer, or distributor other than the person or persons who in fact manufactured, packed, or distributed such device and which thereby falsely purports or is represented to be the product of, or to have been packed or distributed by, such other device manufacturer, packer, or distributor.

"(3) For purposes of subparagraph (2)—

"(A) the term 'manufactured' refers to any of the following activities: manufacture, preparation, propagation, compounding, assembly, or processing; and

"(B) the term 'manufacturer' means a person who is engaged in any of the activities listed in clause (A).".

SEC. 70533. REQUIRING THE STRATEGIC NATIONAL STOCKPILE TO INCLUDE CERTAIN TYPES OF MEDICAL SUPPLIES.

Section 319F–2(a)(1) of the Public Health Service Act (42 U.S.C. 247d–6b(a)(1)) is amended by inserting "(including personal protective equipment, ancillary medical supplies, and other supplies required for the administration of drugs, vaccines and other biological products, medical devices, and diagnostic tests)"' after "other supplies".

SEC. 70534. REPORTING REQUIREMENT FOR DRUG MANUFACTURERS.

(a) Establishments In A Foreign Country.—Section 510(i) of the Federal Food, Drug, and Cosmetic Act (21 U.S.C. 360(i)) is amended by inserting at the end the following new paragraph:

"(5) The requirements of paragraphs (1) and (2) shall apply to establishments within a foreign country engaged in the manufacture, preparation, propagation, compounding, or processing of any drug, including the active pharmaceutical ingredient, that is required to be listed pursuant to subsection (j). Such requirements shall apply regardless of whether the drug, including the active pharmaceutical ingredient, undergoes further manufacture, preparation, propagation, compounding, or processing at a separate establishment outside the United States prior to being imported or offered for import into the United States.".

(b) Listing Of Drugs.—Section 510(j) of the Federal Food, Drug, and Cosmetic Act (21 U.S.C. 360(j)) is amended—

(1) in paragraph (1)—

(A) in subparagraph (D), by striking "and" at the end;

(B) in subparagraph (E), by striking the period at the end and inserting "; and"; and

(C) by adding at the end the following new subparagraph:

"(F) in the case of a drug contained in the applicable list, a certification that the registrant has—

"(i) identified every other establishment where manufacturing is performed for the drug; and

"(ii) notified each known foreign establishment engaged in the manufacture, preparation, propagation, compounding, or processing of the drug, including the active pharmaceutical ingredient, of the inclusion of the drug in the list and the obligation to register.";

(2) by redesignating paragraphs (3) and (4) as paragraphs (4) and (5), respectively; and

(3) by inserting after paragraph (2) the following:

"(3) (A) Subject to subparagraph (B), each person who registers with the Secretary under this section shall report to the Secretary by electronic means in a form and manner as specified by the Secretary, with regard to drugs, once during the month of March of each year, once during the month of June of each year, once during the month of September of each year, and once during the month of December of each year, on the amount of each listed drug that was manufactured, prepared, propagated, compounded, or processed at each establishment registered by such person since the date the person last made a report under this paragraph. Such amount shall include the number of dosage units for each finished drug product intended for distribution in the United States, or amount of active pharmaceutical ingredient intended for distribution in the United States. The Secretary may require information reported under this subparagraph to be further delineated in such manner as the Secretary determines appropriate.

"(B) Notwithstanding subparagraph (A), the Secretary may issue an order exempting certain biological products or categories of biological products licensed under section 351 of the Public Health Service Act from some or all of the reporting requirements under such subparagraph if the Secretary determines that the application of such requirements to such products (or categories thereof) is not necessary to protect the public health.".

(c) Rules Of Construction.—

(1) Nothing in the amendments made by this section shall be construed—

(A) to limit or narrow, in any manner, the meaning or application of the provisions of subsection (i) or (j) of section 510 of the Federal Food, Drug, and Cosmetic Act (21 U.S.C. 360); or

(B) to affect any determination under either such subsection made prior to the date of enactment of this Act.

(2) Nothing in the amendments made by this section shall be construed—

(A) to limit or narrow the ability of the Secretary of Health and Human Services to share confidential commercial information pursuant to a memorandum of understanding, entered into before, on, or after the date of enactment of this section, between the Food and Drug Administration and another Federal department or agency; or

(B) as authorizing the Secretary to disclose any information that is confidential commercial or trade secret information subject to section 552(b)(4) of title 5, United States Code, or section 1905 of title 18, United States Code.

SEC. 70535. NATIONAL CENTERS OF EXCELLENCE IN CONTINUOUS PHARMACEUTICAL MANUFACTURING.

(a) In General.—Section 3016 of the 21st Century Cures Act (21 U.S.C. 399h) is amended to read as follows:

"SEC. 3016. NATIONAL CENTERS OF EXCELLENCE IN CONTINUOUS PHARMACEUTICAL MANUFACTURING.

"(a) In General.—The Secretary of Health and Human Services, acting through the Commissioner of Food and Drugs—

"(1) shall solicit and, beginning not later than one year after the date of enactment of the National Centers of Excellence in Continuous Pharmaceutical Manufacturing Act of 2019, receive requests from institutions of higher education to be designated as a National Center of Excellence in Continuous Pharmaceutical Manufacturing (in this section referred to as a 'National Center of Excellence') to support the advancement and development of continuous manufacturing; and

"(2) shall so designate any institution of higher education that—

"(A) requests such designation; and

"(B) meets the criteria specified in subsection (c).

"(b) Request For Designation.—A request for designation under subsection (a) shall be made to the Secretary at such time, in such manner, and containing such information as the Secretary may require. Any such request shall include a description of how the institution of higher education meets or plans to meet each of the criteria specified in subsection (c).

"(c) Criteria For Designation Described.—The criteria specified in this subsection with respect to an institution of higher education are that the institution has, as of the date of the submission of a request under subsection

(a) by such institution—
"(1) physical and technical capacity for research and development of continuous manufacturing;
"(2) manufacturing knowledge-sharing networks with other institutions of higher education, large and small pharmaceutical manufacturers, generic and nonprescription manufacturers, contract manufacturers, and other entities;
"(3) proven capacity to design and demonstrate new, highly effective technology for use in continuous manufacturing;
"(4) a track record for creating and transferring knowledge with respect to continuous manufacturing;
"(5) the potential to train a future workforce for research on and implementation of advanced manufacturing and continuous manufacturing; and
"(6) experience in participating in and leading a continuous manufacturing technology partnership with other institutions of higher education, large and small pharmaceutical manufacturers, generic and nonprescription manufacturers, contract manufacturers, and other entities—
"(A) to support companies with continuous manufacturing in the United States;
"(B) to support Federal agencies with technical assistance, which may include regulatory and quality metric guidance as applicable, for advanced manufacturing and continuous manufacturing;
"(C) with respect to continuous manufacturing, to organize and conduct research and development activities needed to create new and more effective technology, capture and disseminate expertise, create intellectual property, and maintain technological leadership;
"(D) to develop best practices for designing continuous manufacturing; and
"(E) to assess and respond to the workforce needs for continuous manufacturing, including the development of training programs if needed.
"(d) Termination Of Designation.—The Secretary may terminate the designation of any National Center of Excellence designated under this section if the Secretary determines such National Center of Excellence no longer meets the criteria specified in subsection (c). Not later than 60 days before the effective date of such a termination, the Secretary shall provide written notice to the National Center of Excellence, including the rationale for such termination.
"(e) Conditions For Designation.—As a condition of designation as a National Center of Excellence under this section, the Secretary shall require that an institution of higher education enter into an agreement with the Secretary under which the institution agrees—
"(1) to collaborate directly with the Food and Drug Administration to publish the reports required by subsection (g);
"(2) to share data with the Food and Drug Administration regarding best practices and research generated through the funding under subsection (f);
"(3) to develop, along with industry partners (which may include large

and small biopharmaceutical manufacturers, generic and nonprescription manufacturers, and contract manufacturers) and another institution or institutions designated under this section, if any, a roadmap for developing a continuous manufacturing workforce;

"(4) to develop, along with industry partners and other institutions designated under this section, a roadmap for strengthening existing, and developing new, relationships with other institutions; and

"(5) to provide an annual report to the Food and Drug Administration regarding the institution's activities under this section, including a description of how the institution continues to meet and make progress on the criteria listed in subsection (c).

"(f) Funding.—

"(1) IN GENERAL.—The Secretary shall award funding, through grants, contracts, or cooperative agreements, to the National Centers of Excellence designated under this section for the purpose of studying and recommending improvements to continuous manufacturing, including such improvements as may enable the Centers—

"(A) to continue to meet the conditions specified in subsection (e); and

"(B) to expand capacity for research on, and development of, continuing manufacturing.

"(2) CONSISTENCY WITH FDA MISSION.—As a condition on receipt of funding under this subsection, a National Center of Excellence shall agree to consider any input from the Secretary regarding the use of funding that would—

"(A) help to further the advancement of continuous manufacturing through the National Center of Excellence; and

"(B) be relevant to the mission of the Food and Drug Administration.

"(3) AUTHORIZATION OF APPROPRIATIONS.—There is authorized to be appropriated to carry out this subsection $80,000,000 for the period of fiscal years 2021 through 2025.

"(4) RULE OF CONSTRUCTION.—Nothing in this section shall be construed as precluding a National Center for Excellence designated under this section from receiving funds under any other provision of this Act or any other Federal law.

"(g) Annual Review And Reports.—

"(1) ANNUAL REPORT.—Beginning not later than one year after the date on which the first designation is made under subsection (a), and annually thereafter, the Secretary shall—

"(A) submit to Congress a report describing the activities, partnerships and collaborations, Federal policy recommendations, previous and continuing funding, and findings of, and any other applicable information from, the National Centers of Excellence designated under this section; and

"(B) make such report available to the public in an easily accessible electronic format on the website of the Food and Drug Administration.

"(2) REVIEW OF NATIONAL CENTERS OF EXCELLENCE AND POTENTIAL DESIGNEES.—The Secretary shall periodically review the National Centers of Excellence designated under this section to ensure that such National Centers of Excellence continue to meet the criteria for designation under this section.

"(3) REPORT ON LONG-TERM VISION OF FDA ROLE.—Not later than 2 years after the date on which the first designation is made under subsection (a), the Secretary, in consultation with the National Centers of Excellence designated under this section, shall submit a report to the Congress on the long-term vision of the Department of Health and Human Services on the role of the Food and Drug Administration in supporting continuous manufacturing, including—

"(A) a national framework of principles related to the implementation and regulation of continuous manufacturing;

"(B) a plan for the development of Federal regulations and guidance for how advanced manufacturing and continuous manufacturing can be incorporated into the development of pharmaceuticals and regulatory responsibilities of the Food and Drug Administration; and

"(C) appropriate feedback solicited from the public, which may include other institutions, large and small biopharmaceutical manufacturers, generic and nonprescription manufacturers, and contract manufacturers.

"(h) Definitions.—In this section:

"(1) ADVANCED MANUFACTURING.—The term 'advanced manufacturing' means an approach for the manufacturing of pharmaceuticals that incorporates novel technology, or uses an established technique or technology in a new or innovative way (such as continuous manufacturing where the input materials are continuously transformed within the process by two or more unit operations) that enhances drug quality or improves the manufacturing process.

"(2) CONTINUOUS MANUFACTURING.—The term 'continuous manufacturing'—

"(A) means a process where the input materials are continuously fed into and transformed within the process, and the processed output materials are continuously removed from the system; and

"(B) consists of an integrated process that consists of a series of two or more unit operations.

"(3) INSTITUTION OF HIGHER EDUCATION.—The term 'institution of higher education' has the meaning given such term in section 101(a) of the Higher Education Act of 1965 (20 U.S.C. 1001(a)).

"(4) SECRETARY.—The term 'Secretary' means the Secretary of Health and Human Services, acting through the Commissioner of Food and Drugs.".

(b) Transition Rule.—Section 3016 of the 21st Century Cures Act (21 U.S.C. 399h), as in effect on the day before the date of the enactment of this section, shall apply with respect to grants awarded under such section before such date of enactment.

Subtitle D—Public Health Extenders

SEC. 70541. EXTENSION FOR COMMUNITY HEALTH CENTERS, THE NATIONAL HEALTH SERVICE CORPS, AND TEACHING HEALTH CENTERS THAT OPERATE GME PROGRAMS.

(a) Community Health Centers.—Section 10503(b)(1) of the Patient Protection and Affordable Care Act (42 U.S.C. 254b–2(b)(1)) is amended—

(1) in subparagraph (E), by striking "and" at the end;

(2) in subparagraph (F), by striking ", $4,000,000,000 for fiscal year 2019, and $2,575,342,466 for the period beginning on October 1, 2019, and ending on May 22, 2020; and" and inserting a semicolon; and

(3) by adding at the end the following:

"(G) $4,000,000,000 for each of fiscal years 2019 and 2020; and

"(H) $668,493,151 for the period beginning on October 1, 2020, and ending on November 30, 2020; and".

(b) National Health Service Corps.—Section 10503(b)(2) of the Patient Protection and Affordable Care Act (42 U.S.C. 254b–2(b)(2)) is amended—

(1) in subparagraph (F), by striking "and 2019; and" and inserting "through 2020; and"; and

(2) in subparagraph (G), by striking "$199,589,041 for the period beginning on October 1, 2019, and ending on May 22, 2020" and inserting "$51,808,220 for the period beginning on October 1, 2020, and ending on November 30, 2020."

(c) Teaching Health Centers That Operate Graduate Medical Education Programs.—Section 340H(g)(1) of the Public Health Service Act (42 U.S.C. 256h(g)(1)) is amended—

(1) by striking "and 2019" and inserting "through 2020" and;

(2) by striking "$81,445,205 for the period beginning on October 1, 2019, and ending on May 22, 2020" and inserting "$21,141,096 for the period beginning on October 1, 2020, and ending on November 30, 2020".

SEC. 70542. DIABETES PROGRAMS.

(a) Type I.—Section 330B(b)(2)(D) of the Public Health Service Act (42 U.S.C. 254c–2(b)(2)(D)) is amended by striking "and 2019, and $96,575,342 for the period beginning on October 1, 2019, and ending on May 22, 2020" and inserting "through 2020, and $25,068,494 for the period beginning on October 1, 2020, and ending on November 30, 2020".

(b) Indians.—Section 330C(c)(2)(D) of the Public Health Service Act (42 U.S.C. 254c–3(c)(2)(D)) is amended by striking "and 2019, and $96,575,342 for the period beginning on October 1, 2019, and ending on May 22, 2020" and inserting "through 2020, and $25,068,494 for the period beginning on October 1, 2020, and ending on November 30, 2020".

Subtitle E—Other Extenders

SEC. 70551. EXTENSION OF SEXUAL RISK AVOIDANCE EDUCATION PROGRAM.

Section 510 of the Social Security Act (42 U.S.C. 710) is amended—

(1) in subsection (a)—

(A) in paragraph (1), in the matter preceding subparagraph (A), by striking "and 2019 and for the period beginning October 1, 2019, and ending May 22, 2020" and inserting "through 2020 and for the period beginning on October 1, 2020, and ending on November 30, 2020";

(B) in paragraph (2)(A), by striking "and 2019 and for the period beginning October 1, 2019, and ending May 22, 2020" and inserting "through 2020, and for the period beginning on October 1, 2020, and ending on November 30, 2020"; and

(C) in paragraphs (1), (2)(A), and (2)(B)(i), by striking "with respect to such period, for fiscal year 2020" each place it appears and inserting "with respect to such period, for fiscal year 2021"; and

(2) in subsection (f)(1), by striking "and 2019 and $48,287,671 for the period beginning October 1, 2019, and ending May 22, 2020" and inserting "through 2020, and $12,534,247 for the period beginning on October 1, 2020, and ending on November 30, 2020".

SEC. 70552. EXTENSION OF PERSONAL RESPONSIBILITY EDUCATION PROGRAM.

Section 513 of the Social Security Act (42 U.S.C. 713) is amended—

(1) in subsection (a)(1)—

(A) in subparagraph (A), in the matter preceding clause (i), by striking "through 2019 and for the period beginning October 1, 2019, and ending May 22, 2020" and inserting "through 2020 and for the period beginning on October 1, 2020, and ending November 30, 2020"; and

(B) in subparagraph (B)(i), by striking "beginning October 1, 2019, and ending May 22, 2020" and inserting "beginning on October 1, 2020, and ending November 30, 2020";

(2) in subsection (a)(4)(A), by striking "2019" each place it appears and inserting "2020"; and

(3) in subsection (f), by striking "through 2019 and $48,287,671 for the period beginning October 1, 2019, and ending May 22, 2020" and inserting "through 2020, and $12,534,247 for the period beginning on October 1, 2020, and ending on November 30, 2020".

Subtitle F—Miscellaneous

SEC. 70561. HEALTH PROVIDER LOAN PROGRAM.

(a) In General.—Not later than 30 days after the date of enactment of this title, the Secretary shall establish a program under which loans shall be made to eligible health care organizations to assist such organizations with anticipated revenue loss or higher operating costs as a result of the COVID-19 emergency.

(b) Program Requirements.—The Secretary shall establish standards and guidelines for application, loan amount, repayment, and extension, and shall consider the eligible health care organization's financial condition, service in an area heavily impacted by the COVID-19 emergency, or other factors deemed appropriate.

(c) Eligible Health Care Organizations.—To be eligible for a loan under subsection (a), an entity shall—

(1) be a health care provider or supplier that receives assistance or otherwise participates in the Medicare or Medicaid program under title XVIII or XIX of the Social Security Act (42 U.S.C. 1395 and 1396 et seq.), including a hospital, critical access hospital, skilled nursing facility, physician practice, home health provider, community health center, ambulatory surgical care center, or hospice; and

(2) submit to the Secretary an application at such time, in such manner, and containing such information as the Secretary may require.

(d) Terms And Conditions.—

(1) INTEREST.—A loan under this section shall have a rate of interest of not to exceed 2 percent. Interest shall begin to accrue on the date that is 60 days after the date of origination.

(2) TERM.—The term of a loan under this section shall be 1 year minus one day. A borrower shall have the option to extend such term for a total of not to exceed 19 years. Further extensions may be granted if approval by the Secretary.

(3) SECURITY.—An eligible health care organization shall not be required to provide security for a loan under this section.

(4) PAYMENTS.—Loan payments shall be made on a biannual basis.

(e) Definitions.—In this section:

(1) COVID-19 EMERGENCY.—The term "COVID-19 emergency" means the national emergency declared by the President under the National Emergencies Act (50 U.S.C. 1601 et seq.) with respect to the Coronavirus Disease 2019 (COVID-19).

(2) SECRETARY.—The term "Secretary" means the Secretary of Health and Human Services.

(f) Use Of Certain Funds.—Loan recipients may use funds such recipients were awarded under the Public Health and Social Services Emergency Fund or the Health Provider Assistance Fund established under section 562 to repay loans awarded under this section, provided the funds from the Public Health and Social Services Emergency Fund or the Health Provider Assistance Fund were awarded based on foregone revenue.

(g) Clarification.—No individual, employer, or other entity may be restricted from participating in or benefitting from any exemption or benefit under this section, based on any factor that is unrelated to its qualifications to perform the required services.

(h) Appropriations.—There is authorized to be appropriated, and there is appropriated, to carry out this section, $80,000,000,000 for fiscal year 2020, to remain available until expended.

DIVISION H—EMERGENCY CORONAVIRUS PANDEMIC UNEMPLOYMENT COMPENSATION ACT OF 2020

SEC. 80001. SHORT TITLE.

This division may be cited as the "Emergency Coronavirus Pandemic Unemployment Compensation Act of 2020".

SEC. 80002. TABLE OF CONTENTS.

The table of contents for this division is as follows:

TITLE I—FEDERAL BENEFIT ENHANCEMENTS

SEC. 80101. EMERGENCY INCREASE IN UNEMPLOYMENT COMPENSATION BENEFITS.

(a) Federal-State Agreements.—Any State which desires to do so may enter into and participate in an agreement under this section with the Secretary of Labor (hereinafter in this section referred to as the "Secretary"). Any State which is a party to an agreement under this section may, upon providing 30 days' written notice to the Secretary, terminate such agreement.

(b) Provisions Of Agreement.—

(1) IN GENERAL.—Any agreement under this section shall provide the following:

(A) FEDERAL PANDEMIC UNEMPLOYMENT COMPENSATION.—The State agency of the State will make payments of regular compensation to individuals in amounts and to the extent that they would be determined if the State law of the State were applied, with respect to any week for which the individual is (disregarding this section) otherwise entitled under the State law to receive regular compensation, as if such State law had been modified in a manner such that the amount of regular compensation (including dependents' allowances) payable for any week shall be equal to—

(i) the amount determined under the State law (before the application of this paragraph), plus

(ii) an additional amount of $600 (in this section referred to as "Federal Pandemic Unemployment Compensation").

(B) FEDERAL PANDEMIC SHORT-TIME COMPENSATION.—In the case of a State that provides under the State law for the payment of short-time compensation under a short-time compensation program (as defined in section 3306(v) of the Internal Revenue Code of 1986), the State agency of the State will make payments of compensation (as defined in subsection (h) of such section) to employees participating in such program in amounts and to the extent that they would be determined under such program if the State law of the State were applied, with respect to any week for which the individual is (disregarding this section) otherwise eligible under the program under the State law to receive such compensation, as if such State law had been modified in a manner such that the amount of compensation payable for any week shall be equal to the amount determined under the State law (before the application of this paragraph) plus $300 (in this section referred to as "Federal Pandemic Short-Time Compensation").

(2) ALLOWABLE METHODS OF PAYMENT.—Any Federal Pandemic Unemployment Compensation or Federal Pandemic Short-Time Compensation provided for in accordance with paragraph (1) shall be payable either—

(A) as an amount which is paid at the same time and in the same manner as any compensation otherwise payable for the week involved; or

(B) at the option of the State, by payments which are made separately from, but on the same weekly basis as, any compensation otherwise payable.

(c) Nonreduction Rule.—An agreement under this section shall not apply (or shall cease to apply) with respect to a State upon a determination by the Secretary that the method governing the computation of regular compensation under the State law of that State has been modified in a manner such that the maximum benefit entitlement and the average weekly benefit amount of regular compensation (or short-time compensation in the case of a State described in subsection (b)(1)(B)) which will be payable during the period of the agreement (determined disregarding any Federal Pandemic Unemployment Compensation or Federal Pandemic Short-Time Compensation) will be less than the maximum benefit entitlement and the average weekly benefit amount of regular compensation (or short-time compensation) which would otherwise have been payable during such period under the State law, as in effect on January 1, 2020.

(d) Payments To States.—

(1) IN GENERAL.—

(A) FULL REIMBURSEMENT.—There shall be paid to each State which has entered into an agreement under this section an amount equal to 100 percent of—

(i) the total amount of Federal Pandemic Unemployment Compensation paid to individuals by the State pursuant to such agreement;

(ii) the total amount of Federal Pandemic Short-Time Compensation paid to individuals by the State pursuant to such agreement; and

(iii) any additional administrative expenses incurred by the State by reason of such agreement (as determined by the Secretary).

(B) TERMS OF PAYMENTS.—Sums payable to any State by reason of such State's having an agreement under this section shall be payable, either in advance or by way of reimbursement (as determined by the Secretary), in such amounts as the Secretary estimates the State will be entitled to receive under this section for each calendar month, reduced or increased, as the case may be, by any amount by which the Secretary finds that his estimates for any prior calendar month were greater or less than the amounts which should have been paid to the State. Such estimates may be made on the basis of such statistical, sampling, or other method as may be agreed upon by the Secretary and the State agency of the State involved.

(2) CERTIFICATIONS.—The Secretary shall from time to time certify to the Secretary of the Treasury for payment to each State the sums payable to such State under this section.

(3) APPROPRIATION.—There are appropriated from the general fund of the Treasury, without fiscal year limitation, such sums as may be necessary for purposes of this subsection.

(e) Applicability.—

(1) IN GENERAL.—An agreement entered into under this section shall apply to weeks of unemployment—

(A) beginning on or after March 13, 2020; and

(B) ending on or before January 1, 2021.

(2) TRANSITION RULE FOR INDIVIDUALS REMAINING ENTITLED TO REGULAR COMPENSATION AS OF JUNE 30, 2021.—In the case of any individual who, as of the date specified in paragraph (1)(B), has not yet exhausted all rights to regular compensation under the State law of a

State with respect to a benefit year that began before such date (or short-time compensation in the case of a State described in subsection (b)(1)(B)), Federal Pandemic Unemployment Compensation or Federal Pandemic Short-Time Compensation (as the case may be) shall continue to be payable to such individual for any week beginning on or after such date for which the individual is otherwise eligible for regular compensation (or short-time compensation) with respect to such benefit year.

(3) TERMINATION.—Notwithstanding any other provision of this subsection, no Federal Pandemic Unemployment Compensation or Federal Pandemic Short-Time Compensation shall be payable for any week beginning after June 30, 2021.

(f) Fraud And Overpayments.—

(1) IN GENERAL.—If an individual knowingly has made, or caused to be made by another, a false statement or representation of a material fact, or knowingly has failed, or caused another to fail, to disclose a material fact, and as a result of such false statement or representation or of such nondisclosure such individual has received an amount of Federal Pandemic Unemployment Compensation or Federal Pandemic Short-Time Compensation to which such individual was not entitled, such individual—

(A) shall be ineligible for further Federal Pandemic Unemployment Compensation or Federal Pandemic Short-Time Compensation in accordance with the provisions of the applicable State unemployment compensation law relating to fraud in connection with a claim for unemployment compensation; and

(B) shall be subject to prosecution under section 1001 of title 18, United States Code.

(2) REPAYMENT.—In the case of individuals who have received amounts of Federal Pandemic Unemployment Compensation or Federal Pandemic Short-Time Compensation to which they were not entitled, the State shall require such individuals to repay the amounts of such Federal Pandemic Unemployment Compensation or Federal Pandemic Short-Time Compensation to the State agency, except that the State agency may waive such repayment if it determines that—

(A) the payment of such Federal Pandemic Unemployment Compensation or Federal Pandemic Short-Time Compensation was without fault on the part of any such individual; and

(B) such repayment would be contrary to equity and good conscience.

(3) RECOVERY BY STATE AGENCY.—

(A) IN GENERAL.—The State agency may recover the amount to be repaid, or any part thereof, by deductions from any Federal Pandemic Unemployment Compensation or Federal Pandemic Short-Time Compensation payable to such individual or from any unemployment compensation payable to such individual under any State or Federal unemployment compensation law administered by the State agency or under any other State or Federal law administered by the State agency which provides for the payment of any assistance or allowance with respect to any week of unemployment, during the 3-year period after the date such individuals received the payment of the Federal Pandemic Unemployment Compensation or Federal Pandemic Short-Time Compensation to which they were not entitled, in accordance with the same procedures as apply to the recovery of overpayments of regular unemployment benefits paid by the State.

(B) OPPORTUNITY FOR HEARING.—No repayment shall be required, and no deduction shall be made, until a determination has been made, notice thereof and an opportunity for a fair hearing has been given to the individual, and the determination has become final.

(4) REVIEW.—Any determination by a State agency under this section shall be subject to review in the same manner and to the same extent as determinations under the State unemployment compensation law, and only in that manner and to that extent.

(g) Application To Other Unemployment Benefits.—

(1) IN GENERAL.—Each agreement under this section shall include provisions to provide that the purposes of the preceding provisions of this section shall be applied with respect to unemployment benefits described in subsection (i)(3) to the same extent and in the same manner as if those benefits were regular compensation.

(2) ELIGIBILITY AND TERMINATION RULES.—Federal Pandemic Unemployment Compensation—

(A) shall not be payable, pursuant to this subsection, with respect to any unemployment benefits described in subsection (i)(3) for any week beginning on or after the date specified in subsection (e)(1)(B), except in the case of an individual who was eligible to receive Federal Pandemic Unemployment Compensation in connection with any regular compensation or any unemployment benefits described in subsection (i)(3) for any period of unemployment ending before such date; and

(B) shall in no event be payable for any week beginning after the date specified in subsection (e)(3).

(h) Treatment Of Federal Pandemic Unemployment Compensation And Federal Pandemic Short-Time Compensation Payments.—

(1) PAYMENT TO BE DISREGARDED FOR PURPOSES OF ALL FEDERAL AND FEDERALLY ASSISTED PROGRAMS.—A Federal Pandemic Unemployment Compensation or Federal Pandemic Short-Time Compensation payment shall not be regarded as income and shall not be regarded as a resource for the month of receipt and the following 9 months, for purposes of determining the eligibility of the recipient (or the recipient's spouse or family) for benefits or assistance, or the amount or extent of benefits or assistance, under any Federal program or under any State or local program financed in whole or in part with Federal funds.

(i) Definitions.—For purposes of this section—

(1) the terms "compensation", "regular compensation", "benefit year", "State", "State agency", "State law", and "week" have the respective meanings given such terms under section 205 of the Federal-State Extended Unemployment Compensation Act of 1970 (26 U.S.C. 3304 note);
(2) the term "maximum benefit entitlement" means the amount of regular compensation payable to an individual with respect to the individual's benefit year; and
(3) any reference to unemployment benefits described in this paragraph shall be considered to refer to—
(A) extended compensation (as defined by section 205 of the Federal-State Extended Unemployment Compensation Act of 1970); and
(B) unemployment compensation (as defined by section 85(b) of the Internal Revenue Code of 1986) provided under any program administered by a State under an agreement with the Secretary.

SEC. 80102. TEMPORARY FINANCING OF SHORT-TIME COMPENSATION PAYMENTS IN STATES WITH PROGRAMS IN LAW.
(a) Payments To States.—
(1) IN GENERAL.—Subject to paragraph (3), there shall be paid to a State an amount equal to 100 percent of the amount of short-time compensation paid under a short-time compensation program (as defined in section 3306(v) of the Internal Revenue Code of 1986) under the provisions of the State law.
(2) TERMS OF PAYMENTS.—Payments made to a State under paragraph (1) shall be payable by way of reimbursement in such amounts as the Secretary estimates the State will be entitled to receive under this section for each calendar month, reduced or increased, as the case may be, by any amount by which the Secretary finds that the Secretary's estimates for any prior calendar month were greater or less than the amounts which should have been paid to the State. Such estimates may be made on the basis of such statistical, sampling, or other method as may be agreed upon by the Secretary and the State agency of the State involved.
(3) LIMITATIONS ON PAYMENTS.—
(A) GENERAL PAYMENT LIMITATIONS.—No payments shall be made to a State under this section for short-time compensation paid to an individual by the State during a benefit year in excess of 26 times the amount of regular compensation (including dependents' allowances) under the State law payable to such individual for a week of total unemployment.
(B) EMPLOYER LIMITATIONS.—No payments shall be made to a State under this section for benefits paid to an individual by the State under a short-time compensation program if such individual is employed by the participating employer on a seasonal, temporary, or intermittent basis.
(b) Applicability.—Payments to a State under subsection (a) shall be available for weeks of unemployment—
(1) beginning on or after March 13, 2020; and

(2) ending on or before December 31, 2020.
(c) New Programs.—Subject to paragraphs (1)(B) and (2) of subsection (b), if at any point after the date of the enactment of this Act the State enacts a State law providing for the payment of short-time compensation under a short-time compensation program that meets the definition of such a program under section 3306(v) of the Internal Revenue Code of 1986, the State shall be eligible for payments under this section after the effective date of such enactment.
(d) Funding And Certifications.—
(1) FUNDING.—There are appropriated, out of moneys in the Treasury not otherwise appropriated, such sums as may be necessary for purposes of carrying out this section.
(2) CERTIFICATIONS.—The Secretary shall from time to time certify to the Secretary of the Treasury for payment to each State the sums payable to such State under this section.
(e) Definitions.—In this section:
(1) SECRETARY.—The term "Secretary" means the Secretary of Labor.
(2) STATE; STATE AGENCY; STATE LAW.—The terms "State", "State agency", and "State law" have the meanings given those terms in section 205 of the Federal-State Extended Unemployment Compensation Act of 1970 (26 U.S.C. 3304 note).
(f) Technical Correction To Definition.—Section 3306(v)(6) of the Internal Revenue Code of 1986 (26 U.S.C. 3306) is amended by striking "Workforce Investment Act of 1998" and inserting "Workforce Innovation and Opportunity Act".

SEC. 80103. TEMPORARY FINANCING OF SHORT-TIME COMPENSATION AGREEMENTS.
(a) Federal-State Agreements.—
(1) IN GENERAL.—Any State which desires to do so may enter into, and participate in, an agreement under this section with the Secretary provided that such State's law does not provide for the payment of short-time compensation under a short-time compensation program (as defined in section 3306(v) of the Internal Revenue Code of 1986).
(2) ABILITY TO TERMINATE.—Any State which is a party to an agreement under this section may, upon providing 30 days' written notice to the Secretary, terminate such agreement.
(b) Provisions Of Federal-State Agreement.—
(1) IN GENERAL.—Any agreement under this section shall provide that the State agency of the State will make payments of short-time compensation under a plan approved by the State. Such plan shall provide that payments are made in accordance with the requirements under section 3306(v) of the Internal Revenue Code of 1986.
(2) LIMITATIONS ON PLANS.—

(A) GENERAL PAYMENT LIMITATIONS.—A short-time compensation plan approved by a State shall not permit the payment of short-time compensation to an individual by the State during a benefit year in excess of 26 times the amount of regular compensation (including dependents' allowances) under the State law payable to such individual for a week of total unemployment.

(B) EMPLOYER LIMITATIONS.—A short-time compensation plan approved by a State shall not provide payments to an individual if such individual is employed by the participating employer on a seasonal, temporary, or intermittent basis.

(3) EMPLOYER PAYMENT OF COSTS.—Any short-time compensation plan entered into by an employer must provide that the employer will pay the State an amount equal to one-half of the amount of short-time compensation paid under such plan. Such amount shall be deposited in the State's unemployment fund and shall not be used for purposes of calculating an employer's contribution rate under section 3303(a)(1) of the Internal Revenue Code of 1986.

(c) Payments To States.—

(1) IN GENERAL.—There shall be paid to each State with an agreement under this section an amount equal to—

(A) one-half of the amount of short-time compensation paid to individuals by the State pursuant to such agreement; and

(B) any additional administrative expenses incurred by the State by reason of such agreement (as determined by the Secretary).

(2) TERMS OF PAYMENTS.—Payments made to a State under paragraph (1) shall be payable by way of reimbursement in such amounts as the Secretary estimates the State will be entitled to receive under this section for each calendar month, reduced or increased, as the case may be, by any amount by which the Secretary finds that the Secretary's estimates for any prior calendar month were greater or less than the amounts which should have been paid to the State. Such estimates may be made on the basis of such statistical, sampling, or other method as may be agreed upon by the Secretary and the State agency of the State involved.

(3) FUNDING.—There are appropriated, out of moneys in the Treasury not otherwise appropriated, such sums as may be necessary for purposes of carrying out this section.

(4) CERTIFICATIONS.—The Secretary shall from time to time certify to the Secretary of the Treasury for payment to each State the sums payable to such State under this section.

(d) Applicability.—An agreement entered into under this section shall apply to weeks of unemployment—

(1) beginning on or after March 13, 2020; and

(2) ending on or before December 31, 2020.

(e) Special Rule.—If a State has entered into an agreement under this section and subsequently enacts a State law providing for the payment of short-time compensation under a short-time compensation program that meets the definition of such a program under section 3306(v) of the Internal Revenue Code of 1986, the State—

(1) shall not be eligible for payments under this section for weeks of unemployment beginning after the effective date of such State law; and

(2) subject to paragraphs (1)(B) and (2) of section 2(b), shall be eligible to receive payments under section 2 after the effective date of such State law.

(f) Definitions.—In this section:

(1) SECRETARY.—The term "Secretary" means the Secretary of Labor.

(2) STATE; STATE AGENCY; STATE LAW.—The terms "State", "State agency", and "State law" have the meanings given those terms in section 205 of the Federal-State Extended Unemployment Compensation Act of 1970 (26 U.S.C. 3304 note).

SEC. 80104. EMERGENCY FLEXIBILITY FOR SHORT-TIME COMPENSATION.

Notwithstanding any other law, if a State modifies its unemployment compensation law and policies with respect to availability for work and work search test requirements for short-time compensation on an emergency temporary basis as needed to respond to the spread of COVID–19, such modifications shall be disregarded for the purposes of applying section 303 of the Social Security Act and section 3306(v)(5) of the Internal Revenue Code of 1986 to such State law.

SEC. 80105. GRANTS FOR SHORT-TIME COMPENSATION PROGRAMS.

(a) Grants.—

(1) FOR IMPLEMENTATION OR IMPROVED ADMINISTRATION.—The Secretary shall award grants to States that enact short-time compensation programs (as defined in subsection (i)(2)) for the purpose of implementation or improved administration of such programs.

(2) FOR PROMOTION AND ENROLLMENT.—The Secretary shall award grants to States that are eligible and submit plans for a grant under paragraph (1) for such States to promote and enroll employers in short-time compensation programs (as so defined).

(3) ELIGIBILITY.—

(A) IN GENERAL.—The Secretary shall determine eligibility criteria for the grants under paragraphs (1) and (2).

(B) CLARIFICATION.—A State administering a short-time compensation program that does not meet the definition of a short-time compensation program under section 3306(v) of the Internal Revenue Code of 1986, and a State with an agreement under section 3, shall not be eligible to receive a grant under this section until such time as the State law of the State provides for payments under a short-time compensation program that meets such

definition and such law.
(b) Amount Of Grants.—
(1) IN GENERAL.—The maximum amount available for making grants to a State under paragraphs (1) and (2) shall be equal to the amount obtained by multiplying $100,000,000 (less the amount used by the Secretary under subsection (e)) by the same ratio as would apply under subsection (a)(2)(B) of section 903 of the Social Security Act (42 U.S.C. 1103) for purposes of determining such State's share of any excess amount (as described in subsection (a)(1) of such section) that would have been subject to transfer to State accounts, as of October 1, 2019, under the provisions of subsection (a) of such section.
(2) AMOUNT AVAILABLE FOR DIFFERENT GRANTS.—Of the maximum incentive payment determined under paragraph (1) with respect to a State—
(A) one-third shall be available for a grant under subsection (a)(1); and
(B) two-thirds shall be available for a grant under subsection (a)(2).
(c) Grant Application And Disbursal.—
(1) APPLICATION.—Any State seeking a grant under paragraph (1) or (2) of subsection (a) shall submit an application to the Secretary at such time, in such manner, and complete with such information as the Secretary may require. In no case may the Secretary award a grant under this section with respect to an application that is submitted after December 31, 2020.
(2) NOTICE.—The Secretary shall, within 30 days after receiving a complete application, notify the State agency of the State of the Secretary's findings with respect to the requirements for a grant under paragraph (1) or (2) (or both) of subsection (a).
(3) CERTIFICATION.—If the Secretary finds that the State law provisions meet the requirements for a grant under subsection (a), the Secretary shall thereupon make a certification to that effect to the Secretary of the Treasury, together with a certification as to the amount of the grant payment to be transferred to the State account in the Unemployment Trust Fund (as established in section 904(a) of the Social Security Act (42 U.S.C. 1104(a))) pursuant to that finding. The Secretary of the Treasury shall make the appropriate transfer to the State account within 7 days after receiving such certification.
(4) REQUIREMENT.—No certification of compliance with the requirements for a grant under paragraph (1) or (2) of subsection (a) may be made with respect to any State whose—
(A) State law is not otherwise eligible for certification under section 303 of the Social Security Act (42 U.S.C. 503) or approvable under section 3304 of the Internal Revenue Code of 1986; or
(B) short-time compensation program is subject to discontinuation or is not scheduled to take effect within 12 months of the certification.
(d) Use Of Funds.—The amount of any grant awarded under this section shall be used for the implementation of short-time compensation programs and the

overall administration of such programs and the promotion and enrollment efforts associated with such programs, such as through—
(1) the creation or support of rapid response teams to advise employers about alternatives to layoffs;
(2) the provision of education or assistance to employers to enable them to assess the feasibility of participating in short-time compensation programs; and
(3) the development or enhancement of systems to automate—
(A) the submission and approval of plans; and
(B) the filing and approval of new and on-going short-time compensation claims.
(e) Administration.—The Secretary is authorized to use 0.25 percent of the funds available under subsection (g) to provide for outreach and to share best practices with respect to this section and short-time compensation programs.
(f) Recoupment.—The Secretary shall establish a process under which the Secretary shall recoup the amount of any grant awarded under paragraph (1) or (2) of subsection (a) if the Secretary determines that, during the 5-year period beginning on the first date that any such grant is awarded to the State, the State—
(1) terminated the State's short-time compensation program; or
(2) failed to meet appropriate requirements with respect to such program (as established by the Secretary).
(g) Funding.—There are appropriated for fiscal year 2020, out of moneys in the Treasury not otherwise appropriated, to the Secretary, $100,000,000 to carry out this section, to remain available until December 31, 2020.
(h) Reporting.—The Secretary may establish reporting requirements for States receiving a grant under this section in order to provide oversight of grant funds.
(i) Definitions.—In this section:
(1) SECRETARY.—The term "Secretary" means the Secretary of Labor.
(2) SHORT-TIME COMPENSATION PROGRAM.—The term "short-time compensation program" has the meaning given such term in section 3306(v) of the Internal Revenue Code of 1986.
(3) STATE; STATE AGENCY; STATE LAW.—The terms "State", "State agency", and "State law" have the meanings given those terms in section 205 of the Federal-State Extended Unemployment Compensation Act of 1970 (26 U.S.C. 3304 note).

SEC. 80106. EMERGENCY EXTENDED BENEFIT PERIOD FOR 2020.
(a) In General.—For purposes of section 203 of the Federal-State Extended Unemployment Compensation Act of 1970 (26 U.S.C. 3304 note), and notwithstanding any other provision of such section, an emergency extended benefit period shall be deemed to occur with respect to each State as follows:
(1) in the case of a State with respect to which an extended benefit period is

not in effect (without regard to this section) for the 1st week beginning after the date of enactment of this Act, an emergency extended benefit period is deemed to begin with such week with respect to such State; and

(2) in the case of a State with respect to which an extended benefit period is otherwise in effect (without regard to this section) for such week, an emergency extended benefit period is deemed to begin with the week following the last week of such extended benefit period.

(b) Special Rule With Respect To Certain States.—In the case of a State described in subsection (a)(1) with respect to which an extended benefit period would (but for this section) begin during an emergency extended benefit period, such extended benefit period shall begin with the week following the last week of such emergency extended benefit period.

(c) Additional Funding For Extended Compensation Accounts.—In the case of a State described in (a)(2) or (b), section 202(b)(1) the Federal-State Extended Unemployment Compensation Act of 1970 (26 U.S.C. 3304 note) shall be applied for weeks during an emergency extended benefit period by substituting for each of "50", "thirteen", and "thirty-nine" such higher number as the State determines is necessary to account for such emergency extended benefit period.

(d) Treatment Of Emergency Extended Benefit Period Under FSEUCA.—The provisions of the Federal-State Extended Unemployment Compensation Act of 1970 (26 U.S.C. 3304 note) shall apply to a State with respect to which an emergency extended benefit period is in effect in the same manner as such provisions apply to a State with respect to which an extended benefit period is in effect.

TITLE II—EXPANDED ELIGIBILITY FOR UNEMPLOYMENT COMPENSATION

SEC. 80201. PANDEMIC SELF-EMPLOYMENT AND JOB ENTRANT COMPENSATION.

(a) Federal-State Agreements.—Any State which desires to do so may enter into and participate in an agreement under this section with the Secretary of Labor (hereinafter in this section referred to as the "Secretary"). Any State which is a party to an agreement under this section may, upon providing 30 days' written notice to the Secretary, terminate such agreement.

(b) Provisions Of Agreement.—

(1) PANDEMIC SELF-EMPLOYMENT AND JOB ENTRANT COMPENSATION.—Any agreement under subsection (a) shall provide that the State agency of the State will make payments on a weekly basis (in this section referred to as "Pandemic Self-Employment and Job Entrant Compensation") to unemployed individuals who—

(A) have no rights to regular compensation with respect to a week under

the State law or any other State unemployment compensation law or to compensation under any other Federal law;
(B) are not receiving any State or private paid leave (as defined in subsection (g)) with respect to such week; and
(C) attest that—
(i) the individual is not able or available to work due to COVID–19 with respect to such week (as determined under paragraph (4)); and
(ii) but for COVID–19 (as determined under paragraph (4)), the individual would be able and available to work during such week.
(2) AMOUNT OF PANDEMIC SELF-EMPLOYMENT AND JOB ENTRANT COMPENSATION.—
(A) IN GENERAL.—Except as provided in subparagraph (B), the amount of Pandemic Self-Employment and Job Entrant Compensation payable to an individual for a week under an agreement under subsection (a) shall be $300.
(B) HIGHER PAYMENT FOR CERTAIN INDIVIDUALS.—Notwithstanding subparagraph (A), the amount of Pandemic Self-Employment and Job Entrant Compensation payable to an individual for a week under an agreement under subsection (a) shall be an amount equal to the sum of $600 plus 1⁄4 of the average weekly benefit amount of regular compensation paid to eligible individuals in the State as of January 1, 2020, but only in the case of an individual who attests (and furnishes such supporting documentation as the State agency may request) that—
(i) the individual had net earnings from self-employment (as defined in section 1402(a) of the Internal Revenue Code of 1986) of not less than $2,500 during the 6-month period ending on the date of enactment of this Act; or
(ii) the individual had a contract or other offer of employment suspended or rescinded due to COVID–19.
(3) DURATION OF BENEFIT PAYMENTS.—An individual who becomes entitled to Pandemic Self-Employment and Job Entrant Compensation paid by a State under an agreement under subsection (a) shall receive such benefit for not more than 26 weeks.
(4) NOT ABLE OR AVAILABLE TO WORK DUE TO COVID–19.—For purposes of this subsection, an individual shall be considered to be not able or available to work due to COVID–19 with respect to a week during any part of which the individual is not able or available to work because—
(A) the individual has a current diagnosis of COVID–19;
(B) the individual is under quarantine (including self-imposed quarantine), at the instruction of a health care provider, employer, or a local, State, or Federal official, in order to prevent the spread of COVID–19;
(C) the individual is unable to engage in self-employment (in the case of an individual described in paragraph (2)(B)(i)) or seek suitable employment because of closings or restrictions on movement related to COVID–19;
(D) the individual is engaged in caregiving (without compensation) for an individual who has a current diagnosis of COVID–19 or is under quarantine

as described in subparagraph (B)); or
(E) the individual is engaged in caregiving (without compensation), because of the COVID-19-related closing of a school or other care facility or care program, for a child or other individual unable to provide self-care.
(5) COORDINATION WITH CERTAIN TAX CREDITS.—Notwithstanding paragraph (1), no individual may become entitled to Pandemic Self-Employment and Job Entrant Compensation under an agreement under subsection (a) unless the individual makes an irrevocable election (at such time and in such manner as the Secretary of the Treasury may provide) to have sections 7002 and 7004 of the Families First Coronavirus Response Act not apply with respect to such individual. An individual who makes such an election shall not be treated as an individual to whom a credit is allowable under such sections.
(c) Payments To States.—
(1) IN GENERAL.—
(A) FULL REIMBURSEMENT.—There shall be paid to each State which has entered into an agreement under this section an amount equal to 100 percent of—
(i) the total amount of Pandemic Self-Employment and Job Entrant Compensation paid to individuals by the State pursuant to such agreement; and
(ii) any additional administrative expenses incurred by the State by reason of such agreement (as determined by the Secretary).
(B) TERMS OF PAYMENTS.—Sums payable to any State by reason of such State's having an agreement under this section shall be payable, either in advance or by way of reimbursement (as determined by the Secretary), in such amounts as the Secretary estimates the State will be entitled to receive under this section for each calendar month, reduced or increased, as the case may be, by any amount by which the Secretary finds that his estimates for any prior calendar month were greater or less than the amounts which should have been paid to the State. Such estimates may be made on the basis of such statistical, sampling, or other method as may be agreed upon by the Secretary and the State agency of the State involved.
(2) FUNDING.—
(A) IN GENERAL.—Funds in the extended unemployment compensation account (as established by section 905(a) of the Social Security Act (42 U.S.C. 1105(a)) of the Unemployment Trust Fund (as established by section 904(a) of such Act (42 U.S.C. 1104(a)) shall be used to make payments to States pursuant to paragraph (1).
(B) TRANSFER OF FUNDS.—Notwithstanding any other provision of law, the Secretary of the Treasury shall transfer from the general fund of the Treasury (from funds not otherwise appropriated) to the extended unemployment compensation account such sums as the Secretary of Labor estimates to be necessary to make payments described in subparagraph (A).

There are appropriated from the general fund of the Treasury, without fiscal year limitation, the sums referred to in the preceding sentence and such sums shall not be required to be repaid.

(3) CERTIFICATIONS.—The Secretary shall from time to time certify to the Secretary of the Treasury for payment to each State the sums payable to such State under this section.

(d) Applicability.—

(1) IN GENERAL.—An agreement entered into under this section shall apply with respect to weeks—

(A) beginning on or after March 13, 2020; and

(B) ending on or before January 1, 2021.

(2) TRANSITION RULE FOR INDIVIDUALS REMAINING ENTITLED TO PANDEMIC SELF-EMPLOYMENT AND JOB ENTRANT COMPENSATION AS OF JANUARY 1, 2021.—In the case of any individual who, as of the date specified in paragraph (1)(B), has not yet exhausted all rights to Pandemic Self-Employment and Job Entrant Compensation under the agreement under subsection (a), Pandemic Self-Employment and Job Entrant Compensation shall continue to be payable to such individual for any week beginning on or after such date for which the individual is otherwise eligible for such Pandemic Self-Employment and Job Entrant Compensation.

(3) TERMINATION.—Notwithstanding any other provision of this subsection, no Pandemic Self-Employment and Job Entrant Compensation shall be payable for any week beginning after June 30, 2021.

(e) Fraud And Overpayments.—

(1) IN GENERAL.—If an individual knowingly has made, or caused to be made by another, a false statement or representation of a material fact, or knowingly has failed, or caused another to fail, to disclose a material fact, and as a result of such false statement or representation or of such nondisclosure such individual has received an amount of Pandemic Self-Employment and Job Entrant Compensation to which such individual was not entitled, such individual—

(A) shall be ineligible for further Pandemic Self-Employment and Job Entrant Compensation in accordance with the provisions of the applicable State unemployment compensation law relating to fraud in connection with a claim for unemployment compensation; and

(B) shall be subject to prosecution under section 1001 of title 18, United States Code.

(2) REPAYMENT.—In the case of individuals who have received amounts of Pandemic Self-Employment and Job Entrant Compensation to which they were not entitled, the State shall require such individuals to repay the amounts of such Pandemic Self-Employment and Job Entrant Compensation to the State agency, except that the State agency may waive such repayment if it determines that—

(A) the payment of such Pandemic Self-Employment and Job Entrant

Compensation was without fault on the part of any such individual; and
(B) such repayment would be contrary to equity and good conscience.
(3) RECOVERY BY STATE AGENCY.—
(A) IN GENERAL.—The State agency may recover the amount to be repaid, or any part thereof, by deductions from any Pandemic Self-Employment and Job Entrant Compensation payable to such individual or from any unemployment compensation payable to such individual under any State or Federal unemployment compensation law administered by the State agency or under any other State or Federal law administered by the State agency which provides for the payment of any assistance or allowance with respect to any week of unemployment, during the 3-year period after the date such individuals received the payment of the Pandemic Self-Employment and Job Entrant Compensation to which they were not entitled, in accordance with the same procedures as apply to the recovery of overpayments of regular unemployment benefits paid by the State.
(B) OPPORTUNITY FOR HEARING.—No repayment shall be required, and no deduction shall be made, until a determination has been made, notice thereof and an opportunity for a fair hearing has been given to the individual, and the determination has become final.
(4) REVIEW.—Any determination by a State agency under this section shall be subject to review in the same manner and to the same extent as determinations under the State unemployment compensation law, and only in that manner and to that extent.
(5) DEPOSIT IN STATE UNEMPLOYMENT FUND.—Any amount recovered by a State agency pursuant to this subsection shall be deposited in the account of such State in the Unemployment Trust Fund.
(f) Treatment Of Pandemic Self-Employment And Job Entrant Compensation Payments.—
(1) PAYMENT TO BE DISREGARDED FOR PURPOSES OF ALL FEDERAL AND FEDERALLY ASSISTED PROGRAMS.—A Pandemic Self-Employment and Job Entrant Compensation payment shall not be regarded as income and shall not be regarded as a resource for the month of receipt and the following 9 months, for purposes of determining the eligibility of the recipient (or the recipient's spouse or family) for benefits or assistance, or the amount or extent of benefits or assistance, under any Federal program or under any State or local program financed in whole or in part with Federal funds.
(2) PAYMENT NOT CONSIDERED INCOME FOR PURPOSES OF TAXATION.—A Pandemic Self-Employment and Job Entrant Compensation payment shall not be considered as gross income for purposes of the Internal Revenue Code of 1986.
(g) Definitions.—For purposes of this section—
(1) the terms "compensation" (except as such term is used in subsection (b)(4)), "regular compensation", "State", "State agency", and "State law" have the respective meanings given such terms under section 205 of the Federal-State

Extended Unemployment Compensation Act of 1970 (26 U.S.C. 3304 note); and

(2) the term "State or private paid leave" means a benefit which provides full or partial wage replacement to employees on the basis of specifically defined qualifying events described in section 102 of the Family and Medical Leave Act of 1993 or defined by a written employer policy or State law and which ends either when the qualifying event is no longer applicable or a set period of benefits is exhausted.

TITLE III—RELIEF FOR GOVERNMENTAL AND NONPROFIT ENTITIES

SEC. 80301. EMERGENCY UNEMPLOYMENT RELIEF FOR GOVERNMENTAL ENTITIES AND NONPROFIT ORGANIZATIONS.

(a) Flexibility In Paying Reimbursement.—The Secretary of Labor may issue clarifying guidance to allow States to interpret their State unemployment compensation laws in a manner that would provide maximum flexibility to reimbursing employers as it relates to timely payment and assessment of penalties and interest pursuant to such State laws.

(b) Federal Funding.—Section 903 of the Social Security Act (42 U.S.C. 1103) is amended by adding at the end the following:

"Transfers For Federal Reimbursement Of State Unemployment Funds

"(j) (1) (A) In addition to any other amounts, the Secretary of Labor shall provide for the transfer of funds during the applicable period to the accounts of the States in the Unemployment Trust Fund, by transfer from amounts reserved for that purpose in the Federal unemployment account, in accordance with the succeeding provisions of this subsection.

"(B) The amount of funds transferred to the account of a State under subparagraph (A) during the applicable period shall, as determined by the Secretary of Labor, be equal to one half of the amounts of compensation (as defined in section 3306(h) of the Internal Revenue Code of 1986) attributable under the State law to service to which section 3309(a)(1) of such Code applies that were paid by the State for weeks of unemployment beginning and ending during such period. Such transfers shall be made at such times as the Secretary of Labor considers appropriate.

"(C) Notwithstanding any other law, funds transferred to the account of a State under subparagraph (A) shall be used exclusively to reimburse governmental entities and other organizations described in section 3309(a)(2) of such Code for amounts paid (in lieu of contributions) into the State unemployment fund pursuant to such section.

"(D) For purposes of this paragraph, the term 'applicable period' means the period beginning on March 13, 2020, and ending on December 31, 2020.

"(2) (A) Notwithstanding any other provision of law, the Secretary of the

Treasury shall transfer from the general fund of the Treasury (from funds not otherwise appropriated) to the employment security administration account (as established by section 901 of the Social Security Act) such sums as the Secretary of Labor estimates to be necessary for purposes of making the transfers described in paragraph (1).

"(B) There are appropriated from the general fund of the Treasury, without fiscal year limitation, the sums referred to in subparagraph (A) and such sums shall not be required to be repaid.".

(c) Operating Instructions Or Other Guidance.—The Secretary of Labor may issue any operating instructions or other guidance necessary to carry out the amendments made by this section.

TITLE IV—EMERGENCY ASSISTANCE FOR RAIL WORKERS

SEC. 80401. WAIVER OF THE 7-DAY WAITING PERIOD FOR BENEFITS UNDER THE RAILROAD UNEMPLOYMENT INSURANCE ACT.

(a) No Waiting Week.—With respect to any registration period beginning after the date of enactment of this Act and ending on or before December 31, 2020, subparagraphs (A)(ii) and (B)(ii) of section 2(a)(1) of the Railroad Unemployment Insurance Act (45 U.S.C. 352(a)(1)) shall not apply.

(b) Regulations.—The Railroad Retirement Board may prescribe any operating instructions or regulations necessary to carry out this section.

(c) Appropriations.—Out of any funds in the Treasury not otherwise appropriated, there are appropriated $50,000,000 to cover the costs of additional benefits payable due to the application of subsection (a). Upon the exhaustion of the funds appropriated under this subsection, subsection (a) shall no longer apply with respect to any registration period beginning after the date of exhaustion of funds.

(d) Definitions.—For purposes of this section, "registration period" has the meaning given such term under section 1 of the Railroad Unemployment Insurance Act.

SEC. 80402. ENHANCED BENEFITS UNDER THE RAILROAD UNEMPLOYMENT INSURANCE ACT.

Section 2(a) of the Railroad Unemployment Insurance Act (45 U.S.C. § 352(a)) is amended by adding at the end the following:

"(5) (A) Notwithstanding paragraph (3), subsection (c)(1)(B), and any other limitation on total benefits in this Act, for registration periods beginning on or after April 1, 2020, but on or before December 31, 2020, a recovery benefit in the amount of $1,200 shall be payable to a qualified employee with respect to any registration period in which the employee received unemployment benefits under paragraph (1)(A), and in any registration period in which the employee did not receive unemployment benefits due to the limitation in subsection (c)(1)(B) or due to reaching the maximum number of days of benefits in the benefit year beginning July 1, 2019, under subsection (c)(1)(A), and throughout any continuing period of unemployment beginning on or before December 31, 2020, except that no benefit under this section shall be payable after June 30, 2021. No recovery benefits shall be payable under this section upon the exhaustion of the funds appropriated under subparagraph (B) for payment of benefits under this subparagraph.

"(B) Out of any funds in the Treasury not otherwise appropriated, there are appropriated $950,000,000 to cover the cost of recovery benefits provided under subparagraph (A), to remain available until expended.

"(C) A recovery benefit payable under subparagraph (A) shall not be regarded as income and shall not be regarded as a resource for the month of receipt and the following 9 months, for purposes of determining the eligibility of the recipient (or the recipient's spouse or family) for benefits or assistance, or the amount or extent of benefits or assistance, under any Federal program or under any State or local program financed in whole or in part with Federal funds.".

SEC. 80403. EXTENDED UNEMPLOYMENT BENEFITS UNDER THE RAILROAD UNEMPLOYMENT INSURANCE ACT.

(a) Extension.—Section 2(c)(2)(D)(iii) of the Railroad Unemployment Insurance Act (45 U.S.C. 352(c)(2)(D)(iii)) is amended—

(1) by striking "July 1, 2008" and inserting "July 15, 2019";

(2) by striking "June 30, 2013" and inserting "June 30, 2020"; and

(3) by striking "December 31, 2013" and inserting "December 31, 2020".

(b) Clarification On Authority To Use Funds.—Funds appropriated under either the first or second sentence of clause (iv) of section 2(c)(2)(D) of the Railroad Unemployment Insurance Act shall be available to cover the cost of additional extended unemployment benefits provided under such section 2(c)(2)(D) by reason of the amendments made by subsection (a) as well as to cover the cost of such benefits provided under such section 2(c)(2)(D) as in effect on the day before the date of enactment of this Act.

SEC. 80404. TREATMENT OF PAYMENTS FROM THE RAILROAD UNEMPLOYMENT INSURANCE ACCOUNT.

(a) In General.—Section 256(i)(1) of the Balanced Budget and Emergency Deficit Control Act of 1985 (2 U.S.C. 906(i)(1)) is amended—

(1) in subparagraph (B), by striking "and" at the end;

(2) in subparagraph (C), by inserting "and" at the end; and

(3) by inserting after subparagraph (C) the following new subparagraph:

"(D) any payment made from the Railroad Unemployment Insurance Account (established by section 10 of the Railroad Unemployment Insurance Act) for the purpose of carrying out the Railroad Unemployment Insurance Act, and funds appropriated or transferred to or otherwise deposited in such Account,".

(b) Effective Date.—The treatment of payments made from the Railroad Unemployment Insurance Account pursuant to the amendment made by subsection (a) shall take effect 7 days after the date of enactment of this Act and shall apply only to obligations incurred on or after such effective date for such payments.

DIVISION I—FINANCIAL SERVICES

SEC. 1. SHORT TITLE; TABLE OF CONTENTS.

(a) Short Title.—This division may be cited as the "Financial Protections and Assistance for America's Consumers, States, Businesses, and Vulnerable Populations Act".

(b) Table Of Contents.—The table of contents for this division is as follows:

SEC. 2. REFERENCES TO THIS DIVISION.

In this division, any reference to "this Act" shall be deemed a reference to this division.

SEC. 3. SEVERABILITY.

If any provision of this Act or the application of such provision to any person or circumstance is held to be unconstitutional, the remainder of this Act, and the application of the provisions of this Act, to any person or circumstance shall not be affected thereby.

TITLE I—PROTECTING CONSUMERS, RENTERS, HOMEOWNERS

AND PEOPLE EXPERIENCING HOMELESSNESS

SEC. 101. SUSPENSION OF REQUIREMENTS REGARDING TENANT CONTRIBUTION TOWARD RENT.

(a) Suspension.—Notwithstanding any other provision of law, the obligation of each tenant household of a dwelling unit in assisted housing to pay any contribution toward rent for occupancy in such dwelling unit shall be suspended with respect to such occupancy during the period beginning on the date of the enactment of this Act and ending 6 months after the date of the termination by the Federal Emergency Management Agency of the emergency declared on March 13, 2020, by the President under the Robert T. Stafford Disaster Relief and Emergency Assistance Act (42 U.S.C. 4121 et seq.) relating to the Coronavirus Disease 2019 (COVID–19) pandemic.

(b) Federal Reimbursement Payments.—To the extent that amounts are made available pursuant to subsection (e) for reimbursements under this subsection, the Secretary of Housing and Urban Development or the Secretary of Agriculture, as appropriate, shall—

(1) provide owners of assisted housing and public housing agencies for any amounts in rent not received as a result of subsection (a), plus the amount of any increases in costs of administering and maintaining such housing to the extent only that such increases result from the public health emergency relating to Coronavirus Disease 2019 (COVID–19); and

(2) in the case of public housing agencies providing assistance under section 8(o) of the United States Housing Act of 1937 (42 U.S.C. 1437f(o)), reimburse such agencies in an amount sufficient to cover any increase in housing assistance payments resulting from the suspension of tenant rent payments pursuant to subsection (a), plus the amount of any increases in the cost of administering such assistance to the extent only that such increases result from the public health emergency relating to Coronavirus Disease 2019 (COVID–19).

(c) Prohibitions.—

(1) ON FINES.—No tenant or tenant household may be charged a fine or fee for nonpayment of rent in accordance with subsection (a) and such nonpayment of rent shall not be grounds for any termination of tenancy or eviction.

(2) ON DEBT.—No tenant or tenant household may be treated as accruing any debt by reason of suspension of contribution of rent under subsection (a).

(3) ON REPAYMENT.—held liable for repayment of any amount of rent contribution suspended under subsection (a).

(4) ON CREDIT SCORES.—The nonpayment of rent by a tenant or tenant household shall not be reported to a consumer reporting agency nor shall such nonpayment adversely affect a tenant or member of a tenant household's credit score.

(d) Assisted Housing.—For purposes of this section, the term "assisted housing" means housing or a dwelling unit assisted under—
(1) section 213, 220, 221(d)(3), 221(d)(4), 223(e), 231, or 236 of the National Housing Act (12 U.S.C. 1715l(d)(3), (d)(4), or 1715z–1);
(2) section 101 of the Housing and Urban Development Act of 1965 (12 U.S.C. 1701s);
(3) section 202 of the Housing Act of 1959 (12 U.S.C. 1701q);
(4) section 811 of the Cranston-Gonzales National Affordable Housing Act (42 U.S.C. 8013);
(5) title II of the Cranston-Gonzalez National Affordable Housing Act (42 U.S.C. 12701 et seq.);
(6) subtitle D of title VIII of the Cranston-Gonzalez National Affordable Housing Act (42 U.S.C. 12901 et seq.);
(7) title I of the Housing and Community Development Act of 1974 (42 U.S.C. 5301 et seq.);
(8) section 8 of the United States Housing Act of 1937 (42 U.S.C. 1437f);
(9) the public housing program under title I of the United States Housing Act of 1937 (42 U.S.C. 1437 et seq.); or
(10) section 514, 515, 516, 521(a)(2), 538, or 542 of the Housing Act of 1949 (42 U.S.C. 1484, 1485, 1486, 1490a(a)(2), 1490p–2, 1490r).
(e) Authorization Of Appropriations.—There is authorized to be appropriated such sums as may be necessary to make payments under subsection (b) to all owners of assisted housing and public housing agencies.

SEC. 102. TEMPORARY MORATORIUM ON EVICTION FILINGS.
(a) Congressional Findings.—The Congress finds that—
(1) according to the 2018 American Community Survey, 36 percent of households in the United States—more than 43 million households—are renters;
(2) in 2019 alone, renters in the United States paid $512 billion in rent;
(3) according to the Joint Center for Housing Studies of Harvard University, 20.8 million renters in the United States spent more than 30 percent of their incomes on housing in 2018 and 10.9 million renters spent more than 50 percent of their incomes on housing in the same year;
(4) Moody's Analytics estimates that 27 million jobs in the U.S. economy are at high risk because of COVID–19;
(5) the impacts of the spread of COVID–19, which is now considered a global pandemic, are expected to negatively impact the incomes of potentially millions of renter households, making it difficult for them to pay their rent on time; and
(6) evictions in the current environment would increase homelessness and housing instability which would be counterproductive towards the public health goals of keeping individuals in their homes to the greatest extent possible.

(b) Moratorium.—During the period beginning on the date of the enactment of this Act and ending on the date described in paragraph (1) of subsection (d), the lessor of a covered dwelling may not make, or cause to be made, any filing with the court of jurisdiction to initiate a legal action to recover possession of the covered dwelling from the tenant regardless of cause, except when a tenant perpetrates a serious criminal act that threatens the health, life, or safety of other tenants, owners, or staff of the property in which the covered dwelling is located.

(c) Definitions.—For purposes of this section, the following definitions shall apply:

(1) COVERED DWELLING.—The term "covered dwelling" means a dwelling that is occupied by a tenant—

(A) pursuant to a residential lease; or

(B) without a lease or with a lease terminable at will under State law.

(2) DWELLING.—The term "dwelling" has the meaning given such term in section 802 of the Fair Housing Act (42 U.S.C. 3602) and includes houses and dwellings described in section 803(b) of such Act (42 U.S.C. 3603(b)).

(d) Sunset.—

(1) SUNSET DATE.—The date described in this paragraph is the date of the expiration of the 6-month period that begins upon the termination by the Federal Emergency Management Agency of the emergency declared on March 13, 2020, by the President under the Robert T. Stafford Disaster Relief and Emergency Assistance Act (42 U.S.C. 4121 et seq.) relating to the Coronavirus Disease 2019 (COVID–19) pandemic.

(2) NOTICE TO VACATE AFTER SUNSET DATE.—After the date described in paragraph (1), the lessor of a covered dwelling may not require the tenant to vacate the covered dwelling before the expiration of the 30-day period that begins upon the provision by the lessor to the tenant, after the date described in paragraph (1), of a notice to vacate the covered dwelling.

SEC. 103. SUSPENSION OF OTHER CONSUMER LOAN PAYMENTS.

(a) In General.—During the COVID–19 emergency, a debt collector may not, with respect to a debt of a consumer (other than debt related to a federally related mortgage loan)—

(1) capitalize unpaid interest;

(2) apply a higher interest rate triggered by the nonpayment of a debt to the debt balance;

(3) charge a fee triggered by the nonpayment of a debt;

(4) sue or threaten to sue for nonpayment of a debt;

(5) continue litigation to collect a debt that was initiated before the date of enactment of this section;

(6) submit or cause to be submitted a confession of judgment to any court;

(7) enforce a security interest through repossession, limitation of use, or foreclosure;

(8) take or threaten to take any action to enforce collection, or any adverse action for nonpayment of a debt, or for nonappearance at any hearing relating to a debt;

(9) commence or continue any action to cause or to seek to cause the collection of a debt, including pursuant to a court order issued before the end of the 120-day period following the end of the COVID–19 emergency, from wages, Federal benefits, or other amounts due to a consumer by way of garnishment, deduction, offset, or other seizure;

(10) cause or seek to cause the collection of a debt, including pursuant to a court order issued before the end of the 120-day period following the end of the COVID–19 emergency, by levying on funds from a bank account or seizing any other assets of a consumer;

(11) commence or continue an action to evict a consumer from real or personal property; or

(12) disconnect or terminate service from utility service, including electricity, natural gas, telecommunications or broadband, water, or sewer.

(b) Rule Of Construction.—Nothing in this section may be construed to prohibit a consumer from voluntarily paying, in whole or in part, a debt.

(c) Repayment Period.—After the expiration of the COVID–19 emergency, with respect to a debt described under subsection (a), a debt collector—

(1) may not add to the debt balance any interest or fee prohibited by subsection (a);

(2) shall, for credit with a defined term or payment period, extend the time period to repay the debt balance by 1 payment period for each payment that a consumer missed during the COVID–19 emergency, with the payments due in the same amounts and at the same intervals as the pre-existing payment schedule;

(3) shall, for an open end credit plan (as defined under section 103 of the Truth in Lending Act) or other credit without a defined term, allow the consumer to repay the debt balance in a manner that does not exceed the amounts permitted by formulas under section 170(c) of the Truth in Lending Act and regulations promulgated thereunder;

(4) shall, when the consumer notifies the debt collector, offer reasonable and affordable repayment plans, loan modifications, refinancing, options with a reasonable time in which to repay the debt.

(d) Communications In Connection With The Collection Of A Debt.—

(1) IN GENERAL.—During the COVID–19 emergency, without prior consent of a consumer given directly to a debt collector during the COVID–19 emergency, or the express permission of a court of competent jurisdiction, a debt collector may only communicate in writing in connection with the collection of any debt (other than debt related to a federally related mortgage loan).

(2) REQUIRED DISCLOSURES.—

(A) IN GENERAL.—All written communications described under paragraph

(1) shall inform the consumer that the communication is for informational purposes and is not an attempt to collect a debt.

(B) REQUIREMENTS.—The disclosure required under subparagraph (A) shall be made—

(i) in type or lettering not smaller than 14-point bold type;

(ii) separate from any other disclosure;

(iii) in a manner designed to ensure that the recipient sees the disclosure clearly;

(iv) in English and Spanish and in any additional languages in which the debt collector communicates, including the language in which the loan was negotiated, to the extent known by the debt collector; and

(v) may be provided by first-class mail or electronically, if the borrower has otherwise consented to electronic communication with the debt collector and has not revoked such consent.

(C) ORAL NOTIFICATION.—Any oral notification shall be provided in the language the debt collector otherwise uses to communicate with the borrower.

(D) WRITTEN TRANSLATIONS.—In providing written notifications in languages other than English in this Section, a debt collector may rely on written translations developed by the Bureau of Consumer Financial Protection.

(e) Violations.—

(1) IN GENERAL.—Any person who violates this section shall—

(A) except as provided under subparagraph (B), be subject to civil liability in accordance with section 813 of the Fair Debt Collection Practices Act, as if the person is a debt collector for purposes of that section; and

(B) be liable to the consumer for an amount 10 times the amounts described in such section 813, for each violation.

(2) PREDISPUTE ARBITRATION AGREEMENTS.—Notwithstanding any other provision of law, no predispute arbitration agreement or predispute joint-action waiver shall be valid or enforceable with respect to a dispute brought under this section, including a dispute as to the applicability of this section, which shall be determined under Federal law.

(f) Tolling.—Except as provided in subsection (g)(5), any applicable time limitations, including statutes of limitations, related to a debt under Federal or State law shall be tolled during the COVID–19 emergency.

(g) Claims Of Affected Creditors And Debt Collectors.—

(1) VALUATION OF PROPERTY.—With respect to any action asserting a taking under the Fifth Amendment of the Constitution of the United States as a result of this section or seeking a declaratory judgment regarding the constitutionality of this section, the value of the property alleged to have been taken without just compensation shall be evaluated—

(A) with consideration of the likelihood of full and timely payment of the obligation without the actions taken pursuant to this section; and

(B) without consideration of any assistance provided directly or indirectly to the consumer from other Federal, State, and local government programs instituted or legislation enacted in response to the COVID–19 emergency.

(2) SCOPE OF JUST COMPENSATION.—In an action described in paragraph (1), any assistance or benefit provided directly or indirectly to the person from other Federal, State, and local government programs instituted in or legislation enacted response to the COVID–19 emergency, shall be deemed to be compensation for the property taken, even if such assistance or benefit is not specifically provided as compensation for property taken by this section.

(3) APPEALS.—Any appeal from an action under this section shall be treated under section 158 of title 28, United States Code, as if it were an appeal in a case under title 11, United States Code.

(4) REPOSE.—Any action asserting a taking under the Fifth Amendment to the Constitution of the United States as a result of this section shall be brought within not later than 180 days after the end of the COVID–19 emergency.

(h) Credit Facility For Other Purposes.—

(1) ESTABLISHMENT.—The Board of Governors of the Federal Reserve System shall establish a facility that the Board of Governors shall use to make payments to covered financial institutions to compensate such institutions for documented financial losses caused by the suspension of payments required under this section.

(2) COVERED FINANCIAL INSTITUTION DEFINED.—In this subsection, the term "covered financial institution" means the holder of a loan described under this section.

(i) Definitions.—In this section:

(1) CONSUMER.—The term "consumer" means any individual obligated or allegedly obligated to pay any debt.

(2) COVID–19 EMERGENCY.—The term "COVID–19 emergency" means the period that begins upon the date of the enactment of this Act and ends on the date of the termination by the Federal Emergency Management Agency of the emergency declared on March 13, 2020, by the President under the Robert T. Stafford Disaster Relief and Emergency Assistance Act (42 U.S.C. 4121 et seq.) relating to the Coronavirus Disease 2019 (COVID–19) pandemic.

(3) CREDITOR.—The term "creditor" means—

(A) any person who offers or extends credit creating a debt or to whom a debt is owed or other obligation for payment;

(B) any lessor of real or personal property; or

(C) any provider of utility services.

(4) DEBT.—The term "debt"—

(A) means any obligation or alleged obligation that is or during the COVID emergency becomes past due—

(i) for which the original agreement, or if there is no agreement, the original obligation to pay was created before the COVID emergency, whether or not such obligation has been reduced to judgment; and

(ii) that arises out of a transaction with a consumer; and

(B) does not include a federally related mortgage loan.

(5) DEBT COLLECTOR.—The term "debt collector" means a creditor, and any person or entity that engages in the collection of debt, including the Federal Government and a State government, irrespective of whether the debt is allegedly owed to or assigned to that person or to the entity.

(6) FEDERALLY RELATED MORTGAGE LOAN.—The term "federally related mortgage loan" has the meaning given that term under section 3 of the Real Estate Settlement Procedures Act of 1974 (12 U.S.C. 2602).

SEC. 104. EMERGENCY RENTAL ASSISTANCE.

(a) Authorization Of Appropriations.—There is authorized to be appropriated for grants under the Emergency Solutions Grants program under subtitle B of title IV of the McKinney-Vento Homeless Assistance Act (42 U.S.C. 11371 et seq.) $100,000,000,000 for grants under such subtitle only for providing rental assistance in accordance with section 415(a)(4) of such Act (42 U.S.C. 11374(a)(4)) and this section to respond to needs arising from the emergency declared on March 13, 2020, by the President under the Robert T. Stafford Disaster Relief and Emergency Assistance Act (42 U.S.C. 4121 et seq.) relating to the Coronavirus Disease 2019 (COVID–19) pandemic.

(b) Income Targeting.—For purposes of assistance made available with amounts made available pursuant to subsection (a)—

(1) section 401(1)(A) of the McKinney-Vento Homeless Assistance Act (42 U.S.C. 11360(1)(A)) shall be applied by substituting "80 percent" for "30 percent"; and

(2) each grantee of such amounts shall use not less than 50 percent of the amounts received only for providing assistance for persons or families experiencing homelessness or at risk of homelessness, who have incomes not exceeding 50 percent of the median income for the relevant geographic area; except that the Secretary may waive the requirement under this paragraph if the grantee demonstrates to the satisfaction of the Secretary that the population in the geographic area served by the grantee having such incomes is sufficiently being served with respect to activities eligible for funding with such amounts.

(c) Definition Of At Risk Of Homelessness.—For purposes of assistance made available with amounts made available pursuant to subsection (a), section 401(1) of the McKinney-Vento Homeless Assistance Act shall be applied, during the period that begins on the date of the enactment of this Act and ends upon the expiration of the 6-month period that begins upon the termination by the Federal Emergency Management Agency of the emergency declared on March 13, 2020, by the President under the Robert T. Stafford Disaster Relief and Emergency Assistance Act (42 U.S.C. 4121 et seq.) relating to the Coronavirus Disease 2019 (COVID–19) pandemic, as if subparagraph (C) were repealed.

(d) 3-Year Availability.—Each grantee of amounts made available pursuant to

subsection (a) shall expend—
(1) at least 60 percent of such grant amounts within 2 years of the date that such funds became available to the grantee for obligation; and
(2) 100 percent of such grant amounts within 3 years of such date.
The Secretary may recapture any amounts not expended in compliance with paragraph (1) of this subsection and reallocate such amounts to grantees in compliance with the formula referred to in subsection (h)(1)(A) of this section.
(e) Rent Restrictions.—Paragraph (1) of section 576.106(d) of the Secretary's regulations (24 C.F.R. 576.106(d)(1)) shall be applied, with respect to rental assistance made available with amounts made available pursuant to subsection (a), by substituting "120 percent of the Fair Market Rent" for "the Fair Market Rent" .
(f) Subleases.—Notwithstanding the second sentence of subsection (g) of section 576.106 of the Secretary's regulations (24 C.F.R. 576.106(g)), a program participant may sublet, with rental assistance made available with amounts made available pursuant to subsection (a) of this section, a dwelling unit from a renter of the dwelling unit if there is a legally binding, written lease agreement for such sublease.
(g) Housing Relocation Or Stabilization Activities.—A grantee of amounts made available pursuant to subsection (a) may expend up to 20 percent of its allocation for activities under section 415(a)(5) of the McKinney-Vento Homeless Assistance Act (42 U.S.C. 11374(a)(5)).
(h) Allocation Of Assistance.—
(1) IN GENERAL.—In allocating amounts made available pursuant to subsection (a), the Secretary of Housing and Urban Development shall—
(A) not later than 30 days after the date of the enactment of this Act, allocate any such amounts that do not exceed $50,000,000,000 under the formula specified in subsections (a), (b), and (e) of section 414 of the McKinney-Vento Homeless Assistance Act (42 U.S.C. 11373) to, and notify, each State, metropolitan city, and urban county that is to receive a direct grant of such amounts; and
(B) not later than 120 days after the date of the enactment of this Act, allocate any remaining amounts to eligible grantees by a formula to be developed by the Secretary of Housing and Urban Development that takes into consideration the formula referred to in subparagraph (A) of this paragraph, and the need for emergency rental assistance under this section, including severe housing cost burden among extremely low- and very low-income renters and disruptions in housing and economic conditions, including unemployment.
(2) ALLOCATIONS TO STATES.—A State recipient of an allocation under this section may elect to directly administer up to 50 percent of its allocation to carry out activities eligible under this section.
(3) ELECTION NOT TO ADMINISTER.—If a grantee elects not to receive funds under this section, such funds shall be allocated to the State recipient

in which the grantee is located.
(i) Inapplicability Of Matching Requirement.—Subsection (a) of section 416 of the McKinney-Vento Homeless Assistance Act (42 U.S.C. 11375(a)) shall not apply to any amounts made available pursuant to subsection (a) of this section.
(j) Prohibition On Prerequisites.—None of the funds authorized under this section may be used to require people experiencing homelessness to receive treatment or perform any other prerequisite activities as a condition for receiving shelter, housing, or other services.
(k) Public Hearings.—
(1) INAPPLICABILITY OF IN-PERSON HEARING REQUIREMENTS.—A grantee may not be required to hold in-person public hearings in connection with its citizen participation plan, but shall provide citizens with notice and a reasonable opportunity to comment of not less than 15 days. Following the period that begins upon the date of the enactment of this Act and ends upon the date of the termination by the Federal Emergency Management Agency of the emergency declared on March 13, 2020, by the President under the Robert T. Stafford Disaster Relief and Emergency Assistance Act (42 U.S.C. 4121 et seq.) relating to the Coronavirus Disease 2019 (COVID–19) pandemic, and after the period described in paragraph (2), the Secretary shall direct grantees to resume pre-crisis public hearing requirements.
(2) VIRTUAL PUBLIC HEARINGS.—During the period that national or local health authorities recommend social distancing and limiting public gatherings for public health reasons, a grantee may fulfill applicable public hearing requirements for all grants from funds made available pursuant to this section by carrying out virtual public hearings. Any such virtual hearings shall provide reasonable notification and access for citizens in accordance with the grantee's certifications, timely responses from local officials to all citizen questions and issues, and public access to all questions and responses.
(l) Administration.—Of any amounts made available pursuant to subsection (a), not more than the lesser of 0.5 percent, or $15,000,000, may be used for staffing, training, technical assistance, technology, monitoring, research, and evaluation activities necessary to carry out the program carried out under this section, and such amounts shall remain available until September 30, 2024.

SEC. 105. EMERGENCY HOMELESS ASSISTANCE.
(a) Authorization Of Appropriations.—There is authorized to be appropriated under the Emergency Solutions Grants program under subtitle B of title IV of the McKinney-Vento Homeless Assistance Act (42 U.S.C. 11371 et seq.) $15,500,000,000 for grants under such subtitle in accordance with this section to respond to needs arising from the public health emergency relating to Coronavirus Disease 2019 (COVID–19).
(b) Formula.—Notwithstanding sections 413 and 414 of the McKinney-Vento Homeless Assistance Act (42 U.S.C. 11372, 11373), the Secretary of Housing

and Urban Development (in this Act referred to as the "Secretary") shall allocate amounts made available pursuant to subsection (a) in accordance with a formula to be established by the Secretary that takes into consideration the following factors:

(1) Risk of transmission of coronavirus in a jurisdiction.

(2) Whether a jurisdiction has a high number or rate of sheltered and unsheltered homeless individuals and families.

(3) Economic and housing market conditions in a jurisdiction.

(c) Eligible Activities.—In addition to eligible activities under section 415(a) of the McKinney-Vento Homeless Assistance Act (42 U.S.C. 11374(a), amounts made available pursuant to subsection (a) may also be used for costs of the following activities:

(1) Providing training on infectious disease prevention and mitigation.

(2) Providing hazard pay, including for time worked before the effectiveness of this clause, for staff working directly to prevent and mitigate the spread of coronavirus or COVID–19 among people experiencing or at risk of homelessness.

(3) Reimbursement of costs for eligible activities (including activities described in this paragraph) relating to preventing, preparing for, or responding to the coronavirus or COVID–19 that were accrued before the date of the enactment of this Act.

Use of such amounts for activities described in this paragraph shall not be considered use for administrative purposes for purposes of section 418 of the McKinney-Vento Homeless Assistance Act (42 U.S.C. 11377).

(d) Inapplicability Of Procurement Standards.—To the extent amounts made available pursuant to subsection (a) are used to procure goods and services relating to activities to prevent, prepare for, or respond to the coronavirus or COVID–19, the standards and requirements regarding procurement that are otherwise applicable shall not apply.

(e) Inapplicability Of Habitability And Environmental Review Standards.—Any Federal standards and requirements regarding habitability and environmental review shall not apply with respect to any emergency shelter that is assisted with amounts made available pursuant to subsection (a) and has been determined by a State or local health official, in accordance with such requirements as the Secretary shall establish, to be necessary to prevent and mitigate the spread of coronavirus or COVID–19, such shelters.

(f) Inapplicability Of Cap On Emergency Shelter Activities.—Subsection (b) of section 415 of the McKinney-Vento Homeless Assistance Act shall not apply to any amounts made available pursuant to subsection (a)(1) of this section.

(g) Initial Allocation Of Assistance.—Section 417(b) of the McKinney-Vento Homeless Assistance Act (42 U.S.C. 11376(b)) shall be applied with respect to amounts made available pursuant to subsection (a) by substituting "30-day" for "60-day".

(h) Waivers And Alternative Requirements.—

(1) AUTHORITY.—In administering amounts made available pursuant to subsection (a), the Secretary may waive, or specify alternative requirements for, any provision of any statute or regulation (except for any requirements related to fair housing, nondiscrimination, labor standards, and the environment) that the Secretary administers in connection with the obligation or use by the recipient of such amounts, if the Secretary finds that good cause exists for the waiver or alternative requirement and such waiver or alternative requirement is consistent with the purposes described in this subsection.

(2) EFFECTIVENESS; APPLICABILITY.—Any such waivers shall be deemed to be effective as of the date a State or unit of local government began preparing for coronavirus and shall apply to the use of amounts made available pursuant to subsection (a) and amounts provided in prior appropriation Acts for fiscal year 2020 under the heading "Department of Housing and Urban Development—Community Planning and Development—Community Development Fund" and used by recipients for the purposes described in this subsection.

(3) NOTIFICATION.—The Secretary shall notify the public through the Federal Register or other appropriate means 5 days before the effective date of any such waiver or alternative requirement, and any such public notice may be provided on the Internet at the appropriate Government web site or through other electronic media, as determined by the Secretary.

(4) EXEMPTION.—The use of amounts made available pursuant to subsection (a) shall not be subject to the consultation, citizen participation, or match requirements that otherwise apply to the Emergency Solutions Grants program, except that a recipient shall publish how it has and will utilize its allocation at a minimum on the Internet at the appropriate Government web site or through other electronic media.

(i) Inapplicability Of Matching Requirement.—Subsection (a) of section 416 of the McKinney-Vento Homeless Assistance Act (42 U.S.C. 11375(a)) shall not apply to any amounts made available pursuant to subsection (a) of this section.

(j) Prohibition On Prerequisites.—None of the funds authorized under this section may be used to require people experiencing homelessness to receive treatment or perform any other prerequisite activities as a condition for receiving shelter, housing, or other services.

SEC. 106. PARTICIPATION OF INDIAN TRIBES AND TRIBALLY DESIGNATED HOUSING ENTITIES IN CONTINUUM OF CARE PROGRAM.

(a) In General.—Title IV of the McKinney-Vento Homeless Assistance Act (42 U.S.C. 11360 et seq.) is amended—

(1) in section 401 (42 U.S.C. 11360)—

(A) by redesignating paragraphs (10) through (33) as paragraphs (12) through

(35), respectively;

(B) by redesignating paragraphs (8) and (9) as paragraphs (9) and (10), respectively;

(C) by inserting after paragraph (7) the following:

"(8) FORMULA AREA.—The term 'formula area' has the meaning given the term in section 1000.302 of title 24, Code of Federal Regulations, or any successor regulation.";

(D) in paragraph (9), as so redesignated, by inserting "a formula area," after "nonentitlement area,"; and

(E) by inserting after paragraph (10), as so redesignated, the following:

"(11) INDIAN TRIBE.—The term 'Indian Tribe' has the meaning given the term 'Indian tribe' in section 4 of the Native American Housing Assistance and Self-Determination Act of 1996 (25 U.S.C. 4103)."; and

(2) in subtitle C (42 U.S.C. 11381 et seq.), by adding at the end the following:

"SEC. 435. PARTICIPATION OF INDIAN TRIBES AND TRIBALLY DESIGNATED HOUSING ENTITIES.

"Notwithstanding any other provision of this title, for purposes of this subtitle, an Indian Tribe or tribally designated housing entity (as defined in section 4 of the Native American Housing Assistance and Self-Determination Act of 1996 (25 U.S.C. 4103)) may—

"(1) be a collaborative applicant or eligible entity; or

"(2) receive grant amounts from another entity that receives a grant directly from the Secretary, and use the amounts in accordance with this subtitle.".

(b) Technical And Conforming Amendment.—The table of contents in section 101(b) of the McKinney-Vento Homeless Assistance Act (Public Law 100–77; 101 Stat. 482) is amended by inserting after the item relating to section 434 the following:

"Sec. 435. Participation of Indian Tribes and tribally designated housing entities.".

SEC. 107. HOUSING ASSISTANCE FUND.

(a) Definitions.—In this section:

(1) SECRETARY.—The term "Secretary" means the Secretary of the Treasury.

(2) STATE.—The term "State" means any State of the United States, the District of Columbia, any territory of the United States, Puerto Rico, Guam, American Samoa, the Virgin Islands, and the Northern Mariana Islands.

(b) Establishment Of Fund.—There is established at the Department of the Treasury a Housing Assistance Fund to provide such funds as are allocated in subsection (f) to State housing finance agencies for the purpose of preventing homeowner mortgage defaults, foreclosures, and displacements of individuals and families experiencing financial hardship after January 21, 2020.

(c) Allocation Of Funds.—

(1) IN GENERAL.—The Secretary of the Treasury shall establish such criteria

as are necessary to allocate the funds available within the Housing Assistance Fund to each State. The Secretary shall allocate such funds among all States taking into consideration the number of unemployment claims within a State relative to the nationwide number of unemployment claims.

(2) SMALL STATE MINIMUM.—Each State shall receive no less than $125,000,000 for the purposes established in subsection (b).

(d) Disbursement Of Funds.—

(1) INITIAL DISBURSEMENT.—The Secretary shall disburse to the State housing finance agencies not less than ½ of the amount made available pursuant to this section, and in accordance with the allocations established under subsection (c), not later than 120 days after the date of enactment of this Act. The Secretary or designee shall enter into a contract with each State housing finance agency, which may be amended from time to time, establishing the terms of the use of such funds prior to the disbursement of such funds.

(2) SECOND DISBURSEMENT.—The Secretary shall disburse all funds made available pursuant to this section, and in accordance with the allocations established under subsection (c), not later than 180 days after the date of enactment of this Act.

(e) Permissible Uses Of Fund.—

(1) IN GENERAL.—Funds made available to State housing finance agencies pursuant to this section may be used for the purposes established under subsection (b), which may include—

(A) mortgage payment assistance;

(B) financial assistance to allow a borrower to reinstate their mortgage following a period of forbearance;

(C) principal reduction;

(D) utility payment assistance, including electric, gas, and water payment assistance;

(E) any program established under the Housing Finance Agency Innovation Fund for the Hardest Hit Housing Markets;

(F) reimbursement of funds expended by a State or local government during the period beginning on January 21, 2020, and ending on the date that the first funds are disbursed by the State under the Housing Assistance Fund, for the purpose of providing housing or utility assistance to individuals or otherwise providing funds to prevent foreclosure or eviction of a homeowner or prevent mortgage delinquency or loss of housing or critical utilities as a response to the coronavirus disease 2019 (COVID–19) pandemic; and

(G) any other assistance to prevent eviction, mortgage delinquency or default, foreclosure, or the loss of essential utility services.

(2) ADMINISTRATIVE EXPENSES.—Not greater than 10 percent of the amount allocated to a State pursuant to subsection (c) may be used by a State housing financing agency for administrative expenses. Any amounts allocated to administrative expenses that are no longer necessary for administrative

expenses may be used in accordance with paragraph (1).

(f) Appropriation.—There is authorized to be appropriated for the fiscal year ending September 30, 2020, to remain available until expended or transferred or credited under subsection (h), $35,000,000,000 to the Housing Assistance Fund established under subsection (b).

(g) Use Of Housing Finance Agency Innovation Fund For The Hardest Hit Housing Markets Funds.—A State housing finance agency may reallocate any administrative or programmatic funds it has received as an allocation from the Housing Finance Agency Innovation Fund for the Hardest Hit Housing Markets created pursuant to section 101(a) of the Emergency Economic Stabilization Act of 2008 (12 U.S.C. 5211(a)) that have not been otherwise allocated or disbursed as of the date of enactment of this Act to supplement any administrative or programmatic funds received from the Housing Assistance Fund. Such reallocated funds shall not be considered when allocating resources from the Housing Assistance Fund using the process established under subsection (c) and shall remain available for the uses permitted and under the terms and conditions established by the contract with Secretary created pursuant to subsection (d)(1) and the terms of subsection (h).

(h) Rescission Of Funds.—Any funds that have not been allocated by a State housing finance agency to provide assistance as described under subsection (e) by December 31, 2030, shall be reallocated by the Secretary in the following manner:

(1) 65 percent shall be transferred or credited to the Housing Trust Fund established under section 1338 of the Federal Housing Enterprises Financial Safety and Soundness Act of 1992 (12 U.S.C. 4568); and

(2) 35 percent shall be transferred or credited to the Capital Magnet Fund under section 1339 of the Federal Housing Enterprises Financial Safety and Soundness Act of 1992 (12 U.S.C. 4569).

(i) Reporting Requirements.—The Secretary shall provide public reports not less frequently than quarterly regarding the use of funds provided by the Housing Assistance Funds. Such reports shall include the following data by State and by program within each State, both for the past quarter and throughout the life of the program—

(1) the amount of funds allocated;

(2) the amount of funds disbursed;

(3) the number of households and individuals assisted;

(4) the acceptance rate of applicants;

(5) the average amount of assistance provided per household receiving assistance;

(6) the average length of assistance provided per household receiving assistance;

(7) the income ranges of households for each household receiving assistance; and

(8) the outcome 12 months after the household has received assistance.

SEC. 108. MORTGAGE FORBEARANCE.

(a) Findings.—

(1) FINDINGS.—Congress finds that—

(A) the collection of debts involves the use of the mails and wires and other instrumentalities of interstate commerce;

(B) at times of major disaster or emergency, the income of consumers is often impaired and their necessary daily expenses often increase;

(C) temporary forbearance benefits not only consumer and small business debtors, but also other creditors by avoiding downward collateral price spirals triggered by an increase in foreclosure activity;

(D) without forbearance, many consumers and small businesses are unlikely to be able to pay their obligations according to their original terms and are likely to default on obligations or file for bankruptcy, resulting in reduced recoveries for creditors, and in the case of bankruptcy, no recovery of unaccrued interest;

(E) with forbearance, creditors are likely to realize greater long-term value because consumers and small businesses will be more likely to be able to repay their obligations after the major disaster or emergency has subsided;

(F) the legislative and administrative response to major disasters and emergencies may consist of multiple components divided among different statutes and programs; and

(G) when evaluating whether property has been taken from a person without just compensation, a holistic evaluation of the burdens and benefits of all legislative and administrative responses, including indirect benefits from macroeconomic stabilization, is appropriate.

(2) FURTHER FINDINGS REGARDING MORTGAGE FORBEARANCE.—Congress further finds that—

(A) ensuring that consumers are able to remain in their residences reduces the disruptions and economic harm caused by such disasters and emergencies by ensuring that consumers are able to continue their existing employment, education, childcare, and healthcare arrangements, which are often geographically-based;

(B) temporary forbearance on residential mortgages is therefore critical to fostering economic recovery and stability in the wake of major disasters or emergencies;

(C) temporary mortgage forbearance during a declared disaster benefits not only mortgagors, but also mortgagees because mortgagors' ability to pay is likely to be restored after a disaster or emergency subsides, so forbearance may increase mortgagors' total recovery. Without forbearance, mortgagors are likely to default or file for bankruptcy, resulting in significant losses for mortgagees; and

(D) temporary mortgage forbearance during a declared disaster also benefits the mortgagees of other properties because housing prices are geographically and serially correlated so an increase in foreclosures can drive down the value of collateral for all mortgage lenders, further destabilizing the economy.

(3) FURTHER FINDINGS REGARDING MORTGAGE SERVICERS.—Congress further finds that—

(A) mortgage servicers are often contractually obligated to advance scheduled mortgage payments to securitization investors, irrespective of whether the servicer collects the payment from the mortgagor;

(B) mortgage servicers are often thinly capitalized and with limited capacity for engaging in large scale advancing of payments to securitization investors;

(C) securitization investors have long been aware of servicers' thin capitalization;

(D) in the wake of the 2008 financial crisis, several servicers had difficulty obtaining sufficiently liquidity to make advances;

(E) mortgage servicing is a heavily regulated industry;

(F) in response to the 2008 financial crisis, Congress created a safe harbor for mortgage servicers that undertook loan modifications;

(G) in response to the 2008 financial crisis, the Home Affordable Modification Program paid mortgage servicers to undertake loan modifications;

(H) as part of the 2012 joint State-Federal National Mortgage Settlement, mortgage servicers committed to undertaking loan modifications; and

(I) investors in mortgage securitizations are or should be aware of servicers' thin capitalization, liquidity constraints, the extent and history of servicing regulation and therefore do not have a reasonable expectation that the terms of servicing contracts will be enforceable at times of national financial crisis.

(4) DETERMINATION.—It is the sense of the Congress that, on the basis of the findings described under paragraphs (1), (2), and (3), the Congress determines that the provisions of this Act are necessary and proper for the purpose of carrying into execution the powers of the Congress to regulate commerce among the several States and to establish uniform bankruptcy laws.

(b) Prohibition On Foreclosures And Repossessions During The COVID–19 Emergency.—

(1) PROHIBITION ON FORECLOSURES.—The Real Estate Settlement Procedures Act of 1974 (12 U.S.C. 2601 et seq.) is amended—

(A) in section 3 (12 U.S.C. 2602)—

(i) in paragraph (8), by striking "and" at the end;

(ii) in paragraph (9), by striking the period at the end and inserting "; and"; and

(iii) by adding at the end the following:

"(10) the term 'COVID–19 emergency' means the period that begins upon the date of the enactment of this Act and ends on the date of the termination by the Federal Emergency Management Agency of the emergency declared on March 13, 2020, by the President under the Robert T. Stafford Disaster Relief and Emergency Assistance Act (42 U.S.C. 4121 et seq.) relating to the Coronavirus Disease 2019 (COVID–19) pandemic."; and

(B) in section 6(k)(1) (12 U.S.C. 2605(k)(1))—

(i) in subparagraph (D), by striking "or" at the end;

(ii) by redesignating subparagraph (E) as subparagraph (G); and

(iii) by inserting after subparagraph (D) the following:

"(E) commence or continue any judicial foreclosure action or non-judicial foreclosure process or any action to evict a consumer following a foreclosure during the COVID–19 emergency or the 180-day period following such emergency (except that such prohibition shall not apply to a mortgage secured by a dwelling that the servicer has determined after exercising reasonable diligence is vacant or abandoned);

"(F) fail to toll the time in a foreclosure process on a property during the COVID–19 emergency or the 180-day period following such emergency (except that such prohibition shall not apply to a mortgage secured by a dwelling that the servicer has determined after exercising reasonable diligence is vacant or abandoned); or".

(2) REPOSSESSION PROHIBITION.—During the COVID–19 emergency and for the 180-day period following such emergency, a servicer of a consumer loan secured by a manufactured home or a motor vehicle may not repossess such home or vehicle.

(c) Forbearance Of Residential Mortgage Loan Payments For Single Family Properties (1–4 Units).—Section 6 of the Real Estate Settlement Procedures Act of 1974 (12 U.S.C. 2605) is amended by adding at the end the following:

"(n) Forbearance During The COVID–19 Emergency.—

"(1) CONSUMER RIGHT TO REQUEST A FORBEARANCE.—

"(A) REQUEST FOR FORBEARANCE.—A borrower experiencing a financial hardship during the COVID–19 emergency may request forbearance from any mortgage obligation, regardless of delinquency status, by submitting a request to the borrower's servicer, either orally or in writing, affirming that the borrower is experiencing hardship during the COVID–19 emergency. A borrow shall not be required to provide any additional documentation to receive such forbearance.

"(B) LENGTH OF FORBEARANCE; EXTENSION.—A forbearance requested pursuant to subparagraph (A) shall be provided for a period of 180 days, and may be extended upon request of the borrower for an additional 180 days.

"(C) TREATMENT OF TENANTS.—A borrower receiving a forbearance under this subsection with respect to a mortgage secured by a dwelling that has tenants, whether or not the borrower also lives in the dwelling, shall provide the tenants with rent relief for a period not less than the period covered by the forbearance.

"(2) AUTOMATIC FORBEARANCE FOR DELINQUENT BORROWERS.—

"(A) IN GENERAL.—Notwithstanding any other law governing forbearance relief, during the COVID–19 emergency, any borrower who is or becomes 60 days or more delinquent on a mortgage obligation shall automatically be granted a 180-day forbearance, which may be extended upon request of the borrower for an additional 180 days. Such a borrower may elect to continue making regular payments by notifying the servicer of the mortgage obligation of such election.

"(B) NOTICE TO BORROWER.—The servicer of a mortgage obligation placed in forbearance pursuant to subparagraph (A) shall provide the borrower written notification of the forbearance and its duration as well as information about available loss mitigation options and the right to end the forbearance and resume making regular payments.

"(C) TREATMENT OF PAYMENTS DURING FORBEARANCE.—Any payments made by the borrower during the forbearance period shall be credited to the borrower's account in accordance with section 129F of the Truth in Lending Act (15 U.S.C. 1639f) or as the borrower may otherwise instruct that is consistent with the terms of the mortgage loan contract.

"(3) REQUIREMENTS FOR SERVICERS.—

"(A) NOTIFICATION.—

"(i) IN GENERAL.—Each servicer of a federally related mortgage loan shall notify the borrower of their right to request forbearance under paragraph (1)—

"(I) not later than 14 days after the date of enactment of this subsection; and

"(II) until the end of COVID–19 emergency—

"(aa) on each periodic statement provided to the borrower; and

"(bb) in any oral or written communication by the servicer with or to the borrower.

"(ii) MANNER OF NOTIFICATION.—

"(I) WRITTEN NOTIFICATION.—Any written notification required under this section—

"(aa) shall be provided—

"(AA) in English and Spanish and in any additional languages in which the servicer communicates, including the language in which the loan was negotiated, to the extent known by the servicer; and

"(BB) at least as clearly and conspicuously as the most clear and conspicuous disclosure on the document;

"(bb) shall include the notification of the availability of language assistance and housing counseling produced by the Federal Housing Finance Agency under subsection (o); and

"(cc) may be provided by first-class mail or electronically, if the borrower has otherwise consented to electronic communication with the servicer and has not revoked such consent.

"(II) ORAL NOTIFICATION.—Any oral notification required under clause (i) shall be provided in the language the servicer otherwise uses to communicate with the borrower.

"(III) WRITTEN TRANSLATIONS.—In providing written notifications in languages other than English under subclause (I), a servicer may rely on written translations developed by the Federal Housing Finance Agency or the Bureau.

"(B) OTHER REQUIREMENTS.—

"(i) FORBEARANCE REQUIRED.—Upon receiving a request for forbearance from a consumer under paragraph (1) or placing a borrower in automatic forbearance under paragraph (2), a servicer shall provide the forbearance for not less than 180 days, and an additional 180 days at the request of the borrower, provided that the borrower will have the option to discontinue the forbearance at any time.

"(ii) PROHIBITION ON FEES, PENALTIES, AND INTEREST.—During the period of a forbearance under this subsection, no fees, penalties or additional interest beyond the amounts scheduled or calculated as if the borrower made all contractual payments on time and in full under the terms of the mortgage contract in effect at the time the borrower enters into the forbearance shall accrue.

"(iii) TREATMENT OF ESCROW PAYMENTS.—If a borrower in forbearance under this subsection is required to make payments to an escrow account, the servicer shall pay or advance the escrow disbursements in a timely manner (defined as on or before the deadline to avoid a penalty), regardless of the status of the borrower's payments. The servicer may collect any resulting escrow shortage or deficiency from the borrower after the forbearance period ends, in a lump sum payment, spread over 60 months, or capitalized into the loan, at the borrower's election.".

(d) Notification Of Language Assistance And Housing Counseling.—Section 6 of the Real Estate Settlement Procedures Act of 1974 (12 U.S.C. 2605), as amended by subsection (c), is further amended by adding at the end the following:

"(o) Notification Of Language Assistance And Housing Counseling.—

"(1) IN GENERAL.—The Federal Housing Finance Agency shall, within 30 days of the date of enactment of this Act, make available a document providing notice of the availability of language assistance and housing counseling in substantially the same form, and in at least the same languages, as the existing Language Translation Disclosure.

"(2) MINIMUM REQUIREMENT.—The document described under subsection (a) shall include the notice in at least all the languages for which Federal Housing Finance Agency currently has translations on its existing Language Translation Disclosure available.

"(3) PROVISION TO SERVICERS.—The Federal Housing Finance Agency shall make this document available to servicers to fulfill their requirements under subsection (n).".

(e) United States Department Of Agriculture Direct Loan Program.—Section 505 of the Housing Act of 1949 (42 U.S.C. 1475) is amended—

(1) by redesignating subsection (b) as subsection (c); and

(2) by inserting after subsection (a) the following:

"(b) Loan Modification.—

"(1) IN GENERAL.—The Secretary shall implement a loan modification program to modify the terms of outstanding loans for borrowers who face financial hardship.

"(2) AFFORDABLE PAYMENTS.—The Secretary's loan modification program under paragraph (1) shall be designed so as to provide affordable payments for borrowers. In defining 'affordable payments' the Secretary shall consult definitions of affordability promulgated by the Federal Housing Finance Authority, the Department of Housing and Urban Development, and the Bureau of Consumer Financial Protection.

"(3) ADDITIONAL PROGRAM REQUIREMENTS.—The Secretary's loan modification program under paragraph (1) shall allow for measures including extension of the remaining loan term to up to 480 months and a reduction in interest rate to the market interest rate as defined by regulations of the Secretary. The modification program shall be available for borrowers in a moratorium and for borrowers not already in a moratorium who qualify under the terms established by the Secretary. The Secretary may also establish reasonable additional measures for providing affordable loan modifications to borrowers";

(3) in subsection (c), as so redesignated, by adding at the end the following: "Acceleration of the promissory note and initiation of foreclosure proceedings shall not terminate a borrower's eligibility for a moratorium, loan reamortization, special servicing, or other foreclosure alternative."; and

(4) by adding at the end the following:

"(d) Requirement.—The Secretary shall comply with subsection (k)(1), (n), and (o) of section 6 of the Real Estate Settlement Procedures Act of 1974 with respect to any single-family loans it holds or services.".

(f) Forbearance Of Residential Mortgage Loan Payments For Multifamily Properties (5+ Units).—

(1) IN GENERAL.—During the COVID–19 emergency, a multifamily borrower experiencing a financial hardship due, directly or indirectly, to the COVID–19 emergency may request a forbearance under the terms set forth in this section.

(2) REQUEST FOR RELIEF.—A multifamily borrower may submit a request for forbearance under paragraph (1) to the borrower's servicer, either orally or in writing, affirming that the multifamily borrower is experiencing hardship during the COVID–19 emergency.

(3) FORBEARANCE PERIOD.—

(A) IN GENERAL.—Upon receipt of an oral or written request for forbearance from a multifamily borrower, a servicer shall—

(i) document the financial hardship;

(ii) provide the forbearance for not less than 180 days; and

(iii) provide the forbearance for an additional 180 days upon the request of the borrower at least 30 days prior to the end of the forbearance period described under subparagraph (A).

(B) RIGHT TO DISCONTINUE.—A multifamily borrower shall have the option to discontinue the forbearance at any time.

(4) RENTER PROTECTIONS.—During the term of a forbearance under this section, a multifamily borrower may not—

(A) evict a tenant for nonpayment of rent; or

(B) apply or accrue any fees or other penalties on renters for nonpayment of rent.

(5) OBLIGATION TO BRING THE LOAN CURRENT.—A multifamily borrower shall bring a loan placed in forbearance under this section current within the earlier of—

(A) 12 months after the conclusion of the forbearance period; or

(B) receipt of any business interruption insurance proceeds by the multifamily borrower.

(6) DEFINITION.—For the purposes of this subsection, the term "multifamily borrower" means a borrower of a residential mortgage loan that is secured by a lien against a property comprising five or more dwelling units.

(g) Federal Reserve Credit Facility For Mortgage Servicers.—

(1) IN GENERAL.—The Board of Governors of the Federal Reserve System and the Secretary of the Treasury, pursuant to the authority granted under section 13(3) of the Federal Reserve Act, directly (or indirectly through an intermediary, such as the Federal National Mortgage Association, the Federal Home Loan Mortgage Corporation, the Government National Mortgage Association, an insured depository institution, non-depository lending institution, or a special purpose vehicle)—

(A) shall extend credit to mortgage servicers and other obligated advancing parties that in each case have liquidity needs due to the COVID–19 emergency or compliance with this Act with respect to mortgage loans (the "affected mortgages"); and

(B) may extend further credit to mortgage servicers for other liquidity needs due to the actual or imminent delinquency or default on mortgage loans due to the COVID–19 emergency.

(2) NON-COMPLIANT SERVICERS.—A mortgage servicer shall not be eligible for assistance under paragraph (1) if the provider is in violation of any requirement under this Act, and fails to promptly cure any such violation upon notice or discovery thereof.

(3) PAYMENTS AND PURCHASES.—Credit extended under paragraph (1)

(A) shall be in an amount sufficient to—

(A) cover—

(i) the pass-through payment of principal and interest to mortgage-backed securities holders;

(ii) the payment of taxes and insurance to third parties; and

(iii) the temporary reimbursement of modification costs and fees due to servicers that will be deferred until such time as a forbearance period terminates, due in each case on, or in respect of, such affected mortgage loans or related mortgage-backed securities;

(B) purchase affected mortgages from pools of securitized mortgages

(4) COLLATERAL.—The credit authorized by this section shall be secured by the pledgor's interest in accounts receivable, loans, or related interests resulting from the payment advances made on the affected mortgages by the mortgage servicers.

(5) CREDIT SUPPORT.—The Secretary of the Treasury shall provide credit support to the Board of Governors of the Federal Reserve System for the program required by this section.

(6) CONFLICT WITH OTHER LAWS.—Notwithstanding any Federal or State law to the contrary, the Federal National Mortgage Association, the Federal Home Loan Mortgage Corporation, and the Government National Mortgage Association may permit the pledge or grant of a security interest in the pledgor's interest in such accounts receivable or loans or related interests and honor or permit the enforcement of such pledge or grant in accordance with its terms.

(7) DURATION.—The extension of credit by the Board of Governors of the Federal Reserve System and credit support from the Secretary of the Treasury under this section shall be available until the later of—

(A) 6 months after the end of the COVID–19 emergency; and

(B) the date on which on the Board of Governors of the Federal Reserve System and the Secretary of the Treasury determine such credit and credit support should no longer be available to address the liquidity concern addressed by this section.

(8) AMENDMENTS TO NATIONAL HOUSING ACT.—Section 306(g)(1) of the National Housing Act (12 U.S.C. 1721(g)(1)) is amended—

(A) by inserting the following new sentence after the fourth sentence in the paragraph: "In any case in which (I) the President declares a major disaster or emergency for the nation or any area that in either case has been affected by damage or other adverse effects of sufficient severity and magnitude to warrant major disaster assistance under the Robert T. Stafford Disaster Relief and Emergency Assistance Act or other Federal law, (II) upon request of an Issuer of any security, the Association elects to extend to the Issuer one or more of the disaster assistance or emergency programs that the Association determines to be available to account for the Issuer's failure or anticipated failure to receive from the mortgagor the full amount of principal and interest due, then (III) the Association may elect not to declare the Issuer to be in default because of such request for such disaster or emergency assistance.";

(B) by inserting after the word "issued" in the sixth sentence, as redesignated, the following: "subject to any pledge or grant of security interest of the pledgor's interest in and to any such mortgage or mortgages or any interest therein and the proceeds thereon, which the Association may elect to approve;"; and

(C) by inserting after the word "issued" in the seventh sentence, as redesignated, the following: ", or (D) its approval and honoring of any pledge or grant of security interest of the pledgor's interest in and to any such mortgage or mortgages or any interest therein and proceeds thereon.".

(h) Safe Harbor.—

(1) IN GENERAL.—Notwithstanding any other provision of law, whenever a servicer of residential mortgages of residential mortgage-backed securities—

(A) grants a borrower relief under section 6(n) and 6(p) of the Real Estate Settlement Procedures Act of 1974 with respect to a residential mortgage originated before April 1, 2020, including a mortgage held in a securitization or other investment vehicle, and

(B) the servicer or trustee or issuer owes a duty to investors or other parties regarding the standard for servicing such mortgage,

the servicer shall be deemed to have satisfied the such a duty, and the servicer shall not be liable to any party who is owed such a duty and shall not be subject to any injunction, stay, or other equitable relief to such party, based upon its good faith compliance with the provisions of 6(n) and 6(p) of the Real Estate Settlement Procedures Act of 1974. Any person, including a trustee or issuer, who cooperates with a servicer when such cooperation is necessary for the servicer to implement the provisions of 6(n) and 6(p) of the Real Estate Settlement Procedures Act of 1974 shall be protected from liability in the same manner.

(2) STANDARD INDUSTRY PRACTICE.—Compliance with 6(n) and 6(p) of the Real Estate Settlement Procedures Act of 1974 during the COVID–19 emergency shall constitute standard industry practice for purposes of all Federal and State laws.

(3) DEFINITIONS.—As used in this subsection—

(A) the term "servicer" has the meaning given that term under section 6(i)(2) of the Real Estate Settlement Procedures Act of 1974 (12 U.S.C. 2605(i)(2)); and

(B) the term "securitization vehicle" has the meaning given that term under section 129A(f)(3) of the Truth in Lending Act (15 U.S.C. 1639a(f)(3)).

(4) RULE OF CONSTRUCTION.—No provision of paragraph (1) or (2) shall be construed as affecting the liability of any servicer or person for actual fraud in servicing of a loan or for the violation of a State or Federal law.

(i) Post-Pandemic Mortgage Repayment Options.—Section 6 of the Real Estate Settlement Procedures Act of 1974 (12 U.S.C. 2605), as amended by subsection (d), is further amended by adding at the end the following:

"(p) Post-Pandemic Mortgage Repayment Options.—With respect to a federally related residential mortgage loan, before the end of any forbearance provided under subsection (n), servicers shall—

"(1) evaluate the borrower's ability to return to making regular mortgage payments;

"(2) if the borrower is able to return to making regular mortgage payments at the end of the forbearance period—

"(A) modify the borrower's loan to extend the term for the same period as the length of the forbearance, with all payments that were not made during the forbearance distributed at the same intervals as the borrower's existing payment schedule and evenly distributed across those intervals, with no penalties, late fees, additional interest accrued beyond the amounts scheduled or calculated as if the borrower made all contractual payments on time and in full under the terms of the mortgage contract in effect at the time the borrower entered into the forbearance, and with no modification fee charged to the borrower; or

"(B) if the borrower elects to modify the loan to capitalize a resulting escrow shortage or deficiency, the servicer may modify the borrower's loan by re-amortizing the principal balance and extending the term of the loan sufficient to maintain the regular mortgage payments; and

"(C) notify the borrower in writing of the extension, including provision of a new payment schedule and date of maturity, and that the borrower shall have the election of prepaying the suspended payments at any time, in a lump sum or otherwise;

"(3) if the borrower is financially unable to return to making periodic mortgage payments as provided for in the mortgage contract at the end of the COVID–19 emergency—

"(A) evaluate the borrower for all loan modification options, without regard to whether the borrower has previously requested, been offered, or provided a loan modification or other loss mitigation option and without any requirement that the borrower come current before such evaluation or as a condition of eligibility for such modification, including—

"(i) further extending the borrower's repayment period;

"(ii) reducing the principal balance of the loan; or

"(iii) other modification or loss mitigation options available to the servicer under the terms of any investor requirements and existing laws and policies; and

"(B) if the borrower qualifies for such a modification, the service shall offer a loan with such terms as to provide a loan with such terms as to provide an affordable payment, with no penalties, late fees, additional interest beyond the amounts scheduled or calculated as if the borrower made all contractual payments on time and in full under the terms of the mortgage contract in effect at the time the borrower entered into the forbearance, and with no modification fees charged to the borrower; and

"(4) if a borrower is granted a forbearance on payments that would be owed pursuant to a trial loan modification plan—

"(A) any forbearance of payments shall not be treated as missed or delinquent payments or otherwise negatively affect the borrower's ability to complete their trial plan;

"(B) any past due amounts as of the end of the trial period, including unpaid interest, real estate taxes, insurance premiums, and assessments paid on the borrower's behalf, will be added to the mortgage loan balance, but only to the extent that such charges are not fees associated with the granting of the forbearance, such as late fees, modification fees, or unpaid interest from the period of the forbearance beyond the amounts scheduled or calculated as if the borrower made all contractual payments on time and in full under the terms of the mortgage contract in effect at the time the borrower entered into the forbearance; and

"(C) if the borrower is unable to resume payments on the trial modification at the end of the forbearance period, re-evaluate the borrower for all available loan modifications under paragraph 3, without any requirement that the borrower become current before such evaluation or as a condition of eligibility for such modification.".

(j) Claims Of Affected Investors And Other Parties.—Any action asserting a taking under the Fifth Amendment to the Constitution of the United States as a result of this subsection shall be brought not later than 180 days after the end of the COVID–19 emergency.

(k) Extension Of The GSE Patch.—The Director of the Bureau of Consumer Financial Protection shall revise section 1026.43(e)(4)(iii)(B) of title 12, Code of Federal Regulations, to extend the sunset of the special rule provided under such section 1026.43(e)(4) until January 1, 2022, or such later date as may be determined by the Bureau.

(l) Definitions.—In this section:

(1) COVID–19 EMERGENCY.—The term "COVID–19 emergency" means the period that begins upon the date of the enactment of this Act and ends on the date of the termination by the Federal Emergency Management Agency of the emergency declared on March 13, 2020, by the President under the Robert T. Stafford Disaster Relief and Emergency Assistance Act (42 U.S.C. 4121 et seq.) relating to the Coronavirus Disease 2019 (COVID–19) pandemic.

(2) MANUFACTURED HOME.—The term "manufactured home "has the meaning given that term under section 603 of the National Manufactured Housing Construction and Safety Standards Act of 1974 (42 U.S.C. 5402).

(3) MOTOR VEHICLE.—The term "motor vehicle" has the meaning given that term under Section 1029(f) of the Consumer Financial Protection Act of 2010 (12 U.S.C. 5519(f)).

(4) RESIDENTIAL MORTGAGE LOAN.—The term "residential mortgage loan" means any consumer credit transaction that is secured by a mortgage, deed of trust, or other equivalent consensual security interest on residence consisting of a single dwelling unit that is occupied by the mortgagor.

SEC. 109. BANKRUPTCY PROTECTIONS.

(a) Increasing The Homestead Exemption.—

(1) HOMESTEAD EXEMPTION.—Section 522 of title 11, United States Code, is amended—

(A) in subsection (d)(1), by striking "$15,000" and inserting "$100,000"; and

(B) by adding at the end the following:

"(r) Notwithstanding any other provision of applicable nonbankruptcy law, a debtor in any State may exempt from property of the estate the property described in subsection (d)(1) not to exceed the value in subsection (d)(1) if the exemption for such property permitted by applicable nonbankruptcy law is lower than that amount.".

(b) Effect Of Missed Mortgage Payments On Discharge.—Section 1328 of title 11, United States Code, is amended by adding at the end the following:

"(i) A debtor shall not be denied a discharge under this section because, as of the date of discharge, the debtor did not make 6 or fewer payments directly to the holder of a debt secured by real property.

"(j) Notwithstanding subsections (a) and (b), upon the debtor's request, the court shall grant a discharge of all debts provided for in the plan that are dischargeable under subsection (a) if the debtor—

"(1) has made payments under a confirmed plan for at least 1 year; and

"(2) is experiencing a loss of income or increase in expenses due, directly or indirectly, to the coronavirus disease 2019 (COVID–19) pandemic.".

(c) Modification Of Chapter 13 Plan Due To Hardship Caused By COVID–19 Pandemic.—Section 1329 of title 11, United States Code, is amended by adding at end the following:

"(d) (1) Subject to paragraph (3), for a plan confirmed prior to the date of enactment of this subsection, the plan may be modified upon the request of the debtor if—

"(A) the debtor is experiencing or has experienced a material financial hardship due, directly or indirectly, to the coronavirus disease 2019 (COVID–19) pandemic; and

"(B) the modification is approved after notice and a hearing.

"(2) A modification under paragraph (1) may include extending the period of time for payments on claims not later than 7 years after the date on which the first payment under the original confirmed plan was due.

"(3) Sections 1322(a), 1322(b), 1323(c), and the requirements of section 1325(a) shall apply to any modification under paragraph (1).".

(d) Applicability.—

(1) The amendments made by subsections (a) and (b) shall apply to any case commenced before, on, or after the date of enactment of this Act.

(2) The amendment made by subsection (c) shall apply to any case for which a plan has been confirmed under section 1325 of title 11, United States Code, before the date of enactment of this Act.

SEC. 110. DEBT COLLECTION.

(a) Temporary Debt Collection Moratorium During The COVID–19 Emergency Period.—

(1) IN GENERAL.—The Fair Debt Collection Practices Act (15 U.S.C. 1692 et seq.) is amended by inserting after section 812 the following:

"§ 812A. Temporary debt collection moratorium during the COVID–19

emergency period
“(a) Definitions.—In this section:
“(1) CONSUMER.—The term ‘consumer’ means any natural person obligated or allegedly obligated to pay any debt.
“(2) COVID–19 EMERGENCY PERIOD.—The term ‘COVID–19 emergency period’ means the period that begins upon the date of the enactment of this Act and ends upon the date of the termination by the Federal Emergency Management Administration of the emergency declared on March 13, 2020, by the President under the Robert T. Stafford Disaster Relief and Emergency Assistance Act (42 U.S.C. 4121 et seq.) relating to the Coronavirus Disease 2019 (COVID–19) pandemic.
“(3) CREDITOR.—The term ‘creditor’ means any person who offers or extends credit creating a debt or to whom a debt is owed or other obligation of payment.
“(4) DEBT.—The term ‘debt’—
“(A) means any past due obligation or alleged obligation of a consumer, non-profit organization, or small business to pay money—
“(i) arising out of a transaction in which the money, property, insurance, or services which are the subject of the transaction are primarily for personal, family, business, non-profit, or household purposes, whether or not such obligation has been reduced to judgment;
“(ii) owed to a local, State, or Federal government;
“(B) does not include federally related mortgages (as defined under section 3 of the Real Estate Settlement Procedures Act of 1974) unless a deficiency judgment has been made with respect to such federally related mortgage.
“(5) DEBT COLLECTOR.—The term ‘debt collector’ includes a creditor and any person or entity that engages in the collection of debt (including the Federal Government or a State government) whether or not the debt is allegedly owed to or assigned to that person or entity.
“(6) DEPOSITORY INSTITUTION.—The term ‘depository institution’—
“(A) has the meaning given that term under section 3 of the Federal Deposit Insurance Act; and
“(B) means a Federal or State credit union (as such terms are defined, respectively, under section 101 of the Federal Credit Union Act.)
“(7) NON-PROFIT ORGANIZATION.—The term ‘non-profit organization’ means an organization described in section 501(c)(3) of the Internal Revenue Code of 1986 and exempt from taxation under subsection (a) of such section.
“(8) SMALL BUSINESS.—The term ‘small business’ has the meaning given the term ‘small business concern’ under section 3 of the Small Business Act (15 U.S.C. 632).
“(b) Prohibitions.—Notwithstanding any other provision of law, during COVID–19 emergency period and the 120-day period immediately following, a debt collector is prohibited from—
“(1) capitalizing or adding extra interest or fees triggered by the non-payment

of an obligation by a consumer, small business, or non-profit organization to the balance of an account;

"(2) suing or threatening to sue a consumer, small business, or non-profit for a past-due debt;

"(3) continuing litigation initiated before the date of enactment of this section to collect a debt from a consumer, small business, or non-profit organization;

"(4) enforcing a security interest, including through repossession or foreclosure, against a consumer, small business, or non-profit organization;

"(5) reporting a past due debt of a consumer, small business, or non-profit organization to a consumer reporting agency;

"(6) taking or threatening to take any action to enforce collection, or any adverse action against a consumer, small business, or non-profit organization for non-payment or for non-appearance at any hearings related to a debt;

"(7) except with respect to enforcing an order for child support or spousal support, initiating or continuing any action to cause or to seek to cause the collection of a debt from wages, Federal benefits, or other amounts due to a consumer, small business, or non-profit organization, by way of garnishment, deduction, offset, or other seizure, or to cause or seek to cause the collection of a debt by seizing funds from a bank account or any other assets held by such consumer, small business, or non-profit organization;

"(8) in the case of action or collection described under paragraph (7) that was initiated prior to the beginning of the date of such disaster or emergency, failing to suspend the action or collection until 120 days after the end of the COVID–19 emergency period;

"(9) upon the termination of the incident period for such disaster or emergency, failing to extend the time period to pay an obligation by one payment period for each payment that a consumer, small business, or non-profit organization missed during the incident period, with the payments due in the same amounts and at the same intervals as the pre-existing payment schedule of the consumer, small business, or non-profit organization (as applicable) or, if the debt has no payment periods, allow the consumer, small business, or non-profit a reasonable time in which to repay the debt in affordable payments;

"(10) disconnecting a consumer, small business, or non-profit organization from a utility prepaid or post-paid electricity, natural gas, telecommunications, broadband, water, or sewer service; or

"(11) exercising a right to set off provision contained in any consumer, small business, or non-profit organization account agreement with a depository institution.

"(c) Violation.—Any person who violates a provision of this section shall—

"(1) be treated as a debt collector for purposes of section 813; and

"(2) be liable to the consumer, small business, or non-profit organization an amount equal to 10 times the damages allowed under section 813 for each such violation.".

(2) TABLE OF CONTENTS AMENDMENT.—The table of contents at the

beginning of the Fair Debt Collection Practices Act (15 U.S.C. 1692 et seq.) is amended by inserting after the item relating to section 812 the following new item:

"812A. Temporary debt collection moratorium during the COVID–19 emergency period.".

(b) Confessions Of Judgment Prohibition.—

(1) IN GENERAL.—Chapter 2 of the Truth in Lending Act (15 U.S.C. 1631 et seq.) is amended—

(A) by adding at the end the following:

"§ 140B. Confessions of judgment prohibition

"(a) In General.—During a period described under section 812A(b) of the Fair Debt Collection Practices Act, no person may directly or indirectly take or receive from another person or seek to enforce an obligation that constitutes or contains a cognovit or confession of judgment (for purposes other than executory process in the State of Louisiana), warrant of attorney, or other waiver of the right to notice and the opportunity to be heard in the event of suit or process thereon.

"(b) Exemption.—The exemption in section 104(1) shall not apply to this section.

"(c) Debt Defined.—In this section, the term 'debt' means any obligation of a person to pay to another person money—

"(1) regardless of whether the obligation is absolute or contingent, if the understanding between the parties is that any part of the money shall be or may be returned;

"(2) that includes the right of the person providing the money to an equitable remedy for breach of performance if the breach gives rise to a right to payment; and

"(3) regardless of whether the obligation or right to an equitable remedy described in paragraph (2) has been reduced to judgment or is fixed, contingent, matured, unmatured, disputed, undisputed, secured, or unsecured."; and

(B) in the table of contents for such chapter, by adding at the end the following:

"140B. Confessions of judgment prohibition.".

(2) CONFORMING AMENDMENT.—Section 130(a) of the Truth in Lending Act (15 U.S.C. 1640(a)) is amended by adding at the end the following: "For purposes of this section, the term 'creditor' refers to any person charged with compliance.".

SEC. 111. DISASTER PROTECTION FOR WORKERS' CREDIT.

(a) Purpose.—The purpose of this section, and the amendments made by this section, is to protect consumers' credit from negative impacts as a result of financial hardship due to the coronavirus disease (COVID–19) outbreak and future major disasters.

(b) Reporting Of Information During Major Disasters.—

(1) IN GENERAL.—The Fair Credit Reporting Act is amended by inserting

after section 605B the following:
"§ 605C. Reporting of information during major disasters
"(a) Definitions.—In this section:
"(1) COVID–19 EMERGENCY PERIOD.—The term 'COVID–19 emergency period' means the period beginning on the date of enactment of this section and ending on the later of—
"(A) 120 days after the date of enactment of this section; or
"(B) 120 days after the date of termination by the Federal Emergency Management Administration of the emergency declared on March 13, 2020, by the President under the Robert T. Stafford Disaster Relief and Emergency Assistance Act (42 U.S.C. 4121 et seq.) relating to the Coronavirus Disease 2019 (COVID–19) pandemic.
"(2) COVERED MAJOR DISASTER PERIOD.—The term 'covered major disaster period' means—
"(A) the period beginning on the date on which a major disaster is declared by the President under section 401 of the Robert T. Stafford Disaster Relief and Emergency Assistance Act (42 U.S.C. 5170), under which assistance is authorized under section 408 of such Act (42 U.S.C. 5174), and ending on the date that is 120 days after the end of the incident period designated in such declaration; or
"(B) the period ending 120 days after the date of termination by the Federal Emergency Management Administration of the emergency declared on March 13, 2020, by the President under the Robert T. Stafford Disaster Relief and Emergency Assistance Act (42 U.S.C. 4121 et seq.) relating to the Coronavirus Disease 2019 (COVID–19) pandemic.
"(3) MAJOR DISASTER.—The term 'major disaster' means a major disaster declared by the President under section 401 of the Robert T. Stafford Disaster Relief and Emergency Assistance Act (42 U.S.C. 5170), under which assistance is authorized under section 408 of such Act (42 U.S.C. 5174)
"(b) Moratorium On Furnishing Adverse Information During COVID–19 Emergency Period.—No person may furnish any adverse item of information (except information related to a felony criminal conviction) relating to a consumer that was the result of any action or inaction that occurred during the COVID–19 emergency period.
"(c) Moratorium On Furnishing Adverse Information During Covered Major Disaster Period.—No person may furnish any adverse item of information (except information related to a felony criminal conviction) relating to a consumer that was the result of any action or inaction that occurred during a covered major disaster period if the consumer is a resident of the affected area covered by a declaration made by the President under section 401 of the Robert T. Stafford Disaster Relief and Emergency Assistance Act (42 U.S.C. 5170), under which assistance is authorized under section 408 of such Act (42 U.S.C. 5174).
"(d) Information Excluded From Consumer Reports.—In addition to the

information described in section 605(a), no consumer reporting agency may make any consumer report containing an adverse item of information (except information related to a felony criminal conviction) reported relating to a consumer that was the result of any action or inaction that occurred during the COVID–19 emergency period or a covered major disaster period, and as applicable under subsection (f)(3), for 270 days after the expiration of the applicable period.

"(e) Summary Of Rights.—Not later than 60 days after the date of enactment of this subsection, the Bureau shall update the model summary of rights under section 609(c)(1) to include a description of the right of a consumer to—

"(1) request the deletion of adverse items of information under subsection (f); and

"(2) request a consumer report or score, without charge to the consumer, under subsection (g).

"(f) Deletion Of Adverse Items Of Information Resulting From The Coronavirus Disease (COVID–19) Outbreak And Major Disasters.—

"(1) REPORTING.—

"(A) IN GENERAL.—Not later than 60 days after the date of enactment of this subsection, the Bureau shall create a website for consumers to report, under penalty of perjury, economic hardship as a result of the coronavirus disease (COVID–19) outbreak or a major disaster (if the consumer is a resident of the affected area covered by such major disaster) for the purpose of extending credit report protection for an additional 270 days after the end of the COVID–19 emergency period or covered major disaster period, as applicable.

"(B) DOCUMENTATION.—The Bureau shall—

"(i) not require any documentation from a consumer to substantiate the economic hardship; and

"(ii) provide notice to the consumer that a report under subparagraph (A) is under penalty of perjury.

"(C) REPORTING PERIOD.—A consumer may report economic hardship under subparagraph (A) during the COVID–19 emergency period or a covered major disaster period, as applicable, and for 60 days thereafter.

"(2) DATABASE.—The Bureau shall establish and maintain a secure database that—

"(A) is accessible to each consumer reporting agency described in section 603(p) and nationwide specialty consumer reporting agency for purposes of fulfilling their duties under paragraph (3) to check and automatically delete any adverse item of information (except information related to a felony criminal conviction) reported that occurred during the COVID–19 emergency period or a covered major disaster period with respect to a consumer; and

"(B) contains the information reported under paragraph (1).

"(3) DELETION OF ADVERSE ITEMS OF INFORMATION BY

NATIONWIDE CONSUMER REPORTING AND NATIONWIDE SPECIALTY CONSUMER REPORTING AGENCIES.—

"(A) IN GENERAL.—Each consumer reporting agency described in section 603(p) and each nationwide specialty consumer reporting agency shall, using the information contained in the database established under paragraph (2), delete from the file of each consumer named in the database each adverse item of information (except information related to a felony criminal conviction) that was a result of an action or inaction that occurred during the COVID–19 emergency period or a covered major disaster period up to 270 days following the end of the such period.

"(B) TIMELINE.—Each consumer reporting agency described in section 603(p) and each nationwide specialty consumer reporting agency shall check the database at least weekly and delete adverse items of information as soon as practicable after information that is reported under paragraph (1) appears in the database established under paragraph (2).

"(4) REQUEST FOR DELETION OF ADVERSE ITEMS OF INFORMATION.—

"(A) IN GENERAL.—A consumer who has filed a report of economic hardship with the Bureau may submit a request, without charge to the consumer, to a consumer reporting agency to delete from the consumer's file an adverse item of information (except information related to a felony criminal conviction) that was a result of an action or inaction that occurred during the COVID–19 emergency period or a covered major disaster period up to 270 days following the end of the such period.

"(B) TIMING.—A consumer may submit a request under subparagraph (A), not later than 270-day period described in that subparagraph.

"(C) REMOVAL AND NOTIFICATION.—Upon receiving a request under this paragraph to delete an adverse item of information, a consumer reporting agency shall—

"(i) delete the adverse item of information (except information related to a felony criminal conviction) from the consumer's file; and

"(ii) notify the consumer and the furnisher of the adverse item of information of the deletion.

"(g) Free Credit Report And Scores.—

"(1) IN GENERAL.—During the COVID–19 emergency period or a covered major disaster period and ending 12 months after the expiration of the COVID–19 emergency period or covered major disaster period, as applicable, each consumer reporting agency as described under 603(p) and nationwide specialty consumer reporting agency shall make all disclosures described under section 609 upon request by a consumer, by mail or online, without charge to the consumer and without limitation as to the number of requests. A consumer reporting agency shall also supply a consumer, upon request and without charge, with a credit score that—

"(A) is derived from a credit scoring model that is widely distributed to users by the consumer reporting agency for the purpose of any extension of credit or other transaction designated by the consumer who is requesting the credit score; or

"(B) is widely distributed to lenders of common consumer loan products and predicts the future credit behavior of the consumer.

"(2) TIMING.—A file disclosure or credit score under paragraph (1) shall be provided to the consumer not later than—

"(A) 7 days after the date on which the request is received if the request is made by mail; and

"(B) not later than 15 minutes if the request is made online.

"(3) ADDITIONAL REPORTS.—A file disclosure provided under paragraph (1) shall be in addition to any disclosure requested by the consumer under section 612(a).

"(4) PROHIBITION.—A consumer reporting agency that receives a request under paragraph (1) may not request or require any documentation from the consumer that demonstrates that the consumer was impacted by the coronavirus disease (COVID–19) outbreak or a major disaster (except to verify that the consumer resides in an area covered by the major disaster) as a condition of receiving the file disclosure or score.

"(h) Posting Of Rights.—Not later than 30 days after the date of enactment of this section, each consumer reporting agency shall prominently post and maintain a direct link on the homepage of the public website of the consumer reporting agency information relating to the right of consumers to—

"(1) request the deletion of adverse items of information (except information related to a felony criminal conviction) under subsection (f); and

"(2) request consumer file disclosures and scores, without charge to the consumer, under subsection (g).

"(i) Ban On Reporting Medical Debt Information Related To COVID–19 Or A Major Disaster.—

"(1) FURNISHING BAN.—No person shall furnish adverse information to a consumer reporting agency related to medical debt if such medical debt is with respect to medical expenses related to treatments arising from COVID–19 or a major disaster (whether or not the expenses were incurred during the COVID–19 emergency period or covered major disaster period).

"(2) CONSUMER REPORT BAN.—No consumer reporting agency may made a consumer report containing adverse information related to medical debt if such medical debt is with respect to medical expenses related to treatments arising from COVID–19 or a major disaster (whether or not the expenses were incurred during the COVID–19 emergency period or covered major disaster period).

"(j) Credit Scoring Models.—A person that creates and implements credit scoring models may not treat the absence, omission, or deletion of any information pursuant to this section as a negative factor or negative value in credit scoring models created or implemented by such person.".

(2) TECHNICAL AND CONFORMING AMENDMENT.—The table of contents for the Fair Credit Reporting Act is amended by inserting after the item relating to section 605B the following:

"605C. Reporting of information during major disasters.".

(c) Limitations On New Credit Scoring Models During The COVID–19 Emergency And Major Disasters.—The Fair Credit Reporting Act (15 U.S.C. 1681 et seq.) is amended—

(1) by adding at the end the following:

"§ 630. Limitations on new credit scoring models during the COVID–19 emergency and major disasters

"With respect to a person that creates and implements credit scoring models, such person may not, during the COVID–19 emergency period or a covered major disaster period (as such terms are defined under section 605C), create or implement a new credit scoring model (including a revision to an existing scoring model) if the new credit scoring model would identify a significant percentage of consumers as being less creditworthy when compared to the previous credit scoring models created or implemented by such person."; and

(2) in the table of contents for such Act, by adding at the end the following new item:

"630. Limitations on new credit scoring models during major disasters.".

SEC. 112. STUDENT LOANS.

(a) Payments For Private Education Loan Borrowers As A Result Of The COVID–19 National Emergency.—Section 140 of the Truth in Lending Act (15 U.S.C. 1650) is amended by adding at the end the following new subsection:

"(h) COVID–19 National Emergency Private Education Loan Repayment Assistance.—

"(1) AUTHORITY.—Effective on the date of the enactment of this section, for the duration of the COVID–19 emergency period and the 6-month period immediately following, the Secretary of the Treasury shall, for each borrower of a private education loan, pay the total amount due for such month on the loan, based on the payment plan selected by the borrower or the borrower's loan status.

"(2) NO CAPITALIZATION OF INTEREST.—With respect to any loan in repayment during the COVID–19 national emergency period and the 6-month period immediately following, interest due on a private education loan during such period shall not be capitalized at any time during the COVID–19 national emergency period and the 6-month period immediately following.

"(3) REPORTING TO CONSUMER REPORTING AGENCIES.—During the period in which the Secretary of the Treasury is making payments on a loan under paragraph (1), the Secretary shall ensure that, for the purpose of reporting information about the loan to a consumer reporting agency, any payment made by the Secretary is treated as if it were a regularly scheduled payment made by a borrower.

"(4) NOTICE OF PAYMENTS AND PROGRAM.—Not later than 15 days following the date of enactment of this subsection, and monthly thereafter during the COVID–19 national emergency period and the 6-month period immediately following, the Secretary of the Treasury shall provide a notice to all borrowers of private education loans—

"(A) informing borrowers of the actions taken under this subsection;

"(B) providing borrowers with an easily accessible method to opt out of the benefits provided under this subsection; and

"(C) notifying the borrower that the program under this subsection is a temporary program and will end 6 months after the COVID–19 national emergency period ends.

"(5) SUSPENSION OF INVOLUNTARY COLLECTION.—During the COVID–19 national emergency period and the 6-month period immediately following, the holder of a private education loan shall immediately take action to halt all involuntary collection related to the loan.

"(6) MANDATORY FORBEARANCE.—During the period in which the Secretary of the Treasury is making payments on a loan under paragraph (1), the servicer of such loan shall grant the borrower forbearance as follows:

"(A) A temporary cessation of all payments on the loan other than the payments of interest and principal on the loan that are made under paragraph (1).

"(B) For borrowers who are delinquent but who are not yet in default before the date on which the Secretary begins making payments under paragraph (1), the retroactive application of forbearance to address any delinquency.

"(7) DATA TO IMPLEMENT.—Holders and servicers of private education loans shall report, to the satisfaction of the Secretary of the Treasury, the information necessary to calculate the amount to be paid under this section.

"(8) COVID–19 EMERGENCY PERIOD DEFINED.—In this subsection, the term 'COVID–19 emergency period' means the period that begins upon the date of the enactment of this Act and ends upon the date of the termination by the Federal Emergency Management Administration of the emergency declared on March 13, 2020, by the President under the Robert T. Stafford Disaster Relief and Emergency Assistance Act (42 U.S.C. 4121 et seq.) relating to the Coronavirus Disease 2019 (COVID–19) pandemic.".

(b) Additional Protections For Private Student Loan Borrowers.—

(1) Each private education loan holder who receives any monthly payment pursuant to this section must modify all private education loan contracts that it holds to provide for the same repayment plan and forgiveness terms available to Direct Loans borrowers under 34 C.F.R. § 685.209(c), in effect as of January 1, 2020.

(2) For a borrower who has defaulted on the private education loan under the terms of the promissory note prior to any loan payment made or forbearance

granted under this section, no payment made or forbearance granted under this section shall be considered an event that impacts the calculation of the applicable state statutes of limitation.

(3) A private education loan debt collector, as that term is defined in the Federal Debt Collection Practices Act, may not pressure a borrower to elect to apply the amount to any private education loan. "Pressure" is defined as any communication, recommendation or other similar communication, other than providing basic information about a borrower's options, urging a borrower to make this election. Violation of this provision shall be an unfair practice in violation of 15 U.S.C. § 1692f.

(4) A private education loan debt collector or creditor may not pressure a borrower to elect to apply the amount to any private education loan. "Pressure" is defined as any communication, recommendation or other similar communication, other than providing basic information about a borrower's options, urging a borrower to make this election. Violation of this provision shall be an abusive act or practice as defined by 12 U.S.C. § 5531.

(5) For a borrower who has defaulted on the private education loan, under the terms of the promissory note, prior to any loan payment made under this section, no loan relief provided under this section shall be considered an event that impacts the calculation of the applicable state statutes of limitation.

(c) Minimum Relief For Private Student Loan Borrowers As A Result Of The COVID–19 National Emergency.—

(1) MINIMUM STUDENT LOAN RELIEF AS A RESULT OF THE COVID–19 NATIONAL EMERGENCY.—Not later than 270 days after the last day of the COVID–19 emergency period, the Secretary of the Treasury shall carry out a program under which a qualified borrower, with respect to the private education of loans of such qualified borrower, shall receive in accordance with paragraph (3) an amount equal to the lesser of the following:

(A) The total amount of each private education loan of the borrower; or

(B) $10,000.

(2) NOTIFICATION OF BORROWERS.—Not later than 270 days after the last day of the COVID–19 emergency period, the Secretary of the Treasury shall notify each qualified borrower of—

(A) the requirements to provide loan relief to such borrower under this section; and

(B) the opportunity for such borrower to make an election under paragraph (3)(A) with respect to the application of such loan relief to the covered loans and private education loans of such borrower.

(3) DISTRIBUTION OF FUNDING.—

(A) ELECTION BY BORROWER.—Not later than 45 days after a notice is sent under paragraph (2), a qualified borrower may elect to apply the amount determined with respect to such borrower under paragraph (1) to any private education loan of the borrower.

(B) AUTOMATIC PAYMENT.—

(i) IN GENERAL.—In the case of a qualified borrower who does not make an election under subparagraph (A) before the date described in such paragraph, the Secretary of the Treasury shall apply the amount determined with respect to such borrower under paragraph (1) in order of the private education loan of the qualified borrower with the highest interest rate.
(ii) EQUAL INTEREST RATES.—In case of two or more private education loans described in clause (i) with equal interest rates, the Secretary of the Treasury shall apply the amount determined with respect to such borrower under paragraph (1) first to the loan with the highest principal.
(4) DEFINITIONS.—In this subsection:
(A) COVERED LOAN.—The term "covered loan" means—
(i) a loan made, insured, or guaranteed under part B of title IV of the Higher Education Act of 1965 (20 U.S.C. 1071 et seq.);
(ii) a loan made under part D of title IV of the Higher Education Act of 1965 (20 U.S.C. 1087a et seq.); and
(iii) a Federal Perkins Loan made pursuant to part E of title IV of the Higher Education Act of 1965 (20 U.S.C. 1087aa et seq.).
(B) COVID–19 EMERGENCY PERIOD.—The term "COVID–19 emergency period" means the period that begins upon the date of the enactment of this Act and ends upon the date of the termination by the Federal Emergency Management Administration of the emergency declared on March 13, 2020, by the President under the Robert T. Stafford Disaster Relief and Emergency Assistance Act (42 U.S.C. 4121 et seq.) relating to the Coronavirus Disease 2019 (COVID–19) pandemic.
(C) PRIVATE EDUCATION LOAN.—The term "private education loan" has the meaning given the term in section 140 of the Truth in Lending Act (15 U.S.C. 1650).
(D) QUALIFIED BORROWER.—The term "qualified borrower" means a borrower of a covered loan or a private education loan.
(E) SECRETARIES CONCERNED.—The term "Secretaries concerned" means—
(i) the Secretary of Education, with respect to covered loans and borrowers of such covered loans; and
(ii) the Secretary of the Treasury, with respect to private education loans and borrowers of such private education loans.

SEC. 113. WAIVER OF IN-PERSON APPRAISAL REQUIREMENTS.
(a) Finding.—The Congress finds that as the country continues to grapple with the impact of the spread of COVID–19, several adjustments are needed to ensure that mortgage processing can continue to function without significant delays, despite requirements that would otherwise require in-person interactions.
(b) Waiver.—
(1) IN GENERAL.—Until the end of the COVID–19 emergency, any appraisal

that is conducted for a loan with respect to which applicable law would otherwise require the performance of an interior inspection may be performed without an interior inspection, if—

(A) an exterior inspection is performed in conjunction with other methods to maximize credibility, including verifiable contemporaneous video or photographic documentation by the borrower and borrower observations; and

(B) the applicable lender, guarantor, regulating agency, or insurer may order additional services to include an interior inspection at a later date.

(2) STIPULATION.— An appraiser conducting an appraisal without an interior inspection pursuant to this section shall stipulate an extraordinary assumption that the property's interior quality, condition, and physical characteristics are as described and consistent with the exterior view, and shall employ all available methods to maximize accuracy while maintaining safety.

(c) Rulemaking.—Not later than the end of the 1-week period beginning on the date of enactment of this Act, the Federal Housing Commissioner of the Federal Housing Agency and the Director of the Federal Housing Finance Agency shall issue such rules or guidance as may be necessary to ensure that such agencies, the Federal Home Loan Mortgage Corporation, the Federal National Mortgage Association, and the Federal home loan banks make any adjustments to mortgage processing requirements that may be necessary to provide flexibility to avoid in-person interactions while preserving the goals of the programs and consumer protection.

(d) COVID–19 Emergency Defined.—In this section, the term "COVID–19 emergency" means the period that begins upon the date of the enactment of this Act and ends on the date of the termination by the Federal Emergency Management Agency of the emergency declared on March 13, 2020, by the President under the Robert T. Stafford Disaster Relief and Emergency Assistance Act (42 U.S.C. 4121 et seq.) relating to the Coronavirus Disease 2019 (COVID–19) pandemic.

SEC. 114. SUPPLEMENTAL FUNDING FOR COMMUNITY DEVELOPMENT BLOCK GRANTS.

(a) Funding And Allocations.—

(1) AUTHORIZATION OF APPROPRIATIONS.—There is authorized to be appropriated $12,000,000,000 for assistance in accordance with this section under the community development block grant program under title I of the Housing and Community Development Act of 1974 (42 U.S.C. 5301 et seq.).

(2) INITIAL ALLOCATION.—$6,000,000,000 of the amount made available pursuant to paragraph (1) shall be distributed pursuant to section 106 of such Act (42 U.S.C. 5306) to grantees and such allocations shall be made within 30 days after the date of the enactment of this Act.

(3) SUBSEQUENT ALLOCATION.—

(A) IN GENERAL.—The $6,000,000,000 made available pursuant to paragraph

(1) that remains after allocation pursuant to paragraph (2) shall be allocated, not later than 45 days after the date of the enactment of this Act, directly to States to prevent, prepare for, and respond to coronavirus within the State, including activities within entitlement and nonentitlement communities, based on public health needs, risk of transmission of coronavirus, number of coronavirus cases compared to the national average, and economic and housing market disruptions, and other factors, as determined by the Secretary, using best available data.

(B) TECHNICAL ASSISTANCE.—Of the amount referred to in subparagraph (A), $10,000,000 shall be made available for capacity building and technical assistance to support the use of such amounts to expedite or facilitate infectious disease response.

(4) DIRECT DISTRIBUTION.—Of the amount made available pursuant to paragraph (1), $3,000,000,000 shall be distributed directly to States and units of general local government, at the discretion of the Secretary of Housing and Urban Development (in this section referred to as the "Secretary"), according to a formula based on factors to be determined by the Secretary, prioritizing risk of transmission of coronavirus, number of coronavirus cases compared to the national average, and economic and housing market disruptions resulting from coronavirus.

(5) ROLLING ALLOCATIONS.—Allocations under this subsection may be made on a rolling basis as additional needs develop and data becomes available.

(6) BEST AVAILABLE DATA.—The Secretary shall make all allocations under this subsection based on the best available data at the time of allocation.

(b) Eligible Activities.—Amounts made available pursuant to subsection (a) may be used only for—

(1) eligible activities described in 105(a) of the Housing and Community Development Act of 1974 (42 U.S.C. 5305(a)) relating to preventing, preparing for, or responding to the public health emergency relating to Coronavirus Disease 2019 (COVID–19); and

(2) reimbursement of costs for such eligible activities relating to preventing, preparing for, or responding to Coronavirus Disease 2019 (COVID–19) that were accrued before the date of the enactment of this Act.

(c) Inapplicability Of Public Services Cap.—The limitation under paragraph (8) of section 105(a) of the Housing and Community Development Act of 1974 (42 U.S.C. 5305(a)(8)) on the amount that may be used for activities under such paragraph shall not apply with respect to—

(1) amounts made available pursuant to subsection (a); and

(2) amounts made available in preceding appropriation Acts for fiscal years 2019 and 2020 for carrying out title I of the Housing and Community Development Act of 1974, to the extent such amounts are used for activities described in subsection (b) of this section.

(d) Waivers.—

(1) IN GENERAL.—The Secretary may waive, or specify alternative requirements for, any provision of any statute or regulation that the Secretary administers in connection with the use of amounts made available pursuant to subsection (a)(1) and for fiscal years 2019 and 2020 (except for requirements related to fair housing, nondiscrimination, labor standards, and the environment), if the Secretary finds that good cause exists for the waiver or alternative requirement and such waiver or alternative requirement would not be inconsistent with the overall purpose of title I of the Housing and Community Development Act of 1974, including for the purposes of addressing the impact of coronavirus.

(2) NOTICE.—The Secretary shall notify the public through the Federal Register or other appropriate means 5 days before the effective date of any such waiver or alternative requirement in order for such waiver or alternative requirement to take effect. Such public notice may be provided on the Internet at the appropriate Government web site or through other electronic media, as determined by the Secretary.

(e) Statements Of Activities; Comprehensive Housing Affordability Strategies.—

(1) INAPPLICABILITY OF REQUIREMENTS.—Section 116(b) of such Act (42 U.S.C. 5316(b); relating to submission of final statements of activities not later than August 16 of a given fiscal year) and any implementing regulations shall not apply to final statements submitted in accordance with paragraphs (2) and (3) of section 104 of such Act (42 U.S.C. 5304(a)) and comprehensive housing affordability strategies submitted in accordance with section 105 of the Cranston-Gonzalez National Affordable Housing Act (42 U.S.C. 12705) for fiscal years 2019 and 2020.

(2) NEW REQUIREMENTS.—Final statements and comprehensive housing affordability strategies shall instead be submitted not later than August 16, 2021.

(3) AMENDMENTS.—Notwithstanding subsections (a)(2), (a)(3), and (c) of section 104 of the Housing and Community Development Act of 1974 (42 U.S.C. 5304) and section 105 of the Cranston-Gonzalez National Affordable Housing Act (42 U.S.C. 12705), a grantee may not be required to amend its statement of activities in order to engage in activities to prevent, prepare, and respond to coronavirus or the economic and housing disruption caused by it, but shall make public a report within 180 days of the end of the crisis which fully accounts for such activities.

(f) Public Hearings.—

(1) INAPPLICABILITY OF IN-PERSON HEARING REQUIREMENTS.—A grantee may not be required to hold in-person public hearings in connection with its citizen participation plan, but shall provide citizens with notice and a reasonable opportunity to comment of not less than 15 days.

(2) VIRTUAL PUBLIC HEARINGS.—During the period that national or local health authorities recommend social distancing and limiting public

gatherings for public health reasons, a grantee may fulfill applicable public hearing requirements for all grants from funds made available pursuant to subsection (a)(1) and under the heading "Department of Housing and Urban Development—Community Planning and Development—Community Development Fund" in appropriation Acts for fiscal years 2019 and 2020 by carrying out virtual public hearings. Any such virtual hearings shall provide reasonable notification and access for citizens in accordance with the grantee's certifications, timely responses from local officials to all citizen questions and issues, and public access to all questions and responses.

(g) Duplication Of Benefits.—The Secretary shall ensure there are adequate procedures in place to prevent any duplication of benefits as defined by section 312 of the Robert T. Stafford Disaster Relief and Emergency Assistance Act (42 U.S.C. 5155) and act in accordance with section 1210 of the Disaster Recovery Reform Act of 2018 (division D of Public Law 115–254; 132 Stat. 3442) and section 312 of the Robert T. Stafford Disaster Relief and Emergency Assistance Act (42 U.S.C. 5155).

SEC. 115. COVID–19 EMERGENCY HOUSING RELIEF.

(a) Definition Of COVID–19 Emergency Period.—For purposes of this section, the term "COVID–19 emergency period" means the period that begins upon the date of the enactment of this Act and ends upon the date of the termination by the Federal Emergency Management Agency of the emergency declared on March 13, 2020, by the President under the Robert T. Stafford Disaster Relief and Emergency Assistance Act (42 U.S.C. 4121 et seq.) relating to the Coronavirus Disease 2019 (COVID–19) pandemic.

(b) Suspension Of Community Service, Work, Presence In Unit, And Minimum Rent Requirements And Time Limits On Assistance.—

(1) SUSPENSION.—Notwithstanding any other provision of law, during the COVID–19 emergency period, the following provisions of law and requirements shall not apply:

(A) Section 12(c) of the United States Housing Act of 1937 (42 U.S.C. 1437j(c); relating to community service).

(B) Any work requirement or time limitation on assistance established by a public housing agency participating in the Moving to Work demonstration program authorized under section 204 of the Departments of Veterans Affairs and Housing and Urban Development and Independent Agencies Appropriations Act, 1996 (Public Law 104–134; 110 Stat. 1321).

(C) Paragraph (3) of section 3(a) of the United States Housing Act of 1937 (42 U.S.C. 1437a(a)(3); relating to minimum rental amount).

(D) Section 982.312 of the regulations of the Secretary of Housing and Urban Development (24 C.F.R. 982.312); relating to absence from unit).

(2) PROHIBITION.—No penalty may be imposed nor any adverse action taken for failure on the part of any tenant of public housing or a dwelling unit assisted under section 8 of the United States Housing Act of 1937 (42 U.S.C.

1437f) to comply with the laws and requirements specified in paragraph (1) during the period specified in paragraph (1).

(c) Housing Choice Vouchers.—

(1) SECTION 8 VOUCHERS.—Notwithstanding any other provision of law, the Secretary of Housing and Urban Development shall provide that—

(A) during the COVID–19 emergency period, a public housing agency may not terminate the availability to an eligible household of a housing choice voucher under section 8(o) of the United States Housing Act of 1937 (42 U.S.C. 1437f(o)) for failure to enter into a lease for an assisted dwelling unit;

(B) in the case of any eligible household on whose behalf such a housing choice voucher has been made available, if as of the termination of the COVID–19 emergency period such availability has not terminated (including by reason of subparagraph (A)) and such voucher has not been used to enter into a lease for an assisted dwelling unit, the public housing agency making such voucher available may not terminate such availability until the expiration of the 60-day period beginning upon the termination of the COVID–19 emergency period; and

(C) during the COVID–19 emergency period, clause (i) of section 8(o)(8)(A) of the United States Housing Act of 1937 (42 U.S.C. 1437f(o)(8)A)(i); relating to initial inspection of dwelling units) shall not apply, except that in any case in which an inspection of a dwelling unit for which a housing assistance payment is established is not conducted before an assistance payment is made for such dwelling unit—

(i) such clause shall be applied by substituting "the expiration of the 90-day period beginning on the termination of the COVID–19 emergency period (as such term is defined in section 117(a) of the Financial Protections and Assistance for America's Consumers, States, Businesses, and Vulnerable Populations Act)" for "any assistance payment is made"; and

(ii) the public housing agency shall inform the tenant household and the owner of such dwelling unit of the inspection requirement applicable to such dwelling unit pursuant to clause (i).

(2) RURAL HOUSING VOUCHERS.—Notwithstanding any other provision of law, the Secretary of Agriculture shall provide that the same restrictions and requirements applicable under paragraph (1) to voucher assistance under section 8(o) of the United States Housing Act of 1937 shall apply with respect to voucher assistance under section 542 of the Housing Act of 1949 (42 U.S.C. 1490r). In applying such restrictions and requirements, the Secretary may take into consideration and provide for any differences between such programs while ensuring that the program under such section 542 is carried out in accordance with the purposes of such restrictions and requirements.

(d) Suspension Of Income Reviews.—During the COVID–19 emergency period, the Secretary of Housing and Urban Development and the Secretary of Agriculture shall waive any requirements under law or regulation requiring review of the income of an individual or household for purposes of assistance under a housing assistance program administered by such Secretary, except—

(1) in the case of review of income upon the initial provision of housing assistance; or

(2) if such review is requested by an individual or household due to a loss of income.

(e) Authority To Suspend Or Delay Deadlines.—During the COVID–19 emergency period, the Secretary of Housing and Urban Development and the Secretary of Agriculture may suspend or delay any deadline relating to public housing agencies or owners of housing assisted under a program administered by such Secretary, except any deadline relating to responding to exigent conditions related to health and safety or emergency physical conditions.

(f) Suspension Of Assisted Housing Scoring Activities.—The Secretary of Housing and Urban Development shall suspend scoring under the Section 8 Management Assessment Program and the Public Housing Assessment System during the period beginning upon the date of the enactment of this Act and ending upon expiration of the 90-day period that begins upon the termination of the COVID–19 emergency period.

(g) Requirements Regarding Residual Receipts And Reserve Funds.—

(1) SUSPENSION OF REQUIREMENT TO SUBMIT RESIDUAL RECEIPTS TO HUD.—During the COVID–19 emergency period, any requirements for owners of federally assisted multifamily housing to remit residual receipts to the Secretary of Housing and Urban Development shall not apply.

(2) ELIGIBLE USES OF RESERVE FUNDS.—During the COVID–19 emergency period, any costs of an owner of federally assisted multifamily housing for items, activities, and services related to responding to coronavirus or COVID–19 shall be considered eligible uses for the reserve fund for replacements for such housing.

SEC. 116. SUPPLEMENTAL FUNDING FOR SERVICE COORDINATORS TO ASSIST ELDERLY HOUSEHOLDS.

(a) In General.—There is authorized to be appropriated $300,000,000 for grants under section 676 of the Housing and Community Development Act of 1992 (42 U.S.C. 13632) for costs of providing service coordinators for purposes of coordinating services to prevent, prepare for, or respond to the public health emergency relating to Coronavirus Disease 2019 (COVID–19).

(b) Hiring.—In the hiring of staff using amounts made available pursuant to this section, grantees shall consider and hire, at all levels of employment and to the greatest extent possible, a diverse staff, including by race, ethnicity, gender, and disability status. Each grantee shall submit a report to the Secretary of Housing and Urban Development describing compliance with the preceding sentence not later than the expiration of the 120-day period that begins upon the termination of the emergency declared on March 13, 2020, by the President under the Robert T. Stafford Disaster Relief and Emergency Assistance Act (42 U.S.C. 4121 et seq.) relating to the Coronavirus Disease

2019 (COVID–19) pandemic.

(c) One-Time Grants.—Grants made using amounts made available pursuant to subsection (a) shall not be renewable.

(d) One-Year Availability.—Any amounts made available pursuant to this section that are allocated for a grantee and remaining unexpended upon the expiration of the 12-month period beginning upon such allocation shall be recaptured by the Secretary.

SEC. 117. FAIR HOUSING.

(a) Definition Of COVID–19 Emergency Period.— For purposes of this section, the term "COVID–19 emergency period" means the period that begins upon the date of the enactment of this Act and ends upon the date of the termination by the Federal Emergency Management Agency of the emergency declared on March 13, 2020, by the President under the Robert T. Stafford Disaster Relief and Emergency Assistance Act (42 U.S.C. 4121 et seq.) relating to the Coronavirus Disease 2019 (COVID–19) pandemic.

(b) Fair Housing Activities.—

(1) FHIP; FHAP.—

(A) AUTHORIZATION OF APPROPRIATIONS.—To ensure that fair housing organizations and State and local civil rights agencies have sufficient resources to deal with expected increases in fair housing complaints, to investigate housing discrimination, including financial scams that target protected classes associated with or resulting from the COVID–19 pandemic, and during such pandemic, there is authorized to be appropriated for contracts, grants, and other assistance—

(i) $55,000,000 for the Fair Housing Initiatives Program under section 561 of the Housing and Community Development Act of 1987 (42 U.S.C. 3616a); and

(ii) $35,000,000 for the Fair Housing Assistance Program under the Fair Housing Act (42 U.S.C. 3601 et seq.).

Amounts made available pursuant to this subparagraph may be used by such organizations and agencies to establish the capacity to and to carry out activities and services by telephone and online means, including for individuals with limited English proficiency and individuals with a disability in accordance with requirements under the Americans With Disabilities Act of 1990.

(B) PRIVATE ENFORCEMENT INITIATIVE.—In entering into contracts for private enforcement initiatives under 561(b) of the Housing and Community Development Act of 1987 (42 U.S.C. 3616a(b)) using amounts made available pursuant to subparagraph (A)(i) of this subsection, the Secretary of Housing and Urban Development shall give priority to applications from qualified fair housing enforcement organizations that have at least 2 years of fair housing testing experience.

(C) 3-YEAR AVAILABILITY.—Any amounts made available pursuant subparagraph (A) that are allocated for a grantee and remain unexpended upon the expiration of the 3-year period beginning upon such allocation shall be recaptured by the Secretary.

(2) OFFICE OF FAIR HOUSING AND EQUAL OPPORTUNITY.—There is authorized to be appropriated $200,000,000 for the Office of Fair Housing and Equal Opportunity of the Department of Housing and Urban Development for costs of fully staffing such Office to ensure robust enforcement of the Fair Housing Act during the COVID–19 pandemic, including ensuring that—

(A) assistance provided under this Act is provided and administered in a manner that affirmatively furthers fair housing in accordance with the Fair Housing Act;

(B) such Office has sufficient capacity for intake of housing discrimination complaints by telephone and online mechanisms, including for individuals with limited English proficiency and individuals with a disability in accordance with requirements under the Americans With Disabilities Act of 1990 and section 504 of the Rehabilitation Act of 1973 (29 U.S.C. 794); and

(C) such Office has the capacity to respond to all housing discrimination complaints made during the COVID–19 pandemic within time limitations required under law.

In the hiring of staff using amounts made available pursuant to this subsection, the Secretary of Housing and Urban Development shall consider and hire, at all levels of employment and to the greatest extent possible, a diverse staff, including by race, ethnicity, gender, and disability status. The Secretary shall submit a report to the Congress describing compliance with the preceding sentence on a quarterly basis, for each of the first 4 calendar quarters ending after the date of the enactment of this Act.

(c) Fair Housing Guidance And Education.—

(1) PROHIBITION OF SHOWINGS.—Not later than the expiration of the 30-day period beginning on the date of the enactment of this Act, the Secretary of Housing and Urban Development shall issue guidance for owners of dwelling units assisted under housing assistance programs of the Department prohibiting, during the COVID–19 emergency period, of any showings of occupied assisted dwelling units to prospective tenants.

(2) EDUCATION.—There is authorized to be appropriated $10,000,000 for the Office of Fair Housing and Equal Opportunity of the Department of Housing and Urban Development to carry out a national media campaign to educate the public of increased housing rights during COVID–19 emergency period, that provides that information and materials used in such campaign are available—

(A) in the languages used by communities with limited English proficiency; and

(B) to persons with disabilities.

SEC. 118. HUD COUNSELING PROGRAM AUTHORIZATION.

(a) Findings.—The Congress finds the following:

(1) The spread of COVID–19, which is now considered a global pandemic, is expected to negatively impact the incomes of potentially millions of homeowners, making it difficult for them to pay their mortgages on time.
(2) Housing counseling is critical to ensuring that homeowners have the resources they need to navigate the loss mitigation options available to them while they are experiencing financial hardship.
(b) Authorization.—There is authorized to be appropriated the Secretary of Housing and Urban Development $700,000,000 to carry out counseling services described under section 106 of the Housing and Urban Development Act of 1968 (12 U.S.C. 1701x).

SEC. 119. DEFENSE PRODUCTION ACT OF 1950.
(a) Increase In Authorizations.—
(1) AUTHORIZATIONS.—In addition to amounts otherwise authorized to be appropriated, there is authorized to be appropriated in the aggregate $3,000,000,000 for fiscal year 2020 and 2021 to carry out titles I and III of the Defense Production Act of 1950 to produce medical ventilators, personal protection equipment, and other critically needed medical supplies and to carry out any other actions necessary to respond to the COVID–19 emergency.
(2) CARRYOVER FUNDS.—Section 304(e) of the Defense Production Act of 1950 shall not apply at the close of fiscal year 2020.
(3) COVID–19 EMERGENCY.—In this section, the term "COVID–19 emergency" means the emergency declared on March 13, 2020, by the President under the Robert T. Stafford Disaster Relief and Emergency Assistance Act (42 U.S.C. 4121 et seq.) relating to the Coronavirus Disease 2019 (COVID–19) pandemic.
(b) Strengthening Congressional Oversight; Public Portal.—
(1) IN GENERAL.—Not later than three months after the date of enactment of this Act, and every three months thereafter, the Secretary of Commerce, in coordination with the Secretary of Health and Human Services, the Secretary of Defense, and any other Federal department or agency that has utilized authority under title I or title III of the Defense Production Act of 1950 to respond to the COVID–19 emergency, shall submit a report to the Committee on Financial Services of the House of Representatives and the Committee on Banking, Housing, and Urban Affairs of the Senate—
(A) on the use of such authority and the expenditure of any funds in connection with such authority;
(B) that includes details of each purchase order made using such authorities, including the product and amount of product ordered and the entity that fulfilled the contract.
(2) PUBLIC AVAILABILITY.—The Secretary of Commerce shall place all reports submitted under paragraph (1) on an appropriate website available to the public, in an easily searchable format.
(3) SUNSET.—The requirements under this section shall terminate after the

expenditure of all funds appropriated pursuant to the authorizations under subsection (a).

TITLE II—ASSISTING SMALL BUSINESSES AND COMMUNITY FINANCIAL INSTITUTIONS

SEC. 201. SMALL BUSINESS CREDIT FACILITY.

(a) Establishment.—The Board of Governors of the Federal Reserve System shall establish a credit facility to provide loans to small businesses during the COVID–19 emergency.

(b) Definitions.—In this section:

(1) COVID–19 EMERGENCY.—The term "COVID–19 emergency" means the period that begins upon the date of the enactment of this Act and ends on the date of the termination by the Federal Emergency Management Agency of the emergency declared on March 13, 2020, by the President under the Robert T. Stafford Disaster Relief and Emergency Assistance Act (42 U.S.C. 4121 et seq.) relating to the Coronavirus Disease 2019 (COVID–19) pandemic.

(2) SMALL BUSINESS.—The term "small business" means—

(A) a small business concern (as defined under section 3 of the Small Business Act (15 U.S.C. 632);

(B) a family farm;

(C) an independent contractor; and

(D) any other class of businesses to which the Board of Governors determines loans would promote full employment and price stability.

SEC. 202. SMALL BUSINESS FINANCIAL ASSISTANCE PROGRAM.

(a) In General.—The Secretary of the Treasury shall establish a Small Business Financial Assistance Program under which the Secretary shall provide loans and loan guarantees to small businesses.

(b) Application.—In making loans and loan guarantees under this section, the Secretary shall—

(1) provide a simple application process for borrowers; and

(2) establish clear and easy to understand underwriting standards for such loans.

(c) Zero-Interest Loans.—Loans made by or guaranteed by the Secretary under this section shall be zero-interest loans, if the small business receiving such loan does not involuntarily terminate any employee of the small business during the COVID–19 emergency.

(d) Advance.—

(1) IN GENERAL.—Upon request from an applicant for a loan under this section, the Secretary may provide to such applicant an advance, in cash, to such applicant.

(2) AMOUNT.—An advance provided under paragraph (1) shall be in an amount equal to the revenue of the applicant for the period beginning January

1, 2020 and ending January 31, 2020.

(3) PROCEDURES.—

(A) REVIEW.—The Secretary shall have 1 week from the receipt of a request for an advance under paragraph (1) to conduct a risk assessment of the applicant to determine whether to approve or deny such request.

(B) APPROVAL.—If the Secretary does not deny a request under subparagraph (A), the advance shall be directly deposited into the account identified by the applicant.

(C) REMAINING FUNDS.—Not later than 4 weeks after approving a request of an applicant under subparagraph (A), the Secretary shall disburse the remaining funds to such applicant.

(e) Forgiveness.—If small business that receives a loan or loan guarantee under this section demonstrates to the Secretary that the number of full-time employees of such small business on the date such small business submitted an application under this section is greater than or equal to the number of full-time employees of such small business on the date that is 1 year after the date of such submission, the Secretary shall forgive the remaining outstanding principal and interest on such loan or loan guarantee.

(f) Funding.—The Secretary shall use $50,000,000,000 from the Exchange Stabilization Fund, without further appropriation, to carry out this section.

(g) Definitions.—In this section:

(1) COVID–19 EMERGENCY.—The term "COVID–19 emergency" means the period that—

(A) begins on the declaration of the emergency declared on March 13, 2020, by the President under the Robert T. Stafford Disaster Relief and Emergency Assistance Act (42 U.S.C. 4121 et seq.) relating to the Coronavirus Disease 2019 (COVID–19) pandemic; and

(B) ends on the termination by the Federal Emergency Management Agency of such emergency.

(2) SMALL BUSINESS.—The term "small business" means—

(A) a small business concern (as defined under section 3 of the Small Business Act (15 U.S.C. 632);

(B) a family farm; and

(C) an independent contractor.

SEC. 203. LOAN AND OBLIGATION PAYMENT RELIEF FOR AFFECTED SMALL BUSINESSES AND NON-PROFITS.

(a) In General.—

(1) IN GENERAL.—During the COVID–19 emergency, a debt collector may not, with respect to a debt of a small business or non-profit (other than debt related to a federally related mortgage loan)—

(A) capitalize unpaid interest;

(B) apply a higher interest rate triggered by the nonpayment of a debt to the debt balance;

(C) charge a fee triggered by the nonpayment of a debt;
(D) sue or threaten to sue for nonpayment of a debt;
(E) continue litigation to collect a debt that was initiated before the date of enactment of this section;
(F) submit or cause to be submitted a confession of judgment to any court;
(G) enforce a security interest through repossession, limitation of use, or foreclosure;
(H) take or threaten to take any action to enforce collection, or any adverse action for nonpayment of a debt, or for nonappearance at any hearing relating to a debt;
(I) commence or continue any action to cause or to seek to cause the collection of a debt, including pursuant to a court order issued before the end of the 120-day period following the end of the COVID–19 emergency, from wages, Federal benefits, or other amounts due to a small business or non-profit by way of garnishment, deduction, offset, or other seizure;
(J) cause or seek to cause the collection of a debt, including pursuant to a court order issued before the end of the 120-day period following the end of the COVID–19 emergency, by levying on funds from a bank account or seizing any other assets of a small business or non-profit;
(K) commence or continue an action to evict a small business or non-profit from real or personal property; or
(L) disconnect or terminate service from utility service, including electricity, natural gas, telecommunications or broadband, water, or sewer.
(2) RULE OF CONSTRUCTION.—Nothing in this subsection may be construed to prohibit a small business or non-profit from voluntarily paying, in whole or in part, a debt.
(3) REPAYMENT PERIOD.—After the expiration of the COVID–19 emergency, with respect to a debt described under paragraph (1), a debt collector—
(A) may not add to the debt balance any interest or fee prohibited by paragraph (1);
(B) shall, for credit with a defined term or payment period, extend the time period to repay the debt balance by 1 payment period for each payment that a small business or non-profit missed during the COVID–19 emergency, with the payments due in the same amounts and at the same intervals as the pre-existing payment schedule;
(C) shall, for an open end credit plan (as defined under section 103 of the Truth in Lending Act) or other credit without a defined term, allow the small business or non-profit to repay the debt balance in a manner that does not exceed the amounts permitted by formulas under section 170(c) of the Truth in Lending Act and regulations promulgated thereunder; and
(D) shall, when the small business or non-profit notifies the debt collector, offer reasonable and affordable repayment plans, loan modifications, refinancing, options with a reasonable time in which to repay the debt.

(4) COMMUNICATIONS IN CONNECTION WITH THE COLLECTION OF A DEBT.—

(A) IN GENERAL.—During the COVID–19 emergency, without prior consent of a small business or non-profit given directly to a debt collector during the COVID–19 emergency, or the express permission of a court of competent jurisdiction, a debt collector may only communicate in writing in connection with the collection of any debt (other than debt related to a federally related mortgage loan).

(B) REQUIRED DISCLOSURES.—

(i) IN GENERAL.—All written communications described under subparagraph (A) shall inform the small business or non-profit that the communication is for informational purposes and is not an attempt to collect a debt.

(ii) REQUIREMENTS.—The disclosure required under clause (i) shall be made—

(I) in type or lettering not smaller than 14-point bold type;

(II) separate from any other disclosure;

(III) in a manner designed to ensure that the recipient sees the disclosure clearly;

(IV) in English and Spanish and in any additional languages in which the debt collector communicates, including the language in which the loan was negotiated, to the extent known by the debt collector; and

(V) may be provided by first-class mail or electronically, if the borrower has otherwise consented to electronic communication with the debt collector and has not revoked such consent.

(iii) ORAL NOTIFICATION.—Any oral notification shall be provided in the language the debt collector otherwise uses to communicate with the borrower.

(iv) WRITTEN TRANSLATIONS.—In providing written notifications in languages other than English in this Section, a debt collector may rely on written translations developed by the Bureau of Consumer Financial Protection.

(5) VIOLATIONS.—

(A) IN GENERAL.—Any person who violates this section shall—

(i) except as provided under clause (ii), be subject to civil liability in accordance with section 813 of the Fair Debt Collection Practices Act, as if the person is a debt collector for purposes of that section.

(B) PREDISPUTE ARBITRATION AGREEMENTS.—Notwithstanding any other provision of law, no predispute arbitration agreement or predispute joint-action waiver shall be valid or enforceable with respect to a dispute brought under this section, including a dispute as to the applicability of this section, which shall be determined under Federal law.

(6) TOLLING.—Except as provided in paragraph (7)(D), any applicable time limitations, including statutes of limitations, related to a debt under Federal or State law shall be tolled during the COVID–19 emergency.

(7) CLAIMS OF AFFECTED CREDITORS AND DEBT COLLECTORS.—

(A) VALUATION OF PROPERTY.—With respect to any action asserting a taking under the Fifth Amendment of the Constitution of the United States as a result of this section or seeking a declaratory judgment regarding the constitutionality of this section, the value of the property alleged to have been taken without just compensation shall be evaluated—

(i) with consideration of the likelihood of full and timely payment of the obligation without the actions taken pursuant to this section; and

(ii) without consideration of any assistance provided directly or indirectly to the small business or non-profit from other Federal, State, and local government programs instituted or legislation enacted in response to the COVID–19 emergency.

(B) SCOPE OF JUST COMPENSATION.—In an action described in subparagraph (A), any assistance or benefit provided directly or indirectly to the person from other Federal, State, and local government programs instituted in or legislation enacted response to the COVID–19 emergency, shall be deemed to be compensation for the property taken, even if such assistance or benefit is not specifically provided as compensation for property taken by this section.

(C) APPEALS.—Any appeal from an action under this section shall be treated under section 158 of title 28, United States Code, as if it were an appeal in a case under title 11, United States Code.

(D) REPOSE.—Any action asserting a taking under the Fifth Amendment to the Constitution of the United States as a result of this section shall be brought within not later than 180 days after the end of the COVID–19 emergency.

(8) DEFINITIONS.—In this section:

(A) COVID–19 EMERGENCY.—The term "COVID–19 emergency" means the period that begins upon the date of the enactment of this Act and ends on the date of the termination by the Federal Emergency Management Agency of the emergency declared on March 13, 2020, by the President under the Robert T. Stafford Disaster Relief and Emergency Assistance Act (42 U.S.C. 4121 et seq.) relating to the Coronavirus Disease 2019 (COVID–19) pandemic.

(B) CREDITOR.—The term "creditor" means—

(i) any person who offers or extends credit creating a debt or to whom a debt is owed or other obligation for payment;

(ii) any lessor of real or personal property; or

(iii) any provider of utility services.

(C) DEBT.—The term "debt"—

(i) means any obligation or alleged obligation—

(I) for which the original agreement, or if there is no agreement, the original obligation to pay was created before or during the COVID–19 emergency, whether or not such obligation has been reduced to judgment; and

(II) that arises out of a transaction with a small business or non-profit; and

(ii) does not include a federally related mortgage loan.

(D) DEBT COLLECTOR.—The term "debt collector" means a creditor, and any person or entity that engages in the collection of debt, including the Federal Government and a State government, irrespective of whether the debt is allegedly owed to or assigned to that person or to the entity.

(E) FEDERALLY RELATED MORTGAGE LOAN.—The term "federally related mortgage loan" has the meaning given that term under section 3 of the Real Estate Settlement Procedures Act of 1974 (12 U.S.C. 2602).

(F) NON-PROFIT.—The term "non-profit" means an organization described in section 501(c)(3) of the Internal Revenue Code of 1986 and exempt from taxation under section 501(a) of such Code.

(G) SMALL BUSINESS.—The term "small business" has the meaning given the term "small business concern" under section 3 of the Small Business Act.

(b) Credit Facility For Other Purposes.—The Board of Governors of the Federal Reserve System shall establish a facility that the Board of Governors shall use to make payments to holders of loans or obligations to compensate such holders for documented financial losses—

(1) with respect to a loan made to an individual, small business, or non-profit; and

(2) where such losses were caused by a suspension of payments required under Federal law in connection with the COVID–19 emergency.

SEC. 204. REAUTHORIZATION OF THE STATE SMALL BUSINESS CREDIT INITIATIVE ACT OF 2010.

The State Small Business Credit Initiative Act of 2010 (15 U.S.C. 5701 et seq.) is amended—

(1) by striking "2009 allocation" each place such term appears and inserting "2019 allocation";

(2) by striking "2010 allocation" each place such term appears and inserting "2020 allocation";

(3) by striking "date of enactment of this Act" each place it appears and inserting "date of the enactment of the Small Business Support and Access to Capital Act of 2020";

(4) by striking "date of the enactment of this Act" each place it appears and inserting "date of the enactment of the Small Business Support and Access to Capital Act of 2020";

(5) in section 3003(b)(2)—

(A) in the section heading, by striking "2009 ALLOCATION FORMULA" and inserting striking "2019 ALLOCATION FORMULA";

(B) by striking "2008 State employment decline" each place such term appears and inserting "2018 State employment decline";

(C) in subparagraph (A), by striking "2009 allocation" and inserting "2019 allocation"; and

(D) in subparagraph (C)—

(i) in the subparagraph heading, by striking "2008 STATE EMPLOYMENT

DECLINE DEFINED" and inserting "2018 STATE EMPLOYMENT DECLINE DEFINED";
(ii) in clause (i), by striking "December 2007" and inserting "December 2017"; and
(iii) in clause (ii), by striking "December 2008" and inserting "December 2018";
(6) in section 3003(b)(3)—
(A) in the section heading, by striking "2010 ALLOCATION FORMULA" and inserting striking "2020 ALLOCATION FORMULA";
(B) by striking "2009 unemployment number" each place such term appears and inserting "2019 unemployment number"; and
(C) in subparagraph (C)—
(i) in the subparagraph heading, by striking "2009 UNEMPLOYMENT NUMBER DEFINED" and inserting "2019 UNEMPLOYMENT NUMBER DEFINED"; and
(ii) by striking "December 2009" and inserting "December 2019";
(7) in section 3005(e), by striking "to the Secretary a report" and inserting "to the Secretary and Congress a report";
(8) in section 3007—
(A) in subsection (a)(1), by striking " to the Secretary a report " and inserting "to the Secretary and Congress a report"; and
(B) in subsection (b)—
(i) by striking "March 31, 2011" and inserting "March 31, 2021"; and
(ii) by striking "to the Secretary" and inserting "to the Secretary and Congress"; and
(9) in section 3009—
(A) in subsection (b), by striking "$1,500,000,000" and inserting "$10,000,000,000";
(B) in subsection (c), by adding at the end the following new sentence: "At the end of such period, any amounts that remain unexpended or unobligated shall be transferred to the Community Development Financial Institutions Fund established under section 104(a) of the Riegle Community Development and Regulatory Improvement Act of 1994.".

SEC. 205. FUNDING OF THE INITIATIVE TO BUILD GROWTH EQUITY FUNDS FOR MINORITY BUSINESSES.

(a) Grant.—The Minority Business Development Agency shall provide a grant of $3,000,0000,000 to fully implement the Initiative to Build Growth Equity Funds for Minority Businesses (the "Initiative"; award number MB19OBD8020113), including to use such amounts as capital for the Equity Funds.
(b) Administrative Expenses.—Of the amounts provided under subsection (a), the grant recipient may use not more than 2.25 percent of such amount for administrative expenses, of which—

(1) not more than 1.5 percent per annum may be used for fees to be paid to investment managers for fund investment activities, including deal sourcing, due diligence, investment monitoring, and investment reporting; and

(2) not more than 0.75 percent per annum may be used for fund administration activities by the grant recipient, including fund manager evaluation, selection, monitoring, and overall fund program management.

(c) Treatment Of Interest.—Notwithstanding any other provision of law, with the approval of the Minority Business Development Agency, grant funds made available under subsection (a) may be deposited in interest-bearing accounts pending disbursement, and any interest which accrues may be retained without returning such interest to the Treasury of the United States and interest earned may be obligated and expended for the purposes for which the grant was made available without further appropriation.

(d) Reporting And Audit Requirements.—

(1) REPORTING BY RECIPIENT.—The grant recipient under this section shall issue a report to the Minority Business Development Agency every 6 months detailing the use of grant funds received under this section and any other information that the Minority Business Development Agency may require.

(2) ANNUAL REPORT TO CONGRESS.—The Minority Business Development Agency shall issue an annual report to the Congress containing the information received under paragraph (1) and an analysis of the implementation of the Initiative.

(3) GAO AUDIT.—The Comptroller General of the United States shall, every 2 years, carry out an audit of the Initiative and issue a report to the Congress and the Minority Business Development Agency containing the results of such audit.

(4) FUND MANAGERS.—Fund managers shall annually report on their fund management activities, including—

(A) fund performance;

(B) impacts of capital investments by industry and geography;

(C) racial, ethnic, and gender demographics of minority businesses receiving capital from the Initiative; and

(D) any other ancillary and economic benefits of capital investments from the Initiative.

(e) Funding.—There is authorized to be appropriated to the Minority Business Development Agency $3,000,000,000 to make the grant described under subsection (a).

SEC. 206. COMMUNITY DEVELOPMENT FINANCIAL INSTITUTIONS FUND SUPPLEMENTAL APPROPRIATION AUTHORIZATION.

There is authorized to be appropriated $1,000,000,000 for fiscal year 2020, for providing financial assistance and technical assistance under subparagraphs (A) and (B) of section 108(a)(1) of the Community Development Banking and Financial Institutions Act of 1994 (12 U.S.C. 4707(a)(1)), except that subsections (d) and (e) of such section 108 shall not apply to the provision of such assistance.

SEC. 207. MINORITY DEPOSITORY INSTITUTION.

(a) Sense Of Congress On Funding The Loan-Loss Reserve Fund For Small Dollar Loans.—The sense of Congress is the following:

(1) The Community Development Financial Institutions Fund (the "CDFI Fund") is an agency of the Department of the Treasury, and was established by the Riegle Community Development and Regulatory Improvement Act of 1994. The mission of the CDFI Fund is "to expand economic opportunity for underserved people and communities by supporting the growth and capacity of a national network of community development lenders, investors, and financial service providers". A community development financial institution (a "CDFI") is a specialized financial institution serving low-income communities and a Community Development Entity (a "CDE") is a domestic corporation or partnership that is an intermediary vehicle for the provision of loans, investments, or financial counseling in low-income communities. The CDFI Fund certifies CDFIs and CDEs. Becoming a certified CDFI or CDE allows organizations to participate in various CDFI Fund programs as follows:

(A) The Bank Enterprise Award Program, which provides FDIC-insured depository institutions awards for a demonstrated increase in lending and investments in distressed communities and CDFIs.

(B) The CDFI Program, which provides Financial and Technical Assistance awards to CDFIs to reinvest in the CDFI, and to build the capacity of the CDFI, including financing product development and loan loss reserves.

(C) The Native American CDFI Assistance Program, which provides CDFIs and sponsoring entities Financial and Technical Assistance awards to increase lending and grow the number of CDFIs owned by Native Americans to help build capacity of such CDFIs.

(D) The New Market Tax Credit Program, which provides tax credits for making equity investments in CDEs that stimulate capital investments in low-income communities.

(E) The Capital Magnet Fund, which provides awards to CDFIs and nonprofit affordable housing organizations to finance affordable housing solutions and related economic development activities.

(F) The Bond Guarantee Program, a source of long-term, patient capital for CDFIs to expand lending and investment capacity for community and economic development purposes.

(2) The Department of the Treasury is authorized to create multi-year grant programs designed to encourage low-to-moderate income individuals to establish accounts at federally insured banks, and to improve low-to-moderate income individuals' access to such accounts on reasonable terms.

(3) Under this authority, grants to participants in CDFI Fund programs may

be used for loan-loss reserves and to establish small-dollar loan programs by subsidizing related losses. These grants also allow for the providing recipients with the financial counseling and education necessary to conduct transactions and manage their accounts. These loans provide low-cost alternatives to payday loans and other nontraditional forms of financing that often impose excessive interest rates and fees on borrowers, and lead millions of Americans to fall into debt traps. Small-dollar loans can only be made pursuant to terms, conditions, and practices that are reasonable for the individual consumer obtaining the loan.

(4) Program participation is restricted to eligible institutions, which are limited to organizations listed in section 501(c)(3) of the Internal Revenue Code and exempt from tax under 501(a) of such Code, federally insured depository institutions, community development financial institutions and State, local, or Tribal government entities.

(5) Since its founding, the CDFI Fund has awarded over $3,300,000,000 to CDFIs and CDEs, allocated $54,000,000,000 in tax credits, and $1,510,000,000 in bond guarantees. According to the CDFI Fund, some programs attract as much as $10 in private capital for every $1 invested by the CDFI Fund. The Administration and the Congress should prioritize appropriation of funds for the loan loss reserve fund and technical assistance programs administered by the Community Development Financial Institution Fund, as included in the version of the "Financial Services and General Government Appropriations Act, 2020" (H.R. 3351) that passed the House of Representatives on June, 26, 2019.

(b) Definitions.—In this section:

(1) COMMUNITY DEVELOPMENT FINANCIAL INSTITUTION.—The term "community development financial institution" has the meaning given under section 103 of the Riegle Community Development and Regulatory Improvement Act of 1994 (12 U.S.C. 4702).

(2) MINORITY DEPOSITORY INSTITUTION.—The term "minority depository institution" has the meaning given under section 308 of the Financial Institutions Reform, Recovery, and Enforcement Act of 1989 (12 U.S.C. 1463 note), as amended by this Act.

(c) Inclusion Of Women's Banks In The Definition Of Minority Depository Institution.—Section 308(b)(1) of the Financial Institutions Reform, Recovery, and Enforcement Act of 1989 (12 U.S.C. 1463 note) is amended—

(1) by redesignating subparagraphs (A), (B), and (C) as clauses (i), (ii), and (iii), respectively;

(2) by striking "means any" and inserting the following: means—

"(A) any"; and

(3) in clause (iii) (as so redesignated), by striking the period at the end and inserting "; or"; and

(4) by inserting at the end the following new subparagraph:

"(B) any bank described in clause (i), (ii), or (iii) of section 19(b)(1)(A) of the

Federal Reserve Act—
"(i) more than 50 percent of the outstanding shares of which are held by 1 or more women; and
"(ii) the majority of the directors on the board of directors of which are women.".
(d) Establishment Of Impact Bank Designation.—
(1) IN GENERAL.—Each appropriate Federal banking agency shall establish a program under which a depository institution with total consolidated assets of less than $10,000,000,000 may elect to be designated as an impact bank if 50 percent or more of the loans extended by such covered bank are extended to low-income borrowers.
(2) DESIGNATION.—Based on data obtained through examinations, an appropriate Federal banking agency shall submit a notification to a depository institution stating that the depository institution qualifies for designation as an impact bank.
(3) APPLICATION.—A depository institution that does not receive a notification described in paragraph (2) may submit an application to the appropriate Federal banking agency demonstrating that the depository institution qualifies for designation as an impact bank.
(4) ADDITIONAL DATA OR OVERSIGHT.—A depository institution is not required to submit additional data to an appropriate Federal banking agency or be subject to additional oversight from such an agency if such data or oversight is related specifically and solely for consideration for a designation as an impact bank.
(5) REMOVAL OF DESIGNATION.—If an appropriate Federal banking agency determines that a depository institution designated as an impact bank no longer meets the criteria for such designation, the appropriate Federal banking agency shall rescind the designation and notify the depository institution of such rescission.
(6) RECONSIDERATION OF DESIGNATION; APPEALS.—A depository institution may—
(A) submit to the appropriate Federal banking agency a request to reconsider a determination that such depository institution no longer meets the criteria for the designation; or
(B) file an appeal in accordance with procedures established by the appropriate Federal banking agency.
(7) RULEMAKING.—Not later than 1 year after the date of the enactment of this Act, the appropriate Federal banking agencies shall jointly issue rules to carry out the requirements of this subsection, including by providing a definition of a low-income borrower.
(8) FEDERAL DEPOSIT INSURANCE ACT DEFINITIONS.—In this subsection, the terms "depository institution" and "appropriate Federal banking agency" have the meanings given such terms, respectively, in section 3 of the Federal Deposit Insurance Act (12 U.S.C. 1813).

(e) Minority Depository Institutions Advisory Committees.—

(1) ESTABLISHMENT.—Each covered regulator shall establish an advisory committee to be called the "Minority Depository Institutions Advisory Committee".

(2) DUTIES.—Each Minority Depository Institutions Advisory Committee shall provide advice to the respective covered regulator on meeting the goals established by section 308 of the Financial Institutions Reform, Recovery, and Enforcement Act of 1989 (12 U.S.C. 1463 note) to preserve the present number of covered minority institutions, preserve the minority character of minority-owned institutions in cases involving mergers or acquisitions, provide technical assistance, and encourage the creation of new covered minority institutions. The scope of the work of each such Minority Depository Institutions Advisory Committee shall include an assessment of the current condition of covered minority institutions, what regulatory changes or other steps the respective agencies may be able to take to fulfill the requirements of such section 308, and other issues of concern to minority depository institutions.

(3) MEMBERSHIP.—

(A) IN GENERAL.—Each Minority Depository Institutions Advisory Committee shall consist of no more than 10 members, who—

(i) shall serve for one two-year term;

(ii) shall serve as a representative of a depository institution or an insured credit union with respect to which the respective covered regulator is the covered regulator of such depository institution or insured credit union; and

(iii) shall not receive pay by reason of their service on the advisory committee, but may receive travel or transportation expenses in accordance with section 5703 of title 5, United States Code.

(B) DIVERSITY.—To the extent practicable, each covered regulator shall ensure that the members of Minority Depository Institutions Advisory Committee of such agency reflect the diversity of depository institutions.

(4) MEETINGS.—

(A) IN GENERAL.—Each Minority Depository Institutions Advisory Committee shall meet not less frequently than twice each year.

(B) INVITATIONS.—Each Minority Depository Institutions Advisory Committee shall invite the attendance at each meeting of the Minority Depository Institutions Advisory Committee of—

(i) one member of the majority party and one member of the minority party of the Committee on Financial Services of the House of Representatives and the Committee on Banking, Housing, and Urban Affairs of the Senate; and

(ii) one member of the majority party and one member of the minority party of any relevant subcommittees of such committees.

(5) NO TERMINATION OF ADVISORY COMMITTEES.—The termination requirements under section 14 of the Federal Advisory Committee Act (5 U.S.C. app.) shall not apply to a Minority Depository Institutions Advisory

Committee established pursuant to this subsection.
(6) DEFINITIONS.—In this subsection:
(A) COVERED REGULATOR.—The term "covered regulator" means the Comptroller of the Currency, the Board of Governors of the Federal Reserve System, the Federal Deposit Insurance Corporation, and the National Credit Union Administration.
(B) COVERED MINORITY INSTITUTION.—The term "covered minority institution" means a minority depository institution (as defined in section 308(b) of the Financial Institutions Reform, Recovery, and Enforcement Act of 1989 (12 U.S.C. 1463 note)) or a minority credit union (as defined in section 1204(c) of the Financial Institutions Reform, Recovery, and Enforcement Act of 1989, as amended by this Act).
(C) DEPOSITORY INSTITUTION.—The term "depository institution" has the meaning given under section 3 of the Federal Deposit Insurance Act (12 U.S.C. 1813).
(D) INSURED CREDIT UNION.—The term "insured credit union" has the meaning given in section 101 of the Federal Credit Union Act (12 U.S.C. 1752).
(7) TECHNICAL AMENDMENT.—Section 308(b) of the Financial Institutions Reform, Recovery, and Enforcement Act of 1989 (12 U.S.C. 1463 note) is amended by adding at the end the following new paragraph:
"(3) DEPOSITORY INSTITUTION.—The term 'depository institution' means an 'insured depository institution' (as defined in section 3 of the Federal Deposit Insurance Act (12 U.S.C. 1813)) and an insured credit union (as defined in section 101 of the Federal Credit Union Act (12 U.S.C. 1752)).".
(f) Federal Deposits In Minority Depository Institutions.—
(1) IN GENERAL.—Section 308 of the Financial Institutions Reform, Recovery, and Enforcement Act of 1989 (12 U.S.C. 1463 note) is amended—
(A) by adding at the end the following new subsection:
"(d) Federal Deposits.—The Secretary of the Treasury shall ensure that deposits made by Federal agencies in minority depository institutions and impact banks are fully collateralized or fully insured, as determined by the Secretary. Such deposits shall include reciprocal deposits as defined in section 337.6(e)(2)(v) of title 12, Code of Federal Regulations (as in effect on March 6, 2019)."; and
(B) in subsection (b), as amended by section 6(g), by adding at the end the following new paragraph:
"(4) IMPACT BANK.—The term 'impact bank' means a depository institution designated by an appropriate Federal banking agency pursuant to section 5 of the Ensuring Diversity in Community Banking Act of 2020.".
(2) TECHNICAL AMENDMENTS.—Section 308 of the Financial Institutions Reform, Recovery, and Enforcement Act of 1989 (12 U.S.C. 1463 note) is amended—
(A) in the matter preceding paragraph (1), by striking "section—" and

inserting "section:"; and
(B) in the paragraph heading for paragraph (1), by striking "FINANCIAL" and inserting "DEPOSITORY".
(g) Minority Bank Deposit Program.—
(1) IN GENERAL.—Section 1204 of the Financial Institutions Reform, Recovery, and Enforcement Act of 1989 (12 U.S.C. 1811 note) is amended to read as follows:

"SEC. 1204. EXPANSION OF USE OF MINORITY BANKS AND MINORITY CREDIT UNIONS.
"(a) Minority Bank Deposit Program.—
"(1) ESTABLISHMENT.—There is established a program to be known as the 'Minority Bank Deposit Program' to expand the use of minority banks and minority credit unions.
"(2) ADMINISTRATION.—The Secretary of the Treasury, acting through the Fiscal Service, shall—
"(A) on application by a depository institution or credit union, certify whether such depository institution or credit union is a minority bank or minority credit union;
"(B) maintain and publish a list of all depository institutions and credit unions that have been certified pursuant to subparagraph (A); and
"(C) periodically distribute the list described in subparagraph (B) to—
"(i) all Federal departments and agencies;
"(ii) interested State and local governments; and
"(iii) interested private sector companies.
"(3) INCLUSION OF CERTAIN ENTITIES ON LIST.—A depository institution or credit union that, on the date of the enactment of this section, has a current certification from the Secretary of the Treasury stating that such depository institution or credit union is a minority bank or minority credit union shall be included on the list described under paragraph (2)(B).
"(b) Expanded Use Among Federal Departments And Agencies.—
"(1) IN GENERAL.—Not later than 1 year after the establishment of the program described in subsection (a), the head of each Federal department or agency shall develop and implement standards and procedures to ensure, to the maximum extent possible as permitted by law, the use of minority banks and minority credit unions to serve the financial needs of each such department or agency.
"(2) REPORT TO CONGRESS.—Not later than 2 years after the establishment of the program described in subsection (a), and annually thereafter, the head of each Federal department or agency shall submit to Congress a report on the actions taken to increase the use of minority banks and minority credit unions to serve the financial needs of each such department or agency.
"(c) Definitions.—For purposes of this section:
"(1) CREDIT UNION.—The term 'credit union' has the meaning given the

term 'insured credit union' in section 101 of the Federal Credit Union Act (12 U.S.C. 1752).

"(2) DEPOSITORY INSTITUTION.—The term 'depository institution' has the meaning given the term 'insured depository institution' in section 3 of the Federal Deposit Insurance Act (12 U.S.C. 1813).

"(3) MINORITY.—The term 'minority' means any Black American, Native American, Hispanic American, or Asian American.

"(4) MINORITY BANK.—The term 'minority bank' means a minority depository institution as defined in section 308 of this Act.

"(5) MINORITY CREDIT UNION.—The term 'minority credit union' means any credit union for which more than 50 percent of the membership (including board members) of such credit union are minority individuals, as determined by the National Credit Union Administration pursuant to section 308 of this Act.".

(2) CONFORMING AMENDMENTS.—The following provisions are amended by striking "1204(c)(3)" and inserting "1204(c)":

(A) Section 808(b)(3) of the Community Reinvestment Act of 1977 (12 U.S.C. 2907(b)(3)).

(B) Section 40(g)(1)(B) of the Federal Deposit Insurance Act (12 U.S.C. 1831q(g)(1)(B)).

(C) Section 704B(h)(4) of the Equal Credit Opportunity Act (15 U.S.C. 1691c–2(h)(4)).

(h) Diversity Report And Best Practices.—

(1) ANNUAL REPORT.—Each covered regulator shall submit to Congress an annual report on diversity including the following:

(A) Data, based on voluntary self-identification, on the racial, ethnic, and gender composition of the examiners of each covered regulator, disaggregated by length of time served as an examiner.

(B) The status of any examiners of covered regulators, based on voluntary self-identification, as a veteran.

(C) Whether any covered regulator, as of the date on which the report required under this subsection is submitted, has adopted a policy, plan, or strategy to promote racial, ethnic, and gender diversity among examiners of the covered regulator.

(D) Whether any special training is developed and provided for examiners related specifically to working with banks that serve communities that are predominantly minorities, low income, or rural, and the key focus of such training.

(2) BEST PRACTICES.—Each Office of Minority and Women Inclusion of a covered regulator shall develop, provide to the head of the covered regulator, and make publicly available best practices—

(A) for increasing the diversity of candidates applying for examiner positions, including through outreach efforts to recruit diverse candidate to apply for entry-level examiner positions; and

(B) for retaining and providing fair consideration for promotions within the examiner staff for purposes of achieving diversity among examiners.
(3) COVERED REGULATOR DEFINED.—In this subsection, the term "covered regulator" means the Comptroller of the Currency, the Board of Governors of the Federal Reserve System, the Federal Deposit Insurance Corporation, and the National Credit Union Administration.
(i) Investments In Minority Depository Institutions And Impact Banks.—
(1) CONTROL FOR CERTAIN INSTITUTIONS.—Section 7(j)(8)(B) of the Federal Deposit Insurance Act (12 U.S.C. 1817(j)(8)(B)) is amended to read as follows:
"(B) 'control' means the power, directly or indirectly—
"(i) to direct the management or policies of an insured depository institution; or
"(ii) (I) with respect to an insured depository institution, of a person to vote 25 per centum or more of any class of voting securities of such institution; or
"(II) with respect to an insured depository institution that is an impact bank (as designated pursuant to section 5 of the Ensuring Diversity in Community Banking Act of 2020) or a minority depository institution (as defined in section 308(b) of the Financial Institutions Reform, Recovery, and Enforcement Act of 1989), of an individual to vote 30 percent of more of any class of voting securities of such an impact bank or a minority depository institution.".
(2) RULEMAKING.—The appropriate Federal banking agency (as defined in section 3 of the Federal Deposit Insurance Act (12 U.S.C. 1813)) shall jointly issue rules for de novo minority depository institutions and de novo impact banks (as designated pursuant to section 5) to allow 3 years to meet the capital requirements otherwise applicable to minority depository institutions and impact banks.
(3) REPORT.—Not later than 1 year after the date of the enactment of this Act, the appropriate Federal banking agencies shall jointly submit to Congress a report on—
(A) the principal causes for the low number of de novo minority depository institutions during the 10-year period preceding the date of the report;
(B) the main challenges to the creation of de novo minority depository institutions and de novo impact banks; and
(C) regulatory and legislative considerations to promote the establishment of de novo minority depository institutions and de novo impact banks.
(j) Requirement To Mentor Minority Depository Institutions Or Community Development Financial Institutions To Serve As A Depositary Or Financial Agent.—
(1) IN GENERAL.—Before a large financial institution may be employed as a financial agent of the Department of the Treasury or perform any reasonable duties as depositary of public moneys of the Department of the Treasury, the large financial institution shall demonstrate participation as a mentor in a covered mentor-protege program to a protege firm that is a minority

depository institution or a community development financial institution.

(2) REPORT.—Not later than 6 months after the date of the enactment of this Act and annually thereafter, the Secretary of the Treasury shall submit to Congress a report on participants in a covered mentor-protege program, including an analysis of outcomes of such program.

(3) PROCEDURES.—The Secretary of the Treasury shall publish procedures for compliance with the requirements of this subsection for large financial institutions.

(4) DEFINITIONS.—In this subsection:

(A) COVERED MENTOR-PROTEGE PROGRAM.—The term "covered mentor-protege program" means a mentor-protege program established by the Secretary of the Treasury pursuant to section 45 of the Small Business Act (15 U.S.C. 657r).

(B) LARGE FINANCIAL INSTITUTION.—The term "large financial institution" means any entity—

(i) regulated by the Comptroller of the Currency, the Board of Governors of the Federal Reserve System, the Federal Deposit Insurance Corporation, or the National Credit Union Administration; and

(ii) that has total consolidated assets greater than or equal to $50,000,000,000.

(k) Custodial Deposit Program For Covered Minority Depository Institutions And Impact Banks.—

(1) ESTABLISHMENT.—The Secretary of the Treasury shall establish a custodial deposit program (in this subsection referred to as the "Program") under which a covered bank shall receive monthly deposits from a qualifying account.

(2) APPLICATION.—A covered bank shall submit to the Secretary an application to participate in the Program at such time, in such manner, and containing such information as the Secretary may determine.

(3) PROGRAM OPERATIONS.—

(A) DESIGNATION OF CUSTODIAL ENTITIES.—The Secretary shall designate eligible custodial entities to make monthly deposits with covered banks selected for participation in the Program on behalf of a qualifying account.

(B) CUSTODIAL ACCOUNTS.—

(i) IN GENERAL.—The Secretary shall establish a custodial deposit account for each qualifying account with the eligible custodial entity designated to make deposits with covered banks for each such qualifying account.

(ii) AMOUNT.—The Secretary shall deposit a total amount not greater than 5 percent of a qualifying account into any custodial deposit accounts established under subparagraph (A).

(iii) DEPOSITS WITH PROGRAM PARTICIPANTS.—

(I) MONTHLY DEPOSITS.—Each month, each eligible custodial entity designated by the Secretary shall deposit an amount not greater than the insured amount, in the aggregate, from each custodial deposit account, in a

single covered bank.
(II) LIMITATION.—With respect to the funds of an individual qualifying account, the eligible custodial entity may not deposit an amount greater than the insured amount in a single covered bank.
(III) INSURED AMOUNT DEFINED.—In this clause, the term "insured amount" means the amount that is the greater of—
(aa) the standard maximum deposit insurance amount (as defined in section 11(a)(1)(E) of the Federal Deposit Insurance Act (12 U.S.C. 1821(a)(1)(E))); or
(bb) such higher amount negotiated between the Secretary and the Corporation under which the Corporation will insure all deposits of such higher amount.
(iv) LIMITATIONS.—The total amount of funds deposited under the Program in a covered bank may not exceed the lesser of—
(I) 10 percent of the average amount of deposits held by such covered bank in the previous quarter; or
(II) $100,000,000.
(C) INTEREST.—
(i) IN GENERAL.—Each eligible custodial entity designated by the Secretary shall—
(I) collect interest from each covered bank in which such custodial entity deposits funds pursuant to subparagraph (B); and
(II) disburse such interest to the Secretary each month.
(ii) INTEREST RATE.—The rate of any interest collected under this subparagraph may not exceed 50 percent of the discount window primary credit interest rate most recently published on the Federal Reserve Statistical Release on selected interest rates (daily or weekly), commonly referred to as the H.15 release (commonly known as the "Federal funds rate").
(D) STATEMENTS.—Each eligible custodial entity designated by the Secretary shall submit to the Secretary monthly statements that include the total amount of funds deposited with, and interest rate received from, each covered bank by the eligible custodial entity on behalf of qualifying entities.
(E) RECORDS.—The Secretary shall issue a quarterly report to Congress and make publicly available a record identifying all covered banks participating in the Program and amounts deposited under the Program in covered banks.
(4) REQUIREMENTS RELATING TO DEPOSITS.—Deposits made with covered banks under this subsection may not—
(A) be considered by the Corporation to be funds obtained, directly or indirectly, by or through any deposit broker for deposit into 1 or more deposit accounts (as described under section 29 of the Federal Deposit Insurance Act (12 U.S.C. 1831f)); or
(B) be subject to insurance fees from the Corporation that are greater than insurance fees for typical demand deposits not obtained, directly or indirectly, by or through any deposit broker (commonly known as "core deposits").
(5) MODIFICATIONS.—

(A) IN GENERAL.—The Secretary shall provide a 3-month period for public notice and comment before making any material change to the operation of the Program.

(B) EXCEPTION.—The requirements of subparagraph (A) shall not apply if the Secretary makes a material change to the Program to comply with safety and soundness standards or other law.

(6) TERMINATION.—

(A) BY COVERED BANK.—A covered bank selected for participation in the Program pursuant to paragraph (3) may terminate participation in the Program by providing the Secretary a notification 60 days prior to termination.

(B) BY SECRETARY.—The Secretary may terminate the participation of a covered bank in the Program if the Secretary determines the covered bank—

(i) violated any terms of participation in the Program;

(ii) failed to comply with Federal bank secrecy laws, as documented in writing by the primary regulator of the covered bank;

(iii) failed to remain well capitalized; or

(iv) failed comply with safety and soundness standards, as documented in writing by the primary regulator of the covered bank.

(7) DEFINITIONS.—In this subsection:

(A) CORPORATION.—The term "Corporation" means the Federal Deposit Insurance Corporation.

(B) COVERED BANK.—The term "covered bank" means—

(i) a minority depository institution that is regulated by the Corporation or the National Credit Union Administration that is well capitalized (as defined in section 38(b) of the Federal Deposit Insurance Act (12 U.S.C. 1831o(b))); or

(ii) a depository institution designated pursuant to section 5 of the Ensuring Diversity in Community Banking Act of 2020 that is well capitalized (as defined in section 38(b) of the Federal Deposit Insurance Act (12 U.S.C. 1831o(b))).

(C) ELIGIBLE CUSTODIAL ENTITY.—The term "eligible custodial entity" means—

(i) an insured depository institution (as defined in section 3 of the Federal Deposit Insurance Act (12 U.S.C. 1813)),

(ii) an insured credit union (as defined in section 101 of the Federal Credit Union Act (12 U.S.C. 1752)), or

(iii) or a well capitalized State-chartered trust company,

designated by the Secretary under subsection (k)(3)(A).

(D) FEDERAL BANK SECRECY LAWS.—The term "Federal bank secrecy laws" means—

(i) section 21 of the Federal Deposit Insurance Act (12 U.S.C. 1829b);

(ii) section 123 of Public Law 91–508; and

(iii) subchapter II of chapter 53 of title 31, United States Code.

(E) QUALIFYING ACCOUNT.—The term "qualifying account" means any account established in the Department of the Treasury that—

(i) is controlled by the Secretary; and
(ii) is expected to maintain a balance greater than $200,000,000 for the following calendar month.
(F) SECRETARY.—The term "Secretary" means the Secretary of the Treasury.
(G) WELL CAPITALIZED.—The term "well capitalized" has the meaning given in section 38 of the Federal Deposit Insurance Act (12 U.S.C. 1831o).
(l) Streamlined Community Development Financial Institution Applications And Reporting.—
(1) APPLICATION PROCESSES.—Not later than 12 months after the date of the enactment of this Act and with respect to any person having assets under $3,000,000,000 that submits an application for deposit insurance with the Federal Deposit Insurance Corporation that could also become a community development financial institution, the Federal Deposit Insurance Corporation, in consultation with the Administrator of the Community Development Financial Institutions Fund, shall—
(A) develop systems and procedures to record necessary information to allow the Administrator to conduct preliminary analysis for such person to also become a community development financial institution; and
(B) develop procedures to streamline the application and annual certification processes and to reduce costs for such person to become, and maintain certification as, a community development financial institution that serves low- and moderate-income neighborhoods (as defined under the Community Reinvestment Act of 1977 (12 U.S.C. 2901 et seq.)).
(2) REPORT ON IMPLEMENTATION.—Not later than 18 months after the date of the enactment of this Act, the Federal Deposit Insurance Corporation shall submit to Congress a report describing the systems and procedures required under paragraph (1).
(3) ANNUAL REPORT.—
(A) IN GENERAL.—Section 17(a)(1) of the Federal Deposit Insurance Act (12 U.S.C. 1827(a)(1)) is amended—
(i) in subparagraph (E), by striking "and" at the end;
(ii) by redesignating subparagraph (F) as subparagraph (G);
(iii) by inserting after subparagraph (E) the following new subparagraph:
"(F) applicants for deposit insurance that could also become a community development financial institution (as defined in section 103 of the Riegle Community Development and Regulatory Improvement Act of 1994), a minority depository institution (as defined in section 308 of the Financial Institutions Reform, Recovery, and Enforcement Act of 1989), or an impact bank (as designated pursuant to section 5 of the Ensuring Diversity in Community Banking Act of 2020); and".
(B) APPLICATION.—The amendment made by this paragraph shall apply with respect to the first report to be submitted after the date that is 2 years after the date of the enactment of this Act.
(m) Task Force On Lending To Small Business Concerns.—

(1) IN GENERAL.—Not later than 6 months after the date of the enactment of this Act, the Administrator of the Small Business Administration shall establish a task force to examine methods for improving relationships between the Small Business Administration and community development financial institutions, minority depository institutions, and impact bank (as designated pursuant to section 5 of the Ensuring Diversity in Community Banking Act of 2020) to increase the volume of loans provided by such institutions to small business concerns (as defined under section 3 of the Small Business Act (15 U.S.C. 632)).

(2) REPORT TO CONGRESS.—Not later than 18 months after the establishment of the task force described in paragraph (1), the Administrator of the Small Business Administration shall submit to Congress a report on the findings of such task force.

(n) Assistance To Minority Depository Institutions And Impact Banks.—The Secretary of the Treasury shall establish a program to provide assistance to a minority depository institution or an impact bank (as designated pursuant to section 5 of the Ensuring Diversity in Community Banking Act of 2020) to support growth and development of such minority depository institutions and impact banks, including by providing assistance with obtaining or converting a charter, bylaw amendments, field-of-membership expansion requests, and online training and resources.

SEC. 208. LOANS TO MDIS AND CDFIS.

(a) In General.—During the COVID–19 emergency period, the Board of Governors of the Federal Reserve System shall provide zero-interest loans to minority depository institutions and community development financial institutions to help mitigate the economic impact of COVID–19 in low-income, underserved communities.

(b) Asset Limitation.—Subsection (a) shall only apply to minority depository institutions and community development financial institutions with less than $1,000,000,000 in assets.

(c) Interest To Resume 18 Months After Pandemic.—Notwithstanding subsection (a), the Board of Governors shall charge interest on loans made pursuant to subsection (a) after the end of the 18-month period beginning at the end of the COVID–19 emergency period, at a rate to be determined by the Board of Governors based on the interest amount charged under the discount window lending programs.

(d) COVID–19 Pandemic Defined.—In this section, the term "COVID–19 emergency period" means the period that begins upon the date of the enactment of this Act and ends upon the date of the termination by the Federal Emergency Management Administration of the emergency declared on March 13, 2020, by the President under the Robert T. Stafford Disaster Relief and Emergency Assistance Act (42 U.S.C. 4121 et seq.) relating to the Coronavirus Disease 2019 (COVID–19) pandemic.

SEC. 209. INSURANCE OF TRANSACTION ACCOUNTS.

(a) Banks And Savings Associations.—

(1) AMENDMENTS.—Section 11(a)(1) of the Federal Deposit Insurance Act (12 U.S.C. 1821(a)(1)) is amended—

(A) in subparagraph (B)—

(i) by striking "The net amount" and inserting the following:

"(i) IN GENERAL.—Subject to clause (ii), the net amount"; and

(ii) by adding at the end the following new clauses:

"(ii) AUTHORIZATION FOR INSURANCE FOR TRANSACTION ACCOUNTS.—Notwithstanding clause (i), the Corporation may fully insure the net amount that any depositor at an insured depository institution maintains in a transaction account. Such amount shall not be taken into account when computing the net amount due to such depositor under clause (i).

"(iii) TRANSACTION ACCOUNT DEFINED.—For purposes of this subparagraph, the term 'transaction account' has the meaning given that term under section 19 of the Federal Reserve Act (12 U.S.C. 461)."; and

(B) in subparagraph (C), by striking "subparagraph (B)" and inserting "subparagraph (B)(i)".

(2) PROSPECTIVE REPEAL.—Effective January 1, 2022, section 11(a)(1) of the Federal Deposit Insurance Act (12 U.S.C. 1821(a)(1)), as amended by paragraph (1), is amended—

(A) in subparagraph (B)—

(i) by striking "DEPOSIT.—" and all that follows through "clause (ii), the net amount" and insert "DEPOSIT.—The net amount"; and

(ii) by striking clauses (ii) and (iii); and

(B) in subparagraph (C), by striking "subparagraph (B)(i)" and inserting "subparagraph (B)".

(b) Credit Unions.—

(1) AMENDMENTS.—Section 207(k)(1) of the Federal Credit Union Act (12 U.S.C. 1787(k)(1)) is amended—

(A) in subparagraph (A)—

(i) by striking "Subject to the provisions of paragraph (2), the net amount" and inserting the following:

"(i) NET AMOUNT OF INSURANCE PAYABLE.—Subject to clause (ii) and the provisions of paragraph (2), the net amount"; and

(ii) by adding at the end the following new clauses:

"(ii) AUTHORIZATION FOR INSURANCE FOR TRANSACTION ACCOUNTS.—Notwithstanding clause (i), the Board may fully insure the net amount that any member or depositor at an insured credit union maintains in a transaction account. Such amount shall not be taken into account when computing the net amount due to such member or depositor under clause (i).

"(iii) TRANSACTION ACCOUNT DEFINED.—For purposes of this subparagraph, the term 'transaction account' has the meaning given that term

under section 19 of the Federal Reserve Act (12 U.S.C. 461).”; and
(B) in subparagraph (B), by striking “subparagraph (A)” and inserting “subparagraph (A)(i)”.
(2) PROSPECTIVE REPEAL.—Effective January 1, 2022, section 207(k)(1) of the Federal Credit Union Act (12 U.S.C. 1787(k)(1)), as amended by paragraph (1), is amended—
(A) in subparagraph (A)—
(i) by striking “(I) NET AMOUNT OF INSURANCE PAYABLE.—” and all that follows through “paragraph (2), the net amount” and inserting “Subject to the provisions of paragraph (2), the net amount”; and
(ii) by striking clauses (ii) and (iii); and
(B) in subparagraph (B), by striking “subparagraph (A)(i)” and inserting “subparagraph (A)”.
(c) COVID–19 Emergency Defined.—In this section, the term “COVID–19 emergency” means the period that begins upon the date of the enactment of this Act and ends upon the date of the termination by the Federal Emergency Management Agency of the emergency declared on March 13, 2020, by the President under the Robert T. Stafford Disaster Relief and Emergency Assistance Act (42 U.S.C. 4121 et seq.) relating to the Coronavirus Disease 2019 (COVID–19) pandemic.

TITLE III—SUPPORTING STATE, TERRITORY, AND LOCAL GOVERNMENTS

SEC. 301. MUNI FACILITY.

(a) Amendment To Authority To Buy And Sell Bonds And Notes.—Section 14(b) of the Federal Reserve Act (12 U.S.C. 355) is amended—
(1) in paragraph (1)—
(A) by inserting “and during unusual and exigent circumstances,” before “bonds issued”; and
(B) by striking “of 1933” and all that follows through “assured revenues”; and
(2) by adding at the end the following:
“(3) STATE DEFINED.—In this section, the term ‘State’ means each of the several States, any bi-State agency, the District of Columbia, each territory and possession of the United States, and each federally recognized Indian Tribe.”.
(b) Federal Reserve Authorization To Purchase COVID–19 Related Municipal Issuances.—
(1) AUTHORITY.—Within seven days after the date of enactment of this subsection, the Federal Reserve Board of Governors shall establish a facility to buy and sell, at home or abroad, bills, notes, bonds, and warrants that are issued by any State or political subdivision thereof between March 1, 2020, and July 1, 2021, in order to fund a public health or public service response to the COVID–19 pandemic. The Board of Governors of the Federal Reserve System

may extend the authority under this subsection if the Board determines necessary.

(2) REQUIRED PURCHASES.—The Board of Governors of the Federal Reserve System shall establish policies and procedures to require the direct placement of bills, notes, bonds, and warrants described in paragraph (1) with the Board at an interest cost that does not exceed the Federal funds rate target for short-term interbank lending, within seven days after the date of enactment of this section.

(3) REVIEW OF SPENDING.—During the 3-year period beginning on the date on which all purchases under this section are completed, relevant Federal authorities shall review such purchases to determine if funds were diverted from legitimate public health or public services responses to the COVID–19 pandemic to make such purchase. The relevant Federal authorities shall take appropriate action based on findings of such review.

(4) DEFINITIONS.—In this subsection:

(A) PUBLIC HEALTH OR PUBLIC SERVICE RESPONSE TO THE COVID–19 PANDEMIC.—The term "public health or public service response to the COVID–19 pandemic" means—

(i) the purchase, manufacture, or delivery of medical equipment, facilities, or services—

(I) to treat or quarantine COVID–19 patients;

(II) to protect first responders interacting with such patients; or

(III) to test for COVID–19 infections and track social contacts of patients who have tested positive for the virus;

(ii) the purchase, manufacture, or delivery of basic living supports for individuals who are not COVID–19 patients during periods of voluntary or mandatory social distancing or quarantine designed to prevent the spread of COVID–19; or

(iii) the maintenance and delivery of basic public services to communities responding to the public health or economic effects of the COVID–19 pandemic.

(B) STATE.—The term "State" means each of the several States, any bi-State agency, the District of Columbia, each territory and possession of the United States, and each federally recognized Indian Tribe.

SEC. 302. TEMPORARY WAIVER AND REPROGRAMMING AUTHORITY.

(a) Waiver Authority.—

(1) IN GENERAL.—With respect to a covered grant awarded to a State, territory, or local government by a Federal financial regulator, the Federal financial regulator may, upon request, waive any matching or cost-sharing requirements with respect to such grant until January 1, 2023.

(2) REQUIREMENTS FOR WAIVER RECIPIENTS.—A State, territory, or local government granted a waiver with respect to a grant under subsection (a)

shall waive any matching or cost-sharing requirements that such government imposes on sub-grantees on such grant until January 1, 2023.

(b) Reprogramming Authority.—

(1) IN GENERAL.—With respect to a covered grant awarded to a State, territory, or local government by a Federal financial regulator, the Federal financial regulator may, upon request, permit the State, territory, or local government to reprogram awarded grant funds for purposes related to unemployment, childcare, and healthcare, if the majority of normally funded activities under such grant are not in areas related to unemployment, childcare, and healthcare.

(2) CONSIDERATION FOR FUTURE GRANTS.—Any grantee (or sub-grantee) with respect to which a Federal financial regulator allows to reprogram funds under paragraph (1) shall be given priority by such Federal financial regulator for future awards of the type reprogrammed.

(c) Definitions.—In this section:

(1) COVERED GRANTS.—The term "covered award" means a grant—

(A) that was awarded to a State, territory, or local government before the date of enactment of this Act and under which the State, territory, or local government may still receive additional grant amounts; or

(B) with respect to which the period of performance does not expire before January 1, 2023.

(2) FEDERAL FINANCIAL REGULATOR.—The term "Federal financial regulator" means the Board of Governors of the Federal Reserve System, the Bureau of Consumer Financial Protection, the Department of Housing and Urban Development, the Department of the Treasury (other than the Internal Revenue Service), the Federal Deposit Insurance Corporation, the Office of the Comptroller of the Currency, the National Credit Union Administration, and the Securities and Exchange Commission.

TITLE IV—PROMOTING FINANCIAL STABILITY AND TRANSPARENT MARKETS

SEC. 401. TEMPORARY HALT TO RULEMAKINGS UNRELATED TO COVID–19.

(a) In General.—Until the end of the 30-day period following the end of the COVID–19 emergency period, the Federal financial regulators—

(1) may not adopt or amend any rule, regulation, guidance, or order unless such rule, regulation, guidance, or order is directly related to responding to the COVID–19 emergency; and

(2) shall keep open and extend any ongoing public comment period related to a proposed or final rule, unless such rule is related to responding to the COVID–19 emergency.

(b) Notice And Sunset Of Emergency Actions.—The Federal financial regulators shall—

(1) provide the Committee on Financial Services of the House of Representatives and the Committee on Banking, Housing, and Urban Affairs of the Senate with a notice of any regulatory actions taken during the COVID–19 emergency period, along with an explanation of how such action was necessary and appropriate in response to the COVID–19 emergency; and

(2) limit the period of effectiveness of any action taken in response to the COVID–19 emergency to be not longer than 12-months following the end of the COVID–19 emergency period.

(c) Voting By Regulators.—Any action taken pursuant to this section by a Federal financial regulator headed by a multi-person entity may only be taken by unanimous vote.

(d) Definitions.—In this section:

(1) COVID–19 EMERGENCY PERIOD.—For purposes of this Act, the term "COVID–19 emergency period" means the period that begins upon the date of the enactment of this Act and ends upon the date of the termination by the Federal Emergency Management Agency of the emergency declared on March 13, 2020, by the President under the Robert T. Stafford Disaster Relief and Emergency Assistance Act (42 U.S.C. 4121 et seq.) relating to the Coronavirus Disease 2019 (COVID–19) pandemic.

(2) FEDERAL FINANCIAL REGULATOR.—In this section, the term "Federal financial regulator" means the Board of Governors of the Federal Reserve System, the Bureau of Consumer Financial Protection, the Department of Housing and Urban Development, the Department of the Treasury (other than the Internal Revenue Service), the Federal Deposit Insurance Corporation, the Federal Housing Finance Agency, the Office of the Comptroller of the Currency, the National Credit Union Administration, and the Securities and Exchange Commission.

SEC. 402. TEMPORARY BAN ON STOCK BUYBACKS.

(a) In General.—It shall be unlawful for any issuer, the securities of which are traded on a national securities exchange, to purchase securities of the issuer during the period beginning on the date of enactment of this section and ending 120 days after the end of the COVID–19 emergency period.

(b) Early Termination.—The Securities and Exchange Commission may terminate the prohibition under subsection (a) after the end of the COVID–19 emergency period and before the end of the 120-day period described under subsection (a), if—

(1) the Commission determines such termination is in the public interest; and

(2) immediately notifies the Congress and the public of such determination and the reason for such determination, including on the website of the Commission.

(c) Enforcement; Rulemaking.—

(1) IN GENERAL.—The Securities and Exchange Commission shall have the

authority to enforce this Act and may issue such rules as may be necessary to carry out this Act.

(2) COMMISSION VOTING.—Any action taken by the Commission pursuant to this section may only be taken upon a unanimous vote of the commissioners.

(d) Definitions.—In this section:

(1) COVID–19 EMERGENCY PERIOD.—The term "COVID–19 emergency period" means the period that begins upon the date of the enactment of this Act and ends upon the date of the termination by the Federal Emergency Management Agency of the emergency declared on March 13, 2020, by the President under the Robert T. Stafford Disaster Relief and Emergency Assistance Act (42 U.S.C. 4121 et seq.) relating to the Coronavirus Disease 2019 (COVID–19) pandemic.

(2) OTHER DEFINITIONS.—The terms "issuer", "national securities exchange", and "security" have the meaning given those terms, respectively, under section 3 of the Securities Exchange Act of 1934.

SEC. 403. DISCLOSURES RELATED TO SUPPLY CHAIN DISRUPTION RISK.

Section 13 of the Securities Exchange Act of 1934 (15 U.S.C. 78m) is amended by adding at the end the following:

"(s) Disclosures Related To Supply Chain Disruption Risk.—

"(1) IN GENERAL.—Each issuer required to file an annual report under subsection (a) shall disclose in that report—

"(A) an identification of—

"(i) the risks in the issuer's sourcing of goods, labor, services, and other supply chain related matters, including—

"(I) risks of dependency upon sole sourcing arrangements or sourcing concentrated in one geographic locality;

"(II) shipping risks; and

"(III) risks arising from natural disasters, pandemics, extreme weather, armed conflicts, refugee and related disruptions, trade conflicts or disruptions, and labor wage, safety, and health care practices; and

"(ii) the impacts any risk or disruption identified in clause (i) would have on the issuer's workforce, suppliers, and customers;

"(B) the issuer's business continuity or other contingency plans that will be implemented in the case of a supply chain disruption in order to mitigate such risks and impacts; and

"(C) all other material information.

"(2) UPDATES.—Disclosures required under this subsection shall be updated when there are material changes.".

SEC. 404. DISCLOSURES RELATED TO GLOBAL PANDEMIC RISK.

(a) In General.—Section 13 of the Securities Exchange Act of 1934 (15 U.S.C.

78m), as amended by section 403, is further amended by adding at the end the following:

"(t) Disclosures Related To Global Pandemic Risk.—

"(1) IN GENERAL.—Each issuer required to file current reports under subsection (a) shall, in the event the World Health Organization declares a pandemic, file a report with the Commission containing a description of—

"(A) the risks and exposures to the issuer related to the pandemic, including risks to health and worker safety faced by the issuer's employees and independent contractors;

"(B) the steps the issuer is taking to mitigate such risks and exposures, including measures to protect the workforce, including information related to wages, healthcare, and leave;

"(C) a preliminary view on the effect the pandemic may have on the issuer's business, solvency, and workforce; and

"(D) all other material information.

"(2) UPDATES.—Disclosures required under this subsection shall be updated when there are material changes.

"(3) PUBLIC AVAILABILITY OF REPORTS.—The Commission shall make each report filed to the Commission under paragraph (1) available to the public, including on the website of the Commission.".

(b) Application.—Section 13(t) of the Securities Exchange Act of 1934, as added by subsection (a), shall apply to a pandemic declared by the World Health Organization that is in existence on the date of enactment of this Act or that is declared after the date of enactment of this Act.

SEC. 405. OVERSIGHT OF FEDERAL AID RELATED TO COVID–19.

(a) Congressional COVID–19 Aid Oversight Panel.—

(1) ESTABLISHMENT.—There is hereby established the Congressional COVID–19 Aid Oversight Panel (hereafter in this subsection referred to as the "Oversight Panel") as an establishment in the legislative branch.

(2) DUTIES.—The Oversight Panel shall review the current state of the financial markets and the regulatory system and submit regular reports to Congress on the following:

(A) The use of Federal aid provided during the COVID–19 emergency.

(B) The impact of Federal aid related to COVID–19 on the financial markets and financial institutions.

(3) MEMBERSHIP.—

(A) IN GENERAL.—The Oversight Panel shall consist of 5 members, as follows:

(i) 1 member appointed by the Speaker of the House of Representatives.

(ii) 1 member appointed by the minority leader of the House of Representatives.

(iii) 1 member appointed by the majority leader of the Senate.

(iv) 1 member appointed by the minority leader of the Senate.

(v) 1 member appointed by the Speaker of the House of Representatives and the majority leader of the Senate, after consultation with the minority leader of the Senate and the minority leader of the House of Representatives.

(B) PAY.—Each member of the Oversight Panel shall each be paid at a rate equal to the daily equivalent of the annual rate of basic pay for level I of the Executive Schedule for each day (including travel time) during which such member is engaged in the actual performance of duties vested in the Commission.

(C) PROHIBITION OF COMPENSATION OF FEDERAL EMPLOYEES.—Members of the Oversight Panel who are full-time officers or employees of the United States or Members of Congress may not receive additional pay, allowances, or benefits by reason of their service on the Oversight Panel.

(D) TRAVEL EXPENSES.—Each member shall receive travel expenses, including per diem in lieu of subsistence, in accordance with applicable provisions under subchapter I of chapter 57 of title 5, United States Code.

(E) QUORUM.—Four members of the Oversight Panel shall constitute a quorum but a lesser number may hold hearings.

(F) VACANCIES.—A vacancy on the Oversight Panel shall be filled in the manner in which the original appointment was made.

(G) MEETINGS.—The Oversight Panel shall meet at the call of the Chairperson or a majority of its members.

(4) STAFF.—

(A) IN GENERAL.—The Oversight Panel may appoint and fix the pay of any personnel as the Oversight Panel considers appropriate.

(B) EXPERTS AND CONSULTANTS.—The Oversight Panel may procure temporary and intermittent services under section 3109(b) of title 5, United States Code.

(C) STAFF OF AGENCIES.—Upon request of the Oversight Panel, the head of any Federal department or agency may detail, on a reimbursable basis, any of the personnel of that department or agency to the Oversight Panel to assist it in carrying out its duties under this section.

(5) POWERS.—

(A) HEARINGS AND SESSIONS.—The Oversight Panel may, for the purpose of carrying out this section, hold hearings, sit and act at times and places, take testimony, and receive evidence as the Panel considers appropriate and may administer oaths or affirmations to witnesses appearing before it.

(B) POWERS OF MEMBERS AND AGENTS.—Any member or agent of the Oversight Panel may, if authorized by the Oversight Panel, take any action which the Oversight Panel is authorized to take by this section.

(C) OBTAINING OFFICIAL DATA.—The Oversight Panel may secure directly from any department or agency of the United States information necessary to enable it to carry out this section. Upon request of the Chairperson of the Oversight Panel, the head of that department or agency shall furnish that information to the Oversight Panel.

(D) REPORTS.—The Oversight Panel shall receive and consider all reports required to be submitted to the Oversight Panel under this section.

(6) AUTHORIZATION OF APPROPRIATIONS.—There is authorized to be appropriated to the Oversight Panel such sums as may be necessary for any fiscal year, half of which shall be derived from the applicable account of the House of Representatives, and half of which shall be derived from the contingent fund of the Senate.

(7) SUNSET.—The Oversight Panel established by this subsection shall terminate on the date that is two years following the termination by the Federal Emergency Management Agency of the emergency declared on March 13, 2020, by the President under the Robert T. Stafford Disaster Relief and Emergency Act (42 U.S.C. 4121 et seq.) relating to the Coronavirus Disease 2019 (COVID–19) pandemic.

(8) DEFINITIONS.—In this subsection:

(A) COVID–19 EMERGENCY.—The term "COVID–19 emergency" means the period that begins upon the date of the enactment of this Act and ends one year after the termination by the Federal Emergency Management Agency of the emergency declared on March 13, 2020, by the President under the Robert T. Stafford Disaster Relief and Emergency Act (42 U.S.C. 4121 et seq.) relating to the Coronavirus Disease 2019 (COVID–19) pandemic.

(B) FEDERAL AID.—The term "Federal aid" means any emergency lending provided under section 13(3) of the Federal Reserve Act or any Federal financial support in the form of a grant, loan, or loan guarantee.

(b) Special Inspector General Authority Over Federal Aid Related To COVID–19.—Section 121 of the Emergency Economic Stabilization Act of 2008 (12 U.S.C. 5231) is amended—

(1) in subsection (k)—

(A) in paragraph (1), by striking "or" at the end;

(B) in paragraph (2), by striking the period at the end and inserting "; or"; and

(C) by adding at the end the following:

"(3) the date on which all Federal aid related to the COVID–19 emergency is repaid."; and

(2) by adding at the end the following:

"(l) Responsibility With Respect To Federal Aid Related To COVID–19.—

"(1) IN GENERAL.—The Special Inspector General shall have the same authority and responsibilities with respect to Federal aid provided during the COVID–19 emergency as the Special Inspector General has with respect to financial assistance (including the purchase of troubled assets) provided under this title.

"(2) DEFINITIONS.—In this section:

"(A) COVID–19 EMERGENCY.—The term 'COVID–19 emergency' means the period that begins upon the date of the enactment of this Act and ends one year after the termination by the Federal Emergency Management Agency of the emergency declared on March 13, 2020, by the President under the Robert T. Stafford Disaster Relief and Emergency Act (42 U.S.C. 4121 et seq.) relating

to the Coronavirus Disease 2019 (COVID–19) pandemic.
"(B) FEDERAL AID.—The term 'Federal aid' means any emergency lending provided under section 13(3) of the Federal Reserve Act or any Federal financial support in the form of a grant, loan, or loan guarantee.".

SEC. 406. INTERNATIONAL FINANCIAL INSTITUTIONS.
(a) United States Participation In, And Contributions To, The Nineteenth Replenishment Of The Resources Of The International Development Association.— The International Development Association Act (22 U.S.C. 284 et seq.) is amended by adding at the end the following:

"SEC. 31. NINETEENTH REPLENISHMENT.
"(a) The United States Governor of the International Development Association is authorized to contribute on behalf of the United States $3,004,200,000 to the nineteenth replenishment of the resources of the Association, subject to obtaining the necessary appropriations.
"(b) In order to pay for the United States contribution provided for in subsection (a), there are authorized to be appropriated, without fiscal year limitation, $3,004,200,000 for payment by the Secretary of the Treasury.".
(b) United States Participation In, And Contributions To, The Fifteenth Replenishment Of The Resources Of The African Development Fund.—The African Development Fund Act (22 U.S.C. 290g et seq.) is amended by adding at the end the following:

"SEC. 226. FIFTEENTH REPLENISHMENT.
"(a) The United States Governor of the Fund is authorized to contribute on behalf of the United States $513,900,000 to the fifteenth replenishment of the resources of the Fund, subject to obtaining the necessary appropriations.
"(b) In order to pay for the United States contribution provided for in subsection (a), there are authorized to be appropriated, without fiscal year limitation, $513,900,000 for payment by the Secretary of the Treasury.".
(c) United States Participation In, And Contributions To, The Seventh Capital Increase For The African Development Bank.— The African Development Bank Act (22 U.S.C. 290i et seq.) is amended by adding at the end the following:

"SEC. 1345. SEVENTH CAPITAL INCREASE.
"(a) Subscription Authorized.—
"(1) The United States Governor of the Bank may subscribe on behalf of the United States to 532,023 additional shares of the capital stock of the Bank.
"(2) Any subscription by the United States to the capital stock of the Bank shall be effective only to such extent and in such amounts as are provided in advance in appropriations Acts.
"(b) Limitations On Authorization Of Appropriations.—
"(1) In order to pay for the increase in the United States subscription to the Bank under subsection (a), there are authorized to be appropriated, without

fiscal year limitation, $7,286,587,008 for payment by the Secretary of the Treasury.
"(2) Of the amount authorized to be appropriated under paragraph (1)—
"(A) $437,190,016 shall be for paid in shares of the Bank; and
"(B) $6,849,396,992 shall be for callable shares of the Bank.".

SEC. 407. CONDITIONS ON FEDERAL AID TO CORPORATIONS.
(a) Requirements On All Corporations Until Federal Aid Related To COVID–19 Is Repaid.—Any corporation that receives Federal aid related to COVID–19 shall, until the date on which all such Federal aid is repaid by the corporation to the Federal Government, comply with the following:
(1) RESTRICTIONS ON EXECUTIVE BONUSES.—The corporation may not pay a bonus to any executive of the corporation.
(2) BAN ON EXECUTIVE GOLDEN PARACHUTES.—The corporation may not pay any type of compensation (whether present, deferred, or contingent) to an executive of the corporation, if such compensation is in connection with the termination of employment of the executive.
(3) BAN ON STOCK BUYBACKS.—The corporation may not purchase securities of the corporation.
(4) BAN ON DIVIDENDS.—The corporation may not pay dividends on securities of the corporation.
(5) BAN ON FEDERAL LOBBYING.—The corporation may not carry out any Federal lobbying activities.
(b) Permanent Requirements On Accelerated Filers Receiving Federal Aid Related To COVID–19.—
(1) IN GENERAL.—An accelerated filer that receives Federal aid related to COVID–19 shall permanently comply with the following:
(A) WORKER BOARD REPRESENTATION.—
(i) IN GENERAL.—At least 1/3 of the members of the accelerated filer's directors are chosen by the employees of the accelerated filer in a one-employee-one-vote election process.
(ii) COMPLIANCE DATE.—An accelerated filer shall comply with the requirements under clause (i) not later than the end of the 2-year period beginning on the date of enactment of this Act.
(iii) DEFINITIONS.—In this subparagraph—
(I) the term "director" has the meaning given the term in section 3 of the Securities Exchange Act of 1934 (15 U.S.C. 78c); and
(II) the term "employee" has the meaning given the term in section 2 of the National Labor Relations Act (29 U.S.C. 152).
(B) ADDITIONAL DISCLOSURES.—If the securities of the corporation are traded on a national securities exchange, the corporation shall issue the following disclosures to the Securities and Exchange Commission on a quarterly basis (and make such disclosures available to shareholders of the corporation and the public):

(i) The political spending disclosures required under paragraph (2).

(ii) The human capital management disclosures required under paragraph (3).

(iii) The environmental, social, and governance disclosures required under paragraph (4).

(iv) The Federal aid disclosures required under paragraph (5).

(v) The disclosures of financial performance on a country-by-country basis required under paragraph (6).

(2) POLITICAL SPENDING DISCLOSURES.—

(A) IN GENERAL.—With respect to an accelerated filer, the disclosures required under this paragraph are—

(i) a description of any expenditure for political activities made during the preceding quarter;

(ii) the date of each expenditure for political activities;

(iii) the amount of each expenditure for political activities;

(iv) if the expenditure for political activities was made in support of or opposed to a candidate, the name of the candidate and the office sought by, and the political party affiliation of, the candidate;

(v) the name or identity of trade associations or organizations described in section 501(c) of the Internal Revenue Code of 1986 and exempt from tax under section 501(a) of such Code which receive dues or other payments as described in paragraph (1)(A)(i)(III);

(vi) a summary of each expenditure for political activities made during the preceding year in excess of $10,000, and each expenditure for political activities for a particular election if the total amount of such expenditures for that election is in excess of $10,000;

(vii) a description of the specific nature of any expenditure for political activities the corporation intends to make for the forthcoming fiscal year, to the extent the specific nature is known to the corporation; and

(viii) the total amount of expenditures for political activities intended to be made by the corporation for the forthcoming fiscal year.

(B) DEFINITIONS.—In this paragraph:

(i) EXPENDITURE FOR POLITICAL ACTIVITIES.—The term "expenditure for political activities"—

(I) means—

(aa) an independent expenditure (as defined in section 301(17) of the Federal Election Campaign Act of 1971 (52 U.S.C. 30101(17)));

(bb) an electioneering communication (as defined in section 304(f)(3) of that Act (52 U.S.C. 30104(f)(3))) and any other public communication (as defined in section 301(22) of that Act (52 U.S.C. 30101(22))) that would be an electioneering communication if it were a broadcast, cable, or satellite communication; or

(cc) dues or other payments to trade associations or organizations described in section 501(c) of the Internal Revenue Code of 1986 and exempt from tax under section 501(a) of that Code that are, or could reasonably be anticipated to be, used or transferred to another association or organization for the purposes described in item (aa) or (bb); and

(II) does not include—

(aa) direct lobbying efforts through registered lobbyists employed or hired by the corporation;

(bb) communications by a corporation to its shareholders and executive or administrative personnel and their families; or

(cc) the establishment and administration of contributions to a separate segregated fund to be utilized for political purposes by a corporation.

(ii) EXCEPTION.—The term "corporation" does not include an investment company registered under section 8 of the Investment Company Act of 1940 (15 U.S.C. 80a–8).

(3) HUMAN CAPITAL MANAGEMENT DISCLOSURES.—With respect to an accelerated filer, the disclosures required under this paragraph are the following:

(A) Workforce demographic information, including the number of full-time employees, the number of part-time employees, the number of contingent workers (including temporary and contract workers), and any policies or practices relating to subcontracting, outsourcing, and insourcing.

(B) Workforce stability information, including information about the voluntary turnover or retention rate, the involuntary turnover rate, the internal hiring rate, and the internal promotion rate.

(C) Workforce composition, including data on diversity (including racial and gender composition) and any policies and audits related to diversity.

(D) Workforce skills and capabilities, including information about training of employees (including the average number of hours of training and spending on training per employee per year), skills gaps, and alignment of skills and capabilities with business strategy.

(E) Workforce culture and empowerment, including information about—

(i) policies and practices of the corporation relating to freedom of association and work-life balance initiatives;

(ii) any incidents of verified workplace harassment in the previous 5 fiscal years of the corporation;

(iii) policies and practices of the corporation relating to employee engagement and psychological wellbeing, including management discussion regarding—

(I) the creation of an autonomous work environment;

(II) fostering a sense of purpose in the workforce;

(III) trust in management; and

(IV) a supportive, fair, and constructive workplace.

(F) Workforce health and safety, including information about—

(i) the frequency, severity, and lost time due to injuries, illness, and fatalities;

(ii) the total dollar value of assessed fines under the Occupational Safety and Health Act of 1970;

(iii) the total number of actions brought under section 13 of the Occupational

Safety and Health Act of 1970 to prevent imminent dangers; and

(iv) the total number of actions brought against the corporation under section 11(c) of the Occupational Safety and Health Act of 1970.

(G) Workforce compensation and incentives, including information about—

(i) total workforce compensation, including disaggregated information about compensation for full-time, part-time, and contingent workers;

(ii) policies and practices about how performance, productivity, and sustainability are considered when setting pay and making promotion decisions; and

(iii) policies and practices relating to any incentives and bonuses provided to employees below the named executive level and any policies or practices designed to counter any risks create by such incentives and bonuses.

(H) Workforce recruiting, including information about the quality of hire, new hire engagement rate, and new hire retention rate.

(4) ENVIRONMENTAL, SOCIAL AND GOVERNANCE DISCLOSURES.—With respect to an accelerated filer, the disclosures required under this paragraph are disclosures that satisfy the recommendations of the Task Force on Climate-related Financial Disclosures of the Financial Stability Board as reported in June, 2017.

(5) FEDERAL AID DISCLOSURES.—With respect to an accelerated filer, the disclosure required under this paragraph is a description of how the Federal aid related to COVID–19 received by the corporation is being used to support the corporation's employees.

(6) DISCLOSURES OF FINANCIAL PERFORMANCE ON A COUNTRY-BY-COUNTRY BASIS.—

(A) IN GENERAL.—With respect to an accelerated filer, the disclosures required under this paragraph are the following:

(i) CONSTITUENT ENTITY INFORMATION.—Information on any constituent entity of the corporation, including the following:

(I) The complete legal name of the constituent entity.

(II) The tax jurisdiction, if any, in which the constituent entity is resident for tax purposes.

(III) The tax jurisdiction in which the constituent entity is organized or incorporated (if different from the tax jurisdiction of residence).

(IV) The tax identification number, if any, used for the constituent entity by the tax administration of the constituent entity's tax jurisdiction of residence.

(V) The main business activity or activities of the constituent entity.

(ii) TAX JURISDICTION.—Information on each tax jurisdiction in which one or more constituent entities is resident, presented as an aggregated or consolidated form of the information for the constituent entities resident in each tax jurisdiction, including the following:

(I) Revenues generated from transactions with other constituent entities.

(II) Revenues not generated from transactions with other constituent entities.

(III) Profit or loss before income tax.

(IV) Total income tax paid on a cash basis to all tax jurisdictions.

(V) Total accrued tax expense recorded on taxable profits or losses.

(VI) Stated capital.

(VII) Total accumulated earnings.

(VIII) Total number of employees on a full-time equivalent basis.

(IX) Net book value of tangible assets, which, for purposes of this section, does not include cash or cash equivalents, intangibles, or financial assets.

(iii) SPECIAL RULES.—The information listed in clause (ii) shall be provided, in aggregated or consolidated form, for any constituent entity or entities that have no tax jurisdiction of residence. In addition, if a constituent entity is an owner of a constituent entity that does not have a jurisdiction of tax residence, then the owner's share of such entity's revenues and profits will be aggregated or consolidated with the information for the owner's tax jurisdiction of residence.

(B) DEFINITIONS.—In this paragraph—

(i) the term "constituent entity" means, with respect to an accelerated filer, any separate business entity of the accelerated filer;

(ii) the term "tax jurisdiction"—

(I) means a country or a jurisdiction that is not a country but that has fiscal autonomy; and

(II) includes a territory or possession of the United States that has fiscal autonomy.

(c) Permanent Requirements On All Corporations Receiving Federal Aid Related To COVID–19.—Any corporation that receives Federal aid related to COVID–19 shall permanently comply with the following:

(1) PAID LEAVE FOR WORKERS.—The corporation shall provide at least 14 days of paid leave to workers (employees and contractors, full-time and part-time) who—

(A) are unable to telework;

(B) need to be isolated or quarantined to prevent the spread of COVID–19; or

(C) need time off to care for the needs of family members.

(2) MINIMUM WAGE.—The corporation shall pay each employee (full-time and part-time) of the corporation a wage of not less than $15 an hour, beginning not later than January 1, 2021.

(3) LIMITATION ON CEO AND EXECUTIVE PAY.—The corporation may not have a CEO to median worker pay ratio of greater than 50 to 1 and no officer or employee of the corporation may received higher compensation than the chief executive officer (or any equivalent position).

(d) Requirements On All Corporations Receiving Federal Aid Related To COVID–19 Until The End Of The Emergency.—Any corporation that receives Federal aid related to COVID–19 shall, until the COVID–19 emergency ends, comply with the following:

(1) WORKFORCE LEVELS AND BENEFITS.—The corporation shall maintain at least the same workforce levels and benefits that existed before

the COVID–19 emergency.

(2) MAINTENANCE OF WORKER PAY.—The corporation shall maintain worker (employee or contractor, full-time and part-time) pay throughout the entire duration of the COVID–19 emergency at or above the pay level the worker was earning before the emergency.

(3) MAINTENANCE OF COLLECTIVE BARGAINING AGREEMENTS.—The corporation may not alter any collective bargaining agreement that was in place at the beginning of the COVID–19 emergency.

(e) Enforcement; Rulemaking.—The Securities and Exchange Commission and the Secretary of the Treasury shall have the authority to enforce this section and may issue such rules as may be necessary to carry out this section.

(f) Definitions.—In this section:

(1) ACCELERATED FILER.—The Securities and Exchange Commission shall define the term "accelerated filer" for purposes of this section.

(2) CEO TO MEDIAN WORKER PAY RATIO.—With respect to an accelerated filer, the term "CEO to median worker pay ratio" means the ratio of—

(A) the annual total compensation of the chief executive officer (or any equivalent position) of the corporation; and

(B) the median of the annual total compensation of all employees of the corporation, except the chief executive officer (or any equivalent position) of the corporation.

(3) COVID–19 EMERGENCY.—The term "COVID–19 emergency" means the period that begins upon the date of the enactment of this Act and ends upon the termination by the Federal Emergency Management Agency of the emergency declared on March 13, 2020, by the President under the Robert T. Stafford Disaster Relief and Emergency Act (42 U.S.C. 4121 et seq.) relating to the Coronavirus Disease 2019 (COVID–19).

(4) FEDERAL AID.—The term "Federal aid" means any emergency lending provided under section 13(3) of the Federal Reserve Act or any Federal financial support in the form of a grant, loan, or loan guarantee.

(5) S CORPORATION.—The term "S corporation" has the meaning given that term under section 1361(a) of the Internal Revenue Code of 1986.

(6) SECURITIES TERMS.—The terms "national securities exchange" and "security" have the meaning given those terms, respectively, under section 3 of the Securities Exchange Act of 1934.

SEC. 408. AUTHORITY FOR WARRANTS AND DEBT INSTRUMENTS.

(a) Definitions.—In this section:

(1) ASSET.—The term "asset" means any financial instrument that the Secretary, after consultation with the Chairman of the Board of Governors of the Federal Reserve System, determines the purchase of which or the guarantee of which is necessary to promote economic stability.

(2) COMPANY.—The term "company" means any entity that is not subject to the prohibitions in subsection (e).

(3) SECRETARY.—The term “Secretary” means the Secretary of the Treasury.

(b) Warrant Or Senior Debt Instrument.—The Secretary may not purchase, or make any commitment to purchase, or guarantee, or make any commitment to guarantee, any asset in response to the coronavirus disease (COVID–19) outbreak, unless the Secretary receives from the company from which such assets are to be purchased or are to be guaranteed—

(1) in the case of a company, the securities of which are traded on a national securities exchange, a warrant giving the right to the Secretary to receive senior preferred voting stock; or

(2) in the case of any company other than one described in paragraph (1), a warrant for senior preferred voting stock, or a senior debt instrument from such company.

(c) Terms And Conditions.—The terms and conditions of any warrant or senior debt instrument required under subsection (b) shall meet the following requirements:

(1) PURPOSES.—Such terms and conditions shall, at a minimum, be designed—

(A) to provide for reasonable participation by the Secretary, for the benefit of taxpayers, in equity appreciation in the case of a warrant or other equity security, or a reasonable interest rate premium, in the case of a debt instrument; and

(B) to provide additional protection for the taxpayer against losses from sale of assets by the Secretary and any associated administrative expenses.

(2) TERMS OF SENIOR PREFERRED VOTING STOCK.—With respect to senior preferred voting stock received from a company, the Secretary shall—

(A) have the right to vote on matters brought before the stockholders generally; and

(B) control a percentage of votes equal to the percentage of the total value of the company the government’s share will represent after the investment.

(3) AUTHORITY TO SELL, EXERCISE, OR SURRENDER.—

(A) IN GENERAL.—For the primary benefit of taxpayers, the Secretary may sell, exercise, or surrender a warrant or any senior debt instrument received under this section, based on the conditions established under paragraph (1).

(B) PROCEEDS.—Of any proceeds received through the sale, exercise, or surrender of any warrant or any senior debt instrument—

(i) 65 percent shall be transferred or credited to the Housing Trust Fund established under section 1338 of the Federal Housing Enterprises Financial Safety and Soundness Act of 1992 (12 U.S.C. 4568); and

(ii) 35 percent shall be transferred or credited to the Capital Magnet Fund under section 1339 of the Federal Housing Enterprises Financial Safety and Soundness Act of 1992 (12 U.S.C. 4569).

(4) CONVERSION.—The warrant shall provide that if, after the warrant is received by the Secretary under this section, the company that issued the warrant is no longer listed or traded on a national securities exchange or

securities association, as described in subsection (b)(1), the Secretary will have an option to convert the warrants to senior debt to ensure that the Treasury is appropriately compensated for the value of the warrant, in an amount determined by the Secretary for the primary benefit of taxpayers.
(5) PROTECTIONS.—Any warrant representing securities to be received by the Secretary under this section shall contain anti-dilution provisions of the type employed in capital market transactions, as determined by the Secretary for the primary benefit of taxpayers. Such provisions shall protect the value of the securities from market transactions such as stock splits, stock distributions, dividends, and other distributions, mergers, and other forms of reorganization or recapitalization.
(6) EXERCISE PRICE.—The exercise price for any warrant issued pursuant to this section shall be set by the Secretary, for the primary benefit of taxpayers.
(7) SUFFICIENCY.—The company shall guarantee to the Secretary that it has authorized shares of stock available to fulfill its obligations under this section. Should the company not have sufficient authorized shares, including preferred shares that may carry dividend rights equal to a multiple number of common shares, the Secretary may, to the extent necessary for the primary benefit of taxpayers, accept a senior debt note in an amount, and on such terms as will compensate the Secretary with equivalent value, in the event that a sufficient shareholder vote to authorize the necessary additional shares cannot be obtained.
(d) Exceptions.—The Secretary may establish an exception to the requirements of this section and appropriate alternative requirements for any participating company that is legally prohibited from issuing securities and debt instruments, so as not to allow circumvention of the requirements of this section.
(e) Prohibitions Of Foreign Companies.—
(1) IN GENERAL.—The Secretary may not purchase, or make any commitment to purchase, or guarantee, or make any commitment to guarantee, any asset in response to the coronavirus disease (COVID–19) outbreak from—
(A) any foreign incorporated entity that the Secretary has determined is an inverted domestic corporation or any subsidiary of such entity; or
(B) any joint venture if more than 10 percent of the joint venture (by vote or value) is held by a foreign incorporated entity that the Secretary has determined is an inverted domestic corporation or any subsidiary of such entity.
(2) INVERTED DOMESTIC CORPORATION.—
(A) IN GENERAL.—For purposes of this subsection, a foreign incorporated entity shall be treated as an inverted domestic corporation if, pursuant to a plan (or a series of related transactions)—
(i) the entity completes on or after May 8, 2014, the direct or indirect acquisition of—
(I) substantially all of the properties held directly or indirectly by a domestic corporation; or

(II) substantially all of the assets of, or substantially all of the properties constituting a trade or business of, a domestic partnership; and

(ii) after the acquisition, either—

(I) more than 50 percent of the stock (by vote or value) of the entity is held—

(aa) in the case of an acquisition with respect to a domestic corporation, by former shareholders of the domestic corporation by reason of holding stock in the domestic corporation; or

(bb) in the case of an acquisition with respect to a domestic partnership, by former partners of the domestic partnership by reason of holding a capital or profits interest in the domestic partnership; or

(II) the management and control of the expanded affiliated group which includes the entity occurs, directly or indirectly, primarily within the United States, as determined pursuant to regulations prescribed by the Secretary, and such expanded affiliated group has significant domestic business activities.

(B) EXCEPTION FOR CORPORATIONS WITH SUBSTANTIAL BUSINESS ACTIVITIES IN FOREIGN COUNTRY OF ORGANIZATION.—

(i) IN GENERAL.—A foreign incorporated entity described in subparagraph (A) shall not be treated as an inverted domestic corporation if after the acquisition the expanded affiliated group which includes the entity has substantial business activities in the foreign country in which or under the law of which the entity is created or organized when compared to the total business activities of such expanded affiliated group.

(ii) SUBSTANTIAL BUSINESS ACTIVITIES.—The Secretary shall establish regulations for determining whether an affiliated group has substantial business activities for purposes of clause (i), except that such regulations may not treat any group as having substantial business activities if such group would not be considered to have substantial business activities under the regulations prescribed under section 7874 of the Internal Revenue Code of 1986, as in effect on January 18, 2017.

(C) SIGNIFICANT DOMESTIC BUSINESS ACTIVITIES.—

(i) IN GENERAL.—For purposes of subparagraph (A)(ii)(II), an expanded affiliated group has significant domestic business activities if at least 25 percent of—

(I) the employees of the group are based in the United States;

(II) the employee compensation incurred by the group is incurred with respect to employees based in the United States;

(III) the assets of the group are located in the United States; or

(IV) the income of the group is derived in the United States.

(ii) DETERMINATION.—Determinations pursuant to clause (i) shall be made in the same manner as such determinations are made for purposes of determining substantial business activities under regulations referred to in subparagraph (B) as in effect on January 18, 2017, but applied by treating all references in such regulations to "foreign country" and "relevant foreign country" as references to "the United States". The Secretary may issue regulations decreasing the threshold percent in any of the tests under such regulations for determining if business activities constitute significant domestic business activities for purposes of this subparagraph.

(3) WAIVER.—

(A) IN GENERAL.—The Secretary may waive paragraph (1) if the Secretary determines that the waiver is—

(i) required in the interest of national security; or

(ii) necessary for the efficient or effective administration of Federal or federally funded—

(I) programs that provide health benefits to individuals; or

(II) public health programs.

(B) REPORT TO CONGRESS.—The Secretary shall, not later than 14 days after issuing such waiver, submit a written notification of the waiver to the relevant authorizing committees of Congress and the Committees on Appropriations of the Senate and the House of Representatives.

(4) DEFINITIONS AND SPECIAL RULES.—

(A) DEFINITIONS.—In this subsection, the terms "expanded affiliated group", "foreign incorporated entity", "domestic", and "foreign" have the meaning given those terms in section 835(c) of the Homeland Security Act of 2002 (6 U.S.C. 395(c)).

(B) SPECIAL RULES.—In applying paragraph (2) of this subsection for purposes of paragraph (1) of this subsection, the rules described under 835(c)(1) of the Homeland Security Act of 2002 (6 U.S.C. 395(c)(1)) shall apply.

(5) REGULATIONS REGARDING MANAGEMENT AND CONTROL.—

(A) IN GENERAL.—The Secretary shall, for purposes of this subsection, prescribe regulations for purposes of determining cases in which the management and control of an expanded affiliated group is to be treated as occurring, directly or indirectly, primarily within the United States. The regulations prescribed under the preceding sentence shall apply to periods after May 8, 2014.

(B) EXECUTIVE OFFICERS AND SENIOR MANAGEMENT.—The regulations prescribed under subparagraph (A) shall provide that the management and control of an expanded affiliated group shall be treated as occurring, directly or indirectly, primarily within the United States if substantially all of the executive officers and senior management of the expanded affiliated group who exercise day-to-day responsibility for making decisions involving strategic, financial, and operational policies of the expanded affiliated group are based or primarily located within the United States. Individuals who in fact exercise such day-to-day responsibilities shall be treated as executive officers and senior management regardless of their title.

(f) Preemption.—Any State or Federal laws that prohibit the transactions authorized by this statute, including state or federal laws that prohibit company directors from agreeing to the transactions authorized by this statute, are preempted and superseded by this statute.

SEC. 409. AUTHORIZATION TO PARTICIPATE IN THE NEW ARRANGEMENTS TO BORROW OF THE INTERNATIONAL MONETARY FUND.

Section 17 of the Bretton Woods Agreements Act (22 U.S.C. 286e–2) is amended—

(1) in subsection (a)—

(A) by redesignating paragraphs (3) through (5) as paragraphs (4) through (6) and inserting after paragraph (2) the following:

"(3) In order to carry out the purposes of a one-time decision of the Executive Directors of the International Monetary Fund (the Fund) to expand the resources of the New Arrangements to Borrow, established pursuant to the decision of January 27, 1997 referred to in paragraph (1) above, the Secretary of the Treasury is authorized to make loans, in an amount not to exceed the dollar equivalent of 28,202,470,000 of Special Drawing Rights, in addition to any amounts previously authorized under this section; except that prior to activation of the New Arrangements to Borrow, the Secretary shall report to Congress on whether supplementary resources are needed to forestall or cope with an impairment of the international monetary system and whether the Fund has fully explored other means of funding to the Fund."; and

(B) in paragraph (6) (as so redesignated by subparagraph (A) of this paragraph), by striking "December 16, 2022" and inserting "December 31, 2025"; and

(2) in subsection (e)(1), by inserting "(a)(3)," after "(a)(2),".

SEC. 410. [RESERVED].

[Reserved]

SEC. 411. [RESERVED].

[Reserved]

SEC. 412. INTERNATIONAL FINANCE CORPORATION.

The International Finance Corporation Act (22 U.S.C. 282 et seq.) is amended by adding at the end the following:

"SEC. 18. CAPITAL INCREASES AND AMENDMENT TO THE ARTICLES OF AGREEMENT.

"(a) Votes Authorized.—The United States Governor of the Corporation is authorized to vote in favor of—

"(1) a resolution to increase the authorized capital stock of the Corporation by 16,999,998 shares, to implement the conversion of a portion of the retained earnings of the Corporation into paid-in capital, which will result in the United States being issued an additional 3,771,899 shares of capital stock, without any cash contribution;

"(2) a resolution to increase the authorized capital stock of the Corporation on a general basis by 4,579,995 shares; and

"(3) a resolution to increase the authorized capital stock of the Corporation on a selective basis by 919,998 shares.

"(b) Amendment Of The Articles Of Agreement.—The United States Governor of the Corporation is authorized to agree to and accept an amendment to Article II, Section 2(c)(ii) of the Articles of Agreement of the Corporation that would increase the vote by which the Board of Governors of the Corporation may increase the capital stock of the Corporation from a four-fifths majority to an 85 percent majority.".

SEC. 413. OVERSIGHT AND REPORTS.

(a) Oversight.—

(1) SIGTARP.—As provided for under section 405 of this division, the Special Inspector General for the Troubled Asset Relief Program (SIGTARP) shall have oversight of the Secretary's administration of the loans, loan guarantees, and other investments provided under section 101 of division Y, the use of the funds by eligible businesses, and compliance with the requirements of section 407.

(2) OVERSIGHT PANEL.—As provided for under section 405 of this division, the Congressional COVID–19 Aid Oversight Panel shall have oversight of the Secretary's administration of the loans, loan guarantees, and other investments provided under section 101 of division Y, the use of the funds by eligible businesses, and compliance with the requirements of section 407.

(b) Secretary.—The Secretary shall, with respect to the loans, loan guarantees, and other investments provided under section 101 of division Y, make such reports as are required under section 5302 of title 31, United States Code.

(c) Government Accountability Office.—

(1) STUDY.—The Comptroller General of the United States shall conduct a study on the loans and loan guarantees provided under section 101 of division Y.

(2) REPORT.—Not later than 9 months after the date of enactment of this Act, and annually thereafter through the year succeeding the last year for which loans or loan guarantees provided under section 101 of division Y are in effect, the Comptroller General shall submit to the Committee on Financial Services, the Committee on Appropriations, and the Committee on the Budget of the House of Representatives and the Committee on Banking, Housing, and Urban Affairs, the Committee on Appropriations, and the Committee on the Budget of the Senate a report on the loans and loan guarantees provided under section 101 of division Y.

(d) Diversity Report.—The Congressional COVID–19 Aid Oversight Panel, in conjunction with the SIGTARP, shall collect diversity data from any corporation that receives Federal aid related to COVID–19, and issue a report that will be made publicly available no later than one year after the disbursement of funds. In addition to any other data, the report shall include the following:

(1) EMPLOYEE DEMOGRAPHICS.—The gender, race, and ethnic identity

(and to the extent possible, results disaggregated by ethnic group) of the corporation's employees, as otherwise known or provided voluntarily for the total number of employees (full- and part-time) and the career level of employees (executive and manager versus employees in other roles).

(2) SUPPLIER DIVERSITY.—The number and dollar value invested with minority- and women-owned suppliers (and to the extent possible, results disaggregated by ethnic group), including professional services (legal and consulting) and asset managers, and deposits and other accounts with minority depository institutions, as compared to all vendor investments.

(3) PAY EQUITY.—A comparison of pay amongst racial and ethnic minorities (and to the extent possible, results disaggregated by ethnic group) as compared to their white counterparts and comparison of pay between men and women for similar roles and assignments.

(4) CORPORATE BOARD DIVERSITY.—Corporate board demographic data, including total number of board members, gender, race and ethnic identity of board members (and to the extent possible, results disaggregated by ethnic group), as otherwise known or provided voluntarily, board position titles, as well as any leadership and subcommittee assignments.

(5) DIVERSITY AND INCLUSION OFFICES.—The reporting structure of lead diversity officials, number of staff and budget dedicated to diversity and inclusion initiatives.

(e) Diversity And Inclusion Initiatives.—Any corporation that receives Federal aid related to COVID–19 must maintain officials and budget dedicated to diversity and inclusion initiatives for no less than 5 years after disbursement of funds.

TITLE V—PANDEMIC PLANNING AND GUIDANCE FOR CONSUMERS AND REGULATORS

SEC. 501. FINANCIAL LITERACY EDUCATION COMMISSION EMERGENCY RESPONSE.

(a) Purpose.—The purpose of this section is to provide financial literacy education, including information on access to banking services and other financial products, for individuals seeking information and resources as they recover from any financial distress caused by the coronavirus disease (COVID–19) outbreak and future major disasters.

(b) Financial Literacy And Education Commission Response To The COVID–19 Emergency.—

(1) SPECIAL MEETING.—Not later than the end of the 60-day period beginning on the date of enactment of this section, the Financial Literacy and Education Commission (the "Commission") shall convene a special meeting to discuss and plan assistance related to the financial impacts of the COVID–19 emergency.

(2) UPDATE OF THE COMMISSION'S WEBSITE.—

(A) IN GENERAL.—Not later than the end of the 60-day period beginning on the date of enactment of this section, the Commission shall update the website of the Commission with a full list of tools to help individuals recover from any financial hardship as a result of the COVID–19 emergency.

(B) SPECIFIC REQUIREMENTS.—In performing the update required under subparagraph (A), the Commission shall—

(i) place special emphasis on providing an additional set of tools geared towards women, racial and ethnic minorities, veterans, disabled, and LGBTQ+ communities; and

(ii) provide information in English and Spanish.

(C) INFORMATION FROM MEMBERS.—Not later than the end of the 60-day period beginning on the date of enactment of this section, each Federal department or agency that is a member of the Commission shall provide an update on the website of the Commission disclosing any tools that the department or agency is offering to individuals or to employees of the department or agency related to the COVID–19 emergency.

(3) IMPLEMENTATION REPORT TO CONGRESS.—The Secretary of the Treasury and the Director of the Bureau of Consumer Financial Protection shall, jointly and not later than the end of the 30-day period following the date on which the meeting required under paragraph (1) is held and all updates required under paragraph (2) have been completed, report to Congress on the implementation of this section.

(4) COVID–19 EMERGENCY DEFINED.—In this subsection, the term "COVID–19 emergency" means the emergency declared on March 13, 2020, by the President under the Robert T. Stafford Disaster Relief and Emergency Assistance Act (42 U.S.C. 4121 et seq.) relating to the Coronavirus Disease 2019 (COVID–19) pandemic.

SEC. 502. INTERAGENCY PANDEMIC GUIDANCE FOR CONSUMERS.

(a) Interagency Pandemic Guidance.—

(1) GUIDANCE.—Not later than the end of the 60-day period beginning on the date of enactment of this section, the Federal financial regulators shall issue interagency regulatory guidance on preparedness, flexibility, and relief options for consumers in pandemics and major disasters, such as deferment, forbearance, affordable payment plan options, and other options such as delays on debt collections and wage garnishments.

(2) UPDATES.—The Federal financial regulators shall update the guidance required under paragraph (1) as necessary to keep such guidance current.

(b) Pandemic Preparedness Testing.—

(1) IN GENERAL.—Not later than the end of the 2-year period beginning on the date of enactment of this section, and every 5 years thereafter, the Federal financial regulators shall carry out testing along with the institutions regulated by the Federal financial regulators to determine how effectively such

institutions will be able to respond to a pandemic or major disaster.

(2) REPORT.—After the end of each test required under paragraph (1), the Federal financial regulators shall, jointly, issue a report to Congress containing the results of such test and any regulatory or legislative recommendations the regulators may have to increase pandemic preparedness.

(c) Definitions.—In this section:

(1) FEDERAL FINANCIAL REGULATORS.—The term "Federal financial regulators" means the Board of Governors of the Federal Reserve System, the Bureau of Consumer Financial Protection, the Comptroller of the Currency, the Director of the Federal Housing Finance Agency, the Federal Deposit Insurance Corporation, the National Credit Union Administration, the Secretary of Agriculture, and the Secretary of Housing and Urban Development.

(2) MAJOR DISASTER.—The term "major disaster" means a major disaster declared by the President under section 401 of the Robert T. Stafford Disaster Relief and Emergency Assistance Act (42 U.S.C. 5170), under which assistance is authorized under section 408 of such Act (42 U.S.C. 5174), or section 501 of such Act (42 U.S.C. 5191).

SEC. 503. SEC PANDEMIC GUIDANCE FOR INVESTORS.

(a) Pandemic Guidance.—

(1) GUIDANCE.—Not later than the end of the 60-day period beginning on the date of enactment of this section, the Securities and Exchange Commission shall issue regulatory guidance on preparedness, flexibility, relief, and investor protection for investors in pandemics and major disasters, including relevant disclosures.

(2) UPDATES.—The Commission shall update the guidance required under paragraph (1) as necessary to keep such guidance current.

(b) Pandemic Preparedness Testing.—

(1) IN GENERAL.—Not later than the end of the 60-day period beginning on the date of enactment of this Act, and every 5 years thereafter, the Securities and Exchange Commission shall carry out testing along with the entities regulated by the Commission to determine how effectively such entities will be able to respond to a pandemic or major disaster.

(2) REPORT.—After the end of each test required under paragraph (1), the Commission shall issue a report to Congress containing the results of such test and any regulatory or legislative recommendations the Commission may have to increase pandemic preparedness.

(c) Major Disaster Defined.—In this section, the term "major disaster" means a major disaster declared by the President under section 401 of the Robert T. Stafford Disaster Relief and Emergency Assistance Act (42 U.S.C. 5170), under which assistance is authorized under section 408 of such Act (42 U.S.C. 5174), or section 501 of such Act (42 U.S.C. 5191).

SEC. 504. UPDATES OF THE PANDEMIC INFLUENZA PLAN AND NATIONAL PLANNING FRAMEWORKS.

(a) In General.—Not later than one year following the end of the Declaration of the National Emergency, the President shall ensure that the Pandemic Influenza Plan (2017 Update) and the National Planning Frameworks are updated. The Secretary of the Treasury, in consultation with the Federal financial regulators, shall provide to the President the following:

(1) An assessment of the effectiveness of current plans and strategies to address the economic, financial, and monetary issues arising from a pandemic or other disaster.

(2) A description of the most significant challenges to protecting the economy, the financial system, and consumers, during a pandemic or other disaster, including the specific challenges experienced by women, racial and ethnic minorities, diverse-owned businesses, veterans, and the disabled.

(3) Actions that could be carried out in a crisis, as defined by the preparedness plans described in subsection (a), such as the following:

(A) Significant increases of unemployment insurance benefits (including payment amounts) for all workers under a certain income threshold, including freelancers and the self-employed, during the crisis.

(B) Loan deference, modification, and forbearance mechanisms of all consumer and business payments, allowing long-term repayment plans and excluding no industries, during the crisis.

(C) Suspension of foreclosure and eviction proceedings taken against individuals or businesses during the crisis.

(D) Suspension of all negative consumer credit reporting during the crisis.

(E) Prohibition of debt collection, repossession, and garnishment of wages during the crisis.

(F) Provision of emergency homeless assistance during the crisis.

(G) An increase in Community Development Block Grants during the crisis and to improve community response.

(H) Reduction of hurdles in the form of waivers and authorities to modify existing housing and homelessness programs to facilitate response to the crisis.

(I) Expand the size standards for eligible businesses with access no-interest or low-interest loans through the Small Business Administration during the crisis.

(J) Remove the size standard limits on eligible businesses with access no-interest or low-interest loans through the Small Business Administration during the crisis for businesses that agree to maintain their employment workforce and preserve benefits during the crisis.

(K) Support for additional no-interest or low-interest loans for small businesses through the Small Business Administration during the crisis.

(L) Utilization of the Community Development Financial Institutions (CDFI) Fund to support small businesses as well as low-income communities during the crisis.

(M) Support for State, territory, and local government financing during the crisis.

(N) Waiver of matching requirements for municipal governments during the crisis.

(O) Suspension of requirements relating to minimum distributions for retirement plans and individual retirement accounts for the calendar years of which the crisis is occurring.

(b) Special Consideration For Diversity.—In issuing the updates required under subsection (a), the President shall ensure that consideration is given as to how to minimize the economic impacts of a crisis on women, minorities, diverse-owned businesses, veterans, and the disabled.

(c) Making Plans Public.—The updated plans described in subsection (a) shall be made publicly available, but may have classified information redacted.

(d) Definitions.—In this section:

(1) DECLARATION OF THE NATIONAL EMERGENCY.—The term "Declaration of the National Emergency" means the emergency declared by the President under section 501 of the Robert T. Stafford Disaster Relief and Emergency Assistance Act (42 U.S.C. 5191) relating to the COVID–19 pandemic.

(2) FEDERAL FINANCIAL REGULATOR.—The term "Federal financial regulators" means the Bureau of Consumer Financial Protection, the Federal Deposit Insurance Corporation, the Federal Housing Finance Agency, the Board of Governors of the Federal Reserve System, the Office of the Comptroller of the Currency, the National Credit Union Administration, and the Securities and Exchange Commission.

DIVISION J—EDUCATION RELIEF AND OTHER PROGRAMS

TITLE I—EDUCATION PROVISIONS

SEC. 100101. SHORT TITLE.

This title may be cited as the "COVID–19 Pandemic Education Relief Act of 2020".

SEC. 100102. DEFINITIONS.

In this title:

(1) CORONAVIRUS.—The term "coronavirus" has the meaning given that term in section 506 of the Coronavirus Preparedness and Response Supplemental Appropriations Act, 2020 (Public Law 116–123).

(2) INSTITUTION OF HIGHER EDUCATION.—The term "institution of higher education" has the meaning given that term in section 102 of the Higher Education Act of 1965 (20 U.S.C. 1002).

(3) QUALIFYING EMERGENCY.—The term "qualifying emergency" means—

(A) a public health emergency related to the coronavirus declared by the Secretary of Health and Human Services pursuant to section 319 of the Public Health Service Act (42 U.S.C. 247d);

(B) an event related to the coronavirus for which the President declared a major disaster or an emergency under section 401 or 501, respectively, of the Robert T. Stafford Disaster Relief and Emergency Assistance Act (42 U.S.C. 5170 and 5191); or

(C) a national emergency related to the coronavirus declared by the President under section 201 of the National Emergencies Act (50 U.S.C. 1601 et seq.).

(4) SECRETARY.—The term "Secretary" means the Secretary of Education.

(5) FOREIGN INSTITUTION.—The term "foreign institution" means an institution of higher education located outside the United States that is described in paragraphs (1)(C) and (2) of section 102(a) of the Higher Education Act of 1965 (20 U.S.C. 1002(a)).

SEC. 100103. CAMPUS-BASED AID WAIVERS.

(a) Waiver Of Non-Federal Share Requirement.—Notwithstanding sections 413C(a)(2) and 443(b)(5) of the Higher Education Act of 1965 (20 U.S.C. 1070b–2(a)(2) and 1087–53(b)(5)), with respect to funds made available for award years 2019–2020 and 2020–2021, the Secretary shall waive the requirement that a participating institution of higher education provide a non-Federal share to match Federal funds provided to the institution for the programs authorized pursuant to subpart 3 of part A and part C of title IV of the Higher Education Act of 1965 (20 U.S.C. 1070b et seq. and 1087–51 et seq.) for all awards made under such programs during such award years, except nothing in this subsection shall affect the non-Federal share requirement under section 443(c)(3) of such Act that applies to private for-profit organizations.

(b) Authority To Reallocate.—Notwithstanding sections 413D, 442, and 488 of the Higher Education Act of 1965 (20 U.S.C. 1070b–3, 1087–52, and 1095), during a period of a qualifying emergency, an institution may transfer up to 100 percent of the institution's unexpended allotment under section 442 of such Act to the institution's allotment under section 413D of such Act, but may not transfer any funds from the institution's unexpended allotment under section 413D of such Act to the institution's allotment under section 442 of such Act.

SEC. 100104. USE OF SUPPLEMENTAL EDUCATIONAL OPPORTUNITY GRANTS FOR EMERGENCY AID.

(a) In General.—Notwithstanding section 413B of the Higher Education Act of 1965 (20 U.S.C. 1070b–1), an institution of higher education may reserve any amount of an institution's allocation under subpart 3 of part A of title IV of the Higher Education Act of 1965 (20 U.S.C. 1070b et seq.) for a fiscal year to award, in such fiscal year, emergency financial aid grants to assist undergraduate or graduate students for unexpected expenses and unmet financial need as the result of a qualifying emergency.

(b) Determinations.—In determining eligibility for and awarding emergency financial aid grants under this section, an institution of higher education may—

(1) waive the amount of need calculation under section 471 of the Higher Education Act of 1965 (20 U.S.C. 1087kk);

(2) allow for a student affected by a qualifying emergency to receive funds in an amount that is not more than the maximum Federal Pell Grant for the applicable award year; and

(3) utilize a contract with a scholarship-granting organization designated for the sole purpose of accepting applications from or disbursing funds to students enrolled in the institution of higher education, if such scholarship-granting organization disburses the full allocated amount provided to the institution of higher education to the recipients.

(c) Special Rule.—Any emergency financial aid grants to students under this section shall not be treated as other financial assistance for the purposes of section 471 of the Higher Education Act of 1965 (20 U.S.C. 1087kk).

SEC. 100105. FEDERAL WORK-STUDY DURING A QUALIFYING EMERGENCY.

(a) In General.—In the event of a qualifying emergency, an institution of higher education participating in the program under part C of title IV of the Higher Education Act of 1965 (20 U.S.C. 1087–51 et seq.) may make payments under such part to affected work-study students, for the period of time (not to exceed one academic year) in which affected students were unable to fulfill the students' work-study obligation for all or part of such academic year due to such qualifying emergency, as follows:

(1) Payments may be made under such part to affected work-study students in an amount equal to or less than the amount of wages such students would have been paid under such part had the students been able to complete the work obligation necessary to receive work study funds, as a one time grant or as multiple payments.

(2) Payments shall not be made to any student who was not eligible for work study or was not completing the work obligation necessary to receive work study funds under such part prior to the occurrence of the qualifying emergency.

(3) Any payments made to affected work-study students under this subsection shall meet the matching requirements of section 443 of the Higher Education Act of 1965 (20 U.S.C. 1087–53), unless such matching requirements are waived by the Secretary.

(b) Definition Of Affected Work-Study Student.—In this section, the term "affected work-study student" means a student enrolled at an eligible institution participating in the program under part C of title IV of the Higher Education Act of 1965 (20 U.S.C. 1087–51 et seq.) who—

(1) received a work-study award under section 443 of the Higher Education Act of 1965 (20 U.S.C. 1087–53) for the academic year during which a qualifying emergency occurred;

(2) earned Federal work-study wages from such eligible institution for such academic year; and

(3) was prevented from fulfilling the student's work-study obligation for all or part of such academic year due to such qualifying emergency.

SEC. 100106. ADJUSTMENT OF SUBSIDIZED LOAN USAGE LIMITS.

Notwithstanding section 455(q)(3) of the Higher Education Act of 1965 (20 U.S.C. 1087e(q)(3)), the Secretary shall exclude from a student's period of enrollment for purposes of loans made under part D of title IV of the Higher Education Act of 1965 (20 U.S.C. 1087a et seq.) any semester (or the equivalent) that the student does not complete due to a qualifying emergency, if the Secretary is able to administer such policy in a manner that limits complexity and the burden on the student.

SEC. 100107. EXCLUSION FROM FEDERAL PELL GRANT DURATION LIMIT.

The Secretary shall exclude from a student's Federal Pell Grant duration limit under section 401(c)(5) of the Higher Education Act of 1965 (2 U.S.C. 1070a(c)(5)) any semester (or the equivalent) that the student does not complete due to a qualifying emergency if the Secretary is able to administer such policy in a manner that limits complexity and the burden on the student.

SEC. 100108. INSTITUTIONAL REFUNDS AND FEDERAL STUDENT LOAN FLEXIBILITY.

(a) Institutional Waiver.—

(1) IN GENERAL.—The Secretary shall waive the institutional requirement under section 484B of the Higher Education Act of 1965 (20 U.S.C. 1091b) with respect to the amount of grant or loan assistance (other than assistance received under part C of title IV of such Act) to be returned under such section if a recipient of assistance under title IV of the Higher Education Act of 1965 (20 U.S.C. 1070 et seq.) withdraws from the institution of higher education during the payment period or period of enrollment as a result of a qualifying emergency.

(2) WAIVERS.—The Secretary shall require each institution using a waiver relating to the withdrawal of recipients under this subsection to report the number of such recipients, the amount of grant or loan assistance (other than assistance received under part C of title IV of such Act) associated with each such recipient, and the total amount of grant or loan assistance (other than assistance received under part C of title IV of such Act) for which each institution has not returned assistance under title IV to the Secretary.

(b) Student Waiver.—The Secretary shall waive the amounts that students are required to return under section 484B of the Higher Education Act of 1965 (20 U.S.C. 1091b) with respect to Federal Pell Grants or other grant assistance if the withdrawals on which the returns are based are withdrawals by students who withdrew from the institution of higher education as a result of a qualifying emergency.

(c) Canceling Loan Obligation.—Notwithstanding any other provision of the Higher Education Act of 1965 (20 U.S.C. 1001 et seq.), the Secretary shall cancel the borrower's obligation to repay the entire portion of a loan made under part D of title IV of such Act (20 U.S.C. 1087a et seq.) associated with a payment period for a recipient of such loan who withdraws from the institution of higher education during the payment period as a result of a qualifying emergency.

(d) Approved Leave Of Absence.—Notwithstanding any other provision of the Higher Education Act of 1965 (20 U.S.C. 1001 et seq.), for purposes of receiving assistance under title IV of the Higher Education Act of 1965 (20 U.S.C. 1070 et seq.), an institution of higher education may, as a result of a qualifying emergency, provide a student with an approved leave of absence that does not require the student to return at the same point in the academic program that the student began the leave of absence if the student returns within the same semester (or the equivalent).

SEC. 100109. SATISFACTORY ACADEMIC PROGRESS.

Notwithstanding section 484 of the Higher Education Act of 1965 (20 U.S.C. 1091), in determining whether a student is maintaining satisfactory academic progress for purposes of title IV of the Higher Education Act of 1965 (20

U.S.C. 1070 et seq.), an institution of higher education may, as a result of a qualifying emergency, exclude from the quantitative component of the calculation any attempted credits that were not completed by such student without requiring an appeal by such student.

SEC. 100110. CONTINUING EDUCATION AT AFFECTED FOREIGN INSTITUTIONS.

(a) In General.—Notwithstanding section 481(b) of the Higher Education Act of 1965 (20 U.S.C. 1088(b)), with respect to a foreign institution, in the case of a public health emergency, major disaster or emergency, or national emergency declared by the applicable government authorities in the country in which the foreign institution is located, the Secretary may permit any part of an otherwise eligible program to be offered via distance education for the duration of such emergency or disaster and the following payment period for purposes of title IV of the Higher Education Act of 1965 (20 U.S.C. 1070 et seq.).

(b) Eligibility.—An otherwise eligible program that is offered in whole or in part through distance education by a foreign institution between March 1, 2020, and the date of enactment of this Act shall be deemed eligible for the purposes of part D of title IV of the Higher Education Act of 1965 (20 U.S.C. 1087a et seq.) for the duration of the emergency or disaster affecting the institution as described in subsection (a) and the following payment period for purposes of title IV of the Higher Education Act of 1965 (20 U.S.C. 1070 et seq.). An institution of higher education that uses the authority provided in the previous sentence shall report such use to the Secretary—

(1) for the 2019–2020 award year, not later than June 30, 2020; and

(2) for an award year subsequent to the 2019–2020 award year, not later than 30 days after such use.

(c) Report.—Not later than 180 days after the date of enactment of this Act, and every 180 days thereafter for the duration of the applicable disaster or emergency and the following payment period, the Secretary shall submit to the authorizing committees (as defined in section 103 of the Higher Education Act of 1965 (20 U.S.C. 1003)) a report that identifies each foreign institution that carried out a distance education program authorized under this section.

(d) Written Arrangements.—

(1) IN GENERAL.—Notwithstanding section 102 of the Higher Education Act of 1965 (20 U.S.C. 1002), with respect to a foreign institution, in the case of a public health emergency, major disaster or emergency, or national emergency declared by the applicable government authorities in the country in which the foreign institution is located, the Secretary may allow a foreign institution to enter into a written arrangement with an institution of higher education located in the United States that participates in the Federal Direct Loan Program under part D of title IV of the Higher Education Act of 1965 (20 U.S.C. 1087a et seq.), for the duration of such emergency or disaster and

the following payment period, for the purpose of allowing a student of the foreign institution who is a borrower of a loan made under such part to take courses from the institution of higher education located in the United States.

(2) FORM OF ARRANGEMENTS.—

(A) PUBLIC OR OTHER NONPROFIT INSTITUTIONS.—A foreign institution that is a public or other nonprofit institution may enter into a written arrangement under paragraph (1) only with an institution of higher education described in section 101 of such Act (20 U.S.C. 1001).

(B) OTHER INSTITUTIONS.—A foreign institution that is a graduate medical school, nursing school, or a veterinary school and that is not a public or other nonprofit institution may enter into a written arrangement under paragraph (1) with an institution of higher education described in section 101 or section 102 of such Act (20 U.S.C. 1001 and 1002).

(3) REPORT ON USE.—An institution of higher education that uses the authority described in paragraph (2) shall report such use to the Secretary—

(A) for the 2019–2020 award year, not later than June 30, 2020; and

(B) for an award year subsequent to the 2019–2020 award year, not later than 30 days after such use.

(4) REPORT FROM THE SECRETARY.—Not later than 180 days after the date of enactment of this Act, and every 180 days thereafter for the duration of the applicable disaster or emergency and the following payment period, the Secretary shall submit to the authorizing committees (as defined in section 103 of the Higher Education Act of 1965 (20 U.S.C. 1003)) a report that identifies each foreign institution that entered into a written arrangement authorized under paragraph (1).

SEC. 100111. HBCU CAPITAL FINANCING.

(a) Deferment Period.—

(1) IN GENERAL.—Notwithstanding any provision of title III of the Higher Education Act of 1965 (20 U.S.C. 1051 et seq.), or any regulation promulgated under such title, the Secretary may grant a deferment, for the duration of a qualifying emergency, to an institution of higher education that has received a loan under part D of title III of such Act (20 U.S.C. 1066 et seq.).

(2) TERMS.—During the deferment period granted under this subsection—

(A) the institution of higher education shall not be required to pay any periodic installment of principal or interest required under the loan agreement for such loan; and

(B) the Secretary shall make principal and interest payments otherwise due under the loan agreement.

(3) CLOSING.—At the closing of a loan deferred under this subsection, terms shall be set under which the institution of higher education shall be required to repay the Secretary for the payments of principal and interest made by the Secretary during the deferment, on a schedule that begins upon repayment to the lender in full on the loan agreement, except in no case shall repayment

be required to begin before the date that is 1 full fiscal year after the date that is the end of the qualifying emergency.

(b) Termination Date.—

(1) IN GENERAL.—The authority provided under this section to grant a loan deferment under subsection (a) shall terminate on the date on which the qualifying emergency is no longer in effect.

(2) DURATION.—Any provision of a loan agreement or insurance agreement modified by the authority under this section shall remain so modified for the duration of the period covered by the loan agreement or insurance agreement.

(c) Report.—Not later than 180 days after the date of enactment of this Act, and every 180 days thereafter during the period beginning on the first day of the qualifying emergency and ending on September 30 of the fiscal year following the end of the qualifying emergency, the Secretary shall submit to the authorizing committees (as defined in section 103 of the Higher Education Act of 1965 (20 U.S.C. 1003)) a report that identifies each institution of higher education that received assistance under this section.

SEC. 100112. WAIVER AUTHORITY AND REPORTING REQUIREMENT FOR INSTITUTIONAL AID.

(a) Waiver Authority.—Notwithstanding any other provision of the Higher Education Act of 1965 (U.S.C. 1001 et seq.), unless enacted with specific reference to this section, for any institution of higher education that was receiving assistance under title III, title V, or subpart 4 of part A of title VII of such Act (20 U.S.C. 1051 et seq.; 1101 et seq.; 1136a et seq.) at the time of a qualifying emergency, the Secretary may, for the period beginning on the first day of the qualifying emergency and ending on September 30 of the fiscal year following the end of the qualifying emergency—

(1) waive—

(A) the eligibility data requirements set forth in section 391(d) and 521(e) of the Higher Education Act of 1965 (20 U.S.C. 1068(d) and 1103(e));

(B) the wait-out period set forth in section 313(d) of the Higher Education Act of 1965 (20 U.S.C. 1059(d));

(C) the allotment requirements under paragraphs (2) and (3) of subsection 318(e) of the Higher Education Act of 1965 (20 U.S.C. 1059e(e)), and references to "the academic year preceding the beginning of that fiscal year" in paragraph (1);

(D) the allotment requirements under subsections (b), (c), and (g) of section 324 of the Higher Education Act of 1965 (20 U.S.C. 1063), and references to "the end of the school year preceding the beginning of that fiscal year" under subsection (a) and references to "the academic year preceding such fiscal year" under subsection (h) of such section;

(E) subparagraphs (A), (C), (D), and (E) of section 326(f)(3) of the Higher Education Act of 1965 (20 U.S.C. 1063b(f)(3)), and references to "previous year" under subparagraph (B) of such section;

(F) subparagraphs (A), (C), (D), and (E) of section 723(f)(3) and section 724(f)(3) of the Higher Education Act of 1965 (20 U.S.C. 1136a(f)(3) and 1136b(f)(3)), and references to "previous academic year" under subparagraph (B) of such sections; and
(G) the allotment restriction set forth in section 318(d)(4) and 323(c)(2) of the Higher Education Act of 1965 (20 U.S.C. 1059e(d)(4) and 1062(c)(2)); and
(2) waive or modify any statutory or regulatory provision to ensure that institutions that were receiving assistance under title III, title V, or subpart 4 of part A of title VII of such Act (20 U.S.C. 1051 et seq.; 1101 et seq.; 1136a et seq.) at the time of a qualifying emergency are not adversely affected by any formula calculation for fiscal year 2020 and for the period beginning on the first day of the qualifying emergency and ending on September 30 of the fiscal year following the end of the qualifying emergency, as necessary.
(b) Use Of Unexpended Funds.—Any funds paid to an institution under title III, title V, or subpart 4 of part A of title VII of the Higher Education Act of 1965 (20 U.S.C. 1051 et seq.; 1101 et seq.; 1136a et seq.) and not expended or used for the purposes for which the funds were paid to the institution during the 5-year period following the date on which the funds were first paid to the institution, may be carried over and expended during the succeeding 5-year period.
(c) Report.—Not later than 180 days after the date of enactment of this Act, and every 180 days thereafter for the period beginning on the first day of the qualifying emergency and ending on September 30 of the fiscal year following the end of the qualifying emergency, the Secretary shall submit to the authorizing committees (as defined in section 103 of the Higher Education Act of 1965 (20 U.S.C. 1003)) a report that identifies each institution that received a waiver or modification under this section.

SEC. 100113. AUTHORIZED USES AND OTHER MODIFICATIONS FOR GRANTS.
(a) In General.—The Secretary is authorized to modify the required and allowable uses of funds for grants awarded under part A or B of title III, chapters I or II of subpart 2 of part A of title IV, title V, or subpart 4 of part A of title VII of the Higher Education Act of 1965 (20 U.S.C. 1057 et seq.; 1060 et seq.; 1070a–11 et seq.; 1070a–21 et seq.; 1101 et seq.; 1136a et seq.) to an institution of higher education or other grant recipient (not including individual recipients of Federal student financial assistance), at the request of an institution of higher education or other recipient of a grant (not including individual recipients of Federal student financial assistance) as a result of a qualifying emergency, for the period beginning on the first day of the qualifying emergency and ending on September 30 of the fiscal year following the end of the qualifying emergency.
(b) Matching Requirement Modifications.—Notwithstanding any other provision of the Higher Education Act of 1965 (20 U.S.C. 1001 et seq.),

the Secretary is authorized to modify any Federal share or other financial matching requirement for a grant awarded on a competitive basis, or a grant awarded under part A or B of title III or subpart 4 of part A of title VII of the Higher Education Act of 1965 (20 U.S.C. 1057 et seq.; 1060 et seq.; 1136a et seq.) at the request of an institution of higher education or other grant recipient as a result of a qualifying emergency, for the period beginning on the first day of the qualifying emergency and ending on September 30 of the fiscal year following the end of the qualifying emergency.

(c) Reports.—Not later than 180 days after the date of enactment of this Act, and every 180 days thereafter for the duration of the period beginning on the first day of the qualifying emergency and ending on September 30 of the fiscal year following the end of the qualifying emergency, the Secretary shall submit to the authorizing committees (as defined in section 103 of the Higher Education Act of 1965 (20 U.S.C. 1003)) a report that identifies each institution of higher education or other grant recipient that received a modification under this section.

SEC. 100114. SERVICE OBLIGATIONS FOR TEACHERS.

(a) Teach Grants.—For the purposes of section 420N of the Higher Education Act of 1965 (20 U.S.C. 1070g–2), during a qualifying emergency, the Secretary—

(1) may modify the categories of extenuating circumstances under which a recipient of a grant under subpart 9 of part A of title IV of such Act who is unable to fulfill all or part of the recipient's service obligation may be excused from fulfilling that portion of the service obligation; and

(2) shall consider teaching service that, as a result of a qualifying emergency, is part-time or temporarily interrupted to be full-time service and to fulfill the service obligations under section 420N.

(b) Teacher Loan Forgiveness.—Notwithstanding section 428J or 460 of the Higher Education Act of 1965 (20 U.S.C. 1078–10; 1087j), the Secretary shall waive the requirements under such sections that years of teaching service shall be consecutive if—

(1) the teaching service of a borrower is temporarily interrupted due to a qualifying emergency; and

(2) after the temporary interruption due to a qualifying emergency, the borrower resumes teaching service and completes a total of five years of qualifying teaching service under such sections, including qualifying teaching service performed before, during, and after such qualifying emergency.

SEC. 100115. PAYMENTS FOR STUDENT LOAN BORROWERS AS A RESULT OF A NATIONAL EMERGENCY.

(a) Payments For Student Loan Borrowers During A National Emergency.—

(1) IN GENERAL.—Part G of title IV of the Higher Education Act of 1965 (20 U.S.C. 1088 et seq.) is amended by inserting after section 493D the following:

"SEC. 493E. PAYMENTS FOR STUDENT LOAN BORROWERS DURING A NATIONAL EMERGENCY.

"(a) Definitions.—In this section:

"(1) CORONAVIRUS.—The term 'coronavirus' has the meaning given the term in section 506 of the Coronavirus Preparedness and Response Supplemental Appropriations Act, 2020 (Public Law 116–123).

"(2) INCOME-DRIVEN REPAYMENT.—The term 'income-driven repayment' means—

"(A) income-based repayment authorized under section 493C for loans made, insured, or guaranteed under part B or part D; or

"(B) income contingent repayment authorized under section 455(e) for loans made under part D.

"(3) INVOLUNTARY COLLECTION.—The term 'involuntary collection' means—

"(A) a wage garnishment authorized under section 488A of this Act or section 3720D of title 31, United States Code;

"(B) a reduction of tax refund by amount of debt authorized under section 3720A of title 31, United States Code;

"(C) a reduction of any other Federal benefit payment by administrative offset authorized under section 3716 of title 31, United States Code (including a benefit payment due to an individual under the Social Security Act or any other provision described in subsection (c)(3)(A)(i) of such section); and

"(D) any other involuntary collection activity.

"(4) NATIONAL EMERGENCY.—The term 'national emergency' means—

"(A) a public health emergency related to the coronavirus that is declared by the Secretary of Health and Human Services pursuant to section 319 of the Public Health Service Act (42 U.S.C. 247d); or

"(B) a national emergency related to the coronavirus declared by the President under the National Emergencies Act (50 U.S.C. 1601 et seq.).

"(b) National Emergency Student Loan Repayment Assistance.—

"(1) AUTHORITY.—Beginning on the date of enactment of the Take Responsibility for Workers and Families Act, in the event of a national emergency, the Secretary shall, for each month during the national emergency period and for each borrower of a loan made, insured, or guaranteed under part B, D, or E, pay the total amount due for such month on the loan, based on the payment plan selected by the borrower or the borrower's loan status.

"(2) NO CAPITALIZATION OF INTEREST.—With respect to any loan in repayment during a national emergency period, interest due on loans made, insured, or guaranteed under part B, D, or E during such period shall not be capitalized at any time during the national emergency.

"(3) APPLICABILITY OF PAYMENTS.—Any payment made by the Secretary under this section shall be considered by the Secretary, or by a lender with respect to a loan made, insured, or guaranteed under part B—

"(A) as a qualifying payment under the public service loan forgiveness program under section 455(m), if the borrower would otherwise qualify under such section;

"(B) in the case of a borrower enrolled in an income-driven repayment plan, as a qualifying payment for the purpose of calculating eligibility for loan forgiveness for the borrower in accordance with section 493C(b)(7) or section 455(d)(1)(D), as the case may be; and

"(C) in the case of a borrower in default, as an on-time monthly payment for purposes of loan rehabilitation pursuant to section 428F(a).

"(4) REPORTING TO CONSUMER REPORTING AGENCIES.—During the period in which the Secretary is making payments on a loan under paragraph (1), the Secretary shall ensure that, for the purpose of reporting information about the loan to a consumer reporting agency, any payment made by the Secretary is treated as if it were a regularly scheduled payment made by a borrower.

"(5) NOTICE OF PAYMENTS AND PROGRAM.—Not later than 15 days following the date of enactment of the COVID–19 Pandemic Education Relief Act of 2020, and monthly thereafter during the period of a national emergency, the Secretary shall provide a notice to all borrowers of loans made, insured, or guaranteed under part B, D, or E—

"(A) informing borrowers of the actions taken under this section;

"(B) providing borrowers with an easily accessible method to opt out of the benefits provided under this section; and

"(C) notifying the borrower that the program under this section is a temporary program and will end after the national emergency ends.

"(6) SUSPENSION OF INVOLUNTARY COLLECTION.—Beginning on the date of enactment of the Take Responsibility for Workers and Families Act, in the event of a national emergency, the Secretary, or other holder of a loan made, insured, or guaranteed under part B, D, or E, shall immediately take action to halt all involuntary collection related to the loan until the date on which the national emergency ends.

"(c) Waiver Of Interest During National Emergency.—Notwithstanding any other provision of law, the Secretary shall pay any interest that would otherwise be charged or accrue during a national emergency on any loan made, insured, or guaranteed under part B, D, or E.

"(d) Transition Period.—Upon the termination of a national emergency, the Secretary shall carry out a program to provide for a transition period of 90 days, beginning on the day after the last day of the national emergency, during which—

"(1) the Secretary shall provide not less than 3 notices to borrowers indicating when the borrower's normal payment obligations will resume; and

"(2) any missed payments by a borrower under part B, D, or E shall not—

"(A) result in fees or penalties; or

"(B) be reported to any consumer reporting agency or otherwise impact the borrower's credit history.

"(e) Implementation In FFEL Entities.—To facilitate implementation of this section—

"(1) lenders and guaranty agencies holding loans made, insured, or guaranteed under part B shall report, to the satisfaction of the Secretary, information to verify at the borrower level the amount of payments made under this section; and

"(2) the Secretary shall have the authority to establish a payment schedule for purposes of this section for loans made, insured, or guaranteed under part B and not held by the Secretary.

"(f) Waivers.—In carrying out this section, the Secretary may waive the application of—

"(1) subchapter I of chapter 35 of title 44, United States Code;

"(2) the master calendar requirements under section 482;

"(3) negotiated rulemaking under section 492; and

"(4) the requirement to publish the notices related to the system of records of the agency before implementation required under paragraphs (4) and (11) of section 552a(e) of title 5, United States Code (commonly known as the 'Privacy Act of 1974'), except that the notices shall be published not later than 180 days after the date of enactment of the Take Responsibility for Workers and Families Act".".

(2) FFEL AMENDMENT.—Section 428(c)(8) of the Higher Education Act of 1965 (20 U.S.C. 1078(c)(8)) is amended by striking "and for which" and all that follows through "this subsection".

(3) APPLICABILITY.—The requirement of the Secretary to make payments under section 493E of the Higher Education Act of 1965, as added by paragraph 1, shall apply to payments due after the date of enactment of this Act.

(b) Minimum Relief For Student Loan Borrowers As A Result Of A National Emergency.—Part G of title IV the Higher Education Act of 1965 (20 U.S.C. 1088 et seq.), as amended by subsection (a), is further amended by inserting after section 493E the following:

"SEC. 493F. MINIMUM RELIEF FOR STUDENT LOAN BORROWERS AS A RESULT OF A NATIONAL EMERGENCY.

"(a) Minimum Student Loan Relief As A Result Of A National Emergency.—Not later than 90 days after the conclusion of a national emergency (as defined in section 493E), the Secretary shall, for each borrower of a loan made under part B, D, or E, reduce the total outstanding balance due on all such loans of the borrower, by an amount equal to the lesser of—

"(1) the difference between $10,000 and the total amount of payments made by the Secretary under section 493E(b) on such loans of the borrower during the period of such national emergency; or

"(2) the total amount of outstanding principal and interest due on such loans of the borrower, as of the date of the calculation under this subsection.

"(b) Data To Implement.—Contractors of the Secretary and lenders and guaranty agencies holding loans made, insured, or guaranteed under part B shall report, to the satisfaction of the Secretary, the information necessary to calculate the amount to be applied under subsection (a).".

SEC. 100116. RULE OF CONSTRUCTION.
Except as otherwise provided in this Act or the amendments made by this Act, nothing in this Act shall be construed to provide additional authority to the Secretary of Education to waive any provision of the following:
(1) The Elementary and Secondary Education Act of 1965 (20 U.S.C. 6301 et seq.).
(2) The Individuals with Disabilities Education Act (20 U.S.C. 1400 et seq.).
(3) The Higher Education Act of 1965 (20 U.S.C. 1001 et seq.).
(4) The Carl D. Perkins Career and Technical Education Act of 2006 (20 U.S.C. 2301 et seq.).

TITLE II—OTHER PROGRAMS

SEC. 100202. PROVISIONS RELATED TO THE CORPORATION FOR NATIONAL AND COMMUNITY SERVICE.
(a) Accrual Of Service Hours.—
(1) ACCRUAL THROUGH OTHER SERVICE HOURS.—
(A) IN GENERAL.—Notwithstanding any other provision of the Domestic Volunteer Service Act of 1973 (42 U.S.C. 4950 et seq.) or the National and Community Service Act of 1990 (42 U.S.C. 12501 et seq.), the Corporation for National and Community Service shall allow an individual described in subparagraph (B) to accrue other service hours that will count toward the number of hours needed for the individual's education award.
(B) AFFECTED INDIVIDUALS.—Subparagraph (A) shall apply to any individual serving in a position eligible for an educational award under subtitle D of title I of the National and Community Service Act of 1990 (42 U.S.C. 12601 et seq.)—
(i) who is performing limited service due to COVID–19; or
(ii) whose position has been suspended or placed on hold due to COVID–19.
(2) PROVISIONS IN CASE OF EARLY EXIT.—In any case where an individual serving in a position eligible for an educational award under subtitle D of title I of the National and Community Service Act of 1990 (42 U.S.C. 12601 et seq.) was required to exit the position early at the direction of the Corporation for National and Community Service, the Chief Executive Officer of the Corporation for National and Community Service may—
(A) deem such individual as having met the requirements of the position; and
(B) award the individual the full value of the educational award under such subtitle for which the individual would otherwise have been eligible.
(b) No Required Return Of Grant Funds.—Notwithstanding section 129(l)(3)(A)(i) of the National and Community Service Act of 1990 (42 U.S.C. 12581(l)

(3)(A)(i)), the Chief Executive Officer of the Corporation for National and Community Service may permit fixed-amount grant recipients under such section 129(l) to maintain a pro rata amount of grant funds, at the discretion of the Corporation for National and Community Service, for participants who exited, were suspended, or are serving in a limited capacity due to COVID–19, to enable the grant recipients to maintain operations and to accept participants.

(c) Extension Of Terms And Age Limits.—Notwithstanding any other provision of law, the Corporation for National and Community Service may extend the term of service (for a period not to exceed the 1-year period immediately following the end of the national emergency) or waive any upper age limit (except in no case shall the maximum age exceed 26 years of age) for national service programs carried out by the National Civilian Community Corps under subtitle E of title I of the National and Community Service Act of 1990 (42 U.S.C. 12611 et seq.), and the participants in such programs, for the purposes of—

(1) addressing disruptions due to COVID–19; and

(2) minimizing the difficulty in returning to full operation due to COVID–19 on such programs and participants. DIVISION K—AGRICULTURE PROVISIONS

TITLE I—COMMODITY SUPPORT AND OTHER AGRICULTURE PROGRAMS

SEC. 110101. SUPPLEMENTAL DAIRY MARGIN COVERAGE.

(a) In General.—Of the funds of the Commodity Credit Corporation, the Secretary of Agriculture shall provide supplemental dairy margin coverage payments to eligible dairy operations described in subsection (b) whenever the average actual dairy production margin (as defined in section 1401 of the Agricultural Act of 2014 (7 U.S.C. 9051)) for a month is less than the coverage level threshold selected by such eligible dairy operation under such section 1406.

(b) Eligible Dairy Operation Described.—An eligible dairy operation described in this subsection is a participating dairy operation (as defined in section 1401 of the Agricultural Act of 2014 (7 U.S.C. 9051)) that—

(1) is located in the United States; and

(2) on the date of the enactment of this section, had a production history established under the dairy margin coverage program described in section 1405 of the Agricultural Act of 2014 (7 U.S.C. 9055) of less than 5 million pounds, as determined in accordance with subsection (c) of that Act.

(c) Supplemental Production History Calculation.—For purposes of determining the production history of an eligible dairy operation under this subsection, such an operation's production history shall be equal to—

(1) the production volume of such dairy operation for the 2019 milk marketing year; minus

(2) the production history of such dairy operation established under section 1405 of the Agricultural Act of 2014 (7 U.S.C. 9055).

(d) Coverage Percentage.—

(1) IN GENERAL.—For purposes of calculating payments to be issued under this section, an eligible dairy operation's coverage percentage shall be equal to the coverage percentage selected by such eligible dairy operation under section 1406 of the Agricultural Act of 2014 (7 U.S.C. 9056).

(2) 5-MILLION POUND LIMITATION.—

(A) IN GENERAL.—The Secretary shall not provide supplemental dairy margin coverage on a dairy operation's actual production for calendar year 2019 such that the total covered production history of the operation exceeds 5 million pounds.

(B) DETERMINATION OF AMOUNT.—In calculating the total covered production history of a dairy operation under subparagraph (A), the Secretary shall multiply the coverage percentage selected under section 1406 of the Agricultural Act of 2014 (7 U.S.C. 9056) by the sum of—

(i) The supplemental production history calculated under subsection (c) with respect to such dairy operation; and

(ii) The dairy margin coverage production history described in subsection (c)(2) with respect to such dairy operation.

(e) Premium Cost.—The premium cost for an eligible dairy operation under this section shall be equal to the product of multiplying—

(1) the Tier I premium cost calculated under section 1407(b) of the Agricultural Act of 2014 (7 12 U.S.C. 9057(b)); by

(2) the production history calculation determined under subsection (c) (such that total covered production history does not exceed 5 million pounds).

(f) Regulations.—Not later than 45 days after the date of the enactment of this section, the Secretary shall issue regulations to carry out this section.

(g) Retroactivity.—The authority to carry out this section shall begin on January 1, 2020.

SEC. 110102. TARGETED PURCHASES.

(a) In General.—The Secretary of Agriculture shall utilize not less than $300,000,000 of the funds available under section 32 of the Act of August 24, 1935 (7 U.S.C. 612c) to purchase qualified agricultural products for the purpose of donating the products to food assistance programs, including the Emergency Food Assistance Program, of which the Secretary shall utilize—

(1) not less than $150,000,000 to purchase specialty crops;

(2) not less than $75,000,000 to purchase dairy; and

(3) not less than $75,000,000 to purchase meat and poultry products.

(b) Qualified Agricultural Product Defined.—In this section, the term "qualified agricultural product" means a dairy, meat, or poultry product, or a specialty crop—

(1) that was packaged or marketed for sale to commercial or food service industries;

(2) for which decreased demand exists for such a product due to the COVID–19 outbreak; and

(3) the repurposing of which would be impractical for grocery or retail sale.

TITLE II—SUPPLEMENTAL NUTRITION ASSISTANCE PROGRAM

SEC. 110201. SNAP FUNDING.

There are hereby appropriated to the Secretary of Agriculture, out of any money in the Treasury not otherwise appropriated, such sums as maybe necessary to carry out this title and sections 2301 and 2302 of the Families First Coronavirus Response Act (Public Law 116–127).

SEC. 110202. SNAP ALLOTMENTS.

(a) Nutrition Assistance Allotment Amount.—

(1) VALUE OF BENEFITS.—Notwithstanding any other provision of law, beginning on May 1, 2020, the value of benefits determined under section 8(a) of the Food and Nutrition Act of 2008 (7 U.S.C. 2017(a)), and consolidated block grants for Puerto Rico and American Samoa determined under section 19(a) of such Act (7 U.S.C. 2028(a)), shall be calculated using 115 percent of the June 2019 value of the thrifty food plan (as defined in section 3 of such Act (7 U.S.C. 2012)) if the value of the benefits and block grants would be greater under that calculation than in the absence of this paragraph.

(2) MINIMUM AMOUNT.—

(A) IN GENERAL.—The minimum value of benefits determined under section 8(a) of the Food and Nutrition Act of 2008 (7 U.S.C. 2017(a)) for a household of not more than 2 members shall be $30.

(B) EFFECTIVENESS.—Subparagraph (A) shall remain in effect until the date on which 8 percent of the value of the thrifty food plan for a household containing 1 member, rounded to the nearest whole dollar increment, is equal to or greater than $30.

(b) Requirements For The Secretary.—In carrying out this section, the Secretary shall—

(1) consider the benefit increases described in subsection (a) to be a "mass change";

(2) require a simple process for States to notify households of the increase in benefits;

(3) not include any errors in the implementation of this section in the payment error rate calculated under section 16(c) of the Food and Nutrition Act of 2008 (7 U.S.C. 2025(c));

(4) disregard the additional amount of benefits that a household receives as a result of this section in determining the amount of overissuances under section 13 of the Food and Nutrition Act of 2008 (7 U.S.C. 2022); and

(5) set the tolerance level for excluding small errors for the purposes of section 16(c) of the Food and Nutrition Act of 2008 (7 U.S.C. 2025(c)) at $50 through

September 30, 2021.

(c) Administrative Expenses.—

(1) IN GENERAL.—For the costs of State administrative expenses associated with carrying out this section and administering the supplemental nutrition assistance program established under the Food and Nutrition Act of 2008 (7 U.S.C. 2011 et seq.), the Secretary of Agriculture shall make available $150,000,000 for fiscal year 2020 and $150,000,000 for fiscal year 2021.

(2) TIMING FOR FISCAL YEAR 2020.—Not later than 60 days after the date of the enactment of this section, the Secretary shall make available to States amounts for fiscal year 2020 under paragraph (1).

(3) ALLOCATION OF FUNDS.—Funds described in paragraph (1) shall be made available as grants to State agencies for each fiscal year as follows:

(A) 75 percent of the amounts available for each fiscal year shall be allocated to States based on the share of each State of households that participate in the supplemental nutrition assistance program as reported to the Department of Agriculture for the most recent 12-month period for which data are available, adjusted by the Secretary (as of the date of the enactment of this section) for participation in disaster programs under section 5(h) of the Food and Nutrition Act of 2008 (7 U.S.C. 2014(h)); and

(B) 25 percent of the amounts available for each fiscal year shall be allocated to States based on the increase in the number of households that participate in the supplemental nutrition assistance program as reported to the Department of Agriculture over the most recent 12-month period for which data are available, adjusted by the Secretary (as of the date of the enactment of this section) for participation in disaster programs under section 5(h) of the Food and Nutrition Act of 2008 (7 U.S.C. 2014(h)).

SEC. 110203. SNAP RULES.

No funds (including fees) made available under this Act or any other Act for any fiscal year may be used to finalize, implement, administer, enforce, carry out, or otherwise give effect to—

(1) the final rule entitled "Supplemental Nutrition Assistance Program: Requirements for Able-Bodied Adults Without Dependents" published in the Federal Register on December 5, 2019 (84 Fed. Reg. 66782);

(2) the proposed rule entitled "Revision of Categorical Eligibility in the Supplemental Nutrition Assistance Program (SNAP)" published in the Federal Register on July 24, 2019 (84 Fed. Reg. 35570); or

(3) the proposed rule entitled "Supplemental Nutrition Assistance Program: Standardization of State Heating and Cooling Standard Utility Allowances" published in the Federal Register on October 3, 2019 (84 Fed. Reg. 52809).

SEC. 110204. SNAP HOT FOOD PURCHASES.

During the period beginning 10 days after the date of the enactment of this Act and ending on the termination date of the public health emergency declaration made by the Secretary of Health and Human Services under section 319 of the Public Health Service Act based on an outbreak of coronavirus disease

2019 (COVID–19), the term “food”, as defined in section 3 of the Food and Nutrition Act of 2008 (7 U.S.C. 2012), shall be deemed to exclude “hot foods or hot food products ready for immediate consumption other than those authorized pursuant to clauses (3), (4), (5), (7), (8), and (9) of this subsection,” for purposes of such Act, except that such exclusion is limited to retail food stores authorized to accept and redeem supplemental nutrition assistance program benefits as of the date of enactment of this Act.

SEC. 110205. FOOD DISTRIBUTION PROGRAM ON INDIAN RESERVATIONS.

Any funds provided in the Third Coronavirus Preparedness and Response Supplemental Appropriations Act, 2020 for the Food Distribution Program on Indian Reservations, as authorized by section 4(b) of the Food and Nutrition Act of 2008 (7 U.S.C. 2013(b)), are not subject to the payment of the non-Federal share requirement described in section 4(b)(4)(A) of the Food and Nutrition Act of 2008 (7 U.S.C. 2013(b)(4)(A)).

DIVISION K—AGRICULTURE PROVISIONS

TITLE I—COMMODITY SUPPORT AND OTHER AGRICULTURE PROGRAMS

SEC. 110101. SUPPLEMENTAL DAIRY MARGIN COVERAGE.

(a) In General.—Of the funds of the Commodity Credit Corporation, the Secretary of Agriculture shall provide supplemental dairy margin coverage payments to eligible dairy operations described in subsection (b) whenever the average actual dairy production margin (as defined in section 1401 of the Agricultural Act of 2014 (7 U.S.C. 9051)) for a month is less than the coverage level threshold selected by such eligible dairy operation under such section 1406.

(b) Eligible Dairy Operation Described.—An eligible dairy operation described in this subsection is a participating dairy operation (as defined in section 1401 of the Agricultural Act of 2014 (7 U.S.C. 9051)) that—

(1) is located in the United States; and

(2) on the date of the enactment of this section, had a production history established under the dairy margin coverage program described in section 1405 of the Agricultural Act of 2014 (7 U.S.C. 9055) of less than 5 million pounds, as determined in accordance with subsection (c) of that Act.

(c) Supplemental Production History Calculation.—For purposes of determining the production history of an eligible dairy operation under this subsection, such an operation's production history shall be equal to—

(1) the production volume of such dairy operation for the 2019 milk marketing year; minus

(2) the production history of such dairy operation established under section 1405 of the Agricultural Act of 2014 (7 U.S.C. 9055).

(d) Coverage Percentage.—

(1) IN GENERAL.—For purposes of calculating payments to be issued under this section, an eligible dairy operation's coverage percentage shall be equal to the coverage percentage selected by such eligible dairy operation under section 1406 of the Agricultural Act of 2014 (7 U.S.C. 9056).

(2) 5-MILLION POUND LIMITATION.—

(A) IN GENERAL.—The Secretary shall not provide supplemental dairy margin coverage on a dairy operation's actual production for calendar year 2019 such that the total covered production history of the operation exceeds 5 million pounds.

(B) DETERMINATION OF AMOUNT.—In calculating the total covered production history of a dairy operation under subparagraph (A), the Secretary shall multiply the coverage percentage selected under section 1406 of the Agricultural Act of 2014 (7 U.S.C. 9056) by the sum of—

(i) The supplemental production history calculated under subsection (c) with respect to such dairy operation; and

(ii) The dairy margin coverage production history described in subsection (c) (2) with respect to such dairy operation.

(e) Premium Cost.—The premium cost for an eligible dairy operation under this section shall be equal to the product of multiplying—

(1) the Tier I premium cost calculated under section 1407(b) of the Agricultural Act of 2014 (7 12 U.S.C. 9057(b)); by

(2) the production history calculation determined under subsection (c) (such that total covered production history does not exceed 5 million pounds).

(f) Regulations.—Not later than 45 days after the date of the enactment of this section, the Secretary shall issue regulations to carry out this section.

(g) Retroactivity.—The authority to carry out this section shall begin on January 1, 2020.

SEC. 110102. TARGETED PURCHASES.

(a) In General.—The Secretary of Agriculture shall utilize not less than $300,000,000 of the funds available under section 32 of the Act of August 24, 1935 (7 U.S.C. 612c) to purchase qualified agricultural products for the purpose of donating the products to food assistance programs, including the Emergency Food Assistance Program, of which the Secretary shall utilize—

(1) not less than $150,000,000 to purchase specialty crops;

(2) not less than $75,000,000 to purchase dairy; and

(3) not less than $75,000,000 to purchase meat and poultry products.

(b) Qualified Agricultural Product Defined.—In this section, the term "qualified agricultural product" means a dairy, meat, or poultry product, or a specialty crop—

(1) that was packaged or marketed for sale to commercial or food service industries;

(2) for which decreased demand exists for such a product due to the COVID–19 outbreak; and

(3) the repurposing of which would be impractical for grocery or retail sale.

TITLE II—SUPPLEMENTAL NUTRITION ASSISTANCE PROGRAM

SEC. 110201. SNAP FUNDING.

There are hereby appropriated to the Secretary of Agriculture, out of any money in the Treasury not otherwise appropriated, such sums as maybe necessary to carry out this title and sections 2301 and 2302 of the Families First Coronavirus Response Act (Public Law 116–127).

SEC. 110202. SNAP ALLOTMENTS.

(a) Nutrition Assistance Allotment Amount.—

(1) VALUE OF BENEFITS.—Notwithstanding any other provision of law, beginning on May 1, 2020, the value of benefits determined under section 8(a)

of the Food and Nutrition Act of 2008 (7 U.S.C. 2017(a)), and consolidated block grants for Puerto Rico and American Samoa determined under section 19(a) of such Act (7 U.S.C. 2028(a)), shall be calculated using 115 percent of the June 2019 value of the thrifty food plan (as defined in section 3 of such Act (7 U.S.C. 2012)) if the value of the benefits and block grants would be greater under that calculation than in the absence of this paragraph.
(2) MINIMUM AMOUNT.—
(A) IN GENERAL.—The minimum value of benefits determined under section 8(a) of the Food and Nutrition Act of 2008 (7 U.S.C. 2017(a)) for a household of not more than 2 members shall be $30.
(B) EFFECTIVENESS.—Subparagraph (A) shall remain in effect until the date on which 8 percent of the value of the thrifty food plan for a household containing 1 member, rounded to the nearest whole dollar increment, is equal to or greater than $30.
(b) Requirements For The Secretary.—In carrying out this section, the Secretary shall—
(1) consider the benefit increases described in subsection (a) to be a "mass change";
(2) require a simple process for States to notify households of the increase in benefits;
(3) not include any errors in the implementation of this section in the payment error rate calculated under section 16(c) of the Food and Nutrition Act of 2008 (7 U.S.C. 2025(c));
(4) disregard the additional amount of benefits that a household receives as a result of this section in determining the amount of overissuances under section 13 of the Food and Nutrition Act of 2008 (7 U.S.C. 2022); and
(5) set the tolerance level for excluding small errors for the purposes of section 16(c) of the Food and Nutrition Act of 2008 (7 U.S.C. 2025(c)) at $50 through September 30, 2021.
(c) Administrative Expenses.—
(1) IN GENERAL.—For the costs of State administrative expenses associated with carrying out this section and administering the supplemental nutrition assistance program established under the Food and Nutrition Act of 2008 (7 U.S.C. 2011 et seq.), the Secretary of Agriculture shall make available $150,000,000 for fiscal year 2020 and $150,000,000 for fiscal year 2021.
(2) TIMING FOR FISCAL YEAR 2020.—Not later than 60 days after the date of the enactment of this section, the Secretary shall make available to States amounts for fiscal year 2020 under paragraph (1).
(3) ALLOCATION OF FUNDS.—Funds described in paragraph (1) shall be made available as grants to State agencies for each fiscal year as follows:
(A) 75 percent of the amounts available for each fiscal year shall be allocated to States based on the share of each State of households that participate in the supplemental nutrition assistance program as reported to the Department of Agriculture for the most recent 12-month period for which data are available,

adjusted by the Secretary (as of the date of the enactment of this section) for participation in disaster programs under section 5(h) of the Food and Nutrition Act of 2008 (7 U.S.C. 2014(h)); and

(B) 25 percent of the amounts available for each fiscal year shall be allocated to States based on the increase in the number of households that participate in the supplemental nutrition assistance program as reported to the Department of Agriculture over the most recent 12-month period for which data are available, adjusted by the Secretary (as of the date of the enactment of this section) for participation in disaster programs under section 5(h) of the Food and Nutrition Act of 2008 (7 U.S.C. 2014(h)).

SEC. 110203. SNAP RULES.

No funds (including fees) made available under this Act or any other Act for any fiscal year may be used to finalize, implement, administer, enforce, carry out, or otherwise give effect to—

(1) the final rule entitled "Supplemental Nutrition Assistance Program: Requirements for Able-Bodied Adults Without Dependents" published in the Federal Register on December 5, 2019 (84 Fed. Reg. 66782);

(2) the proposed rule entitled "Revision of Categorical Eligibility in the Supplemental Nutrition Assistance Program (SNAP)" published in the Federal Register on July 24, 2019 (84 Fed. Reg. 35570); or

(3) the proposed rule entitled "Supplemental Nutrition Assistance Program: Standardization of State Heating and Cooling Standard Utility Allowances" published in the Federal Register on October 3, 2019 (84 Fed. Reg. 52809).

SEC. 110204. SNAP HOT FOOD PURCHASES.

During the period beginning 10 days after the date of the enactment of this Act and ending on the termination date of the public health emergency declaration made by the Secretary of Health and Human Services under section 319 of the Public Health Service Act based on an outbreak of coronavirus disease 2019 (COVID–19), the term "food", as defined in section 3 of the Food and Nutrition Act of 2008 (7 U.S.C. 2012), shall be deemed to exclude "hot foods or hot food products ready for immediate consumption other than those authorized pursuant to clauses (3), (4), (5), (7), (8), and (9) of this subsection," for purposes of such Act, except that such exclusion is limited to retail food stores authorized to accept and redeem supplemental nutrition assistance program benefits as of the date of enactment of this Act.

SEC. 110205. FOOD DISTRIBUTION PROGRAM ON INDIAN RESERVATIONS.

Any funds provided in the Third Coronavirus Preparedness and Response Supplemental Appropriations Act, 2020 for the Food Distribution Program on Indian Reservations, as authorized by section 4(b) of the Food and Nutrition Act of 2008 (7 U.S.C. 2013(b)), are not subject to the payment of the non-

Federal share requirement described in section 4(b)(4)(A) of the Food and Nutrition Act of 2008 (7 U.S.C. 2013(b)(4)(A)).

DIVISION L—ACCESS ACT

SEC. 120001. SHORT TITLE.

This division may be cited as the "American Coronavirus/COVID-19 Election Safety and Security Act" or the "ACCESS Act".

SEC. 120002. REQUIREMENTS FOR FEDERAL ELECTION CONTINGENCY PLANS IN RESPONSE TO NATURAL DISASTERS AND EMERGENCIES.

(a) In General.—

(1) ESTABLISHMENT.—Not later than 30 days after the date of the enactment of this Act, each State and each jurisdiction in a State which is responsible for administering elections for Federal office shall establish and make publicly available a contingency plan to enable individuals to vote in elections for Federal office during a state of emergency, public health emergency, or national emergency which has been declared for reasons including—

(A) a natural disaster; or

(B) an infectious disease.

(2) UPDATING.—Each State and jurisdiction shall update the contingency plan established under this subsection not less frequently than every 5 years.

(b) Requirements Relating To Safety.—The contingency plan established under subsection (a) shall include initiatives to provide equipment and resources needed to protect the health and safety of poll workers and voters when voting in person.

(c) Requirements Relating To Recruitment Of Poll Workers.—The contingency plan established under subsection (a) shall include initiatives by the chief State election official and local election officials to recruit poll workers from resilient or unaffected populations, which may include—

(1) employees of other State and local government offices; and

(2) in the case in which an infectious disease poses significant increased health risks to elderly individuals, students of secondary schools and institutions of higher education in the State.

(d) State.—For purposes of this section, the term "State" includes the District of Columbia, the Commonwealth of Puerto Rico, Guam, American Samoa, the United States Virgin Islands, and the Commonwealth of the Northern Mariana Islands.

(e) Enforcement.—

(1) ATTORNEY GENERAL.—The Attorney General may bring a civil action against any State or jurisdiction in an appropriate United States District Court for such declaratory and injunctive relief (including a temporary restraining order, a permanent or temporary injunction, or other order) as may be necessary to carry out the requirements of this section.

(2) PRIVATE RIGHT OF ACTION.—

(A) IN GENERAL.—In the case of a violation of this section, any person who is aggrieved by such violation may provide written notice of the violation to the chief election official of the State involved.

(B) RELIEF.—If the violation is not corrected within 20 days after receipt of a notice under subparagraph (A), or within 5 days after receipt of the notice if the violation occurred within 120 days before the date of an election for Federal office, the aggrieved person may, in a civil action, obtain declaratory or injunctive relief with respect to the violation.

(C) SPECIAL RULE.—If the violation occurred within 5 days before the date of an election for Federal office, the aggrieved person need not provide notice to the chief election official of the State involved under subparagraph (A) before bringing a civil action under subparagraph (B).

(f) Effective Date.—This section shall apply with respect to the regularly scheduled general election for Federal office held in November 2020 and each succeeding election for Federal office.

SEC. 120003. EARLY VOTING AND VOTING BY MAIL.

(a) Requirements.—Title III of the Help America Vote Act of 2002 (52 U.S.C. 21081 et seq.) is amended by adding at the end the following new subtitle:

"Subtitle C—Other Requirements

"SEC. 321. EARLY VOTING.

"(a) Requiring Allowing Voting Prior To Date Of Election.—

"(1) IN GENERAL.—Each State shall allow individuals to vote in an election for Federal office during an early voting period which occurs prior to the date of the election, in the same manner as voting is allowed on such date.

"(2) LENGTH OF PERIOD.—The early voting period required under this subsection with respect to an election shall consist of a period of consecutive days (including weekends) which begins on the 15th day before the date of the election (or, at the option of the State, on a day prior to the 15th day before the date of the election) and ends on the date of the election.

"(b) Minimum Early Voting Requirements.—Each polling place which allows voting during an early voting period under subsection (a) shall—

"(1) allow such voting for no less than 10 hours on each day;

"(2) have uniform hours each day for which such voting occurs; and

"(3) allow such voting to be held for some period of time prior to 9:00 a.m (local time) and some period of time after 5:00 p.m. (local time).

"(c) Location Of Polling Places.—

"(1) PROXIMITY TO PUBLIC TRANSPORTATION.—To the greatest extent practicable, a State shall ensure that each polling place which allows voting during an early voting period under subsection (a) is located within walking distance of a stop on a public transportation route.

"(2) AVAILABILITY IN RURAL AREAS.—The State shall ensure that polling places which allow voting during an early voting period under subsection (a) will be located in rural areas of the State, and shall ensure that such polling places are located in communities which will provide the greatest opportunity for residents of rural areas to vote during the early voting period.

"(d) Standards.—

"(1) IN GENERAL.—The Commission shall issue standards for the administration of voting prior to the day scheduled for a Federal election. Such standards shall include the nondiscriminatory geographic placement of polling places at which such voting occurs.

"(2) DEVIATION.—The standards described in paragraph (1) shall permit States, upon providing adequate public notice, to deviate from any requirement in the case of unforeseen circumstances such as a natural disaster, terrorist attack, or a change in voter turnout.

"(e) Ballot Processing And Scanning Requirements.—

"(1) IN GENERAL.—The State shall begin processing and scanning ballots cast during early voting for tabulation at least 14 days prior to the date of the election involved.

"(2) LIMITATION.—Nothing in this subsection shall be construed to permit a State to tabulate ballots in an election before the closing of the polls on the date of the election.

"(f) Effective Date.—This section shall apply with respect to the regularly scheduled general election for Federal office held in November 2020 and each succeeding election for Federal office.

"SEC. 322. PROMOTING ABILITY OF VOTERS TO VOTE BY MAIL.

"(a) Uniform Availability Of Absentee Voting To All Voters.—

"(1) IN GENERAL.—If an individual in a State is eligible to cast a vote in an election for Federal office, the State may not impose any additional conditions or requirements on the eligibility of the individual to cast the vote in such election by absentee ballot by mail, including—

"(A) requiring any form of identification as a condition of obtaining the absentee ballot; or

"(B) requiring notarization or witness signature or other formal authentication (other than voter attestation) as a condition of the acceptance of the ballot by an election official.

"(2) PERMITTING CERTAIN REQUIREMENTS.—Notwithstanding paragraph (1)—

"(A) a State shall require an individual to meet signature verification in accordance with subsection (b); and

"(B) the State may impose a deadline for requesting the ballot and related voting materials from the appropriate State or local election official and for returning the ballot to the appropriate State or local election official.

"(b) Requiring Signature Verification.—

"(1) REQUIREMENT.—A State may not accept and process an absentee ballot submitted by any individual with respect to an election for Federal office unless the State verifies the identification of the individual by comparing the individual's signature on the absentee ballot with the individual's signature on the official list of registered voters in the State, in accordance with such procedures as the State may adopt (subject to the requirements of paragraph (2)).

"(2) DUE PROCESS REQUIREMENTS.—

"(A) NOTICE AND OPPORTUNITY TO CURE DISCREPANCY.—If an individual submits an absentee ballot and the appropriate State or local election official determines that a discrepancy exists between the signature on such ballot and the signature of such individual on the official list of registered voters in the State, such election official, prior to making a final determination as to the validity of such ballot, shall make a good faith effort to immediately notify such individual by mail, telephone, and (if available) electronic mail that—

"(i) a discrepancy exists between the signature on such ballot and the signature of such individual on the official list of registered voters in the State;

"(ii) such individual may provide the official with information to cure such discrepancy, either in person, by telephone, or by electronic methods; and

"(iii) if such discrepancy is not cured prior to the expiration of the 7-day period which begins on the date of the election, such ballot will not be counted.

"(B) OPPORTUNITY TO PROVIDE MISSING SIGNATURE.—If an individual submits an absentee ballot without a signature, the State shall notify the individual and give the individual an opportunity to provide the missing signature on a form proscribed by the State.

"(C) OTHER REQUIREMENTS.—An election official may not make a determination that a discrepancy exists between the signature on an absentee ballot and the signature of the individual who submits the ballot on the official list of registered voters in the State unless—

"(i) at least 2 election officials make the determination; and

"(ii) each official who makes the determination has received training in procedures used to verify signatures.

"(3) REPORT.—

"(A) IN GENERAL.—Not later than 120 days after the end of a Federal election cycle, each chief State election official shall submit to Congress a report containing the following information for the applicable Federal election cycle in the State:

"(i) The number of ballots invalidated due to a discrepancy under this subsection.

"(ii) Description of attempts to contact voters to provide notice as required by this subsection.

"(iii) Description of the cure process developed by such State pursuant to this subsection, including the number of ballots determined valid as a result of such process.

"(B) FEDERAL ELECTION CYCLE DEFINED.—For purposes of this subsection, the term 'Federal election cycle' means the period beginning on January 1 of any odd numbered year and ending on December 31 of the following year.

"(c) Methods And Timing For Transmission Of Ballots And Balloting Materials To Voters.—

"(1) METHOD FOR REQUESTING BALLOT.—In addition to such other methods as the State may establish for an individual to request an absentee ballot, the State shall permit an individual to submit a request for an absentee ballot online. The State shall be considered to meet the requirements of this paragraph if the website of the appropriate State or local election official allows an absentee ballot request application to be completed and submitted online and if the website permits the individual—

"(A) to print the application so that the individual may complete the application and return it to the official; or

"(B) request that a paper copy of the application be transmitted to the individual by mail or electronic mail so that the individual may complete the application and return it to the official.

"(2) ENSURING DELIVERY PRIOR TO ELECTION.—If an individual requests to vote by absentee ballot in an election for Federal office, the appropriate State or local election official shall ensure that the ballot and relating voting materials are received by the individual prior to the date of the election so long as the individual's request is received by the official not later than 5 days (excluding Saturdays, Sundays, and legal public holidays) before the date of the election, except that nothing in this paragraph shall preclude a State or local jurisdiction from allowing for the acceptance and processing of ballot requests submitted or received after such required period.

"(3) SPECIAL RULES IN CASE OF EMERGENCY PERIODS.—

"(A) AUTOMATIC MAILING OF ABSENTEE BALLOTS TO ALL VOTERS.—If the area in which an election is held is in an area in which an emergency or disaster which is described in subparagraph (A) or (B) of section 1135(g)(1) of the Social Security Act (42 U.S.C. 1320b–5(g)(1)) is declared during the period described in subparagraph (C)—

"(i) paragraphs (1) and (2) shall not apply with respect to the election; and

"(ii) not later than 2 weeks before the date of the election, the appropriate State or local election official shall transmit absentee ballots and balloting materials for the election to all individuals who are registered to vote in such election.

"(B) AFFIRMATION.—If an individual receives an absentee ballot from a State or local election official pursuant to subparagraph (A) and returns the voted ballot to the official, the ballot shall not be counted in the election unless the individual includes with the ballot a signed affirmation that—

"(i) the individual has not and will not cast another ballot with respect to the election; and

"(ii) acknowledges that a material misstatement of fact in completing the ballot may constitute grounds for conviction of perjury.

"(C) PERIOD DESCRIBED.—The period described in this subparagraph with respect to an election is the period which begins 120 days before the date of the election and ends 30 days before the date of the election.

"(D) APPLICATION TO NOVEMBER 2020 GENERAL ELECTION.— Because of the public health emergency declared pursuant to section 319 of the Public Health Service Act (42 U.S.C. 247d) resulting from the COVID–19 pandemic, the special rules set forth in this paragraph shall apply with respect to the regularly scheduled general election for Federal office held in November 2020 in each State.

"(d) Accessibility For Individuals With Disabilities.—The State shall ensure that all absentee ballots and related voting materials in elections for Federal office are accessible to individuals with disabilities in a manner that provides the same opportunity for access and participation (including with privacy and independence) as for other voters.

"(e) Requirements For Envelopes.—

"(1) PREPAYMENT OF POSTAGE.—Consistent with regulations of the United States Postal Service, the State or the unit of local government responsible for the administration of an election for Federal office shall prepay the postage on any ballot in the election which is cast by mail.

"(2) USE OF SELF-SEALING ENVELOPE.—The State or unit of local government shall provide with any absentee ballot transmitted to a voter by mail a self-sealing return envelope.

"(f) Uniform Deadline For Acceptance Of Mailed Ballots.—If a ballot submitted by an individual by mail with respect to an election for Federal office in a State is postmarked on or before the date of the election, the State may not refuse to accept or process the ballot on the grounds that the individual did not meet a deadline for returning the ballot to the appropriate State or local election official.

"(g) Methods Of Returning Ballots.—

"(1) IN GENERAL.—The State shall permit an individual to whom a ballot in an election was provided under this section to cast the ballot by delivering the ballot at such times and to such locations as the State may establish, including—

"(A) permitting the individual to deliver the ballot to a polling place on the date of the election; and

"(B) permitting the individual to deliver the ballot to a designated ballot drop-off location.

"(2) PERMITTING VOTERS TO DESIGNATE OTHER PERSON TO RETURN BALLOT.—The State—

"(A) shall permit a voter to designate any person to return a voted and sealed absentee ballot to the post office, a ballot drop-off location, tribally designated building, or election office so long as the person designated to return the ballot does not receive any form of compensation based on the number of ballots that the person has returned and no individual, group, or organization provides compensation on this basis; and

"(B) may not put any limit on how many voted and sealed absentee ballots any designated person can return to the post office, a ballot drop off location, tribally designated building, or election office.

"(h) Ballot Processing And Scanning Requirements.—

"(1) IN GENERAL.—The State shall begin processing and scanning ballots cast by mail for tabulation at least 14 days prior to the date of the election involved.

"(2) LIMITATION.—Nothing in this subsection shall be construed to permit a State to tabulate ballots in an election before the closing of the polls on the date of the election.

"(i) Rule Of Construction.—Nothing in this section shall be construed to affect the authority of States to conduct elections for Federal office through the use of polling places at which individuals cast ballots.

"(j) No Effect On Ballots Submitted By Absent Military And Overseas Voters; Treatment Of Blank Absentee Ballots Transmitted To Certain Voters.—Nothing in this section may be construed to affect the treatment of any ballot submitted by an individual who is entitled to vote by absentee ballot under the Uniformed and Overseas Citizens Absentee Voting Act (52 U.S.C. 20301 et seq.), and any blank absentee ballot transmitted to an individual by mail or electronically in accordance with section 102(f) of such Act shall be treated in the same manner as any other absentee ballot for purposes of this section.

"(k) Effective Date.—This section shall apply with respect to the regularly scheduled general election for Federal office held in November 2020 and each succeeding election for Federal office.

"SEC. 323. ABSENTEE BALLOT TRACKING PROGRAM.

"(a) Requirement.—Each State shall carry out a program to track and confirm the receipt of absentee ballots in an election for Federal office under which the State or local election official responsible for the receipt of voted absentee ballots in the election carries out procedures to track and confirm the receipt of such ballots, and makes information on the receipt of such ballots available to the individual who cast the ballot, by means of online access using the Internet site of the official's office.

"(b) Information On Whether Vote Was Counted.—The information referred to under subsection (a) with respect to the receipt of an absentee ballot shall include information regarding whether the vote cast on the ballot was counted, and, in the case of a vote which was not counted, the reasons therefor.

"(c) Use Of Toll-Free Telephone Number By Officials Without Internet Site.—A program established by a State or local election official whose office does not have an Internet site may meet the requirements of subsection (a) if the official has established a toll-free telephone number that may be used by an individual who cast an absentee ballot to obtain the information on the receipt of the voted absentee ballot as provided under such subsection.

"(d) Effective Date.—This section shall apply with respect to the regularly scheduled general election for Federal office held in November 2020 and each succeeding election for Federal office.

"SEC. 324. RULES FOR COUNTING PROVISIONAL BALLOTS.

"(a) Statewide Counting Of Provisional Ballots.—

"(1) IN GENERAL.—For purposes of section 302(a)(4), notwithstanding the precinct or polling place at which a provisional ballot is cast within the State, the appropriate election official shall count each vote on such ballot for each election in which the individual who cast such ballot is eligible to vote.

"(2) EFFECTIVE DATE.—This subsection shall apply with respect to the regularly scheduled general election for Federal office held in November 2020 and each succeeding election for Federal office.

"(b) Uniform And Nondiscriminatory Standards.—

"(1) IN GENERAL.—Consistent with the requirements of section 302, each State shall establish uniform and nondiscriminatory standards for the issuance, handling, and counting of provisional ballots.

"(2) EFFECTIVE DATE.—This subsection shall apply with respect to the regularly scheduled general election for Federal office held in November 2020 and each succeeding election for Federal office.

"SEC. 325. COVERAGE OF COMMONWEALTH OF NORTHERN MARIANA ISLANDS.

"In this subtitle, the term 'State' includes the Commonwealth of the Northern Mariana Islands.

"SEC. 326. MINIMUM REQUIREMENTS FOR EXPANDING ABILITY OF INDIVIDUALS TO VOTE.

"The requirements of this subtitle are minimum requirements, and nothing in this subtitle may be construed to prevent a State from establishing standards which promote the ability of individuals to vote in elections for Federal office, so long as such standards are not inconsistent with the requirements of this subtitle or other Federal laws.".

(b) Conforming Amendment Relating To Issuance Of Voluntary Guidance By Election Assistance Commission.—Section 311(b) of such Act (52 U.S.C. 21101(b)) is amended—

(1) by striking "and" at the end of paragraph (2);

(2) by striking the period at the end of paragraph (3) and inserting "; and"; and

(3) by adding at the end the following new paragraph:

"(4) in the case of the recommendations with respect to subtitle C, June 30, 2020.".

(c) Enforcement.—

(1) COVERAGE UNDER EXISTING ENFORCEMENT PROVISIONS.—Section 401 of such Act (52 U.S.C. 21111) is amended by striking "and 303" and inserting "303, and subtitle C of title III".

(2) AVAILABILITY OF PRIVATE RIGHT OF ACTION.—Title IV of such (52 U.S.C. 21111 et seq.) is amended by adding at the end the following new section:

“SEC. 403. PRIVATE RIGHT OF ACTION FOR VIOLATIONS OF CERTAIN REQUIREMENTS.

“(a) In General.—In the case of a violation of subtitle C of title III, section 402 shall not apply and any person who is aggrieved by such violation may provide written notice of the violation to the chief election official of the State involved.

“(b) Relief.—If the violation is not corrected within 20 days after receipt of a notice under subsection (a), or within 5 days after receipt of the notice if the violation occurred within 120 days before the date of an election for Federal office, the aggrieved person may, in a civil action, obtain declaratory or injunctive relief with respect to the violation.

“(c) Special Rule.—If the violation occurred within 5 days before the date of an election for Federal office, the aggrieved person need not provide notice to the chief election official of the State involved under subsection (a) before bringing a civil action under subsection (b).”.

(d) Clerical Amendment.—The table of contents of such Act is amended—

(1) by adding at the end of the items relating to title III the following:

“Subtitle C—Other Requirements

“Sec. 321. Early voting.

“Sec. 322. Promoting ability of voters to vote by mail.

“Sec. 323. Absentee ballot tracking program.

“Sec. 324. Rules for counting provisional ballots.

“Sec. 325. Coverage of Commonwealth of Northern Mariana Islands.

“Sec. 326. Minimum requirements for expanding ability of individuals to vote.”; and

(2) by adding at the end of the items relating to title IV the following new item:

“Sec. 403. Private right of action for violations of certain requirements. ”.

SEC. 120004. POSTAGE-FREE ABSENTEE BALLOTS.

(a) In General.—Chapter 34 of title 39, United States Code, is amended by adding after section 3406 the following:

“§ 3407. Absentee ballots

“(a) Any absentee ballot for any election for Federal office shall be carried expeditiously, with postage prepaid by the State or unit of local government responsible for the administration of the election.

“(b) As used in this section, the term ‘absentee ballot’ means any ballot transmitted by a voter by mail in an election for Federal office, but does not include any ballot covered by section 3406.”.

(b) Clerical Amendment.—The table of sections for chapter 34 of such title is amended by inserting after the item relating to section 3406 the following:

“3407. Absentee ballots carried free of postage.”.

SEC. 120005. REQUIRING TRANSMISSION OF BLANK ABSENTEE BALLOTS UNDER UOCAVA TO CERTAIN VOTERS.

(a) In General.—The Uniformed and Overseas Citizens Absentee Voting Act (52 U.S.C. 20301 et seq.) is amended by inserting after section 103B the following new section:

"SEC. 103C. TRANSMISSION OF BLANK ABSENTEE BALLOTS TO CERTAIN OTHER VOTERS.

"(a) In General.—

"(1) STATE RESPONSIBILITIES.—Subject to paragraph (2), each State shall transmit blank absentee ballots by mail and electronically to qualified individuals in the same manner and under the same terms and conditions under which the State transmits such ballots to absent uniformed services voters and overseas voters under section 102(f).

"(2) REQUIREMENTS.—Any blank absentee ballot transmitted to a qualified individual under this section—

"(A) must comply with the language requirements under section 203 of the Voting Rights Act of 1965 (52 U.S.C. 10503); and

"(B) must comply with the disability requirements under section 508 of the Rehabilitation Act of 1973 (29 U.S.C. 794d).

"(3) AFFIRMATION.—The State may not transmit a ballot to a qualified individual under this section unless the individual provides the State with a signed affirmation in electronic form that—

"(A) the individual is a qualified individual (as defined in subsection (b));

"(B) the individual has not and will not cast another ballot with respect to the election; and

"(C) acknowledges that a material misstatement of fact in completing the ballot may constitute grounds for conviction of perjury.

"(4) CLARIFICATION REGARDING FREE POSTAGE.—An absentee ballot obtained by a qualified individual under this section shall be considered balloting materials as defined in section 107 for purposes of section 3406 of title 39, United States Code.

"(5) PROHIBITING REFUSAL TO ACCEPT BALLOT FOR FAILURE TO MEET CERTAIN REQUIREMENTS.—A State shall not refuse to accept and process any otherwise valid blank absentee ballot which was transmitted to a qualified individual under this section and used by the individual to vote in the election solely on the basis of the following:

"(A) Notarization or witness signature requirements.

"(B) Restrictions on paper type, including weight and size.

"(C) Restrictions on envelope type, including weight and size.

"(b) Qualified Individual.—

"(1) IN GENERAL.—In this section, except as provided in paragraph (2), the term 'qualified individual' means any individual who is otherwise qualified to vote in an election for Federal office and who meets any of the following

requirements:
"(A) The individual—
"(i) has requested an absentee ballot from the State or jurisdiction in which such individual is registered to vote; and
"(ii) has not received such absentee ballot at least 2 days before the date of the election.
"(B) The individual—
"(i) resides in an area of a State with respect to which an emergency or public health emergency has been declared by the chief executive of the State or of the area involved within 5 days of the date of the election under the laws of the State due to reasons including a natural disaster, including severe weather, or an infectious disease; and
"(ii) has not requested an absentee ballot.
"(C) The individual expects to be absent from such individual's jurisdiction on the date of the election due to professional or volunteer service in response to a natural disaster or emergency as described in subparagraph (B).
"(D) The individual is hospitalized or expects to be hospitalized on the date of the election.
"(E) The individual is an individual with a disability (as defined in section 3 of the Americans with Disabilities Act of 1990 (42 U.S.C. 12102)) and resides in a State which does not offer voters the ability to use secure and accessible remote ballot marking. For purposes of this subparagraph, a State shall permit an individual to self-certify that the individual is an individual with a disability.
"(2) EXCLUSION OF ABSENT UNIFORMED SERVICES AND OVERSEAS VOTERS.—The term 'qualified individual' shall not include an absent uniformed services voter or an overseas voter.
"(c) State.—For purposes of this section, the term 'State' includes the District of Columbia, the Commonwealth of Puerto Rico, Guam, American Samoa, the United States Virgin Islands, and the Commonwealth of the Northern Mariana Islands.
"(d) Effective Date.—This section shall apply with respect to the regularly scheduled general election for Federal office held in November 2020 and each succeeding election for Federal office.".
(b) Conforming Amendment.—Section 102(a) of such Act (52 U.S.C. 20302(a)) is amended—
(1) by striking "and" at the end of paragraph (10);
(2) by striking the period at the end of paragraph (11) and inserting "; and"; and
(3) by adding at the end the following new paragraph:
"(12) meet the requirements of section 103C with respect to the provision of blank absentee ballots for the use of qualified individuals described in such section.".
(c) Clerical Amendments.—The table of contents of such Act is amended by inserting the following after section 103:

"Sec. 103A. Procedures for collection and delivery of marked absentee ballots of absent overseas uniformed services voters.
"Sec. 103B. Federal voting assistance program improvements.
"Sec. 103C. Transmission of blank absentee ballots to certain other voters.".

SEC. 120006. VOTER REGISTRATION.
(a) Requiring Availability Of Internet For Voter Registration.—
(1) REQUIRING AVAILABILITY OF INTERNET FOR REGISTRATION.—The National Voter Registration Act of 1993 (52 U.S.C. 20501 et seq.) is amended by inserting after section 6 the following new section:

"SEC. 6A. INTERNET REGISTRATION.
"(a) Requiring Availability Of Internet For Online Registration.—
"(1) AVAILABILITY OF ONLINE REGISTRATION AND CORRECTION OF EXISTING REGISTRATION INFORMATION.—Each State, acting through the chief State election official, shall ensure that the following services are available to the public at any time on the official public websites of the appropriate State and local election officials in the State, in the same manner and subject to the same terms and conditions as the services provided by voter registration agencies under section 7(a):
"(A) Online application for voter registration.
"(B) Online assistance to applicants in applying to register to vote.
"(C) Online completion and submission by applicants of the mail voter registration application form prescribed by the Election Assistance Commission pursuant to section 9(a)(2), including assistance with providing a signature as required under subsection (c).
"(D) Online receipt of completed voter registration applications.
"(b) Acceptance Of Completed Applications.—A State shall accept an online voter registration application provided by an individual under this section, and ensure that the individual is registered to vote in the State, if—
"(1) the individual meets the same voter registration requirements applicable to individuals who register to vote by mail in accordance with section 6(a)(1) using the mail voter registration application form prescribed by the Election Assistance Commission pursuant to section 9(a)(2); and
"(2) the individual meets the requirements of subsection (c) to provide a signature in electronic form (but only in the case of applications submitted during or after the second year in which this section is in effect in the State).
"(c) Signature Requirements.—
"(1) IN GENERAL.—For purposes of this section, an individual meets the requirements of this subsection as follows:
"(A) In the case of an individual who has a signature on file with a State agency, including the State motor vehicle authority, that is required to provide voter registration services under this Act or any other law, the individual consents to the transfer of that electronic signature.

"(B) If subparagraph (A) does not apply, the individual submits with the application an electronic copy of the individual's handwritten signature through electronic means.

"(C) If subparagraph (A) and subparagraph (B) do not apply, the individual executes a computerized mark in the signature field on an online voter registration application, in accordance with reasonable security measures established by the State, but only if the State accepts such mark from the individual.

"(2) TREATMENT OF INDIVIDUALS UNABLE TO MEET REQUIREMENT.—If an individual is unable to meet the requirements of paragraph (1), the State shall—

"(A) permit the individual to complete all other elements of the online voter registration application;

"(B) permit the individual to provide a signature at the time the individual requests a ballot in an election (whether the individual requests the ballot at a polling place or requests the ballot by mail); and

"(C) if the individual carries out the steps described in subparagraph (A) and subparagraph (B), ensure that the individual is registered to vote in the State.

"(3) NOTICE.—The State shall ensure that individuals applying to register to vote online are notified of the requirements of paragraph (1) and of the treatment of individuals unable to meet such requirements, as described in paragraph (2).

"(d) Confirmation And Disposition.—

"(1) CONFIRMATION OF RECEIPT.—Upon the online submission of a completed voter registration application by an individual under this section, the appropriate State or local election official shall send the individual a notice confirming the State's receipt of the application and providing instructions on how the individual may check the status of the application.

"(2) NOTICE OF DISPOSITION.—Not later than 7 days after the appropriate State or local election official has approved or rejected an application submitted by an individual under this section, the official shall send the individual a notice of the disposition of the application.

"(3) METHOD OF NOTIFICATION.—The appropriate State or local election official shall send the notices required under this subsection by regular mail, and, in the case of an individual who has provided the official with an electronic mail address, by both electronic mail and regular mail.

"(e) Provision Of Services In Nonpartisan Manner.—The services made available under subsection (a) shall be provided in a manner that ensures that, consistent with section 7(a)(5)—

"(1) the online application does not seek to influence an applicant's political preference or party registration; and

"(2) there is no display on the website promoting any political preference or party allegiance, except that nothing in this paragraph may be construed to prohibit an applicant from registering to vote as a member of a political party.

"(f) Protection Of Security Of Information.—In meeting the requirements of this section, the State shall establish appropriate technological security measures to prevent to the greatest extent practicable any unauthorized access to information provided by individuals using the services made available under subsection (a).
"(g) Accessibility Of Services.—A state shall ensure that the services made available under this section are made available to individuals with disabilities to the same extent as services are made available to all other individuals.
"(h) Use Of Additional Telephone-Based System.—A State shall make the services made available online under subsection (a) available through the use of an automated telephone-based system, subject to the same terms and conditions applicable under this section to the services made available online, in addition to making the services available online in accordance with the requirements of this section.
"(i) Nondiscrimination Among Registered Voters Using Mail And Online Registration.—In carrying out this Act, the Help America Vote Act of 2002, or any other Federal, State, or local law governing the treatment of registered voters in the State or the administration of elections for public office in the State, a State shall treat a registered voter who registered to vote online in accordance with this section in the same manner as the State treats a registered voter who registered to vote by mail.".
(2) SPECIAL REQUIREMENTS FOR INDIVIDUALS USING ONLINE REGISTRATION.—
(A) TREATMENT AS INDIVIDUALS REGISTERING TO VOTE BY MAIL FOR PURPOSES OF FIRST-TIME VOTER IDENTIFICATION REQUIREMENTS.—Section 303(b)(1)(A) of the Help America Vote Act of 2002 (52 U.S.C. 21083(b)(1)(A)) is amended by striking "by mail" and inserting "by mail or online under section 6A of the National Voter Registration Act of 1993".
(B) REQUIRING SIGNATURE FOR FIRST-TIME VOTERS IN JURISDICTION.—Section 303(b) of such Act (52 U.S.C. 21083(b)) is amended—
(i) by redesignating paragraph (5) as paragraph (6); and
(ii) by inserting after paragraph (4) the following new paragraph:
"(5) SIGNATURE REQUIREMENTS FOR FIRST-TIME VOTERS USING ONLINE REGISTRATION.—
"(A) IN GENERAL.—A State shall, in a uniform and nondiscriminatory manner, require an individual to meet the requirements of subparagraph (B) if—
"(i) the individual registered to vote in the State online under section 6A of the National Voter Registration Act of 1993; and
"(ii) the individual has not previously voted in an election for Federal office in the State.
"(B) REQUIREMENTS.—An individual meets the requirements of this

subparagraph if—

"(i) in the case of an individual who votes in person, the individual provides the appropriate State or local election official with a handwritten signature; or

"(ii) in the case of an individual who votes by mail, the individual submits with the ballot a handwritten signature.

"(C) INAPPLICABILITY.—Subparagraph (A) does not apply in the case of an individual who is—

"(i) entitled to vote by absentee ballot under the Uniformed and Overseas Citizens Absentee Voting Act (52 U.S.C. 20302 et seq.);

"(ii) provided the right to vote otherwise than in person under section 3(b)(2)(B)(ii) of the Voting Accessibility for the Elderly and Handicapped Act (52 U.S.C. 20102(b)(2)(B)(ii)); or

"(iii) entitled to vote otherwise than in person under any other Federal law.".

(C) CONFORMING AMENDMENT RELATING TO EFFECTIVE DATE.—Section 303(d)(2)(A) of such Act (52 U.S.C. 21083(d)(2)(A)) is amended by striking "Each State" and inserting "Except as provided in subsection (b)(5), each State".

(3) CONFORMING AMENDMENTS.—

(A) TIMING OF REGISTRATION.—Section 8(a)(1) of the National Voter Registration Act of 1993 (52 U.S.C. 20507(a)(1)) is amended—

(i) by striking "and" at the end of subparagraph (C);

(ii) by redesignating subparagraph (D) as subparagraph (E); and

(iii) by inserting after subparagraph (C) the following new subparagraph:

"(D) in the case of online registration through the official public website of an election official under section 6A, if the valid voter registration application is submitted online not later than the lesser of 28 days, or the period provided by State law, before the date of the election (as determined by treating the date on which the application is sent electronically as the date on which it is submitted); and".

(B) INFORMING APPLICANTS OF ELIGIBILITY REQUIREMENTS AND PENALTIES.—Section 8(a)(5) of such Act (52 U.S.C. 20507(a)(5)) is amended by striking "and 7" and inserting "6A, and 7".

(b) Same Day Registration.—

(1) IN GENERAL.—Subtitle C of title III of the Help America Vote Act of 2002, as added by section 3(a), is amended—

(A) by redesignating sections 325 and 326 as sections 326 and 327; and

(B) by inserting after section 324 the following new section:

"SEC. 325. SAME DAY REGISTRATION.

"(a) In General.—

"(1) REGISTRATION.—Each State shall permit any eligible individual on the day of a Federal election and on any day when voting, including early voting, is permitted for a Federal election—

"(A) to register to vote in such election at the polling place using a form that meets the requirements under section 9(b) of the National Voter Registration Act of 1993 (or, if the individual is already registered to vote, to revise any of the individual's voter registration information); and

"(B) to cast a vote in such election.

"(2) EXCEPTION.—The requirements under paragraph (1) shall not apply to a State in which, under a State law in effect continuously on and after the date of the enactment of this section, there is no voter registration requirement for individuals in the State with respect to elections for Federal office.

"(b) Eligible Individual.—For purposes of this section, the term 'eligible individual' means, with respect to any election for Federal office, an individual who is otherwise qualified to vote in that election.

"(c) Effective Date.—Each State shall be required to comply with the requirements of subsection (a) for the regularly scheduled general election for Federal office occurring in November 2020 and for any subsequent election for Federal office.".

(2) CLERICAL AMENDMENT.—The table of contents of such Act, as amended by section 3, is amended—

(A) by redesignating the items relating to sections 325 and 326 as relating to sections 326 and 327; and

(B) by inserting after the item relating to section 324 the following new item: "Sec. 325. Same day registration.".

(c) Prohibiting State From Requiring Applicants To Provide More Than Last 4 Digits Of Social Security Number.—

(1) FORM INCLUDED WITH APPLICATION FOR MOTOR VEHICLE DRIVER'S LICENSE.—Section 5(c)(2)(B)(ii) of the National Voter Registration Act of 1993 (52 U.S.C. 20504(c)(2)(B)(ii)) is amended by striking the semicolon at the end and inserting the following: ", and to the extent that the application requires the applicant to provide a Social Security number, may not require the applicant to provide more than the last 4 digits of such number;".

(2) NATIONAL MAIL VOTER REGISTRATION FORM.—Section 9(b)(1) of such Act (52 U.S.C. 20508(b)(1)) is amended by striking the semicolon at the end and inserting the following: ", and to the extent that the form requires the applicant to provide a Social Security number, the form may not require the applicant to provide more than the last 4 digits of such number;".

(3) EFFECTIVE DATE.—The amendments made by this subsection shall apply with respect to the regularly scheduled general election for Federal office held in November 2020 and each succeeding election for Federal office.

SEC. 120007. ACCOMMODATIONS FOR VOTERS RESIDING IN INDIAN LANDS.

(a) Accommodations Described.—

(1) DESIGNATION OF BALLOT PICKUP AND COLLECTION LOCATIONS.—Given the widespread lack of residential mail delivery in

Indian Country, an Indian Tribe may designate buildings as ballot pickup and collection locations with respect to an election for Federal office at no cost to the Indian Tribe. An Indian Tribe may designate one building per precinct located within Indian lands. The applicable State or political subdivision shall collect ballots from those locations. The applicable State or political subdivision shall provide the Indian Tribe with accurate precinct maps for all precincts located within Indian lands 60 days before the election.

(2) PROVISION OF MAIL-IN AND ABSENTEE BALLOTS.—The State or political subdivision shall provide mail-in and absentee ballots with respect to an election for Federal office to each individual who is registered to vote in the election who resides on Indian lands in the State or political subdivision involved without requiring a residential address or a mail-in or absentee ballot request.

(3) USE OF DESIGNATED BUILDING AS RESIDENTIAL AND MAILING ADDRESS.—The address of a designated building that is a ballot pickup and collection location with respect to an election for Federal office may serve as the residential address and mailing address for voters living on Indian lands if the tribally designated building is in the same precinct as that voter. If there is no tribally designated building within a voter's precinct, the voter may use another tribally designated building within the Indian lands where the voter is located. Voters using a tribally designated building outside of the voter's precinct may use the tribally designated building as a mailing address and may separately designate the voter's appropriate precinct through a description of the voter's address, as specified in section 9428.4(a)(2) of title 11, Code of Federal Regulations.

(4) LANGUAGE ACCESSIBILITY.—In the case of a State or political subdivision that is a covered State or political subdivision under section 203 of the Voting Rights Act of 1965 (52 U.S.C. 10503), that State or political subdivision shall provide absentee or mail-in voting materials with respect to an election for Federal office in the language of the applicable minority group as well as in the English language, bilingual election voting assistance, and written translations of all voting materials in the language of the applicable minority group, as required by section 203 of the Voting Rights Act of 1965 (52 U.S.C. 10503), as amended by subsection (b).

(5) CLARIFICATION.—Nothing in this section alters the ability of an individual voter residing on Indian lands to request a ballot in a manner available to all other voters in the State.

(6) DEFINITIONS.—In this section:

(A) INDIAN.—The term "Indian" has the meaning given the term in section 4 of the Indian Self-Determination and Education Assistance Act (25 U.S.C. 5304).

(B) INDIAN LANDS.—The term "Indian lands" includes—

(i) any Indian country of an Indian Tribe, as defined under section 1151 of title 18, United States Code;

(ii) any land in Alaska owned, pursuant to the Alaska Native Claims Settlement Act (43 U.S.C. 1601 et seq.), by an Indian Tribe that is a Native village (as defined in section 3 of that Act (43 U.S.C. 1602)) or by a Village Corporation that is associated with an Indian Tribe (as defined in section 3 of that Act (43 U.S.C. 1602));

(iii) any land on which the seat of the Tribal Government is located; and

(iv) any land that is part or all of a Tribal designated statistical area associated with an Indian Tribe, or is part or all of an Alaska Native village statistical area associated with an Indian Tribe, as defined by the Census Bureau for the purposes of the most recent decennial census.

(C) INDIAN TRIBE.—The term “Indian Tribe” has the meaning given the term “Indian tribe” in section 4 of the Indian Self-Determination and Education Assistance Act (25 U.S.C. 5304).

(D) TRIBAL GOVERNMENT.—The term “Tribal Government” means the recognized governing body of an Indian Tribe.

(7) ENFORCEMENT.—

(A) ATTORNEY GENERAL.—The Attorney General may bring a civil action in an appropriate district court for such declaratory or injunctive relief as is necessary to carry out this subsection.

(B) PRIVATE RIGHT OF ACTION.—

(i) A person or Tribal Government who is aggrieved by a violation of this subsection may provide written notice of the violation to the chief election official of the State involved.

(ii) An aggrieved person or Tribal Government may bring a civil action in an appropriate district court for declaratory or injunctive relief with respect to a violation of this subsection, if—

(I) that person or Tribal Government provides the notice described in clause (i); and

(II) (aa) in the case of a violation that occurs more than 120 days before the date of an election for Federal office, the violation remains and 90 days or more have passed since the date on which the chief election official of the State receives the notice under clause (i); or

(bb) in the case of a violation that occurs 120 days or less before the date of an election for Federal office, the violation remains and 20 days or more have passed since the date on which the chief election official of the State receives the notice under clause (i).

(iii) In the case of a violation of this section that occurs 30 days or less before the date of an election for Federal office, an aggrieved person or Tribal Government may bring a civil action in an appropriate district court for declaratory or injunctive relief with respect to the violation without providing notice to the chief election official of the State under clause (i).

(b) Bilingual Election Requirements.—Section 203 of the Voting Rights Act of 1965 (52 U.S.C. 10503) is amended—

(1) in subsection (b)(3)(C), by striking “1990” and inserting “2010”; and

(2) by striking subsection (c) and inserting the following:
"(c) Provision Of Voting Materials In The Language Of A Minority Group.—
"(1) IN GENERAL.—Whenever any State or political subdivision subject to the prohibition of subsection (b) of this section provides any registration or voting notices, forms, instructions, assistance, or other materials or information relating to the electoral process, including ballots, it shall provide them in the language of the applicable minority group as well as in the English language.
"(2) EXCEPTIONS.—
"(A) IN GENERAL.—
"(i) In the case of a minority group that is not American Indian or Alaska Native and the language of that minority group is oral or unwritten, the State or political subdivision shall only be required to furnish, in the covered language, oral instructions, assistance, translation of voting materials, or other information relating to registration and voting.
"(ii) In the case of a minority group that is American Indian or Alaska Native, the State or political subdivision shall only be required to furnish in the covered language oral instructions, assistance, or other information relating to registration and voting, including all voting materials, if the Tribal Government of that minority group has certified that the language of the applicable American Indian or Alaska Native language is presently unwritten or the Tribal Government does not want written translations in the minority language.
"(3) WRITTEN TRANSLATIONS FOR ELECTION WORKERS.—Notwithstanding paragraph (2), the State or political division may be required to provide written translations of voting materials, with the consent of any applicable Indian Tribe, to election workers to ensure that the translations from English to the language of a minority group are complete, accurate, and uniform.".
(c) Effective Date.—This section and the amendments made by this section shall apply with respect to the regularly scheduled general election for Federal office held in November 2020 and each succeeding election for Federal office.

SEC. 120008. PAYMENTS BY ELECTION ASSISTANCE COMMISSION TO STATES TO ASSIST WITH COSTS OF COMPLIANCE.
(a) Availability Of Grants.—Subtitle D of title II of the Help America Vote Act of 2002 (52 U.S.C. 21001 et seq.) is amended by adding at the end the following new part:
"PART 7—PAYMENTS TO ASSIST WITH COSTS OF COMPLIANCE WITH ACCESS ACT

"SEC. 297. PAYMENTS TO ASSIST WITH COSTS OF COMPLIANCE WITH ACCESS ACT.
"(a) Availability And Use Of Payments.—
"(1) IN GENERAL.—The Commission shall make a payment to each eligible

State to assist the State with the costs of complying with the American Coronavirus/COVID–19 Election Safety and Security Act and the amendments made by such Act, including the provisions of such Act and such amendments which require States to pre-pay the postage on absentee ballots and balloting materials.

"(2) PUBLIC EDUCATION CAMPAIGNS.—For purposes of this part, the costs incurred by a State in carrying out a campaign to educate the public about the requirements of the American Coronavirus/COVID–19 Election Safety and Security Act and the amendments made by such Act shall be included as the costs of complying with such Act and such amendments.

"(b) Primary Elections.—

"(1) PAYMENTS TO STATES.—In addition to any payments under subsection (a), the Commission shall make a payment to each eligible State to assist the State with the costs incurred in voluntarily electing to comply with the American Coronavirus/COVID–19 Election Safety and Security Act and the amendments made by such Act with respect to primary elections for Federal office held in the State in 2020.

"(2) STATE POLITICAL PARTY-RUN PRIMARIES.—In addition to any payments under paragraph (1), in the case of a State voluntarily electing to comply with the American Coronavirus/COVID–19 Election Safety and Security Act and the amendments made by such Act with respect to primary elections for Federal office held in the State in 2020, the Commission shall make a payment to each eligible political party of the State for the costs incurred by the party in transmitting absentee ballots and balloting materials with respect to such elections (including the costs relating to pre-paying the postage on the return envelopes for such ballots and materials).

"(c) Pass-Through Of Funds To Local Jurisdictions.—

"(1) IN GENERAL.—If a State receives a payment under this part for costs that include costs incurred by a local jurisdiction or Tribal government within the State, the State shall pass through to such local jurisdiction or Tribal government a portion of such payment that is equal to the amount of the costs incurred by such local jurisdiction or Tribal government.

"(2) TRIBAL GOVERNMENT DEFINED.—In this subsection, the term 'Tribal Government' means the recognized governing body of an Indian tribe (as defined in section 4 of the Indian Self-Determination and Education Assistance Act (25 U.S.C. 5304).

"(d) Schedule Of Payments.—As soon as practicable after the date of the enactment of this part and not less frequently than once each calendar year thereafter, the Commission shall make payments under this part.

"(e) Coverage Of Commonwealth Of Northern Mariana Islands.—In this part, the term 'State' includes the Commonwealth of the Northern Mariana Islands.

"(f) Limitation.—No funds may be provided to a State under this part for costs attributable to the electronic return of marked ballots by any voter.

"SEC. 297A. AMOUNT OF PAYMENT.

"(a) In General.—Except as provided in section 297C, the amount of a payment made to an eligible State for a year under this part shall be determined by the Commission.

"(b) Continuing Availability Of Funds After Appropriation.—A payment made to an eligible State or eligible unit of local government under this part shall be available without fiscal year limitation.

"SEC. 297B. REQUIREMENTS FOR ELIGIBILITY.

"(a) Application.—Except as provided in section 297C, each State that desires to receive a payment under this part for a fiscal year, and each political party of a State that desires to receive a payment under section 297(b)(2), shall submit an application for the payment to the Commission at such time and in such manner and containing such information as the Commission shall require.

"(b) Contents Of Application.—Each application submitted under subsection (a) shall—

"(1) describe the activities for which assistance under this part is sought; and

"(2) provide such additional information and certifications as the Commission determines to be essential to ensure compliance with the requirements of this part.

"SEC. 297C. SPECIAL RULES FOR PAYMENTS FOR ELECTIONS SUBJECT TO EMERGENCY RULES.

"(a) Submission Of Estimated Costs.—If the special rules in the case of an emergency period under section 322(c)(3) apply to an election, not later than the applicable deadline under subsection (c), the State shall submit to the Commission a request for a payment under this part, and shall include in the request the State's estimate of the costs the State expects to incur in the administration of the election which are attributable to the application of such special rules to the election.

"(b) Payment.—Not later than 7 days after receiving a request from the State under subsection (a), the Commission shall make a payment to the State in an amount equal to the estimate provided by the State in the request.

"(c) Applicable Deadline.—The applicable deadline under this paragraph with respect to an election is—

"(1) with respect to the regularly scheduled general election for Federal office held in November 2020, 15 days after the date of the enactment of this part; and

"(2) with respect to any other election, 15 days after the emergency or disaster described in section 322(c)(3) is declared.

"SEC. 297D. AUTHORIZATION OF APPROPRIATIONS.

"There are authorized to be appropriated for payments under this part—

"(1) in the case of payments made under section 297C, such sums as may be necessary for fiscal year 2020 and each succeeding fiscal year; and

"(2) in the case of any other payments, such sums as may be necessary for fiscal year 2020.

"SEC. 297E. REPORTS.

"(a) Reports By Recipients.—Not later than 6 months after the end of each fiscal year for which an eligible State received a payment under this part, the State shall submit a report to the Commission on the activities conducted with the funds provided during the year.

"(b) Reports By Commission To Committees.—With respect to each fiscal year for which the Commission makes payments under this part, the Commission shall submit a report on the activities carried out under this part to the Committee on House Administration of the House of Representatives and the Committee on Rules and Administration of the Senate.".

(b) Clerical Amendment.—The table of contents of such Act is amended by adding at the end of the items relating to subtitle D of title II the following:

"PART 7—PAYMENTS TO ASSIST WITH COSTS OF COMPLIANCE WITH ACCESS ACT

"Sec. 297. Payments to assist with costs of compliance with Access Act.

"Sec. 297A. Amount of payment.

"Sec. 297B. Requirements for eligibility.

"Sec. 297C. Authorization of appropriations.

"Sec. 297D. Reports.".

SEC. 120009. GRANTS TO STATES FOR CONDUCTING RISK-LIMITING AUDITS OF RESULTS OF ELECTIONS.

(a) Availability Of Grants.—Subtitle D of title II of the Help America Vote Act of 2002 (52 U.S.C. 21001 et seq.), as amended by section 8(a), is further amended by adding at the end the following new part:

"PART 8—GRANTS FOR CONDUCTING RISK-LIMITING AUDITS OF RESULTS OF ELECTIONS

"SEC. 298. GRANTS FOR CONDUCTING RISK-LIMITING AUDITS OF RESULTS OF ELECTIONS.

"(a) Availability Of Grants.—The Commission shall make a grant to each eligible State to conduct risk-limiting audits as described in subsection (b) with respect to the regularly scheduled general elections for Federal office held in November 2020 and each succeeding election for Federal office.

"(b) Risk-Limiting Audits Described.—In this part, a 'risk-limiting audit' is a post-election process—

"(1) which is conducted in accordance with rules and procedures established by the chief State election official of the State which meet the requirements of subsection (c); and

"(2) under which, if the reported outcome of the election is incorrect, there is at least a predetermined percentage chance that the audit will replace the incorrect outcome with the correct outcome as determined by a full, hand-to-eye tabulation of all votes validly cast in that election that ascertains voter intent manually and directly from voter-verifiable paper records.

"(c) Requirements For Rules And Procedures.—The rules and procedures established for conducting a risk-limiting audit shall include the following elements:

"(1) Rules for ensuring the security of ballots and documenting that prescribed procedures were followed.

"(2) Rules and procedures for ensuring the accuracy of ballot manifests produced by election agencies.

"(3) Rules and procedures for governing the format of ballot manifests, cast vote records, and other data involved in the audit.

"(4) Methods to ensure that any cast vote records used in the audit are those used by the voting system to tally the election results sent to the chief State election official and made public.

"(5) Procedures for the random selection of ballots to be inspected manually during each audit.

"(6) Rules for the calculations and other methods to be used in the audit and to determine whether and when the audit of an election is complete.

"(7) Procedures and requirements for testing any software used to conduct risk-limiting audits.

"(d) Definitions.—In this part, the following definitions apply:

"(1) The term 'ballot manifest' means a record maintained by each election agency that meets each of the following requirements:

"(A) The record is created without reliance on any part of the voting system used to tabulate votes.

"(B) The record functions as a sampling frame for conducting a risk-limiting audit.

"(C) The record contains the following information with respect to the ballots cast and counted in the election:

"(i) The total number of ballots cast and counted by the agency (including undervotes, overvotes, and other invalid votes).

"(ii) The total number of ballots cast in each election administered by the agency (including undervotes, overvotes, and other invalid votes).

"(iii) A precise description of the manner in which the ballots are physically stored, including the total number of physical groups of ballots, the numbering system for each group, a unique label for each group, and the number of ballots in each such group.

"(2) The term 'incorrect outcome' means an outcome that differs from the outcome that would be determined by a full tabulation of all votes validly cast in the election, determining voter intent manually, directly from voter-verifiable paper records.

"(3) The term 'outcome' means the winner of an election, whether a candidate or a position.

"(4) The term 'reported outcome' means the outcome of an election which is determined according to the canvass and which will become the official, certified outcome unless it is revised by an audit, recount, or other legal process.

"SEC. 298A. ELIGIBILITY OF STATES.

"A State is eligible to receive a grant under this part if the State submits to the Commission, at such time and in such form as the Commission may require, an application containing—

"(1) a certification that, not later than 5 years after receiving the grant, the State will conduct risk-limiting audits of the results of elections for Federal office held in the State as described in section 298;

"(2) a certification that, not later than one year after the date of the enactment of this section, the chief State election official of the State has established or will establish the rules and procedures for conducting the audits which meet the requirements of section 298(c);

"(3) a certification that the audit shall be completed not later than the date on which the State certifies the results of the election;

"(4) a certification that, after completing the audit, the State shall publish a report on the results of the audit, together with such information as necessary to confirm that the audit was conducted properly;

"(5) a certification that, if a risk-limiting audit conducted under this part leads to a full manual tally of an election, State law requires that the State or election agency shall use the results of the full manual tally as the official results of the election; and

"(6) such other information and assurances as the Commission may require.

"SEC. 298B. AUTHORIZATION OF APPROPRIATIONS.

"There are authorized to be appropriated for grants under this part $20,000,000 for fiscal year 2020, to remain available until expended.".

(b) Clerical Amendment.—The table of contents of such Act, as amended by section 8(b), is further amended by adding at the end of the items relating to subtitle D of title II the following:

"PART 8—GRANTS FOR CONDUCTING RISK-LIMITING AUDITS OF RESULTS OF ELECTIONS

"Sec. 298. Grants for conducting risk-limiting audits of results of elections.

"Sec. 298A. Eligibility of States.

"Sec. 298B. Authorization of appropriations.

(c) GAO Analysis Of Effects Of Audits.—

(1) ANALYSIS.—Not later than 6 months after the first election for Federal office is held after grants are first awarded to States for conducting risk-limiting audits under part 8 of subtitle D of title II of the Help America Vote Act of 2002 (as added by subsection (a)) for conducting risk-limiting audits

of elections for Federal office, the Comptroller General of the United States shall conduct an analysis of the extent to which such audits have improved the administration of such elections and the security of election infrastructure in the States receiving such grants.

(2) REPORT.—The Comptroller General of the United States shall submit a report on the analysis conducted under subsection (a) to the appropriate congressional committees.

SEC. 120010. ADDITIONAL APPROPRIATIONS FOR THE ELECTION ASSISTANCE COMMISSION.

(a) In General.—In addition to any funds otherwise appropriated to the Election Assistance Commission for fiscal year 2020, there is authorized to be appropriated $3,000,000 for fiscal year 2020 in order for the Commission to provide additional assistance and resources to States for improving the administration of elections.

(b) Availability Of Funds.—Amounts appropriated pursuant to the authorization under this subsection shall remain available without fiscal year limitation.

DIVISION M—OVERSIGHT AND ACCOUNTABILITY

SEC. 130001. CORONAVIRUS ACCOUNTABILITY AND TRANSPARENCY COMMITTEE.

(a) Establishment Of The Coronavirus Accountability And Transparency Committee.—There is established the Coronavirus Accountability and Transparency Committee within the Council of the Inspectors General on Integrity and Efficiency to coordinate and support Inspectors General in conducting oversight of covered funds to detect and prevent fraud, waste, and abuse.

(b) Composition Of Committee.—

(1) CHAIRPERSON.—The Chairperson of the Committee shall be an Inspector General, identified in paragraph (2)(A) with experience managing oversight of large organizations and expenditures and shall be selected by the Chair of the Council of the Inspectors General on Integrity and Efficiency.

(2) MEMBERS.—The members of the Committee shall include—

(A) the Inspectors General of the Departments of Commerce, Defense, Education, Health and Human Services, Homeland Security, Labor, Transportation, Treasury, Treasury Inspector General for Tax Administration, Veterans Affairs, and the Small Business Administration; and

(B) any other Inspector General as designated by the Chair of the Council of the Inspectors General on Integrity and Efficiency.

(c) Functions Of The Committee.—

(1) FUNCTIONS.—

(A) IN GENERAL.—The Committee shall coordinate and assist Inspectors General in the oversight of covered funds and the response of the Executive Branch to the Coronavirus Pandemic in order to prevent fraud, waste, and abuse.

(B) SPECIFIC FUNCTIONS.—The functions of the Committee shall include—

(i) developing a strategic plan to ensure Inspectors General effectively and efficiently conduct comprehensive oversight over all aspects of the covered funds and the response by the Executive Branch to the Coronavirus;

(ii) serving as a liaison to the Director of the Office of Management and Budget, Secretary of the Treasury, and other officials responsible for implementing this Act;

(iii) supporting audits and investigations of covered funds to determine whether wasteful spending, poor contract or grant management, or other abuses are occurring and referring matters the Committee considers appropriate for audit or investigation to the Inspector General for the agency that disbursed the covered funds or more than one Inspector General, as appropriate;

(iv) supporting reviews of contracts, grants, and other assistance that use using covered funds or that are otherwise related to Coronavirus by assessing whether—

(I) the contracts, grants, and other assistance meet applicable standards;

(II) the contracts, grants, and other assistance adequately specify the purpose of the contract, grant, or other assistance, as well as applicable measures of performance; and

(III) there are sufficient qualified acquisition and grant personnel overseeing the use of covered funds; and

(v) reviewing whether there are appropriate mechanisms for interagency collaboration relating to covered funds, including coordinating and collaborating to the extent practicable with State and local government entities.

(2) REPORTS.—

(A) REPORTS.—The Committee shall submit to the President and Congress, including the appropriate congressional committees, timely alerts on current or potential management and funding problems that require immediate attention. The Committee also shall submit to Congress such other reports as the Committee considers appropriate on the use and benefits of covered funds and the response of the Executive Branch to the Coronavirus.

(B) BIANNUAL REPORTS.—The Committee shall submit reports every six months to the President and the appropriate congressional committees, summarizing the findings of the Committee and Inspectors General of agencies. The Committee may submit additional reports as appropriate.

(C) PUBLIC AVAILABILITY.—

(i) IN GENERAL.—All reports submitted under this paragraph shall be made publicly available and posted on the website established by subsection (e).

(ii) REDACTIONS.—Any portion of a report submitted under this paragraph may be redacted when made publicly available, if that portion would disclose information that is not subject to disclosure under sections 552 and 552a of title 5, United States Code.

(3) RECOMMENDATIONS.—

(A) IN GENERAL.—The Committee, in coordination with the member Inspectors General, shall make recommendations to agencies and to Congress, including the appropriate committees, on measures to prevent fraud, waste, and abuse relating to covered funds.

(B) RESPONSIVE REPORTS.—Not later than 30 days after receipt of a recommendation under subparagraph (A), an agency shall submit a report to the President, the congressional committees of jurisdiction, and the appropriate congressional committees, on—

(i) whether the agency agrees or disagrees with the recommendations; and

(ii) any specific action or action plan the agency will take to implement the recommendations.

(d) Powers And Authorities Of The Committee.—

(1) IN GENERAL.—The Committee shall coordinate and support investigations, audits and reviews of spending of covered funds to avoid

duplication and overlap of work and ensure that there are not gaps in oversight activities by the member Inspectors General. If a gap in oversight is identified, the Committee shall request that an Inspector General or more than one Inspector General, designated by the Chair, conduct the appropriate audit or review.

(2) AUDITS AND INVESTIGATIONS.—The Committee may—

(A) provide all necessary support to an Inspector General or Inspectors General in the conduct of investigations, audits, evaluations, and reviews relating to covered funds and Coronavirus response; and

(B) collaborate on investigations, audits and reviews relating to covered funds and Coronavirus response with any Inspector General of an agency or more than one Inspectors General.

(3) AUTHORITIES.—

(A) AUDITS AND INVESTIGATIONS.—In providing assistance to Inspectors General in the conduct of investigations, audits and reviews, the Committee shall have the authorities provided under section 6 of the Inspector General Act of 1978 (5 U.S.C. App.). The Committee may issue subpoenas to compel the testimony of persons and may enforce subpoenas in the event of a refusal to obey by order of any appropriate United States district court as provided for Inspector General subpoenas under section 6 of the Inspector General Act of 1978 (5 U.S.C. App.).

(B) STANDARDS AND GUIDELINES.—The Committee shall carry out the powers under paragraphs (1) and (2) in accordance with section 4(b)(1) of the Inspector General Act of 1978 (5 U.S.C. App.).

(C) REPORT OF REFUSALS.—Whenever information or assistance requested by the Committee or an Inspector General, is unreasonably refused or not provided, the Committee shall immediately report the circumstances to the appropriate committees.

(D) INFORMATION AND ASSISTANCE.—Upon request of the Committee for information or assistance from any agency or other entity of the Federal Government, or any recipient under this Act, the head of such entity shall, insofar as is practicable and not in contravention of any existing law, and consistent with section 6 of the Inspector General Act of 1978, as amended, furnish such information or assistance to the Committee.

(4) CONTRACTS.—The Council may enter into contracts to enable the Committee to discharge its duties under this Act, including contracts for audits, studies, analyses, and other services with public agencies and private persons, and make such payments as may be necessary to carry out the duties of the Committee.

(5) TRANSFER OF FUNDS.—The Council may transfer funds appropriated to the Council under this section for administrative support services and any audits, investigations, reviews, or other activities to any office of Inspector General.

(6) EMPLOYMENT AND PERSONNEL AUTHORITIES.—

(A) IN GENERAL.—

(i) AUTHORITIES.—The Council may exercise the authorities of subsections (b) through (i) of section 3161 of title 5, United States Code, (without regard to subsection (a) of that section) to carry out the Committee's functions under this section.

(ii) APPLICATION.—For purposes of exercising the authorities described under clause (i), the term "Chairperson of the Council" shall be substituted for the term "head of a temporary organization".

(iii) CONSULTATION.—In exercising the authorities described under clause (i), the Chairperson shall consult with members of the Committee.

(iv) EMPLOYMENT AUTHORITIES.—In exercising the employment authorities under subsection (b) of section 3161 of title 5, United States Code, paragraph (2) of subsection (b) of section 3161 of that title (relating to periods of appointments) shall not apply and no period of appointment may exceed the date on which the Committee terminates under subsection (i).

(v) DETAIL OF PERSONNEL.—In addition to the authority provided by subsection (c) of section 3161 of title 5, United States Code, upon the request of an Inspector General, the Council may detail, on a nonreimbursable basis, any personnel of the Committee to that Inspector General to assist in carrying out any audit or investigation referred to the Inspector General by the Committee.

(vi) REHIRING ANNUITANTS.—The Committee may employ annuitants covered by section 9902(g) of title 5, United States Code, for purposes of the oversight of covered funds or the Coronavirus response. The employment of annuitants under this subparagraph shall be subject to the provisions of section 9902(g) of title 5, United States Code, as if the Committee was the Department of Defense.

(vii) COMPETITIVE STATUS.—A person employed by the Committee shall acquire competitive status for appointment to any position in the competitive service for which the employee possesses the required qualifications upon the completion of 2 years of continuous service as an employee under this subsection. No person who is first employed more than 2 years after the date of the enactment of this Act may acquire competitive status under this authority.

(e) Committee Website.—

(1) ESTABLISHMENT.—The Committee shall utilize www.Oversight.gov to establish and maintain, no later than 30 days after the enactment of this Act, a public-facing website for accountability and transparency in the use of covered funds.

(2) PURPOSE.—The website established and maintained under paragraph (1) shall provide information relating to implementation of this Act and provide connections to other government websites with related information.

(3) CONTENT AND FUNCTION.—In establishing the website established and maintained under paragraph (1), the Committee shall ensure the website—

(A) provides materials explaining what this Act means for citizens in plain

language and shall be regularly updated;
(B) provides accountability information, including findings from audits, investigations, or reviews conducted by the Committee, Inspectors General, and the Government Accountability Office;
(C) provides data made available in a searchable, sortable, downloadable, and machine-readable format;
(D) provides—
(i) data on how funds provided under this Act are spent including through relevant economic, financial, grant, subgrant, contract, subcontract, loan, and other relevant information with a unique, trackable identification number for each project where applicable; and
(ii) information about the process that was used for the award of loans, grants, or contracts, and for contracts over $150,000, an explanation of the contract agreement where applicable;
(E) includes searchable, sortable, downloadable, machine-readable reports on covered funds obligated by month to each State and congressional district where applicable;
(F) includes detailed information on Federal Government contracts, grants, and loans that expend covered funds, using, where applicable, the data elements required by the Digital Access and Transparency Act (Public Law 113–101), and shall allow for aggregate reporting on awards below $50,000 or to individuals, as prescribed by the Director of the Office of Management and Budget;
(G) includes appropriate links to other government websites with information concerning covered funds, including Federal agency and State websites;
(H) provides information on Federal allocations of formula grants and awards of competitive grants using covered funds;
(I) provides, if applicable, information on Federal allocations of mandatory and other entitlement programs by State, county, or other appropriate geographical unit;
(J) be enhanced and updated as necessary to carry out the purposes of this section; and
(K) presents the data such that funds subawarded by recipients are not double counted in search results, data visualizations or other reports.
(4) WAIVER.—The Committee may exclude posting contractual or other information on the website on a case-by-case basis when necessary to protect information that is not subject to disclosure under sections 552 and 552a of title 5, United States Code.
(f) Independence Of Inspectors General.—
(1) INDEPENDENT AUTHORITY.—Nothing in this section shall affect the independent authority of an Inspector General or the Comptroller General to determine whether to conduct an audit or investigation of covered funds.
(2) REQUESTS BY COMMITTEE.—If the Committee requests that an Inspector General conduct or refrain from conducting an audit or investigation

and such Inspector General rejects such request in whole or in part, such Inspector General shall, not later than 30 days after rejecting the request, submit a report to the appropriate congressional committees. The report shall state the reasons that such Inspector General has rejected the request in whole or in part.

(g) Coordination With The Comptroller General And State Auditors.—The Committee shall coordinate its oversight activities with the Comptroller General of the United States and State and local auditors.

(h) Authorization Of Appropriations.—For the purposes of carrying out the mission of the Council of the Inspectors General on Integrity and Efficiency under section 11 of the Inspector General Act of 1978 (5 U.S.C. App.) and to carry out this section, there are authorized to be appropriated into the revolving fund described in subsection (c)(3)(B) of such section, out of any amount in the Treasury not otherwise appropriated, $100,000,000 to carry out the duties and functions of the Council.

(i) Termination Of The Committee.—The Committee and its authorities and responsibilities shall terminate on the later of—

(1) the date the last grant administered under this Act is expended;

(2) the date the last contract administered under this Act expires;

(3) the date the last loan or loan guarantee provided under this Act matures or expires, as appropriate; or

(4) the date the last instrument or asset acquired by the Federal Government has been sold or transferred out of the ownership or control of the Federal Government, or otherwise disposed of.

(j) Definitions.—In this section:

(1) COMMITTEE.—The term "Committee" means the Coronavirus Accountability and Transparency Committee established in subsection (a).

(2) COVERED FUNDS.—The term "covered funds" means any funds that are made available, in any form, under this Act.

(3) RECIPIENT.—The term "recipient" means a recipient of Federal funds under this Act.

(4) APPROPRIATE CONGRESSIONAL COMMITTEES.—The term "appropriate congressional committees" means the Committees on Appropriations and Homeland Security of the Senate and Committees on Appropriations and Oversight and Reform in the House of Representatives.

SEC. 130002. GAO OVERSIGHT AND AUDIT AUTHORITY.

(a) Authority.—The Comptroller General shall conduct monitoring and oversight of the exercise of authorities under this Act or any other Act to prepare for, respond to, and recover from the Coronavirus pandemic and the effect of the pandemic on the health, economy, and public and private institutions of the United States, including public health and homeland security efforts by the Federal Government and the use of selected funds under this or any other Act related to the Coronavirus pandemic.

(b) Briefings And Reports.—In conducting monitoring and oversight under subsection (a), the Comptroller General shall—

(1) during the period beginning on the date of enactment of this Act and ending on the date on which the national emergency declared by the President under the National Emergencies Act (50 U.S.C. 1601 et seq.) with respect to the Coronavirus Disease 2019 expires, offer regular briefings on not less frequently than a monthly basis to the appropriate congressional committees regarding Federal public health and homeland security efforts;

(2) publish reports regarding the ongoing monitoring and oversight efforts, which, along with any audits and investigations conducted by the Comptroller General, shall be submitted to the appropriate congressional committees and posted on the website of the Government Accountability Office—

(A) not later than 90 days after the date of enactment of this Act, every other month thereafter until the date that is 1 year after the date of enactment of this Act; and

(B) after the period described in subparagraph (A), on a periodic basis; and

(3) submit to the appropriate congressional committees additional reports as warranted by the findings of the monitoring and oversight activities of the Comptroller General.

(c) Access To Information.—

(1) RIGHT OF ACCESS.—In conducting monitoring and oversight activities under this section, the Comptroller General shall have access to records, upon request, of any Federal, State, or local agency, contractor, grantee, recipient, or subrecipient pertaining to any Federal effort or assistance of any type related to Coronavirus under this Act or any other Act, including private entities receiving such assistance.

(2) COPIES.—The Comptroller General may make and retain copies of any records accessed under paragraph (1) as the Comptroller General determines appropriate.

(3) INTERVIEWS.—In addition to such other authorities as are available, the Comptroller General or a designee of the Comptroller General may interview Federal, State, or local officials, contractor staff, grantee staff, recipients, or subrecipients pertaining to any Federal effort or assistance of any type related to Coronavirus under this or any other Act, including private entities receiving such assistance.

(4) INSPECTION OF FACILITIES.—As determined necessary by the Comptroller General, the Government Accountability Office may inspect facilities at which Federal, State, or local officials, contractor staff, grantee staff, or recipients or subrecipients carry out their responsibilities related to Coronavirus.

(5) ENFORCEMENT.—Access rights under this subsection shall be subject to enforcement consistent with section 716 of title 31, United States Code.

(d) Relationship To Existing Authority.—Nothing in this section shall be construed to limit, amend, supersede, or restrict in any manner any existing

authority of the Comptroller General.
(e) Definitions.—In this section:
(1) APPROPRIATE CONGRESSIONAL COMMITTEES.—The term "appropriate congressional committees" means—
(A) the Committee on Appropriations of the Senate;
(B) the Committee on Homeland Security and Governmental Affairs of the Senate;
(C) the Committee on Health, Education, Labor, and Pensions of the Senate;
(D) the Committee on Appropriations of the House of Representatives;
(E) the Committee on Homeland Security of the House of Representatives;
(F) the Committee on Oversight and Reform of the House of Representatives; and
(G) the Committee on Energy and Commerce of the House of Representatives.
(2) COMPTROLLER GENERAL.—The term "Comptroller General" means the Comptroller General of the United States.

DIVISION N—U.S. POSTAL SERVICE PROVISIONS

SEC. 140001. ELIMINATION OF USPS DEBT; ADDITIONAL BORROWING AUTHORITY.

(a) In General.—Notwithstanding any other provision of law—

(1) any outstanding debt of the United States Postal Service owed to the Treasury pursuant to sections 2005 and 2011 of title 5, United States Code, on the date of the enactment of this Act is hereby cancelled; and

(2) after the date of the enactment of this Act, the United States Postal Service is authorized to borrow money from the Treasury in an amount not to exceed $15,000,000,000 to carry out the duties and responsibilities of the Postal Service, including those under title 39, United States Code, and the Secretary of the Treasury shall lend up to such amount at the request of the Postal Service.

(b) Repeal Of Fiscal Year Borrowing Limit.—Section 2005(a)(1) of title 39, United States Code, is amended by striking "In any one fiscal year," and all that follows through the period.

SEC. 140002. PRIORITIZATION OF DELIVERY FOR MEDICAL PURPOSES DURING COVID–19 EMERGENCY.

Notwithstanding any other provision of law, the United States Postal Service—

(1) shall prioritize delivery of postal products for medical purposes during the emergency, declared by the President under section 501 of the Robert T. Stafford Disaster Relief and Emergency Assistance Act (42 U.S.C. 5191) on March 13, 2020, based on the outbreak of COVID–19;

(2) may establish temporary delivery points, in such form and manner as the Postal Service determines necessary, to protect employees of the Postal Service and individuals receiving deliveries from the Postal Service; and

(3) may institute flexible delivery, in such form and manner as the Postal Service determines necessary, in the event operations or employees of the Postal Service are impacted by the COVID–19 outbreak described in paragraph (1).

DIVISION O—FEDERAL WORKFORCE PROVISIONS

SEC. 150001. REIMBURSEMENT FOR CHILD AND FAMILY CARE FOR FEDERAL EMPLOYEES DURING COVID–19 PANDEMIC.

(a) In General.—During the period beginning on the date of enactment of this Act and ending on December 31, 2020, any employee who is unable to care for a dependent child of the employee or a relative of the employee who has COVID–19 as a result of the employee being required to report to their duty station (either permanent or temporary) or to telework shall be entitled to reimbursement for the costs of such care.

(b) Application.—

(1) IN GENERAL.—Any payment provided by operation of subsection (a) shall be paid on a monthly basis, with payments being made to the employee on the last day of each month.

(2) SUBMISSION OF RECEIPTS.—For purposes of determining reimbursement amounts, each employee shall submit to their employing office receipts or other documents as the office may require.

(3) LIMIT.—Reimbursement may not be paid to any employee under this section for any month in an amount greater than $2,000 per child or relative.

(c) Definitions.—In this section—

(1) the term "employee" means any individual occupying a position in the civil service (as that term is defined in section 2101(1) of title 5, United States Code); and

(2) the terms "dependent child" and "relative" have the meaning given those terms in paragraphs (2) and (16), respectively, of section 109 of the Ethics in Government Act of 1978 (5 U.S.C. App. 109(2)).

SEC. 150002. FEDERAL CONTRACTOR REIMBURSEMENT.

Not later than 10 calendar days after the date of the enactment of this Act, the Director of the Office of Management and Budget, in consultation with the Administrator of the Office of Federal Procurement Policy, shall issue guidance to the head of each executive agency to provide equitable adjustment for any contractor under a contract with the Federal Government whose work was disrupted as a result of measures taken with respect to COVID–19. For purposes of this section, work disruption shall include denial of access to Federal facilities, supply chain disruptions, use of annual leave by individuals employed to fulfill the contract, and furloughs of individuals employed to fulfill the contract.

SEC. 150003. WEATHER AND SAFETY LEAVE FOR COVID–19.

(a) In General.—Beginning on the date of enactment of this Act and ending on December 31, 2020, subsection (b)(3) of section 6329c of title 5, United States Code, shall be applied by substituting "approved location, including by reason of the inability to travel or access work stations as a result of COVID–19" for "approved location".

(b) Approved Location.—Such section is amended in subsection (a)—

(1) by striking "and" at the end of paragraph (1);

(2) by striking the period at the end of paragraph (2) and inserting "; and"; and

(3) by adding at the end the following:

"(3) the term 'approved location' means any location at which an employee has been approved to perform work, including any Federal office, a teleworking site, or other location as determined by the head of the agency at which the employee is employed.".

(c) Rule Of Construction.—Notwithstanding subparagraph (B) of subsection (a)(2) of such section, intermittent employees described in such subparagraph shall be eligible for the leave provided by operation of subsection (a) of this section.

SEC. 150004. COVID–19 TELEWORKING REQUIREMENTS FOR FEDERAL EMPLOYEES.

(a) Mandated Telework.—

(1) IN GENERAL.—Effective immediately upon the date of enactment of this Act, the head of any Federal agency shall require any employee of such agency who is authorized to telework under chapter 65 of title 5, United States Code, or any other provision of law to telework during the period beginning on the date of enactment of this Act and ending on December 31, 2020.

(2) DEFINITIONS.—In this subsection—

(A) the term "employee" means any individual occupying a position in the civil service (as that term is defined in section 2101(1) of title 5, United States Code); and

(B) the term "telework" has the meaning given that term in section 6501(3) of such title.

(b) Telework Participation Goals.—Chapter 65 of title 5, United States Code, is amended as follows:

(1) In section 6502—

(A) in subsection (b)—

(i) in paragraph (4), by striking "and" at the end;

(ii) in paragraph (5), by striking the period at the end and inserting a semicolon; and

(iii) by adding at the end the following:

"(6) include annual goals for increasing the percent of employees of the executive agency participating in teleworking—

"(A) three or more days per pay period;

"(B) one or 2 days per pay period;

"(C) once per month; and

"(D) on an occasional, episodic, or short-term basis; and

"(7) include methods for collecting data on, setting goals for, and reporting costs savings to the executive agency achieved through teleworking,

consistent with the guidance developed under section 150004(c) of the Take Responsibility for Workers and Families Act."; and
(B) by adding at the end the following:
"(d) Notification For Reduction In Teleworking Participation.—Not later than 30 days before the date that an executive agency implements or modifies a teleworking plan that would reduce the percentage of employees at the agency who telework, the head of the executive agency shall provide written notification, including a justification for the reduction in telework participation and a description of how the agency will pay for any increased costs resulting from that reduction, to—
"(1) the Director of the Office of Personnel Management;
"(2) the Committee on Oversight and Reform of the House of Representatives; and
"(3) the Committee on Homeland Security and Governmental Affairs of the Senate.
"(e) Prohibition On Agency-Wide Limits On Teleworking.—An agency may not prohibit any delineated period of teleworking participation for all employees of the agency, including the periods described in subparagraphs (A) through (D) of subsection (b)(6). The agency shall make any teleworking determination with respect to an employee or group of employees at the agency on a case-by-case basis.".
(2) In section 6506(b)(2)—
(A) in subparagraph (F)(vi), by striking "and" at the end;
(B) in subparagraph (G), by striking the period at the end and inserting a semicolon; and
(C) by adding at the end the following:
"(H) agency cost savings achieved through teleworking, consistent with the guidance developed under section 2(c) of the Telework Metrics and Cost Savings Act; and
"(I) a detailed explanation of a plan to increase the Government-wide teleworking participation rate above such rate applicable to fiscal year 2016, including agency-level plans to maintain or improve such rate for each of the teleworking frequency categories listed under subparagraph (A)(iii).".
(c) Guidance.—Not later than 90 days after the date of the enactment of this Act, the Director of the Office of Personnel Management, in collaboration with the Chief Human Capital Officer Council, shall establish uniform guidance for agencies on how to collect data on, set goals for, and report cost savings achieved through, teleworking. Such guidance shall account for cost savings related to travel, energy use, and real estate.
(d) Technical Correction.—Section 6506(b)(1) of title 5, United States Code, is amended by striking "with Chief" and inserting "with the Chief".

SEC. 150005. PAY DIFFERENTIAL FOR DUTY RELATED TO COVID–19.

(a) In General.—Section 5545 of title 5, United States Code, is amended by adding at the end the following:

"(e) (1) The Office shall establish a schedule or schedules of pay differentials for duty during which an employee is exposed to an individual who has (or who has been exposed to) COVID–19.

"(2) Under such regulations as the Office may prescribe, during the period beginning on March 15, 2020, and ending on September 30, 2020, an employee to whom chapter 51 and subchapter III of chapter 53 applies, and an employee appointed under chapter 73 or 74 of title 38, is entitled to be paid the differential under paragraph (1) for any period in which the employee is carrying out the duty described in such paragraph.".

(b) TSA Employees.—Section 111(d)(2) of the Aviation and Transportation Security Act (49 U.S.C. 44935 note) is amended by adding at the end the following:

"(C) HAZARDOUS DUTY PAY FOR COVID–19.—The provisions of section 5545(e) of title 5, United States Code, shall to apply to any individual appointed under paragraph (1).".

SEC. 150006. WORKERS' COMPENSATION FOR CERTAIN FEDERAL EMPLOYEES WHO CONTRACT COVID-19.

(a) In General.—Chapter 81 of title 5, United States Code, is amended by—

(1) by redesigating section 8152 as section 8153; and

(2) by inserting after section 8151 the following:

"§ 8152. Workers' compensation for certain Federal employees who contract COVID-19

"(a) Any employee described in subsection (b) who is diagnosed with COVID-19 (as defined in ____) during the period between January 30, 2020, and January 30, 2022, shall, upon application, presumptively be entitled to disability compensation, medical services, and any other benefit provided under this chapter.

"(b) An employee described in this subsection is any of the following:

"(1) An employee whose duties involve the provision of health care or protection of public health performance of duties in a health care facility or operation.

"(2) A first responder.

"(3) A law enforcement officer (as that term is defined in section 8331(20) or 8401(17)).

"(4) A transportation security officer.

"(5) An employee of the United States Postal Service, Department of Veterans Affairs, Veterans Health Administration, and Indian Health Services.

"(6) Any employee carrying out duties that require substantial contact with the public.

"(7) Any employee whose duties include a recognized risk of exposure to the coronavirus (as that term is defined in section 506 of the Coronavirus

Preparedness and Response Supplemental Appropriations Act, 2020).".

(b) Clerical Amendment.—The table of sections for such chapter is amended—

(1) by redesignating the item relating to section 8152 as section 8153; and

(2) by inserting after the item relating to section 8151 the following:

"8152. Workers' compensation for certain Federal employees who contract COVID-19.".

DIVISION P—FEDERAL EMPLOYEE COLLECTIVE BARGAINING AND OFFICIAL TIME

SEC. 160001. SHORT TITLE.

This division may be cited as the "Protecting Collective Bargaining and Official Time for Federal Workers Act".

SEC. 160002. FINDINGS.

Congress finds the following:

(1) Federal Unions play a critical role in protecting the rights of Federal workers by allowing members to have a collective voice on the job and in the legislative process, advance issues for working families, ensure equal opportunities for all workers, and raise the standards by which all professional and technical workers are employed.

(2) Collective bargaining is essential to the union process, because it provides mutual agreement between all parties that fosters harmonious relationships between the Federal Government and its employees and protects the interest of both parties.

(3) The current administration has acted through Executive Orders and official memorandums to dismantle Federal Unions and undermine their collective bargaining rights across the Federal workforce and these directives have already negatively impacted labor contracts, both signed and under active negotiation.

(4) These orders set an aggressive schedule for unions to engage in collective bargaining, while also slashing the unions official time for performing union duties by over 91 percent in some cases. These actions are limiting the ability for unions to prepare for negotiations and perform their legally required employee representational duties.

(5) Section 7101(a) of title 5, United States Code, states, "Congress finds that labor organizations and collective bargaining in the civil service are in the public interest.". Attempting to eliminate the Union by eliminating almost all its official time repudiates the statutory position that unions are in the public interest.

(6) Through these orders, agencies are required to comply with artificial bargaining schedules, which undermine good faith negotiations and divert the decision-making to an impasse panel, which has no union representation on it and does not represent both parties.

(7) Collectively, the administration's actions have violated Congressional intent, undermined the ability of unions to engage in collective bargaining, and threatened the rights and benefits of millions of Federal workers.

SEC. 160003. NULLIFICATION OF EXECUTIVE ORDERS RELATING TO FEDERAL EMPLOYEE COLLECTIVE BARGAINING.

Each of the following Executive Orders and presidential memorandum are

rescinded and shall have no force or effect:
(1) Executive Order 13837 (relating to the use of official time).
(2) Executive Order 13836 (relating to Federal collective bargaining).
(3) Executive Order 13839 (relating to the Merit Systems Protection Board).
(4) The Presidential Memorandum on the Delegation of Certain Authority under the Federal Service Labor-Management Relations Statute, issued to the Secretary of Defense on January 29, 2020.

DIVISION Q—VETERAN CORONAVIRUS RESPONSE ACT OF 2020

SEC. 170001. SHORT TITLE.

This division may be cited as the "Student Veteran Coronavirus Response Act of 2020".

SEC. 170002. PAYMENT OF WORK-STUDY ALLOWANCES DURING EMERGENCY SITUATIONS.

Section 3485 of title 38, United States Code, is amended by adding at the end the following new subsection:

"(f) (1) In case of an individual who is in receipt of work-study allowance pursuant to an agreement described in subsection (a)(3) as of the date on which an emergency situation occurs and who is unable to continue to perform qualifying work-study activities described in subsection (a)(4) by reason of the emergency situation—

"(A) the Secretary may continue to pay work-study allowance under this section or make deductions described in subsection (e)(1) during the period of such emergency situation, notwithstanding the inability of the individual to perform such work-study activities by reason of such emergency situation; and

"(B) at the option of the individual, the Secretary shall extend the agreement described in subsection (a)(3) with the individual for any subsequent period of enrollment initiated during the emergency situation, notwithstanding the inability of the individual to perform work-study activities described in subsection (a)(4) by reason of such emergency situation.

"(2) The amount of work-study allowance payable to an individual under paragraph (1)(A) during the period of an emergency situation shall be an amount determined by the Secretary but may not exceed the amount that would be payable under subsection (a)(2) if the individual worked 25 hours per week paid during such period.".

SEC. 170003. PAYMENT OF ALLOWANCES TO VETERANS ENROLLED IN EDUCATIONAL INSTITUTIONS CLOSED FOR EMERGENCY SITUATIONS.

(a) Temporary Provision.—

(1) IN GENERAL.—During the period beginning on March 1, 2020, and ending on December 21, 2020, the Secretary may pay allowances to an eligible veteran or eligible person under section 3680(a)(2)(A) of title 38, United States Code, if the veteran or person is enrolled in a program or course of education that—

(A) is provided by an educational institution that is closed by reason of an emergency situation; or

(B) is suspended by reason of an emergency situation.

(2) AMOUNT OF ALLOWANCE.—The total number of weeks for which

allowances may be paid under this section may not exceed four weeks.

(3) NOT COUNTED FOR PURPOSES OF LIMITATION.—Any amount paid under this section shall not be counted for purposes of the limitation on allowanced under section 3680(a)(2)(A) of title 38, United States Code.

(b) Permanent Provision.—Section 3680(a)(2) of title 38, United States Code, is amended—

(1) in subparagraph (A), by striking "12-month" and inserting "six-month"; and

(2) in subparagraph (B)—

(A) by striking "or following" and inserting "during periods following"; and

(B) by inserting after "section 3699(b)(1)(B) of this title," the following: ", or during periods when a course of study or program of education is temporarily closed or terminated by reason of an emergency situation,".

SEC. 170004. PROHIBITION OF CHARGE TO ENTITLEMENT OF STUDENTS UNABLE TO PURSUE A PROGRAM OF EDUCATION DUE TO AN EMERGENCY SITUATION.

Section 3699(b)(1) of title 38, United States Code, is amended—

(1) in subparagraph (A), by striking "or" at the end;

(2) in subparagraph (B)(ii), by striking "and" at the end and inserting "or" ; and

(3) by adding at the end the following new subparagraph:

"(C) the temporary closure of an educational institution or the temporary closure or termination of a course or program of education by reason of an emergency situation; and".

SEC. 170005. EXTENSION OF TIME LIMITATIONS FOR USE OF ENTITLEMENT.

(a) Montgomery GI Bill.—Section 3031 of title 38, United States Code, is amended by adding at the end the following new subsection:

"(i) In the case of an individual eligible for educational assistance under this chapter who is prevented from pursuing the individual's chosen program of education before the expiration of the 10-year period for the use of entitlement under this chapter otherwise applicable under this section because the educational institution closed (temporarily or permanently) under an established policy based on an Executive order of the President or due to an emergency situation, such 10-year period—

"(1) shall not run during the period the individual is so prevented from pursuing such program; and

"(2) shall again begin running on the first day after the individual is able to resume pursuit of a program of education with educational assistance under this chapter.".

(b) Post-9/11 Educational Assistance.—

(1) IN GENERAL.—Section 3321(b)(1) of such title is amended—

(A) by inserting "(A)" before "Subsections";

(B) by striking "and (d)" and inserting "(d), and (i)"; and by adding at the end the following new subparagraph:

"(B) Subsection (i) of section 3031 shall apply with respect to the running of the 15-year period described in paragraphs (4)(A) and (5)(A) of this subsection in the same manner as such subsection applies under section 3031 with respect to the running of the 10-year period described in section 3031(a).".

(2) TRANSFER PERIOD.—Section 3319(h)(5) is amended—

(A) in subparagraph (A) by inserting "or (C)" after "subparagraph (B)"; and

(B) by adding at the end the following new subparagraph:

"(C) EMERGENCY SITUATIONS.—In any case in which the Secretary determines that an individual to whom entitlement is transferred under this section has been prevented from pursuing the individual's chosen program of education before the individual attains the age of 26 years because the educational institution closed (temporarily or permanently) under an established policy based on an Executive order of the President or due to an emergency situation, the Secretary shall extend the period during which the individual may use such entitlement for a period equal to the number of months that the individual was so prevented from pursuing the program of education, as determined by the Secretary.".

(c) Vocational Rehabilitation And Training.—

(1) PERIOD FOR USE.—Section 3103 of such title is amended—

(A) in subsection (a), by striking "or (e)" and inserting "(e), or (g)"; and

(B) by adding at the end the following new subsection:

"(g) In any case in which the Secretary determines that a veteran has been prevented from participating in a vocational rehabilitation program under this chapter within the twelve-year period of eligibility prescribed in subsection (a) by reason of an Executive order of the President or due to an emergency situation, such twelve-year period—

"(1) shall not run during the period the individual is so prevented from participating such program; and

"(2) shall again begin running on the first day after the individual is able to resume participation in such program.".

(2) DURATION OF PROGRAM.—Section 3105(b) of such title is amended—

(A) in paragraph (1), by striking "paragraph (2)" and inserting "paragraphs (2) and (3)"; and

(B) by adding at the end the following new paragraph:

"(3) (A) In any case in which the Secretary determines that a veteran has been prevented from participating in counseling and placement and postplacement services described in section 3104(a)(2) and (5) of this title by reason of an Executive order of the President or due to an emergency situation, the Secretary shall extend the period during which the Secretary may provide such counseling and placement and postplacement services for the veteran for a period equal to the number of months that the veteran was so prevented from participating in such counseling and services, as determined by the Secretary.

"(B) In any case in which the Secretary determines that a veteran has been prevented from participating in a vocational rehabilitation program under this chapter by reason of an Executive order of the President or due to an emergency situation, the Secretary shall extend the period of the veteran's vocational rehabilitation program for a period equal to the number of months that the veteran was so prevented from participating in the vocational rehabilitation program, as determined by the Secretary.".

(d) Educational Assistance For Members Of The Selected Reserve.—Section 16133(b) of title 10, United States Code, is amended by adding at the end the following new paragraph:

"(5) In any case in which the Secretary concerned determines that a person entitled to educational assistance under this chapter has been prevented from using such person's entitlement by reason of an Executive order of the President or due to an emergency situation, the Secretary concerned shall extend the period of entitlement prescribed in subsection (a) for a period equal to the number of months that the person was so prevented from using such entitlement, as determined by the Secretary.".

SEC. 170006. RESTORATION OF ENTITLEMENT TO REHABILITATION PROGRAMS FOR VETERANS AFFECTED BY SCHOOL CLOSURE OR DISAPPROVAL.

(a) Entitlement.—Section 3699 of title 38, United States Code, is amended by striking "chapter 30," each time it appears and inserting "chapter 30, 31,".

(b) Payment Of Subsistence Allowances.—Section 3680(a)(2)(B) of title 38, United States Code, is amended—

(1) by inserting "or a subsistence allowance described in section 3108" before ", during"; and

(2) by inserting "or allowance" after "such a stipend".

(c) Effective Date.—The amendments made by this section shall apply as if included in the enactment of section 109 of the Harry W. Colmery Veterans Educational Assistance Act of 2017 (Public Law 115–48; 131 Stat. 978).

SEC. 170007. EXTENSION OF PAYMENT OF VOCATIONAL REHABILITATION SUBSISTENCE ALLOWANCES.

In the case of any veteran who the Secretary of Veterans Affairs determines is satisfactorily following a program of employment services provided under section 3104(a)(5) of title 38, United States Code, during period beginning on March 1, 2020, and ending on December 21, 2020, the Secretary may pay the veteran a subsistence allowance, as prescribed in section 3108 of such title for full-time training for the type of program that the veteran was pursuing, for two additional months.

SEC. 170008. INCREASE OF AMOUNT OF DEPARTMENT OF VETERANS AFFAIRS PAYMENTS FOR AID AND ATTENDANCE DURING EMERGENCY PERIOD RESULTING FROM COVID–19 PANDEMIC.

(a) In General.—During the covered period, the Secretary of Veterans Affairs shall apply each of the following provisions of title 38, United States Code, by substituting for the dollar amount in such provision the amount equal to 125 percent of the dollar amount that was in effect under such provision on the date of the enactment of this Act:

(1) Subsections (l), (m), and (r) of section 1114.

(2) Paragraphs (1) and (2) of subsection (d) of section 1521.

(3) Paragraphs (2) and (4) of subsection (f) of section 1521.

(b) Covered Period.—In this section, the covered period is the period that begins on the date of the enactment of this Act and ends 60 days after the last day of the emergency period (as defined in section 1135(g)(1) of the Social Security Act (42 U.S.C. 1320b–5(g)(1))) resulting from the COVID–19 pandemic.

SEC. 170009. TREATMENT OF WORK INJURY COMPENSATION CLAIMS FILED BY EMPLOYEES OF THE DEPARTMENT OF VETERANS AFFAIRS FOR COVID–19.

(a) Eligibility.—Notwithstanding section 7425(b) of title 38, United States Code, or any other provision of law, each employee of the Department of Veterans Affairs (including employees under chapter 74 of such title) shall be treated as an employee under chapter 81 of title 5, United States Code, for purposes of making claims under such chapter relating to coronavirus disease 2019 (COVID–19).

(b) Presumption.—If an employee of the Department of Veterans Affairs described in subsection (a) contracts coronavirus disease 2019 (COVID–19), such disease shall be presumed to have been proximately caused by the employment of the employee for purposes of claims made under chapter 81 of title 5, United States Code.

SEC. 170010. DEFERRAL OF CERTAIN DEBTS ARISING FROM LAWS ADMINISTERED BY THE SECRETARY OF VETERANS AFFAIRS.

(a) In General.—With regard to a covered debt, the Secretary of Veterans Affairs, during the covered period, may not take any of the following actions:

(1) Collect a payment (including by the offset of any payment by the Secretary).

(2) Record such a debt.

(3) Issue notice of such a debt to an individual or a consumer reporting agency.

(4) Allow any interest to accrue.

(5) Apply any administrative fee.

(b) Exception.—Notwithstanding subsection (a), the Secretary may collect a payment regarding a covered debt (including interest or any administrative

fee) from an individual who elects to make such a payment during the covered period.
(c) Definitions.—In this section:
(1) The term "consumer reporting agency" has the meaning given that term in section 5701 of title 38, United States Code.
(2) The term "covered debt" means a debt owed—
(A) by an individual to the United States; and
(B) arising from a covered law.
(3) The term "covered law" means any law administered by the Secretary of Veterans Affairs through—
(A) the Under Secretary for Health; or
(B) the Under Secretary of Benefits.
(4) The term "covered period" means—
(A) the COVID–19 emergency period; and
(B) the 60 days immediately following the date of the end of the COVID–19 emergency period.
(5) The term "COVID–19 emergency period" means the emergency period described in section 1135(g)(1)(B) of the Social Security Act (42 U.S.C. 1320b–5(g)(1)(B)).

DIVISION R—AVIATION WORKER RELIEF

SEC. 1. SHORT TITLE; TABLE OF CONTENTS.

(a) Short Title.—This division may be cited as the "Aviation Worker Relief Act of 2020".

(b) Table Of Contents.—The table of contents for this division is as follows:

SEC. 2. DEFINITIONS.

Unless otherwise specified, the terms in section 40102(a) of title 49, United States Code, shall apply to this division, except that—

(1) the term "contractor" means a person that performs airport ground support or catering functions under contract with a passenger air carrier; and

(2) the term "employee" means an individual, other than a corporate officer, who is employed by an air carrier or contractor.

TITLE I—AVIATION WORKER RELIEF

SEC. 101. PANDEMIC RELIEF FOR AVIATION WORKERS.

(a) Financial Assistance.—Notwithstanding any other provision of law, the President shall take the following actions to preserve aviation jobs and compensate airline industry workers:

(1) Issue grants that shall exclusively be used for the continuation of payment of employee wages, salaries, and benefits to—

(A) specified entities, in an aggregate amount equal to $37,000,000,000; and

(B) contractors of air carriers, in an aggregate amount equal to $3,000,000,000.

(2) Subject to section 102(c), issue unsecured loans and loan guarantees to air carriers in amounts that do not, in the aggregate, exceed $21,000,000,000.

(b) Assurances.—To be eligible for assistance under this section, an air carrier shall enter into an agreement with the Secretary of Transportation, or otherwise certify, as determined appropriate by the President, that such air carrier shall comply with any actions required under this division.

(c) Administrative Expenses.—Notwithstanding any other provision of law, the Secretary may use $100,000,000 of the funds made available under section 101(a)(2) for costs and administrative expenses associated with the provision of loans or guarantees authorized under such section.

(d) Specified Entity Defined.—In this section, the term "specified entity"

means—
(1) an air carrier that is authorized to conduct operations under part 121 of title 14, Code of Federal Regulations; or
(2) an air carrier that is authorized to conduct operations under part 135 of title 14, Code of Federal Regulations, that—
(A) transports passengers by aircraft on a scheduled basis; or
(B) transports property or mail by aircraft on a scheduled or unscheduled basis.

SEC. 102. PROCEDURES FOR FINANCIAL ASSISTANCE.
(a) Awardable Amounts.—The President shall disburse grants under section 101(a)(1)—
(1) to a specified entity (as such term is defined in section 101(d)), in an amount equal to the salaries and benefits reported by the air carrier to the Department of Transportation pursuant to part 241 of title 14, Code of Federal Regulations, for the period from April 1, 2019, through September 30, 2019;
(2) to a specified entity (as such term is defined in section 101(d)) that does not transmit reports under such part 241, in an amount that such air carrier certifies, using sworn financial statements or other appropriate data, as the amount of wages, salaries, benefits, and other compensation that such air carrier paid the employees of such air carrier during the period from April 1, 2019, through September 30, 2019; and
(3) to a contractor, in an amount that the contractor certifies, using sworn financial statements or other appropriate data, as the amount of wages, salaries, benefits, and other compensation that such contractor paid the employees of such contractor during the period from April 1, 2019, through September 30, 2019.
(b) Deadlines And Procedures.—
(1) PROCEDURES.—The President shall publish streamlined and expedited procedures—
(A) not later than 5 days after the date of enactment of this Act for air carriers and contractors to submit requests for compensation under section 101(a)(1); and
(B) not later than 30 days after the date of enactment of this Act for air carriers to submit requests for loans and loan guarantees under section 101(a)(2).
(2) ISSUANCE OF GRANTS.—The President shall award initial grants under section 101(a)(1) not later than 10 days after the date of enactment of this Act.
(3) DISCRETIONARY GRANTS.—For any funds made available under paragraph (1) of section 101(a) that remain available after the issuance of grants pursuant to paragraph (2) of such section, the President shall determine an appropriate method for the timely distribution of the remaining funds in an equitable manner to air carriers for the payment of employee wages, salaries, and benefits.
(c) Interest Rates.—A loan issued under section 101(a)(2) shall provide for

repayment with no interest for a period of at least 1 year after the loan is issued. The President may otherwise provide for repayment at an interest rate commensurate with the level of risk associated with the loan.

(d) Priority Of Government Claim.—In any proceeding initiated by or against an air carrier under chapter 7 or 11 of title 11, United States Code, with outstanding debt on a loan provided under section 101(a)(2), any claim by the Government with respect to such debt shall assume the highest status of any other claim against such air carrier, whether secured or unsecured.

(e) Audits.—The inspector general of the Department of Transportation may audit certifications under subsection (a)(2).

SEC. 103. TERMS AND CONDITIONS.

(a) Share Repurchases.—

(1) IN GENERAL.—Notwithstanding any other provision of law, an air carrier receiving assistance under section 101 may not purchase an equity interest of such air carrier on a national securities exchange.

(2) DEFINITIONS.—In this subsection:

(A) EXCHANGE.—The term "exchange" has the meaning given the terms in section 3 of the Securities Exchange Act of 1934 1(15 U.S.C. 78c).

(B) NATIONAL SECURITIES EXCHANGE.—The term "national securities exchange" means an exchange registered under section 6 of the Securities Exchange Act of 1934 (15 U.S.C. 78f).

(b) Prohibition On Use Of Funds For Payments To Shareholders Or Bondholders.—An air carrier receiving financial assistance under section 101 may not use the proceeds of such assistance to make any distribution of funds to shareholders or bondholders, including stock dividends.

(c) Executive Compensation.—

(1) IN GENERAL.—The President may provide financial assistance under section 101 to an air carrier only if such air carrier enters into a legally binding agreement with the President that, during the 10-year period following the date of enactment of this Act, the air carrier's chief executive officer will receive, from the air carrier—

(A) during any 12 consecutive months of such 10-year period, total compensation not in excess of an amount that is 50 times the median compensation earned by all employees of such air carrier in calendar year 2019; and

(B) severance pay or other benefits upon termination of employment with the air carrier not in excess of the maximum total compensation received from the air carrier in calendar year 2019.

(2) TOTAL COMPENSATION DEFINED.—In this subsection, the term "total compensation" includes salary, bonuses, awards of stock, and other financial benefits provided by an air carrier to an officer or employee of the air carrier.

(d) Financial Protection Of Government.—

(1) IN GENERAL.—To the extent to which any participating air carrier accepts financial assistance, in the form of accepting the proceeds of any loans guaranteed by the government under this title, the President is authorized to enter into contracts under which the Government, contingent on the financial success of the participating corporation, participate in the gains of the participating corporation or its security holders through the use of such instruments as warrants, stock options, common or preferred stock, or other appropriate equity instruments.

(2) DEPOSITS IN TREASURY.—All amounts collected by the President under this subsection shall be deposited in the Treasury as miscellaneous receipts.

(e) Air Carrier Maintenance Outsourcing.—

(1) IN GENERAL.—A passenger air carrier receiving assistance under section 101 may not apply the proceeds of such assistance toward a contract for heavy maintenance work at a facility located outside of the United States if such contract would increase the proportion of maintenance work performed outside of the United States to all maintenance work performed by or on behalf of such air carrier at any location.

(2) DEFINITION.—In this section, the term "heavy maintenance work" has the meaning given the term in section 44733(g)(1) of title 49, United States Code.

SEC. 104. REPORTS.

(a) Report.—Not later than October 1, 2020, the President shall submit to the Committee on Transportation and Infrastructure of the House of Representatives and the Committee on Commerce, Science, and Transportation of the Senate a report on the financial status of the air carrier industry, including a description of each grant or loan issued under section 101.

(b) Update.—Not later than the last day of the 1-year period following the date of enactment of this Act, the President shall update and submit to the Committee on Transportation and Infrastructure of the House of Representatives and the Committee on Commerce, Science, and Transportation of the Senate the report described in subsection (a).

SEC. 105. COORDINATION.

In implementing this title with respect to air carriers, the Secretary shall coordinate with the Secretary of Transportation.

TITLE II—LABOR PROTECTIONS

SEC. 201. ASSISTANCE IRRESPECTIVE OF LABOR COSTS.

The President, or any department, agency, or actor of the Federal government, may not condition the provision of any financial assistance under section 101(a) of this division or section 13 of the Federal Reserve Act (12 U.S.C. 261

et seq.) on an air carrier's implementation of measures to reduce labor costs or to enter into negotiations with the certified bargaining representative of a craft or class of employees of the air carrier under section 2 of the Railway Labor Act (45 U.S.C. 152) regarding pay or other terms and conditions of employment.

SEC. 202. COLLECTIVE BARGAINING AND SNAP-BACK.

(a) In General.—Notwithstanding any other provision of law, any contractual relief or reduction to rates of pay, rules, and working conditions agreed to by the authorized representatives of the employees of an air carrier, or otherwise imposed on such employees, during or as result of the pandemic of the coronavirus COVID–19 by an air carrier that receives financial assistance under section 101 shall be terminated within 6 months, unless the authorized representatives of the employees choose to make an alternative agreement with the air carrier.

(b) Definition Of Authorized Representative.—In this section, the term "authorized representative" means an exclusive representative of employees within the meaning of section of the Railway Labor Act (45 U.S.C. 152).

SEC. 203. PROTECTION OF ORGANIZING ACTIVITY.

A person receiving financial assistance under section 101 shall remain neutral in any communications with employees with respect to any efforts of an employee to organize, recruit, or assist in the organizing a labor organization.

SEC. 204. WORKING AND TRAVEL CONDITIONS.

A person receiving financial assistance under section 101 shall adhere to guidance published by the Centers for Disease Control and Prevention and applicable public health authorities for the duration of the national emergency declared by the President under the National Emergencies Act (50 U.S.C. 1601 et seq.) related to the pandemic of the coronavirus COVID–19 for providing safe conditions for employees and passengers, including providing employees with adequate and sufficient personal protective equipment and ensuring all aircraft and facilities owned or operated by such person are clean and sanitary.

SEC. 205. LABOR UNION REPRESENTATION ON AIR CARRIER BOARDS.

An air carrier receiving financial assistance under section 101 shall designate at least one seat on the air carrier's board of directors for an individual who is a member or officer of a labor organization representing air carrier employees, with such individual to be named by such organization.

SEC. 206. FURLOUGHED WORKER PROTECTIONS.

An air carrier receiving financial assistance under section 101 shall take such action as is necessary to ensure that, with respect to the national emergency declared by the President under the National Emergencies Act (50 U.S.C. 1601 et seq.) related to the pandemic of the coronavirus COVID–19—

(1) if an employee of such air carrier was provided health insurance benefits or other welfare benefits described in subparagraph (A) or (B) of section 3(1) of the Employee Retirement Income Security Act of 1974 (29 U.S.C. 1002(1)) from the air carrier prior to such emergency, such employee shall retain such benefits at an equivalent rate for the duration of such emergency;

(2) employees of such air carrier are credited any furlough time taken as a result of the pandemic for years of service for purposes of any employee benefit plan (as defined in section 3(3) of the Employee Retirement Income Security Act of 1974 (29 U.S.C. 1002(3)) with respect to which the employee is a participant; and

(3) an employee of such air carrier who is voluntarily or involuntarily furloughed as a result of the national emergency declared by the President under the National Emergencies Act (50 U.S.C. 1601 et seq.) related to the pandemic of the coronavirus COVID–19 may, upon reemployment or recall to such air carrier, be entitled to the following benefits under an employee pension benefit plan that such employee would have received if the employee had remained continuously employed with the air carrier, similar to benefit rights under subchapter II of chapter 43 of title 38, United States Code:

(A) An employee shall be treated as not having incurred a break in service with the employer or employers maintaining the plan by reason of the furlough.

(B) The period of furlough shall be deemed to constitute service with the employer or employers maintaining the plan for purposes of vesting, participation, and determining the employee's benefit accruals.

(C) An employee shall be entitled to make-up missed employee contributions or elective deferrals that could have been made to a qualified defined contribution plan during the period of furlough. Makeup contributions under this paragraph may be made during the period beginning on the date of recall and whose duration is three times the period of the furlough, such payment period not to exceed 5 years.

(D) The employer reemploying or recalling such employee shall contribute all employer contributions that the employer would have made on behalf of such employee to qualified defined contribution plans, including plans commonly known as 401(k) plans, if the employee had remained continuously employed.

(E) If employer contributions to a plan are contingent on the employee making an employee contribution or elective deferral, the employer contribution is required only to the extent the employee makes the payment to the plan with respect to such contributions or deferrals. No such payment may exceed the amount the employee would have been permitted or required to contribute had the employee remained continuously employed by the employer throughout the period of service. Any payment to the plan described in this paragraph shall be made during the period beginning on the date of recall and whose duration is three times the period of the person's furlough, such payment period not to exceed 5 years.

SEC. 207. HEALTHCARE FOR UNPROTECTED WORKERS.

(a) In General.—The Secretary may not provide any financial assistance under this Act to an air carrier unless the air carrier enters into a legally binding agreement with the Secretary that the air carrier will provide, and will require any contractor, subcontractor, or affiliate of the air carrier, including any contractor, subcontractor, or affiliate that performs airline catering services, to provide, to all employees, including airline catering employees, health insurance benefits equal to or greater than the hourly health and welfare fringe benefit rate published by the Department of Labor pursuant to the McNamara-O'Hara Service Contract Act of 1965 (41 U.S.C. 6710–6707) and section 4.52 of title 29, Code of Federal Regulations, for all hours worked by each such employee.

(b) Effective Period.—Subsection (a) shall apply to an air carrier receiving assistance under section 101 for the 5-year period beginning on the date on which such assistance was awarded.

(c) Definitions.—

(1) AIRLINE CATERING EMPLOYEE.—The term "airline catering employee" means an employee who performs airline catering services.

(2) AIRLINE CATERING SERVICES.—The term "airline catering services" means preparation, assembly, or both, of food, beverages, provisions and related supplies for delivery, and the delivery of such items, directly to aircraft or to a location on or near airport property for subsequent delivery to aircraft.

SEC. 208. EMPLOYEE WAGES AND LEAVE.

(a) Wages.—Section 6 of the Fair Labor Standards Act of 1938 (29 U.S.C. 206) is amended by adding at the end the following:

"(h) Employees In Industries Saved With Taxpayer Dollars.—

"(1) IN GENERAL.—Notwithstanding any other provision of law, subject to the requirements of this subsection, the wage rate in effect under subsection (a)(1) with respect to an employee of an employer described in paragraph (2), or any individual who provides labor or services for remuneration for such employer, regardless of whether the individual is classified as an independent contractor or otherwise by such employer, shall be not less than $15.00 per hour.

"(2) EMPLOYER.—An employer described in this paragraph is an employer who—

"(A) receives financial assistance under section 101 of the Aviation Worker Relief Act of 2020; or

"(B) who provides goods or services under a contract to an employer who receives financial assistance under such section.

"(3) TREATMENT OF NON-EMPLOYEES.—An individual who provides labor or services for remuneration to an employer as described in paragraph (1) shall be treated as an employee for the purposes of sections 10 through 17 of this Act.

"(4) PERIOD OF APPLICATION.—This subsection shall apply to an employer described in paragraph (2) for the 10-year period beginning on the date such assistance was awarded.".

(b) Benefits And Leave.— Notwithstanding any other provision of law, an air carrier receiving financial assistance under section 101 shall, for the duration of the national emergency declared by the President under the National Emergencies Act (50 U.S.C. 1601 et seq.) related to the pandemic of the coronavirus COVID–19—

(1) satisfy all funding obligations under part 3 of title I of the Employee Retirement Income Security Act of 1974 (29 U.S.C. 1081 et seq.) with respect to each plan to which such part applies and to which the air carrier is obligated to contribute for plan years beginning or ending during the duration of such emergency;

(2) provide employees with a guaranteed wage for every workweek that provides each employee continued payments in the amount of 100 percent of the employee's full wages and for the employee's total expected hours per workweek in the event that the employee is terminated, furloughed, experiences a reduction in work hours, or otherwise suffers any loss of such wages during such period; and

(3) provide paid medical or sick leave and paid family leave to encourage employees who are diagnosed with or experiencing symptoms of COVID–19 or are under quarantine relating to the coronavirus pandemic, or caring for a dependent or any individual experiencing such symptoms or under such a quarantine.

SEC. 209. LIMITATION ON REJECTION OF COLLECTIVE BARGAINING AGREEMENTS.

(a) Definitions.—

(1) COVERED AIR CARRIER.—The term "covered air carrier" means an air carrier that receives Federal financial assistance.

(2) COVERED PERIOD.—The term "covered period", with respect to a covered air carrier, means the period—

(A) beginning on the date on which the covered air carrier first receives Federal financial assistance; and

(B) ending on the date that is 10 years after the date on which the covered air carrier last receives Federal financial assistance.

(3) DEBTOR IN POSSESSION.—The term "debtor in possession" has the meaning given such term in section 1101 of title 11, United States Code.

(4) FEDERAL FINANCIAL ASSISTANCE.—The term "Federal financial assistance" means financial assistance or a credit instrument received from the Federal Government under this Act.

(5) TRUSTEE.—The term "trustee" means a trustee appointed in a case commenced by, or commenced against, a covered air carrier under title 11, United States Code.

(b) Limitation.—If a covered air carrier commences a case or if an involuntary case is commenced against a covered air carrier under title 11, United States Code, during the covered period with respect to the covered air carrier, the covered air carrier, the debtor in possession, or the trustee may not seek a rejection of, or interim relief from, a collective bargaining agreement under—
(1) section 1113 of title 11, United States Code; or
(2) any other provision of law.

SEC. 210. INCREASED WAGE PRIORITY.
Section 507(a) of title 11, United States Code, is amended—
(1) in paragraph (4)—
(A) by redesignating subparagraphs (A) and (B) as clauses (i) and (ii), respectively;
(B) in the matter preceding clause (i), as so redesignated, by inserting "(A)" before "Fourth";
(C) in subparagraph (A), as so designated, in the matter preceding clause (i), as so redesignated—
(i) by striking "$10,000" and inserting "$20,000";
(ii) by striking "within 180 days"; and
(iii) by striking "or the date of the cessation of the debtor's business, whichever occurs first,"; and
(D) by adding at the end the following:
"(B) Severance pay described in subparagraph(A)(i) shall be deemed earned in full upon the layoff or termination of employment of the individual to whom the severance is owed.";
(2) in paragraph (5)—
(A) in subparagraph (A)—
(i) by striking "within 180 days"; and
(ii) by striking "or the date of the cessation of the debtor's business, whichever occurs first"; and
(B) by striking subparagraph (B) and inserting the following:
"(B) for each such plan, to the extent of the number of employees covered by each such plan, multiplied by $20,000.".

SEC. 211. REJECTION OF COLLECTIVE BARGAINING AGREEMENTS.
(a) In General.—Section 1113 of title 11, United States Code, is amended by striking subsections (a) through (f) and inserting the following:
"(a) The debtor in possession, or the trustee if one has been appointed under this chapter, other than a trustee in a case covered by subchapter IV of this chapter and by title I of the Railway Labor Act (45 U.S.C. 151 et seq.), may reject a collective bargaining agreement only in accordance with this section. In this section, a reference to the trustee includes the debtor in possession.
"(b) No provision of this title shall be construed to permit the trustee to unilaterally terminate or alter any provision of a collective bargaining

agreement before complying with this section. The trustee shall timely pay all monetary obligations arising under the terms of the collective bargaining agreement. Any such payment required to be made before a plan confirmed under section 1129 is effective has the status of an allowed administrative expense under section 503.

"(c) (1) If the trustee seeks modification of a collective bargaining agreement, the trustee shall provide notice to the labor organization representing the employees covered by the collective bargaining agreement that modifications are being proposed under this section, and shall promptly provide an initial proposal for modifications to the collective bargaining agreement. Thereafter, the trustee shall confer in good faith with the labor organization, at reasonable times and for a reasonable period in light of the complexity of the case, in attempting to reach mutually acceptable modifications of the collective bargaining agreement.

"(2) The initial proposal and subsequent proposals by the trustee for modification of a collective bargaining agreement shall be based upon a business plan for the reorganization of the debtor, and shall reflect the most complete and reliable information available. The trustee shall provide to the labor organization all information that is relevant for negotiations. The court may enter a protective order to prevent the disclosure of information if disclosure could compromise the position of the debtor with respect to the competitors in the industry of the debtor, subject to the needs of the labor organization to evaluate the proposals of the trustee and any application for rejection of the collective bargaining agreement or for interim relief pursuant to this section.

"(3) In consideration of Federal policy encouraging the practice and process of collective bargaining and in recognition of the bargained-for expectations of the employees covered by the collective bargaining agreement, modifications proposed by the trustee—

"(A) shall be proposed only as part of a program of workforce and nonworkforce cost savings devised for the reorganization of the debtor, including savings in management personnel costs;

"(B) shall be limited to modifications designed to achieve a specified aggregate financial contribution for the employees covered by the collective bargaining agreement (taking into consideration any labor cost savings negotiated within the 12-month period before the filing of the petition), and shall be not more than the minimum savings essential to permit the debtor to exit bankruptcy, such that confirmation of a plan of reorganization is not likely to be followed by the liquidation, or the need for further financial reorganization, of the debtor (or any successor to the debtor) in the short term; and

"(C) shall not be disproportionate or overly burden the employees covered by the collective bargaining agreement, either in the amount of the cost savings sought from such employees or the nature of the modifications.

"(d) (1) If, after a period of negotiations, the trustee and the labor organization have not reached an agreement over mutually satisfactory modifications, and further negotiations are not likely to produce mutually satisfactory modifications, the trustee may file a motion seeking rejection of the collective bargaining agreement after notice and a hearing. Absent agreement of the parties, no such hearing shall be held before the expiration of the 21-day period beginning on the date on which notice of the hearing is provided to the labor organization representing the employees covered by the collective bargaining agreement. Only the debtor and the labor organization may appear and be heard at such hearing. An application for rejection shall seek rejection effective upon the entry of an order granting the relief.

"(2) In consideration of Federal policy encouraging the practice and process of collective bargaining and in recognition of the bargained-for expectations of the employees covered by the collective bargaining agreement, the court may grant a motion seeking rejection of a collective bargaining agreement only if, based on clear and convincing evidence—

"(A) the court finds that the trustee has complied with the requirements of subsection (c);

"(B) the court has considered alternative proposals by the labor organization and has concluded that such proposals do not meet the requirements of subsection (c)(3)(B);

"(C) the court finds that further negotiations regarding the proposal of the trustee or an alternative proposal by the labor organization are not likely to produce an agreement;

"(D) the court finds that implementation of the proposal of the trustee shall not—

"(i) cause a material diminution in the purchasing power of the employees covered by the collective bargaining agreement;

"(ii) adversely affect the ability of the debtor to retain an experienced and qualified workforce; or

"(iii) impair the labor relations of the debtor such that the ability to achieve a feasible reorganization would be compromised; and

"(E) the court concludes that rejection of the collective bargaining agreement and immediate implementation of the proposal of the trustee is essential to permit the debtor to exit bankruptcy, such that confirmation of a plan of reorganization is not likely to be followed by liquidation, or the need for further financial reorganization, of the debtor (or any successor to the debtor) in the short term.

"(3) If the trustee has implemented a program of incentive pay, bonuses, or other financial returns for insiders, senior executive officers, or the twenty next most highly compensated employees or consultants providing services to the debtor during the bankruptcy, or such a program was implemented within 180 days before the date of the filing of the petition, the court shall presume that the trustee has failed to satisfy the requirements of subsection (c)(3)(C).

"(4) In no case shall the court enter an order rejecting a collective bargaining agreement that would result in modifications to a level lower than the level proposed by the trustee in the proposal found by the court to have complied with the requirements of this section.

"(5) At any time after the date on which an order rejecting a collective bargaining agreement is entered, or in the case of a collective bargaining agreement entered into between the trustee and the labor organization providing mutually satisfactory modifications, at any time after that collective bargaining agreement has been entered into, the labor organization may apply to the court for an order seeking an increase in the level of wages or benefits, or relief from working conditions, based upon changed circumstances. The court shall grant the request only if the increase or other relief is not inconsistent with the standard set forth in paragraph (2)(E).

"(e) During a period during which a collective bargaining agreement at issue under this section continues in effect and a motion for rejection of the collective bargaining agreement has been filed, if essential to the continuation of the business of the debtor or in order to avoid irreparable damage to the estate, the court, after notice and a hearing, may authorize the trustee to implement interim changes in the terms, conditions, wages, benefits, or work rules provided by the collective bargaining agreement. Any hearing under this subsection shall be scheduled in accordance with the needs of the trustee. The implementation of such interim changes shall not render the application for rejection moot and may be authorized for not more than 14 days in total.

"(f) (1) Rejection of a collective bargaining agreement constitutes a breach of the collective bargaining agreement, and shall be effective no earlier than the entry of an order granting such relief.

"(2) Notwithstanding paragraph (1), solely for purposes of determining and allowing a claim arising from the rejection of a collective bargaining agreement, rejection shall be treated as rejection of an executory contract under section 365(g) and shall be allowed or disallowed in accordance with section 502(g)(1). No claim for rejection damages shall be limited by section 502(b)(7). Economic self-help by a labor organization shall be permitted upon a court order granting a motion to reject a collective bargaining agreement under subsection (d) or pursuant to subsection (e), and no provision of this title or of any other provision of Federal or State law may be construed to the contrary.

"(g) The trustee shall provide for the reasonable fees and costs incurred by a labor organization under this section, upon request and after notice and a hearing.

"(h) A collective bargaining agreement that is assumed shall be assumed in accordance with section 365.".

(b) Prohibition On Modification Of Retiree Benefits.—Section 1114 of title 11, United States Code, is further amended by adding at the end the following:

"(n) Notwithstanding any other provision in this title, the trustee may not modify retiree benefits if the debtor is an air carrier, as such term is defined in section 40102 of title 49, United States Code, or an affiliate of such air carrier, that received assistance under the Aviation Worker Relief Act of 2020.".

TITLE III—AIRLINE INDUSTRY FINANCIAL OVERSIGHT

SEC. 301. CREATION OF OFFICE OF AIRLINE INDUSTRY FINANCIAL OVERSIGHT.

(a) In General.—There is hereby established, within the Office of the Secretary of Transportation, the Office of Airline Industry Financial Oversight.
(b) Director Of Office.—The office established under this section shall be headed by a Director, who shall be a career employee of the Department of Transportation and selected on the basis of such individual's knowledge of financial markets, airline operations, and finance, and such other qualifications as the Secretary considers relevant.

SEC. 302. RESPONSIBILITIES OF OFFICE OF AIRLINE INDUSTRY FINANCIAL OVERSIGHT.

The Director of the Office of Airline Industry Financial Oversight shall—
(1) assess, not less than once every 12 months, the financial fitness of each passenger air carrier conducting operations under part 121 of title 14, Code of Federal Regulations;
(2) determine and prescribe minimum capital and funding requirements for each such air carrier to ensure that no air carrier would be reasonably likely to become insolvent as the result of a substantial reduction in demand for air travel following the occurrence of a terror attack, pandemic, or other national or global event that reduces economic activity;
(3) require each such air carrier to conduct an annual stress test to determine the extent of financial stress that the air carrier can withstand before becoming financially insolvent, using at least 3 sets of assumptions regarding the severity of financial stress and to report the results of such test to the Office for analysis;
(4) based on an analysis of the stress tests performed under paragraph (3), annually adjust the minimum capital and funding requirements imposed under paragraph (2); and
(5) impose such other requirements, including through the issuance of regulations, as the director determines necessary to ensure the continued operations of air carriers despite an event described in paragraph (2).

SEC. 303. ACCESS TO INFORMATION.

(a) In General.—In discharging the responsibilities enumerated in section 302, the director or employees of the office may inspect such financial records in an air carrier's possession as the director or employees of the office deem appropriate.
(b) Protection Of Trade Secrets.—The Director and employees of the Office of Airline Industry Financial Oversight shall protect, from public disclosure,

any material containing trade secrets in the Office's custody, in accordance with section 1905 of title 18, United States Code.

SEC. 304. REPORTS TO CONGRESS.

Not later than February 1 of each calendar year, the Director of the office established under section 301 shall submit to the Committee on Transportation and Infrastructure of the House of Representatives and the Committee on Commerce, Science, and Transportation of the Senate a report describing each action taken under section 302 during the preceding calendar year.

SEC. 305. RULEMAKING AUTHORITY.

The Secretary may issue such regulations as the Secretary determines are necessary to implement the requirements of this title.

SEC. 306. AUTHORIZATION OF APPROPRIATIONS.

There is authorized to be appropriated to the Secretary of Transportation $3,000,000 for each of fiscal years 2020 through 2023 to carry out this title to remain available until expended.

TITLE IV—AIRPORT RELIEF

SEC. 401. EMERGENCY PANDEMIC FUNDING FOR AIRPORTS.

(a) In General.—There is authorized to be appropriated, from the General Fund of the Treasury, $10,000,000,000 for the Secretary of Transportation to issue grants to airport sponsors for the purposes of emergency response, cleaning, sanitization, janitorial services, staffing, workforce retention, paid leave, procurement of protective health equipment and training for employees and contractors, debt service payments, infrastructure projects and airport operations.

(b) Methodology For Disbursement.—Funds shall be apportioned as set forth in clauses (i) and (ii) of section 47114(c)(1)(C) of title 49, United States Code, and there shall be no maximum apportionment limit. Funds provided under this section shall not be subject to reduced apportionment under section 47114(f) of such title. Any remaining funds shall be distributed to sponsors based on each airport's passenger enplanements compared to total passenger enplanements of all airports, for the most recent calendar year the Secretary apportioned funds pursuant to section 47114(c).

(c) High-Need Airports.—The Secretary shall set aside 2 percent of the remaining funds described in subsection (b) to provide grants to commercial service airports or general aviation airports that demonstrate the highest financial need.

(d) Workforce Retention.—

(1) IN GENERAL.—Except as otherwise provided in this subsection, all airports receiving funds under subsection (a) shall continue to employ,

through December 31, 2020, at least 90 percent of the number of individuals employed by the airport as of the date of enactment of this Act.
(2) WAIVER.—The Secretary may waive the workforce retention requirement under this subsection 120 days after the date of enactment of this Act if the Secretary determines—
(A) the airport is experiencing economic hardship as a direct result of the requirement; or
(B) the requirement reduces aviation safety or security.
(3) SMALL AIRPORTS.—This subsection shall not apply to nonhub airports or nonprimary airports receiving funds under subsection (c).
(e) Relief To Airport Concessions.—An airport sponsor must use at least 2 percent of any funds received under subsection (a) to provide financial relief to airport concessionaires experiencing economic hardship (in terms of rent, minimum annual guarantees, lease obligations, or other fees). With respect to funds under this subsection, airport sponsors must show good faith efforts to provide relief to small business concerns owned and controlled by socially and economically disadvantaged businesses, as such term is defined under section 47113 of title 49, United States Code.
(f) Cost Share.—The Federal share payable of the costs for which a grant is made under this section or under the Consolidated Appropriations Act, 2020 (Public Law 116–94) shall be 100 percent.
(g) Quality Assurance.—The Secretary shall institute adequate policies, procedures and internal controls to prevent waste, fraud, abuse and program mismanagement for the distribution of funds under this section.
(h) Availability.—Sums authorized to be appropriated under this sections shall remain available for 3 fiscal years.
(i) Limitations.—The funds made available under this section shall not be subject to any limitation on obligations set forth in an appropriations Act as applied to the heading "Grants-in-Aid for Airports".
(j) Administrative Costs.—The Secretary may retain up to 0.1 percent of the funds provided under this section to fund the award and oversight of grants made under this heading.
(k) Definitions.—In this section:
(1) AIRPORT CONCESSION.—the term "airport concession" means a business, other than air carrier, located on an airport that is engaged in the sale of consumer goods or services to the public under an agreement with an airport, another concessionaire, or the owner or lessee of a terminal.
(2) AIRPORT; GENERAL AVIATION AIRPORT; NONHUB AIRPORT; SPONSOR.—The terms "airport", "general aviation airport", "nonhub airport", and "sponsor" have the meanings given those terms in section 47102 of title 49, United States Code.
(3) COMMERCIAL SERVICE AIRPORT.—The term "commercial service airport" means a public use airport that reported at least 2500 passenger boardings at such airport during fiscal year 2018.

SEC. 402. MAINTAINING PRE-CRISIS AIRPORT IMPROVEMENT PROGRAM LEVELS.

Section 47114(c)(1) of title 49, United States Code, is amended by adding at the end the following:

"(J) SPECIAL RULE FOR FISCAL YEARS 2021 THROUGH 2023.—Notwithstanding subparagraph (A), the Secretary shall apportion to a sponsor of an airport under that subparagraph for each of fiscal years 2021 through 2023 an amount based on the number of passenger boardings at the airport during calendar year 2018 if the number of passenger boardings at the airport during calendar year 2018 are higher than the number of passenger boardings that would be otherwise calculated under subparagraph (A).".

SEC. 403. NATIONAL AVIATION PREPAREDNESS PLAN.

(a) In General.—The Secretary of Transportation, in coordination with the Secretary of Health and Human Services, the Secretary of Homeland Security and other appropriate stakeholders, shall develop a national aviation preparedness plan for communicable disease outbreaks.

(b) Contents Of Plan.—A plan developed under subsection (a) shall, at a minimum—

(1) require involvement from multiple airports on a national level;

(2) provide airports and air carriers with an adaptable and scalable framework with which to align their individual plans;

(3) improve coordination among airports, air carriers, Customs and Border Patrol, the Centers for Disease Control and Prevention, and other appropriate Federal stakeholders on developing policies that increase the effectiveness of screening, quarantining, and contact-tracing with respect to inbound passengers; and

(4) fully incorporate elements referenced in the recommendation of the Comptroller General of the United States to the Secretary of Transportation contained in Report No. GAO 16–127.

TITLE V—SMALL COMMUNITY AIR SERVICE

SEC. 501. CONTINUATION OF CERTAIN AIR SERVICE.

(a) Action Of Secretary.—The Secretary of Transportation shall take appropriate action to ensure that all communities that receive scheduled air service before March 1, 2020, continue to receive adequate air transportation service and that essential air service to small communities continues without interruption and in a manner that maintains well-functioning heath care supply chains, including medical device, medical supplies, and pharmaceutical supply chains.

(b) Antitrust Immunity.—The Secretary may grant an exemption under section 41308 of title 49, United States Code, to 2 air carriers for the limited purpose of such cooperation as is necessary to ensure that small communities continue to receive an adequate level of air transportation service.

SEC. 502. TOLLING OF EAS LIMITATIONS.

The Secretary may not order the termination of essential air service on the basis of the applicable place failing to meet the definition of an eligible place under subparagraph (B) or (C) of section 41731(a)(1) of title 49, United States Code, if such community was otherwise an eligible place as defined under section 41731 of such title on March 1, 2020.

SEC. 503. SUNSET.

The requirements of this title, and any order issued by the Secretary under this title, shall sunset on the day that is 6 months after the last effective date of a national emergency declared by the President under the National Emergencies Act (50 U.S.C. 1601 et seq.) related to the pandemic of the coronavirus COVID–19.

TITLE VI—CONSUMER PROTECTIONS

SEC. 601. AIRLINE PRICE GOUGING DURING DISASTER OR EMERGENCY.

(a) In General.—Section 41712 of title 49, United States Code, is amended by adding at the end the following:

"(d) Airfare Pricing And Fees During Disaster Or Other Emergency.—

"(1) IN GENERAL.—It shall be an unfair or deceptive practice under subsection (a) for any ticket agent, air carrier, foreign air carrier, or other person selling or offering to sell a ticket for air transportation on a covered flight to—

"(A) impose any unreasonable increase in the price of such ticket, as compared to the ticket price in effect on the day on which a flight becomes a covered flight; and

"(B) charge any fee for a change to, or cancellation of, such ticket, or for any difference in fare for an itinerary change.

"(2) COVERED FLIGHT DEFINED.—In this subsection, the term 'covered flight' means a flight of an air carrier or foreign air carrier departing from, or arriving at, an airport located in an area with respect to which—

"(A) a major disaster or emergency declared by the President under the Robert T. Stafford Disaster Relief and Emergency Assistance Act (42 U.S.C. 5121 et seq.) is in effect and State or local authorities have ordered a mandatory evacuation;

"(B) a public health emergency declared pursuant to section 319 of the Public Health Service Act (42 U.S.C. 247d) is in effect;

"(C) a national emergency declared by the President under the National Emergencies Act (50 U.S.C. 1601 et seq.) is in effect; or

"(D) a restriction on air travel is in effect, including restrictions on nonessential air transportation or nationwide bans imposed on air transportation during a disaster, emergency, or pandemic.

"(3) SAVINGS PROVISION.—Nothing in this subsection, or the amendment made by this subsection, may be construed to limit or otherwise affect any responsibility of any ticket agent, air carrier, or foreign air carrier or other person offering to sell a ticket for air transportation during a major disaster or emergency.".

SEC. 602. AIRLINE REFUNDS DURING NATIONAL DISASTERS OR EMERGENCIES.

(a) In General.—Not later than 30 days after the date of enactment of this Act, the Secretary of Transportation shall require that any covered seller who sells a ticket for a passenger to take a covered flight, and either such flight is cancelled by the air carrier or such ticket is canceled by the passenger, such covered seller shall promptly offer the passenger a choice of—

(1) a full monetary refund for such ticket, including any ancillary fees paid; and

(2) an alternative compensation method determined appropriate by the covered seller, including credit, voucher, or other mechanism to compensate a passenger.

(b) Credit Or Voucher.—An alternative compensation method provided pursuant to subsection (a)(2) may not expire for at least 1 year date of the covered flight.

(c) Definitions.—In this section, the following definitions apply:

(1) COVERED FLIGHT.—The term "covered flight" has the meaning given to such term in section 41712(d) of title 49, United States Code.

(2) COVERED SELLER.—The term "covered seller" means a ticket agent, air carrier, foreign air carrier, or other person offering to sell a ticket for air transportation.

SEC. 603. CONDITIONS ON AIRLINE ANCILLARY FEES.

(a) In General.—Not later than 90 days after the date of enactment of this Act, the Secretary of Transportation shall require covered air carriers to report to the Secretary of Transportation, not less than quarterly, all ancillary revenues collected by the air carrier during the quarter for which the report is provided.

(b) Contents.—In implementing the requirement under subsection (a), the Secretary shall require reporting of ancillary revenues from, at a minimum, the following optional fees or charges:

(1) Booking fees, including fees for telephone reservations.

(2) Fees for priority check-in and security screening.

(3) Fees for the transportation of carry-on, first checked, second checked, excess, and oversized or overweight baggage.

(4) Fees for transportation of in-flight medical equipment.

(5) Fees for in-flight entertainment, beverages, and food.

(6) Fees for internet access.
(7) Fees for seating assignments.
(8) Fees for reservation cancellation and change.
(9) Charges for lost tickets.
(10) Revenue from the sale of travel insurance
(11) Fees for unaccompanied minor and passenger assistance.
(12) Fees for pets.
(c) Definitions.—In this section, the following definitions apply:
(1) ANCILLARY REVENUES.—The term "ancillary revenues" means charges paid by airline passengers that are not included in the standard ticket fare.
(2) COVERED AIR CARRIER.—
(A) IN GENERAL.—The term "covered air carrier" means an air carrier covered under part 241 of title 14, Code of Federal Regulations.
(B) EXCLUSION.—The term "covered air carrier" excludes air carriers with annual revenues of less than $20,000,000.

TITLE VII—ENVIRONMENTAL PROTECTIONS

SEC. 701. SUSTAINABLE AVIATION FUEL DEVELOPMENT PROGRAM.

(a) In General.—The Secretary of Transportation, in consultation with the Department of Agriculture and the Environmental Protection Agency, shall make competitive grants to eligible entities to offset the cost of a project to develop, transport, or store sustainable aviation fuels that would reduce United States greenhouse gas emissions.
(b) Selection.—In making grants under subsection (a), the Secretary shall consider—
(1) the anticipated public benefits of the project;
(2) the potential to increase the commercial application of sustainable aviation fuels among the United States commercial aviation and aerospace industry;
(3) the potential greenhouse gases emitted from the project;
(4) the potential for new job creation; and
(5) the potential the project has in reducing United States greenhouse gas emissions associated with air travel.
(c) Authorization Of Appropriations.—There are authorized to be appropriated $200,000,000 for each of the fiscal years 2021 through 2026 to carry out this section.
(d) Report.—Not later than October 1, 2026, the Secretary shall submit to the Committee on Commerce, Science, and Transportation, the Committee on Environment and Public Works, and the Committee on Agriculture, Nutrition, and Forestry of the Senate, and the Committee on Transportation and Infrastructure, the Committee on Energy and Commerce, and the Committee on Agriculture of the House of Representatives, a report describing

the results of the grant program authorized by this section. The report shall include the following:

(1) A description of the entities and projects that received grants under this section.

(2) Description of whether the program is leading to an increase in commercial application of sustainable aviation fuels by United States aviation and aerospace industry stakeholders.

(3) The economic impacts resulting from the grants to and operation of the project.

(e) Eligibility.—Entities eligible to receive a grant under this section shall include State and local governments, nongovernmental entities, air carriers, airports, and businesses engaged in the development, transportation, or storage of sustainable aviation fuels.

(f) Definition Of Sustainable Aviation Fuel.—The term "sustainable aviation fuel" means liquid fuel consisting of synthesized hydrocarbons which meets the requirements of ASTM International Standard D7566 or ASTM International Standard D1655, Annex A1, subsection A.1.2.2, and is derived from biomass (as defined in section 45K(c)(3) of the Internal Revenue Code of 1986), waste streams, or gaseous carbon oxides, conforms to the standards, recommended practices and guidance agreed to by the United States pursuant to the European Union Emissions Trading Scheme Prohibition Act of 2011 (Public Law 112–200) for addressing aircraft emissions, and achieves at least a 30 percent reduction in greenhouse gas emissions on a lifecycle basis compared to conventional jet fuel.

SEC. 702. AIRLINE ASSISTANCE TO RECYCLE AND SAVE PROGRAM.

(a) Establishment.—Not later than 90 days after the date of enactment of this Act, the Secretary shall establish and carry out a program, to be known as the "Airline Assistance to Recycle and Save Program", under which the Secretary shall purchase high-polluting aircraft from air carriers in exchange for commitments from such air carriers to purchase fuel-efficient aircraft.

(b) Application.—To be eligible for the program established under subsection (a), an air carrier shall submit to the Secretary an application at such time, in such manner, and containing such information as the Secretary may require, including a description of an high-polluting aircraft of the air carrier.

(c) Program Requirements.—

(1) LIST OF ELIGIBLE AIRCRAFT.—In carrying out the program established under subsection (a), the Secretary, in consultation with the Administrator, shall prepare, maintain, publicize, and make available through a publicly available website, lists of aircraft that are—

(A) high-polluting aircraft; and

(B) fuel-efficient aircraft that are on the market or in production.

(2) COMMITMENT REQUIREMENT.—In carrying out the program established under subsection (a), the Secretary shall issue such regulations

as are necessary to set requirements for the commitment to purchase a fuel-efficient aircraft described in subsection (a), including a timing requirement for the purchase of a fuel-efficient aircraft.

(d) Use Of Purchased Aircraft.—Notwithstanding any other provision of law, the Secretary may sell, to an air carrier or eligible foreign air carrier, parts or components of aircraft purchased under this division.

(e) Regulations.—Not later than 30 days after the date of enactment of this Act, the Secretary shall issue such regulations as are necessary to carry out this section.

(f) Authorization Of Appropriations.—There is authorized to carry out the program established under this section $1,000,000,000 and such sums shall remain available until expended.

(g) Definitions.—In this section:

(1) ADMINISTRATOR.—The term "Administrator" means the Administrator of the Environmental Protection Agency.

(2) AIRCRAFT MANUFACTURER.—The term "aircraft manufacturer" has the meaning given such term in section 44301 of title 49, United States Code.

(3) ELIGIBLE FOREIGN AIR CARRIER.—

(A) IN GENERAL.—The term "eligible foreign air carrier" means a foreign air carrier as such term is defined in section 40102 of title 49, United States Code.

(B) EXCLUSION.—The term "eligible foreign air carrier" does not include a foreign air carrier that—

(i) is domiciled in a country that is a state sponsor of terrorism; or

(ii) has a majority ownership interest of individuals or entities domiciled in a country that is a state sponsor of terrorism.

(4) SECRETARY.—The term "Secretary" means the Secretary of Transportation.

(5) STATE SPONSOR OF TERRORISM.—The term "state sponsor of terrorism" means a country the government of which the Secretary of State determines has repeatedly provided support for international terrorism pursuant to—

(A) section 1754(c)(1)(A) of the Export Control Reform Act of 2018 (50 U.S.C. 4318(c)(1)(A));

(B) section 620A of the Foreign Assistance Act of 1961 (22 U.S.C. 2371);

(C) section 40 of the Arms Export Control Act (22 U.S.C. 2780); or

(D) any other provision of law.

SEC. 703. EXPANSION OF VOLUNTARY AIRPORT LOW EMISSION PROGRAM.

Section 40117 of title 49, United States Code, is amended—

(1) in subsection (a)(3)(G) by striking "if the airport is located in an air quality nonattainment area (as defined in section 171(2) of the Clean Air Act (42 U.S.C. 7501(2)) or a maintenance area referred to in section 175A of such act (42 U.S.C. 7505a)"; and

(2) in subsection (b) by adding at the end the following:

"(8) PRIORITY OF PROJECTS.—In carrying out this section, the Secretary shall prioritize funding for airports in areas located in an air quality nonattainment area (as defined in section 171(2) of the Clean Air Act (42 U.S.C. 7501(2)) or a maintenance area referred to in section 175A of such act (42 U.S.C. 7505a).".

SEC. 704. AIRLINE CARBON EMISSIONS OFFSETS AND GOALS.

(a) Carbon Offsetting Program.—

(1) IN GENERAL.—Not later than 90 days after the enactment of this Act, the Administrator of the Federal Aviation Administration shall require each air carrier receiving assistance under section 101, to fully offset the annual carbon emissions of such air carriers for domestic flights beginning in 2025.

(2) VERIFICATION.—In issuing regulations and guidance to carry out to paragraph (1), the Administrator shall develop standards and practices to ensure the use of carbon offsets by air carriers are real, additional, permanent, verifiable, and not double counted and align with standards, recommended practices, assessment tools, and guidance agreed to by the United States pursuant to the European Union Emissions Trading Scheme Prohibition Act of 2011 (Public Law 112–200) for addressing aircraft emissions.

(3) AUDITING.—An air carrier covered under this subsection shall take reasonable and continuous measures to ensure any carbon offsets credited to, or purchased by, such carrier continue to be accurate.

(4) CERTIFICATION.—The Administrator shall annually certify that an air carrier's carbon offsetting program aligns with the standards developed pursuant to paragraph (2).

(b) Carbon Emissions Goal.—

(1) IN GENERAL.—The Administrator of the Federal Aviation Administration, with the concurrence of the Administrator of the Environmental Protection Agency, shall require each air carrier receiving assistance under section 101 to—

(A) make and achieve a binding commitment to reduce the greenhouse gas emissions attributable to the domestic flights of such air carrier in every calendar year, beginning with 2021, on a path consistent with a 25 percent reduction in the aviation sector's emissions from 2019 levels by 2035, and a 50 percent reduction in the sector's emissions from 2019 levels by 2050, applying the standards, recommended practices, and guidance agreed to by the United States pursuant to the European Union Emissions Trading Scheme Prohibition Act of 2011 (Public Law 112–200) for addressing aircraft emissions; and

(B) submit to the Administrator, annually, a report containing a plan for meeting the commitment described in subparagraph (A) and evidence of compliance with such commitment, including the annual emissions of the air carrier, use of alternative fuels, and any other means of implementing such commitment.

(2) CERTIFICATION.—

(A) IN GENERAL.—Not later than 5 years after the date of enactment of this Act, and not less frequently than every 5 years thereafter, the Administrator shall certify each air carrier covered under this subsection that is taking such actions as are necessary to meet the requirements established pursuant to paragraph (1).

(B) REMEDIATION.—With respect to any air carrier covered under this subsection that the Administrator does not certify under subparagraph (A), the Administrator, in consultation with such air carrier, shall, not later than 180 days after the last date on which a certification could have been made under such subparagraph, develop a plan to ensure such air carrier meets the requirements established pursuant to paragraph (1).

(3) PUBLIC INFORMATION.—The Secretary shall make publicly available the reports described in paragraph (1).

(4) LIMITATION.—Nothing in this subsection shall affect or alter the authorities and responsibilities to address greenhouse gases under any other provision of law.

(c) International Competitiveness.—In issuing regulations to carry out to subsection (b) and (c), the Administrator shall create a mechanism that ensures foreign air carriers that enter the national airspace system have an equivalent emissions reductions target or programs such that the United States airline industry is not at a competitive disadvantage.

SEC. 705. RESEARCH AND DEVELOPMENT OF SUSTAINABLE AVIATION FUELS.

There is authorized to be appropriated to the Federal Aviation Administration $100,000,000 for each of fiscal years 2021 through 2026 for research and development of sustainable aviation fuels.

SEC. 706. IMPROVING CONSUMER INFORMATION REGARDING RELEASE OF GREENHOUSE GASES FROM FLIGHTS.

(a) In General.—Not later than January 1, 2023, the Secretary of Transportation shall develop and implement, by regulation, a program to require air carriers that receive assistance under section 101 provide passengers with information regarding greenhouse gas emissions resulting from each individual flight that is—

(1) customized to account for such emissions associated with each aircraft and the flight route of such aircraft; and

(2) made available on the first display of any website selling any ticket for such flight, following a search of a requested itinerary in a format that is easily visible to the purchaser.

(b) Public Reporting.—The Secretary shall publish monthly data and information that anonymously aggregates and analyzes the information provided to individual passengers under to subsection (a). Such information and data shall—

(1) be accessible to the public on the internet; and

(2) identify and quantify the greenhouse gas emissions and relative climate change impact of each passenger air carrier that receives assistance under section 101.

SEC. 707. STUDY ON CERTAIN CLIMATE CHANGE MITIGATION EFFORTS.

(a) In General.—Not later than 90 days after the date of enactment of this Act, the Secretary of Transportation shall seek to enter into an agreement with the National Academies of Sciences, Engineering, and Medicine (referred to in this section as the "National Academies") to conduct a study on climate change mitigation efforts with respect to the civil aviation and aerospace industries.

(b) Study Contents.—In conducting the study under subsection (a), the National Academies shall—

(1) identify climate change mitigation efforts, including efforts relating to emerging technologies, in the civil aviation and aerospace industries;

(2) develop and apply an appropriate indicator for assessing the effectiveness of such efforts;

(3) identify gaps in such efforts;

(4) identify barriers preventing expansion of such efforts; and

(5) develop recommendations with respect to such efforts.

(c) Reports.—

(1) FINDINGS OF STUDY.—Not later than 1 year after the date on which the Secretary enters into an agreement for a study pursuant to subsection (a), the Secretary shall submit to the appropriate congressional committees the findings of the study.

(2) ASSESSMENT.—Not later than 180 days after the date on which the Secretary submits the findings pursuant to paragraph (1), the Secretary, acting through the Administrator of the Federal Aviation Administration, shall submit to the appropriate congressional committees a report that contains an assessment of the findings.

(d) Authorization Of Appropriations.—There is authorized to be appropriated to the Secretary to carry out this section $1,500,000.

(e) Definitions.—In this section:

(1) APPROPRIATE CONGRESSIONAL COMMITTEES.—The term "appropriate congressional committees" means the Committee on Transportation and Infrastructure of the House of Representatives, the Committee on Commerce, Science, and Transportation of the Senate, and other congressional committees determined appropriate by the Secretary.

(2) CLIMATE CHANGE MITIGATION EFFORTS.—The term "climate change mitigation efforts" means efforts, including the use of technologies, materials, processes, or practices, that contribute to the reduction of

greenhouse gas emissions.

TITLE VIII—MISCELLANEOUS

SEC. 801. SEPARABILITY.

If any provision of this division (including any amendment made by this division) or the application thereof to any person or circumstance is held invalid, the remainder of this division (including any amendment made by this division) and the application thereof to other persons or circumstances shall not be affected thereby.

SEC. 802. APPLICATION OF LAW.

Chapter 83 of title 41, United States Code, shall not apply with respect to purchases made in response to—

(1) the public health emergency declared on January 31, 2020 under section 319 of the Public Health Service Act (42 U.S.C. 247d); or

(2) the emergency declared by the President on March 13, 2020, under section 501 of the Robert T. Stafford Disaster Relief and Emergency Assistance Act (42 U.S.C. 5191) and under any subsequent major disaster declaration under section 401 of such Act that supersedes such emergency declaration.

DIVISION S—SMALL BUSINESS ADMINISTRATION

SEC. 190001. DEFINITIONS.

In this division—

(1) the terms "Administration" and "Administrator" mean the Small Business Administration and the Administrator thereof, respectively;

(2) the term "covered small business concern" means a small business concern that has experienced, as a result of COVID–19—

(A) supply chain disruptions, including changes in—

(i) quantity and lead time, including the number of shipments of components and delays in shipments;

(ii) quality, including shortages in supply for quality control reasons; and

(iii) technology, including a compromised payment network;

(B) staffing challenges;

(C) a decrease in sales or customers; or

(D) a closure; and

(3) the term "small business concern" has the meaning given the term in section 3 of the Small Business Act (15 U.S.C. 636).

SEC. 190002. PAYCHECK PROTECTION PROGRAM.

(a) In General.—Section 7(a) of the Small Business Act (15 U.S.C. 636(a)) is amended—

(1) in paragraph (2)—

(A) in subparagraph (A), in the matter preceding clause (i), by striking "and (E)" and inserting "(E), and (F)"; and

(B) by adding at the end the following:

"(F) PARTICIPATION IN THE PAYCHECK PROTECTION PROGRAM.—In an agreement to participate in a loan on a deferred basis under paragraph (36), the participation by the Administration shall be 100 percent."; and

(2) by adding at the end the following:

"(36) PAYCHECK PROTECTION PROGRAM.—

"(A) DEFINITIONS.—In this paragraph—

"(i) the terms 'appropriate Federal banking agency' and 'insured depository institution' have the meanings given those terms in section 3 of the Federal Deposit Insurance Act (12 U.S.C. 1813);

"(ii) the term 'covered loan' means a loan made under this paragraph during the covered period;

"(iii) the term 'covered period' means the period beginning on February 15, 2020 and ending on June 30, 2020;

"(iv) the term 'eligible recipient' means an individual or entity that is eligible to receive a covered loan;

"(v) the term 'eligible self-employed individual' has the meaning given the term in section 7002(b) of the Families First Coronavirus Response Act (Public Law 116–127);

"(vi) the term 'nonprofit organization' means an organization that is described in section 501(c)(3) of the Internal Revenue Code of 1986 and that is exempt from taxation under section 501(a) of such Code;

"(vii) the term 'payroll costs'—

"(I) means—

"(aa) the sum of payments of any compensation with respect to employees that is a—

"(AA) salary or wage;

"(BB) payment of cash tip or equivalent;

"(CC) payment for vacation, parental, family, medical, or sick leave;

"(DD) allowance for dismissal or separation;

"(EE) payment required for the provisions of group health care benefits, including insurance premiums;

"(FF) payment of any retirement benefit; or

"(GG) payment of State or local tax assessed on the compensation of employees; and

"(bb) the sum of payments of any compensation to a sole proprietor or independent contractor that is a wage, commission, or similar compensation and that is in an amount that is not more than $100,000 in 1 year, as prorated for the covered period; and

"(II) shall not include—

"(aa) the compensation of an individual employee in excess of an annual salary of $100,000, as prorated for the covered period;

"(bb) taxes imposed or withheld under chapters 21, 22, or 24 of the Internal Revenue Code of 1986 during the covered period;

"(cc) any compensation of an employee whose principal place of residence is outside of the United States;

"(dd) qualified sick leave wages for which a credit is allowed under section 7001 of the Families First Coronavirus Response Act (Public Law 116–127); or

"(ee) qualified family leave wages for which a credit is allowed under section 7003 of the Families First Coronavirus Response Act (Public Law 116–127); and

"(viii) the term 'veterans organization' means an organization that is described in paragraph (19) of section 501(c) of the Internal Revenue Code that is exempt from taxation under section 501(a) of such Code.

"(B) SMALL BUSINESS INTERRUPTION LOANS.—Except as otherwise provided in this paragraph, the Administrator may guarantee covered loans under the same terms, conditions, and processes as a loan made under this subsection.

"(C) REGISTRATION OF LOANS.—Not later than 15 days after the date on which a loan is made under this paragraph, the Administration shall register the loan using the TIN (as defined in section 7701 of the Internal Revenue Code of 1986) assigned to the borrower.

"(D) INCREASED ELIGIBILITY FOR CERTAIN SMALL BUSINESSES AND ORGANIZATIONS.—

"(i) IN GENERAL.—During the covered period, in addition to small business concerns, any business concern, nonprofit organization, or veterans organization shall be eligible to receive a covered loan if the business concern, nonprofit organization, or veterans organization employs not more than the greater of—

"(I) 500 employees; or

"(II) if applicable, the size standard in number of employees established by the Administration for the industry in which the business concern, nonprofit organization, or veterans organization operates.

"(ii) INCLUSION OF SOLE PROPRIETORS, INDEPENDENT CONTRACTORS, AND ELIGIBLE SELF-EMPLOYED INDIVIDUALS.—

"(I) IN GENERAL.—During the covered period, individuals who operate under a sole proprietorship or as an independent contractor and eligible self-employed individuals shall be eligible to receive a covered loan.

"(II) DOCUMENTATION.—An eligible self-employed individual seeking a covered loan shall submit payroll tax filings reported to the Internal Revenue Service. An independent contractor shall submit Forms 1099–MISC received. A sole proprietorship shall submit schedules from their tax return filed (or to be filed) showing their income and expenses from their sole proprietorship.

"(iii) BUSINESS CONCERNS WITH MORE THAN 1 PHYSICAL LOCATION.—During the covered period, any business concern that employs not more than 500 employees per physical location of the business concern and that is assigned a North American Industry Classification System code beginning with 72 at the time of disbursal shall be eligible to receive a covered loan.

"(iv) WAIVER OF AFFILIATION RULES.—During the covered period, the provisions applicable to affiliations under section 121.103 of title 13, Code of Federal Regulations, or any successor regulation, are waived with respect to eligibility for a covered loan for—

"(I) any business concern with not more than 500 employees that, as of the date on which the covered loan is disbursed, is assigned a North American Industry Classification System code beginning with 72;

"(II) any business concern operating as a franchise that is assigned a franchise identifier code by the Administration; and

"(III) any business concern that receives financial assistance from a company licensed under section 301 of the Small Business Investment Act of 1958 (15 U.S.C. 681).

"(E) MAXIMUM LOAN AMOUNT.—During the covered period, with respect to a covered loan, the maximum loan amount shall be the lesser of—

"(i) (I) the product obtained by multiplying—

"(aa) the average total monthly payments by the applicant for payroll costs, costs related mortgage payments, rent (including under a lease agreement), and utilities incurred during the 1-year period before the date on which the loan is made, except that, in the case of an applicant that is seasonal employer, as determined by the Administrator, the average total monthly payments for payroll shall be for the 12-week period beginning February 15, 2019, or at the election of the eligible recipient, March 1, 2019, and ending June 30, 2019; by

"(bb) 4; or

"(II) if requested by an otherwise eligible recipient that was not in business during the period beginning on February 15, 2019 and ending on June 30, 2019, the product obtained by multiplying—

"(aa) the average total monthly payments by the applicant for payroll costs, costs related mortgage payments, rent (including under a lease agreement), and utilities incurred during the period beginning on January 1, 2020 and ending on February 29, 2020; by

"(bb) 4; or

"(ii) $10,000,000.

"(F) ALLOWABLE USES OF COVERED LOANS.—

"(i) IN GENERAL.—During the covered period, an eligible recipient may, in addition to the allowable uses of a loan made under this subsection, use the proceeds of the covered loan for—

"(I) payroll costs;

"(II) costs related to the continuation of group health care benefits during periods of paid sick, medical, or family leave, and insurance premiums;

"(III) employee salaries, commissions, or similar compensations;

"(IV) mortgage payments;

"(V) rent (including rent under a lease agreement);

"(VI) utilities; and

"(VII) interest on any other debt obligations that were incurred before the covered period.

"(ii) DELEGATED AUTHORITY.—

"(I) IN GENERAL.—For purposes of making covered loans for the purposes described in clause (i), a lender approved under this paragraph shall be considered to have delegated authority to make and approve covered loans, subject to the provisions of this paragraph.

"(II) CONSIDERATIONS.—In evaluating the eligibility of a borrower for a covered loan with the terms described in this paragraph, a lender shall consider whether the borrower—

"(aa) was in operation on February 15, 2020;

"(bb)(AA) had employees for whom the borrower paid salaries and payroll taxes; or

"(BB) paid independent contractors, as reported on a Form 1099–MISC; and

"(cc) is substantially impacted by public health restrictions related to the Coronavirus 2019 (COVID–19).

"(iii) ADDITIONAL LENDERS.—The authority to make loans under this paragraph shall be extended to additional lenders determined by the Administrator and the Secretary of the Treasury to have the necessary qualifications to process, close, disburse and service loans made with the guarantee of the Administration.

"(iv) LIMITATION.—An eligible recipient of a covered loan for purposes of paying payroll costs and other obligations described in this subparagraph shall not be eligible to receive an economic injury disaster loan under subsection (b)(2) for the same purpose.

"(G) BORROWER REQUIREMENTS.—

"(i) CERTIFICATION.—An eligible recipient applying for a covered loan shall make a good faith certification—

"(I) that the uncertainty of current economic conditions makes necessary the loan request to support the ongoing operations of the eligible recipient; and

"(II) acknowledging that funds will be used to retain workers and maintain payroll or make mortgage payments, lease payments, and utility payments.

"(ii) FULL-TIME EQUIVALENT EMPLOYEES.—An eligible recipient of a covered loan shall maintain an average monthly number of full-time equivalent employees (as defined in section 45R(d)(2) of the Internal Revenue Code of 1986) during the covered period that is not less than the average monthly number of full-time equivalent employees during the applicable period described in subclause (I)(aa) or subclause (II)(aa) of subparagraph (E)(i).

"(H) FEE WAIVER.—During the covered period, with respect to a covered loan—

"(i) in lieu of the fee otherwise applicable under paragraph (23)(A), the Administrator shall collect no fee; and

"(ii) in lieu of the fee otherwise applicable under paragraph (18)(A), the Administrator shall collect no fee.

"(I) CREDIT ELSEWHERE.—During the covered period, the requirement that a small business concern is unable to obtain credit elsewhere, as defined in section 3(h), shall not apply to a covered loan.

"(J) COLLATERAL AND PERSONAL GUARANTEE REQUIREMENTS.—During the covered period, with respect to a covered loan—

"(i) no collateral shall be required for the covered loan; and

"(ii) no personal guarantee shall be required for the covered loan.

"(K) MATURITY FOR LOANS WITH REMAINING BALANCE AFTER APPLICATION OF FORGIVENESS.—With respect to a covered loan that has a remaining balance after reduction based on the loan forgiveness amount under section 1105 of the CARES Act—

"(i) the remaining balance shall continue to be guaranteed by the Administration under this subsection; and

"(ii) the covered loan shall have a maximum maturity of 10 years from the date on which the borrower applies for loan forgiveness under that section.

"(L) INTEREST RATE REQUIREMENTS.—During the covered period, a covered loan shall bear an interest rate not to exceed 4 percent.

"(M) SUBSIDY RECOUPMENT FEE.—Notwithstanding any other provision of law, a covered loan shall not be subject to a subsidy recoupment fee.

"(N) LOAN DEFERMENT.—

"(i) DEFINITION OF IMPACTED BORROWER.—

"(I) IN GENERAL.—In this subparagraph, the term 'impacted borrower' means an eligible recipient that—

"(aa) is in operation on February 15, 2020; and

"(bb) has an application for a covered loan that is approved or pending approval on or after the date of enactment of this paragraph.

"(II) PRESUMPTION.—For purposes of this subparagraph, an impacted borrower is presumed to have been adversely impacted by COVID–19.

"(ii) DEFERRAL.—During the covered period, the Administrator shall—

"(I) consider each eligible recipient that applies for a covered loan to be an impacted borrower; and

"(II) require lenders under this subsection to provide complete payment deferment relief for impacted borrowers with covered loans for a period of less than 6 months, including payment of principal, interest, and fees.

"(iii) SECONDARY MARKET.—During the covered period, with respect to a covered loan that is sold on the secondary market, if an investor declines to approve a deferral requested by a lender under clause (ii), the Administrator shall exercise the authority to purchase the loan so that the impacted borrower may receive a deferral for a period of not less than 6 months starting on the date on which the loan is disbursed.

"(iv) GUIDANCE.—Not later than 30 days after the date of enactment of this paragraph, the Administrator shall provide guidance to lenders under this paragraph on the deferment process described in this subparagraph.

"(O) SECONDARY MARKET SALES.—A covered loan shall not be eligible to be sold in the secondary market until the covered recipient of the covered loan has requested the loan forgiveness authorized under section 1105 of the CARES Act and the Administrator has finally determined the amount of any forgiveness to which the eligible recipient is entitled and has made payment to the lender. Any remaining balance on the loan after the application of that payment may be sold in the secondary market.

"(P) REGULATORY CAPITAL REQUIREMENTS.—

"(i) RISK WEIGHT.—With respect to the appropriate Federal banking agencies applying capital requirements under their respective risk-based capital requirements, a covered loan shall receive a risk weight of zero percent.

"(ii) TEMPORARY RELIEF FROM TDR DISCLOSURES.—Notwithstanding any other provision of law, an insured depository institution that modifies a covered loan in relation to COVID–19-related difficulties in a troubled debt restructuring on or after March 13, 2020, shall not be required to comply with the Financial Accounting Standards Board Accounting Standards Codification Subtopic 310–40 ('Receivables – Troubled Debt Restructurings by Creditors') for purposes of compliance with the requirements of the Federal Deposit Insurance Act (12 U.S.C. 1811 et seq.), until such time and under such circumstances as the appropriate Federal banking agency determines

appropriate.
"(Q) REIMBURSEMENT FOR PROCESSING.—
"(i) IN GENERAL.—The Administrator shall reimburse a lender authorized to make a covered loan at a rate of 5 percent of the balance of the financing outstanding at the time of disbursement of the covered loan.
"(ii) TIMING.—A reimbursement described in clause (i) shall be made not later than 5 days after the disbursement of the covered loan.
"(R) DUPLICATION.—Nothing in this paragraph shall prohibit a recipient of an economic injury disaster loan made under subsection (b)(2) during the period beginning on February 15, 2020 and ending on March 31, 2020 from receiving assistance under this paragraph.".
(b) Commitments For 7(a) Loans.—During the period beginning on February 15, 2020 and ending on June 30, 2020—
(1) the amount authorized for commitments for general business loans authorized under section 7(a) of the Small Business Act (15 U.S.C. 636(a)), including loans made under paragraph (36) of such section, as added by subsection (a), shall be $349,000,000,000; and
(2) the amount authorized for commitments for such loans under the heading "BUSINESS LOANS PROGRAM ACCOUNT" under the heading "Small Business Administration" under title V of the Consolidated Appropriations Act, 2020 (Public Law 116–93; 133 Stat. 2475) shall not apply.
(c) Express Loans.—
(1) IN GENERAL.—Section 7(a)(31)(D) of the Small Business Act (15 U.S.C. 636(a)(31)(D)) is amended by striking "$350,000" and inserting "$1,000,000".
(2) PROSPECTIVE REPEAL.—Effective on January 1, 2021, section 7(a)(31)(D) of the Small Business Act (15 U.S.C. 636(a)(31)(D)) is amended by striking "$1,000,000" and inserting "$350,000".
(d) Exception To Guarantee Fee Waiver For Veterans.—Section 7(a)(31)(G) of the Small Business Act (15 U.S.C. 636(a)(31)(G)) is amended—
(1) by striking clause (ii); and
(2) by redesignating clause (iii) as clause (ii).
(e) Interim Rule.—On and after the date of enactment of this Act, the interim final rule published by the Administrator entitled "Express Loan Programs: Affiliation Standards" (85 Fed. Reg. 7622 (February 10, 2020)) shall have no force or effect.

SEC. 190003. ENTREPRENEURIAL DEVELOPMENT.
(a) Definitions.—In this section—
(1) the term "resource partner" means—
(A) a small business development center; and
(B) a women's business center;
(2) the term "small business development center" has the meaning given the term in section 3 of the Small Business Act (15 U.S.C. 632); and
(3) the term "women's business center" means a women's business center

described in section 29 of the Small Business Act (15 U.S.C. 656).

(b) Education, Training, And Advising Grants.—

(1) IN GENERAL.—The Administration may provide financial assistance in the form of grants to resource partners to provide education, training, and advising to covered small business concerns.

(2) USE OF FUNDS.—Grants under this subsection shall be used for the education, training, and advising of covered small business concerns and their employees on—

(A) accessing and applying for resources provided by the Administration and other Federal resources relating to access to capital and business resiliency;

(B) the hazards and prevention of the transmission and communication of COVID–19 and other communicable diseases;

(C) the potential effects of COVID–19 on the supply chains, distribution, and sale of products of covered small business concerns and the mitigation of those effects;

(D) the management and practice of telework to reduce possible transmission of COVID–19;

(E) the management and practice of remote customer service by electronic or other means;

(F) the risks of and mitigation of cyber threats in remote customer service or telework practices;

(G) the mitigation of the effects of reduced travel or outside activities on covered small business concerns during COVID–19 or similar occurrences; and

(H) any other relevant business practices necessary to mitigate the economic effects of COVID–19 or similar occurrences.

(3) GRANT DETERMINATION.—

(A) SMALL BUSINESS DEVELOPMENT CENTERS.—The Administration shall award 80 percent of funds authorized to carry out this subsection to small business development centers, which shall be awarded pursuant to a formula jointly developed, negotiated, and agreed upon, with full participation of both parties, between the association formed under section 21(a)(3)(A) of the Small Business Act (15 U.S.C. 648(a)(3)(A)) and the Administration.

(B) WOMEN'S BUSINESS CENTERS.—The Administration shall award 20 percent of funds authorized to carry out this subsection to women's business centers, which shall be awarded pursuant to a process established by the Administration in consultation with recipients of assistance.

(C) NO MATCHING FUNDS REQUIRED.—Matching funds shall not be required for any grant under this subsection.

(4) GOALS AND METRICS.—

(A) IN GENERAL.—Goals and metrics for the funds made available under this subsection shall be jointly developed, negotiated, and agreed upon, with full participation of both parties, between the resource partners and the Administrator, which shall—

(i) take into consideration the extent of the circumstances relating to the spread of COVID–19, or similar occurrences, that affect covered small business concerns located in the areas covered by the resource partner, particularly in rural areas or economically distressed areas;

(ii) generally follow the use of funds outlined in paragraph (2), but shall not restrict the activities of resource partners in responding to unique situations; and

(iii) encourage resource partners to develop and provide services to covered small business concerns.

(B) PUBLIC AVAILABILITY.—The Administrator shall make publicly available the methodology by which the Administrator and resource partners jointly develop the metrics and goals described in subparagraph (A).

(c) Resource Partner Association Grants.—

(1) IN GENERAL.—The Administrator may provide grants to an association or associations representing resource partners under which the association or associations shall establish a single centralized hub for COVID–19 information, which shall include—

(A) 1 online platform that consolidates resources and information available across multiple Federal agencies for small business concerns related to COVID–19; and

(B) a training program to educate resource partner counselors, members of the Service Corps of Retired Executives established under section 8(b)(1)(B) of the Small Business Act (15 U.S.C. 637(b)(1)(B)), and counselors at veterans business outreach centers described in section 32 of the Small Business Act (15 U.S.C. 657b) on the resources and information described in subparagraph (A).

(2) GOALS AND METRICS.—Goals and metrics for the funds made available under this subsection shall be jointly developed, negotiated, and agreed upon, with full participation of both parties, between the association or associations receiving a grant under this subsection and the Administrator.

(d) Report.—Not later than 6 months after the date of enactment of this Act, and annually thereafter, the Administrator shall submit to the Committee on Small Business and Entrepreneurship of the Senate and the Committee on Small Business of the House of Representatives a report that describes—

(1) with respect to the initial year covered by the report—

(A) the programs and services developed and provided by the Administration and resource partners under subsection (b);

(B) the initial efforts to provide those services under subsection (b); and

(C) the online platform and training developed and provided by the Administration and the association or associations under subsection (c); and

(2) with respect to the subsequent years covered by the report—

(A) with respect to the grant program under subsection (b)—

(i) the efforts of the Administrator and resource partners to develop services to assist covered small business concerns;

(ii) the challenges faced by owners of covered small business concerns in accessing services provided by the Administration and resource partners;

(iii) the number of unique covered small business concerns that were served by the Administration and resource partners; and

(iv) other relevant outcome performance data with respect to covered small business concerns, including the number of employees affected, the effect on sales, the disruptions of supply chains, and the efforts made by the Administration and resource partners to mitigate these effects; and

(B) with respect to the grant program under subsection (c)—

(i) the efforts of the Administrator and the association or associations to develop and evolve an online resource for small business concerns; and

(ii) the efforts of the Administrator and the association or associations to develop a training program for resource partner counselors, including the number of counselors trained.

SEC. 190004. WAIVER OF MATCHING FUNDS REQUIREMENT UNDER THE WOMEN'S BUSINESS CENTER PROGRAM.

During the 3-month period beginning on the date of enactment of this Act, the requirement relating to obtaining cash contributions from non-Federal sources under section 29(c)(1) of the Small Business Act (15 U.S.C. 656(c)(1)) is waived for any recipient of assistance under such section 29.

SEC. 190005. LOAN FORGIVENESS.

(a) Definitions.—In this section—

(1) the term "covered loan" means a loan guaranteed under paragraph (36) of section 7(a) of the Small Business Act (15 U.S.C. 636(a)), as added by section 1102;

(2) the term "covered mortgage obligation" means any indebtedness or debt instrument incurred in the ordinary course of business that—

(A) is a liability of the borrower;

(B) is a mortgage on real or personal property; and

(C) was incurred before February 15, 2020;

(3) the term "covered period" means the 8-week period beginning on date of the origination of a covered loan;

(4) the term "covered rent obligation" means rent obligated under a leasing agreement in force before February 15, 2020;

(5) the term "covered utility payment" means payment for a service for the distribution of electricity, gas, water, transportation, telephone, or internet access for which service began before February 15, 2020;

(6) the term "eligible recipient" means the recipient of a covered loan;

(7) the term "expected forgiveness amount" means the amount of principal that a lender reasonably expects a borrower to expend during the covered period on the sum of any—

(A) payroll costs;

(B) payments of interest on any covered mortgage obligation (which shall not

include any prepayment of or payment of principal on a covered mortgage obligation);
(C) payments on any covered rent obligation; and
(D) covered utility payments; and
(8) the term "payroll costs" has the meaning given that term in paragraph (36) of section 7(a) of the Small Business Act (15 U.S.C. 636(a)), as added by section 190002(a)(2) of this division.
(b) Forgiveness.—An eligible recipient shall be eligible for forgiveness of indebtedness on a covered loan in an amount equal to the sum of the following costs incurred and payments made during the covered period:
(1) Payroll costs.
(2) Any payment of interest on any covered mortgage obligation (which shall not include any prepayment of or payment of principal on a covered mortgage obligation).
(3) Any payment on any covered rent obligation.
(4) Any covered utility payment.
(c) Treatment Of Amounts Forgiven.—
(1) IN GENERAL.—Amounts which have been forgiven under this section shall be considered canceled indebtedness by a lender authorized under section 7(a) of the Small Business Act (15 U.S.C. 636(a)).
(2) PURCHASE OF GUARANTEES.—For purposes of the purchase of the guarantee for a covered loan by the Administrator, amounts which are forgiven under this section shall be treated in accordance with the procedures that are otherwise applicable to a loan guaranteed under section 7(a) of the Small Business Act (15 U.S.C. 636(a)).
(3) REMITTANCE.—Not later than 90 days after the date on which the amount of forgiveness under this section is determined, the Administrator shall remit to the lender an amount equal to the amount of forgiveness, plus any interest accrued through the date of payment.
(4) ADVANCE PURCHASE OF COVERED LOAN.—
(A) REPORT.—A lender authorized under section 7(a) of the Small Business Act (15 U.S.C. 636(a)) may report to the Administrator an expected forgiveness amount on a covered loan or on a pool of covered loans of up to 100 percent of the principal on the covered loan or pool of covered loans, respectively.
(B) PURCHASE.—The Administrator shall purchase the expected forgiveness amount described in subparagraph (A) as if the amount were the principal amount of a loan guaranteed under section 7(a) of the Small Business Act 636(a).
(C) TIMING.—Not later than 5 days after the date on which the Administrator receives a report under subparagraph (A), the Administrator shall purchase the expected forgiveness amount under subparagraph (B) with respect to each covered loan to which the report relates.
(d) Limits On Amount Of Forgiveness.—
(1) AMOUNT MAY NOT EXCEED PRINCIPAL.—The amount of loan

forgiveness under this section shall not exceed the principal amount of the financing made available under the applicable covered loan.

(2) REDUCTION BASED ON REDUCTION IN NUMBER OF EMPLOYEES.—

(A) IN GENERAL.—The amount of loan forgiveness under this section shall be reduced, but not increased, by multiplying the amount described in subsection (b) by the quotient obtained by dividing—

(i) the average number of full-time equivalent employees per month employed by the eligible recipient during the covered period; by

(ii) (I) the average number of full-time equivalent employees per month employed by the eligible recipient during the period beginning on February 15, 2019 and ending on June 30, 2019;

(II) if the eligible recipient was not in operation before June 30, 2019, the average number of full-time equivalent employees per month employed by the eligible recipient during the period beginning on January 1, 2020 and ending on February 29, 2020; or

(III) in the case of an eligible recipient that is seasonal employer, as determined by the Administrator, the average number of full-time equivalent employees per month employed by the eligible recipient during the period beginning on February 15, 2019 and ending on June 30, 2019.

(B) CALCULATION OF AVERAGE NUMBER OF EMPLOYEES.—For purposes of subparagraph (A), the average number of full-time equivalent employees shall be determined by calculating the average number of full-time equivalent employees for each pay period falling within a month.

(3) REDUCTION RELATING TO SALARY AND WAGES.—

(A) IN GENERAL.—The amount of loan forgiveness under this section shall be reduced by the amount of any reduction in total salary or wages of any employee described in subparagraph (B) during the covered period that is in excess of 25 percent of the total salary or wages of the employee during the most recent full quarter during which the employee was employed before the covered period.

(B) EMPLOYEES DESCRIBED.—An employee described in this subparagraph is any employee who did not receive, during any single pay period during 2019, wages or salary at an annualized rate of pay in an amount more than $100,000.

(4) EXCEPTION FOR TIPPED WORKERS.—An eligible recipient with tipped employees described in section 3(m)(2)(A) of the Fair Labor Standards Act of 1938 (29 U.S.C. 203(m)(2)(A)) may receive forgiveness for additional wages paid to those employees.

(5) EXEMPTION FOR RE-HIRES.—

(A) IN GENERAL.—In a circumstance described in subparagraph (B), the amount of loan forgiveness under this section shall be determined without regard to a reduction in the number of full-time equivalent employees of an eligible recipient or a reduction in the salary of 1 or more employees of the eligible recipient, as applicable, during the period beginning on February 15, 2020 and ending on April 1, 2020.

(B) CIRCUMSTANCES.—A circumstance described in this subparagraph is a circumstance—

(i) in which—

(I) during the period beginning on February 15, 2020 and ending on April 1, 2020, there is a reduction, as compared to February 15, 2020, in the number of full-time equivalent employees of an eligible recipient; and

(II) not later than June 30, 2020, the eligible employer has eliminated the reduction in the number of full-time equivalent employees;

(ii) in which—

(I) during the period beginning on February 15, 2020 and ending on April 1, 2020, there is a reduction, as compared to February 15, 2020, in the salary or wages of 1 or more employees of the eligible recipient; and

(II) not later than June 30, 2020, the eligible employer has eliminated the reduction in the salary or wages of such employees; or

(iii) in which the events described in clause (i) and (ii) occur.

(e) Application.—An eligible recipient seeking loan forgiveness under this section shall submit to the lender that originated the covered loan an application, which shall include—

(1) documentation verifying the number of full-time equivalent employees on payroll and pay rates for the periods described in subsection (d), including—

(A) payroll tax filings reported to the Internal Revenue Service; and

(B) State income, payroll, and unemployment insurance filings;

(2) documentation, including cancelled checks, payment receipts, transcripts of accounts, or other documents verifying payments on covered mortgage obligations, payments on covered lease obligations, and covered utility payments;

(3) a certification from a representative of the eligible recipient authorized to make such certifications that—

(A) the documentation presented is true and correct; and

(B) the amount for which forgiveness is requested was used to retain employees, make interest payments on a covered mortgage obligation, make payments on a covered rent obligation, or make covered utility payments; and

(4) any other documentation the Administrator determines necessary.

(f) Prohibition On Forgiveness Without Documentation.—No eligible recipient shall receive forgiveness under this section without submitting to the lender that originated the covered loan the documentation required under subsection (e).

(g) Decision.—Not later than 60 days after the date on which a lender receives an application for loan forgiveness under this section from an eligible recipient, the lender shall issue a decision on the an application.

(h) Safe Harbor.—If a lender determines that an eligible recipient has accurately verified the payments for payroll costs, payments on covered mortgage obligations, payments on covered lease obligations, or covered utility payments during covered period—

(1) an enforcement action may not be taken against the lender under section 47(e) of the Small Business Act (15 U.S.C. 657t(e)) relating to loan forgiveness for the payments for payroll costs, payments on covered mortgage obligations, payments on covered lease obligations, or covered utility payments, as the case may be; and

(2) the lender shall not be subject to any penalties by the Administrator relating to loan forgiveness for the payments for payroll costs, payments on covered mortgage obligations, payments on covered lease obligations, or covered utility payments, as the case may be.

(i) Taxability.—Canceled indebtedness under this section shall be excluded from gross income for purposes of the Internal Revenue Code of 1986.

(j) Rule Of Construction.—The cancellation of indebtedness on a covered loan under this section shall not otherwise modify the terms and conditions of the covered loan.

(k) Regulations.—Not later than 30 days after the date of enactment of this Act, the Administrator shall issue guidance and regulations implementing this section.

SEC. 190006. MINORITY BUSINESS DEVELOPMENT AGENCY.

(a) Definitions.—In this section—

(1) the term "Agency" means the Minority Business Development Agency of the Department of Commerce; and

(2) the term "minority business center" means a Business Center of the Agency.

(b) Education, Training, And Advising Grants.—

(1) IN GENERAL.—The Agency may provide financial assistance in the form of grants to minority business centers to provide education, training, and advising to covered small business concerns.

(2) USE OF FUNDS.—Grants under this section shall be used for the education, training, and advising of covered small business concerns and their employees on—

(A) accessing and applying for resources provided by the Agency and other Federal resources relating to access to capital and business resiliency;

(B) the hazards and prevention of the transmission and communication of COVID–19 and other communicable diseases;

(C) the potential effects of COVID–19 on the supply chains, distribution, and sale of products of covered small business concerns and the mitigation of those effects;

(D) the management and practice of telework to reduce possible transmission of COVID–19;

(E) the management and practice of remote customer service by electronic or other means;

(F) the risks of and mitigation of cyber threats in remote customer service or telework practices;

(G) the mitigation of the effects of reduced travel or outside activities on covered small business concerns during COVID–19 or similar occurrences; and

(H) any other relevant business practices necessary to mitigate the economic effects of COVID–19 or similar occurrences.

(3) NO MATCHING FUNDS REQUIRED.—Matching funds shall not be required for any grant under this section.

(4) GOALS AND METRICS.—

(A) IN GENERAL.—Goals and metrics for the funds made available under this section shall be jointly developed, negotiated, and agreed upon, with full participation of both parties, between the minority business centers and the Agency, which shall—

(i) take into consideration the extent of the circumstances relating to the spread of COVID–19, or similar occurrences, that affect covered small business concerns located in the areas covered by the minority business centers, particularly in rural areas or economically distressed areas;

(ii) generally follow the use of funds outlined in paragraph (2), but shall not restrict the activities of minority business centers in responding to unique situations; and

(iii) encourage minority business centers to develop and provide services to covered small business concerns.

(B) PUBLIC AVAILABILITY.—The Agency shall make publicly available the methodology by which the Agency and minority business centers jointly develop the metrics and goals described in subparagraph (A).

(5) AUTHORIZATION OF APPROPRIATIONS.—There is authorized to be appropriated $10,000,000 to carry out this section, to remain available until expended.

(c) Waivers.—

(1) IN GENERAL.—Notwithstanding any other provision of law or regulation, the Agency may, during the 3-month period that begins on the date of enactment of this Act, waive any matching requirement imposed on a minority business center or specialty center of the Agency under a cooperative agreement between such a center and the Agency if the applicable center is unable to raise funds, or has suffered a loss of revenue, because of the effects of COVID–19.

(2) REMAINING COMPLIANT.—Notwithstanding any provision of a cooperative agreement between the Agency and a minority business center, if, during the period beginning on the date of enactment of this Act and ending on September 30, 2021, such a center decides not to collect fees because of the economic consequences of COVID–19, the center shall be considered to be in compliance with that agreement if—

(A) the center notifies the Agency with respect to that decision, which the

center may provide through electronic mail; and
(B) the Agency, not later than 15 days after the date on which the center provides notice to the Agency under subparagraph (A)—
(i) confirms receipt of the notification under subparagraph (A); and
(ii) accepts the decision of the center.

SEC. 190007. CONTRACTING.
(a) Definition.—In this section, the term "covered entity" means a small business concern or nonprofit organization—
(1) that is a party to a contract with a Federal agency; and
(2) for which the contractor performance is adversely impacted as a result of COVID–19.
(b) Promotion Of Small Business Contracting.—
(1) SMALL BUSINESS CONTRACTING RELIEF.—
(A) IN GENERAL.—Notwithstanding any other provision of law or regulation, and except as provided in subparagraph (B), during the period beginning on the date of enactment of this Act and ending on September 30, 2021, the head of the Federal agency with which a covered entity has a contract shall provide the covered entity with the greater of—
(i) 30 additional days to carry out the responsibilities of the covered entity under the contract; or
(ii) an additional amount of time to carry out the responsibilities of the covered entity under the contract that the head of the Federal agency determines to be appropriate after taking into consideration the severity of the adverse impact experienced by the covered entity.
(B) EXCLUSION OF MISSION-CRITICAL CONTRACTS.—Subparagraph (A) shall not apply to any contract that the head of the Federal agency that is a party to the contract determines is critical to carrying out the mission of the Federal agency.
(2) PAYMENT CONTINUATION.—If the performance of all or any part of the work of a Federal goods or services contract with a contractor that is a small business concern or a nonprofit organization in force and effect during the period beginning on the date of enactment of this Act and ending on September 30, 2021, is unavoidably delayed or interrupted by the inability of the employees of the small business concern or nonprofit organization, as applicable, to access Government facilities, systems, or other Government-provided resources due to restrictions related to COVID–19 that have been imposed by any authority or due to orders or instructions issued by the contracting agency in response to COVID–19—
(A) the Government shall pay the small business concern or nonprofit organization, as applicable, upon the submission of the documentation required by the contract and according to the terms specified in the contract, the prices stipulated in the contract for goods or services as if the small business concern or nonprofit organization, as applicable, had rendered and

the Government accepted the goods or services; and

(B) contractor delivery schedules shall be revised and the small business concern or nonprofit organization, as applicable, shall be eligible for equitable adjustments based on the revised schedules.

(3) PROMPT PAYMENTS.—Notwithstanding any other provision of law or regulation, during any period in which the President invokes the authorities of the Defense Production Act of 1950 (50 U.S.C. 4501 et seq.), for any payment due by the head of a Federal agency on a contract for an item of property or service provided—

(A) with respect to a prime contractor (as defined in section 8701 of title 41, United States Code) that is a small business concern or nonprofit organization, the head of the Federal agency shall, to the fullest extent permitted by law and to the maximum extent practicable, establish an accelerated payment date of 15 days after a proper invoice for the amount due is received; and

(B) with respect to a prime contractor (as defined in section 8701 of title 41, United States Code) that subcontracts with a small business concern or nonprofit organization, the head of the Federal agency shall, to fullest extent permitted by law and to the maximum extent practicable, establish an accelerated payment date of 15 days after receipt of a proper invoice for the amount due if the prime contractor agrees to make payments to the subcontractor in accordance with the accelerated payment date, to the maximum extent practicable, without any further consideration from or fees charged to the subcontractor.

(4) BAR ON MULTIPLE FORMS OF CONTRACT RELIEF.—A small business concern or nonprofit organization may not receive a modification of terms or assistance under more than 1 paragraph of this subsection with respect to any single contract.

(c) Resolicitation Of Contracts With Small Business Concerns.—During fiscal years 2021 and 2022, a Federal agency shall not cancel a contract in which the prime contractor (as defined in section 8701 of title 41, United States Code) is a small business concern that defaulted on the terms of the contract directly or indirectly due to the COVID–19 unless the Director of Small and Disadvantaged Business Utilization of the Federal agency certifies that—

(1) the contract is mission-critical;

(2) resolicitation of the contract would allow a faster delivery than the small business concern could provide; and

(3) the resolicitation of the contract is, to the greatest extent possible, awarded to another small business concern.

(d) 8(a) Extension.—The Administrator of the Small Business Administration shall allow a small business concern participating in the program established under section 8(a) of the Small Business Act on the date of enactment of this section, to extend such participation by a period of 1 year from the date of the concern's admission to the program.

SEC. 190008. UNITED STATES TREASURY PROGRAM MANAGEMENT AUTHORITY.

(a) Authority To Include Additional Financial Institutions.—The Department of the Treasury, in consultation with the Administration, the Farm Credit Administration, and the other Federal financial regulatory agencies (as defined in section 313(r) of title 31, United States Code), shall establish criteria for insured depository institutions (as defined in section 3 of the Federal Deposit Insurance Act (12 U.S.C. 1813)), institutions of the Farm Credit System chartered under the Farm Credit Act of 1971 (12 U.S.C. 2001 et seq.), and other lenders that do not already participate in lending under programs of the Administration, to participate in the small business interruption loans program to provide loans under this section until the date on which the national emergency declared by the President under the National Emergencies Act (50 U.S.C. 1601 et seq.) with respect to the Coronavirus Disease 2019 (COVID–19) expires.

(b) Safety And Soundness.—An insured depository institution (as defined in section 3 of the Federal Deposit Insurance Act (12 U.S.C. 1813)), institution of the Farm Credit System chartered under the Farm Credit Act of 1971 (12 U.S.C. 2001 et seq.), or other lender may only participate in the program established under this section if participation does not affect the safety and soundness of the institution or lender.

(c) Regulations For Lenders And Loans.—

(1) IN GENERAL.—The Secretary of the Treasury, in consultation with the Administrator, shall issue regulations and guidance in order to direct additional lenders under this section and establish terms and conditions for small business interruption loans under this section, including terms concerning compensation, underwriting standards, interest rates, and maturity.

(2) REQUIREMENTS.—The terms and conditions established under paragraph (1) shall provide for the following:

(A) A rate of interest that does not exceed the maximum permissible rate of interest available on a loan of comparable maturity under paragraph (36) of section 7(a) of the Small Business Act (15 U.S.C. 636(a)), as added by section 190002(a)(2) of this division.

(B) Terms and conditions that, to the maximum extent practicable, are the same as the terms and conditions required under the following provisions of paragraph (36) of section 7(a) of the Small Business Act (15 U.S.C. 636(a)), as added by section 190002(a) of this division:

(i) Subparagraph (D), pertaining to borrower eligibility.

(ii) Subparagraph (E), pertaining to the maximum loan amount.

(iii) Subparagraph (F)(i), pertaining to allowable uses of program loans.

(iv) Subparagraph (H), pertaining to fee waivers.

(v) Subparagraph (N), pertaining to loan deferment.

(C) A guarantee percentage that, to the maximum extent practicable, is the same as the guarantee percentage required under subparagraph (F) of section 7(a)(2) of the Small Business Act (15 U.S.C. 636(a)(2)), as added by section 190002 of this division.

(D) Loan forgiveness under terms and conditions that, to the maximum extent practicable, are the same as the terms and conditions for loan forgiveness under section 190005 of this division.

(d) Additional Regulations Generally.—The Secretary of the Treasury may issue regulations and guidance as may be necessary to carry out the purposes of this section.

(e) Certification.—As a condition of receiving a loan under this section, a borrower shall certify under terms acceptable to the Secretary of the Treasury that the borrower—

(1) does not have an application pending for a loan under section 7(a) of the Small Business Act (15 U.S.C. 636(a)); and

(2) has not received such a loan during the period beginning on February 15, 2020 and ending on December 31, 2020.

(f) Program Administration.—Under the infrastructure of the Department of the Treasury and with guidance from the Secretary of the Treasury, the Administrator shall administer the program established under this section, including the making and purchasing of guarantees on loans under the program, until the date on which the national emergency declared by the President under the National Emergencies Act (50 U.S.C. 1601 et seq.) with respect to the Coronavirus Disease 2019 (COVID–19) expires.

(g) Criminal Penalties.—A loan under this section shall be deemed to be a loan under the Small Business Act (15 U.S.C. 631 et seq.) for purposes of section 16 of such Act (15 U.S.C. 645).

SEC. 190009. EMERGENCY ECONOMIC INJURY GRANTS FOR ADDITIONAL COVERED ENTITIES.

(a) In General.—The Administrator of the Small Business Administration shall provide grants to additional covered entities that have suffered a substantial economic injury (as defined in section 7(b)(2) of the Small Business Act (15 U.S.C. 636(b)(2))), directly or indirectly, as a result of the public health emergency declared because of COVID–19.

(b) Additional Covered Entity Defined.—The term "additional covered entity" means—

(1) a business concern that employs not more than 500 employees per physical location of the business concern and that is assigned a North American Industry Classification System code beginning with 71; 72; 44; 45; and 812930;

(2) a small business concern (as defined under section 3 of the Small Business Act (15 U.S.C. 632)); and

(3) if such person was in operation on or before January 31, 2020—

(A) a individual who operates under a sole proprietorship or as an independent contractor;

(B) a cooperative that employs not more than 500 employees per physical location of the cooperative;
(C) an ESOP (as defined in section 3(q)(6) of the Small Business Act (15 U.S.C. 632(q)(6))) that employs not more than 500 employees per physical location of the ESOP;
(D) an organization serving veterans or members of the Armed Forces (as defined in section 501(c)(19) of the Internal Revenue Code of 1986, that is exempt from taxation under subsection (a) of such section);
(E) a private non-profit organization that employs not more than 500 employees per physical location of the organization; or
(F) a start-up small business concern that employs not more than 500 employees per physical location of the concern.
(c) Process.—The Administrator shall use the existing direct loan application process administered under section 7(b) of the Small Business Act (15 U.S.C. 636(b)) to disburse grant funds, to greatest extent possible, within 3 days after receiving an application from an additional covered entity.
(d) Verification.—Before disbursing amounts under this subsection, the Administrator shall verify that the applicant is an additional covered entity.
(e) Exemption From Affiliation Rules.—For the purposes of this section, the Administrator of the Small Business Administration shall suspend the application of the affiliation rules of the Administration during the period beginning on January 31, 2020 and ending on September 30, 2021, except that individual affiliates may not exceed the current small business size standard for the industry in which the affiliate operates, and any group of affiliates may not receive more than 3 times the maximum allowable grant amount under subsection (f).
(f) Amount Of Grant.—The amount of a grant provided under this section shall be not more than $10,000.
(g) Use Of Funds.—An additional covered entity that receives a grant under this section may use the grant funds to address the direct effects of the COVID–19 pandemic, including—
(1) payroll support, including paid sick, medical, or family leave and costs related to the continuation of health care benefits;
(2) maintaining payroll to retain employees during business disruptions or substantial slowdowns;
(3) meeting increased costs to obtain materials unavailable from the original source of the additional covered entity due to interrupted supply chains;
(4) making payments under a lease or mortgage loan, or a contract for utility services, related to a place of operation of the additional covered entity;
(5) repaying obligations that cannot be met due to revenue losses; and
(6) other expenses, as deemed appropriate by the Administrator.
(h) Eligibility For Additional Assistance.—An additional covered entity that receives a grant under this section may also apply for a loan under subsections (a) or (b) of section 7 of the Small Business Act (15 U.S.C. 636).

(i) Procedures.—The Administrator shall establish procedures to verify and document the compliance of an additional covered entity that receives a grant under this section with the requirements under this section in order to prevent waste, fraud, and abuse of such grant funds.

(j) Report.—Not later than March 31, 2022, the Administrator of the Small Business Administration shall submit to Congress a report that includes—

(1) the number of grants made under this section, disaggregated by the number of grants made—

(A) in an amount less than or equal to $1,000;

(B) in an amount greater than $2,000 but less than or equal to $3,000;

(C) in an amount greater than $3,000 but less than or equal to $4,000;

(D) in an amount greater than $4,000 but less than or equal to $5,000;

(E) in an amount greater than $5,000 but less than or equal to $6,000;

(F) in an amount greater than $6,000 but less than or equal to $7,000;

(G) in an amount greater than $7,000 but less than or equal to $8,000;

(H) in an amount greater than $8,000 but less than or equal to $9,000; and

(I) in an amount greater than $9,000 but less than or equal to $10,000;

(2) the average amount of a grant award;

(3) an analysis of the program established under this section and recommendations for improvement;

(4) the average time from receipt of an application to approval of grant under this section; and

(5) the average time from approval of grant to disbursement of grant funds.

(k) Authorization Of Appropriations.—There is authorized to be appropriated $100,000,000,000 to the Administrator to carry out this section.

(l) Termination.—The authority to carry out grants under this section shall terminate on September 30, 2021.

SEC. 190010. RESOURCES AND SERVICES IN LANGUAGES OTHER THAN ENGLISH.

(a) In General.—The Administrator shall provide the resources and services made available by the Administration to small business concerns in the 10 most commonly spoken languages, other than English, in the United States, which shall include Mandarin, Cantonese, Japanese, and Korean.

(b) Authorization Of Appropriations.—There is authorized to be appropriated to the Administrator $25,000,000 to carry out this section.

SEC. 190011. SUBSIDY FOR CERTAIN LOAN PAYMENTS.

(a) Definition Of Covered Loan.—In this section, the term "covered loan" means a loan that is—

(1) guaranteed by the Administration under—

(A) section 7(a) of the Small Business Act (15 U.S.C. 636(a)), including a loan made under the Community Advantage Pilot Program of the Administration; or

(B) title V of the Small Business Investment Act of 1958 (15 U.S.C. 695 et seq.); or
(2) made by an intermediary to a small business concern using loans or grants received under section 7(m) of the Small Business Act (15 U.S.C. 636(m)).
(b) Sense Of Congress.—It is the sense of Congress that—
(1) all borrowers are adversely affected by COVID–19;
(2) relief payments by the Administration are appropriate for all borrowers; and
(3) in addition to the relief provided under this division, the Administration should encourage lenders to provide payment deferments, when appropriate, and to extend the maturity of covered loans, so as to avoid balloon payments or any requirement for increases in debt payments resulting from deferments provided by lenders during the period of the national emergency declared by the President under the National Emergencies Act (50 U.S.C. 1601 et seq.) with respect to the Coronavirus Disease 2019 (COVID–19).
(c) Principal And Interest Payments.—
(1) IN GENERAL.—The Administrator shall pay the principal, interest, and any associated fees that are owed on a covered loan in a regular servicing status—
(A) with respect to a covered loan made before the date of enactment of this Act and not on deferment, for the 6-month period beginning with the next payment due on the covered loan;
(B) with respect to a covered loan made before the date of enactment of this Act and on deferment, for the 6-month period beginning with the next payment due on the covered loan after the deferment period; and
(C) with respect to a covered loan made during the period beginning on the date of enactment of this Act and ending on the date that is 6 months after such date of enactment, for the 6-month period beginning with the first payment due on the covered loan.
(2) TIMING OF PAYMENT.—The Administrator shall begin making payments under paragraph (1) on a covered loan not later than 30 days after the date on which the first such payment is due.
(3) APPLICATION OF PAYMENT.—Any payment made by the Administrator under paragraph (1) shall be applied to the covered loan such that the borrower is relieved of the obligation to pay that amount.
(d) Other Requirements.—The Administrator shall—
(1) communicate and coordinate with the Federal Deposit Insurance Corporation, the Office of the Comptroller of the Currency, and State bank regulators to encourage those entities to not require lenders to increase their reserves on account of receiving payments made by the Administrator under subsection (c);
(2) waive statutory limits on maximum loan maturities for any covered loan durations where the lender provides a deferral and extends the maturity of covered loans during the 1-year period following the date of enactment of

this Act; and
(3) when necessary to provide more time because of the potential of higher volumes, travel restrictions, and the inability to access some properties during the COVID–19 pandemic, extend lender site visit requirements to—
(A) not more than 60 days (which may be extended at the discretion of the Administration) after the occurrence of an adverse event, other than a payment default, causing a loan to be classified as in liquidation; and
(B) not more than 90 days after a payment default.
(e) Rule Of Construction.—Nothing in this section may be construed to limit the authority of the Administrator to make payments pursuant to subsection (c) with respect to a covered loan solely because the covered loan has been sold in the secondary market.
(f) Authorization Of Appropriations.—There is authorized to be appropriated to the Administrator $16,800,000,000 to carry out this section.

SEC. 190012. TEMPORARY FEE REDUCTIONS.
(a) Purpose.—The purpose of the section is to waive borrower and lender fees on loans, including a permanent fix to waive fees for veterans and their spouses.
(b) Administrative Fee Waiver.—
(1) IN GENERAL.—During the period beginning on the date of enactment of this Act and ending on September 30, 2021, and to the extent that the cost of such elimination or reduction of fees is offset by appropriations, with respect to each loan guaranteed under section 7(a) of the Small Business Act (15 U.S.C. 636(a)) (including a recipient of assistance under the Community Advantage Pilot Program of the Administration) for which an application is approved or pending approval on or after the date of enactment of this Act, the Administrator shall—
(A) in lieu of the fee otherwise applicable under section 7(a)(23)(A) of the Small Business Act (15 U.S.C. 636(a)(23)(A)), collect no fee or reduce fees to the maximum extent possible; and
(B) in lieu of the fee otherwise applicable under section 7(a)(18)(A) of the Small Business Act (15 U.S.C. 636(a)(18)(A)), collect no fee or reduce fees to the maximum extent possible.
(2) APPLICATION OF FEE ELIMINATIONS OR REDUCTIONS.—To the extent that amounts are made available to the Administrator for the purpose of fee eliminations or reductions under paragraph (1), the Administrator shall—
(A) first use any amounts provided to eliminate or reduce fees paid by small business borrowers under clauses (i) through (iii) of section 7(a)(18)(A) of the Small Business Act (15 U.S.C. 636(a)(18)(A)), to the maximum extent possible; and
(B) then use any amounts provided to eliminate or reduce fees under 7(a)(23)(A) of the Small Business Act (15 U.S.C. 636(a)(23)(A)).

(c) Exception To Guarantee Fee Waiver For Veterans.—Section 7(a)(31)(G) of the Small Business Act (15 U.S.C. 636(a)(31)(G)) is amended—

(1) by striking clause (ii); and

(2) by redesignating clause (iii) as clause (ii).

(d) Temporary Fee Elimination For The 504 Loan Program.—

(1) IN GENERAL.—During the period beginning on the date of enactment of this section and ending on September 30, 2021, and to the extent the cost of such elimination in fees is offset by appropriations, with respect to each project or loan guaranteed by the Administrator pursuant to title V of the Small Business Investment Act of 1958 (15 U.S.C. 695 et seq.) for which an application is approved or pending approval on or after the date of enactment of this section—

(A) the Administrator shall, in lieu of the fee otherwise applicable under section 503(d)(2) of the Small Business Investment Act of 1958 (15 U.S.C. 697(d)(2)), collect no fee; and

(B) a development company shall, in lieu of the processing fee described under section 120.971(a)(1) of title 13, Code of Federal Regulations (relating to fees paid by borrowers), or any successor thereto, collect no fee.

(2) REIMBURSEMENT FOR WAIVED FEES.—

(A) IN GENERAL.—To the extent that the cost of such payments is offset by appropriations, the Administrator shall reimburse each development company that does not collect a processing fee pursuant to paragraph (1)(B).

(B) AMOUNT.—The payment to a development company under subparagraph (A) shall be in an amount equal to 1.5 percent of the net debenture proceeds for which the development company does not collect a processing fee pursuant to paragraph (1)(B).

SEC. 190013. GUARANTEE AMOUNTS.

(a) Purpose.—The purpose of this section is to increase loan guarantee amounts in order to mitigate risk for lenders and keep credit flowing, including an emphasis on underserved borrowers.

(b) 7(A) Loan Guarantees.—

(1) IN GENERAL.—Section 7(a)(2)(A) of the Small Business Act (15 U.S.C. 636(a)(2)(A)) is amended by striking "), such participation by the Administration shall be equal to" and all that follows through the period at the end and inserting "or the Community Advantage Pilot Program of the Administration), such participation by the Administration shall be equal to 90 percent of the balance of the financing outstanding at the time of disbursement of the loan.".

(2) TERMINATION.—Effective September 30, 2021, section 7(a)(2)(A) of the Small Business Act (15 U.S.C. 636(a)(2)(A)), as amended by paragraph (1), is amended to read as follows:

"(A) IN GENERAL.—Except as provided in subparagraphs (B), (D), and (E), in an agreement to participate in a loan on a deferred basis under this subsection (including a loan made under the Preferred Lenders Program), such participation by the Administration shall be equal to—

"(i) 75 percent of the balance of the financing outstanding at the time of disbursement of the loan, if such balance exceeds $150,000; or

"(ii) 85 percent of the balance of the financing outstanding at the time of disbursement of the loan, if such balance is less than or equal to $150,000.".

(c) Express Loan Guarantee Amounts And Loan Size Increases.—

(1) TEMPORARY MODIFICATION.—Section 7(a)(31) of the Small Business Act (15 U.S.C. 636(a)(31)) is amended—

(A) in subparagraph (A)(iv), by striking "with a guaranty rate of not more than 50 percent." and inserting the following: with a guarantee rate—

"(I) for a loan in an amount less than or equal to $350,000, of not more than 90 percent; and

"(II) for a loan in an amount greater than $350,000, of not more than 75 percent."; and

(B) in subparagraph (D), by striking "$350,000" and inserting "$1,000,000".

(2) INCREASE IN AVAILABILITY.—Effective September 30, 2021, section 7(a)(31) of the Small Business Act (15 U.S.C. 636(a)(31)), as amended by paragraph (1), is amended—

(A) in subparagraph (A)(iv), by striking "guarantee rate" and all that follows through the period at the end and inserting "guarantee rate of not more than 50 percent."; and

(B) in subparagraph (D), by striking "$1,000,000" and inserting "$500,000".

SEC. 190014. MAXIMUM LOAN AMOUNT AND PROGRAM LEVELS FOR 7(a) LOANS.

(a) Purpose.—The purpose of this section is to temporarily increase the maximum loan size in order to expand the reach of this long-term capital.

(b) Maximum Loan Amount.—During the period beginning on the date of enactment of this section and ending on September 30, 2021, with respect to any loan guaranteed under section 7(a) of the Small Business Act (15 U.S.C. 636(a)) for which an application is approved or pending approval on or after the date of enactment of this section, the maximum loan amount shall be $10,000,000.

(c) Program Levels.—During each of fiscal years 2020 and 2021, commitments for general business loans authorized under section 7(a) of the Small Business Act (15 U.S.C. 636(a)) shall not exceed $75,000,000,000.

(d) Collateral Requirements.—During the period beginning on the date of enactment of this section and ending September 30, 2021, with respect to each loan guaranteed under section 7(a) of the Small Business Act (15 U.S.C. 636(a))—

(1) no collateral shall be required on loans of $100,000 and less made under this section; and

(2) the Administration shall establish appropriate collateral standards for

loans over $100,000 made under this section except that when a loan over $350,000 is not fully secured by business assets, the Administration shall not require that loan guarantors as described in subparagraph (3) pledge personally owned assets including personal residences and other personally owned real estate as additional collateral on the loan.

(e) Personal Guarantee.—During the period beginning on the date of enactment of this section and ending September 30, 2021, with respect to each loan guaranteed under section 7(a) of the Small Business Act (15 U.S.C. 636(a)), no personal guarantee shall be required on loans to cooperatives.

SEC. 190015. MAXIMUM LOAN AMOUNT FOR 504 LOANS.

(a) Purpose.—The purpose of this section is to make refinancing of fixed assets more flexible for small business concerns seeking immediate financing and relief from the COVID–19 crisis.

(b) Temporary Increase.—During the period beginning on the date of enactment of this section and ending on September 30, 2021, with respect to each project or loan guaranteed by the Administrator pursuant to title V of the Small Business Investment Act of 1958 (15 U.S.C. 695 et seq.) for which an application is approved or pending approval on or after the date of enactment of this section, the maximum portion of a loan that is backed by the CDC shall be $10,000,000.

(c) Permanent Increase For Small Manufacturers.—Effective on October 1, 2021, section 502(2)(A)(iii) of the Small Business Investment Act of 1958 (15 U.S.C. 696(2)(A)(iii)) is amended by striking "$5,500,000" and inserting "$10,000,000".

(d) Refinancing Not Involving Expansions.—

(1) IN GENERAL.—Section 502(7) of the Small Business Investment Act of 1958 (15 U.S.C. 696(7)) is amended by adding at the end the following:

"(C) REFINANCING NOT INVOLVING EXPANSIONS.—

"(i) DEFINITIONS.—In this subparagraph—

"(I) the term 'borrower' means a small business concern that submits an application to a development company for financing under this subparagraph;

"(II) the term 'eligible fixed asset' means tangible property relating to which the Administrator may provide financing under this section; and

"(III) the term 'qualified debt' means indebtedness—

"(aa) that—

"(AA) was incurred not less than 2 years before the date of the application for assistance under this subparagraph;

"(BB) is a commercial loan;

"(CC) the proceeds of which were used to acquire an eligible fixed asset;

"(DD) was incurred for the benefit of the small business concern; and

"(EE) is collateralized by eligible fixed assets; and

"(bb) for which the borrower has been current on all payments for not less than 1 year before the date of the application.

"(ii) AUTHORITY.—A project that does not involve the expansion of a small business concern may include the refinancing of qualified debt if—

"(I) the amount of the financing is not more than 90 percent of the value of the collateral for the financing, except that, if the appraised value of the eligible fixed assets serving as collateral for the financing is less than the amount equal to 125 percent of the amount of the financing, the borrower may provide additional cash or other collateral to eliminate any deficiency;

"(II) the borrower has been in operation for all of the 2-year period ending on the date of the loan;

"(III) the financing will provide a substantial benefit to the borrower when prepayment penalties, financing fees, and other financing costs are accounted for; and

"(IV) for a financing for which the Administrator determines there will be an additional cost attributable to the refinancing of the qualified debt, the borrower agrees to pay a fee in an amount equal to the anticipated additional cost.

"(iii) FINANCING FOR BUSINESS EXPENSES.—

"(I) FINANCING FOR BUSINESS EXPENSES.—The Administrator may provide financing to a borrower that receives financing that includes a refinancing of qualified debt under clause (ii), in addition to the refinancing under clause (ii), to be used solely for the payment of business expenses.

"(II) APPLICATION FOR FINANCING.—An application for financing under subclause (I) shall include—

"(aa) a specific description of the expenses for which the additional financing is requested; and

"(bb) an itemization of the amount of each expense.

"(III) CONDITION ON ADDITIONAL FINANCING.—A borrower may not use any part of the financing under this clause for non-business purposes.

"(iv) LOANS BASED ON JOBS.—

"(I) JOB CREATION AND RETENTION GOALS.—

"(aa) IN GENERAL.—The Administrator may provide financing under this subparagraph for a borrower that meets the job creation goals under subsection (d) or (e) of section 501.

"(bb) ALTERNATE JOB RETENTION GOAL.—The Administrator may provide financing under this subparagraph to a borrower that does not meet the goals described in item (aa) in an amount that is not more than the product obtained by multiplying the number of employees of the borrower by $75,000.

"(II) NUMBER OF EMPLOYEES.—For purposes of subclause (I), the number of employees of a borrower is equal to the sum of—

"(aa) the number of full-time employees of the borrower on the date on which the borrower applies for a loan under this subparagraph; and

"(bb) the product obtained by multiplying—

"(AA) the number of part-time employees of the borrower on the date on which the borrower applies for a loan under this subparagraph; by

"(BB) the quotient obtained by dividing the average number of hours each part time employee of the borrower works each week by 40.

"(v) NONDELEGATION.—Notwithstanding section 508(e), the Administrator may not permit a premier certified lender to approve or disapprove an application for assistance under this subparagraph.

"(vi) TOTAL AMOUNT OF LOANS.—The Administrator may provide not more than a total of $7,500,000,000 of financing under this subparagraph for each fiscal year.".

(2) CONFORMING AMENDMENT.—Section 521 of division E of the Consolidated Appropriations Act, 2016 (15 U.S.C. 696 note) is repealed.

(e) 504 Debt Refinance With Expansion.—Section 502(7)(B) of the Small Business Investment Act of 1948 (15 U.S.C. 696(7)(B)) is amended, in the matter preceding clause (i), by striking "50" and inserting "100".

"(c) Express Program.—An accredited lender certified company, may, with respect to a covered loan, take any of the following actions with respect to the loan:

"(1) Any action described in any of subparagraphs (A) through (J) of subsection (b)(1).

"(2) If the borrower is not delinquent with respect to the loan payments—

"(A) permit the loan to subordinate to a new third party lender loan for the purposes of refinancing that third party lender loan, except that no refinanced amount with respect to the loan may be increased in order to provide cash to the borrower;

"(B) permit a new party to assume responsibility for the loan if the original borrower remains on the loan as the original guarantor;

"(C) obtain force placed insurance coverage for the loan if the borrower has allowed insurance coverage with respect to the loan to lapse; and

"(D) endorse an insurance check with respect to the property that is financed by the loan in an amount that is less than $100,000.

"(3) Certify that the loan is compliant with the appraisal requirements and environmental policies and procedures applicable to the loan under Standard Operating Procedure 50 10 5(K) of the Administration, effective April 1, 2019, or any successor Standard Operating Procedure.

"(d) Definitions.—In this section—

"(1) the term 'accredited lender certified company' means a certified development company that meets the requirements under section 507(b), including a certified development company that the Administration has designated as an accredited lender under such section 507(b); and

"(2) the term 'covered loan'—

"(A) means a loan made under subsection (a) in an amount that is not more than $500,000; and

"(B) does not include a loan made to a borrower that is a franchise that, or is in an industry that, has a high rate of default, as annually determined by the

Administrator.".

SEC. 190016. ECONOMIC INJURY DISASTER LOANS IMPROVEMENTS.

(a) Approval And Ability To Repay For Certain Loans.—With respect to a loan made under section 7(b)(2) of the Small Business Act (15 U.S.C. 636(b)(2)) in response to the COVID–19 pandemic that does not exceed $350,000, the Administrator—

(1) may approve an applicant based solely on the credit score of the applicant and shall not require an applicant to submit a tax return or a tax return transcript for such approval; or

(2) use alternative appropriate methods to determine an applicant's ability to repay.

(b) Emergencies Involving Federal Primary Responsibility Qualifying For Small Business Administration Assistance.—Section 7(b)(2) of the Small Business Act (15 U.S.C. 636(b)(2)) is amended—

(1) in subparagraph (A), by striking "or" at the end;

(2) in subparagraph (B), by striking "or" at the end;

(3) in subparagraph (C), by striking "or" at the end;

(4) by redesignating subparagraph (D) as subparagraph (E);

(5) by inserting after subparagraph (C) the following:

"(D) an emergency involving Federal primary responsibility determined to exist by the President under the section 501(b) of the Robert T. Stafford Disaster Relief and Emergency Assistance Act (42 U.S.C. 5191(b)); or"; and

(6) in subparagraph (E), as so redesignated—

(A) by striking "or (C)" and inserting "(C), or (D)";

(B) by striking "disaster declaration" each place it appears and inserting "disaster or emergency declaration";

(C) by striking "disaster has occurred" and inserting "disaster or emergency has occurred";

(D) by striking "such disaster" and inserting "such disaster or emergency"; and

(E) by striking "disaster stricken" and inserting "disaster- or emergency-stricken"; and

(7) in the flush matter following subparagraph (E) (as so redesignated), by striking the period at the end and inserting the following: ": Provided further, that for purposes of subparagraph (D), the Administrator shall deem that such an emergency affects each State or subdivision thereof (including counties), and that each State or subdivision has sufficient economic damage to small business concerns to qualify for assistance under this paragraph and the Administrator shall accept applications for such assistance immediately.".

(c) Credit Elsewhere; No Personal Guarantee.—The flush matter following subparagraph (E) (as so redesignated) of section 7(b)(2) of the Small Business Act (15 U.S.C. 636(b)(2)) is amended by striking "That no loan or guarantee" and all that follows through "credit elsewhere" and inserting the following:

"With respect to a loan made under this paragraph to a cooperative, the Administrator shall not require a personal guarantee for such a loan".

(d) Eligibility Of Cooperatives.—Section 7(b)(2) of the Small Business Act (15 U.S.C. 636(b)(2)) is amended by striking "small agricultural cooperative" and inserting "small cooperative".

(e) Additional Amounts.—

(1) IN GENERAL.—The Administrator of the Small Business Administration may increase by 20 percent the amount received by an eligible small business concern under section 7(b)(2) of the Small Business Act (15 U.S.C. 636(b)(2)) to cover continuity-of-operations and risk mitigation improvements, including telework capability, offsite record keeping, redundancy, the administrative costs of establishing paid sick leave, and presenteeism prevention.

(2) DEFINITION.—In this section, the term "eligible small business concern" means a small business concern that—

(A) meets the applicable size standard established under section 3 of the Small Business Act (15 U.S.C. 632); and

(B) is receiving assistance under section 7(b)(2) of the Small Business Act (15 U.S.C. 636(b)(2)) related to COVID–19.

(f) Authorization Of Appropriations.—There is authorized to be appropriated to the Administrator to carry out the loan program under section 7(b)(2) of the Small Business Act (15 U.S.C. 636(b)(2))—

(1) $177,000,000 for administration costs; and

(2) $25,000,000,000 to provide loans or other assistance.

SEC. 190017. RECOVERY ASSISTANCE FOR MICROBUSINESSES.

(a) Purpose.—The purpose of this section is to allow lenders to deploy more capital, give borrowers more time to repay, increase rural lending, and cut technical assistance red tape.

(b) Loans To Intermediaries.—

(1) IN GENERAL.—Section 7(m) of the Small Business Act (15 U.S.C. 636(m)) is amended—

(A) in paragraph (3)(C)—

(i) by striking "and $6,000,000" and inserting "$10,000,000, in the aggregate,"; and

(ii) by inserting before the period at the end the following: ", and $4,500,000 in any of those remaining years";

(B) in paragraph (4)—

(i) in subparagraph (A), by striking "subparagraph (C)" each place that term appears and inserting "subparagraphs (C) and (G)";

(ii) in subparagraph (C), by amending clause (i) to read as follows:

"(i) IN GENERAL.—In addition to grants made under subparagraph (A) or (G), each intermediary shall be eligible to receive a grant equal to 5 percent of the total outstanding balance of loans made to the intermediary under this subsection if—

"(I) the intermediary provides not less than 25 percent of its loans to small business concerns located in or owned by one or more residents of an economically distressed area; or

"(II) the intermediary has a portfolio of loans made under this subsection—

"(aa) that averages not more than $10,000 during the period of the intermediary's participation in the program; or

"(bb) of which not less than 25 percent is serving rural areas during the period of the intermediary's participation in the program."; and

(iii) by adding at the end the following:

"(G) GRANT AMOUNTS BASED ON APPROPRIATIONS.—In any fiscal year in which the amount appropriated to make grants under subparagraph (A) is sufficient to provide to each intermediary that receives a loan under paragraph (1)(B)(i) a grant of not less than 25 percent of the total outstanding balance of loans made to the intermediary under this subsection, the Administration shall make a grant under subparagraph (A) to each intermediary of not less than 25 percent and not more than 30 percent of that total outstanding balance for the intermediary."; and

(C) by striking paragraph (7) and inserting the following:

"(7) PROGRAM FUNDING FOR MICROLOANS.—Under the program authorized by this subsection, the Administration may fund, on a competitive basis, not more than 300 intermediaries.".

(2) ADJUSTMENT TO MICROLOAN LIMITS.—Effective on October 1, 2021, section 7(m)(3)(C) of the Small Business Act (15 U.S.C. 636(m)(3)(C)), as amended by paragraph (1)(A), is further amended—

(A) by striking "$10,000,000" and by inserting "$7,000,000" and

(B) by striking "$4,500,000" and inserting "$3,000,000".

(c) Temporary Waiver Of Technical Assistance Grants Matching Requirements And Flexibility On Pre- And Post-Loan Assistance.—During the period beginning on the date of enactment of this section and ending on September 30, 2021, the Administration shall waive—

(1) the requirement to contribute non-Federal funds under section 7(m)(4)(B) of the Small Business Act (15 U.S.C. 636(m)(4)(B)); and

(2) the limitation on amounts allowed to be expended to provide information and technical assistance under clause (i) of section 7(m)(4)(E) of the Small Business Act (15 U.S.C. 636(m)(4)(E)) and entering into third party contracts to provide technical assistance under clause (ii) of such section 7(m)(4)(E).

(d) Temporary Duration Of Loans To Borrowers.—

(1) IN GENERAL.—During the period beginning on the date of enactment of this section and ending on September 30, 2021, the duration of a loan made by an eligible intermediary under section 7(m) of the Small Business Act (15 U.S.C. 636(m))—

(A) to an existing borrower may be extended to not more than 8 years; and

(B) to a new borrower may be not more than 8 years.

(2) REVERSION.—On and after October 1, 2021, the duration of a loan

made by an eligible intermediary to a borrower under section 7(m) of the Small Business Act (15 U.S.C. 636(m)) shall be 7 years or such other amount established by the Administrator.

(e) Program Levels.—Section 20 of the Small Business Act (15 U.S.C. 631 note) is amended by adding at the end the following:

"(h) Microloan Program.—For each of fiscal years 2021 through 2025, the Administration is authorized to make—

"(1) $80,000,000 in technical assistance grants, as provided in section 7(m); and

"(2) $110,000,000 in direct loans, as provided in section 7(m).".

SEC. 190018. ADDITIONAL LEVERAGE FOR SMALL BUSINESSES AFFECTED BY THE COVID–19 OUTBREAK.

(a) In General.—Section 303(b)(2) of the Small Business Investment Act of 1958 (15 U.S.C. 683(b)(2)) is amended by adding at the end the following:

"(E) ADDITIONAL LEVERAGE BASE ON INVESTMENT.—

"(i) EXCLUSION OF AMOUNTS.—In calculating the outstanding leverage of a company for purposes of subparagraph (A) or (B), the Administrator shall exclude the amount of leverage outstanding to covered small businesses, not to exceed an amount equal to $100,000,000, if the amount excluded is used exclusively for working capital purposes.

"(ii) COVERED SMALL BUSINESS DEFINED.—In this subparagraph, the term 'covered small business' means a small business concern is located in a State or territory of the United States with at least one confirmed or presumed positive case of COVID–19.".

(b) Application.—Notwithstanding any other provision of law, for purposes of additional leverage requested under subparagraph (E) of section 303(b)(2) of the Small Business Investment Act of 1958, as added by subsection (a), the Administrator shall approve or deny such request within 14 calendar days of receipt by the Administrator of the request.

SEC. 190019. STATE TRADE EXPANSION PROGRAM.

(a) Reimbursement.—The Administrator of the Small Business Administration shall reimburse any recipient of assistance under section 22(l) of the Small Business Act (15 U.S.C. 649(l)) for financial losses relating to a foreign trade mission or a trade show exhibition that was cancelled solely due to a public health emergency declared due to COVID–19.

(b) Budget Plan Revisions.—Section 22(l)(3) of the Small Business Act (15 U.S.C. 649(l)(3)) is amended—

(1) in subparagraph (D)(i), by inserting ", including a budget plan for use of funds awarded under this subsection" before the period at the end; and

(2) by adding at the end the following new subparagraph:

"(E) BUDGET PLAN REVISIONS.—

"(i) IN GENERAL.—A State receiving a grant under this subsection may revise the budget plan of the State submitted under subparagraph (D) after the disbursal of grant funds if—

"(I) the revision complies with allowable uses of grant funds under this subsection; and

"(II) such State submits notification of the revision to the Associate Administrator.

"(ii) EXCEPTION.—If a revision under clause (i) reallocates 10 percent or more of the amounts described in the budget plan of the State submitted under subparagraph (D), the State may not implement the revised budget plan without the approval of the Associate Administrator, unless the Associate Administrator fails to approve or deny the revised plan within 10 days after receipt of such revised plan.".

SEC. 190020. EMERGENCY RULEMAKING AUTHORITY.

Not later than 15 days after the date of enactment of this Act, the Administrator shall issue regulations to carry out this division and the amendments made by this division without regard to the notice requirements under section 553(b) of title 5, United States Code.

DIVISION T—REVENUE PROVISIONS

SEC. 1. SHORT TITLE; TABLE OF CONTENTS.

(a) Short Title.—This division may be cited as the "Emergency Pension Plan Relief Act of 2020".

(b) Table Of Contents.—The table of contents of this division is as follows:

TITLE I—HEALTH-RELATED TAX RELIEF

SEC. 101. PAYROLL CREDIT FOR COVID–19 CHARITY CARE PROVIDED BY HOSPITALS.

(a) In General.—In the case of an employer which is an eligible hospital, there shall be allowed as a credit against the tax imposed by section 3111(a) of the Internal Revenue Code of 1986 for each calendar quarter an amount equal to 90 percent of the COVID-related charity care furnished by such hospital during such calendar quarter.

(b) Limitations And Refundability.—

(1) CREDIT LIMITED TO CERTAIN EMPLOYMENT TAXES.—The credit allowed by subsection (a) with respect to any calendar quarter shall not exceed the tax imposed by section 3111(a) of such Code for such calendar quarter (reduced by any credits allowed under subsection (e) or (f) of section 3111 of such Code, or under section 7001 or 7003 of the Families First Coronavirus Response Act, for such quarter) on the wages paid with respect

to the employment of all employees of the employer.

(2) REFUNDABILITY OF EXCESS CREDIT.—

(A) IN GENERAL.—If the amount of the credit under subsection (a) exceeds the limitation of paragraph (1) for any calendar quarter, such excess shall be treated as an overpayment that shall be refunded under sections 6402(a) and 6413(b) of such Code.

(B) TREATMENT OF PAYMENTS.—For purposes of section 1324 of title 31, United States Code, any amounts due to an employer under this paragraph shall be treated in the same manner as a refund due from a credit provision referred to in subsection (b)(2) of such section.

(c) Eligible Hospital.—For purposes of this section, the term "eligible hospital" means a subsection (d) hospital as defined in section 1886(d)(1)(B) of the Social Security Act (42 U.S.C. 1395ww(d)(1)(B)) or a critical access hospital (as defined in section 1861(mm)(1) of such Act (42 U.S.C. 1395x(mm)(1)).

(d) COVID-Related Charity Care.—For purposes of this section—

(1) IN GENERAL.—The term "COVID-related charity care" means, with respect to any eligible hospital, so much of the specified charity care furnished by such hospital as relates to items and services furnished in the United States for the treatment of COVID–19 or a related condition.

(2) SPECIFIED CHARITY CARE.—The term "specified charity care" means, with respect to an eligible hospital, the cost of charity care of such hospital as defined for purposes of the Medicare Cost Report Worksheet S–10.

(e) Special Rules.—

(1) DENIAL OF DOUBLE BENEFIT.—For purposes of chapter 1 of the Internal Revenue Code of 1986, any deduction otherwise allowable under such chapter for any COVID-related charity care shall be reduced by the amount of the credit allowed under this section with respect to such care.

(2) DOCUMENTATION.—No credit shall be allowed under this section unless the employer maintains such documentation as the Secretary of the Treasury (or the Secretary's delegate) may prescribe to establish such employer's eligibility for the credit allowed under this section (and the amount thereof).

(3) ELECTION NOT TO HAVE SECTION APPLY.—This section shall not apply with respect to any employer for any calendar quarter if such employer elects (at such time and in such manner as the Secretary of the Treasury (or the Secretary's delegate) may prescribe) not to have this section apply.

(4) CERTAIN TERMS.—Any term used in this section which is also used in chapter 21 of such Code shall have the same meaning as when used in such chapter.

(f) Regulations.—The Secretary of the Treasury (or the Secretary's delegate) shall prescribe such regulations or other guidance as may be necessary to carry out the purposes of this section, including—

(1) regulations or other guidance (prescribed after consultation with the Secretary of Health and Human Services) which identify specific items and

services which are considered for purposes of subsection (d)(1) to be for the treatment of COVID–19 or a related condition;

(2) regulations or other guidance to effectuate the purposes of the limitations under this section;

(3) regulations or other guidance to minimize compliance and record-keeping burdens under this section;

(4) regulations or other guidance providing for a waiver of penalties for the failure to deposit taxes imposed under section 3111(a) of such Code in anticipation of the allowance of the credit allowed under this section;

(5) regulations or other guidance for recapturing the benefit of credits determined under this section in cases where there is a subsequent adjustment to the credit determined under subsection (a); and

(6) regulations or other guidance regarding the treatment of certified professional employer organizations, as described in section 3511 of such Code.

(g) Application Of Section.—

(1) IN GENERAL.—This section shall apply only to COVID-related charity care which is furnished during the period beginning on February 1, 2020, and ending on December 31, 2020.

(2) TREATMENT OF CERTAIN CARE FURNISHED BEFORE DATE OF ENACTMENT.—For purposes of this section, any COVID-related charity care which is furnished after January 31, 2020, and before the calendar quarter which includes the date of the enactment of this Act shall be treated as having been furnished in such calendar quarter.

(h) Transfers To Federal Old-Age And Survivors Insurance Trust Fund.—There are hereby appropriated to the Federal Old-Age and Survivors Insurance Trust Fund and the Federal Disability Insurance Trust Fund established under section 201 of the Social Security Act (42 U.S.C. 401) amounts equal to the reduction in revenues to the Treasury by reason of this section (without regard to this subsection). Amounts appropriated by the preceding sentence shall be transferred from the general fund at such times and in such manner as to replicate to the extent possible the transfers which would have occurred to such Trust Fund had this section not been enacted.

(i) Coordination With DSH Payments.—Section 1886(r) of the Social Security Act (42 U.S.C. 1395ww(r)) is amended—

(1) n paragraph (2), by inserting "subject to paragraph (4)," before "for fiscal year 2014"; and

(2) by adding at the end the following new paragraph:

"(4) SPECIAL RULE FOR COVID-RELATED CHARITY CARE.—The Secretary shall, beginning in the first fiscal year in which the factor described in paragraph (2)(C) is calculated based on a cost reporting period that includes any portion of calendar year 2020, exclude the amount of the payroll credit for COVID–19 charity care allowed under section 101(a) of the Emergency Pension Plan Relief Act of 2020 provided to a subsection (d) hospital, from the calculation of such factor.".

SEC. 102. PAYROLL CREDIT FOR COVID–19 HOSPITAL FACILITY EXPENDITURES.

(a) In General.—In the case of an employer which is an eligible hospital, there shall be allowed as a credit against the tax imposed by section 3111(a) of the Internal Revenue Code of 1986 for each calendar quarter an amount equal to 90 percent of the COVID–19 hospital facility expenditures paid or incurred by such hospital during such calendar quarter.

(b) Limitations And Refundability.—

(1) CREDIT LIMITED TO CERTAIN EMPLOYMENT TAXES.—The credit allowed by subsection (a) with respect to any calendar quarter shall not exceed the tax imposed by section 3111(a) of such Code for such calendar quarter (reduced by any credits allowed under subsection (e) or (f) of section 3111 of such Code, under section 7001 or 7003 of the Families First Coronavirus Response Act, or under the preceding section of this Act, for such quarter) on the wages paid with respect to the employment of all employees of the employer.

(2) REFUNDABILITY OF EXCESS CREDIT.—

(A) IN GENERAL.—If the amount of the credit under subsection (a) exceeds the limitation of paragraph (1) for any calendar quarter, such excess shall be treated as an overpayment that shall be refunded under sections 6402(a) and 6413(b) of such Code.

(B) TREATMENT OF PAYMENTS.—For purposes of section 1324 of title 31, United States Code, any amounts due to an employer under this paragraph shall be treated in the same manner as a refund due from a credit provision referred to in subsection (b)(2) of such section.

(c) Eligible Hospital.—For purposes of this section, the term "eligible hospital" means a subsection (d) hospital as defined in section 1886(d)(1)(B) of the Social Security Act (42 U.S.C. 1395ww(d)(1)(B)) or a critical access hospital (as defined in section 1861(mm)(1) of such Act (42 U.S.C. 1395x(mm)(1))).

(d) COVID–19 Hospital Facility Expenditures.—For purposes of this section—

(1) IN GENERAL.—The term "COVID–19 hospital facility expenditures" means amounts paid or incurred by an eligible hospital for—

(A) the purchase or construction of a temporary structure in the United States for specified COVID-related purposes,

(B) the lease of any structure in the United States for specified COVID-related purposes if the term of such lease is not greater than 2 years,

(C) the retrofitting of any existing permanent structure in the United States for specified COVID-related purposes, and

(D) any property for use in a structure described in subparagraph (A), (B), or (C) for specified COVID-related purposes if such property is of a character which is subject to the allowance for depreciation provided in section 167 of

the Internal Revenue Code of 1986.
(2) SPECIFIED COVID-RELATED PURPOSES.—The term "specified COVID-related purposes" means the diagnosis, prevention, or treatment of COVID–19 or a related condition.
(3) TEMPORARY STRUCTURE.—The term "temporary structure" means a tent or such other structure which by its design or nature is not suitable to serve as a permanent structure.
(4) COORDINATION WITH GOVERNMENT GRANTS.—The COVID–19 hospital facility expenditures taken into account under this section by any eligible hospital shall be reduced by any amounts provided by any Federal, State, or local government for purposes of making or reimbursing such expenditures.
(e) Special Rules.—
(1) DENIAL OF DOUBLE BENEFIT.—For purposes of the Internal Revenue Code of 1986—
(A) the basis of any property with respect to which a credit is allowed under this section shall be reduced by the amount of such credit, and
(B) such reduction shall be taken into account before determining the amount of any deduction, or allowance for depreciation or amortization, with respect to such property for purposes of such Code.
(2) RECAPTURE OF GAIN.—If an eligible hospital disposes of any property with respect to which a credit was allowed under this section and any gain is determined on such disposition under section 1001 of such Code, the tax imposed under chapter 1 of such Code on such hospital shall be increased by the amount of such gain. The preceding sentence shall apply without regard to whether such eligible hospital is otherwise exempt from, or not subject to, the taxes otherwise imposed under such chapter.
(3) DOCUMENTATION.—No credit shall be allowed under this section unless the employer maintains such documentation as the Secretary of the Treasury (or the Secretary's delegate) may prescribe to establish such employer's eligibility for the credit allowed under this section (and the amount thereof).
(4) ELECTION NOT TO HAVE SECTION APPLY.—This section shall not apply with respect to any employer for any calendar quarter if such employer elects (at such time and in such manner as the Secretary of the Treasury (or the Secretary's delegate) may prescribe) not to have this section apply.
(5) CERTAIN TERMS.—Any term used in this section which is also used in chapter 21 of such Code shall have the same meaning as when used in such chapter.
(f) Regulations.—The Secretary of the Treasury (or the Secretary's delegate) shall prescribe such regulations or other guidance as may be necessary to carry out the purposes of this section, including—
(1) regulations or other guidance to effectuate the purposes of the limitations under this section,

(2) regulations or other guidance to minimize compliance and record-keeping burdens under this section,

(3) regulations or other guidance providing for a waiver of penalties for the failure to deposit taxes imposed under section 3111(a) in anticipation of the allowance of the credit allowed under this section,

(4) regulations or other guidance for recapturing the benefit of credits determined under this section in cases where there is a subsequent adjustment to the credit determined under subsection (a),

(5) regulations or other guidance (prescribed after consultation with the Secretary of Health and Human Services) which identify specific items and services which are considered for purposes of subsection (d)(2) to be for specified COVID-related purposes, and

(6) regulations or other guidance regarding the treatment of certified professional employer organizations, as described in section 3511 of such Code.

(g) Application Of Section.—

(1) IN GENERAL.—This section shall apply only to COVID–19 hospital facility expenditures which are paid or incurred during the period beginning on February 1, 2020, and ending on December 31, 2020.

(2) TREATMENT OF CERTAIN EXPENDITURES MADE BEFORE DATE OF ENACTMENT.—For purposes of this section, any COVID–19 hospital facility expenditures which are paid or incurred after January 31, 2020, and before the calendar quarter which includes the date of the enactment of this Act shall be treated as having been furnished in such calendar quarter.

(h) Transfers To Federal Old-Age And Survivors Insurance Trust Fund.—There are hereby appropriated to the Federal Old-Age and Survivors Insurance Trust Fund and the Federal Disability Insurance Trust Fund established under section 201 of the Social Security Act (42 U.S.C. 401) amounts equal to the reduction in revenues to the Treasury by reason of this section (without regard to this subsection). Amounts appropriated by the preceding sentence shall be transferred from the general fund at such times and in such manner as to replicate to the extent possible the transfers which would have occurred to such Trust Fund had this section not been enacted.

SEC. 103. RESTORATION OF LIMITATIONS ON RECONCILIATION OF TAX CREDITS FOR COVERAGE UNDER A QUALIFIED HEALTH PLAN WITH ADVANCE PAYMENTS OF SUCH CREDIT.

(a) In General.—Section 36B(f)(2)(B)(i) of the Internal Revenue Code of 1986 is amended to read as follows:

"(i) IN GENERAL.—In the case of a taxpayer whose household income is less than 500 percent of the poverty line for the size of the family involved for the taxable year, the amount of the increase under subparagraph (A) shall in no event exceed the applicable dollar amount determined in accordance with the following table (one-half of such amount in the case of a taxpayer whose tax is determined under section 1(c) for the taxable year):

"If the household income (expressed as a percent of poverty line) is:	The applicable dollar amount is:
Less than 200%	$600
At least 200% but less than 250%	$1,000
At least 250% but less than 300%	$1,500
At least 300% but less than 350%	$2,000
At least 350% but less than 400%	$2,500
At least 400% but less than 450%	$3,000
At least 450% but less than 500%	$3,500.".

(b) Effective Date.—The amendments made by this section shall apply to taxable years beginning after December 31, 2019.

SEC. 104. IMPROVING AFFORDABILITY BY REDUCING PREMIUM COSTS FOR CONSUMERS.

(a) In General.—Section 36B(b)(3)(A) of the Internal Revenue Code of 1986 is amended to read as follows:

"(A) APPLICABLE PERCENTAGE.—The applicable percentage for any taxable year shall be the percentage such that the applicable percentage for any taxpayer whose household income is within an income tier specified in the following table shall increase, on a sliding scale in a linear manner, from the initial premium percentage to the final premium percentage specified in such table for such income tier:

"In the case of household income (expressed as a percent of poverty line) within the following income tier:	The initial premiumpercentage is—	The final premium percentage is—
Over 100.0 percent up to 150.0 percent	0.0	0.0
150.0 percent up to 200.0 percent	0.0	3.0
200.0 percent up to 250.0 percent	3.0	4.0
250.0 percent up to 300.0 percent	4.0	6.0
300.0 percent up to 400.0 percent	6.0	8.5
400.0 percent and higher	8.5	8.5".

(b) Conforming Amendment.—Section 36B(c)(1)(A) of the Internal Revenue Code of 1986 is amended by striking "but does not exceed 400 percent".

(c) Effective Date.—The amendments made by this section shall apply to taxable years beginning after December 31, 2020.

TITLE II—ECONOMIC STIMULUS

Subtitle A—Economic Assistance Payments

SEC. 201. 2020 ECONOMIC ASSISTANCE PAYMENTS TO INDIVIDUALS.

(a) In General.—Subchapter B of chapter 65 of the Internal Revenue Code of 1986 is amended by adding at the end the following new section:

"SEC. 6431. 2020 ECONOMIC ASSISTANCE PAYMENTS TO INDIVIDUALS.

"(a) In General.—In the case of an eligible individual, there shall be allowed as a credit against the tax imposed by subtitle A for the first taxable year beginning in 2020 an amount equal to the economic assistance amount determined for such taxable year.

"(b) Economic Assistance Amount.—For purposes of this section, the term 'economic assistance amount' means, with respect to any taxpayer for any taxable year, the sum of—

"(1) $1,500 ($3,000 in the case of a joint return), plus

"(2) $1,500 multiplied by the number of qualifying children (within the meaning of section 24(c)) of the taxpayer for such taxable year (not in excess of 3 such children).

"(c) Phaseout Based On Adjusted Gross Income.—

"(1) IN GENERAL.—The amount of the credit allowed by subsection (a) (determined without regard to this subsection and subsection (f)) shall be reduced (but not below zero) by the amount which bears the same ratio to such amount as—

"(A) the excess (if any) of the adjusted gross income for the taxpayer's first taxable year beginning in 2020 over the applicable phaseout amount, bears to

"(B) 50 percent of the applicable phaseout amount.

"(2) APPLICABLE PHASEOUT AMOUNT.—For purposes of this subsection, the term 'applicable phaseout amount' means—

"(A) $150,000 in the case of a joint return or a surviving spouse (as defined in section 2(a)),

"(B) $112,500 in the case of a head of household (as defined in section 2(b)), and

"(C) $75,000 in any other case.

"(3) ADJUSTED GROSS INCOME.—For purposes of this subsection (other than this paragraph), the term 'adjusted gross income' means adjusted gross income determined without regard to sections 911, 931, and 933.

"(d) Eligible Individual.—For purposes of this section, the term 'eligible individual' means any individual other than—

"(1) any nonresident alien individual,

"(2) any individual with respect to whom a deduction under section 151 is allowable to another taxpayer for a taxable year beginning in the calendar year in which the individual's taxable year begins, and

"(3) an estate or trust.

"(e) Special Rules.—

"(1) CREDIT TREATED AS REFUNDABLE.—The credit allowed by subsection (a) shall be treated as allowed by subpart C of part IV of subchapter A of chapter 1.

"(2) TREATMENT OF CREDIT AND ADVANCE PAYMENTS.—For purposes of section 1324 of title 31, United States Code, any credit under subsection (a) and any credit or refund under subsection (g) shall be treated in the same manner as a refund due from a credit provision referred to in subsection (b)(2) of such section.

"(3) IDENTIFICATION NUMBER REQUIREMENT.—An individual shall not be taken into account in determining the amount of the credit allowed under subsection (a) unless the taxpayer identification number of such individual is included on the return of tax for the taxable year.

"(f) Coordination With Advance Refunds Of Credit.—

"(1) REDUCTION OF REFUNDABLE CREDIT.—The amount of the credit which would (but for this paragraph) be allowable under subsection (a) shall be reduced (but not below zero) by the aggregate refunds and credits made or allowed to the taxpayer under subsection (g) and the aggregate payments to which the taxpayer (or a qualifying child (within the meaning of section 24(c)) of the taxpayer) is entitled under section 202 of the COVID-19 Tax Relief Act of 2020. Any failure to so reduce the credit shall be treated as arising out of a mathematical or clerical error and assessed according to section 6213(b)(1).

"(2) RECAPTURE OF PAYMENTS IN EXCESS OF REFUNDABLE CREDIT.—

"(A) IN GENERAL.—If the sum of the aggregate refunds and credits made or allowed to the taxpayer under subsection (g) and the aggregate payments to which the taxpayer (or a qualifying child (within the meaning of section 24(c)) of the taxpayer) is entitled under section 202 of the COVID-19 Tax Relief Act of 2020 exceeds the credit allowed under subsection (a) (determined without regard to paragraph (1)), the tax imposed under chapter 1 for the taxpayer's first taxable year beginning in 2020 shall be increased by the amount of such excess.

"(B) ELECTION TO SPREAD RECAPTURE OVER 3 YEARS.—In the case of a taxpayer who elects (at such time and in such manner as the Secretary may provide) the application of this subparagraph, subparagraph (A) shall not apply and the tax imposed under chapter 1 shall be increased by 1⁄3 of the excess described in subparagraph (A) in the taxpayer's first taxable year beginning in 2020 and in each of the 2 immediately following taxable years.

"(C) CERTAIN TAXPAYERS NOT SUBJECT TO RECAPTURE.—In the case of a taxpayer that is not required to file a return with respect to income taxes under subtitle A for the taxpayer's first taxable year beginning in 2020, subparagraph (A) shall not apply.

"(3) JOINT RETURNS.—In the case of a refund or credit made or allowed under subsection (g) with respect to a joint return, half of such refund or credit shall be treated as having been made or allowed to each individual filing such return.

"(g) Advance Refunds And Credits.—

"(1) IN GENERAL.—Each taxpayer who was an eligible individual for such taxpayer's first taxable year beginning in 2019 shall be treated as having made a payment against the tax imposed by chapter 1 for such first taxable year in an amount equal to the economic assistance amount (as defined subsection (b)) determined for the applicable prior taxable year.

"(2) APPLICABLE PRIOR TAXABLE YEAR.—For purposes of this subsection, the term 'applicable prior taxable year' means—

"(A) the taxpayer's first taxable year beginning in 2019, or

"(B) if information regarding such taxable year is not available to the Secretary (determined without regard to subsection (h)(1)), the taxpayer's first taxable year beginning in 2018.

"(3) TIMING OF PAYMENTS.—

"(A) IN GENERAL.—The Secretary shall, subject to the provisions of this title, refund or credit any overpayment attributable to paragraph (1) as rapidly as possible.

"(B) TERMINATION OF PAYMENT AUTHORITY.—No refund or credit shall be made or allowed under this subsection after December 31, 2020.

"(4) COORDINATION WITH PAYMENTS TO SOCIAL SECURITY ADMINISTRATION RECIPIENTS.—This subsection shall not apply with respect to any taxpayer entitled to a payment under section 202 of the COVID-19 Tax Relief Act of 2020.

"(5) NO INTEREST.—No interest shall be allowed on any overpayment attributable to this section.

"(6) INFORMATION PROVIDED TO TAXPAYERS.—As soon as practicable, the Secretary shall—

"(A) make best efforts to inform every taxpayer that amounts received pursuant to this subsection may be subject to recapture under subsection (f)(2), and

"(B) develop an Internet tool allowing taxpayers to determine the amount of such recapture using input from the taxpayer.

"(h) Regulations.—The Secretary shall prescribe such regulations or other guidance as may be necessary or appropriate to carry out the purposes of this section, including—

"(1) regulations or other guidance providing taxpayers with respect to whom information for neither taxable year described in subsection (g)(2) is available to the Secretary the opportunity to provide the Secretary information sufficient to allow the Secretary to determine the amount of the credit or refund for such taxpayer under subsection (g), and

"(2) regulations or other guidance providing for the proper treatment of joint returns and taxpayers with qualifying children if any individual taken into account under this section with respect to such joint return or by such taxpayer is an eligible individual (as defined in section 202(b) of the COVID-19 Tax Relief Act of 2020.

"(i) Outreach.—The Secretary shall carry out a robust and comprehensive outreach program to ensure that all taxpayers described in subsection (h)(1) learn of their eligibility for the advance refunds and credits under subsection (g); are advised of the opportunity to receive such advance refunds and credits

as provided under subsection (h)(1); and are provided assistance in applying for such advance refunds and credits. In conducting such outreach program, the Secretary shall coordinate with other government, State, and local agencies; federal partners; and community-based nonprofit organizations that regularly interface with such taxpayers.".
(b) Treatment Of Certain Possessions.—
(1) PAYMENTS TO POSSESSIONS WITH MIRROR CODE TAX SYSTEMS.—The Secretary of the Treasury shall pay to each possession of the United States which has a mirror code tax system amounts equal to the loss (if any) to that possession by reason of the amendments made by this section. Such amounts shall be determined by the Secretary of the Treasury based on information provided by the government of the respective possession.
(2) PAYMENTS TO OTHER POSSESSIONS.—The Secretary of the Treasury shall pay to each possession of the United States which does not have a mirror code tax system amounts estimated by the Secretary of the Treasury as being equal to the aggregate benefits (if any) that would have been provided to residents of such possession by reason of the amendments made by this section if a mirror code tax system had been in effect in such possession. The preceding sentence shall not apply unless the respective possession has a plan, which has been approved by the Secretary of the Treasury, under which such possession will promptly distribute such payments to its residents.
(3) COORDINATION WITH CREDIT ALLOWED AGAINST UNITED STATES INCOME TAXES.—No credit shall be allowed against United States income taxes under section 6431 of the Internal Revenue Code of 1986 (as amended by this section), nor shall any credit or refund be made or allowed under subsection (g) of such section, to any person—
(A) to whom a credit is allowed against taxes imposed by the possession by reason of the amendments made by this section, or
(B) who is eligible for a payment under a plan described in paragraph (2).
(4) MIRROR CODE TAX SYSTEM.—For purposes of this subsection, the term "mirror code tax system" means, with respect to any possession of the United States, the income tax system of such possession if the income tax liability of the residents of such possession under such system is determined by reference to the income tax laws of the United States as if such possession were the United States.
(c) Administrative Provisions.—
(1) DEFINITION OF DEFICIENCY.—Section 6211(b)(4)(A) of the Internal Revenue Code of 1986 is amended by striking "168(k)(4)" and inserting "168(k)(4), and 6431".
(2) MATHEMATICAL OR CLERICAL ERROR AUTHORITY.—Section 6213(g)(2) of such Code is amended—
(A) by inserting "or section 6431 (relating to economic assistance payments to individuals)" before the comma at the end of subparagraph (H), and
(B) by striking "or 32" in subparagraph (L) and inserting "32, or 6431".

(3) EXEMPTION FROM OFFSETS.—So much of any overpayment, credit, refund, or payment as is attributable to the application of section 6431 of the Internal Revenue Code of 1986 shall not be subject to reduction, offset, or levy under section 6331 or subsections (c), (d), (e), or (f) of section 6402 of such Code or under section 3716 or 3720A of title 31, United States Code.

(4) TREATMENT OF CREDIT AND ADVANCE PAYMENTS.—For purposes of section 1324 of title 31, United States Code, any credit under section 6431(a) of the Internal Revenue Code of 1986, any credit or refund under section 6431(g) of such Code, and any payment under subsection (b) of this section, shall be treated in the same manner as a refund due from a credit provision referred to in subsection (b)(2) of such section 1324.

(d) Appropriations To Carry Out This Section.—

(1) IN GENERAL.—Immediately upon the enactment of this Act, the following sums are appropriated, out of any money in the Treasury not otherwise appropriated, for the fiscal year ending September 30, 2020—

(A) For an additional amount for "Department of the Treasury—Bureau of Fiscal Services—Salaries and Expenses", $78,650,000, to remain available until September 30, 2021.

(B) For an additional amount for "Department of the Treasury—Internal Revenue Service—Taxpayer Services", $148,700,000, to remain available until September 30, 2021.

(2) REPORTS.—No later than 15 days after enactment of this Act, the Secretary of the Treasury shall submit a plan to the Committees on Appropriations of the House of Representatives and the Senate detailing the expected use of the funds provided by paragraph (1). Beginning 90 days after enactment of this Act, the Secretary of the Treasury shall submit a quarterly report to the Committees on Appropriations of the House of Representatives and the Senate detailing the actual expenditure of funds provided by paragraph (1) and the expected expenditure of such funds in the subsequent quarter.

(3) TRANSFER AUTHORITY.—In addition to the authority provided in section 101 of title I of division C of Public Law 116–93, the funds provided to the Internal Revenue Service in paragraph (1) may be transferred among accounts of the Internal Revenue Service to prevent, prepare for, and respond to coronavirus. On the date of any such transfer, the Commissioner shall notify the Committees on Appropriations of the House of Representatives and Senate of such transfer.

SEC. 202. ECONOMIC ASSISTANCE PAYMENTS TO CERTAIN FEDERAL BENEFICIARIES.

(a) Payment Authorities And Amounts.—

(1) BASE AMOUNT PAYMENTS.—Subject to subsection (c), the Secretary of the Treasury shall disburse a base amount payment to each individual who, as of the date of the enactment of this Act, is an eligible individual. Such payment shall be in the amount that would be paid under section 6431(b) of

the Internal Revenue Code of 1986 for a single taxpayer with no qualifying children.

(2) INCOME SUPPLEMENT AMOUNT PAYMENTS.—Subject to subsection (c), the Secretary of the Treasury shall disburse income supplement amount payments to each individual who, as of the date of the enactment of this Act, is an eligible individual. The total of such payments to each such individual shall equal the amount defined in 6431(c)(1)(B)(ii) for a single taxpayer with no qualifying children.

(b) Eligible Individual.—

(1) IN GENERAL.—For purposes of subsection (a), an "eligible individual" is an individual who, for the last month that ends prior to the date of enactment of this Act—

(A) is entitled to a social security insurance benefit described in paragraph (2); or

(B) is eligible for a supplemental security income benefit described in paragraph (3).

(2) SOCIAL SECURITY BENEFIT DESCRIBED.—For purposes of paragraph (1), a social security insurance benefit described in this paragraph is any monthly insurance benefit payable under title II of the Social Security Act (42 U.S.C. 401 et seq.) (other than child's insurance benefits payable under section 202(d)(1)(B)(i) of such Act (42 U.S.C. 402(d)(1)(B)(i)), including payments made pursuant to subsections (g) or (i)(7) of section 223 of such Act (42 U.S.C. 423).

(3) SUPPLEMENTAL SECURITY INCOME BENEFIT DESCRIBED.—For purposes of paragraph (1), a supplemental security income benefit described in this paragraph is a monthly benefit payable under title XVI of the Social Security Act (42 U.S.C. 1381 et seq.) (other than a benefit to an individual described in section 1611(e)(1)(B) or section 1614(a)(3)(C) of such Act (42 U.S.C. 1382(e)(1)(B); 1382c(a)(3)(C)), including—

(A) payments made pursuant to section 1619(a) (42 U.S.C. 1382h) or subsections (a)(4), (a)(7), or (p)(7) of section 1631 (42 U.S.C. 1383) of such Act; and

(B) State supplementary payments of the type referred to in section 1616(a) of such Act (42 U.S.C. 1382e(a)) (or payments of the type described in section 212(a) of Public Law 93–66) which are paid by the Commissioner under an agreement referred to in such section 1616(a) (or section 212(a) of Public Law 93–66).

(4) LIMITATION.—Notwithstanding paragraph (1), no individual shall be considered an eligible individual for purposes of subsection (a) if, for the last month that ends prior to the date of enactment of this Act—

(A) the individual is entitled to a social security insurance benefit described in paragraph (2) that was not payable for such month by reason of subsection (x) or (y) of section 202 the Social Security Act (42 U.S.C. 402) or section 1129A of such Act (42 U.S.C. 1320a–8a); or

(B) the individual is eligible for a supplemental security income benefit described in paragraph (3) that was not payable for such month by reason of subsection (e)(1)(A) or (e)(4) of section 1611 (42 U.S.C. 1382) or section 1129A of such Act (42 U.S.C. 1320a–8a).

(c) Limitations On Payments.—

(1) RESIDENCY REQUIREMENT.—A payment under this section shall be made only to individuals who reside in 1 of the 50 States, the District of Columbia, Puerto Rico, Guam, the United States Virgin Islands, American Samoa, or the Northern Mariana Islands, or who are utilizing a foreign or domestic Army Post Office or Fleet Post Office address. For purposes of the preceding sentence, the determination of the individual's residence shall be based on the address of record, as of the date of certification under subsection (d) for a payment under this section, under a program specified in paragraph (b).

(2) TIMING AND MANNER OF PAYMENTS.—

(A) TIMING OF BASE AMOUNT PAYMENT.—The Secretary of the Treasury shall commence disbursing payments under subsection (a)(1) at the earliest practicable date but in no event later than 90 days after the date of enactment of this Act.

(B) TIMING OF INCOME SUPPLEMENT AMOUNT PAYMENTS.—The Secretary of the Treasury shall disburse payments under subsection (a)(2) on a periodic basis in coordination with the timing of refunds and credits made under section 6431(h)(3)(B) of the Internal Revenue Code of 1986.

(C) ELECTRONIC DISBURSEMENT.—The Secretary of the Treasury may disburse any payment electronically to an individual in such manner as if such payment were a benefit payment made to such individual under the applicable program described in paragraph (2) or (3) of subsection (b).

(D) NOTICES.—The Commissioner of Social Security shall send one or more notices, as appropriate, in connection with such payments. Such notices shall include the information described in section 6431(h)(7)(A) of the Internal Revenue Code of 1986 relating to such payments being subject to recapture.

(d) Identification Of Recipients.—The Commissioner of Social Security shall certify the individuals entitled to receive payments under this section and provide the Secretary of the Treasury with the information needed to disburse such payments. A certification of an individual for payment shall be unaffected by any subsequent determination or redetermination of the individual's entitlement to, or eligibility for, a benefit specified in paragraph (2) or (3) of subsection (b).

(e) Treatment Of Payments.—

(1) PAYMENT DISREGARDED FOR PURPOSES OF ALL FEDERAL AND FEDERALLY ASSISTED PROGRAMS.—A payment under subsection (a) shall not be regarded as income or as a resource for any month for purposes of determining the eligibility of the recipient (or the recipient's spouse or family) for benefits or assistance, or the amount or extent of benefits or assistance,

under any Federal program or under any State or local program financed in whole or in part with Federal funds.

(2) PAYMENT NOT CONSIDERED INCOME FOR PURPOSES OF TAXATION.—A payment under subsection (a) shall not be considered as gross income for purposes of the Internal Revenue Code of 1986.

(3) PAYMENTS PROTECTED FROM ASSIGNMENT.—The provisions of sections 207 and 1631(d)(1) of the Social Security Act (42 U.S.C. 407, 1383(d)(1)) shall apply to any payment made under subsection (a) as if such payment was a benefit payment made to such individual under the applicable program described in paragraph (2) or (3) of subsection (b).

(4) PAYMENTS PROTECTED FROM OFFSET AND RECLAMATION.—Notwithstanding paragraph (3), a payment under subsection (a) shall not be subject to any reduction, offset, or levy pursuant to—

(A) section 3716 or 3720A of title 31, United States Code;

(B) section 6331 of the Internal Revenue Code of 1986; or

(C) subsection (c), (d), (e), or (f) of section 6402 of the Internal Revenue Code of 1986.

(f) Payment To Representative Payees.—

(1) IN GENERAL.—In any case in which an individual who is entitled to a payment under subsection (a) and whose benefit described in subsection (b) is paid to a representative payee, the payment under subsection (a) shall be made to the individual's representative payee and the entire payment shall be used only for the benefit of the individual who is entitled to the payment.

(2) ENFORCEMENT.—Section 1129(a)(3) of the Social Security Act (42 U.S.C. 1320a–8(a)(3)) shall apply to any payment under subsection (a) in the same manner as such section applies to a payment under title II or XVI of such Act.

(g) Coordination.—The Secretary of the Treasury and the Commissioner of Social Security shall coordinate with respect to any payments made under this section or section 6431(h) of the Internal Revenue Code of 1986.

(h) Appropriation.—Out of any money in the Treasury not otherwise appropriated, there is appropriated to the Commissioner of Social Security such sums as may be necessary for payments to individuals certified by the Commissioner of Social Security as entitled to receive a payment under this section, to remain available until expended.

Subtitle B—Earned Income Tax Credit

SEC. 211. STRENGTHENING THE EARNED INCOME TAX CREDIT FOR INDIVIDUALS WITH NO QUALIFYING CHILDREN.

(a) Special Rules For 2020 And 2021.—Section 32 of the Internal Revenue Code of 1986 is amended by adding at the end the following new subsection:

"(n) Special Rules For Individuals Without Qualifying Children.—In the case of any taxable year beginning in 2020 or 2021—

"(1) DECREASE IN MINIMUM AGE FOR CREDIT.—

"(A) IN GENERAL.—Subsection (c)(1)(A)(ii)(II) shall be applied by substituting 'the applicable minimum age' for 'age 25'.

"(B) APPLICABLE MINIMUM AGE.—For purposes of this paragraph, the term 'applicable minimum age' means—

"(i) except as otherwise provided in this subparagraph, age 19,

"(ii) in the case of a full-time student (other than a qualified former foster youth or a qualified homeless youth), age 25, and

"(iii) in the case of a qualified former foster youth or qualified homeless youth, age 18.

"(C) FULL-TIME STUDENT.—For purposes of this paragraph, the term 'full-time student' means, with respect to any taxable year, an individual who is an eligible student (as defined in section 25A(b)(3)) during at least 5 calendar months during the taxable year.

"(D) QUALIFIED FORMER FOSTER YOUTH.—For purposes of this paragraph, the term 'qualified former foster youth' means an individual who—

"(i) on or after the date that such individual attained age 14, was in foster care provided under the supervision or administration of a State or tribal agency administering (or eligible to administer) a plan under part B or part E of the Social Security Act (without regard to whether Federal assistance was provided with respect to such child under such part E), and

"(ii) provides (in such manner as the Secretary may provide) consent for State and tribal agencies which administer a plan under part B or part E of the Social Security Act to disclose to the Secretary information related to the status of such individual as a qualified former foster youth.

"(E) QUALIFIED HOMELESS YOUTH.—For purposes of this paragraph, the term 'qualified homeless youth' means, with respect to any taxable year, an individual who—

"(i) is certified by a local educational agency or a financial aid administrator during such taxable year as being either an unaccompanied youth who is a homeless child or youth, or as unaccompanied, at risk of homelessness, and self-supporting. Terms used in the preceding sentence which are also used in section 480(d)(1) of the Higher Education Act of 1965 shall have the same meaning as when used in such section, and

"(ii) provides (in such manner as the Secretary may provide) consent for local educational agencies and financial aid administrators to disclose to the Secretary information related to the status of such individual as a qualified homeless youth.

"(2) INCREASE IN MAXIMUM AGE FOR CREDIT.—Subsection (c)(1)(A)(ii)(II) shall be applied by substituting 'age 66' for 'age 65'.

"(3) INCREASE IN CREDIT AND PHASEOUT PERCENTAGES.—The table contained in subsection (b)(1) shall be applied by substituting '15.3' for '7.65' each place it appears therein.

"(4) INCREASE IN EARNED INCOME AND PHASEOUT AMOUNTS.—

"(A) IN GENERAL.—The table contained in subsection (b)(2)(A) shall be

applied—
"(i) by substituting '$9,570' for '$4,220', and
"(ii) by substituting '$11,310' for '$5,280'.
"(B) COORDINATION WITH INFLATION ADJUSTMENT.—
"(i) IN GENERAL.—In the case of any taxable year beginning after 2019, the $9,570 and $11,310 amounts in subparagraph (A) shall each be increased by an amount equal to—
"(I) such dollar amount, multiplied by
"(II) the cost-of-living adjustment determined under section 1(f)(3) for the calendar year in which the taxable year begins, determined by substituting '2018' for '2016' in subparagraph (A)(ii) thereof.
"(ii) ROUNDING.—If any increase under clause (i) is not a multiple of $10, such increase shall be rounded to the nearest multiple of $10.
"(iii) COORDINATION WITH OTHER INFLATION ADJUSTMENT.—Subsection (j) shall not apply to any dollar amount specified in this paragraph.".
(b) Information Return Matching.—As soon as practicable, the Secretary of the Treasury (or the Secretary's delegate) shall develop and implement procedures for checking an individual's claim for a credit under section 32 of the Internal Revenue Code of 1986, by reason of subsection (n)(1) thereof, against any information return made with respect to such individual under section 6050S (relating to returns relating to higher education tuition and related expenses).
(c) Effective Date.—The amendment made by this section shall apply to taxable years beginning after December 31, 2019.

SEC. 212. TAXPAYER ELIGIBLE FOR CHILDLESS EARNED INCOME CREDIT IN CASE OF QUALIFYING CHILDREN WHO FAIL TO MEET CERTAIN IDENTIFICATION REQUIREMENTS.
(a) In General.—Section 32(c)(1) of the Internal Revenue Code of 1986 is amended by striking subparagraph (F).
(b) Effective Date.—The amendment made by this section shall apply to taxable years beginning after the date of the enactment of this Act.

SEC. 213. CREDIT ALLOWED IN CASE OF CERTAIN SEPARATED SPOUSES.
(a) In General.—Section 32(d) of the Internal Revenue Code of 1986 is amended—
(1) by striking "Married Individuals.—In the case of" and inserting the following: "Married Individuals.—
"(1) IN GENERAL.—In the case of", and
(2) by adding at the end the following new paragraph:
"(2) DETERMINATION OF MARITAL STATUS.—For purposes of this section—
"(A) IN GENERAL.—Except as provided in subparagraph (B), marital status

shall be determined under section 7703(a).

"(B) SPECIAL RULE FOR SEPARATED SPOUSE.—An individual shall not be treated as married if such individual—

"(i) is married (as determined under section 7703(a)) and does not file a joint return for the taxable year,

"(ii) lives with a qualifying child of the individual for more than one-half of such taxable year, and

"(iii) (I) during the last 6 months of such taxable year, does not have the same principal place of abode as the individual's spouse, or

"(II) has a decree, instrument, or agreement (other than a decree of divorce) described in section 121(d)(3)(C) with respect to the individual's spouse and is not a member of the same household with the individual's spouse by the end of the taxable year.".

(b) Conforming Amendments.—

(1) Section 32(c)(1)(A) of such Code is amended by striking the last sentence.

(2) Section 32(c)(1)(E)(ii) of such Code is amended by striking "(within the meaning of section 7703)".

(3) Section 32(d)(1) of such Code, as amended by subsection (a), is amended by striking "(within the meaning of section 7703)".

(c) Effective Date.—The amendments made by this section shall apply to taxable years beginning after the date of the enactment of this Act.

SEC. 214. ELIMINATION OF DISQUALIFIED INVESTMENT INCOME TEST.

(a) In General.—Section 32 of the Internal Revenue Code of 1986 is amended by striking subsection (i).

(b) Conforming Amendments.—

(1) Section 32(j)(1) of such Code is amended by striking "subsections (b)(2) and (i)(1)" and inserting "subsection (b)(2)".

(2) Section 32(j)(1)(B)(i) of such Code is amended by striking "subsections (b)(2)(A) and (i)(1)" and inserting "subsection (b)(2)(A)".

(3) Section 32(j)(2) of such Code is amended—

(A) by striking subparagraph (B), and

(B) by striking "ROUNDING.—" and all that follows through "If any dollar amount" and inserting the following: "ROUNDING.—If any dollar amount".

(c) Effective Date.—The amendments made by this section shall apply to taxable years beginning after the date of the enactment of this Act.

SEC. 215. APPLICATION OF EARNED INCOME TAX CREDIT IN POSSESSIONS OF THE UNITED STATES.

(a) In General.—Chapter 77 of the Internal Revenue Code of 1986 is amended by adding at the end the following new section:

"SEC. 7530. APPLICATION OF EARNED INCOME TAX CREDIT TO

POSSESSIONS OF THE UNITED STATES.
"(a) Puerto Rico.—
"(1) IN GENERAL.—With respect to calendar year 2021 and each calendar year thereafter, the Secretary shall, except as otherwise provided in this subsection, make payments to Puerto Rico equal to—
"(A) the specified matching amount for such calendar year, plus
"(B) in the case of calendar years 2021 through 2025, the lesser of—
"(i) the expenditures made by Puerto Rico during such calendar year for education efforts with respect to individual taxpayers and tax return preparers relating to the earned income tax credit, or
"(ii) $1,000,000.
"(2) REQUIREMENT TO REFORM EARNED INCOME TAX CREDIT.—The Secretary shall not make any payments under paragraph (1) with respect to any calendar year unless Puerto Rico has in effect an earned income tax credit for taxable years beginning in or with such calendar year which (relative to the earned income tax credit which was in effect for taxable years beginning in or with calendar year 2019) increases the percentage of earned income which is allowed as a credit for each group of individuals with respect to which such percentage is separately stated or determined in a manner designed to substantially increase workforce participation.
"(3) SPECIFIED MATCHING AMOUNT.—For purposes of this subsection—
"(A) IN GENERAL.—The term 'specified matching amount' means, with respect to any calendar year, the lesser of—
"(i) the excess (if any) of—
"(I) the cost to Puerto Rico of the earned income tax credit for taxable years beginning in or with such calendar year, over
"(II) the base amount for such calendar year, or
"(ii) the product of 3, multiplied by the base amount for such calendar year.
"(B) BASE AMOUNT.—
"(i) BASE AMOUNT FOR 2021.—In the case of calendar year 2021, the term 'base amount' means the greater of—
"(I) the cost to Puerto Rico of the earned income tax credit for taxable years beginning in or with calendar year 2019 (rounded to the nearest multiple of $1,000,000), or
"(II) $200,000,000.
"(ii) INFLATION ADJUSTMENT.—In the case of any calendar year after 2021, the term 'base amount' means the dollar amount determined under clause (i) increased by an amount equal to—
"(I) such dollar amount, multiplied by—
"(II) the cost-of-living adjustment determined under section 1(f)(3) for such calendar year, determined by substituting 'calendar year 2020' for 'calendar year 2016' in subparagraph (A)(ii) thereof.
Any amount determined under this clause shall be rounded to the nearest multiple of $1,000,000.

"(4) RULES RELATED TO PAYMENTS AND REPORTS.—

"(A) TIMING OF PAYMENTS.—The Secretary shall make payments under paragraph (1) for any calendar year—

"(i) after receipt of the report described in subparagraph (B) for such calendar year, and

"(ii) except as provided in clause (i), within a reasonable period of time before the due date for individual income tax returns (as determined under the laws of Puerto Rico) for taxable years which began on the first day of such calendar year.

"(B) ANNUAL REPORTS.—With respect to calendar year 2021 and each calendar year thereafter, Puerto Rico shall provide to the Secretary a report which shall include—

"(i) an estimate of the costs described in paragraphs (1)(B)(i) and (3)(A)(i)(I) with respect to such calendar year, and

"(ii) a statement of such costs with respect to the preceding calendar year.

"(C) ADJUSTMENTS.—

"(i) IN GENERAL.—In the event that any estimate of an amount is more or less than the actual amount as later determined and any payment under paragraph (1) was determined on the basis of such estimate, proper payment shall be made by, or to, the Secretary (as the case may be) as soon as practicable after the determination that such estimate was inaccurate. Proper adjustment shall be made in the amount of any subsequent payments made under paragraph (1) to the extent that proper payment is not made under the preceding sentence before such subsequent payments.

"(ii) ADDITIONAL REPORTS.—The Secretary may require such additional periodic reports of the information described in subparagraph (B) as the Secretary determines appropriate to facilitate timely adjustments under clause (i).

"(D) DETERMINATION OF COST OF EARNED INCOME TAX CREDIT.—For purposes of this subsection, the cost to Puerto Rico of the earned income tax credit shall be determined by the Secretary on the basis of the laws of Puerto Rico and shall include reductions in revenues received by Puerto Rico by reason of such credit and refunds attributable to such credit, but shall not include any administrative costs with respect to such credit.

"(E) PREVENTION OF MANIPULATION OF BASE AMOUNT.—No payments shall be made under paragraph (1) if the earned income tax credit as in effect in Puerto Rico for taxable years beginning in or with calendar year 2019 is modified after the date of the enactment of this subsection.

"(b) Possessions With Mirror Code Tax Systems.—

"(1) IN GENERAL.—With respect to calendar year 2021 and each calendar year thereafter, the Secretary shall, except as otherwise provided in this subsection, make payments to the Virgin Islands, Guam, and the Commonwealth of the Northern Mariana Islands equal to—

"(A) 75 percent of the cost to such possession of the earned income tax credit

for taxable years beginning in or with such calendar year, plus
"(B) in the case of calendar years 2021 through 2025, the lesser of—
"(i) the expenditures made by such possession during such calendar year for education efforts with respect to individual taxpayers and tax return preparers relating to such earned income tax credit, or
"(ii) $50,000.
"(2) APPLICATION OF CERTAIN RULES.—Rules similar to the rules of subparagraphs (A), (B), (C), and (D) of subsection (a)(4) shall apply for purposes of this subsection.
"(c) American Samoa.—
"(1) IN GENERAL.—With respect to calendar year 2021 and each calendar year thereafter, the Secretary shall, except as otherwise provided in this subsection, make payments to American Samoa equal to—
"(A) the lesser of—
"(i) 75 percent of the cost to American Samoa of the earned income tax credit for taxable years beginning in or with such calendar year, or
"(ii) $12,000,000, plus
"(B) in the case of calendar years 2021 through 2025, the lesser of—
"(i) the expenditures made by American Samoa during such calendar year for education efforts with respect to individual taxpayers and tax return preparers relating to such earned income tax credit, or
"(ii) $50,000.
"(2) REQUIREMENT TO ENACT AND MAINTAIN AN EARNED INCOME TAX CREDIT.—The Secretary shall not make any payments under paragraph (1) with respect to any calendar year unless American Samoa has in effect an earned income tax credit for taxable years beginning in or with such calendar year which allows a refundable tax credit to individuals on the basis of the taxpayer's earned income which is designed to substantially increase workforce participation.
"(3) INFLATION ADJUSTMENT.—In the case of any calendar year after 2021, the $12,000,000 amount in paragraph (1)(A)(ii) shall be increased by an amount equal to—
"(A) such dollar amount, multiplied by—
"(B) the cost-of-living adjustment determined under section 1(f)(3) for such calendar year, determined by substituting 'calendar year 2020' for 'calendar year 2016' in subparagraph (A)(ii) thereof.
Any increase determined under this clause shall be rounded to the nearest multiple of $100,000.
"(4) APPLICATION OF CERTAIN RULES.—Rules similar to the rules of subparagraphs (A), (B), (C), and (D) of subsection (a)(4) shall apply for purposes of this subsection.
"(d) Treatment Of Payments.—For purposes of section 1324 of title 31, United States Code, the payments under this section shall be treated in the same manner as a refund due from a credit provision referred to in subsection (b)

(2) of such section.".

(b) Clerical Amendment.—The table of sections for chapter 77 of such Code is amended by adding at the end the following new item:

"Sec. 7529. Application of earned income tax credit to possessions of the United States.".

Subtitle C—Child Tax Credit

SEC. 221. CHILD TAX CREDIT FULLY REFUNDABLE FOR 2020 THROUGH 2025.

(a) In General.—Section 24(h)(5) of the Internal Revenue Code of 1986 is amended to read as follows:

"(5) REFUNDABLE CREDIT.—The increase determined under the first sentence of subsection (d)(1) shall be the amount determined under subparagraph (A) of such subsection (determined without regard to paragraph (4) of this subsection).".

(b) Effective Date.—The amendment made by this section shall apply to taxable years beginning after December 31, 2019.

SEC. 222. APPLICATION OF CHILD TAX CREDIT IN POSSESSIONS.

(a) In General.—Section 24 of the Internal Revenue Code of 1986 is amended by adding at the end the following new subsection:

"(i) Application Of Credit In Possessions.—

"(1) MIRROR CODE POSSESSIONS.—

"(A) IN GENERAL.—The Secretary shall pay to each possession of the United States with a mirror code tax system amounts equal to the loss to that possession by reason of the application of this section (determined without regard to this subsection) with respect to taxable years beginning after 2019. Such amounts shall be determined by the Secretary of the Treasury based on information provided by the government of the respective possession.

"(B) COORDINATION WITH CREDIT ALLOWED AGAINST UNITED STATES INCOME TAXES.—No credit shall be allowed under this section for any taxable year to any individual to whom a credit is allowable against taxes imposed by a possession with a mirror code tax system by reason of the application of this section in such possession for such taxable year.

"(C) MIRROR CODE TAX SYSTEM.—For purposes of this paragraph, the term 'mirror code tax system' means, with respect to any possession of the United States, the income tax system of such possession if the income tax liability of the residents of such possession under such system is determined by reference to the income tax laws of the United States as if such possession were the United States.

"(2) PUERTO RICO.—In the case of any bona fide resident of Puerto Rico (within the meaning of section 937(a))—

"(A) the credit determined under this section shall be allowable to such resident,

"(B) in the case of any taxable year beginning after December 31, 2021, and before January 1, 2027, the increase determined under the first sentence of subsection (d)(1) shall be the lesser of—

"(i) the amount determined under subsection (d)(1)(A) (determined without regard to subsection (h)(4)), or

"(ii) the dollar amount in effect under subsection (h)(5), and

"(C) in the case of any taxable year after December 31, 2026, the increase determined under the first sentence of subsection (d)(1) shall be the amount determined under subsection (d)(1)(A).

"(3) AMERICAN SAMOA.—

"(A) IN GENERAL.—The Secretary shall pay to American Samoa amounts estimated by the Secretary as being equal to the aggregate benefits that would have been provided to residents of American Samoa by reason of the application of this section for taxable years beginning after 2019 if the provisions of this section had been in effect in American Samoa.

"(B) DISTRIBUTION REQUIREMENT.—Subparagraph (A) shall not apply unless American Samoa has a plan, which has been approved by the Secretary, under which American Samoa will promptly distribute such payments to the residents of American Samoa in a manner which replicates to the greatest degree practicable the benefits that would have been so provided to each such resident.

"(C) COORDINATION WITH CREDIT ALLOWED AGAINST UNITED STATES INCOME TAXES.—

"(i) IN GENERAL.—In the case of a taxable year with respect to which a plan is approved under subparagraph (B), this section (other than this subsection) shall not apply to any individual eligible for a distribution under such plan.

"(ii) APPLICATION OF SECTION IN EVENT OF ABSENCE OF APPROVED PLAN.—In the case of a taxable year with respect to which a plan is not approved under subparagraph (B), rules similar to the rules of paragraph (2) shall apply with respect to bona fide residents of American Samoa (within the meaning of section 937(a)).

"(4) TREATMENT OF PAYMENTS.—The payments made under this subsection shall be treated in the same manner for purposes of section 1324(b)(2) of title 31, United States Code, as refunds due from the credit allowed under this section.".

(b) Effective Date.—The amendment made by this section shall apply to taxable years beginning after December 31, 2019.

SEC. 223. INCREASED CHILD TAX CREDIT.

(a) In General.—Section 24(h)(2) of the Internal Revenue Code of 1986 is amended to read to as follows:

"(2) CREDIT AMOUNT.—Subsection (a) shall be applied by substituting '$3,000 ($3,600 in the case of a qualifying child who has not attained age 6 as of the close of the calendar year in which the taxable year of the taxpayer begins)' for '$1,000'".

(b) Effective Date.—The amendment made by this section shall apply to taxable years beginning after December 31, 2019.

Subtitle D—Dependent Care Assistance

SEC. 231. REFUNDABILITY AND ENHANCEMENT OF CHILD AND DEPENDENT CARE TAX CREDIT.

(a) In General.—Section 21 of the Internal Revenue Code of 1986 is amended by adding at the end the following new subsection:

"(g) Special Rules For 2020 And 2021.—In the case of any taxable year beginning in 2020 or 2021—

"(1) CREDIT MADE REFUNDABLE.—In the case of an individual other than a nonresident alien, the credit allowed under subsection (a) shall be treated as a credit allowed under subpart C (and not allowed under this subpart).

"(2) INCREASE IN APPLICABLE PERCENTAGE.—Subsection (a)(2) shall be applied—

"(A) by substituting '50 percent' for '35 percent', and

"(B) by substituting '$120,000' for '$15,000'.

"(3) INCREASE IN DOLLAR LIMIT ON AMOUNT CREDITABLE.—Subsection (c) shall be applied—

"(A) by substituting '$6,000' for '$3,000' in paragraph (1) thereof, and

"(B) by substituting 'twice the amount in effect under paragraph (1)' for '$6,000' in paragraph (2) thereof.

"(4) INFLATION ADJUSTMENT OF DOLLAR AMOUNTS.—In the case of any taxable year beginning after 2020, the $120,000 amount in paragraph (2)(B) and the $6,000 amount in paragraph (3)(A) shall each be increased by an amount equal to—

"(A) such dollar amount, multiplied by

"(B) the cost-of-living adjustment determined under section 1(f)(3) for the calendar year in which the taxable year begins, determined by substituting '2019' for '2016' in subparagraph (A)(ii) thereof.

If any increase determined under this paragraph is not a multiple of $100, such increase shall be rounded to the next lowest multiple of $100.

"(5) INCOME LIMITATION.—

"(A) IN GENERAL.—Paragraphs (1) through (4) of this subsection shall not apply to any taxpayer for any taxable year if the modified adjusted gross income of such taxpayer for such taxable year exceeds $1,000,000.

"(B) MODIFIED ADJUSTED GROSS INCOME.—For purposes of this paragraph, the term 'modified adjusted gross income' means adjusted gross income determined without regard to sections 911, 931, and 933.".

(b) Conforming Amendment.—Section 1324(b)(2) of title 31, United States Code, is amended by inserting "21 (by reason of subsection (g) thereof)," before "25A".

(c) Coordination With Possession Tax Systems.—Section 21(g)(1) of the

Internal Revenue Code of 1986 (as added by this section) shall not apply to any person—

(1) to whom a credit is allowed against taxes imposed by a possession with a mirror code tax system by reason of the application of section 21 of such Code in such possession for such taxable year, or

(2) to whom a credit would be allowed against taxes imposed by a possession which does not have a mirror code tax system if the provisions of section 21 of such Code had been in effect in such possession for such taxable year.

(d) Effective Date.—The amendments made by this section shall apply to taxable years beginning after December 31, 2019.

SEC. 232. INCREASE IN EXCLUSION FOR EMPLOYER-PROVIDED DEPENDENT CARE ASSISTANCE.

(a) In General.—Section 129(a)(2) of the Internal Revenue Code of 1986 is amended by adding at the end the following new subparagraph:

"(D) SPECIAL RULE FOR 2021 AND 2022.—In the case of any taxable year beginning in 2021 or 2022—

"(i) IN GENERAL.—Subparagraph (A) shall be applied be substituting '$10,500 (half such dollar amount' for '$5,000 ($2,500'.

"(ii) INFLATION ADJUSTMENT.—In the case of any taxable year beginning after 2021, the $10,500 amount in clause (i) shall be increased by an amount equal to—

"(I) such dollar amount, multiplied by

"(II) the cost-of-living adjustment determined under section 1(f)(3) for the calendar year in which the taxable year begins, determined by substituting '2020' for '2016' in subparagraph (A)(ii) thereof.

Any increase determined under the preceding sentence which is not a multiple of $50, shall be rounded to the nearest multiple of $50.".

(b) Effective Date.—The amendment made by this section shall apply to taxable years beginning after December 31, 2020.

Subtitle E—Net Operating Losses

SEC. 241. FIVE-YEAR CARRYBACK OF NET OPERATING LOSSES AND TEMPORARY SUSPENSION OF TAXABLE INCOME LIMITATION.

(a) In General.—Section 172 of the Internal Revenue Code of 1986 is amended by redesignating subsection (g) as subsection (h) and by inserting after subsection (f) the following new subsection:

"(g) Special Rules For 2018, 2019, and 2020.—For purposes of this section—

"(1) FIVE-YEAR CARRYBACK.—

"(A) IN GENERAL.—Any net operating loss arising in a taxable year beginning after December 31, 2017, and before January 1, 2021—

"(i) shall be a net operating loss carryback to each of the 5 taxable years preceding the taxable year of such loss (but not to any taxable year beginning before January 1, 2015), and

"(ii) subparagraphs (B) and (C)(i) of subsection (b)(1) shall not apply.
"(B) ELECTION OUT.—A taxpayer may elect not to have subparagraph (A) apply for any taxable year. Such election shall be made in such manner as may be prescribed by the Secretary, and shall be made—
"(i) in the case of any election relating to a net operating loss arising in a taxable year beginning in 2018 or 2019, by the due date (including extension of time) for filing the return for the taxpayer's first taxable year ending after the date of the enactment of this subparagraph.
"(ii) in the case of any election relating to a net operating loss arising in a taxable year beginning in 2020, by the due date (including extensions of time) for such taxable year.
Any such election, once made, shall be irrevocable.
"(2) SUSPENSION OF NET OPERATING LOSS LIMITATION.—For taxable years beginning after December 31, 2017, and before January 1, 2021, the amount of the deduction allowed under subsection (a) shall be the aggregate of the net operating loss carryovers to such year, plus the net operating loss carrybacks to such year.
"(3) DISQUALIFIED TAXPAYER.—Paragraphs (1) and (2) shall not apply with respect to any taxable year in which the taxpayer is a disqualified taxpayer. Any taxpayer who is a disqualified taxpayer in the first taxable year ending after the date of the enactment of this paragraph, shall be treated as a disqualified taxpayer for taxable years beginning on or after January 1, 2018.
"(4) DEFINITIONS.—For purposes of this subsection—
"(A) DISQUALIFIED TAXPAYER.—A taxpayer is a disqualified taxpayer with respect to a taxable year if—
"(i) in the case of a taxable year ending after December 31, 2019, and beginning before January 1, 2021, the taxpayer (or any related person) is not allowed a deduction under this chapter for the taxable year by reason of section 162(m) or section 280G, or
"(ii) the taxpayer (or any related person) is a specified corporation for the taxable year.
"(B) SPECIFIED CORPORATION.—
"(i) IN GENERAL.—The term 'specified corporation' means, with respect to any taxable year, a corporation the aggregate distributions (including redemptions) of which during any taxable year ending after December 31, 2017, exceed the sum of applicable stock issued of such corporation and 5 percent of the fair market value of the stock of such corporation as of the last day of the taxable year.
"(ii) APPLICABLE STOCK ISSUED.—The term 'applicable stock issued' means, with respect to any corporation, the aggregate value of stock issued by the corporation during any taxable year ending after December 31, 2017, in exchange for money or property other than stock in such corporation.
"(iii) CERTAIN PREFERRED STOCK DISREGARDED.—For purposes of clause (i), stock described in section 1504(a)(4), and distributions (including

redemptions) with respect to such stock, shall be disregarded.

"(C) RELATED PERSON.—A person is a related person to a taxpayer if the related person bears a relationship to the taxpayer specified in section 267(b) or section 707(b)(1).

"(5) SPECIAL RULE FOR LIFE INSURANCE COMPANIES.—In the case of a net operating loss of a life insurance company which arises in a taxable year beginning after December 31, 2017, and before January 1, 2021, and which is a net operating loss carryback to a taxable year beginning before January 1, 2018, such net operating loss shall be treated as an operations loss deduction under subchapter L (as in effect before the enactment of Public Law 115–97) with respect to such taxable year in the same manner as a loss arising in a taxable year beginning before January 1, 2018.".

(b) Coordination With Taxable Year For Which Deferred Foreign Income Treated As Subpart F Income.—Section 965(n) of such Code is amended by adding at the end the following new paragraph:

"(4) DEEMED ELECTION IN CASE OF CERTAIN NET OPERATING LOSS CARRYBACKS.—In the case of a net operating loss carryback to such taxable year by reason of section 172(g)(1), the taxpayer shall be treated as having elected the application of this subsection for such taxable year.".

(c) Conforming Amendment.—Section 172(b)(1) of such Code is amended by inserting "and subsection (g)" after "this paragraph".

(d) Regulatory Authority.—The Secretary of the Treasury (or the Secretary's delegate) shall prescribe such regulations or other guidance as are necessary or appropriate to prevent the abuse of the purposes of the amendments made by this section, including—

(1) anti-stuffing rules, anti-churning rules (including rules relating to sale-leasebacks), and rules similar to the rules under section 1091 of the Internal Revenue Code of 1986 relating to losses from wash sales,

(2) rules applying this subsection to successor corporations and in cases where a taxpayer becomes, or ceases to be, a member of an affiliated group filing a consolidated return under section 1501 of such Code,

(3) rules treating members of an affiliated group filing a consolidated return under section 1501 of such Code as a single corporation, and

(4) rules to prevent the avoidance of this section through related parties, pass-through entities, and intermediaries.

(e) Special Rules.—Rules similar to the rules of subparagraphs (B) and (D) of section 172(b)(1) of the Internal Revenue Code of 1986, as in effect on the day before the date of the enactment of Public Law 115–97, shall apply to any net operating loss to which the amendment made by this section applies. The Secretary of the Treasury (or the Secretary's delegate) shall prescribe such regulations or other guidance as are necessary or appropriate to effect the purposes of such subparagraphs with respect to any such net operating losses.

(f) Effective Date.—

(1) NET OPERATING LOSS LIMITATION.—Except as provided in paragraph

(2), the amendments made by subsections (a) shall apply to—

(A) taxable years beginning after December 31, 2017, and

(B) taxable years beginning on or before December 31, 2017, to which net operating losses arising in taxable years beginning after December 31, 2017, are carried.

(2) CARRYBACKS.—In the case of the amendments made by subsections (b) and (c), and so much of subsection (a) as relates to the carryback of net operating losses, such amendments shall apply to net operating losses arising in taxable years ending after December 31, 2017, and beginning before January 1, 2021.

Subtitle F—Employee Retention Credit

SEC. 251. PAYROLL CREDIT FOR CERTAIN EMPLOYERS AFFECTED BY COVID–19.

(a) In General.—In the case of an eligible employer, there shall be allowed as a credit against the tax imposed by section 3111(a) or 3221(a) of the Internal Revenue Code of 1986 for each calendar quarter an amount equal to 80 percent of the qualified wages allocable to the inoperable trade or business with respect to each employee of such employer for such calendar quarter.

(b) Limitations And Refundability.—

(1) WAGES TAKEN INTO ACCOUNT.—The amount of qualified wages with respect to any employee which may be taken into account under subsection (a) by the eligible employer for all calendar quarters shall not exceed $10,000.

(2) CREDIT LIMITED TO EMPLOYMENT TAXES.—The credit allowed by subsection (a) with respect to any calendar quarter shall not exceed the tax imposed by section 3111(a) or 3221(a) of the Internal Revenue Code of 1986 for such calendar quarter (reduced by any credits allowed under subsections (e) and (f) of section 3111 and sections 7001 and 7003 of the Families First Coronavirus Response Act) on the wages paid with respect to the employment of all the employees of the eligible employer.

(3) REFUNDABILITY OF EXCESS CREDIT.—

(A) IN GENERAL.—If the amount of the credit under subsection (a) exceeds the limitation of paragraph (2) for any calendar quarter, such excess shall be treated as an overpayment that shall be refunded under sections 6402(a) and 6413(b) of such Code.

(B) TREATMENT OF PAYMENTS.—For purposes of section 1324 of title 31, United States Code, any amounts due to the employer under this paragraph shall be treated in the same manner as a refund due from a credit provision referred to in subsection (b)(2) of such section.

(c) Definitions.—For purposes of this section—

(1) ELIGIBLE EMPLOYER.—The term "eligible employer" means an employer—

(A) which conducted an active trade or business on January 31, 2020,

(B) with respect to which such trade or business is an inoperable trade or business after January 31, 2020 during any calendar quarter, and

(C) which had either—

(i) no more than 1,500 full-time equivalent employees (as defined in section 45R(d)(2) of the Internal Revenue Code of 1986) for calendar year 2019, or

(ii) no more than $41.5 million in gross receipts in calendar year 2019.

(2) INOPERABLE TRADE OR BUSINESS.—The term "inoperable trade or business" means any trade or business of an eligible employer for which gross receipts for the calendar quarter are less than 80 percent of gross receipts for the same calendar quarter for the prior year.

(3) QUALIFIED WAGES.—The term "qualified wages" means wages (as defined in section 3121(a) of such Code) or compensation (as defined in section 3231(e) of such Code) paid or incurred by an eligible employer with respect to an employee on any day after January 31, 2020 and before December 31, 2020 that falls during the designated period, except that such term shall not include any wages taken into account under section 7001 or section 7003 of the Families First Coronavirus Response Act.

(4) DESIGNATED PERIOD.—The term "designated period" means the period—

(A) beginning in the calendar quarter in which the trade or business became an inoperable trade or business, and

(B) ending in the calendar quarter for which the gross receipts of the trade or business of the eligible employer are greater than 90 percent of gross receipts for the same calendar quarter for the prior year.

Such term shall include wages paid or incurred without regard to whether the employee performs no services, performs services at a different place of employment, or performs services during the period in which the eligible employer is an inoperable trade or business.

(d) Aggregation Rule.—All persons treated as a single employer under subsection (a) or (b) of section 52 of such Code, or subsection (m) or (o) of section 414 of such Code, shall be treated as one eligible employer for purposes of this section.

(e) Denial Of Double Benefit.—For purposes of chapter 1 of such Code, the gross income of the employer for the taxable year which includes the last day of any calendar quarter with respect to which a credit is allowed under this section shall be increased by the amount of such credit.

(f) Special Rule For Third-Party Payors.—Any credit allowed under this section shall be treated as a credit described in section 3511(d)(2) of such Code.

(g) Election Not To Have Section Apply.—This section shall not apply with respect to any eligible employer for any calendar quarter if such employer elects (at such time and in such manner as the Secretary of the Treasury (or the Secretary's delegate) may prescribe) not to have this section apply.

(h) Employee Not Taken Into Account More Than Once.—An employee shall not be treated as an employee for purposes of this section for any period with respect to any employer if such employer is allowed a credit under section 51 of such Code with respect to such employee for such period.

(i) Regulations.—The Secretary of the Treasury (or the Secretary's delegate) shall prescribe such regulations or other guidance as may be necessary to carry out the purposes of this section, including—

(1) regulations or other guidance providing for waiver of penalties for failure to deposit amounts in anticipation of the allowance of the credit allowed under this section,

(2) regulations or other guidance regarding the form and manner for recapturing credits under this section,

(3) regulations or other guidance to prevent the avoidance of the purposes of this section,

(4) regulations or other guidance describing proper calculation of gross receipts for purposes of subsection (c) for eligible employers that did not operate a trade or business in prior calendar quarters, and

(5) regulations or other guidance regarding the application of the credit under subsection (a) to third party payors (including professional employer organizations, certified professional employer organizations, or agents under section 3504 of such Code), including regulations or other guidance allowing such payors to submit documentation necessary to substantiate the eligible employer status of employers that use such payors.

(j) Transfers To Federal Old-Age And Survivors Insurance Trust Fund.—There are hereby appropriated to the Federal Old-Age and Survivors Insurance Trust Fund and the Federal Disability Insurance Trust Fund established under section 201 of the Social Security Act (42 U.S.C. 401) and the Social Security Equivalent Benefit Account established under section 15A(a) of the Railroad Retirement Act of 1974 (45 U.S.C. 14 231n–1(a)) amounts equal to the reduction in revenues to the Treasury by reason of this section (without regard to this subsection). Amounts appropriated by the preceding sentence shall be transferred from the general fund at such times and in such manner as to replicate to the extent possible the transfers which would have occurred to such Trust Fund or Account had this section not been enacted.

Subtitle G—Credits For Paid Sick And Family Leave

SEC. 261. EXTENSION OF CREDITS.

Sections 7001(g), 7002(e), 7003(g), and 7004(e) of Public Law 116–127 are each amended by striking "2020" and inserting "2021".

SEC. 262. REPEAL OF REDUCED RATE OF CREDIT FOR CERTAIN LEAVE.

(a) Payroll Credit.—Section 7001(b) of Public Law 116–127 is amended by striking "$200 ($511 in the case of any day any portion of which is paid sick time described in paragraph (1), (2), or (3) of section 5102(a) of the Emergency Paid Sick Leave Act)" and inserting "$511".

(b) Self-Employed Credit.—
(1) IN GENERAL.—Section 7002(c)(1)(B) of Public Law 116–127 is amended to read as follows:
"(B) the lesser of—
"(i) $511, or
"(ii) the average daily self-employment income of the individual for the taxable year.".
(2) CONFORMING AMENDMENT.—Section 7002(d)(3) of Public Law 116–127 is amended by striking "$2,000 ($5,110 in the case of any day any portion of which is paid sick time described in paragraph (1), (2), or (3) of section 5102(a) of the Emergency Paid Sick Leave Act)" and inserting "$5,110".

SEC. 263. FEDERAL, STATE, AND LOCAL GOVERNMENTS ALLOWED TAX CREDITS FOR PAID SICK AND PAID FAMILY AND MEDICAL LEAVE.
(a) Credit For Required Paid Sick Leave.—Section 7001(e) of Public Law 116–127 is amended by striking paragraph (4).
(b) Credit For Required Paid Family Leave.—Section 7003(e) of Public Law 116–127 is amended by striking paragraph (4).

SEC. 264. CREDITS NOT ALLOWED TO CERTAIN LARGE EMPLOYERS.
(a) Credit For Required Paid Sick Leave.—
(1) IN GENERAL.—Section 7001(a) of Public Law 116–127 is amended by striking "In the case of an employer" and inserting "In the case of an eligible employer".
(2) ELIGIBLE EMPLOYER.—Section 7001(c) of Public Law 116–127 is amended by striking "For purposes of this section, the term" and all that precedes it and inserting the following:
"(c) Definitions.—For purposes of this section—
"(1) ELIGIBLE EMPLOYER.—The term 'eligible employer' means any employer other an applicable large employer (as defined in section 4980H(c)(2), determined by substituting '500' for '50' each place it appears in subparagraphs (A) and (B) thereof and without regard to subparagraphs (D) and (F) thereof). For purposes of the preceding sentence, the Government of the United States, the government of any State or political subdivision thereof, or any agency or instrumentality of any of the foregoing, shall not be treated as an applicable large employer.
"(2) QUALIFIED SICK LEAVE WAGES.—The term".
(b) Credit For Required Paid Family Leave.—
(1) IN GENERAL.—Section 7003(a) of Public Law 116–127 is amended by striking "In the case of an employer" and inserting "In the case of an eligible employer".
(2) ELIGIBLE EMPLOYER.—Section 7003(c) of Public Law 116–127 is

amended by striking "For purposes of this section, the term" and all that precedes it and inserting the following:

"(c) Definitions.—For purposes of this section—

"(1) ELIGIBLE EMPLOYER.—The term 'eligible employer' means any employer other an applicable large employer (as defined in section 4980H(c)(2), determined by substituting '500' for '50' each place it appears in subparagraphs (A) and (B) thereof and without regard to subparagraphs (D) and (F) thereof). For purposes of the preceding sentence, the Government of the United States, the government of any State or political subdivision thereof, or any agency or instrumentality of any of the foregoing, shall not be treated as an applicable large employer.

"(2) QUALIFIED FAMILY LEAVE WAGES.—The term".

SEC. 265. EFFECTIVE DATE.

The amendments made by this title shall take effect as if included in the provisions of Public Law 116–127 to which they relate.

TITLE III—ADMINISTRATIVE

SEC. 301. DELAY OF CERTAIN DEADLINES.

(a) Filing Deadlines For 2019.—In the case of any return required to be filed for a taxable year ending in 2019, including for purposes of section 6151(a) of the Internal Revenue Code of 1986, section 6072(a) of such Code shall be applied—

(1) by substituting "July" for "April", and

(2) by substituting "the seventh month" for "the fourth month".

(b) Estimated Tax Payments For Individuals.—

(1) IN GENERAL.—In the case of an individual, the due date for any required installment under section 6654 of the Internal Revenue Code of 1986 which (but for the application of this section) would be due during the applicable period shall not be due before October 15, 2020, and all such installments shall be treated as one installment due on such date. The Secretary of the Treasury (or the Secretary's delegate) shall prescribe such regulations or other guidance as may be necessary to carry out the purposes of this subsection.

(2) APPLICABLE PERIOD.—For purposes of this subsection, the applicable period is the period beginning on the date of the enactment of this Act and ending before October 15, 2020.

TITLE IV—RETIREMENT PROVISIONS

SEC. 401. SPECIAL RULES FOR USE OF RETIREMENT FUNDS.

(a) Tax-Favored Withdrawals From Retirement Plans.—

(1) IN GENERAL.—Section 72(t) of the Internal Revenue Code of 1986 shall not apply to any coronavirus-related distribution.

(2) AGGREGATE DOLLAR LIMITATION.—

(A) IN GENERAL.—For purposes of this subsection, the aggregate amount of distributions received by an individual which may be treated as coronavirus-related distributions for any taxable year shall not exceed $100,000.

(B) TREATMENT OF PLAN DISTRIBUTIONS.—If a distribution to an individual would (without regard to subparagraph (A)) be a coronavirus-related distribution, a plan shall not be treated as violating any requirement of the Internal Revenue Code of 1986 merely because the plan treats such distribution as a coronavirus-related distribution, unless the aggregate amount of such distributions from all plans maintained by the employer (and any member of any controlled group which includes the employer) to such individual exceeds $100,000.

(C) CONTROLLED GROUP.—For purposes of subparagraph (B), the term "controlled group" means any group treated as a single employer under subsection (b), (c), (m), or (o) of section 414 of the Internal Revenue Code of 1986.

(3) AMOUNT DISTRIBUTED MAY BE REPAID.—

(A) IN GENERAL.—Any individual who receives a coronavirus-related distribution may, at any time during the 3-year period beginning on the day after the date on which such distribution was received, make 1 or more contributions in an aggregate amount not to exceed the amount of such distribution to an eligible retirement plan of which such individual is a beneficiary and to which a rollover contribution of such distribution could be made under section 402(c), 403(a)(4), 403(b)(8), 408(d)(3), or 457(e)(16), of the Internal Revenue Code of 1986, as the case may be.

(B) TREATMENT OF REPAYMENTS OF DISTRIBUTIONS FROM ELIGIBLE RETIREMENT PLANS OTHER THAN IRAS.—For purposes of the Internal Revenue Code of 1986, if a contribution is made pursuant to subparagraph (A) with respect to a coronavirus-related distribution from an eligible retirement plan other than an individual retirement plan, then the taxpayer shall, to the extent of the amount of the contribution, be treated as having received the coronavirus-related distribution in an eligible rollover distribution (as defined in section 402(c)(4) of such Code) and as having transferred the amount to the eligible retirement plan in a direct trustee to trustee transfer within 60 days of the distribution.

(C) TREATMENT OF REPAYMENTS OF DISTRIBUTIONS FROM IRAS.—For purposes of the Internal Revenue Code of 1986, if a contribution is made pursuant to subparagraph (A) with respect to a coronavirus-related distribution from an individual retirement plan (as defined by section 7701(a)(37) of such Code), then, to the extent of the amount of the contribution, the coronavirus-related distribution shall be treated as a distribution described in section 408(d)(3) of such Code and as having been transferred to the eligible retirement plan in a direct trustee to trustee transfer within 60 days of the distribution.

(4) DEFINITIONS.—For purposes of this subsection—

(A) CORONAVIRUS-RELATED DISTRIBUTION.—Except as provided in paragraph (2), the term "coronavirus-related distribution" means any distribution from an eligible retirement plan made—

(i) on or after January 1, 2020, and before December 31, 2020,

(ii) to an individual—

(I) who is diagnosed with the virus SARS–CoV–2 or with coronavirus disease 2019 (COVID–19) by a test approved by the Centers for Disease Control and Prevention,

(II) whose spouse or dependent (as defined in section 152 of the Internal Revenue Code of 1986) is diagnosed with such virus or disease by such a test, or

(III) who experiences adverse financial consequences as a result of being quarantined, being furloughed or laid off or having work hours reduced due to such virus or disease, being unable to work due to lack of child care due to such virus or disease, closing or reducing hours of a business owned or operated by the individual due to such virus or disease, or other factors as determined by the Secretary of the Treasury (or the Secretary's delegate).

(B) EMPLOYEE CERTIFICATION.—The administrator of an eligible retirement plan may rely on an employee's certification that the employee satisfies the conditions of subparagraph (A)(ii) in determining whether any distribution is a coronavirus-related distribution.

(C) ELIGIBLE RETIREMENT PLAN.—The term "eligible retirement plan" has the meaning given such term by section 402(c)(8)(B) of the Internal Revenue Code of 1986.

(5) INCOME INCLUSION SPREAD OVER 3-YEAR PERIOD.—

(A) IN GENERAL.—In the case of any coronavirus-related distribution, unless the taxpayer elects not to have this paragraph apply for any taxable year, any amount required to be included in gross income for such taxable year shall be so included ratably over the 3-taxable-year period beginning with such taxable year.

(B) SPECIAL RULE.—For purposes of subparagraph (A), rules similar to the rules of subparagraph (E) of section 408A(d)(3) of the Internal Revenue Code of 1986 shall apply.

(6) SPECIAL RULES.—

(A) EXEMPTION OF DISTRIBUTIONS FROM TRUSTEE TO TRUSTEE TRANSFER AND WITHHOLDING RULES.—For purposes of sections 401(a)(31), 402(f), and 3405 of the Internal Revenue Code of 1986, coronavirus-related distributions shall not be treated as eligible rollover distributions.

(B) CORONAVIRUS-RELATED DISTRIBUTIONS TREATED AS MEETING PLAN DISTRIBUTION REQUIREMENTS.—For purposes of the Internal Revenue Code of 1986, a coronavirus-related distribution shall be treated as meeting the requirements of sections 401(k)(2)(B)(i), 403(b)(7)(A)(i), 403(b)(11), and 457(d)(1)(A) of such Code.

(b) Loans From Qualified Plans.—

(1) INCREASE IN LIMIT ON LOANS NOT TREATED AS DISTRIBUTIONS.—In the case of any loan from a qualified employer plan (as defined under section 72(p)(4) of the Internal Revenue Code of 1986) to a qualified individual made during the 180-day period beginning on the date of the enactment of this Act—

(A) clause (i) of section 72(p)(2)(A) of such Code shall be applied by substituting "$100,000" for "$50,000", and

(B) clause (ii) of such section shall be applied by substituting "the present value of the nonforfeitable accrued benefit of the employee under the plan" for "one-half of the present value of the nonforfeitable accrued benefit of the employee under the plan".

(2) DELAY OF REPAYMENT.—In the case of a qualified individual with an outstanding loan (on or after the date of the enactment of this Act) from a qualified employer plan (as defined in section 72(p)(4) of the Internal Revenue Code of 1986)—

(A) if the due date pursuant to subparagraph (B) or (C) of section 72(p)(2) of such Code for any repayment with respect to such loan occurs during the period beginning on the date of the enactment of this Act and ending on December 31, 2020, such due date shall be delayed for 1 year (or, if later, until the date which is 180 days after the date of the enactment of this Act),

(B) any subsequent repayments with respect to any such loan shall be appropriately adjusted to reflect the delay in the due date under subparagraph (A) and any interest accruing during such delay, and

(C) in determining the 5-year period and the term of a loan under subparagraph (B) or (C) of section 72(p)(2) of such Code, the period described in subparagraph (A) of this paragraph shall be disregarded.

(3) QUALIFIED INDIVIDUAL.—For purposes of this subsection, the term "qualified individual" means any individual who is described in subsection (a)(4)(A)(ii).

(c) Provisions Relating To Plan Amendments.—

(1) IN GENERAL.—If this subsection applies to any amendment to any plan or annuity contract, such plan or contract shall be treated as being operated in accordance with the terms of the plan during the period described in paragraph (2)(B)(i).

(2) AMENDMENTS TO WHICH SUBSECTION APPLIES.—

(A) IN GENERAL.—This subsection shall apply to any amendment to any plan or annuity contract which is made—

(i) pursuant to any provision of this section, or pursuant to any regulation issued by the Secretary of the Treasury or the Secretary of Labor (or the delegate of either such Secretary) under any provision of this section, and

(ii) on or before the last day of the first plan year beginning on or after January 1, 2022, or such later date as the Secretary of the Treasury (or the Secretary's delegate) may prescribe.

In the case of a governmental plan (as defined in section 414(d) of the Internal Revenue Code of 1986), clause (ii) shall be applied by substituting the date which is 2 years after the date otherwise applied under clause (ii).

(B) CONDITIONS.—This subsection shall not apply to any amendment unless—

(i) during the period—

(I) beginning on the date that this section or the regulation described in subparagraph (A)(i) takes effect (or in the case of a plan or contract amendment not required by this section or such regulation, the effective date specified by the plan), and

(II) ending on the date described in subparagraph (A)(ii) (or, if earlier, the date the plan or contract amendment is adopted),

the plan or contract is operated as if such plan or contract amendment were in effect, and

(ii) such plan or contract amendment applies retroactively for such period.

SEC. 402. SINGLE-EMPLOYER PLAN FUNDING RULES.

(a) Delay In Payment Of Minimum Required Contributions.—In the case of any minimum required contribution (as determined under section 430(a) of the Internal Revenue Code of 1986 and section 303(a) of the Employee Retirement Income Security Act of 1974 (29 U.S.C. 1083(a))) which (but for this section) would otherwise be due under section 430(j) of such Code (including quarterly contributions under paragraph (3) thereof) and section 303(j) of such Act (29 U.S.C. 1083(j)) (including quarterly contributions under paragraph (3) thereof) during calendar year 2020—

(1) such contributions shall not be required to be made until January 1, 2021, and

(2) the amount of each such minimum required contribution shall be increased by interest accruing for the period between the original due date (without regard to this section) for the contribution and the payment date, at the effective rate of interest for the plan for the plan year which includes such payment date.

(b) Benefit Restriction Status.—For purposes of section 436 of the Internal Revenue Code of 1986 and section 206(g) of the Employee Retirement Income Security Act of 1974 (29 U.S.C. 1056(g)), a plan sponsor may elect to treat the plan's adjusted funding target attainment percentage for the last plan year ending before January 1, 2020, as the adjusted funding target attainment percentage for plan years which include calendar year 2020.

SEC. 403. TEMPORARY WAIVER OF REQUIRED MINIMUM DISTRIBUTION RULES FOR CERTAIN RETIREMENT PLANS AND ACCOUNTS.

(a) In General.—Section 401(a)(9) of the Internal Revenue Code of 1986 is amended by adding at the end the following new subparagraph:

"(I) TEMPORARY WAIVER OF MINIMUM REQUIRED DISTRIBUTION.—
"(i) IN GENERAL.—The requirements of this paragraph shall not apply for calendar year 2020 to—
"(I) a defined contribution plan which is described in this subsection or in section 403(a) or 403(b),
"(II) a defined contribution plan which is an eligible deferred compensation plan described in section 457(b) but only if such plan is maintained by an employer described in section 457(e)(1)(A), or
"(III) an individual retirement plan.
"(ii) SPECIAL RULE FOR REQUIRED BEGINNING DATES IN 2020.—Clause (i) shall apply to any distribution which is required to be made in calendar year 2020 by reason of—
"(I) a required beginning date occurring in such calendar year, and
"(II) such distribution not having been made before January 1, 2020.
"(iii) SPECIAL RULES REGARDING WAIVER PERIOD.—For purposes of this paragraph—
"(I) the required beginning date with respect to any individual shall be determined without regard to this subparagraph for purposes of applying this paragraph for calendar years after 2020,
"(II) if clause (ii) of subparagraph (B) applies, the 5-year period described in such clause shall be determined without regard to calendar year 2020,
"(III) if clause (iii) of subparagraph (E) applies, the 10-year period described in such clause shall be determined without regard to calendar year 2020, and
"(IV) if clause (i) of subparagraph (H) applies, the 10-year period described in such clause shall be determined without regard to calendar year 2020.".
(b) Eligible Rollover Distributions.—Section 402(c)(4) of the Internal Revenue Code of 1986 is amended by striking "2009" each place it appears in the last sentence and inserting "2020".
(c) Effective Dates.—
(1) IN GENERAL.—The amendments made by this section shall apply for calendar years beginning after December 31, 2019.
(2) PROVISIONS RELATING TO PLAN OR CONTRACT AMENDMENTS.—
(A) IN GENERAL.—If this paragraph applies to any pension plan or contract amendment, such pension plan or contract shall not fail to be treated as being operated in accordance with the terms of the plan during the period described in subparagraph (B)(ii) solely because the plan operates in accordance with this section.
(B) AMENDMENTS TO WHICH PARAGRAPH APPLIES.—
(i) IN GENERAL.—This paragraph shall apply to any amendment to any pension plan or annuity contract which—
(I) is made pursuant to the amendments made by this section, and
(II) is made on or before the last day of the first plan year beginning on or after January 1, 2022.
In the case of a governmental plan, subclause (II) shall be applied by

substituting '2024' for '2022'.

(ii) CONDITIONS.—This paragraph shall not apply to any amendment unless during the period beginning on the effective date of the amendment and ending on December 31, 2020, the plan or contract is operated as if such plan or contract amendment were in effect.

SEC. 404. MODIFICATION OF SPECIAL RULES FOR MINIMUM FUNDING STANDARDS FOR COMMUNITY NEWSPAPER PLANS.

(a) Amendment To Internal Revenue Code Of 1986.—Subsection (m) of section 430 of the Internal Revenue Code of 1986, as added by the Setting Every Community Up for Retirement Enhancement Act of 2019, is amended to read as follows:

"(m) Special Rules For Community Newspaper Plans.—

"(1) IN GENERAL.—An eligible newspaper plan sponsor of a plan under which no participant has had the participant's accrued benefit increased (whether because of service or compensation) after April 2, 2019, may elect to have the alternative standards described in paragraph (4) apply to such plan.

"(2) ELIGIBLE NEWSPAPER PLAN SPONSOR.—The term 'eligible newspaper plan sponsor' means the plan sponsor of—

"(A) any community newspaper plan, or

"(B) any other plan sponsored, as of April 2, 2019, by a member of the same controlled group of a plan sponsor of a community newspaper plan if such member is in the trade or business of publishing 1 or more newspapers.

"(3) ELECTION.—An election under paragraph (1) shall be made at such time and in such manner as prescribed by the Secretary. Such election, once made with respect to a plan year, shall apply to all subsequent plan years unless revoked with the consent of the Secretary.

"(4) ALTERNATIVE MINIMUM FUNDING STANDARDS.—The alternative standards described in this paragraph are the following:

"(A) INTEREST RATES.—

"(i) IN GENERAL.—Notwithstanding subsection (h)(2)(C) and except as provided in clause (ii), the first, second, and third segment rates in effect for any month for purposes of this section shall be 8 percent.

"(ii) NEW BENEFIT ACCRUALS.—Notwithstanding subsection (h)(2), for purposes of determining the funding target and normal cost of a plan for any plan year, the present value of any benefits accrued or earned under the plan for a plan year with respect to which an election under paragraph (1) is in effect shall be determined on the basis of the United States Treasury obligation yield curve for the day that is the valuation date of such plan for such plan year.

"(iii) UNITED STATES TREASURY OBLIGATION YIELD CURVE.—For purposes of this subsection, the term 'United States Treasury obligation yield curve' means, with respect to any day, a yield curve which shall be prescribed by the Secretary for such day on interest-bearing obligations of the United States.

"(B) SHORTFALL AMORTIZATION BASE.—

"(i) PREVIOUS SHORTFALL AMORTIZATION BASES.—The shortfall amortization bases determined under subsection (c)(3) for all plan years preceding the first plan year to which the election under paragraph (1) applies (and all shortfall amortization installments determined with respect to such bases) shall be reduced to zero under rules similar to the rules of subsection (c)(6).

"(ii) NEW SHORTFALL AMORTIZATION BASE.—Notwithstanding subsection (c)(3), the shortfall amortization base for the first plan year to which the election under paragraph (1) applies shall be the funding shortfall of such plan for such plan year (determined using the interest rates as modified under subparagraph (A)).

"(C) DETERMINATION OF SHORTFALL AMORTIZATION INSTALLMENTS.—

"(i) 30-YEAR PERIOD.—Subparagraphs (A) and (B) of subsection (c)(2) shall be applied by substituting '30-plan-year' for '7-plan-year' each place it appears.

"(ii) NO SPECIAL ELECTION.—The election under subparagraph (D) of subsection (c)(2) shall not apply to any plan year to which the election under paragraph (1) applies.

"(D) EXEMPTION FROM AT-RISK TREATMENT.—Subsection (i) shall not apply.

"(5) COMMUNITY NEWSPAPER PLAN.—For purposes of this subsection—

"(A) IN GENERAL.—The term 'community newspaper plan' means any plan to which this section applies maintained as of December 31, 2018, by an employer which—

"(i) maintains the plan on behalf of participants and beneficiaries with respect to employment in the trade or business of publishing 1 or more newspapers which were published by the employer at any time during the 11-year period ending on the date of the enactment of this subsection,

"(ii) (I) is not a company the stock of which is publicly traded (on a stock exchange or in an over-the-counter market), and is not controlled, directly or indirectly, by such a company, or

"(II) is controlled, directly or indirectly, during the entire 30-year period ending on the date of the enactment of this subsection by individuals who are members of the same family, and does not publish or distribute a daily newspaper that is carrier-distributed in printed form in more than 5 States, and

"(iii) is controlled, directly or indirectly—

"(I) by 1 or more persons residing primarily in a State in which the community newspaper has been published on newsprint or carrier-distributed,

"(II) during the entire 30-year period ending on the date of the enactment of this subsection by individuals who are members of the same family,

"(III) by 1 or more trusts, the sole trustees of which are persons described in subclause (I) or (II), or

"(IV) by a combination of persons described in subclause (I), (II), or (III).

"(B) NEWSPAPER.—The term 'newspaper' does not include any newspaper (determined without regard to this subparagraph) to which any of the following apply:

"(i) Is not in general circulation.

"(ii) Is published (on newsprint or electronically) less frequently than 3 times per week.

"(iii) Has not ever been regularly published on newsprint.

"(iv) Does not have a bona fide list of paid subscribers.

"(C) CONTROL.—A person shall be treated as controlled by another person if such other person possesses, directly or indirectly, the power to direct or cause the direction and management of such person (including the power to elect a majority of the members of the board of directors of such person) through the ownership of voting securities.

"(6) CONTROLLED GROUP.—For purposes of this subsection, the term 'controlled group' means all persons treated as a single employer under subsection (b), (c), (m), or (o) of section 414 as of the date of the enactment of this subsection.".

(b) Amendment To Employee Retirement Income Security Act Of 1974.—Subsection (m) of section 303 of the Employee Retirement Income Security Act of 1974 (29 U.S.C. 1083(m)), as added by the Setting Every Community Up for Retirement Enhancement Act of 2019, is amended to read as follows:

"(m) Special Rules For Community Newspaper Plans.—

"(1) IN GENERAL.—An eligible newspaper plan sponsor of a plan under which no participant has had the participant's accrued benefit increased (whether because of service or compensation) after April 2, 2019, may elect to have the alternative standards described in paragraph (4) apply to such plan.

"(2) ELIGIBLE NEWSPAPER PLAN SPONSOR.—The term 'eligible newspaper plan sponsor' means the plan sponsor of—

"(A) any community newspaper plan, or

"(B) any other plan sponsored, as of April 2, 2019, by a member of the same controlled group of a plan sponsor of a community newspaper plan if such member is in the trade or business of publishing 1 or more newspapers.

"(3) ELECTION.—An election under paragraph (1) shall be made at such time and in such manner as prescribed by the Secretary of the Treasury. Such election, once made with respect to a plan year, shall apply to all subsequent plan years unless revoked with the consent of the Secretary of the Treasury.

"(4) ALTERNATIVE MINIMUM FUNDING STANDARDS.—The alternative standards described in this paragraph are the following:

"(A) INTEREST RATES.—

"(i) IN GENERAL.—Notwithstanding subsection (h)(2)(C) and except as provided in clause (ii), the first, second, and third segment rates in effect for any month for purposes of this section shall be 8 percent.

"(ii) NEW BENEFIT ACCRUALS.—Notwithstanding subsection (h)(2), for purposes of determining the funding target and normal cost of a plan for any plan year, the present value of any benefits accrued or earned under the plan for a plan year with respect to which an election under paragraph (1) is in effect shall be determined on the basis of the United States Treasury obligation yield curve for the day that is the valuation date of such plan for such plan year.

"(iii) UNITED STATES TREASURY OBLIGATION YIELD CURVE.—For purposes of this subsection, the term 'United States Treasury obligation yield curve' means, with respect to any day, a yield curve which shall be prescribed by the Secretary of the Treasury for such day on interest-bearing obligations of the United States.

"(B) SHORTFALL AMORTIZATION BASE.—

"(i) PREVIOUS SHORTFALL AMORTIZATION BASES.—The shortfall amortization bases determined under subsection (c)(3) for all plan years preceding the first plan year to which the election under paragraph (1) applies (and all shortfall amortization installments determined with respect to such bases) shall be reduced to zero under rules similar to the rules of subsection (c)(6).

"(ii) NEW SHORTFALL AMORTIZATION BASE.—Notwithstanding subsection (c)(3), the shortfall amortization base for the first plan year to which the election under paragraph (1) applies shall be the funding shortfall of such plan for such plan year (determined using the interest rates as modified under subparagraph (A)).

"(C) DETERMINATION OF SHORTFALL AMORTIZATION INSTALLMENTS.—

"(i) 30-YEAR PERIOD.—Subparagraphs (A) and (B) of subsection (c)(2) shall be applied by substituting '30-plan-year' for '7-plan-year' each place it appears.

"(ii) NO SPECIAL ELECTION.—The election under subparagraph (D) of subsection (c)(2) shall not apply to any plan year to which the election under paragraph (1) applies.

"(D) EXEMPTION FROM AT-RISK TREATMENT.—Subsection (i) shall not apply.

"(5) COMMUNITY NEWSPAPER PLAN.—For purposes of this subsection—

"(A) IN GENERAL.—The term 'community newspaper plan' means a plan to which this section applies maintained as of December 31, 2018, by an employer which—

"(i) maintains the plan on behalf of participants and beneficiaries with respect to employment in the trade or business of publishing 1 or more newspapers which were published by the employer at any time during the 11-year period ending on the date of the enactment of this subsection,

"(ii) (I) is not a company the stock of which is publicly traded (on a stock exchange or in an over-the-counter market), and is not controlled, directly or indirectly, by such a company, or

"(II) is controlled, directly, or indirectly, during the entire 30-year period ending on the date of the enactment of this subsection by individuals who are members of the same family, and does not publish or distribute a daily newspaper that is carrier-distributed in printed form in more than 5 States, and

"(iii) is controlled, directly, or indirectly—

"(I) by 1 or more persons residing primarily in a State in which the community newspaper has been published on newsprint or carrier-distributed,

"(II) during the entire 30-year period ending on the date of the enactment of this subsection by individuals who are members of the same family,

"(III) by 1 or more trusts, the sole trustees of which are persons described in subclause (I) or (II), or

"(IV) by a combination of persons described in subclause (I), (II), or (III).

"(B) NEWSPAPER.—The term 'newspaper' does not include any newspaper (determined without regard to this subparagraph) to which any of the following apply:

"(i) Is not in general circulation.

"(ii) Is published (on newsprint or electronically) less frequently than 3 times per week.

"(iii) Has not ever been regularly published on newsprint.

"(iv) Does not have a bona fide list of paid subscribers.

"(C) CONTROL.—A person shall be treated as controlled by another person if such other person possesses, directly or indirectly, the power to direct or cause the direction and management of such person (including the power to elect a majority of the members of the board of directors of such person) through the ownership of voting securities.

"(6) CONTROLLED GROUP.—For purposes of this subsection, the term 'controlled group' means all persons treated as a single employer under subsection (b), (c), (m), or (o) of section 414 of the Internal Revenue Code of 1986 as of the date of the enactment of this subsection.

"(7) EFFECT ON PREMIUM RATE CALCULATION.—Notwithstanding any other provision of law or any regulation issued by the Pension Benefit Guaranty Corporation, in the case of a plan for which an election is made to apply the alternative standards described in paragraph (3), the additional premium under section 4006(a)(3)(E) shall be determined as if such election had not been made.".

(c) Effective Date.—The amendments made by this section shall apply to plan years ending after December 31, 2017.

SEC. 405. APPLICATION OF COOPERATIVE AND SMALL EMPLOYER CHARITY PENSION PLAN RULES TO CERTAIN CHARITABLE EMPLOYERS WHOSE PRIMARY EXEMPT PURPOSE IS PROVIDING SERVICES WITH RESPECT TO MOTHERS AND CHILDREN.

(a) Employee Retirement Income Security Act Of 1974.—Section 210(f)(1) of the Employee Retirement Income Security Act of 1974 (29 U.S.C. 1060(f)(1)) is amended—

(1) by striking "or" at the end of subparagraph (B);

(2) by striking the period at the end of subparagraph (C)(iv) and inserting "; or"; and

(3) by inserting after subparagraph (C) the following new subparagraph:

"(D) that, as of January 1, 2000, was maintained by an employer—

"(i) described in section 501(c)(3) of the Internal Revenue Code of 1986,

"(ii) who has been in existence since at least 1938,

"(iii) who conducts medical research directly or indirectly through grant making, and

"(iv) whose primary exempt purpose is to provide services with respect to mothers and children.".

(b) Internal Revenue Code Of 1986.—Section 414(y)(1) of the Internal Revenue Code of 1986 is amended—

(1) by striking "or" at the end of subparagraph (B);

(2) by striking the period at the end of subparagraph (C)(iv) and inserting "; or"; and

(3) by inserting after subparagraph (C) the following new subparagraph:

"(D) that, as of January 1, 2000, was maintained by an employer—

"(i) described in section 501(c)(3),

"(ii) who has been in existence since at least 1938,

"(iii) who conducts medical research directly or indirectly through grant making, and

"(iv) whose primary exempt purpose is to provide services with respect to mothers and children.".

(c) Effective Date.—The amendments made by this section shall apply to plan years beginning after December 31, 2018.

SEC. 406. EXTENDED AMORTIZATION FOR SINGLE EMPLOYER PLANS.

(a) 15-Year Amortization Under The Internal Revenue Code Of 1986.—Section 430(c) of the Internal Revenue Code of 1986 is amended by adding at the end the following new paragraph:

"(8) 15-YEAR AMORTIZATION.—With respect to plan years beginning after December 31, 2019—

"(A) the shortfall amortization bases for all plan years preceding the first plan year beginning after December 31, 2019 (and all shortfall amortization installments determined with respect to such bases) shall be reduced to zero, and

"(B) subparagraphs (A) and (B) of paragraph (2) shall each be applied by substituting '15-plan-year period' for '7-plan-year period'.".

(b) 15-Year Amortization Under The Employee Retirement Income Security Act Of 1974.—Section 303(c) of the Employee Retirement Income Security

Act of 1974 (29 U.S.C. 1083(c)) is amended by adding at the end the following new paragraph:

"(8) 15-YEAR AMORTIZATION.—With respect to plan years beginning after December 31, 2019—

"(A) the shortfall amortization bases for all plan years preceding the first plan year beginning after December 31, 2019 (and all shortfall amortization installments determined with respect to such bases) shall be reduced to zero, and

"(B) subparagraphs (A) and (B) of paragraph (2) shall each be applied by substituting '15-plan-year period' for '7-plan-year period'.".

(c) Effective Date.—The amendments made by this section shall apply to plan years beginning after December 31, 2019.

SEC. 407. EXTENSION OF PENSION FUNDING STABILIZATION PERCENTAGES FOR SINGLE EMPLOYER PLANS.

(a) Amendments To Internal Revenue Code Of 1986.—

(1) IN GENERAL.—The table contained in subclause (II) of section 430(h)(2)(C)(iv) of the Internal Revenue Code of 1986 is amended to read as follows:

"If the calendar year is:	The applicable minimum percentage is:	The applicable maximum percentage is:
Any year in the period starting in 2012 and ending in 2019	90%	110%
Any year in the period starting in 2020 and ending in 2025	95%	105%
2026	90%	110%
2027	85%	115%
2028	80%	120%
2029	75%	125%
After 2029	70%	130%.".

(2) FLOOR ON 25-YEAR AVERAGES.—Subclause (I) of section 430(h)(2)(C)(iv) of such Code is amended by adding at the end the following: "Notwithstanding anything in this subclause, if the average of the first, second, or third segment rate for any 25-year period is less than 5 percent, such average shall be deemed to be 5 percent.".

(b) Amendments To Employee Retirement Income Security Act Of 1974.—

(1) IN GENERAL.—The table contained in subclause (II) of section 303(h)(2)(C)(iv) of the Employee Retirement Income Security Act of 1974 (29 U.S.C. 1083(h)(2)(C)(iv)(II)) is amended to read as follows:

"If the calendar year is:	The applicable minimum percentage is:	The applicable maximum percentage is:
Any year in the period starting in 2012 and ending in 2019	90%	110%

Any year in the period starting in 2020 and ending in 2025 9 5 %
105%
2026 90% 110%
2027 85% 115%
2028 80% 120%
2029 75% 125%
After 2029 70% 130%.".

(2) CONFORMING AMENDMENTS.—

(A) IN GENERAL.—Section 101(f)(2)(D) of such Act (29 U.S.C. 1021(f)(2)(D)) is amended—

(i) in clause (i) by striking "and the Bipartisan Budget Act of 2015" both places it appears and inserting ", the Bipartisan Budget Act of 2015, and the Emergency Pension Plan Relief Act of 2020", and

(ii) in clause (ii) by striking "2023" and inserting "2029".

(B) STATEMENTS.—The Secretary of Labor shall modify the statements required under subclauses (I) and (II) of section 101(f)(2)(D)(i) of such Act to conform to the amendments made by this section.

(3) FLOOR ON 25-YEAR AVERAGES.—Subclause (I) of section 303(h)(2)(C)(iv) of such Act (29 U.S.C. 1083(h)(2)(C)(iv)(II)) is amended by adding at the end the following: "Notwithstanding anything in this subclause, if the average of the first, second, or third segment rate for any 25-year period is less than 5 percent, such average shall be deemed to be 5 percent.".

(c) Effective Date.—The amendments made by this section shall apply with respect to plan years beginning after December 31, 2019.

TITLE V—REHABILITATION FOR MULTIEMPLOYER PENSIONS

SEC. 501. SHORT TITLE.

This title may be cited as the "Rehabilitation for Multiemployer Pensions Act of 2020".

SEC. 502. PENSION REHABILITATION ADMINISTRATION; ESTABLISHMENT; POWERS.

(a) Establishment.—There is established in the Department of the Treasury an agency to be known as the "Pension Rehabilitation Administration".

(b) Director.—

(1) ESTABLISHMENT OF POSITION.—There shall be at the head of the Pension Rehabilitation Administration a Director, who shall be appointed by the President.

(2) TERM.—

(A) IN GENERAL.—The term of office of the Director shall be 5 years.

(B) SERVICE UNTIL APPOINTMENT OF SUCCESSOR.—An individual serving as Director at the expiration of a term may continue to serve until a successor is appointed.

(3) POWERS.—

(A) APPOINTMENT OF DEPUTY DIRECTORS, OFFICERS, AND EMPLOYEES.—The Director may appoint Deputy Directors, officers, and employees, including attorneys, in accordance with chapter 51 and subchapter III of chapter 53 of title 5, United States Code.

(B) CONTRACTING.—

(i) IN GENERAL.—The Director may contract for financial and administrative services (including those related to budget and accounting, financial reporting, personnel, and procurement) with the General Services Administration, or such other Federal agency as the Director determines appropriate, for which payment shall be made in advance, or by reimbursement, from funds of the Pension Rehabilitation Administration in such amounts as may be agreed upon by the Director and the head of the Federal agency providing the services.

(ii) SUBJECT TO APPROPRIATIONS.—Contract authority under clause (i) shall be effective for any fiscal year only to the extent that appropriations are available for that purpose.

SEC. 503. PENSION REHABILITATION TRUST FUND.

(a) In General.—Subchapter A of chapter 98 of the Internal Revenue Code of 1986 is amended by adding at the end the following new section:

"SEC. 9512. PENSION REHABILITATION TRUST FUND.

"(a) Creation Of Trust Fund.—There is established in the Treasury of the United States a trust fund to be known as the 'Pension Rehabilitation Trust Fund' (hereafter in this section referred to as the 'Fund'), consisting of such amounts as may be appropriated or credited to the Fund as provided in this section and section 9602(b).

"(b) Transfers To Fund.—

"(1) AMOUNTS ATTRIBUTABLE TO TREASURY BONDS.—There shall be credited to the Fund the amounts transferred under section 506 of the Rehabilitation for Multiemployer Pensions Act of 2020.

"(2) LOAN INTEREST AND PRINCIPAL.—

"(A) IN GENERAL.—The Director of the Pension Rehabilitation Administration established under section 502 of the Rehabilitation for Multiemployer Pensions Act of 2020 shall deposit in the Fund any amounts received from a plan as payment of interest or principal on a loan under section 504 of such Act.

"(B) INTEREST.—For purposes of subparagraph (A), the term 'interest' includes points and other similar amounts.

"(3) AVAILABILITY OF FUNDS.—Amounts credited to or deposited in the Fund shall remain available until expended.

"(c) Expenditures From Fund.—Amounts in the Fund are available without further appropriation to the Pension Rehabilitation Administration—

"(1) for the purpose of making the loans described in section 504 of the Rehabilitation for Multiemployer Pensions Act of 2020,

"(2) for the payment of principal and interest on obligations issued under section 506 of such Act, and

"(3) for administrative and operating expenses of such Administration.".

(b) Clerical Amendment.—The table of sections for subchapter A of chapter 98 of the Internal Revenue Code of 1986 is amended by adding at the end the following new item:

"Sec. 9512. Pension Rehabilitation Trust Fund.".

SEC. 504. LOAN PROGRAM FOR MULTIEMPLOYER DEFINED BENEFIT PLANS.

(a) Loan Authority.—

(1) IN GENERAL.—The Pension Rehabilitation Administration established under section 2 is authorized—

(A) to make loans to multiemployer plans (as defined in section 414(f) of the Internal Revenue Code of 1986) which are defined benefit plans (as defined in section 414(j) of such Code) and—

(i) (I) which are in critical and declining status (within the meaning of section 432(b)(6) of such Code and section 305(b)(6) of the Employee Retirement and Income Security Act) as of the date of the enactment of this section, or during the 2-year period beginning on such date, or

(II) with respect to which a suspension of benefits has been approved under section 432(e)(9) of such Code and section 305(e)(9) of such Act as of such date or during such period;

(ii) which as of such date of enactment, or during such period, are in critical status (within the meaning of section 432(b)(2) of such Code and section 305(b)(2) of such Act), have a modified funded percentage of less than 40 percent, and have a ratio of active to inactive participants which is less than 2 to 5; or

(iii) which are insolvent for purposes of section 418E of such Code as of such date of enactment, or during such period, if they became insolvent after December 16, 2014, and have not been terminated; and

(B) subject to subsection (b), to establish appropriate terms for such loans.

For purposes of subparagraph (A)(ii), the term "modified funded percentage" means the percentage equal to a fraction the numerator of which is current value of plan assets (as defined in section 3(26) of such Act) and the denominator of which is current liabilities (as defined in section 431(c)(6)(D) of such Code and section 304(c)(6)(D) of such Act).

(2) CONSULTATION.—The Director of the Pension Rehabilitation Administration shall consult with the Secretary of the Treasury, the Secretary of Labor, and the Director of the Pension Benefit Guaranty Corporation before making any loan under paragraph (1), and shall share with such persons the application and plan information with respect to each such loan.

(3) ESTABLISHMENT OF LOAN PROGRAM.—

(A) IN GENERAL.—A program to make the loans authorized under this section shall be established not later than May 31, 2020, with guidance regarding such program to be promulgated by the Director of the Pension Rehabilitation Administration, in consultation with the Director of the Pension Benefit Guaranty Corporation, the Secretary of the Treasury, and the Secretary of Labor, not later than August 31, 2020.

(B) LOANS AUTHORIZED BEFORE PROGRAM DATE.—Without regard to whether the program under subparagraph (A) has been established, a plan may apply for a loan under this section before either date described in such subparagraph, and the Pension Rehabilitation Administration shall approve the application and make the loan before establishment of the program if necessary to avoid any suspension of the accrued benefits of participants.

(b) Loan Terms.—

(1) IN GENERAL.—The terms of any loan made under subsection (a) shall state that—

(A) the plan shall make payments of interest on the loan for a period of 29 years beginning on the date of the loan (or 19 years in the case of a plan making the election under subsection (c)(5));

(B) final payment of interest and principal shall be due in the 30th year after the date of the loan (except as provided in an election under subsection (c)(5)); and

(C) as a condition of the loan, the plan sponsor stipulates that—

(i) except as provided in clause (ii), the plan will not increase benefits, allow any employer participating in the plan to reduce its contributions, or accept any collective bargaining agreement which provides for reduced contribution rates, during the 30-year period described in subparagraphs (A) and (B);

(ii) in the case of a plan with respect to which a suspension of benefits has been approved under section 432(e)(9) of the Internal Revenue Code of 1986 and section 305(e)(9) of the Employee Retirement Income Security Act of 1974, or under section 418E of such Code, before the loan, the plan will reinstate the suspended benefits (or will not carry out any suspension which has been approved but not yet implemented);

(iii) the plan sponsor will comply with the requirements of section 6059A of the Internal Revenue Code of 1986;

(iv) the plan will continue to pay all premiums due under section 4007 of the Employee Retirement Income Security Act of 1974; and

(v) the plan and plan administrator will meet such other requirements as the Director of the Pension Rehabilitation Administration provides in the loan terms.

The terms of the loan shall not make reference to whether the plan is receiving financial assistance under section 4261(d) of the Employee Retirement Income Security Act of 1974 (29 U.S.C. 1431(d)) or to any adjustment of the loan amount under subsection (d)(2)(A)(ii).

(2) INTEREST RATE.—Except as provided in the second sentence of this paragraph and subsection (c)(5), loans made under subsection (a) shall have as low an interest rate as is feasible. Such rate shall be determined by the Pension Rehabilitation Administration and shall—

(A) not be lower than the rate of interest on 30-year Treasury securities on the first day of the calendar year in which the loan is issued; and

(B) not exceed the greater of—

(i) a rate 0.2 percentage points higher than such rate of interest on such date; or

(ii) the rate necessary to collect revenues sufficient to administer the program under this section.

(c) Loan Application.—

(1) IN GENERAL.—In applying for a loan under subsection (a), the plan sponsor shall—

(A) demonstrate that, except as provided in subparagraph (C)—

(i) the loan will enable the plan to avoid insolvency for at least the 30-year period described in subparagraphs (A) and (B) of subsection (b)(1) or, in the case of a plan which is already insolvent, to emerge from insolvency within and avoid insolvency for the remainder of such period; and

(ii) the plan is reasonably expected to be able to pay benefits and the interest on the loan during such period and to accumulate sufficient funds to repay the principal when due;

(B) provide the plan's most recently filed Form 5500 as of the date of application and any other information necessary to determine the loan amount under subsection (d);

(C) stipulate whether the plan is also applying for financial assistance under section 4261(d) of the Employee Retirement Income Security Act of 1974 (29 U.S.C. 1431(d)) in combination with the loan to enable the plan to avoid insolvency and to pay benefits, or is already receiving such financial assistance as a result of a previous application;

(D) state in what manner the loan proceeds will be invested pursuant to subsection (d), the person from whom any annuity contracts under such subsection will be purchased, and the person who will be the investment manager for any portfolio implemented under such subsection; and

(E) include such other information and certifications as the Director of the Pension Rehabilitation Administration shall require.

(2) STANDARD FOR ACCEPTING ACTUARIAL AND PLAN SPONSOR DETERMINATIONS AND DEMONSTRATIONS IN THE APPLICATION.—In evaluating the plan sponsor's application, the Director of the Pension Rehabilitation Administration shall accept the determinations and demonstrations in the application unless the Director, in consultation with the Director of the Pension Benefit Guaranty Corporation, the Secretary of the Treasury, and the Secretary of Labor, concludes that any such determinations or demonstrations in the application (or any underlying assumptions) are

clearly erroneous or are inconsistent with any rules issued by the Director pursuant to subsection (g).
(3) REQUIRED ACTIONS; DEEMED APPROVAL.—The Director of the Pension Rehabilitation Administration shall approve any application under this subsection within 90 days after the submission of such application unless such application is incomplete or the Director makes a conclusion described in paragraph (2) with respect to the application. An application shall be deemed approved unless, within such 90 days, the Director notifies the plan sponsor of the denial of such application and the reasons for such denial. Any approval or denial of an application by the Director of the Pension Rehabilitation Administration shall be treated as a final agency action for purposes of section 704 of title 5, United States Code. The Pension Rehabilitation Administration shall make the loan pursuant to any application promptly after the approval of such application.
(4) CERTAIN PLANS REQUIRED TO APPLY.—The plan sponsor of any plan with respect to which a suspension of benefits has been approved under section 432(e)(9) of the Internal Revenue Code of 1986 and section 305(e)(9) of the Employee Retirement Income Security Act of 1974 or under section 418E of such Code, before the date of the enactment of this Act shall apply for a loan under this section. The Director of the Pension Rehabilitation Administration shall provide for such plan sponsors to use the simplified application under subsection (d)(2)(B).
(5) INCENTIVE FOR EARLY REPAYMENT.—The plan sponsor may elect at the time of the application to repay the loan principal, along with the remaining interest, at least as rapidly as equal installments over the 10-year period beginning with the 21st year after the date of the loan. In the case of a plan making this election, the interest on the loan shall be reduced by 0.5 percentage points.
(d) Loan Amount And Use.—
(1) AMOUNT OF LOAN.—
(A) IN GENERAL.—Except as provided in subparagraph (B) and paragraph (2), the amount of any loan under subsection (a) shall be, as demonstrated by the plan sponsor on the application under subsection (c), the amount needed to purchase annuity contracts or to implement a portfolio described in paragraph (3)(C) (or a combination of the two) sufficient to provide benefits of participants and beneficiaries of the plan in pay status, and terminated vested benefits, at the time the loan is made.
(B) PLANS WITH SUSPENDED BENEFITS.—In the case of a plan with respect to which a suspension of benefits has been approved under section 432(e)(9) of the Internal Revenue Code of 1986 and section 305(e)(9) of the Employee Retirement Income Security Act of 1974 (29 U.S.C. 1085(e)(9)) or under section 418E of such Code—
(i) the suspension of benefits shall not be taken into account in applying subparagraph (A); and

(ii) the loan amount shall be the amount sufficient to provide benefits of participants and beneficiaries of the plan in pay status and terminated vested benefits at the time the loan is made, determined without regard to the suspension, including retroactive payment of benefits which would otherwise have been payable during the period of the suspension.

(2) COORDINATION WITH PBGC FINANCIAL ASSISTANCE.—

(A) IN GENERAL.—In the case of a plan which is also applying for financial assistance under section 4261(d) of the Employee Retirement Income Security Act of 1974 (29 U.S.C. 1431(d))—

(i) the plan sponsor shall submit the loan application and the application for financial assistance jointly to the Pension Rehabilitation Administration and the Pension Benefit Guaranty Corporation with the information necessary to determine the eligibility for and amount of the loan under this section and the financial assistance under section 4261(d) of such Act; and

(ii) if such financial assistance is granted, the amount of the loan under subsection (a) shall not exceed an amount equal to the excess of—

(I) the amount determined under paragraph (1)(A) or (1)(B)(ii) (whichever is applicable); over

(II) the amount of such financial assistance.

(B) PLANS ALREADY RECEIVING PBGC ASSISTANCE.—The Director of the Pension Rehabilitation Administration shall provide for a simplified application for the loan under this section which may be used by an insolvent plan which has not been terminated and which is already receiving financial assistance (other than under section 4261(d) of such Act) from the Pension Benefit Guaranty Corporation at the time of the application for the loan under this section.

(3) USE OF LOAN FUNDS.—

(A) IN GENERAL.—Notwithstanding section 432(f)(2)(A)(ii) of the Internal Revenue Code of 1986 and section 305(f)(2)(A)(ii) of such Act, the loan received under subsection (a) shall only be used to purchase annuity contracts which meet the requirements of subparagraph (B) or to implement a portfolio described in subparagraph (C) (or a combination of the two) to provide the benefits described in paragraph (1).

(B) ANNUITY CONTRACT REQUIREMENTS.—The annuity contracts purchased under subparagraph (A) shall be issued by an insurance company which is licensed to do business under the laws of any State and which is rated A or better by a nationally recognized statistical rating organization, and the purchase of such contracts shall meet all applicable fiduciary standards under the Employee Retirement Income Security Act of 1974.

(C) PORTFOLIO.—

(i) IN GENERAL.—A portfolio described in this subparagraph is—

(I) a cash matching portfolio or duration matching portfolio consisting of investment grade (as rated by a nationally recognized statistical rating organization) fixed income investments, including United States dollar-denominated public or private debt obligations issued or guaranteed by the United States or a foreign issuer, which are tradeable in United States currency and are issued at fixed or zero coupon rates; or

(II) any other portfolio prescribed by the Secretary of the Treasury in regulations which has a similar risk profile to the portfolios described in subclause (I) and is equally protective of the interests of participants and beneficiaries.

Once implemented, such a portfolio shall be maintained until all liabilities to participants and beneficiaries in pay status, and terminated vested participants, at the time of the loan are satisfied.

(ii) FIDUCIARY DUTY.—Any investment manager of a portfolio under this subparagraph shall acknowledge in writing that such person is a fiduciary under the Employee Retirement Income Security Act of 1974 with respect to the plan.

(iii) TREATMENT OF PARTICIPANTS AND BENEFICIARIES.—Participants and beneficiaries covered by a portfolio under this subparagraph shall continue to be treated as participants and beneficiaries of the plan, including for purposes of title IV of the Employee Retirement Income Security Act of 1974.

(D) ACCOUNTING.—

(i) IN GENERAL.—Annuity contracts purchased and portfolios implemented under this paragraph shall be used solely to provide the benefits described in paragraph (1) until all such benefits have been paid and shall be accounted for separately from the other assets of the plan.

(ii) OVERSIGHT OF NON-ANNUITY INVESTMENTS.—

(I) IN GENERAL.—Any portfolio implemented under this paragraph shall be subject to oversight by the Pension Rehabilitation Administration, including a mandatory triennial review of the adequacy of the portfolio to provide the benefits described in paragraph (1) and approval (to be provided within a reasonable period of time) of any decision by the plan sponsor to change the investment manager of the portfolio.

(II) REMEDIAL ACTION.—If the oversight under subclause (I) determines an inadequacy, the plan sponsor shall take remedial action to ensure that the inadequacy will be cured within 2 years of such determination.

(E) OMBUDSPERSON.—The Participant and Plan Sponsor Advocate established under section 4004 of the Employee Retirement Income Security Act of 1974 shall act as ombudsperson for participants and beneficiaries on behalf of whom annuity contracts are purchased or who are covered by a portfolio under this paragraph.

(e) Collection Of Repayment.—Except as provided in subsection (f), the Pension Rehabilitation Administration shall make every effort to collect repayment of loans under this section in accordance with section 3711 of title 31, United States Code.

(f) Loan Default.—If a plan is unable to make any payment on a loan under this section when due, the Pension Rehabilitation Administration shall negotiate with the plan sponsor revised terms for repayment (including installment payments over a reasonable period or forgiveness of a portion of the loan principal), but only to the extent necessary to avoid insolvency in the subsequent 18 months.

(g) Authority To Issue Rules, Etc.—The Director of the Pension Rehabilitation Administration, in consultation with the Director of the Pension Benefit Guaranty Corporation, the Secretary of the Treasury, and the Secretary of Labor, is authorized to issue rules regarding the form, content, and process of applications for loans under this section, actuarial standards and assumptions to be used in making estimates and projections for purposes of such applications, and assumptions regarding interest rates, mortality, and distributions with respect to a portfolio described in subsection (d)(3)(C).

(h) Report To Congress On Status Of Certain Plans With Loans.—Not later than 1 year after the first loan is made under this section, and annually thereafter, the Director of the Pension Rehabilitation Administration shall submit to the Committee on Ways and Means and the Committee on Education and Labor of the House of Representatives, and the Committee on Finance and the Committee on Health, Education, Labor, and Pensions of the Senate, a report identifying any plan that—

(1) has failed to make any scheduled payment on a loan under this section;

(2) has negotiated revised terms for repayment of such loan (including any installment payments or forgiveness of a portion of the loan principal); or

(3) the Director has determined is no longer reasonably expected to be able to—

(A) pay benefits and the interest on the loan; or

(B) accumulate sufficient funds to repay the principal when due.

Such report shall include the details of any such failure, revised terms, or determination, as the case may be.

(i) Coordination With Taxation Of Unrelated Business Income.—Subparagraph (A) of section 514(c)(6) of the Internal Revenue Code of 1986 is amended—

(1) by striking "or" at the end of clause (i);

(2) by striking the period at the end of clause (ii)(II) and inserting ", or"; and

(3) by adding at the end the following new clause:

"(iii) indebtedness with respect to a multiemployer plan under a loan made by the Pension Rehabilitation Administration pursuant to section 504 of the Rehabilitation for Multiemployer Pensions Act of 2020.".

SEC. 505. COORDINATION WITH WITHDRAWAL LIABILITY AND FUNDING RULES.

(a) Amendment To Internal Revenue Code Of 1986.—Section 432 of the Internal Revenue Code of 1986 is amended by adding at the end the following new subsection:

"(k) Special Rules For Plans Receiving Pension Rehabilitation Loans.—

"(1) DETERMINATION OF WITHDRAWAL LIABILITY.—

"(A) IN GENERAL.—If any employer participating in a plan at the time the plan receives a loan under section 504(a) of the Rehabilitation for Multiemployer Pensions Act of 2020 withdraws from the plan before the end of the 30-year period beginning on the date of the loan, the withdrawal liability of such employer shall be determined under the Employee Retirement Income Security Act of 1974—

"(i) by applying section 4219(c)(1)(D) of the Employee Retirement Income Security Act of 1974 as if the plan were terminating by the withdrawal of every employer from the plan, and

"(ii) by determining the value of nonforfeitable benefits under the plan at the time of the deemed termination by using the interest assumptions prescribed for purposes of section 4044 of the Employee Retirement Income Security Act of 1974, as prescribed in the regulations under section 4281 of the Employee Retirement Income Security Act of 1974 in the case of such a mass withdrawal.

"(B) ANNUITY CONTRACTS AND INVESTMENT PORTFOLIOS PURCHASED WITH LOAN FUNDS.—Annuity contracts purchased and portfolios implemented under section 504(d)(3) of the Rehabilitation for Multiemployer Pensions Act of 2020 shall not be taken into account as plan assets in determining the withdrawal liability of any employer under subparagraph (A), but the amount equal to the greater of—

"(i) the benefits provided under such contracts or portfolios to participants and beneficiaries, or

"(ii) the remaining payments due on the loan under section 504(a) of such Act,

shall be taken into account as unfunded vested benefits in determining such withdrawal liability.

"(2) COORDINATION WITH FUNDING REQUIREMENTS.—In the case of a plan which receives a loan under section 504(a) of the Rehabilitation for Multiemployer Pensions Act of 2020—

"(A) annuity contracts purchased and portfolios implemented under section 504(d)(3) of such Act, and the benefits provided to participants and beneficiaries under such contracts or portfolios, shall not be taken into account in determining minimum required contributions under section 412,

"(B) payments on the interest and principal under the loan, and any benefits owed in excess of those provided under such contracts or portfolios, shall be taken into account as liabilities for purposes of such section, and

"(C) if such a portfolio is projected due to unfavorable investment or actuarial experience to be unable to fully satisfy the liabilities which it covers, the amount of the liabilities projected to be unsatisfied shall be taken into account as liabilities for purposes of such section.".

(b) Amendment To Employee Retirement Income Security Act Of 1974.—Section 305 of the Employee Retirement Income Security Act of 1974 (29 U.S.C. 1085) is amended by adding at the end the following new subsection:

"(k) Special Rules For Plans Receiving Pension Rehabilitation Loans.—

"(1) DETERMINATION OF WITHDRAWAL LIABILITY.—

"(A) IN GENERAL.—If any employer participating in a plan at the time the plan receives a loan under section 504(a) of the Rehabilitation for Multiemployer Pensions Act of 2020 withdraws from the plan before the end of the 30-year period beginning on the date of the loan, the withdrawal liability of such employer shall be determined—

"(i) by applying section 4219(c)(1)(D) as if the plan were terminating by the withdrawal of every employer from the plan, and

"(ii) by determining the value of nonforfeitable benefits under the plan at the time of the deemed termination by using the interest assumptions prescribed for purposes of section 4044, as prescribed in the regulations under section 4281 in the case of such a mass withdrawal.

"(B) ANNUITY CONTRACTS AND INVESTMENT PORTFOLIOS PURCHASED WITH LOAN FUNDS.—Annuity contracts purchased and portfolios implemented under section 504(d)(3) of the Rehabilitation for Multiemployer Pensions Act of 2020 shall not be taken into account in determining the withdrawal liability of any employer under subparagraph (A), but the amount equal to the greater of—

"(i) the benefits provided under such contracts or portfolios to participants and beneficiaries, or

"(ii) the remaining payments due on the loan under section 504(a) of such Act,

shall be taken into account as unfunded vested benefits in determining such withdrawal liability.

"(2) COORDINATION WITH FUNDING REQUIREMENTS.—In the case of a plan which receives a loan under section 504(a) of the Rehabilitation for Multiemployer Pensions Act of 2020—

"(A) annuity contracts purchased and portfolios implemented under section 504(d)(3) of such Act, and the benefits provided to participants and beneficiaries under such contracts or portfolios, shall not be taken into account in determining minimum required contributions under section 302,

"(B) payments on the interest and principal under the loan, and any benefits owed in excess of those provided under such contracts or portfolios, shall be taken into account as liabilities for purposes of such section, and

"(C) if such a portfolio is projected due to unfavorable investment or actuarial experience to be unable to fully satisfy the liabilities which it covers, the amount of the liabilities projected to be unsatisfied shall be taken into account as liabilities for purposes of such section.".

SEC. 506. ISSUANCE OF TREASURY BONDS.

The Secretary of the Treasury shall from time to time transfer from the general fund of the Treasury to the Pension Rehabilitation Trust Fund established under section 9512 of the Internal Revenue Code of 1986 such amounts as are necessary to fund the loan program under section 504 of this Act, including from proceeds from the Secretary's issuance of obligations under chapter 31 of title 31, United States Code.

SEC. 507. REPORTS OF PLANS RECEIVING PENSION REHABILITATION LOANS.

(a) In General.—Subpart E of part III of subchapter A of chapter 61 of the Internal Revenue Code of 1986 is amended by adding at the end the following new section:

"SEC. 6059A. REPORTS OF PLANS RECEIVING PENSION REHABILITATION LOANS.

"(a) In General.—In the case of a plan receiving a loan under section 504(a) of the Rehabilitation for Multiemployer Pensions Act of 2020, with respect to the first plan year beginning after the date of the loan and each of the 29 succeeding plan years, not later than the 90th day of each such plan year the plan sponsor shall file with the Secretary a report (including appropriate documentation and actuarial certifications from the plan actuary, as required by the Secretary) that contains—

"(1) the funded percentage (as defined in section 432(j)(2)) as of the first day of such plan year, and the underlying actuarial value of assets (determined with regard, and without regard, to annuity contracts purchased and portfolios implemented with proceeds of such loan) and liabilities (including any amounts due with respect to such loan) taken into account in determining such percentage,

"(2) the market value of the assets of the plan (determined as provided in paragraph (1)) as of the last day of the plan year preceding such plan year,

"(3) the total value of all contributions made by employers and employees during the plan year preceding such plan year,

"(4) the total value of all benefits paid during the plan year preceding such plan year,

"(5) cash flow projections for such plan year and the 9 succeeding plan years, and the assumptions used in making such projections,

"(6) funding standard account projections for such plan year and the 9 succeeding plan years, and the assumptions relied upon in making such projections,

"(7) the total value of all investment gains or losses during the plan year preceding such plan year,

"(8) any significant reduction in the number of active participants during the plan year preceding such plan year, and the reason for such reduction,

"(9) a list of employers that withdrew from the plan in the plan year preceding such plan year, and the resulting reduction in contributions,

"(10) a list of employers that paid withdrawal liability to the plan during the plan year preceding such plan year and, for each employer, a total assessment of the withdrawal liability paid, the annual payment amount, and the number of years remaining in the payment schedule with respect to such withdrawal liability,

"(11) any material changes to benefits, accrual rates, or contribution rates during the plan year preceding such plan year, and whether such changes relate to the terms of the loan,

"(12) details regarding any funding improvement plan or rehabilitation plan and updates to such plan,

"(13) the number of participants during the plan year preceding such plan year who are active participants, the number of participants and beneficiaries in pay status, and the number of terminated vested participants and beneficiaries,

"(14) the amount of any financial assistance received under section 4261 of the Employee Retirement Income Security Act of 1974 to pay benefits during the preceding plan year, and the total amount of such financial assistance received for all preceding years,

"(15) the information contained on the most recent annual funding notice submitted by the plan under section 101(f) of the Employee Retirement Income Security Act of 1974,

"(16) the information contained on the most recent annual return under section 6058 and actuarial report under section 6059 of the plan, and

"(17) copies of the plan document and amendments, other retirement benefit or ancillary benefit plans relating to the plan and contribution obligations under such plans, a breakdown of administrative expenses of the plan, participant census data and distribution of benefits, the most recent actuarial valuation report as of the plan year, copies of collective bargaining agreements, and financial reports, and such other information as the Secretary, in consultation with the Director of the Pension Rehabilitation Administration, may require.

"(b) Electronic Submission.—The report required under subsection (a) shall be submitted electronically.

"(c) Information Sharing.—The Secretary shall share the information in the report under subsection (a) with the Secretary of Labor and the Director of the Pension Benefit Guaranty Corporation.

"(d) Report To Participants, Beneficiaries, And Employers.—Each plan sponsor required to file a report under subsection (a) shall, before the expiration of the time prescribed for the filing of such report, also provide a summary (written in a manner so as to be understood by the average plan participant) of the information in such report to participants and beneficiaries in the plan and to each employer with an obligation to contribute to the plan.".

(b) Penalty.—Subsection (e) of section 6652 of the Internal Revenue Code of 1986 is amended—

(1) by inserting ", 6059A (relating to reports of plans receiving pension rehabilitation loans)" after "deferred compensation)";

(2) by inserting "($100 in the case of failures under section 6059A)" after "$25"; and

(3) by adding at the end the following: "In the case of a failure with respect to section 6059A, the amount imposed under this subsection shall not be paid from the assets of the plan.".

(c) Clerical Amendment.—The table of sections for subpart E of part III of subchapter A of chapter 61 of the Internal Revenue Code of 1986 is amended by adding at the end the following new item:

"Sec. 6059A. Reports of plans receiving pension rehabilitation loans.".

SEC. 508. PBGC FINANCIAL ASSISTANCE.

(a) In General.—Section 4261 of the Employee Retirement Income Security Act of 1974 (29 U.S.C. 1431) is amended by adding at the end the following new subsection:

"(d) (1) The plan sponsor of a multiemployer plan—

"(A) which is in critical and declining status (within the meaning of section 305(b)(6)) as of the date of the enactment of this subsection or during the 2-year period beginning on such date, or with respect to which a suspension of benefits has been approved under section 305(e)(9) as of such date;

"(B) which, as of such date of enactment or during such period, is in critical status (within the meaning of section 305(b)(2)), has a modified funded percentage of less than 40 percent (as defined in section 504(a)(1) of the Rehabilitation for Multiemployer Pensions Act of 2020), and has a ratio of active to inactive participants which is less than 2 to 5; or

"(C) which is insolvent for purposes of section 418E of the Internal Revenue Code of 1986 as of such date of enactment or during such period, if the plan became insolvent after December 16, 2014, and has not been terminated, and which is applying for a loan under section 504(a) of the Rehabilitation for Multiemployer Pensions Act of 2020 may also apply to the corporation for financial assistance under this subsection, by jointly submitting such applications in accordance with section 504(d)(2) of such Act. The application for financial assistance under this subsection shall demonstrate, based on projections by the plan actuary, that after the receipt of the anticipated loan amount under section 4(a) of such Act, the plan will still become (or remain) insolvent within the 30-year period beginning on the date of the loan.

"(2) In reviewing an application under paragraph (1), the corporation shall review the determinations and demonstrations submitted with the loan application under section 504(c) of the Rehabilitation for Multiemployer Pensions Act of 2020 and provide guidance regarding such determinations and demonstrations prior to approving any application for financial assistance under this subsection. The corporation may deny any application if any such determinations or demonstrations (or any underlying assumptions) are clearly erroneous, or inconsistent with rules issued by the corporation, and the plan and the corporation are unable to reach agreement on such determinations or demonstrations. The corporation shall prescribe any such rules or guidance not later than August 31, 2020.

"(3) In the case of a plan described in paragraph (1)(A) or (1)(B), the total financial assistance provided under this subsection shall be an amount equal to the smallest portion of the loan amount with respect to the plan under paragraph (1)(A) or (1)(B)(ii) of section 504(d) of the Rehabilitation for Multiemployer Pensions Act of 2020 (determined without regard to paragraph (2) thereof) that, if provided as financial assistance under this subsection instead of a loan, would allow the plan to avoid the projected insolvency.

"(4) In the case of a plan described in paragraph (1)(C), the financial assistance provided pursuant to such application under this subsection shall be the present value of the amount (determined by the plan actuary and submitted on the application) that, if such amount were paid by the corporation in combination with the loan and any other assistance being provided to the plan by the corporation at the time of the application, would enable the plan to emerge from insolvency and avoid any other insolvency projected under paragraph (1).

"(5) (A) (i) Except as provided in subparagraph (B), if the corporation determines at the time of approval, or at the beginning of any plan year beginning thereafter, that the plan's 5-year expenditure projection (determined without regard to loan payments described in clause (iii)(III)) exceeds the fair market value of the plan's assets, the corporation shall (subject to the total amount of financial assistance approved under this subsection) provide such assistance in an amount equal to the lesser of—

"(I) the amount by which the plan's 5-year expenditure projection exceeds such fair market value; or

"(II) the plan's expected expenditures for the plan year.

"(ii) For purposes of this subparagraph, the term '5-year expenditure projection' means, with respect to any plan for a plan year, an amount equal to 500 percent of the plan's expected expenditures for the plan year.

"(iii) For purposes of this subparagraph, the term 'expected expenditures' means, with respect to any plan for a plan year, an amount equal to the sum of—

"(I) expected benefit payments for the plan year;

"(II) expected administrative expense payments for the plan year; plus

"(III) payments on the loan scheduled during the plan year pursuant to the terms of the loan under section 504(b) of the Rehabilitation for Multiemployer Pensions Act of 2020.

"(iv) For purposes of this subparagraph, in the case of any plan year during which a plan is approved for a loan under section 504 of such Act, but has not yet received the proceeds, such proceeds shall be included in determining the fair market value of the plan's assets for the plan year. The preceding sentence shall not apply in the case of any plan that for the plan year beginning in 2015 was certified pursuant to section 305(b)(3) as being in critical and declining status, and had more than 300,000 participants.

"(B) The financial assistance under this subsection shall be provided in a lump sum if the plan sponsor demonstrates in the application, and the corporation determines, that such a lump sum payment is necessary for the plan to avoid the insolvency to which the application relates. In the case of a plan described in paragraph (1)(C), such lump sum shall be provided not later than December 31, 2020.

"(6) Subsections (b) and (c) shall apply to financial assistance under this subsection as if it were provided under subsection (a), except that the terms for repayment under subsection (b)(2) shall not require the financial assistance to be repaid before the date on which the loan under section 504(a) of the Rehabilitation for Multiemployer Pensions Act of 2020 is repaid in full.

"(7) The corporation may forgo repayment of the financial assistance provided under this subsection if necessary to avoid any suspension of the accrued benefits of participants.".

(b) Appropriations.—There is appropriated to the Director of the Pension Benefit Guaranty Corporation such sums as may be necessary for each fiscal year to provide the financial assistance described in section 4261(d) of the Employee Retirement Income Security Act of 1974 (29 U.S.C. 1431(d)) (as added by this section) (including necessary administrative and operating expenses relating to such assistance).

DIVISION U—CONSUMER PROTECTION AND TELECOMMUNICATIONS PROVISIONS

TITLE I—COVID-19 PRICE GOUGING PREVENTION

SEC. 101. SHORT TITLE.

This title may be cited as the "COVID-19 Price Gouging Prevention Act".

SEC. 102. PREVENTION OF PRICE GOUGING.

(a) In General.—For the duration of a public health emergency declared pursuant to section 319 of the Public Health Service Act (42 U.S.C. 247d) as a result of confirmed cases of 2019 novel coronavirus (COVID–19), including any renewal thereof, it shall be unlawful for any person to sell or offer for sale a good or service at a price that—

(1) is unconscionably excessive; and

(2) indicates the seller is using the circumstances related to such public health emergency to increase prices unreasonably.

(b) Factors For Consideration.—In determining whether a person has violated subsection (a), there shall be taken into account, with respect to the price at which such person sold or offered for sale the good or service, factors that include the following:

(1) Whether such price grossly exceeds the average price at which the same or a similar good or service was sold or offered for sale by such person—

(A) during the 90-day period immediately preceding January 31, 2020; or

(B) during the same 90-day period of the previous year.

(2) Whether such price grossly exceeds the average price at which the same or a similar good or service was readily obtainable from other similarly situated competing sellers before January 31, 2020.

(3) Whether such price reasonably reflects additional costs, not within the control of such person, that were paid, incurred, or reasonably anticipated by such person, or reasonably reflects the profitability of forgone sales or additional risks taken by such person, to produce, distribute, obtain, or sell such good or service under the circumstances.

(c) Enforcement.—

(1) ENFORCEMENT BY FEDERAL TRADE COMMISSION.—

(A) UNFAIR OR DECEPTIVE ACTS OR PRACTICES.—A violation of subsection (a) shall be treated as a violation of a regulation under section 18(a)(1)(B) of the Federal Trade Commission Act (15 U.S.C. 57a(a)(1)(B)) regarding unfair or deceptive acts or practices.

(B) POWERS OF COMMISSION.—The Commission shall enforce subsection (a) in the same manner, by the same means, and with the same jurisdiction, powers, and duties as though all applicable terms and provisions of the Federal Trade Commission Act (15 U.S.C. 41 et seq.) were incorporated into and made a part of this section. Any person who violates such subsection shall be subject

to the penalties and entitled to the privileges and immunities provided in the Federal Trade Commission Act.
(2) EFFECT ON OTHER LAWS.—Nothing in this section shall be construed in any way to limit the authority of the Commission under any other provision of law.
(3) ENFORCEMENT BY STATE ATTORNEYS GENERAL.—
(A) IN GENERAL.—If the chief law enforcement officer of a State, or an official or agency designated by a State, has reason to believe that any person has violated or is violating subsection (a), the attorney general, official, or agency of the State, in addition to any authority it may have to bring an action in State court under its consumer protection law, may bring a civil action in any appropriate United States district court or in any other court of competent jurisdiction, including a State court, to—
(i) enjoin further such violation by such person;
(ii) enforce compliance with such subsection;
(iii) obtain civil penalties; and
(iv) obtain damages, restitution, or other compensation on behalf of residents of the State.
(B) NOTICE AND INTERVENTION BY THE FTC.—The attorney general of a State shall provide prior written notice of any action under subparagraph (A) to the Commission and provide the Commission with a copy of the complaint in the action, except in any case in which such prior notice is not feasible, in which case the attorney general shall serve such notice immediately upon instituting such action. The Commission shall have the right—
(i) to intervene in the action;
(ii) upon so intervening, to be heard on all matters arising therein; and
(iii) to file petitions for appeal.
(C) LIMITATION ON STATE ACTION WHILE FEDERAL ACTION IS PENDING.—If the Commission has instituted a civil action for violation of this section, no State attorney general, or official or agency of a State, may bring an action under this paragraph during the pendency of that action against any defendant named in the complaint of the Commission for any violation of this section alleged in the complaint.
(D) RELATIONSHIP WITH STATE-LAW CLAIMS.—If the attorney general of a State has authority to bring an action under State law directed at acts or practices that also violate this section, the attorney general may assert the State-law claim and a claim under this section in the same civil action.
(4) SAVINGS CLAUSE.—Nothing in this section shall preempt or otherwise affect any State or local law.
(d) Definitions.—In this section:
(1) COMMISSION.—The term “Commission” means the Federal Trade Commission.
(2) GOOD OR SERVICE.—The term “good or service” means a good or service offered in commerce, including—

(A) food, beverages, water, ice, a chemical, or a personal hygiene product;
(B) any personal protective equipment for protection from or prevention of contagious diseases, filtering facepiece respirators, medical supplies (including medical testing supplies), cleaning supplies, disinfectants, sanitizers; or
(C) any healthcare service, cleaning service, or delivery service.
(3) STATE.—The term "State" means each of the several States, the District of Columbia, each commonwealth, territory, or possession of the United States, and each federally recognized Indian Tribe.

TITLE II—E-RATE SUPPORT FOR WI-FI HOTSPOTS AND CONNECTED DEVICES

SEC. 201. E-RATE SUPPORT FOR WI-FI HOTSPOTS AND CONNECTED DEVICES DURING EMERGENCY PERIODS RELATING TO COVID-19.

(a) Regulations Required.—Not later than 7 days after the date of the enactment of this Act, the Commission shall promulgate regulations providing for the provision, during an emergency period described in subsection (b) and from amounts made available from the Emergency Connectivity Fund established under subsection (i)(1), of universal service support under section 254(h)(1)(B) of the Communications Act of 1934 (47 U.S.C. 254(h)(1)(B)) to an elementary school, secondary school, or library eligible for support under such section, as well as a tribal elementary school, tribal secondary school, or tribal library designated as eligible to receive support under such regulations by an Indian tribe that is eligible for support under section 261 of the Library Services and Technology Act (20 U.S.C. 9161), for—
(1) providing Wi-Fi hotspots to—
(A) in the case of a school, students and staff of such school for use at locations that include locations other than such school; and
(B) in the case of a library, patrons of such library for use at locations that include locations other than such library;
(2) providing connected devices to students and staff or patrons (as the case may be) for use as described in subparagraph (A) or (B) of paragraph (1); and
(3) providing mobile broadband internet access service through such Wi-Fi hotspots or connected devices.
(b) Emergency Periods Described.—An emergency period described in this subsection is the duration of a public health emergency declared pursuant to section 319 of the Public Health Service Act (42 U.S.C. 247d) as a result of COVID-19, including any renewal thereof.
(c) Service Requirement For Connected Devices.—If a school or library provides a connected device to a student, staff member, or patron using universal service support under the regulations required by subsection (a) and such connected device is only capable of connecting to broadband internet

access service through the use of Wi-Fi, such school or library shall also provide to such student, staff member, or patron a Wi-Fi hotspot and mobile broadband internet access service through such Wi-Fi hotspot.

(d) Treatment Of Wi-Fi Hotspots And Connected Devices After Emergency Period.—The Commission shall provide in the regulations required by subsection (a) that, in the case of a school or library that purchases Wi-Fi hotspots or connected devices using support received under such regulations, such school or library—

(1) may, after the emergency period with respect to which such support is received, use such Wi-Fi hotspots or connected devices for such purposes as such school or library considers appropriate, subject to any restrictions provided in such regulations (or any successor regulation); and

(2) may not sell or otherwise transfer in exchange for any thing of value such Wi-Fi hotspots or connected devices.

(e) Prioritization Of Support.—The Commission shall provide in the regulations required by subsection (a) that a school or library shall prioritize the provision of Wi-Fi hotspots or connected devices and associated mobile broadband internet access service for which support is received under such regulations to students and staff or patrons (as the case may be) that the school or library believes do not otherwise have access to broadband internet access service at the residences of such students and staff or patrons.

(f) Certification Requirements.—The Commission shall provide in the regulations required by subsection (a) that—

(1) Wi-Fi hotspots and connected devices for which support is received under such regulations shall be treated as computers for purposes of the certification requirements of paragraphs (5) and (6) of section 254(h) of the Communications Act of 1934 (47 U.S.C. 254(h)); and

(2) notwithstanding the requirements of such paragraphs relating to the timing of certifications, the certifications required by such paragraphs shall be made with respect to such Wi-Fi hotspots and connected devices as a condition of receiving such support.

(g) Rule Of Construction.—Nothing in this section shall be construed to affect any authority the Commission may have under section 254(h)(1)(B) of the Communications Act of 1934 (47 U.S.C. 254(h)(1)(B)) to allow universal service support under such section to be used for the purposes described in subsection (a) other than as required by such subsection.

(h) Exemptions.—

(1) NOTICE AND COMMENT RULEMAKING REQUIREMENTS.—Section 553 of title 5, United States Code, shall not apply to a regulation promulgated under subsection (a) or a rulemaking to promulgate such a regulation.

(2) PAPERWORK REDUCTION ACT REQUIREMENTS.—A collection of information conducted or sponsored under the regulations required by subsection (a), or under section 254 of the Communications Act of 1934 (47

U.S.C. 254) in connection with universal service support provided under such regulations, shall not constitute a collection of information for the purposes of subchapter I of chapter 35 of title 44, United States Code (commonly referred to as the Paperwork Reduction Act).

(i) Emergency Connectivity Fund.—

(1) ESTABLISHMENT.—There is established in the Treasury of the United States a fund to be known as the Emergency Connectivity Fund.

(2) AUTHORIZATION OF APPROPRIATIONS.—There is authorized to be appropriated to the Emergency Connectivity Fund, out of any money in the Treasury not otherwise appropriated, $2,000,000,000 for fiscal year 2020, to remain available through fiscal year 2021.

(3) USE OF FUNDS.—Amounts in the Emergency Connectivity Fund shall be available to the Commission to provide universal service support under the regulations required by subsection (a).

(4) RELATIONSHIP TO UNIVERSAL SERVICE CONTRIBUTIONS.—Universal service support provided under the regulations required by subsection (a) shall be provided from amounts made available under paragraph (3) and not from contributions under section 254(d) of the Communications Act of 1934 (47 U.S.C. 254(d)).

(j) Exception To Gift Restrictions.—Not later than 7 days after the date of the enactment of this Act, the Commission shall amend section 54.503(d) of title 47, Code of Federal Regulations, so as to provide that such section does not apply in the case of a gift or other thing of value that is solicited, accepted, offered, or provided during an emergency period described in subsection (b) for the purpose of responding to needs arising from the emergency.

(k) Definitions.—In this section:

(1) BROADBAND INTERNET ACCESS SERVICE.—The term "broadband internet access service" has the meaning given such term in section 8.1(b) of title 47, Code of Federal Regulations (or any successor regulation).

(2) COMMISSION.—The term "Commission" means the Federal Communications Commission.

(3) CONNECTED DEVICE.—The term "connected device" means a laptop computer, tablet computer, or similar device that is capable of connecting to mobile broadband internet access service, either by receiving such service directly or through the use of Wi-Fi.

(4) WI-FI.—The term "Wi-Fi" means a wireless networking protocol based on Institute of Electrical and Electronics Engineers standard 802.11 (or any successor standard).

(5) WI-FI HOTSPOT.—The term "Wi-Fi hotspot" means a device that is capable of—

(A) receiving mobile broadband internet access service; and

(B) sharing such service with another device through the use of Wi-Fi.

TITLE III—EMERGENCY LIFELINE BENEFIT FOR BROADBAND

SERVICE

SEC. 301. EMERGENCY LIFELINE BENEFIT FOR BROADBAND SERVICE DURING EMERGENCY PERIODS RELATING TO COVID–19.

(a) Promulgation Of Regulations Required.—Not later than 7 days after the date of the enactment of this Act, the Commission shall promulgate regulations for the provision of an emergency lifeline broadband benefit described and in accordance with the requirements of this section.

(b) Requirements.—The regulations promulgated pursuant to subsection (a) shall establish the following:

(1) Regardless of whether a household or any consumer in the household receives support under subpart E of part 54 of title 47, Code of Federal Regulations, a household is eligible for the provision of Tier I service or Tier II service, supported by the emergency lifeline broadband benefit, during an emergency period if—

(A) the household includes at least one qualifying low-income consumer who meets the qualifications in paragraphs (a) and (b) of section 54.409 of title 47, Code of Federal Regulations, or any successor regulation; or

(B) the household receives benefits from the National School Lunch Program's free or reduced cost lunch program.

(2) A provider of broadband internet access service shall apply to the Commission for the reimbursement described in paragraph (6) for each eligible household that requests the emergency lifeline broadband benefit and receives Tier I or Tier II service from the provider.

(3) Within five business days of receiving a request from a broadband internet service provider, the Commission shall determine and issue a decision whether it is in the public interest—

(A) to allow such provider to provide Tier I or Tier II service supported by the emergency lifeline broadband benefit, and

(B) to allow the provider to use its own verification processes to determine whether a household is eligible to receive the emergency lifeline broadband benefit according to the eligibility criteria in paragraph (1), if such processes are reasonable and sufficient to avoid waste, fraud, and abuse.

(4) The Commission shall adopt reasonable recordkeeping and retention requirements for recipients of reimbursements from the funds made available in subsection (f), which requirements shall be in lieu of any reporting, record keeping, retention and compliance requirements as set forth in subpart E of part 54 of title 47, Code of Federal Regulations.

(5) The emergency period may be extended within a State or any portion thereof if the Governor of the State provides written, public notice to the Commission stipulating that an extension is necessary in furtherance of the recovery related to COVID–19. The Commission shall, within 24 hours after receiving such notice, post the notice on the Commission's public website.

(6) The Commission shall reimburse providers of broadband internet access service from funds made available in subsection (f) in the following amounts:
(A) The broadband internet access service provider shall receive $50.00 per month, or an amount equal to the monthly charge for service and equipment if such charge is less than $50.00 per month, for each eligible household that requests the emergency lifeline broadband benefit and receives the Tier I service.
(B) The broadband internet access service provider shall receive $30.00 per month, or an amount equal to the monthly charge for service and equipment if such charge is less than $30.00 per month, for each eligible household that requests the emergency lifeline broadband benefit and receives Tier II service.
(7) To receive a reimbursement under paragraph (6), a broadband internet access service provider shall certify to the Commission—
(A) the number of eligible households that requested the emergency lifeline broadband benefit and received Tier I service—
(i) monthly for the duration of the emergency period; or
(ii) for each month of the emergency period, collectively, after the expiration of the emergency period under paragraph (5);
(B) the number of eligible households that requested the emergency lifeline broadband benefit and received Tier II service—
(i) monthly for the duration of the emergency period; or
(ii) for each month of the emergency period, collectively, after the expiration of the emergency period under paragraph (5);
(C) that the reimbursement sought for providing Tier I service or Tier II service to an eligible household did not exceed the provider's rate for that offering, or similar offerings, for households that are not eligible households subscribing to the same or substantially similar service;
(D) that eligible households for which the provider is seeking reimbursement for providing Tier I or Tier II service using the emergency lifeline broadband benefit—
(i) were not charged for the Tier I service or Tier II service; and
(ii) were not disqualified from receiving the emergency lifeline broadband service based on past or present arrearages; and
(E) that the eligibility of eligible households is verified in accordance with the requirements adopted by the Commission pursuant to paragraph (3).
(c) Eligible Providers.—The Commission may provide a reimbursement to a broadband internet access service provider under this section without requiring such provider to be designated as an eligible telecommunications carrier under section 214(e) of the Communications Act of 1934 (47 U.S.C. 214(e)) and notwithstanding section 254(e) of the Communications Act of 1934 (47 U.S.C. 254(e)).
(d) Rule Of Construction.—Nothing in this section shall affect the collection, distribution, or administration of the Lifeline Assistance Program governed by the rules set forth in subpart E of part 54 of title 47, Code of Federal

Regulations.

(e) Exemptions.—

(1) NOTICE AND COMMENT RULEMAKING REQUIREMENTS.—Section 553 of title 5, United States Code, shall not apply to a regulation promulgated under subsection (a) or a rulemaking to promulgate such a regulation.

(2) PAPERWORK REDUCTION ACT REQUIREMENTS.—A collection of information conducted or sponsored under the regulations required by subsection (a), or under section 254 of the Communications Act of 1934 (47 U.S.C. 254) in connection with universal service support provided under such regulations, shall not constitute a collection of information for the purposes of subchapter I of chapter 35 of title 44, United States Code (commonly referred to as the Paperwork Reduction Act).

(f) Emergency Broadband Connectivity Fund.—

(1) ESTABLISHMENT.—There is established in the Treasury of the United States a fund to be known as the Emergency Broadband Connectivity Fund.

(2) AUTHORIZATION OF APPROPRIATIONS.—There is authorized to be appropriated to the Emergency Broadband Connectivity Fund, out of any money in the Treasury not otherwise appropriated, $1,000,000,000 for fiscal year 2020, to remain available through fiscal year 2021.

(3) USE OF FUNDS.—Amounts in the Emergency Broadband Connectivity Fund shall be available to the Commission to provide reimbursements for Tier I service or Tier II service provided to eligible households under the regulations required pursuant to subsection (a).

(4) RELATIONSHIP TO UNIVERSAL SERVICE CONTRIBUTIONS.—Reimbursements provided under the regulations required by subsection (a) shall be provided from amounts made available under paragraph (3) and not from contributions under section 254(d) of the Communications Act of 1934 (47 U.S.C. 254(d)).

(g) Definitions.—In this section:

(1) BROADBAND INTERNET ACCESS SERVICE.—The term “broadband internet access service” has the meaning given such term in section 8.1(b) of title 47, Code of Federal Regulations (or any successor regulation).

(2) COMMISSION.—The term “Commission” means the Federal Communications Commission.

(3) ELIGIBLE HOUSEHOLD.—The term “eligible household” means a household that meets the requirements described in subsection (b)(1).

(4) EMERGENCY PERIOD.—The term “emergency period” means the duration of a public health emergency declared pursuant to section 319 of the Public Health Service Act (42 U.S.C. 247d) as a result of COVID–19, including any renewal thereof.

(5) TIER I SERVICE.—The term “Tier I service” means broadband internet access service that, at a minimum, provides a download speed of 100 megabits per second, an upload speed of 10 megabits per second, and latency that is

sufficiently low to allow real-time, interactive applications, with no data caps or additional fees for the provision of such service, except taxes and other governmental fees.

(6) TIER II SERVICE.—The term "Tier II service" means broadband internet access service that, at a minimum, provides a download speed of 25 megabits per second, an upload speed of 3 megabits per second, and latency that is sufficiently low to allow real-time, interactive applications, with no data caps or additional fees for the provision of such service, except taxes and other governmental fees.

TITLE IV—CONTINUED CONNECTIVITY

SEC. 401. CONTINUED CONNECTIVITY DURING EMERGENCY PERIODS RELATING TO COVID–19.

Title VII of the Communications Act of 1934 (47 U.S.C. 601 et seq.) is amended by adding at the end the following:

"SEC. 723. CONTINUED CONNECTIVITY DURING EMERGENCY PERIODS RELATING TO COVID–19.

"(a) In General.—During an emergency period described in subsection (b), it shall be unlawful—

"(1) for a provider of advanced telecommunications service or voice service to—

"(A) terminate, reduce, or change such service provided to any individual customer or small business because of the inability of the individual customer or small business to pay for such service if the individual customer or small business certifies to such provider that such inability to pay is a result of disruptions caused by the public health emergency to which such emergency period relates; or

"(B) impose late fees on any individual customer or small business because of the inability of the individual customer or small business to pay for such service if the individual customer or small business certifies to such provider that such inability to pay is a result of disruptions caused by the public health emergency to which such emergency period relates;

"(2) for a provider of advanced telecommunications service to, during such emergency period—

"(A) employ a limit on the amount of data allotted to an individual customer or small business during such emergency period, except that such provider may engage in reasonable network management; or

"(B) charge an individual customer or small business an additional fee for exceeding the limit on the data allotted to an individual customer or small business; or

"(3) for a provider of advanced telecommunications service that had functioning Wi-Fi hotspots available to subscribers in public places on the day before the beginning of such emergency period to fail to make service provided by such Wi-Fi hotspots available to the public at no cost during such emergency period.

"(b) Waiver.—Upon a petition by a provider advanced telecommunications service or voice service, the provisions in subsection (a) may be suspended or waived by the Commission at any time, in whole or in part, for good cause shown.

"(c) Emergency Periods Described.—An emergency period described in this subsection is any portion beginning on or after the date of the enactment of this section of the duration of a public health emergency declared pursuant to section 319 of the Public Health Service Act (42 U.S.C. 247d) as a result of COVID–19, including any renewal thereof.

"(d) Definitions.—In this section:

"(1) ADVANCED TELECOMMUNICATIONS SERVICE.—The term 'advanced telecommunications service' means a service that provides advanced telecommunications capability (as defined in section 706 of the Telecommunications Act of 1996 (47 U.S.C. 1302)).

"(2) BROADBAND INTERNET ACCESS SERVICE.—The term 'broadband internet access service' has the meaning given such term in section 8.1(b) of title 47, Code of Federal Regulations (or any successor regulation).

"(3) INDIVIDUAL CUSTOMER.—The term 'individual customer' means an individual who contracts with a mass-market retail provider of advanced telecommunications service or voice service to provide service to such individual.

"(4) REASONABLE NETWORK MANAGEMENT.—The term 'reasonable network management'—

"(A) means the use of a practice that—

"(i) has a primarily technical network management justification; and

"(ii) is primarily used for and tailored to achieving a legitimate network management purpose, taking into account the particular network architecture and technology of the service; and

"(B) does not include other business practices.

"(5) SMALL BUSINESS.—The term 'small business' has the meaning given such term under section 601(3) of title 5, United States Code.

"(6) VOICE SERVICE.—The term 'voice service' has the meaning given such term under section 227(e)(8) of the Communications Act of 1934 (47 U.S.C. 227(e)(8)).

"(7) WI-FI.—The term 'Wi-Fi' means a wireless networking protocol based on Institute of Electrical and Electronics Engineers standard 802.11 (or any successor standard).

"(8) WI-FI HOTSPOT.—The term 'Wi-Fi hotspot' means a device that is capable of—

"(A) receiving mobile broadband internet access service; and

"(B) sharing such service with another device through the use of Wi-Fi.".

TITLE V—DON'T BREAK UP THE T-BAND

SEC. 501. REPEAL OF REQUIREMENT TO REALLOCATE AND AUCTION T-BAND SPECTRUM.

(a) Repeal.—Section 6103 of the Middle Class Tax Relief and Job Creation Act of 2012 (47 U.S.C. 1413) is repealed.

(b) Clerical Amendment.—The table of contents in section 1(b) of such Act is amended by striking the item relating to section 6103.

DIVISION V—GROW ACT

SEC. 101. SHORT TITLE.

This division may be cited as the "Giving Retirement Options to Workers Act of 2020" or the "GROW Act".

SEC. 102. COMPOSITE PLANS.

(a) Amendment To The Employee Retirement Income Security Act Of 1974.—

(1) IN GENERAL.—Title I of the Employee Retirement Income Security Act of 1974 (29 U.S.C. 1001 et seq.) is amended by adding at the end the following:

"PART 8—COMPOSITE PLANS AND LEGACY PLANS

"SEC. 801. COMPOSITE PLAN DEFINED.

"(a) In General.—For purposes of this Act, the term 'composite plan' means a pension plan—

"(1) which is a multiemployer plan that is neither a defined benefit plan nor a defined contribution plan;

"(2) the terms of which provide that the plan is a composite plan for purposes of this title with respect to which not more than one multiemployer defined benefit plan is treated as a legacy plan within the meaning of section 805, unless there is more than one legacy plan following a merger of composite plans under section 806;

"(3) which provides systematically for the payment of benefits—

"(A) objectively calculated pursuant to a formula enumerated in the plan document with respect to plan participants after retirement, for life; and

"(B) in the form of life annuities, except for benefits which under section 203(e) may be immediately distributed without the consent of the participant;

"(4) for which the plan contributions for the first plan year are at least 120 percent of the normal cost for the plan year;

"(5) which requires—

"(A) an annual valuation of the liability of the plan as of a date within the plan year to which the valuation refers or within one month prior to the beginning of such year;

"(B) an annual actuarial determination of the plan's current funded ratio and projected funded ratio under section 802(a);

"(C) corrective action through a realignment program pursuant to section 803 whenever the plan's projected funded ratio is below 120 percent for the plan year; and

"(D) an annual notification to each participant describing the participant's benefits under the plan and explaining that such benefits may be subject to reduction under a realignment program pursuant to section 803 based on the plan's funded status in future plan years; and

"(6) the board of trustees of which includes at least one retiree or beneficiary in pay status during each plan year following the first plan year in which at least 5 percent of the participants in the plan are retirees or beneficiaries in pay status.

"(b) Transition From A Multiemployer Defined Benefit Plan.—

"(1) IN GENERAL.—The plan sponsor of a defined benefit plan that is a multiemployer plan may, subject to paragraph (2), amend the plan to incorporate the features of a composite plan as a component of the multiemployer plan separate from the defined benefit plan component, except in the case of a defined benefit plan for which the plan actuary has certified under section 305(b)(3) that the plan is or will be in critical status for the plan year in which such amendment would become effective or for any of the succeeding 5 plan years.

"(2) REQUIREMENTS.—Any amendment pursuant to paragraph (1) to incorporate the features of a composite plan as a component of a multiemployer plan shall—

"(A) apply with respect to all collective bargaining agreements providing for contributions to the multiemployer plan on or after the effective date of the amendment;

"(B) apply with respect to all participants in the multiemployer plan for whom contributions are made to the multiemployer plan on or after the effective date of the amendment;

"(C) specify that the effective date of the amendment is—

"(i) the first day of a specified plan year following the date of the adoption of the amendment, except that the plan sponsor may alternatively provide for a separate effective date with respect to each collective bargaining agreement under which contributions to the multiemployer plan are required, which shall occur on the first day of the first plan year beginning after the termination, or if earlier, the re-opening, of each such agreement, or such earlier date as the parties to the agreement and the plan sponsor of the multiemployer plan shall agree to; and

"(ii) not later than the first day of the fifth plan year beginning on or after the date of the adoption of the amendment;

"(D) specify that, as of the amendment's effective date, no further benefits shall accrue under the defined benefit component of the multiemployer plan; and

"(E) specify that, as of the amendment's effective date, the plan sponsor of the multiemployer plan shall be the plan sponsor of both the composite plan component and the defined benefit plan component of the plan.

"(3) SPECIAL RULES.—If a multiemployer plan is amended pursuant to paragraph (1)—

"(A) the requirements of this title and title IV shall be applied to the composite plan component and the defined benefit plan component of the multiemployer plan as if each such component were maintained as a separate plan; and

"(B) the assets of the composite plan component and the defined benefit plan component of the plan shall be held in a single trust forming part of the plan under which the trust instrument expressly provides—

"(i) for separate accounts (and appropriate records) to be maintained to reflect the interest which each of the plan components has in the trust, including separate accounting for additions to the trust for the benefit of each plan component, disbursements made from each plan component's account in the trust, investment experience of the trust allocable to that account, and administrative expenses (whether direct expenses or shared expenses allocated proportionally), and permits, but does not require, the pooling of some or all of the assets of the two plan components for investment purposes; and

"(ii) that the assets of each of the two plan components shall be held, invested, reinvested, managed, administered and distributed for the exclusive benefit of the participants and beneficiaries of each such plan component, and in no event shall the assets of one of the plan components be available to pay benefits due under the other plan component.

"(4) NOT A TERMINATION EVENT.—Notwithstanding section 4041A, an amendment pursuant to paragraph (1) to incorporate the features of a composite plan as a component of a multiemployer plan does not constitute termination of the multiemployer plan.

"(5) NOTICE TO THE SECRETARY.—

"(A) NOTICE.—The plan sponsor of a composite plan shall provide notice to the Secretary of the intent to establish the composite plan (or, in the case of a composite plan incorporated as a component of a multiemployer plan as described in paragraph (1), the intent to amend the multiemployer plan to incorporate such composite plan) at least 30 days prior to the effective date of such establishment or amendment.

"(B) CERTIFICATION.—In the case of a composite plan incorporated as a component of a multiemployer plan as described in paragraph (1), such notice shall include a certification by the plan actuary under section 305(b)(3) that the effective date of the amendment occurs in a plan year for which the multiemployer plan is not in critical status for that plan year and any of the succeeding 5 plan years.

"(6) REFERENCES TO COMPOSITE PLAN COMPONENT.—As used in this part, the term 'composite plan' includes a composite plan component added to a defined benefit plan pursuant to paragraph (1).

"(7) RULE OF CONSTRUCTION.—Paragraph (2)(A) shall not be construed as preventing the plan sponsor of a multiemployer plan from adopting an amendment pursuant to paragraph (1) because some collective bargaining agreements are amended to cease any covered employer's obligation to contribute to the multiemployer plan before or after the plan amendment is effective. Paragraph (2)(B) shall not be construed as preventing the plan sponsor of a multiemployer plan from adopting an amendment pursuant to paragraph (1) because some participants cease to have contributions made to the multiemployer plan on their behalf before or after the plan amendment is effective.

"(c) Coordination With Funding Rules.—Except as otherwise provided in this title, sections 302, 304, and 305 shall not apply to a composite plan.

"(d) Treatment Of A Composite Plan.—For purposes of this Act (other than sections 302 and 4245), a composite plan shall be treated as if it were a defined benefit plan unless a different treatment is provided for under applicable law.

"SEC. 802. FUNDED RATIOS; ACTUARIAL ASSUMPTIONS.

"(a) Certification Of Funded Ratios.—

"(1) IN GENERAL.—Not later than the one-hundred twentieth day of each plan year of a composite plan, the plan actuary of the composite plan shall certify to the Secretary, the Secretary of the Treasury, and the plan sponsor the plan's current funded ratio and projected funded ratio for the plan year.

"(2) DETERMINATION OF CURRENT FUNDED RATIO AND PROJECTED FUNDED RATIO.—For purposes of this section:

"(A) CURRENT FUNDED RATIO.—The current funded ratio is the ratio (expressed as a percentage) of—

"(i) the value of the plan's assets as of the first day of the plan year; to

"(ii) the plan actuary's best estimate of the present value of the plan liabilities as of the first day of the plan year.

"(B) PROJECTED FUNDED RATIO.—The projected funded ratio is the current funded ratio projected to the first day of the fifteenth plan year following the plan year for which the determination is being made.

"(3) CONSIDERATION OF CONTRIBUTION RATE INCREASES.—For purposes of projections under this subsection, the plan sponsor may anticipate contribution rate increases beyond the term of the current collective bargaining agreement and any agreed-to supplements, up to a maximum of 2.5 percent per year, compounded annually, unless it would be unreasonable under the circumstances to assume that contributions would increase by that amount.

"(b) Actuarial Assumptions And Methods.—For purposes of this part:

"(1) IN GENERAL.—All costs, liabilities, rates of interest and other factors under the plan shall be determined for a plan year on the basis of actuarial assumptions and methods—

"(A) each of which is reasonable (taking into account the experience of the plan and reasonable expectations);

"(B) which, in combination, offer the actuary's best estimate of anticipated experience under the plan; and

"(C) with respect to which any change from the actuarial assumptions and methods used in the previous plan year shall be certified by the plan actuary and the actuarial rationale for such change provided in the annual report required by section 103.

"(2) FAIR MARKET VALUE OF ASSETS.—The value of the plan's assets shall be taken into account on the basis of their fair market value.

"(3) DETERMINATION OF NORMAL COST AND PLAN LIABILITIES.—A

plan's normal cost and liabilities shall be based on the most recent actuarial valuation required under section 801(a)(5)(A) and the unit credit funding method.

"(4) TIME WHEN CERTAIN CONTRIBUTIONS DEEMED MADE.—Any contributions for a plan year made by an employer after the last day of such plan year, but not later than two and one-half months after such day, shall be deemed to have been made on such last day. For purposes of this paragraph, such two and one-half month period may be extended for not more than six months under regulations prescribed by the Secretary of the Treasury.

"(5) ADDITIONAL ACTUARIAL ASSUMPTIONS.—Except where otherwise provided in this part, the provisions of section 305(b)(3)(B) shall apply to any determination or projection under this part.

"SEC. 803. REALIGNMENT PROGRAM.

"(a) Realignment Program.—

"(1) ADOPTION.—In any case in which the plan actuary certifies under section 802(a) that the plan's projected funded ratio is below 120 percent for the plan year, the plan sponsor shall adopt a realignment program under paragraph (2) not later than 210 days after the due date of the certification required under such section 802(a). The plan sponsor shall adopt an updated realignment program for each succeeding plan year for which a certification described in the preceding sentence is made.

"(2) CONTENT OF REALIGNMENT PROGRAM.—

"(A) IN GENERAL.—A realignment program adopted under this paragraph is a written program which consists of all reasonable measures, including options or a range of options to be undertaken by the plan sponsor or proposed to the bargaining parties, formulated, based on reasonably anticipated experience and reasonable actuarial assumptions, to enable the plan to achieve a projected funded ratio of at least 120 percent for the following plan year.

"(B) INITIAL PROGRAM ELEMENTS.—Reasonable measures under a realignment program described in subparagraph (A) may include any of the following:

"(i) Proposed contribution increases.

"(ii) A reduction in the rate of future benefit accruals, so long as the resulting rate is not less than 1 percent of the contributions on which benefits are based as of the start of the plan year (or the equivalent standard accrual rate as described in section 305(e)(6)).

"(iii) A modification or elimination of adjustable benefits of participants that are not in pay status before the date of the notice required under subsection (b)(1).

"(iv) Any other lawfully available measures not specifically described in this subparagraph or subparagraph (C) or (D) that the plan sponsor determines are reasonable.

"(C) ADDITIONAL PROGRAM ELEMENTS.—If the plan sponsor has

determined that all reasonable measures available under subparagraph (B) will not enable the plan to achieve a projected funded ratio of at least 120 percent for the following plan year, such reasonable measures may also include—

"(i) a reduction of accrued benefits that are not in pay status by the date of the notice required under subsection (b)(1); or

"(ii) a reduction of any benefits of participants that are in pay status before the date of the notice required under subsection (b)(1) other than core benefits as defined in paragraph (4).

"(D) ADDITIONAL REDUCTIONS.—In the case of a composite plan for which the plan sponsor has determined that all reasonable measures available under subparagraphs (B) and (C) will not enable the plan to achieve a projected funded ratio of at least 120 percent for the following plan year, such reasonable measures may also include—

"(i) a further reduction in the rate of future benefit accruals without regard to the limitation applicable under subparagraph (B)(ii); or

"(ii) a reduction of core benefits,

provided that such reductions shall be equitably distributed across the participant and beneficiary population, taking into account factors, with respect to participants and beneficiaries and their benefits, that may include one or more of the factors listed in subclauses (I) through (X) of section 305(e)(9)(D)(vi), to the extent necessary to enable the plan to achieve a projected funded ratio of at least 120 percent for the following plan year, or at the election of the plan sponsor, a projected funded ratio of at least 100 percent for the following plan year and a current funded ratio of at least 90 percent.

"(3) ADJUSTABLE BENEFIT DEFINED.—For purposes of this part, the term 'adjustable benefit' means—

"(A) benefits, rights, and features under the plan, including post-retirement death benefits, 60-month guarantees, disability benefits not yet in pay status, and similar benefits;

"(B) any early retirement benefit or retirement-type subsidy (within the meaning of section 204(g)(2)(A)) and any benefit payment option (other than the qualified joint and survivor annuity); and

"(C) benefit increases that were adopted (or, if later, took effect) less than 60 months before the first day such realignment program took effect.

"(4) CORE BENEFIT DEFINED.—For purposes of this part, the term 'core benefit' means a participant's accrued benefit payable in the normal form of an annuity commencing at normal retirement age, determined without regard to—

"(A) any early retirement benefits, retirement-type subsidies, or other benefits, rights, or features that may be associated with that benefit; and

"(B) any cost-of-living adjustments or benefit increases effective after the date of retirement.

"(5) COORDINATION WITH CONTRIBUTION INCREASES.—

"(A) IN GENERAL.—A realignment program may provide that some or all of the benefit modifications described in the program will only take effect if the bargaining parties fail to agree to specified levels of increases in contributions to the plan, effective as of specified dates.

"(B) INDEPENDENT BENEFIT MODIFICATIONS.—If a realignment program adopts any changes to the benefit formula that are independent of potential contribution increases, such changes shall take effect not later than 180 days after the first day of the first plan year that begins following the adoption of the realignment program.

"(C) CONDITIONAL BENEFIT MODIFICATIONS.—If a realignment program adopts any changes to the benefit formula that take effect only if the bargaining parties fail to agree to contribution increases, such changes shall take effect not later than the first day of the first plan year beginning after the third anniversary of the date of adoption of the realignment program.

"(D) REVOCATION OF CERTAIN BENEFIT MODIFICATIONS.—Benefit modifications described in subparagraph (C) may be revoked, in whole or in part, and retroactively or prospectively, when contributions to the plan are increased, as specified in the realignment program, including any amendments thereto. The preceding sentence shall not apply unless the contribution increases are to be effective not later than the fifth anniversary of the first day of the first plan year that begins after the adoption of the realignment program.

"(b) Notice.—

"(1) IN GENERAL.—In any case in which it is certified under section 802(a) that the projected funded ratio is less than 120 percent, the plan sponsor shall, not later than 30 days after the date of the certification, provide notification of the current and projected funded ratios to the participants and beneficiaries, the bargaining parties, and the Secretary. Such notice shall include—

"(A) an explanation that contribution rate increases or benefit reductions may be necessary;

"(B) a description of the types of benefits that might be reduced; and

"(C) an estimate of the contribution increases and benefit reductions that may be necessary to achieve a projected funded ratio of 120 percent.

"(2) NOTICE OF BENEFIT MODIFICATIONS.—

"(A) IN GENERAL.—No modifications may be made that reduce the rate of future benefit accrual or that reduce core benefits or adjustable benefits unless notice of such reduction has been given at least 180 days before the general effective date of such reduction for all participants and beneficiaries to—

"(i) plan participants and beneficiaries;

"(ii) each employer who has an obligation to contribute to the composite plan; and

"(iii) each employee organization which, for purposes of collective bargaining, represents plan participants employed by such employers.

"(B) CONTENT OF NOTICE.—The notice under subparagraph (A) shall contain—

"(i) sufficient information to enable participants and beneficiaries to understand the effect of any reduction on their benefits, including an illustration of any affected benefit or subsidy, on an annual or monthly basis that a participant or beneficiary would otherwise have been eligible for as of the general effective date described in subparagraph (A); and

"(ii) information as to the rights and remedies of plan participants and beneficiaries as well as how to contact the Department of Labor for further information and assistance, where appropriate.

"(C) FORM AND MANNER.—Any notice under subparagraph (A)—

"(i) shall be provided in a form and manner prescribed in regulations of the Secretary of Labor;

"(ii) shall be written in a manner so as to be understood by the average plan participant.

"(3) MODEL NOTICES.—The Secretary shall—

"(A) prescribe model notices that the plan sponsor of a composite plan may use to satisfy the notice requirements under this subsection; and

"(B) by regulation enumerate any details related to the elements listed in paragraph (1) that any notice under this subsection must include.

"(4) DELIVERY METHOD.—Any notice under this part shall be provided in writing and may also be provided in electronic form to the extent that the form is reasonably accessible to persons to whom the notice is provided.

"SEC. 804. LIMITATION ON INCREASING BENEFITS.

"(a) Level Of Current Funded Ratios.—Except as provided in subsections (c), (d), and (e), no plan amendment increasing benefits or establishing new benefits under a composite plan may be adopted for a plan year unless—

"(1) the plan's current funded ratio is at least 110 percent (without regard to the benefit increase or new benefits);

"(2) taking the benefit increase or new benefits into account, the current funded ratio is at least 100 percent and the projected funded ratio for the current plan year is at least 120 percent;

"(3) in any case in which, after taking the benefit increase or new benefits into account, the current funded ratio is less than 140 percent and the projected funded ratio is less than 140 percent, the benefit increase or new benefits are projected by the plan actuary to increase the present value of the plan's liabilities for the plan year by not more than 3 percent; and

"(4) expected contributions for the current plan year are at least 120 percent of normal cost for the plan year, determined using the unit credit funding method and treating the benefit increase or new benefits as in effect for the entire plan year.

"(b) Additional Requirements Where Core Benefits Reduced.—If a plan has been amended to reduce core benefits pursuant to a realignment program under section 803(a)(2)(D), such plan may not be subsequently amended to increase core benefits unless the amendment—

"(1) increases the level of future benefit payments only; and

"(2) provides for an equitable distribution of benefit increases across the participant and beneficiary population, taking into account the extent to which the benefits of participants were previously reduced pursuant to such realignment program.

"(c) Exception To Comply With Applicable Law.—Subsection (a) shall not apply in connection with a plan amendment if the amendment is required as a condition of qualification under part I of subchapter D of chapter 1 of the Internal Revenue Code of 1986 or to comply with other applicable law.

"(d) Exception Where Maximum Deductible Limit Applies.—Subsection (a) shall not apply in connection with a plan amendment if and to the extent that contributions to the composite plan would not be deductible for the plan year under section 404(a)(1)(E) of the Internal Revenue Code of 1986 if the plan amendment is not adopted.

"(e) Exception For Certain Benefit Modifications.—Subsection (a) shall not apply in connection with a plan amendment under section 803(a)(5)(C), regarding conditional benefit modifications.

"(f) Treatment Of Plan Amendments.—For purposes of this section—

"(1) if two or more plan amendments increasing benefits or establishing new benefits are adopted in a plan year, such amendments shall be treated as a single amendment adopted on the last day of the plan year;

"(2) all benefit increases and new benefits adopted in a single amendment are treated as a single benefit increase, irrespective of whether the increases and new benefits take effect in more than one plan year; and

"(3) increases in contributions or decreases in plan liabilities which are scheduled to take effect in future plan years may be taken into account in connection with a plan amendment if they have been agreed to in writing or otherwise formalized by the date the plan amendment is adopted.

"SEC. 805. COMPOSITE PLAN RESTRICTIONS TO PRESERVE LEGACY PLAN FUNDING.

"(a) Treatment As A Legacy Plan.—

"(1) IN GENERAL.—For purposes of this part and parts 2 and 3, a defined benefit plan shall be treated as a legacy plan with respect to the composite plan under which the employees who were eligible to accrue a benefit under the defined benefit plan become eligible to accrue a benefit under such composite plan.

"(2) COMPONENT PLANS.—In any case in which a defined benefit plan is amended to add a composite plan component pursuant to section 801(b), paragraph (1) shall be applied by substituting 'defined benefit component' for 'defined benefit plan' and 'composite plan component' for 'composite plan.'

"(3) ELIGIBLE TO ACCRUE A BENEFIT.—For purposes of paragraph (1), an employee is considered eligible to accrue a benefit under a composite plan as of the first day in which the employee completes an hour of service under a collective bargaining agreement that provides for contributions to and accruals under the composite plan in lieu of accruals under the legacy plan.

"(4) COLLECTIVE BARGAINING AGREEMENT.—As used in this part, the term 'collective bargaining agreement' includes any agreement under which an employer has an obligation to contribute to a plan.

"(5) OTHER TERMS.—Any term used in this part which is not defined in this part and which is also used in section 305 shall have the same meaning provided such term in such section.

"(b) Restrictions On Acceptance By Composite Plan Of Agreements And Contributions.—

"(1) IN GENERAL.—The plan sponsor of a composite plan shall not accept or recognize a collective bargaining agreement (or any modification to such agreement), and no contributions may be accepted and no benefits may be accrued or otherwise earned under the agreement—

"(A) in any case in which the plan actuary of any defined benefit plan that would be treated as a legacy plan with respect to such composite plan has certified under section 305(b)(3) that such defined benefit plan is or will be in critical status for the plan year in which such agreement would take effect or for any of the succeeding 5 plan years; and

"(B) unless the agreement requires each employer who is a party to such agreement, including employers whose employees are not participants in the legacy plan, to provide contributions to the legacy plan with respect to such composite plan in a manner that satisfies the transition contribution requirements of subsection (d).

"(2) NOTICE.—Not later than 30 days after a determination by a plan sponsor of a composite plan that an agreement fails to satisfy the requirements described in paragraph (1), the plan sponsor shall provide notification of such failure and the reasons for such determination—

"(A) to the parties to the agreement;

"(B) to active participants of the composite plan who have ceased to accrue or otherwise earn benefits with respect to service with an employer pursuant to paragraph (1); and

"(C) to the Secretary, the Secretary of the Treasury, and the Pension Benefit Guaranty Corporation.

"(3) LIMITATION ON RETROACTIVE EFFECT.—This subsection shall not apply to benefits accrued before the date on which notice is provided under paragraph (2).

"(c) Restriction On Accrual Of Benefits Under A Composite Plan.—

"(1) IN GENERAL.—In any case in which an employer, under a collective bargaining agreement entered into after the date of enactment of the Giving Retirement Options to Workers Act of 2020, ceases to have an obligation to contribute to a multiemployer defined benefit plan, no employees employed by the employer may accrue or otherwise earn benefits under any composite plan, with respect to service with that employer, for a 60-month period beginning on the date on which the employer entered into such collective bargaining agreement.

"(2) NOTICE OF CESSATION OF OBLIGATION.—Within 30 days of determining that an employer has ceased to have an obligation to contribute to a legacy plan with respect to employees employed by an employer that is or will be contributing to a composite plan with respect to service of such employees, the plan sponsor of the legacy plan shall notify the plan sponsor of the composite plan of that cessation.

"(3) NOTICE OF CESSATION OF ACCRUALS.—Not later than 30 days after determining that an employer has ceased to have an obligation to contribute to a legacy plan, the plan sponsor of the composite plan shall notify the bargaining parties, the active participants affected by the cessation of accruals, the Secretary, the Secretary of the Treasury, and the Pension Benefit Guaranty Corporation of the cessation of accruals, the period during which such cessation is in effect, and the reasons therefor.

"(4) LIMITATION ON RETROACTIVE EFFECT.—This subsection shall not apply to benefits accrued before the date on which notice is provided under paragraph (3).

"(d) Transition Contribution Requirements.—

"(1) IN GENERAL.—A collective bargaining agreement satisfies the transition contribution requirements of this subsection if the agreement—

"(A) authorizes payment of contributions to a legacy plan at a rate or rates equal to or greater than the transition contribution rate established by the legacy plan under paragraph (2); and

"(B) does not provide for—

"(i) a suspension of contributions to the legacy plan with respect to any period of service; or

"(ii) any new direct or indirect exclusion of younger or newly hired employees of the employer from being taken into account in determining contributions owed to the legacy plan.

"(2) TRANSITION CONTRIBUTION RATE.—

"(A) IN GENERAL.—The transition contribution rate for a plan year is the contribution rate that, as certified by the actuary of the legacy plan in accordance with the principles in section 305(b)(3)(B), is reasonably expected to be adequate—

"(i) to fund the normal cost for the plan year;

"(ii) to amortize the plan's unfunded liabilities in level annual installments over 25 years, beginning with the plan year in which the transition contribution rate is first established; and

"(iii) to amortize any subsequent changes in the legacy plan's unfunded liability due to experience gains or losses (including investment gains or losses, gains or losses due to contributions greater or less than the contributions made under the prior transition contribution rate, and other actuarial gains or losses), changes in actuarial assumptions, changes to the legacy plan's benefits, or changes in funding method over a period of 15 plan years beginning with the plan year in which such change in unfunded liability is incurred.

The transition contribution rate for any plan year may not be less than the transition contribution rate for the plan year in which such rate is first established.

"(B) MULTIPLE RATES.—If different rates of contribution are payable to the legacy plan by different employers or for different classes of employees, the certification shall specify a transition contribution rate for each such employer.

"(C) RATE APPLICABLE TO EMPLOYER.—

"(i) IN GENERAL.—Except as provided by clause (ii), the transition contribution rate applicable to an employer for a plan year is the rate in effect for the plan year of the legacy plan that commences on or after 180 days before the earlier of—

"(I) the effective date of the collective bargaining agreement pursuant to which the employer contributes to the legacy plan; or

"(II) 5 years after the last plan year for which the transition contribution rate applicable to the employer was established or updated.

"(ii) EXCEPTION.—The transition contribution rate applicable to an employer for the first plan year beginning on or after the commencement of the employer's obligation to contribute to the composite plan is the rate in effect for the plan year of the legacy plan that commences on or after 180 days before such first plan year.

"(D) EFFECT OF LEGACY PLAN FINANCIAL CIRCUMSTANCES.—If the plan actuary of the legacy plan has certified under section 305 that the plan is in endangered or critical status for a plan year, the transition contribution rate for the following plan year is the rate determined with respect to the employer under the legacy plan's funding improvement or rehabilitation plan under section 305, if greater than the rate otherwise determined, but in no event greater than 75 percent of the sum of the contribution rates applicable to the legacy plan and the composite plan for the plan year.

"(E) OTHER ACTUARIAL ASSUMPTIONS AND METHODS.—Except as provided in subparagraph (A), the determination of the transition contribution rate for a plan year shall be based on actuarial assumptions and methods consistent with the minimum funding determinations made under section 304 (or, if applicable, section 305) with respect to the legacy plan for the plan year.

"(F) ADJUSTMENTS IN RATE.—The plan sponsor of a legacy plan from time to time may adjust the transition contribution rate or rates applicable to an employer under this paragraph by increasing some rates and decreasing others if the actuary certifies that such adjusted rates in combination will produce projected contribution income for the plan year beginning on or after the date of certification that is not less than would be produced by the transition contribution rates in effect at the time of the certification.

"(G) NOTICE OF TRANSITION CONTRIBUTION RATE.—The plan sponsor of a legacy plan shall provide notice to the parties to collective bargaining agreements pursuant to which contributions are made to the legacy plan of changes to the transition contribution rate requirements at least 30 days before the beginning of the plan year for which the rate is effective.

"(H) NOTICE TO COMPOSITE PLAN SPONSOR.—Not later than 30 days after a determination by the plan sponsor of a legacy plan that a collective bargaining agreement provides for a rate of contributions that is below the transition contribution rate applicable to one or more employers that are parties to the collective bargaining agreement, the plan sponsor of the legacy plan shall notify the plan sponsor of any composite plan under which employees of such employer would otherwise be eligible to accrue a benefit.

"(3) CORRECTION PROCEDURES.—Pursuant to standards prescribed by the Secretary, the plan sponsor of a composite plan shall adopt rules and procedures that give the parties to the collective bargaining agreement notice of the failure of such agreement to satisfy the transition contribution requirements of this subsection, and a reasonable opportunity to correct such failure, not to exceed 180 days from the date of notice given under subsection (b)(2).

"(4) SUPPLEMENTAL CONTRIBUTIONS.—A collective bargaining agreement may provide for supplemental contributions to the legacy plan for a plan year in excess of the transition contribution rate determined under paragraph (2), regardless of whether the legacy plan is in endangered or critical status for such plan year.

"(e) Nonapplication Of Composite Plan Restrictions.—

"(1) IN GENERAL.—The provisions of subsections (a), (b), and (c) shall not apply with respect to a collective bargaining agreement, to the extent the agreement, or a predecessor agreement, provides or provided for contributions to a defined benefit plan that is a legacy plan, as of the first day of the first plan year following a plan year for which the plan actuary certifies that the plan is fully funded, has been fully funded for at least three out of the immediately preceding 5 plan years, and is projected to remain fully funded for at least the following 4 plan years.

"(2) DETERMINATION OF FULLY FUNDED.—A plan is fully funded for purposes of paragraph (1) if, as of the valuation date of the plan for a plan year, the value of the plan's assets equals or exceeds the present value of the plan's liabilities, determined in accordance with the rules prescribed by the Pension Benefit Guaranty Corporation under sections 4219(c)(1)(D) and 4281 for multiemployer plans terminating by mass withdrawal, as in effect for the date of the determination, except the plan's reasonable assumption regarding the starting date of benefits may be used.

"(3) OTHER APPLICABLE RULES.—Except as provided in paragraph (2), actuarial determinations and projections under this section shall be based on the rules in section 305(b)(3) and section 802(b).

"SEC. 806. MERGERS AND ASSET TRANSFERS OF COMPOSITE PLANS.

"(a) In General.—Assets and liabilities of a composite plan may only be merged with, or transferred to, another plan if—

"(1) the other plan is a composite plan;

"(2) the plan or plans resulting from the merger or transfer is a composite plan;

"(3) no participant's accrued benefit or adjustable benefit is lower immediately after the transaction than it was immediately before the transaction; and

"(4) the value of the assets transferred in the case of a transfer reasonably reflects the value of the amounts contributed with respect to the participants whose benefits are being transferred, adjusted for allocable distributions, investment gains and losses, and administrative expenses.

"(b) Legacy Plan.—

"(1) IN GENERAL.—After a merger or transfer involving a composite plan, the legacy plan with respect to an employer that is obligated to contribute to the resulting composite plan is the legacy plan that applied to that employer immediately before the merger or transfer.

"(2) MULTIPLE LEGACY PLANS.—If an employer is obligated to contribute to more than one legacy plan with respect to employees eligible to accrue benefits under more than one composite plan and there is a merger or transfer of such legacy plans, the transition contribution rate applicable to the legacy plan resulting from the merger or transfer with respect to that employer shall be determined in accordance with the provisions of section 805(d)(2)(B).".

(2) PENALTIES.—

(A) CIVIL ENFORCEMENT OF FAILURE TO COMPLY WITH REALIGNMENT PROGRAM.—Section 502(a) of such Act (29 U.S.C. 1132(a)) is amended—

(i) in paragraph (10), by striking "or" at the end;

(ii) in paragraph (11), by striking the period at the end and inserting "; or"; and

(iii) by adding at the end the following:

"(12) in the case of a composite plan required to adopt a realignment program under section 803, if the plan sponsor—

"(A) has not adopted a realignment program under that section by the deadline established in such section; or

"(B) fails to update or comply with the terms of the realignment program in accordance with the requirements of such section,

by the Secretary, by an employer that has an obligation to contribute with respect to the composite plan, or by an employee organization that represents active participants in the composite plan, for an order compelling the plan sponsor to adopt a realignment program, or to update or comply with the terms of the realignment program, in accordance with the requirements of such section and the realignment program.".

(B) CIVIL PENALTIES.—Section 502(c) of such Act (29 U.S.C. 1132(c)) is amended—

(i) by moving paragraphs (8), (10), and (12) each 2 ems to the left;

(ii) by redesignating paragraphs (9) through (12) as paragraphs (12) through (15), respectively; and

(iii) by inserting after paragraph (8) the following:

"(9) The Secretary may assess against any plan sponsor of a composite plan a civil penalty of not more than $1,100 per day for each violation by such sponsor—

"(A) of the requirement under section 802(a) on the plan actuary to certify the plan's current or projected funded ratio by the date specified in such subsection; or

"(B) of the requirement under section 803 to adopt a realignment program by the deadline established in that section and to comply with its terms.

"(10) (A) The Secretary may assess against any plan sponsor of a composite plan a civil penalty of not more than $100 per day for each violation by such sponsor of the requirement under section 803(b) to provide notice as described in such section, except that no penalty may be assessed in any case in which the plan sponsor exercised reasonable diligence to meet the requirements of such section and—

"(i) the plan sponsor did not know that the violation existed; or

"(ii) the plan sponsor provided such notice during the 30-day period beginning on the first date on which the plan sponsor knew, or in exercising reasonable due diligence should have known, that such violation existed.

"(B) In any case in which the plan sponsor exercised reasonable diligence to meet the requirements of section 803(b)—

"(i) the total penalty assessed under this paragraph against such sponsor for a plan year may not exceed $500,000; and

"(ii) the Secretary may waive part or all of such penalty to the extent that the payment of such penalty would be excessive or otherwise inequitable relative to the violation involved.

"(11) The Secretary may assess against any plan sponsor of a composite plan a civil penalty of not more than $100 per day for each violation by such sponsor of the notice requirements under sections 801(b)(5) and 805(b)(2).".

(3) CONFORMING AMENDMENT.—The table of contents in section 1 of such Act (29 U.S.C. 1001 note) is amended by inserting after the item relating to section 734 the following:

"PART 8—COMPOSITE PLANS AND LEGACY PLANS

"Sec. 801. Composite plan defined.
"Sec. 802. Funded ratios; actuarial assumptions.
"Sec. 803. Realignment program.
"Sec. 804. Limitation on increasing benefits.

(b) Amendment To The Internal Revenue Code Of 1986.—

(1) IN GENERAL.—Part III of subchapter D of chapter 1 of the Internal Revenue Code of 1986 is amended by adding at the end the following:

"Subpart C—Composite Plans And Legacy Plans

"SEC. 437. COMPOSITE PLAN DEFINED.

"(a) In General.—For purposes of this title, the term 'composite plan' means a pension plan—

"(1) which is a multiemployer plan that is neither a defined benefit plan nor a defined contribution plan,

"(2) the terms of which provide that the plan is a composite plan for purposes of this title with respect to which not more than one multiemployer defined benefit plan is treated as a legacy plan within the meaning of section 440A, unless there is more than one legacy plan following a merger of composite plans under section 440B,

"(3) which provides systematically for the payment of benefits—

"(A) objectively calculated pursuant to a formula enumerated in the plan document with respect to plan participants after retirement, for life, and

"(B) in the form of life annuities, except for benefits which under section 411(a)(11) may be immediately distributed without the consent of the participant,

"(4) for which the plan contributions for the first plan year are at least 120 percent of the normal cost for the plan year,

"(5) which requires—

"(A) an annual valuation of the liability of the plan as of a date within the plan year to which the valuation refers or within one month prior to the beginning of such year,

"(B) an annual actuarial determination of the plan's current funded ratio and projected funded ratio under section 438(a),

"(C) corrective action through a realignment program pursuant to section 439 whenever the plan's projected funded ratio is below 120 percent for the plan year, and

"(D) an annual notification to each participant describing the participant's benefits under the plan and explaining that such benefits may be subject to reduction under a realignment program pursuant to section 439 based on the plan's funded status in future plan years, and

"(6) the board of trustees of which includes at least one retiree or beneficiary in pay status during each plan year following the first plan year in which at least 5 percent of the participants in the plan are retirees or beneficiaries in pay status.

"(b) Transition From A Multiemployer Defined Benefit Plan.—

"(1) IN GENERAL.—The plan sponsor of a defined benefit plan that is a multiemployer plan may, subject to paragraph (2), amend the plan to incorporate the features of a composite plan as a component of the multiemployer plan separate from the defined benefit plan component, except in the case of a defined benefit plan for which the plan actuary has certified under section 432(b)(3) that the plan is or will be in critical status for the plan year in which such amendment would become effective or for any of the succeeding 5 plan years.

"(2) REQUIREMENTS.—Any amendment pursuant to paragraph (1) to incorporate the features of a composite plan as a component of a multiemployer plan shall—

"(A) apply with respect to all collective bargaining agreements providing for contributions to the multiemployer plan on or after the effective date of the amendment,

"(B) apply with respect to all participants in the multiemployer plan for whom contributions are made to the multiemployer plan on or after the effective date of the amendment,

"(C) specify that the effective date of the amendment is—

"(i) the first day of a specified plan year following the date of the adoption of the amendment, except that the plan sponsor may alternatively provide for a separate effective date with respect to each collective bargaining agreement under which contributions to the multiemployer plan are required, which shall occur on the first day of the first plan year beginning after the termination, or if earlier, the re-opening, of each such agreement, or such earlier date as the parties to the agreement and the plan sponsor of the multiemployer plan shall agree to, and

"(ii) not later than the first day of the fifth plan year beginning on or after the date of the adoption of the amendment,

"(D) specify that, as of the amendment's effective date, no further benefits shall accrue under the defined benefit component of the multiemployer plan, and

"(E) specify that, as of the amendment's effective date, the plan sponsor of the multiemployer plan shall be the plan sponsor of both the composite plan component and the defined benefit plan component of the plan.

"(3) SPECIAL RULES.—If a multiemployer plan is amended pursuant to paragraph (1)—

"(A) the requirements of this title shall be applied to the composite plan component and the defined benefit plan component of the multiemployer plan as if each such component were maintained as a separate plan, and

"(B) the assets of the composite plan component and the defined benefit plan component of the plan shall be held in a single trust forming part of the plan under which the trust instrument expressly provides—

"(i) for separate accounts (and appropriate records) to be maintained to reflect the interest which each of the plan components has in the trust, including separate accounting for additions to the trust for the benefit of each plan component, disbursements made from each plan component's account in the trust, investment experience of the trust allocable to that account, and administrative expenses (whether direct expenses or shared expenses allocated proportionally), and permits, but does not require, the pooling of some or all of the assets of the two plan components for investment purposes, and

"(ii) that the assets of each of the two plan components shall be held, invested, reinvested, managed, administered and distributed for the exclusive benefit of the participants and beneficiaries of each such plan component, and in no event shall the assets of one of the plan components be available to pay benefits due under the other plan component.

"(4) NOT A TERMINATION EVENT.—Notwithstanding section 4041A of the Employee Retirement Income Security Act of 1974, an amendment pursuant to paragraph (1) to incorporate the features of a composite plan as a component of a multiemployer plan does not constitute termination of the multiemployer plan.

"(5) NOTICE TO THE SECRETARY.—

"(A) NOTICE.—The plan sponsor of a composite plan shall provide notice to the Secretary of the intent to establish the composite plan (or, in the case of a composite plan incorporated as a component of a multiemployer plan as described in paragraph (1), the intent to amend the multiemployer plan to incorporate such composite plan) at least 30 days prior to the effective date of such establishment or amendment.

"(B) CERTIFICATION.—In the case of a composite plan incorporated as a component of a multiemployer plan as described in paragraph (1), such notice shall include a certification by the plan actuary under section 432(b)(3) that the effective date of the amendment occurs in a plan year for which the multiemployer plan is not in critical status for that plan year and any of the succeeding 5 plan years.

"(6) REFERENCES TO COMPOSITE PLAN COMPONENT.—As used in this subpart, the term 'composite plan' includes a composite plan component added to a defined benefit plan pursuant to paragraph (1).

"(7) RULE OF CONSTRUCTION.—Paragraph (2)(A) shall not be construed as preventing the plan sponsor of a multiemployer plan from adopting an amendment pursuant to paragraph (1) because some collective bargaining agreements are amended to cease any covered employer's obligation to contribute to the multiemployer plan before or after the plan amendment is effective. Paragraph (2)(B) shall not be construed as preventing the plan sponsor of a multiemployer plan from adopting an amendment pursuant to paragraph (1) because some participants cease to have contributions made to the multiemployer plan on their behalf before or after the plan amendment is effective.

"(c) Coordination With Funding Rules.—Except as otherwise provided in this title, sections 412, 431, and 432 shall not apply to a composite plan.

"(d) Treatment Of A Composite Plan.—For purposes of this title (other than sections 412 and 418E), a composite plan shall be treated as if it were a defined benefit plan unless a different treatment is provided for under applicable law.

"SEC. 438. FUNDED RATIOS; ACTUARIAL ASSUMPTIONS.

"(a) Certification Of Funded Ratios.—

"(1) IN GENERAL.—Not later than the one-hundred twentieth day of each plan year of a composite plan, the plan actuary of the composite plan shall certify to the Secretary, the Secretary of Labor, and the plan sponsor the plan's current funded ratio and projected funded ratio for the plan year.

"(2) DETERMINATION OF CURRENT FUNDED RATIO AND PROJECTED FUNDED RATIO.—For purposes of this section—

"(A) CURRENT FUNDED RATIO.—The current funded ratio is the ratio (expressed as a percentage) of—

"(i) the value of the plan's assets as of the first day of the plan year, to

"(ii) the plan actuary's best estimate of the present value of the plan liabilities as of the first day of the plan year.

"(B) PROJECTED FUNDED RATIO.—The projected funded ratio is the current funded ratio projected to the first day of the fifteenth plan year following the plan year for which the determination is being made.

"(3) CONSIDERATION OF CONTRIBUTION RATE INCREASES.—For purposes of projections under this subsection, the plan sponsor may anticipate contribution rate increases beyond the term of the current collective bargaining agreement and any agreed-to supplements, up to a maximum of 2.5 percent per year, compounded annually, unless it would be unreasonable under the circumstances to assume that contributions would increase by that amount.

"(b) Actuarial Assumptions And Methods.—For purposes of this part—

"(1) IN GENERAL.—All costs, liabilities, rates of interest, and other factors under the plan shall be determined for a plan year on the basis of actuarial assumptions and methods—

"(A) each of which is reasonable (taking into account the experience of the plan and reasonable expectations),

"(B) which, in combination, offer the actuary's best estimate of anticipated experience under the plan, and

"(C) with respect to which any change from the actuarial assumptions and methods used in the previous plan year shall be certified by the plan actuary and the actuarial rationale for such change provided in the annual report required by section 6058.

"(2) FAIR MARKET VALUE OF ASSETS.—The value of the plan's assets shall be taken into account on the basis of their fair market value.

"(3) DETERMINATION OF NORMAL COST AND PLAN LIABILITIES.—A plan's normal cost and liabilities shall be based on the most recent actuarial valuation required under section 437(a)(5)(A) and the unit credit funding method.

"(4) TIME WHEN CERTAIN CONTRIBUTIONS DEEMED MADE.—Any contributions for a plan year made by an employer after the last day of such plan year, but not later than two and one-half months after such day, shall be deemed to have been made on such last day. For purposes of this paragraph, such two and one-half month period may be extended for not more than six months under regulations prescribed by the Secretary.

"(5) ADDITIONAL ACTUARIAL ASSUMPTIONS.—Except where otherwise provided in this subpart, the provisions of section 432(b)(3)(B) shall apply to any determination or projection under this subpart.

"SEC. 439. REALIGNMENT PROGRAM.

"(a) Realignment Program.—

"(1) ADOPTION.—In any case in which the plan actuary certifies under section 438(a) that the plan's projected funded ratio is below 120 percent for the plan year, the plan sponsor shall adopt a realignment program under paragraph (2) not later than 210 days after the due date of the certification required under section 438(a). The plan sponsor shall adopt an updated realignment program for each succeeding plan year for which a certification described in the preceding sentence is made.

"(2) CONTENT OF REALIGNMENT PROGRAM.—

"(A) IN GENERAL.—A realignment program adopted under this paragraph is a written program which consists of all reasonable measures, including options or a range of options to be undertaken by the plan sponsor or proposed to the bargaining parties, formulated, based on reasonably anticipated experience and reasonable actuarial assumptions, to enable the plan to achieve a projected funded ratio of at least 120 percent for the following plan year.

"(B) INITIAL PROGRAM ELEMENTS.—Reasonable measures under a realignment program described in subparagraph (A) may include any of the following:

"(i) Proposed contribution increases.

"(ii) A reduction in the rate of future benefit accruals, so long as the resulting rate shall not be less than 1 percent of the contributions on which benefits are based as of the start of the plan year (or the equivalent standard accrual rate as described in section 432(e)(6)).

"(iii) A modification or elimination of adjustable benefits of participants that are not in pay status before the date of the notice required under subsection (b)(1).

"(iv) Any other legally available measures not specifically described in this subparagraph or subparagraph (C) or (D) that the plan sponsor determines are reasonable.

"(C) ADDITIONAL PROGRAM ELEMENTS.—If the plan sponsor has determined that all reasonable measures available under subparagraph (B) will not enable the plan to achieve a projected funded ratio of at least 120 percent the following plan year, such reasonable measures may also include—

"(i) a reduction of accrued benefits that are not in pay status by the date of the notice required under subsection (b)(1), or

"(ii) a reduction of any benefits of participants that are in pay status before the date of the notice required under subsection (b)(1) other than core benefits as defined in paragraph (4).

"(D) ADDITIONAL REDUCTIONS.—In the case of a composite plan for which the plan sponsor has determined that all reasonable measures available under subparagraphs (B) and (C) will not enable the plan to achieve a projected funded ratio of at least 120 percent for the following plan year, such reasonable measures may also include—

"(i) a further reduction in the rate of future benefit accruals without regard to the limitation applicable under subparagraph (B)(ii), or

"(ii) a reduction of core benefits,

provided that such reductions shall be equitably distributed across the participant and beneficiary population, taking into account factors, with respect to participants and beneficiaries and their benefits, that may include one or more of the factors listed in subclauses (I) through (X) of section 432(e)(9)(D)(vi), to the extent necessary to enable the plan to achieve a projected funded ratio of at least 120 percent for the following plan year, or at the election of the plan sponsor, a projected funded ratio of at least 100 percent for the following plan year and a current funded ratio of at least 90 percent.

"(3) ADJUSTABLE BENEFIT DEFINED.—For purposes of this subpart, the term 'adjustable benefit' means—

"(A) benefits, rights, and features under the plan, including post-retirement death benefits, 60-month guarantees, disability benefits not yet in pay status, and similar benefits,

"(B) any early retirement benefit or retirement-type subsidy (within the meaning of section 411(d)(6)(B)(i)) and any benefit payment option (other than the qualified joint and survivor annuity), and

"(C) benefit increases that were adopted (or, if later, took effect) less than 60 months before the first day such realignment program took effect.

"(4) CORE BENEFIT DEFINED.—For purposes of this subpart, the term 'core benefit' means a participant's accrued benefit payable in the normal form of an annuity commencing at normal retirement age, determined without regard to—

"(A) any early retirement benefits, retirement-type subsidies, or other benefits, rights, or features that may be associated with that benefit, and

"(B) any cost-of-living adjustments or benefit increases effective after the date of retirement.

"(5) COORDINATION WITH CONTRIBUTION INCREASES.—

"(A) IN GENERAL.—A realignment program may provide that some or all of the benefit modifications described in the program will only take effect if the bargaining parties fail to agree to specified levels of increases in contributions to the plan, effective as of specified dates.

"(B) INDEPENDENT BENEFIT MODIFICATIONS.—If a realignment program adopts any changes to the benefit formula that are independent of potential contribution increases, such changes shall take effect not later than 180 days following the first day of the first plan year that begins following the adoption of the realignment program.

"(C) CONDITIONAL BENEFIT MODIFICATIONS.—If a realignment program adopts any changes to the benefit formula that take effect only if the bargaining parties fail to agree to contribution increases, such changes shall take effect not later than the first day of the first plan year beginning after the third anniversary of the date of adoption of the realignment program.

"(D) REVOCATION OF CERTAIN BENEFIT MODIFICATIONS.—Benefit modifications described in paragraph (3) may be revoked, in whole or in part, and retroactively or prospectively, when contributions to the plan are increased, as specified in the realignment program, including any amendments thereto. The preceding sentence shall not apply unless the contribution increases are to be effective not later than the fifth anniversary of the first day of the first plan year that begins after the adoption of the realignment program.

"(b) Notice.—

"(1) IN GENERAL.—In any case in which it is certified under section 438(a) that the projected funded ratio is less than 120 percent, the plan sponsor shall, not later than 30 days after the date of the certification, provide notification of the current and projected funded ratios to the participants and beneficiaries, the bargaining parties, and the Secretary. Such notice shall include—

"(A) an explanation that contribution rate increases or benefit reductions may be necessary,

"(B) a description of the types of benefits that might be reduced, and

"(C) an estimate of the contribution increases and benefit reductions that may be necessary to achieve a projected funded ratio of 120 percent.

"(2) NOTICE OF BENEFIT MODIFICATIONS.—

"(A) IN GENERAL.—No modifications may be made that reduce the rate of future benefit accrual or that reduce core benefits or adjustable benefits unless notice of such reduction has been given at least 180 days before the general effective date of such reduction for all participants and beneficiaries to—

"(i) plan participants and beneficiaries,

"(ii) each employer who has an obligation to contribute to the composite plan, and

"(iii) each employee organization which, for purposes of collective bargaining, represents plan participants employed by such employers.

"(B) CONTENT OF NOTICE.—The notice under subparagraph (A) shall contain—

"(i) sufficient information to enable participants and beneficiaries to understand the effect of any reduction on their benefits, including an illustration of any affected benefit or subsidy, on an annual or monthly basis that a participant or beneficiary would otherwise have been eligible for as of the general effective date described in subparagraph (A), and

"(ii) information as to the rights and remedies of plan participants and beneficiaries as well as how to contact the Department of Labor for further information and assistance, where appropriate.

"(C) FORM AND MANNER.—Any notice under subparagraph (A)—

"(i) shall be provided in a form and manner prescribed in regulations of the Secretary of Labor,

"(ii) shall be written in a manner so as to be understood by the average plan participant.

"(3) MODEL NOTICES.—The Secretary shall—

"(A) prescribe model notices that the plan sponsor of a composite plan may use to satisfy the notice requirements under this subsection, and

"(B) by regulation enumerate any details related to the elements listed in paragraph (1) that any notice under this subsection must include.

"(4) DELIVERY METHOD.—Any notice under this part shall be provided in writing and may also be provided in electronic form to the extent that the form is reasonably accessible to persons to whom the notice is provided.

"SEC. 440. LIMITATION ON INCREASING BENEFITS.

"(a) Level Of Current Funded Ratios.—Except as provided in subsections (c), (d), and (e), no plan amendment increasing benefits or establishing new benefits under a composite plan may be adopted for a plan year unless—

"(1) the plan's current funded ratio is at least 110 percent (without regard to the benefit increase or new benefits),

"(2) taking the benefit increase or new benefits into account, the current funded ratio is at least 100 percent and the projected funded ratio for the current plan year is at least 120 percent,

"(3) in any case in which, after taking the benefit increase or new benefits into account, the current funded ratio is less than 140 percent or the projected funded ratio is less than 140 percent, the benefit increase or new benefits are projected by the plan actuary to increase the present value of the plan's liabilities for the plan year by not more than 3 percent, and

"(4) expected contributions for the current plan year are at least 120 percent of normal cost for the plan year, determined using the unit credit funding method and treating the benefit increase or new benefits as in effect for the entire plan year.

"(b) Additional Requirements Where Core Benefits Reduced.—If a plan has been amended to reduce core benefits pursuant to a realignment program under section 439(a)(2)(D), such plan may not be subsequently amended to increase core benefits unless the amendment—

"(1) increases the level of future benefit payments only, and

"(2) provides for an equitable distribution of benefit increases across the participant and beneficiary population, taking into account the extent to which the benefits of participants were previously reduced pursuant to such realignment program.

"(c) Exception To Comply With Applicable Law.—Subsection (a) shall not apply in connection with a plan amendment if the amendment is required as a condition of qualification under part I of subchapter D of chapter 1 or to comply with other applicable law.

"(d) Exception Where Maximum Deductible Limit Applies.—Subsection (a) shall not apply in connection with a plan amendment if and to the extent that contributions to the composite plan would not be deductible for the plan year under section 404(a)(1)(E) if the plan amendment is not adopted. The Secretary of the Treasury shall issue regulations to implement this paragraph.

"(e) Exception For Certain Benefit Modifications.—Subsection (a) shall not apply in connection with a plan amendment under section 439(a)(5)(C), regarding conditional benefit modifications.

"(f) Treatment Of Plan Amendments.—For purposes of this section—

"(1) if two or more plan amendments increasing benefits or establishing new benefits are adopted in a plan year, such amendments shall be treated as a single amendment adopted on the last day of the plan year,

"(2) all benefit increases and new benefits adopted in a single amendment are treated as a single benefit increase, irrespective of whether the increases and new benefits take effect in more than one plan year, and

"(3) increases in contributions or decreases in plan liabilities which are scheduled to take effect in future plan years may be taken into account in connection with a plan amendment if they have been agreed to in writing or otherwise formalized by the date the plan amendment is adopted.

"SEC. 440A. COMPOSITE PLAN RESTRICTIONS TO PRESERVE LEGACY PLAN FUNDING.

"(a) Treatment As A Legacy Plan.—

"(1) IN GENERAL.—For purposes of this subchapter, a defined benefit plan shall be treated as a legacy plan with respect to the composite plan under which the employees who were eligible to accrue a benefit under the defined benefit plan become eligible to accrue a benefit under such composite plan.

"(2) COMPONENT PLANS.—In any case in which a defined benefit plan is amended to add a composite plan component pursuant to section 437(b), paragraph (1) shall be applied by substituting 'defined benefit component' for 'defined benefit plan' and 'composite plan component' for 'composite plan'.

"(3) ELIGIBLE TO ACCRUE A BENEFIT.—For purposes of paragraph (1), an employee is considered eligible to accrue a benefit under a composite plan as of the first day in which the employee completes an hour of service under a collective bargaining agreement that provides for contributions to and accruals under the composite plan in lieu of accruals under the legacy plan.

"(4) COLLECTIVE BARGAINING AGREEMENT.—As used in this subpart, the term 'collective bargaining agreement' includes any agreement under which an employer has an obligation to contribute to a plan.

"(5) OTHER TERMS.—Any term used in this subpart which is not defined in this part and which is also used in section 432 shall have the same meaning provided such term in such section.

"(b) Restrictions On Acceptance By Composite Plan Of Agreements And Contributions.—

"(1) IN GENERAL.—The plan sponsor of a composite plan shall not accept or recognize a collective bargaining agreement (or any modification to such agreement), and no contributions may be accepted and no benefits may be accrued or otherwise earned under the agreement—

"(A) in any case in which the plan actuary of any defined benefit plan that would be treated as a legacy plan with respect to such composite plan has certified under section 432(b)(3) that such defined benefit plan is or will be in critical status for the plan year in which such agreement would take effect or for any of the succeeding 5 plan years, and

"(B) unless the agreement requires each employer who is a party to such agreement, including employers whose employees are not participants in the legacy plan, to provide contributions to the legacy plan with respect to such composite plan in a manner that satisfies the transition contribution requirements of subsection (d).

"(2) NOTICE.—Not later than 30 days after a determination by a plan sponsor of a composite plan that an agreement fails to satisfy the requirements described in paragraph (1), the plan sponsor shall provide notification of such failure and the reasons for such determination to—

"(A) the parties to the agreement,

"(B) active participants of the composite plan who have ceased to accrue or otherwise earn benefits with respect to service with an employer pursuant to paragraph (1), and

"(C) the Secretary of Labor, the Secretary of the Treasury, and the Pension Benefit Guaranty Corporation.

"(3) LIMITATION ON RETROACTIVE EFFECT.—This subsection shall not apply to benefits accrued before the date on which notice is provided under paragraph (2).

"(c) Restriction On Accrual Of Benefits Under A Composite Plan.—

"(1) IN GENERAL.—In any case in which an employer, under a collective bargaining agreement entered into after the date of enactment of the Giving Retirement Options to Workers Act of 2020, ceases to have an obligation to contribute to a multiemployer defined benefit plan, no employees employed by the employer may accrue or otherwise earn benefits under any composite plan, with respect to service with that employer, for a 60-month period beginning on the date on which the employer entered into such collective bargaining agreement.

"(2) NOTICE OF CESSATION OF OBLIGATION.—Within 30 days of determining that an employer has ceased to have an obligation to contribute to a legacy plan with respect to employees employed by an employer that is or will be contributing to a composite plan with respect to service of such employees, the plan sponsor of the legacy plan shall notify the plan sponsor of the composite plan of that cessation.

"(3) NOTICE OF CESSATION OF ACCRUALS.—Not later than 30 days after determining that an employer has ceased to have an obligation to contribute to a legacy plan, the plan sponsor of the composite plan shall notify the bargaining parties, the active participants affected by the cessation of accruals, the Secretary, the Secretary of Labor, and the Pension Benefit Guaranty Corporation of the cessation of accruals, the period during which such cessation is in effect, and the reasons therefor.

"(4) LIMITATION ON RETROACTIVE EFFECT.—This subsection shall not apply to benefits accrued before the date on which notice is provided under paragraph (3).

"(d) Transition Contribution Requirements.—

"(1) IN GENERAL.—A collective bargaining agreement satisfies the transition contribution requirements of this subsection if the agreement—

"(A) authorizes for payment of contributions to a legacy plan at a rate or rates equal to or greater than the transition contribution rate established under paragraph (2), and

"(B) does not provide for—

"(i) a suspension of contributions to the legacy plan with respect to any period of service, or

"(ii) any new direct or indirect exclusion of younger or newly hired employees of the employer from being taken into account in determining contributions owed to the legacy plan.

"(2) TRANSITION CONTRIBUTION RATE.—

"(A) IN GENERAL.—The transition contribution rate for a plan year is the contribution rate that, as certified by the actuary of the legacy plan in accordance with the principles in section 432(b)(3)(B), is reasonably expected to be adequate—

"(i) to fund the normal cost for the plan year,

"(ii) to amortize the plan's unfunded liabilities in level annual installments over 25 years, beginning with the plan year in which the transition contribution rate is first established, and

"(iii) to amortize any subsequent changes in the legacy plan's unfunded liability due to experience gains or losses (including investment gains or losses, gains or losses due to contributions greater or less than the contributions made under the prior transition contribution rate, and other actuarial gains or losses), changes in actuarial assumptions, changes to the legacy plan's benefits, or changes in funding method over a period of 15 plan years beginning with the plan year in which such change in unfunded liability is incurred.

The transition contribution rate for any plan year may not be less than the transition contribution rate for the plan year in which such rate is first established.

"(B) MULTIPLE RATES.—If different rates of contribution are payable to the legacy plan by different employers or for different classes of employees, the certification shall specify a transition contribution rate for each such employer.

"(C) RATE APPLICABLE TO EMPLOYER.—

"(i) IN GENERAL.—Except as provided by clause (ii), the transition contribution rate applicable to an employer for a plan year is the rate in effect for the plan year of the legacy plan that commences on or after 180 days before the earlier of—

"(I) the effective date of the collective bargaining agreement pursuant to which the employer contributes to the legacy plan, or

"(II) 5 years after the last plan year for which the transition contribution rate applicable to the employer was established or updated.

"(ii) EXCEPTION.—The transition contribution rate applicable to an employer for the first plan year beginning on or after the commencement of the employer's obligation to contribute to the composite plan is the rate in effect for the plan year of the legacy plan that commences on or after 180 days before such first plan year.

"(D) EFFECT OF LEGACY PLAN FINANCIAL CIRCUMSTANCES.—If the plan actuary of the legacy plan has certified under section 432 that the plan is in endangered or critical status for a plan year, the transition contribution rate for the following plan year is the rate determined with respect to the employer under the legacy plan's funding improvement or rehabilitation plan under section 432, if greater than the rate otherwise determined, but in no event greater than 75 percent of the sum of the contribution rates applicable to the legacy plan and the composite plan for the plan year.

"(E) OTHER ACTUARIAL ASSUMPTIONS AND METHODS.—Except as provided in subparagraph (A), the determination of the transition contribution rate for a plan year shall be based on actuarial assumptions and methods consistent with the minimum funding determinations made under section 431 (or, if applicable, section 432) with respect to the legacy plan for the plan year.

"(F) ADJUSTMENTS IN RATE.—The plan sponsor of a legacy plan from time to time may adjust the transition contribution rate or rates applicable to an employer under this paragraph by increasing some rates and decreasing others if the actuary certifies that such adjusted rates in combination will produce projected contribution income for the plan year beginning on or after the date of certification that is not less than would be produced by the transition contribution rates in effect at the time of the certification.

"(G) NOTICE OF TRANSITION CONTRIBUTION RATE.—The plan sponsor of a legacy plan shall provide notice to the parties to collective bargaining agreements pursuant to which contributions are made to the legacy plan of changes to the transition contribution rate requirements at least 30 days before the beginning of the plan year for which the rate is effective.

"(H) NOTICE TO COMPOSITE PLAN SPONSOR.—Not later than 30 days after a determination by the plan sponsor of a legacy plan that a collective bargaining agreement provides for a rate of contributions that is below the transition contribution rate applicable to one or more employers that are parties to the collective bargaining agreement, the plan sponsor of the legacy plan shall notify the plan sponsor of any composite plan under which employees of such employer would otherwise be eligible to accrue a benefit.

"(3) CORRECTION PROCEDURES.—Pursuant to standards prescribed by the Secretary of Labor, the plan sponsor of a composite plan shall adopt rules and procedures that give the parties to the collective bargaining agreement notice of the failure of such agreement to satisfy the transition contribution requirements of this subsection, and a reasonable opportunity to correct such failure, not to exceed 180 days from the date of notice given under subsection (b)(2).

"(4) SUPPLEMENTAL CONTRIBUTIONS.—A collective bargaining agreement may provide for supplemental contributions to the legacy plan for a plan year in excess of the transition contribution rate determined under paragraph (2), regardless of whether the legacy plan is in endangered or critical status for such plan year.

"(e) Nonapplication Of Composite Plan Restrictions.—

"(1) IN GENERAL.—The provisions of subsections (a), (b), and (c) shall not apply with respect to a collective bargaining agreement, to the extent the agreement, or a predecessor agreement, provides or provided for contributions to a defined benefit plan that is a legacy plan, as of the first day of the first plan year following a plan year for which the plan actuary certifies that the plan is fully funded, has been fully funded for at least three out of the immediately preceding 5 plan years, and is projected to remain fully funded for at least the following 4 plan years.

"(2) DETERMINATION OF FULLY FUNDED.—A plan is fully funded for purposes of paragraph (1) if, as of the valuation date of the plan for a plan year, the value of the plan's assets equals or exceeds the present value of the plan's liabilities, determined in accordance with the rules prescribed by the Pension Benefit Guaranty Corporation under sections 4219(c)(1)(D) and 4281 of Employee Retirement Income and Security Act for multiemployer plans terminating by mass withdrawal, as in effect for the date of the determination, except the plan's reasonable assumption regarding the starting date of benefits may be used.

"(3) OTHER APPLICABLE RULES.—Except as provided in paragraph (2), actuarial determinations and projections under this section shall be based on the rules in section 432(b)(3) and section 438(b).

"SEC. 440B. MERGERS AND ASSET TRANSFERS OF COMPOSITE PLANS.

"(a) In General.—Assets and liabilities of a composite plan may only be merged with, or transferred to, another plan if—

"(1) the other plan is a composite plan,

"(2) the plan or plans resulting from the merger or transfer is a composite plan,

"(3) no participant's accrued benefit or adjustable benefit is lower immediately after the transaction than it was immediately before the transaction, and

"(4) the value of the assets transferred in the case of a transfer reasonably reflects the value of the amounts contributed with respect to the participants whose benefits are being transferred, adjusted for allocable distributions, investment gains and losses, and administrative expenses.

"(b) Legacy Plan.—

"(1) IN GENERAL.—After a merger or transfer involving a composite plan, the legacy plan with respect to an employer that is obligated to contribute to the resulting composite plan is the legacy plan that applied to that employer immediately before the merger or transfer.

"(2) MULTIPLE LEGACY PLANS.—If an employer is obligated to contribute to more than one legacy plan with respect to employees eligible to accrue benefits under more than one composite plan and there is a merger or transfer of such legacy plans, the transition contribution rate applicable to the legacy plan resulting from the merger or transfer with respect to that employer shall be determined in accordance with the provisions of section 440A(d)(2)(B).".

(2) CLERICAL AMENDMENT.—The table of subparts for part III of subchapter D of chapter 1 of the Internal Revenue Code of 1986 is amended by adding at the end the following new item:

"SUBPART C. COMPOSITE PLANS AND LEGACY PLANS

(c) Effective Date.—The amendments made by this section shall apply to plan years beginning after the date of the enactment of this Act.

SEC. 103. APPLICATION OF CERTAIN REQUIREMENTS TO COMPOSITE PLANS.

(a) Amendments To The Employee Retirement Income Security Act Of 1974.—

(1) TREATMENT FOR PURPOSES OF FUNDING NOTICES.—Section 101(f) of the Employee Retirement Income Security Act of 1974 (29 U.S.C. 1021(f)) is amended—

(A) in paragraph (1) by striking "title IV applies" and inserting "title IV applies or which is a composite plan"; and

(B) by adding at the end the following:

"(5) APPLICATION TO COMPOSITE PLANS.—The provisions of this

subsection shall apply to a composite plan only to the extent prescribed by the Secretary in regulations that take into account the differences between a composite plan and a defined benefit plan that is a multiemployer plan.".

(2) TREATMENT FOR PURPOSES OF ANNUAL REPORT.—Section 103 of the Employee Retirement Income Security Act of 1974 (29 U.S.C. 1023) is amended—

(A) in subsection (d) by adding at the end the following sentence: "The provisions of this subsection shall apply to a composite plan only to the extent prescribed by the Secretary in regulations that take into account the differences between a composite plan and a defined benefit plan that is a multiemployer plan.";

(B) in subsection (f) by adding at the end the following:

"(3) ADDITIONAL INFORMATION FOR COMPOSITE PLANS.—With respect to any composite plan—

"(A) the provisions of paragraph (1)(A) shall apply by substituting 'current funded ratio and projected funded ratio (as such terms are defined in section 802(a)(2))' for 'funded percentage' each place it appears; and

"(B) the provisions of paragraph (2) shall apply only to the extent prescribed by the Secretary in regulations that take into account the differences between a composite plan and a defined benefit plan that is a multiemployer plan."; and

(C) by adding at the end the following:

"(h) Composite Plans.—A multiemployer plan that incorporates the features of a composite plan as provided in section 801(b) shall be treated as a single plan for purposes of the report required by this section, except that separate financial statements and actuarial statements shall be provided under paragraphs (3) and (4) of subsection (a) for the defined benefit plan component and for the composite plan component of the multiemployer plan.".

(3) TREATMENT FOR PURPOSES OF PENSION BENEFIT STATEMENTS.—Section 105(a) of the Employee Retirement Income Security Act of 1974 (29 U.S.C. 1025(a)) is amended by adding at the end the following:

"(4) COMPOSITE PLANS.—For purposes of this subsection, a composite plan shall be treated as a defined benefit plan to the extent prescribed by the Secretary in regulations that take into account the differences between a composite plan and a defined benefit plan that is a multiemployer plan.".

(b) Amendments To The Internal Revenue Code Of 1986.—Section 6058 of the Internal Revenue Code of 1986 is amended by redesignating subsection (f) as subsection (g) and by inserting after subsection (e) the following:

"(f) Composite Plans.—A multiemployer plan that incorporates the features of a composite plan as provided in section 437(b) shall be treated as a single plan for purposes of the return required by this section, except that separate financial statements shall be provided for the defined benefit plan component and for the composite plan component of the multiemployer plan.".

(c) Effective Date.—The amendments made by this section shall apply to plan years beginning after the date of the enactment of this Act.

SEC. 104. TREATMENT OF COMPOSITE PLANS UNDER TITLE IV.

(a) Definition.—Section 4001(a) of the Employee Retirement Income Security Act of 1974 (29 U.S.C. 1301(a)) is amended by striking the period at the end of paragraph (21) and inserting a semicolon and by adding at the end the following:

"(22) COMPOSITE PLAN.—The term 'composite plan' has the meaning set forth in section 801.".

(b) Composite Plans Disregarded For Calculating Premiums.—Section 4006(a) of such Act (29 U.S.C. 1306(a)) is amended by adding at the end the following:

"(9) The composite plan component of a multiemployer plan shall be disregarded in determining the premiums due under this section from the multiemployer plan.".

(c) Composite Plans Not Covered.—Section 4021(b)(1) of such Act (29 U.S.C. 1321(b)(1)) is amended by striking "Act" and inserting "Act, or a composite plan, as defined in paragraph (43) of section 3 of this Act".

(d) No Withdrawal Liability.—Section 4201 of such Act (29 U.S.C. 1381) is amended by adding at the end the following:

"(c) Contributions by an employer to the composite plan component of a multiemployer plan shall not be taken into account for any purpose under this title.".

(e) No Withdrawal Liability For Certain Plans.—Section 4201 of such Act (29 U.S.C. 1381) is further amended by adding at the end the following:

"(d) Contributions by an employer to a multiemployer plan described in the except clause of section 3(35) of this Act pursuant to a collective bargaining agreement that specifically designates that such contributions shall be allocated to the separate defined contribution accounts of participants under the plan shall not be taken into account with respect to the defined benefit portion of the plan for any purpose under this title (including the determination of the employer's highest contribution rate under section 4219), even if, under the terms of the plan, participants have the option to transfer assets in their separate defined contribution accounts to the defined benefit portion of the plan in return for service credit under the defined benefit portion, at rates established by the plan sponsor.

"(e) A legacy plan created under section 805 shall be deemed to have no unfunded vested benefits for purposes of this part, for each plan year following a period of 5 consecutive plan years for which—

"(1) the plan was fully funded within the meaning of section 805 for at least 3 of the plan years during that period, ending with a plan year for which the plan is fully funded;

"(2) the plan had no unfunded vested benefits for at least 3 of the plan years during that period, ending with a plan year for which the plan is fully funded;

and

"(3) the plan is projected to be fully funded and to have no unfunded vested benefits for the following four plan years.".

(f) No Withdrawal Liability For Employers Contributing To Certain Fully Funded Legacy Plans.—Section 4211 of such Act (29 U.S.C. 1382) is amended by adding at the end the following:

"(g) No amount of unfunded vested benefits shall be allocated to an employer that has an obligation to contribute to a legacy plan described in subsection (e) of section 4201 for each plan year for which such subsection applies.".

(g) No Obligation To Contribute.—Section 4212 of such Act (29 U.S.C. 1392) is amended by adding at the end the following:

"(d) No Obligation To Contribute.—An employer shall not be treated as having an obligation to contribute to a multiemployer defined benefit plan within the meaning of subsection (a) solely because—

"(1) in the case of a multiemployer plan that includes a composite plan component, the employer has an obligation to contribute to the composite plan component of the plan;

"(2) the employer has an obligation to contribute to a composite plan that is maintained pursuant to one or more collective bargaining agreements under which the multiemployer defined benefit plan is or previously was maintained; or

"(3) the employer contributes or has contributed under section 805(d) to a legacy plan associated with a composite plan pursuant to a collective bargaining agreement but employees of that employer were not eligible to accrue benefits under the legacy plan with respect to service with that employer.".

(h) No Inference.—Nothing in the amendment made by subsection (e) shall be construed to create an inference with respect to the treatment under title IV of the Employee Retirement Income Security Act of 1974, as in effect before such amendment, of contributions by an employer to a multiemployer plan described in the except clause of section 3(35) of such Act that are made before the effective date of subsection (e) specified in subsection (h)(2).

(i) Effective Date.—

(1) IN GENERAL.—Except as provided in subparagraph (2), the amendments made by this section shall apply to plan years beginning after the date of the enactment of this Act.

(2) SPECIAL RULE FOR SECTION 414(k) MULTIEMPLOYER PLANS.—The amendment made by subsection (e) shall apply only to required contributions payable for plan years beginning after the date of the enactment of this Act.

SEC. 105. CONFORMING CHANGES.

(a) Definitions.—Section 3 of the Employee Retirement Income Security Act of 1974 (29 U.S.C. 1002) is amended—

(1) in paragraph (35), by inserting "or a composite plan" after "other than an

individual account plan"; and
(2) by adding at the end the following:
"(43) The term 'composite plan' has the meaning given the term in section 801(a).".
(b) Special Funding Rule For Certain Legacy Plans.—
(1) AMENDMENT TO EMPLOYEE RETIREMENT INCOME SECURITY ACT OF 1974.—Section 304(b) of the Employee Retirement Income Security Act of 1974 (29 U.S.C. 1084(b)) is amended by adding at the end the following:
"(9) SPECIAL FUNDING RULE FOR CERTAIN LEGACY PLANS.—In the case of a multiemployer defined benefit plan that has adopted an amendment under section 801(b), in accordance with which no further benefits shall accrue under the multiemployer defined benefit plan, the plan sponsor may combine the outstanding balance of all charge and credit bases and amortize that combined base in level annual installments (until fully amortized) over a period of 25 plan years beginning with the plan year following the date all benefit accruals ceased.".
(2) AMENDMENT TO INTERNAL REVENUE CODE OF 1986.—Section 431(b) of the Internal Revenue Code of 1986 is amended by adding at the end the following:
"(9) SPECIAL FUNDING RULE FOR CERTAIN LEGACY PLANS.—In the case of a multiemployer defined benefit plan that has adopted an amendment under section 437(b), in accordance with which no further benefits shall accrue under the multiemployer defined benefit plan, the plan sponsor may combine the outstanding balance of all charge and credit bases and amortize that combined base in level annual installments (until fully amortized) over a period of 25 plan years beginning with the plan year following the date on which all benefit accruals ceased.".
(c) Benefits After Merger, Consolidation, Or Transfer Of Assets.—
(1) AMENDMENT TO EMPLOYEE RETIREMENT INCOME SECURITY ACT OF 1974.—Section 208 of the Employee Retirement Income Security Act of 1974 (29 U.S.C. 1058) is amended—
(A) by striking so much of the first sentence as precedes "may not merge" and inserting the following:
"(1) IN GENERAL.—Except as provided in paragraph (2), a pension plan may not merge, and"; and
(B) by striking the second sentence and adding at the end the following:
"(2) SPECIAL REQUIREMENTS FOR MULTIEMPLOYER PLANS.—Paragraph (1) shall not apply to any transaction to the extent that participants either before or after the transaction are covered under a multiemployer plan to which title IV of this Act applies or a composite plan.".
(2) AMENDMENTS TO INTERNAL REVENUE CODE OF 1986.—
(A) QUALIFICATION REQUIREMENT.—Section 401(a)(12) of the Internal Revenue Code of 1986 is amended—
(i) by striking "(12) A trust" and inserting the following:

"(12) BENEFITS AFTER MERGER, CONSOLIDATION, OR TRANSFER OF ASSETS.—

"(A) IN GENERAL.—Except as provided in subparagraph (B), a trust";

(ii) by striking the second sentence; and

(iii) by adding at the end the following:

"(B) SPECIAL REQUIREMENTS FOR MULTIEMPLOYER PLANS.—Subparagraph (A) shall not apply to any multiemployer plan with respect to any transaction to the extent that participants either before or after the transaction are covered under a multiemployer plan to which title IV of the Employee Retirement Income Security Act of 1974 applies or a composite plan.".

(B) ADDITIONAL QUALIFICATION REQUIREMENT.—Paragraph (1) of section 414(l) of such Code is amended—

(i) by striking "(1) IN GENERAL" and all that follows through "shall not constitute" and inserting the following:

"(1) BENEFIT PROTECTIONS: MERGER, CONSOLIDATION, TRANSFER.—

"(A) IN GENERAL.—Except as provided in subparagraph (B), a trust which forms a part of a plan shall not constitute"; and

(ii) by striking the second sentence; and

(iii) by adding at the end the following:

"(B) SPECIAL REQUIREMENTS FOR MULTIEMPLOYER PLANS.—Subparagraph (A) does not apply to any multiemployer plan with respect to any transaction to the extent that participants either before or after the transaction are covered under a multiemployer plan to which title IV of the Employee Retirement Income Security Act of 1974 applies or a composite plan.".

(d) Requirements For Status As A Qualified Plan.—

(1) REQUIREMENT THAT ACTUARIAL ASSUMPTIONS BE SPECIFIED.—Section 401(a)(25) of the Internal Revenue Code of 1986 is amended by inserting "(in the case of a composite plan, benefits objectively calculated pursuant to a formula)" after "definitely determinable benefits".

(2) MISSING PARTICIPANTS IN TERMINATING COMPOSITE PLAN.—Section 401(a)(34) of the Internal Revenue Code of 1986 is amended by striking ", a trust" and inserting "or a composite plan, a trust".

(e) Deduction For Contributions To A Qualified Plan.—Section 404(a)(1) of the Internal Revenue Code of 1986 is amended by redesignating subparagraph (E) as subparagraph (F) and by inserting after subparagraph (D) the following:

"(E) COMPOSITE PLANS.—

"(i) IN GENERAL.—In the case of a composite plan, subparagraph (D) shall not apply and the maximum amount deductible for a plan year shall be the excess (if any) of—

"(I) 160 percent of the greater of—

"(aa) the current liability of the plan determined in accordance with the

principles of section 431(c)(6)(D), or
"(bb) the present value of plan liabilities as determined under section 438, over
"(II) the fair market value of the plan's assets, projected to the end of the plan year.
"(ii) SPECIAL RULES FOR PREDECESSOR MULTIEMPLOYER PLAN TO COMPOSITE PLAN.—
"(I) IN GENERAL.—Except as provided in subclause (II), if an employer contributes to a composite plan with respect to its employees, contributions by that employer to a multiemployer defined benefit plan with respect to some or all of the same group of employees shall be deductible under sections 162 and this section, subject to the limits in subparagraph (D).
"(II) TRANSITION CONTRIBUTION.—The full amount of a contribution to satisfy the transition contribution requirement (as defined in section 440A(d)) and allocated to the legacy defined benefit plan for the plan year shall be deductible for the employer's taxable year ending with or within the plan year.".
(f) Minimum Vesting Standards.—
(1) YEARS OF SERVICE UNDER COMPOSITE PLANS.—
(A) EMPLOYEE RETIREMENT INCOME SECURITY ACT OF 1974.— Section 203 of the Employee Retirement Income Security Act of 1974 (29 U.S.C. 1053) is amended by inserting after subsection (f) the following:
"(g) Special Rules For Computing Years Of Service Under Composite Plans.—
"(1) IN GENERAL.—In determining a qualified employee's years of service under a composite plan for purposes of this section, the employee's years of service under a legacy plan shall be treated as years of service earned under the composite plan. For purposes of such determination, a composite plan shall not be treated as a defined benefit plan pursuant to section 801(d).
"(2) QUALIFIED EMPLOYEE.—For purposes of this subsection, an employee is a qualified employee if the employee first completes an hour of service under the composite plan (determined without regard to the provisions of this subsection) within the 12-month period immediately preceding or the 24-month period immediately following the date the employee ceased to accrue benefits under the legacy plan.
"(3) CERTIFICATION OF YEARS OF SERVICE.—For purposes of paragraph (1), the plan sponsor of the composite plan shall rely on a written certification by the plan sponsor of the legacy plan of the years of service the qualified employee completed under the defined benefit plan as of the date the employee satisfies the requirements of paragraph (2), disregarding any years of service that had been forfeited under the rules of the defined benefit plan before that date.
"(h) Special Rules For Computing Years Of Service Under Legacy Plans.—
"(1) IN GENERAL.—In determining a qualified employee's years of service under a legacy plan for purposes of this section, and in addition to any service under applicable regulations, the employee's years of service under a

composite plan shall be treated as years of service earned under the legacy plan. For purposes of such determination, a composite plan shall not be treated as a defined benefit plan pursuant to section 801(d).

"(2) QUALIFIED EMPLOYEE.—For purposes of this subsection, an employee is a qualified employee if the employee first completes an hour of service under the composite plan (determined without regard to the provisions of this subsection) within the 12-month period immediately preceding or the 24-month period immediately following the date the employee ceased to accrue benefits under the legacy plan.

"(3) CERTIFICATION OF YEARS OF SERVICE.—For purposes of paragraph (1), the plan sponsor of the legacy plan shall rely on a written certification by the plan sponsor of the composite plan of the years of service the qualified employee completed under the composite plan after the employee satisfies the requirements of paragraph (2), disregarding any years of service that has been forfeited under the rules of the composite plan.".

(B) INTERNAL REVENUE CODE OF 1986.—Section 411(a) of the Internal Revenue Code of 1986 is amended by adding at the end the following:

"(14) SPECIAL RULES FOR DETERMINING YEARS OF SERVICE UNDER COMPOSITE PLANS.—

"(A) IN GENERAL.—In determining a qualified employee's years of service under a composite plan for purposes of this subsection, the employee's years of service under a legacy plan shall be treated as years of service earned under the composite plan. For purposes of such determination, a composite plan shall not be treated as a defined benefit plan pursuant to section 437(d).

"(B) QUALIFIED EMPLOYEE.—For purposes of this paragraph, an employee is a qualified employee if the employee first completes an hour of service under the composite plan (determined without regard to the provisions of this paragraph) within the 12-month period immediately preceding or the 24-month period immediately following the date the employee ceased to accrue benefits under the legacy plan.

"(C) CERTIFICATION OF YEARS OF SERVICE.—For purposes of subparagraph (A), the plan sponsor of the composite plan shall rely on a written certification by the plan sponsor of the legacy plan of the years of service the qualified employee completed under the legacy plan as of the date the employee satisfies the requirements of subparagraph (B), disregarding any years of service that had been forfeited under the rules of the defined benefit plan before that date.

"(15) SPECIAL RULES FOR COMPUTING YEARS OF SERVICE UNDER LEGACY PLANS.—

"(A) IN GENERAL.—In determining a qualified employee's years of service under a legacy plan for purposes of this section, and in addition to any service under applicable regulations, the employee's years of service under a composite plan shall be treated as years of service earned under the legacy plan. For purposes of such determination, a composite plan shall not be treated as a defined benefit plan pursuant to section 437(d).

"(B) QUALIFIED EMPLOYEE.—For purposes of this paragraph, an employee is a qualified employee if the employee first completes an hour of service under the composite plan (determined without regard to the provisions of this paragraph) within the 12-month period immediately preceding or the 24-month period immediately following the date the employee ceased to accrue benefits under the legacy plan.

"(C) CERTIFICATION OF YEARS OF SERVICE.—For purposes of subparagraph (A), the plan sponsor of the legacy plan shall rely on a written certification by the plan sponsor of the composite plan of the years of service the qualified employee completed under the composite plan after the employee satisfies the requirements of subparagraph (B), disregarding any years of service that has been forfeited under the rules of the composite plan.".

(2) REDUCTION OF BENEFITS.—

(A) EMPLOYEE RETIREMENT INCOME SECURITY ACT OF 1974.—Section 203(a)(3)(E)(ii) of the Employee Retirement Income Security Act of 1974 (29 U.S.C. 1053(a)(3)(E)(ii)) is amended—

(i) in subclause (I) by striking "4244A" and inserting "305(e), 803,"; and

(ii) in subclause (II) by striking "4245" and inserting "305(e), 4245,".

(B) INTERNAL REVENUE CODE OF 1986.—Section 411(a)(3)(F) of the Internal Revenue Code of 1986 is amended—

(i) in clause (i) by striking "section 418D or under section 4281 of the Employee Retirement Income Security Act of 1974" and inserting "section 432(e) or 439 or under section 4281 of the Employee Retirement Income Security Act of 1974"; and

(ii) in clause (ii) by inserting "or 432(e)" after "section 418E".

(3) ACCRUED BENEFIT REQUIREMENTS.—

(A) EMPLOYEE RETIREMENT INCOME SECURITY ACT OF 1974.—Section 204(b)(1)(B)(i) of the Employee Retirement Income Security Act of 1974 (29 U.S.C. 1054(b)(1)(B)(i)) is amended by inserting ", including an amendment reducing or suspending benefits under section 305(e), 803, 4245 or 4281," after "any amendment to the plan".

(B) INTERNAL REVENUE CODE OF 1986.—Section 411(b)(1)(B)(i) of the Internal Revenue Code of 1986 is amended by inserting ", including an amendment reducing or suspending benefits under section 418E, 432(e), or 439, or under section 4281 of the Employee Retirement Income Security Act of 1974," after "any amendment to the plan".

(4) ADDITIONAL ACCRUED BENEFIT REQUIREMENTS.—

(A) EMPLOYEE RETIREMENT INCOME SECURITY ACT OF 1974.—Section 204(b)(1)(H)(v) of the Employee Retirement Income Security Act of 1974 (29 U.S.C. 1053(b)(1)(H)(v)) is amended by inserting before the period at the end the following: ", or benefits are reduced or suspended under section 305(e), 803, 4245, or 4281".

(B) INTERNAL REVENUE CODE OF 1986.—Section 411(b)(1)(H)(iv) of

the Internal Revenue Code of 1986 is amended—
(i) in the heading by striking "BENEFIT" and inserting "BENEFIT AND THE SUSPENSION AND REDUCTION OF CERTAIN BENEFITS"; and
(ii) in the text by inserting before the period at the end the following: ", or benefits are reduced or suspended under section 418E, 432(e), or 439, or under section 4281 of the Employee Retirement Income Security Act of 1974".
(5) ACCRUED BENEFIT NOT TO BE DECREASED BY AMENDMENT.—
(A) EMPLOYEE RETIREMENT INCOME SECURITY ACT OF 1974.—Section 204(g)(1) of the Employee Retirement Income Security Act of 1974 (29 U.S.C. 1053(g)(1)) is amended by inserting after "302(d)(2)" the following: ", 305(e), 803, 4245,".
(B) INTERNAL REVENUE CODE OF 1986.—Section 411(d)(6)(A) of the Internal Revenue Code of 1986 is amended by inserting after "412(d)(2)," the following: "418E, 432(e), or 439,".
(g) Certain Funding Rules Not Applicable.—
(1) EMPLOYEE RETIREMENT INCOME SECURITY ACT OF 1974.—Section 305 of the Employee Retirement Income Security Act of 1974 (29 U.S.C. 1085) is amended by adding at the end the following:
"(k) Legacy Plans.—Sections 302, 304, and 305 shall not apply to an employer that has an obligation to contribute to a plan that is a legacy plan within the meaning of section 805(a) solely because the employer has an obligation to contribute to a composite plan described in section 801 that is associated with that legacy plan.".
(2) INTERNAL REVENUE CODE OF 1986.—Section 432 of the Internal Revenue Code of 1986 is amended by adding at the end the following:
"(k) Legacy Plans.—Sections 412, 431, and 432 shall not apply to an employer that has an obligation to contribute to a plan that is a legacy plan within the meaning of section 440A(a) solely because the employer has an obligation to contribute to a composite plan described in section 437 that is associated with that legacy plan.".
(h) Termination Of Composite Plan.—Section 403(d) of the Employee Retirement Income Security Act of 1974 (29 U.S.C. 1103(d) is amended—
(1) in paragraph (1), by striking "regulations of the Secretary." and inserting "regulations of the Secretary, or as provided in paragraph (3)."; and
(2) by adding at the end the following:
"(3) Section 4044(a) of this Act shall be applied in the case of the termination of a composite plan by—
"(A) limiting the benefits subject to paragraph (3) thereof to benefits as defined in section 802(b)(3)(B); and
"(B) including in the benefits subject to paragraph (4) all other benefits (if any) of individuals under the plan that would be guaranteed under section 4022A if the plan were subject to title IV.".
(i) Good Faith Compliance Prior To Guidance.—Where the implementation of any provision of law added or amended by this division is subject to

issuance of regulations by the Secretary of Labor, the Secretary of the Treasury, or the Pension Benefit Guaranty Corporation, a multiemployer plan shall not be treated as failing to meet the requirements of any such provision prior to the issuance of final regulations or other guidance to carry out such provision if such plan is operated in accordance with a reasonable, good faith interpretation of such provision.

SEC. 106. EFFECTIVE DATE.

Unless otherwise specified, the amendments made by this division shall apply to plan years beginning after the date of the enactment of this Act.

DIVISION W—OTHER MATTERS

SEC. 240001. SMALL BUSINESS DEBTOR REORGANIZATION.
(a) In General.—Section 1182(1) of title 11, United States Code, is amended to read as follows:
"(1) DEBTOR.—The term 'debtor'—
"(A) subject to subparagraph (B), means a person engaged in commercial or business activities (including any affiliate of such person that is also a debtor under this title and excluding a person whose primary activity is the business of owning single asset real estate) that has aggregate noncontingent liquidated secured and unsecured debts as of the date of the filing of the petition or the date of the order for relief in an amount not more than $7,500,000 (excluding debts owed to 1 or more affiliates or insiders) not less than 50 percent of which arose from the commercial or business activities of the debtor; and
"(B) does not include—
"(i) any member of a group of affiliated debtors that has aggregate noncontingent liquidated secured and unsecured debts in an amount greater than $7,500,000 (excluding debt owed to 1 or more affiliates or insiders);
"(ii) any debtor that is a corporation subject to the reporting requirements under section 13 or 15(d) of the Securities Exchange Act of 1934 (15 U.S.C. 78m, 78o(d)); or
"(iii) any debtor that is an affiliate of an issuer, as defined in section 3 of the Securities Exchange Act of 1934 (15 U.S.C. 78c).".
(b) Applicability Of Chapters.—Section 103(i) of title 11, United States Code, is amended by striking "small business debtor" and inserting "debtor (as defined in section 1182)".
(c) Application Of Amendment.—The amendment made by subsection (a) shall apply only with respect to cases commenced under title 11, United States Code, on or after the date of enactment of this Act.
(d) Technical Corrections.—
(1) DEFINITION OF SMALL BUSINESS DEBTOR.—Section 101(51D)(B)(iii) of title 11, United States Code, is amended to read as follows:
"(iii) any debtor that is an affiliate of an issuer (as defined in section 3 of the Securities Exchange Act of 1934 (15 U.S.C. 78c)).".
(2) UNCLAIMED PROPERTY.—Section 347(b) of title 11, United States Code, is amended by striking "1194" and inserting "1191".
(e) Sunset.—On the date that is 1 year after the date of enactment of this Act, section 1182(1) of title 11, United States Code, is amended to read as follows:
"(1) DEBTOR.—The term 'debtor' means a small business debtor.".

SEC. 240002. BANKRUPTCY RELIEF.
(a) In General.—
(1) EXCLUSION FROM CURRENT MONTHLY INCOME.—Section 101(10A)(B)(ii) of title 11, United States Code, is amended—

(A) in subclause (III), by striking "; and" and inserting a semicolon;

(B) in subclause (IV), by striking the period at the end and inserting "; and"; and

(C) by adding at the end the following:

"(V) Payments made under Federal law relating to the national emergency declared by the President under the National Emergencies Act (50 U.S.C. 1601 et seq.) with respect to the coronavirus disease 2019 (COVID–19).".

(2) CONFIRMATION OF PLAN.—Section 1325(b)(2) of title 11, United States Code, is amended by inserting "payments made under Federal law relating to the national emergency declared by the President under the National Emergencies Act (50 U.S.C. 1601 et seq.) with respect to the coronavirus disease 2019 (COVID–19)," after "other than".

(3) MODIFICATION OF PLAN AFTER CONFIRMATION.—Section 1329 of title 11, United States Code, is amended by adding at end the following:

"(d) (1) Subject to paragraph (3), for a plan confirmed prior to the date of enactment of this subsection, the plan may be modified upon the request of the debtor if—

"(A) the debtor is experiencing or has experienced a material financial hardship due, directly or indirectly, to the coronavirus disease 2019 (COVID–19) pandemic; and

"(B) the modification is approved after notice and a hearing.

"(2) A plan modified under paragraph (1) may not provide for payments over a period that expires more than 7 years after the time that the first payment under the original confirmed plan was due.

"(3) Sections 1322(a), 1322(b), 1323(c), and the requirements of section 1325(a) shall apply to any modification under paragraph (1).".

(4) APPLICABILITY.—

(A) The amendments made by paragraphs (1) and (2) shall apply to any case commenced before, on, or after the date of enactment of this Act.

(B) The amendment made by paragraph (3) shall apply to any case for which a plan has been confirmed under section 1325 of title 11, United States Code, before the date of enactment of this Act.

(b) Sunset.—

(1) IN GENERAL.—

(A) EXCLUSION FROM CURRENT MONTHLY INCOME.—Section 101(10A)(B)(ii) of title 11, United States Code, is amended—

(i) in subclause (III), by striking the semicolon at the end and inserting "; and";

(ii) in subclause (IV), by striking "; and" and inserting a period; and

(iii) by striking subclause (V).

(B) CONFIRMATION OF PLAN.—Section 1325(b)(2) of title 11, United States Code, is amended by striking "payments made under Federal law relating to the national emergency declared by the President under the National Emergencies Act (50 U.S.C. 1601 et seq.) with respect to the coronavirus disease 2019 (COVID–19),".

(C) MODIFICATION OF PLAN AFTER CONFIRMATION.—Section 1329 of title 11, United States Code, is amended by striking subsection (d).
(2) EFFECTIVE DATE.—The amendments made by paragraph (1) shall take effect on the date that is 1 year after the date of enactment of this Act.

DIVISION X—OTHER MATTERS

SEC. 199991. HOME ENERGY AND WATER SERVICE CONTINUITY.

Any entity receiving financial assistance pursuant to the Take Responsibility for Workers and Families Act shall, to the maximum extent practicable, establish or maintain in effect policies to ensure that no home energy service or public water system service to an individual or household, which is provided or regulated by such entity, is disconnected or interrupted during the emergency period described in section 1135(g)(1)(B) of the Social Security Act. For purposes of this section, the term "home energy service" means a service to provide home energy, as such term is defined in section 2604 of the Low-Income Home Energy Assistance Act of 1981, and electric service, as that term is used in the Public Utility Regulatory Policies Act of 1978, and the term "public water system" has the meaning given that term in section 1401 of the Safe Drinking Water Act. Nothing in this section shall be construed to require forgiveness of outstanding debt owed to an entity or to absolve an individual of any obligation to an entity for service.

SEC. 199992. LOW-INCOME HOUSEHOLD DRINKING WATER AND WASTEWATER ASSISTANCE.

(a) Authorization Of Appropriations.—There is authorized to be appropriated $1,500,000,000 to the Secretary to carry out this section. Such sums shall remain available until expended.

(b) Low-Income Household Drinking Water And Wastewater Assistance.—The Secretary shall make grants to States and Indian Tribes to assist low-income households, particularly those with the lowest incomes, that pay a high proportion of household income for drinking water and wastewater services.

(c) Use Of LIHEAP Resources.—In carrying out this section, the Secretary, States, and Indian Tribes, as applicable, shall use the existing processes, procedures, policies, and systems in place to carry out the Low-Income Home Energy Assistance Act of 1981, as the Secretary determines appropriate, including by using the application and approval process under such Act to the maximum extent practicable.

(d) Allotment.—

(1) FACTORS.—The Secretary shall allot amounts appropriated pursuant to this section to a State or Indian Tribe taking into account—

(A) the percentage of households in the State, or under the jurisdiction of the Indian Tribe, that are low-income, as determined by the Secretary;

(B) the average State or Tribal drinking water and wastewater service rates; and

(C) the extent to which the State or Indian Tribe has been impacted by the public health emergency.

(2) NOTIFICATION TO CONGRESS.—Not later than 15 days after

determining an amount to allot to each State or Indian Tribe pursuant to paragraph (1), and prior to making grants under this section, the Secretary shall notify Congress of such allotment amounts.
(e) Determination Of Low-Income Households.—
(1) MINIMUM DEFINITION OF LOW-INCOME.—In determining whether a household is considered low-income for the purposes of this section, a State or Indian Tribe shall—
(A) ensure that, at a minimum, all households within 150 percent of the Federal poverty line are included as low-income households; and
(B) consider households that have not previously received assistance under the Low-Income Home Energy Assistance Act of 1981 in the same manner as households that have previously received such assistance.
(2) HOUSEHOLD DOCUMENTATION REQUIREMENTS.—States and Indian Tribes shall—
(A) to the maximum extent practicable, seek to limit the income history documentation requirements for determining whether a household is considered low-income for the purposes of this section; and
(B) for the purposes of income eligibility, accept proof of job loss or severe income loss dated after February 29, 2020, such as a layoff or furlough notice or verification of application of unemployment benefits, as sufficient to demonstrate lack of income for an individual or household.
(f) Applications.—Each State or Indian Tribe desiring to receive a grant under this section shall submit an application to the Secretary, in such form as the Secretary shall require.
(g) State Agreements With Drinking Water And Wastewater Providers.—To the maximum extent practicable, a State that receives a grant under this section shall enter into agreements with community water systems, private utilities, municipalities, nonprofit organizations associated with providing drinking water, wastewater, and other social services to rural and small communities, and Indian Tribes, to assist in identifying low-income households and to carry out this section.
(h) Administrative Costs.—A State or Indian Tribe that receives a grant under this section may use up to 15 percent of the granted amounts for administrative costs.
(i) Federal Agency Coordination.—In carrying out this section, the Secretary shall coordinate with the Administrator of the Environmental Protection Agency and consult with other Federal agencies with authority over the provision of drinking water and wastewater services.
(j) Audits.—The Secretary shall require each State and Indian Tribe receiving a grant under this section to undertake periodic audits and evaluations of expenditures made by such State or Indian Tribe pursuant to this section.
(k) Reports To Congress.—The Secretary shall submit to Congress a report on the results of activities carried out pursuant to this section—
(1) not later than 1 year after the date of enactment of this section; and

(2) upon disbursement of all funds appropriated pursuant to this section.
(l) Definitions.—In this section:
(1) COMMUNITY WATER SYSTEM.—The term "community water system" has the meaning given such term in section 1401 of the Safe Drinking Water Act (42 U.S.C. 300f).
(2) INDIAN TRIBE.—The term "Indian Tribe" means any Indian Tribe, band, group, or community recognized by the Secretary of the Interior and exercising governmental authority over a Federal Indian reservation.
(3) MUNICIPALITY.—The term "municipality" has the meaning given such term in section 502 of the Federal Water Pollution Control Act (33 U.S.C. 1362).
(4) PUBLIC HEALTH EMERGENCY.—The term "public health emergency" means the public health emergency described in section 1135(g)(1)(B) of the Social Security Act.
(5) SECRETARY.—The term "Secretary" means the Secretary of Health and Human Services.
(6) STATE.—The term "State" means a State, the District of Columbia, the Commonwealth of Puerto Rico, the Virgin Islands of the United States, Guam, American Samoa, and the Commonwealth of the Northern Mariana Islands.

SEC. 199993. DELAY OF STRATEGIC PETROLEUM RESERVE SALE.
(a) Bipartisan Budget Act Of 2015.—Section 404 of the Bipartisan Budget Act of 2015 (42 U.S.C. 6239 note) is amended—
(1) in subsection (e), by striking "2020" and inserting "2022"; and
(2) in subsection (g), by striking "2020" and inserting "2022".
(b) Further Consolidated Appropriations Act, 2020.—Title III of division C of the Further Consolidated Appropriations Act, 2020 (Public Law 116–94) is amended in the matter under the heading "Department of Energy—Energy Programs—Strategic Petroleum Reserve" by striking "Provided, That" and all that follows through the period at the end and inserting the following: "Provided, That, as authorized by section 404 of the Bipartisan Budget Act of 2015 (Public Law 114–74; 42 U.S.C. 6239 note), the Secretary of Energy shall draw down and sell not to exceed a total of $450,000,000 of crude oil from the Strategic Petroleum Reserve in fiscal year 2020, fiscal year 2021, or fiscal year 2022: Provided further, That the proceeds from such drawdown and sale shall be deposited into the 'Energy Security and Infrastructure Modernization Fund' during the fiscal year in which the sale occurs and shall be made available in such fiscal year, to remain available until expended, for necessary expenses to carry out the Life Extension II project for the Strategic Petroleum Reserve.".

SEC. 199994. EXPANSION OF DOL AUTHORITY TO POSTPONE CERTAIN DEADLINES.
Section 518 of the Employee Retirement Income Security Act of 1974 (29

U.S.C. 1148) is amended by striking "or a terroristic or military action (as defined in section 692(c)(2) of such Code), the Secretary may" and inserting "a terroristic or military action (as defined in section 692(c)(2) of such Code), or a public health emergency declared by the Secretary of Health and Human Services pursuant to section 319 of the Public Health Service Act, the Secretary may".

SEC. 199995. PROVIDING BUREAU OF THE CENSUS ACCESS TO INSTITUTIONS OF HIGHER EDUCATION.

(a) In General.—Notwithstanding any other provision of law, including section 444 of the General Education Provisions Act (commonly known as the "Family Educational Rights and Privacy Act of 1974"), an institution of higher education may, in furtherance of a full and accurate decennial census of population count, provide to the Bureau of the Census information requested by the Bureau for purposes of enumeration for the 2020 decennial Census.

(b) Application.—

(1) INFORMATION.—Only information requested on the official 2020 decennial census of population form may be provided to the Bureau of the Census pursuant to this section. No institution of higher education may provide any information to the Bureau on the immigration or citizenship status of any individual.

(2) GROUP QUARTERS.—Only students who, according to guidance from the Bureau, are living in group quarters may be included in the data provided to the Bureau under this section.

(3) NOTICE REQUIRED.—Before information can be provided to the Bureau, the institution of higher education shall give public notice of the categories of information which it plans to provide and shall allow 10 days after such notice has been given for a parent or student to inform the institution that any or all of the information designated should not be released without the parent or student's prior consent. No institution of higher education shall provide the Bureau with the information of any individual who has objected or whose legal guardian has objected to the provision of such information.

(4) USE OF INFORMATION.—Information provided to the Bureau pursuant to this section may only be used for the purposes of enumeration for the 2020 decennial census of population.

(c) Sunset.—The authority provided in this section shall expire on December 31, 2020.

(d) Definitions.—In this section:

(1) GROUP QUARTERS.—The term "group quarters" means housing units owned or operated by an institution of higher education.

(2) INSTITUTION OF HIGHER EDUCATION.—The term "institution of higher education" has the meaning given that term in section 102 of the Higher Education Act of 1965 (20 U.S.C. 1002).

SEC. 199996. TEMPORARY FISCAL RELIEF FOR STATES AND LOCALITIES.

(a) In General.—The Social Security Act (42 U.S.C. 301 et seq.) is amended by inserting after title V the following:

"TITLE VI—TEMPORARY FISCAL RELIEF FOR STATES AND LOCALITIES

"SEC. 601. TEMPORARY FISCAL RELIEF FOR STATES AND LOCALITIES.

"(a) Appropriation.—

"(1) IN GENERAL.—Out of any money in the Treasury of the United States not otherwise appropriated, there are appropriated for fiscal year 2020, $200,000,000,000 for making payments to States, Indian Tribes, and units of local government under this section.

"(2) RESERVATION OF FUNDS.—Of the amount appropriated under paragraph (10, the Secretary shall reserve—

"(A) $1,000,000,000 of such amount for making payments to the United States Virgin Islands, Guam, the Commonwealth of the Northern Mariana Islands, or American Samoa; and

"(B) $10,000,000,000 of such amount for making payments to Indian Tribes.

"(b) Payments.—

"(1) IN GENERAL.—Subject to paragraph (2), from the amount appropriated under paragraph (1) of subsection (a) for fiscal year 2020 which remains after the application of paragraph (2) of that subsection, the Secretary shall, not later than the later of the date that is 15 days after the date of enactment of this section or the date that a State or Indian Tribe provides the certification required by subsection (f) for fiscal year 2020, pay each State or Indian Tribe the amount determined for the State or Indian Tribe for fiscal year 2020 under subsection (c).

"(2) DIRECT PAYMENTS TO UNITS OF LOCAL GOVERNMENT.—The Secretary shall establish a process under which, not later than 15 days after the date of enactment of this section, a unit of local government located in a State for which the amount of the payment determined for the State under subsection (c) for fiscal year 2020 exceeds the minimum payment amount under paragraph (2) of that subsection, may submit the certification required by subsection (f) to the Secretary and be paid directly the amount determined for such unit of local government under subsection (c).

"(c) Determination Of Payment Amounts.—

"(1) STATES.—Subject to the succeeding paragraphs of this subsection, the amount paid to a State other than a State that is a territory specified in subsection (a)(2)(A) under this section for fiscal year 2020 shall be the amount equal to the relative population proportion amount described in paragraph

(4) for such fiscal year.

"(2) STATE MINIMUM PAYMENT.—No State that is 1 of the 50 States, the District of Columbia, or the Commonwealth of Puerto Rico, shall receive a payment under this section for fiscal year 2020 that is less than, $2,500,000,000.

"(3) DIRECT PAYMENTS TO UNITS OF LOCAL GOVERNMENT.—If a unit of local government of a State submits the certification required by subsection (f) for purposes of receiving a direct payment from the Secretary under subsection (b)(2), the Secretary shall reduce the amount determined for a State under paragraph (1) or (2) (as applicable) by the relative unit of local government population proportion (as defined in paragraph (6)).

"(4) RELATIVE POPULATION PROPORTION AMOUNT.—The relative population proportion amount described in this paragraph is the product of—

"(A) the amount appropriated under paragraph (1) of subsection (a) for fiscal year 2020 which remains after the application of paragraph (2) of that subsection; and

"(B) the relative State population proportion (as defined in paragraph (5)).

"(5) RELATIVE STATE POPULATION PROPORTION DEFINED.—For purposes of paragraph (4)(B), the term 'relative State population proportion' means, with respect to a State, the amount equal to the quotient of—

"(A) the population of the State; and

"(B) the total population of all States.

"(6) RELATIVE UNIT OF LOCAL GOVERNMENT POPULATION PROPORTION DEFINED.—For purposes of paragraph (3), the term 'relative unit of local government population proportion' means, with respect to a unit of local government, the amount equal to the quotient of—

"(A) the population of the unit of local government; and

"(B) the total population of the State in which the unit of local government is located.

"(7) CERTAIN TERRITORIES.—The amount paid to a State that is a territory specified in subsection (a)(2)(A) under this section for fiscal year 2020, shall be the amount equal to the product of the amount set aside under subsection (a)(2)(A) for such fiscal year and each such territory's share of the total population among all such territories, as determined by the Secretary.

"(8) INDIAN TRIBES.—From the amount set aside under subsection (a)(2)(B) for fiscal year 2020, the Secretary shall determine and pay an amount to each Indian Tribe that submits the certification required under subsection (f) for fiscal year 2020 based on lost revenues of each such Indian Tribe (or a tribally-owned entity of such Tribe) relative to revenues received in the aggregate in fiscal year 2019 by the Indian Tribe (tribally-owned entity), and in such manner as the Secretary determines appropriate to ensure that all amounts available under such subsection for fiscal year 2020 are distributed to eligible Indian Tribes.

"(9) PRO RATE ADJUSTMENTS.—The Secretary shall adjust on a pro rat basis the amount of the payments determined under this subsection without regard to this paragraph to the extent necessary to comply with the requirements of this subsection.

"(10) DATA.—For purposes of this section, the Secretary shall determine the population of a State or unit of local government based on the most recent year for which data are available from the Bureau of the Census.

"(d) Payments Made In Two Parts.—The Secretary shall pay the amounts determined under subsection (c) for States, territories specified in subsection (a)(2)(A), and Indian Tribes (and if applicable, local units of government) as follows:

"(1) The Secretary shall make initial payments in accordance with the deadlines specified in subsection (b) consisting of—

"(A) in the case of a State for which the amount of payment is determined under paragraph (1) or (2) of subsection (c), 50 percent of the amount determined for the State under paragraph (1) of that subsection (taking into account payments to units of local government, if applicable, under subsections (b)(2) and (c)(3)) or 100 percent of the payment amount specified in paragraph (2) of that subsection, whichever is greater; and

"(B) in the case of a territory specified in subsection (a)(2)(A) or an Indian Tribe 100 percent of the amount determined for such territory or Indian Tribe under paragraph (7) or (8), respectively, of subsection (c).

"(2) In the case of a State for which the initial payment is 50 percent of the amount determined for the State under subsection (c)(1), the Secretary shall pay the State the remaining 50 percent of such amount on the earlier of—

"(A) the 1st day of the month succeeding the first month that beings after the date of enactment of this section for which the national employment-to-population ratio is below 60 percent or the seasonally adjusted national unemployment rate (U–3) determined by the Bureau of Labor Statistics of the Department of Labor for the applicable calendar month as initially reported and prior to any subsequent revisions (rounded to the nearest tenth of a percentage point) exceeds 5.0 percent; or

"(B) July 1, 2020.

A unit of local government for which a direct payment may be made under subsections (b)(2) and (c)(3) shall be paid at the same time and in the percentages as the State in which such government is located.

"(e) Use Of Funds.—

"(1) IN GENERAL.—Subject to paragraphs (2) and (3), a State, Indian Tribe, or unit of local government shall use the funds provided under a payment made under this section to cover only those costs of the State, Indian Tribe, or unite of local government, such as costs to administer and provide benefits under State unemployment insurance law, that are attributable to the public health emergency with respect to the Coronavirus Disease 2019 (COVID–19) that were not accounted for in the budget most recently approved as of the date of enactment of this section for the State, Indian Tribe, or unit of local government and that were incurred during the period that begins on March

1, 2020, and ends on February 28, 2021.

"(2) EXCEPTION.—Nothwithstanding paragraph (1), a State, Indian Tribe, or unit of local government may use funds provided under a payment made under this section for costs attributable to the public health emergency with respect to the Coronavirus Disease 2019 (COVID–19) or to provide essential government services accounted for in the budget most recently approved as of the date of enactment of this section for the State, Indian Tribe, or unit of local government that, without the use of such funds, the State, Indian Tribe, or unit of local government would be unable to provide because of decreased or delayed revenues during the period described in paragraph (1).

"(3) LIMITATIONS.—A State, Indian Tribe, or unit of local government may not use funds provided under a payment made under this section to—

"(A) supplant expenditures permitted under the most recently approved budget for the State, Indian Tribe, or unit of local government for which the State, Indian Tribe, or unit of local government has funds immediately available; or

"(B) provide any kind of tax cut, rebate, deduction, credit, or any other tax benefit, or to reduce or eliminate any other fee imposed by the State, Indian Tribe, or unit of local government, during the period described in paragraph (1).

"(f) Certification.—In order to receive a payment under this section for a fiscal year, a State, Indian Tribe, or unit of local government shall provide the Secretary with a certification signed by the Governor of the State or the Chief Executive for the Indian Tribe or unit of local government that the State's, Indian Tribe's, or unit of local government's proposed uses of the funds are consistent with subsection (e).

"(g) Recoupment.—If the Comptroller General of the United States determines that a State, Indian Tribe, or unit of local government has failed to comply with subparagraph (B) of subsection (e)(3), the Secretary shall establish a process for recouping from the State, Indian Tribe, or unit of local government an amount equal to the amount of funds used in violation of such subparagraph. Amounts recovered by the Secretary under this subsection shall be used as follows:

"(1) 65 percent of such amounts shall be transferred or credited to the Housing Trust Fund established under section 1338 of the Federal Housing Enterprises Financial Safety and Soundness Act of 1992 (12 U.S.C. 4568); and

"(2) 35 percent of such amounts shall be transferred or credited to the Capital Magnet Fund established under section 1339 of the Federal Housing Enterprises Financial Safety and Soundness Act of 1992 (12 U.S.C. 4569).

"(h) Definitions.—In this section:

"(1) INDIAN TRIBE.—The term 'Indian tribe' has the meaning given that term in section 4(e) of the Indian Self-Determination and Education Assistance Act (25 U.S.C. 5304(e)).

"(2) SECRETARY.—The term 'Secretary' means the Secretary of the Treasury.

"(3) STATE.—The term 'State' means the 50 States, the District of Columbia, the Commonwealth of Puerto Rico, the United States Virgin Islands, Guam, the Commonwealth of the Northern Mariana Islands, and American Samoa.

"(4) UNIT OF LOCAL GOVERNMENT.—The term 'unit of local government' means a county, municipality, town, township, village, parish, borough, or other unit of general government below the State level with a population that exceeds 500,000.

"(i) Emergency Designation.—

"(1) IN GENERAL.—The amounts provided by this section are designated as an emergency requirement pursuant to section 4(g) of the Statutory Pay-As-You-Go-Act of 2010 (2 U.S.C. 933(g)).

"(2) DESIGNATION IN SENATE.—In the Senate, this section is designated as an emergency requirement pursuant to section 4112(a) of H. Con. Res. 71 (115th Congress), the concurrent resolution on the budget for fiscal year 2018.".

SEC. 199997. BUDGETARY EFFECTS.

(a) Statutory PAYGO Scorecards.—The budgetary effects of division B and each succeeding division shall not be entered on either PAYGO scorecard maintained pursuant to section 4(d) of the Statutory Pay-As-You-Go Act of 2010.

(b) Senate PAYGO Scorecards.—The budgetary effects of division B and each succeeding division shall not be entered on any PAYGO scorecard maintained for purposes of section 4106 of H. Con. Res. 71 (115th Congress).

(c) Classification Of Budgetary Effects.—Notwithstanding Rule 3 of the Budget Scorekeeping Guidelines set forth in the joint explanatory statement of the committee of conference accompanying Conference Report 105–217 and section 250(c)(8) of the Balanced Budget and Emergency Deficit Control Act of 1985, the budgetary effects of division B and each succeeding division shall not be estimated—

(1) for purposes of section 251 of such Act; and

(2) for purposes of paragraph (4)(C) of section 3 of the Statutory Pay-As-You-Go Act of 2010 as being included in an appropriation Act.

SEC. 199998. AIRCRAFT GREENHOUSE GAS EMISSION STANDARDS.

(a) In General.—Not later than 18 months after the date of enactment of this Act, the Administrator of the Environmental Protection Agency shall promulgate final regulations establishing emission standards for emissions of greenhouse gases from both new and in-service aircraft pursuant to section 231 of the Clean Air Act (42 U.S.C. 7571).

(b) Soliciting Comments.—In proposing such regulations, the Administrator of the Environmental Protection Agency shall solicit comments on—

(1) the minimum greenhouse gas emission standards established by the International Civil Aviation Organization; and

(2) relative to such minimum standards, greenhouse gas emission standards that would achieve greater reductions in greenhouse gas emissions.

DIVISION Y—ADDITIONAL OTHER MATTERS

SEC. 101. EMERGENCY RELIEF THROUGH LOANS AND LOAN GUARANTEES.

(a) In General.—Notwithstanding any other provision of law, to provide liquidity related to losses incurred as a direct result of coronavirus, the Secretary is authorized to make loans, loan guarantees, and other investments in support of eligible businesses (including women-owned, minority-owned, veteran-owned and rural businesses, and mortgage servicers), States, any bi-State agency, the District of Columbia, territories, municipalities, and federally recognized Tribes that do not, in the aggregate, exceed $250,000,000,000 and provide the subsidy amounts necessary for such loans and loan guarantees in accordance with the provisions of the Federal Credit Reform Act of 1990 (2 U.S.C. 661 et seq.).

(c) Loans And Loan Guarantees.—

(1) IN GENERAL.—The Secretary shall review and decide on applications for loans and loan guarantees under this section and may enter into agreements to make or guarantee loans to one or more obligors if the Secretary determines, in the Secretary's discretion, that—

(A) the obligor is a eligible business for which credit is not reasonably available at the time of the transaction;

(B) the intended obligation by the obligor is prudently incurred; and

(C) the loan is sufficiently secured.

(2) TERMS AND LIMITATIONS.—

(A) FORMS; TERMS AND CONDITIONS.—Subject to section 407 of division I of this Act, a loan or loan guarantee shall be issued under this section in such form and on such terms and conditions and contain such covenants, representatives, warranties, and requirements (including requirements for audits) as the Secretary determines appropriate. Any loans made by the Secretary under this section shall be at a rate not less than a rate determined by the Secretary taking into consideration the current average yield on outstanding marketable obligations of the United States of comparable maturity.

(B) PROCEDURES.—As soon as practicable, but in no case later than 10 days after the date of enactment of this Act, the Secretary shall publish procedures for application and minimum requirements, which may be supplemented by the Secretary in the Secretary's discretion, for the making of loans and loan guarantees under this section.

(3) FEDERAL RESERVE PROGRAMS OR FACILITIES.—

(A) TERMS AND CONDITIONS.—

(i) IN GENERAL.—The Secretary may make a loan, loan guarantee, or other investment under this section as part of a program or facility established by the Board of Governors of the Federal Reserve System for the purpose of providing liquidity to the financial system that purchases obligations or other interests directly from issuers of such obligations or other interests only to the extent required under a contractual obligation in effect as of the date of enactment of this Act, the issuer of such obligations or interests agrees not to repurchase any outstanding equity interests while the loan, loan guarantee, or other interest under this section is outstanding.

(ii) PROGRAMS AND FACILITIES AUTHORIZED UNDER THIS ACT.—Programs and facilities described under clause (i) include those established by the Board of Governors pursuant to the authority provided under section 105(h), 110(g), 201, or 203.

(B) LOAN FORGIVENESS.—The principal amount of any obligation issued by an eligible business, State, the District of Columbia, territory, or municipality that is acquired under a program or facility under this section shall not be reduced through loan forgiveness.

(C) FEDERAL RESERVE ACT REQUIREMENTS APPLY.—For the avoidance of doubt, any applicable requirements under section 13(3) of the Federal Reserve Act (12 U.S.C. 343(3)), including requirements relating to loan collateralization, taxpayer protection, and borrower solvency, shall apply with respect to any obligation or other interest issued by an eligible business, State, the District of Columbia, territory, or municipality that is acquired under a program or facility under this section.

(d) Addressing Persistent Poverty In Counties.—In carrying out the authorities provided by this section, the Secretary shall, to the greatest extent possible, ensure that at least 10 percent of the loans, loan guarantees, and other investments provided under this sections are used to support counties with a poverty rate of at least 20 percent over the last 30 years. The Secretary is also authorized to provide technical assistance to such countries to encourage participation in the program.

(e) Financial Protection Of Government.—

(1) IN GENERAL.—To the extent feasible and practicable, the Secretary shall ensure that the Federal Government is compensated for the risk assumed in making loans and loan guarantees under this section.

(2) GOVERNMENT PARTICIPATION IN GAINS.—If an eligible business receives a loan or loan guarantee from the Federal Government under this section, subject to Section 408 of Division I, the Secretary shall enter into contracts under which the Federal Government, contingent on the financial success of the eligible business, would participate in the gains of the eligible business or its security holders through the use of such instruments as warrants, stock options, common or preferred stock, or other appropriate equity instruments.

(f) Deposit Of Proceeds.—Amounts collected by the Secretary under this section, including the proceeds of investments, earnings, and interest collected, shall be deposited in the Treasury as miscellaneous receipts.

(g) Administrative Expenses.—Notwithstanding any other provision of law, the Secretary may use $100,000,000 of the funds made available under this section to pay costs and administrative expenses associated with the provision of direct loans or guarantees authorized under this section.

(h) Transparency Of Financial Assistance.—The Secretary shall provide a weekly report to the Congress, including the House Committee on Financial Services and the Senate Committee on Banking, Housing, and Urban Affairs, providing a detailed description of the status of the implementation of this section, including providing a list of recipients and amounts of any loan, loan guarantee, or investment. The Secretary shall make each report immediately available to the public.

(i) Certification Of The Secretary.—The Secretary shall certify to Congress in the report described in subsection (h) that any corporation that receives aid pursuant to this section does not provide a direct financial benefit to the President of the United States or to any company in which the President owns a controlling interest.

(j) Conforming Amendment.—Section 5302(a)(1) of title 31, United States Code, is amended—

(1) by striking "and" before "section 3"; and

(2) by inserting "Financial Protections and Assistance for America's Consumers, States, Businesses, and Vulnerable Populations Act," before "and for investing".

SEC. 102. LIMITATION ON CERTAIN EMPLOYEE COMPENSATION.

(a) In General.—The Secretary may only enter into a loan or loan agreement under section 101(a) of this division with an eligible business after the eligible business enters into a legally binding agreement with the Secretary that, during the period beginning March 1, 2020, and ending March 1, 2022 or the termination of the loan or loan agreement under section 101(a) of this division, which is later, no officer or employee of the eligible business—

(1) will receive from the eligible business total compensation which exceeds $425,000, during any 12 consecutive months of such period; and

(2) will receive from the eligible business severance pay or other benefits upon termination of employment with the eligible business which exceeds twice the compensation described in paragraph (1).

(b) Total Compensation Defined.—In this section, the term "total compensation" includes salary, bonuses, awards of stock, and other financial benefits provided by an eligible business to an officer or employee of the eligible business.

SEC. 103. REQUIREMENT TO PROVIDE EMPLOYEE HEALTH INSURANCE BENEFITS.

(a) In General.—The Secretary may not provide any loans or loan guarantees under paragraph (1), (2), or (3) of section 4101(b) to an eligible business, unless the eligible business certifies that the eligible business currently provides, or will provide within 60 days from receipt of the loan or loan guarantee, and any contractor, subcontractor, or affiliate of the eligible business, currently provides, or will provide within 60 days from receipt of the loan or loan guarantee, to any employee based in the United States, health insurance benefits equal to or greater than the hourly health and welfare fringe benefit rate published by the Department of Labor pursuant to the McNamara-O'Hara Service Contract Act of 1965 (41 U.S.C. 6710–6707) and section 4.52 of title 28, Code of Federal Regulations, for all hours worked by each employee, and shall continue to do so for at least the 5-year period after any loan or loan guarantee provided to the eligible business under this subtitle ends.

SEC. 104. PROHIBITION ON OUTSOURCING AND REQUIREMENT FOR ON-SHORING.

(a) In General.—The Secretary may not provide any loan, or enter into a loan guarantee to an eligible business under of section 4101(b) unless the eligible business enters into a legally binding agreement with the Secretary that during the 5-year period beginning on the date on which the eligible business receives the funds or, in the case of a loan, during the period of the loan and for 5 years after that period, the eligible business shall—

(1) not outsource to any other business, including through contracting, any job, function, or labor that was previously performed by direct employees of the eligible business who were laid off or furloughed after January 1, 2020;

(2) on-shore to a State any job, function, or labor that—

(A) the eligible business needs additional employees, contractors, or hours of labor to fulfill; and

(B) arise after the date on which the legally binding agreement is executed; and

(3) require that any contractor supplying goods or services to the eligible business under a contract comply with the paragraphs (1) and (2).

(b) Suspension Of Assistance.—If an eligible business does not comply with the requirements under subsection (a), the Secretary—

(1) shall suspend all financial assistance to the eligible business; and

(2) may not provide any additional financial assistance to the eligible business until the date on which the eligible business complies with all such requirements.

SEC. 105. REQUIREMENT TO BE NEUTRAL IN UNION ORGANIZING CAMPAIGNS.

(a) Railway Labor Act.—Section 2 of the Railway Labor Act (45 U.S.C. 152) is amended by adding at the end the following:

"Thirteenth. Any carrier by air (including carriers by air) who received a loan or loan guarantee under paragraph (1), (2), or (3) of section 4101(b) of the Coronavirus Economic Stabilization Act of 2020 shall not, during the term of the loan or guarantee, and for the 5-year period beginning on the date on which the loan or guarantee is repaid—

"(1) require or coerce an employee of the carrier to attend or participate in such carrier's campaign activities unrelated to the employee's job duties, including activities that would be subject to the requirements under section 203(b) of the Labor-Management Reporting and Disclosure Act of 1959 (29 U.S.C. 433(b)) as though the carrier by air were an employer under that Act; or

"(2) engage any person or entity to carry out the activities described in paragraph (1), or provide other related services to employees.

"Fourteenth. Any carrier by air (including carriers by air) who received a loan or loan guarantee under paragraph (1), (2), or (3) of section 4101(b) of the Coronavirus Economic Stabilization Act of 2020 shall, during the term of the loan or guarantee, and for the 5-year period beginning on the date on which the loan or guarantee is repaid, remain neutral during any organizing campaign for a representative by the employees of the carrier.".

(b) National Labor Relations Act.—Section 8(a)(5) of the National Labor Relations Act (29 U.S.C. 158(a)(5)) is amended—

(1) by striking "to refuse" and inserting "(A) to refuse";

(2) by striking the period at the end and inserting "; or"; and

(3) by adding at the end the following:

"(B) in the case of any employer who received a loan or loan guarantee under paragraph (1), (2), or (3) of section 4101(b) of the Coronavirus Economic Stabilization Act of 2020, any other employer who provides goods or services under a contract to such an employer, or any other employer who provides goods or services to a person subject to the Railway Labor Act (45 U.S.C. 151 et seq.) who received a loan or loan guarantee under such a paragraph of such section 4101(b)—

"(i) to, during the term of the loan or guarantee, and for the 5-year period beginning on the date on which the loan or guarantee is repaid, require or coerce an employee to attend or participate in such employer's campaign activities unrelated to the employee's job duties, including activities that are subject to the requirements under section 203(b) of the Labor-Management Reporting and Disclosure Act of 1959 (29 U.S.C. 433(b));

"(ii) to, during the term of the loan or guarantee, and for the 5-year period beginning on the date on which the loan or guarantee is repaid, engage any person or entity to carry out the activities described in clause (i), or provide other related services to employees; or

"(iii) to, during the term of the loan or guarantee, and for the 5-year period beginning on the date on which the loan or guarantee is repaid, fail to remain neutral during any organizing campaign by the employees of the employer on behalf of representation by a labor organization.".

SEC. 106. MAINTENANCE OF EMPLOYEE RETIREMENT PLANS.

(a) In General.—The Secretary shall only make a loan, or enter into a loan guarantee, under paragraph (1), (2), or (3) of section 4101(b) to an eligible business after the eligible business enters into a legally binding agreement with the Secretary that, during the period beginning March 1, 2020, and ending 5 years after the repayment of any such loan—

(1) the eligible business will not amend any plan described in section 401(a) of the Internal Revenue Code of 1986 maintained by the eligible business to eliminate coverage of any employee under such plan who was eligible in the plan year immediately preceding the plan year in which the eligible business enters into a loan agreement under paragraph (1), (2), or (3) of section 4101(b) of this Act; and

(2) the eligible business will maintain all accrual rates (including any matching contributions or nonelective employer contributions) for any plan described in section 401(a) of such Code maintained by the eligible employer at a rate equal to the rate under such plan for the plan year immediately preceding the plan year in which the eligible business enters into a loan agreement under paragraph (1), (2), or (3) of section 4101(b) of this Act.

(b) Affiliates Of Eligible Business.—Any businesses treated as a single employer under the rules of subsection (b), (c), (m), or (o) of section 414 of the Internal Revenue Code (applied as modified by section 415(h) of the Internal Revenue Code) shall be treated as a single employer for purposes of this section.

SEC. 107. EXPANSION OF ELIGIBILITY FOR HEALTH CARE TAX CREDIT; EXTENSION OF CREDIT.

(a) Expansion Of Eligibility.—

(1) IN GENERAL.—Paragraph (1) of section 35(c) of the Internal Revenue Code of 1986 is amended by striking "and" at the end of subparagraph (B), by striking the period at the end of subparagraph (C) and inserting ", and", and by adding at the end the following new subparagraph:

"(D) an eligible national defense or infrastructure worker.".

(2) ELIGIBLE NATIONAL DEFENSE OR INFRASTRUCTURE WORKER.—Subsection (c) of section 35 of the Internal Revenue Code of 1986 is amended by adding at the end the following new paragraph:

"(5) ELIGIBLE NATIONAL DEFENSE OR INFRASTRUCTURE WORKER.—

"(A) IN GENERAL.—The term 'eligible national defense or infrastructure worker' means an individual who—

"(i) as of January 31, 2020, was employed in a critical industry,

"(ii) who filed for unemployment compensation (as defined in section 85(b)) after January 31, 2020, and before the applicable date, and

"(iii) who is covered under qualified health insurance described in subsection (e)(1)(A).

"(B) CRITICAL INDUSTRY.—For purposes of this paragraph, the term 'critical industry' means—

"(i) an industry related to critical national infrastructure or national defense, or

"(ii) a critical industry which is severely distressed in connection with the coronavirus national emergency, as determined by the Secretary, including the airport, air carrier (as defined in section 40102 of title 49, United States

Code), and aerospace industries.

"(C) APPLICABLE DATE.—For purposes of this paragraph, the term 'applicable date' means the earlier of—

"(i) the date which is 6 months after the last day on which the coronavirus national emergency declaration is in effect, or

"(ii) January 1, 2023.

"(D) CORONAVIRUS NATIONAL EMERGENCY.—For purposes of this paragraph—

"(i) IN GENERAL.—The coronavirus national emergency is the emergency with respect to which the President made the declarations described in clause (ii).

"(ii) DECLARATIONS.—The last day on which the coronavirus national emergency declaration is in effect is the later of—

"(I) the last day on which the declaration of the emergency involving Federal primary responsibility determined to exist by the President under the section 501(b) of the Robert T. Stafford Disaster Relief and Emergency Assistance Act (42 U.S.C. 5191(b)) with respect to coronavirus disease 2019 (COVID-19) is in effect; or

"(II) the last day on which the declaration of the national emergency declared by the President under the National Emergencies Act (50 U.S.C. 1601 et seq.) with respect to coronavirus disease 2019 (COVID-19) is in effect.".

(3) ADVANCE PAYMENT OF CREDIT.—Paragraph (1) of section 7527(d) of the Internal Revenue Code of 1986 is amended by striking "or" at the end of subparagraph (A), by striking the period at the end of subparagraph (B) and inserting ", or", and by adding at the end the following new subparagraph:

"(C) in the case of an eligible national defense or infrastructure worker (as defined in section 35(c)(5)), is certified by the Secretary (or by any other person or entity designated by the Secretary) (in consultation with the Secretary of Transportation (or any other person or entity designated by such Secretary), in the case of a worker in aviation- or aerospace-related industries).".

(4) EFFECTIVE DATE.—The amendments made by this subsection shall apply to months beginning after January 31, 2020.

(b) Extension Of Credit.—

(1) IN GENERAL.—Subparagraph (B) of section 35(b)(1) of the Internal Revenue Code of 1986 is amended by striking "January 1, 2021" and inserting "January 1, 2023".

(2) EFFECTIVE DATE.—The amendment made by this subsection shall apply to months beginning after December 31, 2020.

SEC. 108. DEFINITIONS.

In this division:

(1) COVERED LOSS.—The term "covered loss" includes losses, direct or incremental, incurred as a result of COVID–19, as determined by the

Secretary.

(2) ELIGIBLE BUSINESS.—The term "eligible business" means a United States business that has incurred covered losses such that the continued operations of the business are jeopardized, as determined by the Secretary, and that has not otherwise applied for or received economic relief in the form of loans or loan guarantees provided under any other provision of this Act.

(3) SECRETARY.—The term "Secretary" means the Secretary of the Treasury, or the designee of the Secretary of the Treasury.

SEC. 109. RULE OF CONSTRUCTION.

Nothing in this division shall be construed to allow the Secretary to provide relief to eligible businesses except in the form of secured loans and loan guarantees as provided in this title and under terms and conditions that are in the interest of the Federal Government.

Other Books by Thirteen Colony Press

The FBI Confidential Source Failure by U.S. Department of Justice

Read the Office of the Inspector General's report on the FBI's deficiencies in its handling of classified human sources. This Inspector General identified multiple areas that the Federal Bureau of Investigation failed to properly vet confidential secret sources used for investigation. The Inspector discovered that FBI analysts were pressured into not identifying red flags about these sources, possibly tainting the counterintelligence investigation of the Trump campaign. This information was used to secure warrants for monitoring Trump campaign officials.

The Clinton Email Server Report by U.S. State Department

The U.S. Justice Department assigned Robert Mueller and a team of agents in the spring of 2017 to investigate accusations of collusion between President Donald Trump and Russian operatives. This is the complete text of the declassified, redacted report.

The Mueller Report by Robert Mueller

The U.S. Justice Department assigned Robert Mueller and a team of agents in the spring of 2017 to investigate accusations of collusion between President Donald Trump and Russian operatives. This is the complete text of the declassified, redacted report.

Other Books by Sastrugi Press

2024 Total Eclipse State Series by Aaron Linsdau

Sastrugi Press has published state-specific and country guides for the 2024 total eclipse crossing over North America. Check the Sastrugi Press website for the available eclipse books for Texas, Arkansas, Oklahoma, Missouri, Kentucky, Illinois, Indiana, Ohio, Pennsylvania, New York, Vermont, New Hampshire, Maine, Mexico, and Canada.

www.sastrugipress.com/eclipse

50 Wildlife Hotspots by Moose Henderson

Find out where to find animals and photograph them in Grand Teton National Park from a professional wildlife photographer. This unique guide shares the secret locations with the best chance at spotting wildlife.

A Small Pile of Feathers by Gerry Spence

Gerry Spence reveals his spiritual, loving, and sometimes humorous sides, depicted in his devotion to family and to preserving the wild places he writes of as though they were inscribed on his own bones and in his own blood.

Adventure Expedition One by Aaron Linsdau and Terry Williams M.D.

How do you set off on your first epic expedition? Where should you even start? This book has practical advice to help you begin planning your first trek. Dreaming, planning, training, doing, and returning alive are all covered in this guide.

Alaska: Illustrated Guide for the Curious by Nikki Mann and Jeff Wohl

This friendly, illustrated field guide presents interesting and educational information on Alaska's most common land and marine creatures and their habitats. With this book you can learn bear safety, edible berries, tracking, how glaciers are shaping Alaska, the creatures in a tidepool, and so much more. Curious explorers of all ages will enjoy referencing this vibrant guide as you explore the wonder of Alaska.

Along the Sylvan Trail by Julianne Couch

Along the Sylvan Trail dips into the lives of linked characters as they confront futures that aren't clearly dictated by conventional planning. The conflicts of the small town change and pressure residents of Sylvan Grove to look beyond their world to the outside.

Antarctic Tears by Aaron Linsdau

What would make someone give up a high-paying career to ski alone across Antarctica to the South Pole? This inspirational true story will make readers both cheer and cry. Fighting skin-freezing temperatures, infections, and emotional breakdown, Aaron Linsdau exposes the harsh realities of the world's largest wilderness. Discover what drives someone to the brink of destruction to pursue a dream.

Cache Creek by Susan Marsh

Five minutes from the hubbub of Jackson's town square, Cache Creek offers the chance for hikers to immerse themselves in wild nature. It is a popular hiking, biking, and cross-country ski area on the outskirts of Jackson Hole, Wyoming.

Cloudshade by Lori Howe, Ph.D.

The poems of Cloudshade breathe with the vivid, fragrant essence of life in every season on America's high plains. Extraordinarily relatable, the poems of Cloudshade swing wide a door to life in the West, both for lovers of poetry and for those who don't normally read poems.

The Diary of a Dude Wrangler by Struthers Burt

The dude ranch world of Struthers Burt was a romantic destination in the early twentieth century. They transported people back to the Wild West. These ranches were and still are popular destinations. Experience the old west through this dude rancher's writing.

Journeys to the Edge by Randall Peeters, Ph.D.

What is it like to climb Mount Everest? Is it possible for you to actually make the ascent? It requires dreaming big and creating a personal vision to climb the mountains in your life. Randall Peeters shares his successes and failures and gives you some directly applicable guidelines on how you can create a vision for your life.

Lost at Windy Corner by Aaron Linsdau

Windy Corner on Denali has claimed lives, fingers, and toes. What would make someone brave lethal weather, crevasses, and slick ice to attempt to summit North America's highest mountain? The author shares the lessons Denali teaches on managing goals and risks. Apply the message to build resilience and overcome adversity.

Sagebrush Alley by Patricia Jones

What's worse than having a stalker? Being pursued by a second one who has already killed. Attempting to complete her studies, Dana Cameron has to avoid becoming a murder victim. She becomes tangled in a struggle for life trapped in a claustrophobic nightmare.

Sleeping Dogs Don't Lie by Michael McCoy

A young Native American boy is taken from his home after tragedy strikes, grows up in middle America, and through his first real adult summer searches for Wyoming artifacts, falls in with the subversive Dog Soldiers Resurrected, and attempts single-handedly to solve the mystery behind the murder of his treasured coworker.

So I Said by Gerry Spence

The collected sayings of Gerry Spence prods readers into thinking about their own vision of the world. As a lawyer with decades of experience in defending the defenseless, he's fought against giants. His insights provide a grander vision of how the nearly invisible world of the justice system in *So I Said.*

The Burqa Cave by Dean Petersen

Still haunted by Iraq, Tim Ross finds solace teaching high school in Wyoming. That is, until freshman David Jenkins reveals the murder of a lost local girl. Will Tim be able to overcome his demons to stop the murderer?

Voices at Twilight by Lori Howe, Ph.D.

Voices at Twilight is a guide that takes readers on a visual tour of twelve past and present Wyoming ghost towns. Contained within are travel directions, GPS coordinates, and tips for intrepid readers.www.sastrugipress.com

Do you enjoy classic literature? Sastrugi Press has a classic series just for you. Visit our webpage and find more quality books like this one at www.sastrugipress.com/classics/.

Visit Sastrugi Press on the web at www.sastrugipress.com to purchase the above titles in bulk. They are also available from your local bookstore or online retailers in print, e-book, or audiobook form. Thank you for choosing Sastrugi Press.

Made in United States
North Haven, CT
04 November 2026

21766913R00404